Essays on Roman Satire

PRINCETON SERIES OF COLLECTED ESSAYS

This series was initiated in response to requests from students and teachers who want the best essays of leading scholars available in a convenient format. Each book in this series serves scholarship by gathering in one place previously published articles representing the valuable contribution of a noted authority to his field. The format allows for the addition of a preface or introduction and an index to enhance the collection's usefulness. Photoreproduction of the essays keeps costs to a minimum and thus makes possible publication in a relatively inexpensive form.

William S. Anderson

ESSAYS ON ROMAN SATIRE

PRINCETON UNIVERSITY PRESS

PRINCETON, NEW JERSEY

CONTENTS

PREFACE

THE FIFTEEN papers collected here represent my engagement with Roman satire over the span of two decades. Having become thoroughly delighted with the poems of Juvenal while studying at Cambridge University for a second B.A., I returned to Yale University determined to make that satirist the focus of my doctoral dissertation. It proved to be a perfect subject, highly rewarding while I was writing the thesis and richly productive of material for further research and publication. After I had narrowed my topic, I entitled the dissertation "The Rhetoric of Juvenal"; it earned me the Ph.D. in June 1954. My methodology, which continued to underlie later studies, sprang from the assumption that Juvenal wrote artistically controlled and elaborated poetry (hence my pleasure), which should repay careful poetic analysis. I reacted strongly against earlier critics who believed that satire was primarily a social document and the direct expression of social protest. Such critics, when studying Juvenal, accepted his indignation as a spontaneous, unadorned passion and tended to investigate the social, economic, historical, and personal circumstances that led to the eruption of Juvenal's anger. However, the more they worked with the Satires, the less satisfactory seemed the material for their critical theories. It is obvious, first of all, that Juvenal's poems do not provide a reliable series of data on the conditions of Rome in the early second century, and, second, that he uses literary tactics that are anything but spontaneous. For over a century, under the influence of Romantic critics, the word *rhetoric* had been the antithesis of *spontaneous* and was viewed as the hallmark of bad poetry—in the case of Juvenal, of bad satire. What I attempted to show in the dissertation was that rhetoric lay at the heart of Juvenal's most admired Satires, that it was an essential and highly successful element of a very conscious art. In other words, I tried to convert the pejorative term *rhetoric* into a neutral descriptive term of literary practices and then to define the special qualities of the unique satiric rhetoric devised by Juvenal.

In one way or another, all my papers on satire have continued to argue the thesis that Roman satire is primarily an art form that merits careful literary analysis, that the accurate social documentation and the autobiographical aspects behind the satirist's engagement, while certainly relevant (if they could be ascertained), are secondary aspects of the final literary product. During a marvelous year of further research at the

vii

American Academy in Rome in 1955, I expanded my coverage to include the three other Latin poetic satirists—Lucilius, Horace, and Persius—and then I published two of these papers, an analysis of Satire 6 of Juvenal as an intelligently designed poem and an interpretation of *Satire* I, 9 of Horace as a witty elaboration of mock-epic battle. Both appeared in 1956.

These papers are the fifth and eleventh in this collection, for I have not adopted a chronological arrangement here, but preferred to organize the papers according to topic. After a discussion of some of the critical issues involved in interpreting the four poetic satirists, I have placed six papers on Horace, two on Persius, and six more on Juvenal. Let me spend a little time reviewing the problems of each paper and the connections among them.

In "Roman Satirists and Literary Criticism," I explore the difficulties that poets from Lucilius to Juvenal have caused critics by their strategy of first-person presentation and their regular claim to be telling the truth, whether with a smile like Horace, with a snarl like Lucilius and Juvenal, or with a sardonic laugh like Persius. In order to avoid preoccupation with the psyche of the speaker in the Satires and to direct our attention to the poetic talent that creates a largely objective voice of social protest, I recommend the merits of the critical distinction used by students of English satire: the poet Horace or Juvenal should not be identified totally with the character in the Satires who makes the social commentary. That character, or *persona* (to use the Latin term for mask and emphasize the possibilities of dramatic fiction), must be plausible, but he is also subject to criticism by design of the poet. Thus, when Juvenal develops a long tirade against marriage in Satire 6, we need not, with Highet and others, assume that he himself was motivated by hatred of women (because of a disastrous experience with a wife?), but rather that he projected this rather conventional misogyny on a created character.

In "The Roman Socrates: Horace and His Satires," I give a general review of Horace's artistry as a satiric poet and then concentrate on ways in which he modulates the presentation of his *persona* in the two separate Books of Satires that he published at an interval of five years, in 35 and 30 B.C., respectively. Working to distinguish his poetry from the domination of Lucilius, Horace forged a compressed but flexible personal style that functioned integrally with a dramatic role for his speaker: a smiling teacher of the truth about important ethical matters, who differed strikingly from the free-swinging sensationalistic scandalmonger and retailer of choice anecdotes (even about himself) that Lucilius had contrived. In order to give that *persona* maximum objectivity as a planned character whose connections with the actual Horace are imprecise, I suggest that

Horace deliberately created a role for his speaker that would remind his audience of a recognizable Greek type: the ironic Socrates gently teasing his young friends to reexamine their presuppositions and to work more seriously toward an ethically committed life. What makes Horace's dramatic achievement especially impressive is the way he altered his presentation of the satirist's *persona* as he began work on Book II of the Satires. Whereas in Book I he merely gives the impression of a conversation— but actually lets his Socratic speaker dominate the discussion and with a laugh address his ironic ideas directly to us—in Book II he contrives a dramatic context that more convincingly reproduces conversation, and he assigns his satirist the subordinate role in the discussion, primarily as a dramatic audience and occasional interlocutor for a fanatic companion, who treats our satirist and us to a flood of inept teaching. Resemblances to the settings of several Platonic dialogues suggest that Horace has redefined his methods of satire and now employs the more indirect tactics and greater irony of Socrates' greatest pupil, Plato.

In "Autobiography and Art in Horace," I pursue in greater detail, over the whole range of Horace's poetic career, the interrelationship of subjective material and literary purposes. For the purposes of the Satires, it is sufficient to focus on the significant manner in which we are introduced to Horace's father in two centrally located poems of Book I, namely, 4 and 6. In I, 4, Horace's father serves to guarantee the ingenuous function of the eithical teaching in the Book, specifically, of the examples that Horace cites from the behavior of others. We get the picture of a simple, honest, somewhat authoritarian parent who has the best interests of his son at heart, and it seems that Horace has adopted the honest naiveté of the father. Horace's purpose is different in I, 6, and so he employs new details about his father to support a disquisition on the vanity of political ambition and the delights of serene Epicurean leisure. This time, he emphasizes the fact that his father had originally been a slave and had somehow, at some point, earned his freedom. That means social inferiority for the old man and a heritage of social shame for the son. Children of such parentage often, as we have seen in America in the driving ambition and great economic and public successes of immigrants' offspring, react against their parents, try to deny and escape them, and plunge into the rat race toward the most obvious public distinction. Horace, however, reverses the expected pattern and amazes us by crediting his father not only for the skills by which he has advanced to success but also for the ethical quality of his success, one that is free from the burdens of political ambition. Thus, the ex-slave has himself grasped the significance of moral freedom and so liberated his son. Having used his father in two rather different ways to support the particular themes of two separate poems and the cumulatively achieved *persona* he seeks in Book I of the Satires, Horace has no further need of the old man and does not refer to him again except momentarily in the final poem of his first collection of Epistles, which were published some fifteen years after these Satires. In the lyric Odes, which occupied his attention for a decade after the Satires, the *persona* needs no homespun ex-slave father, for he has been taken under the special protection of the Muses of lyric poetry.

In the following pair of papers, I examine particular aspects of poetic craftsmanship that contribute to the success of two rather special Satires of Book I, namely, the adjacent anecdotal poems 8 and 9. The argument of "The Form, Purpose, and Position of Horace's *Satire* I, 8" aims at defining the special features of the poem, especially the characterization of its striking narrator, a statue of Priapus, and linking them thematically with the other poems of Book I. I suggest that Priapus and his story about a "dangerous encounter" with witches and his "miraculous escape" constitute a laughable parallel to the pattern of *Satire* I, 9 and that his gross "revenge" upon these malevolent witches in the form of a thunderous but harmless fart offers us an amusing counterpart to the effect of Horace's smiling personal criticism. Just as it is vital to define the function of the unique speaker of I, 8, so it is important to establish with precision the artistic characterization of the first-person speaker of I, 9. In this latter Satire, the speaker is our familiar satirist himself, who describes his encounter with the man who is conventionally called the "bore." Closer examination, however, shows that Horace presents his companion as far more menacing than a "bore": he is ruthlessly ambitious, eager to push his way into the circle of Maecenas, and he reduces everything and everyone to crass political terms. Such a person constitutes a grave menace to Maecenas's circle, which embraces friendships and cultural interests and Epicurean leisure as well as useful political goals, and he looms for the poor satirist as a murderous enemy. In order to elaborate the basic antagonism between the ruthless political climber and the inoffensive helplessness of the satirist's mild Epicureanism, Horace develops the encounter amusingly in terms of a Homeric confrontation of heroes on the field of battle, and he turns his speaker, to cite my title, into an "unwilling warrior." The reader will observe that in this publication of 1956, although I was already focusing on the artistic representation of the satiric speaker, I did not yet employ the distinction between Horace and his *persona*; hence, the reference to *Horace*, the unwilling warrior.

This characterization of the Horatian satirist as an inoffensive fellow, the helpless victim of another's aggressiveness, and the general smiling indulgence of Horatian satire differ so strikingly from the proclaimed indignation of Juvenal, that it raises the question whether Juvenal thought of the *Sermones* as a significant model for his work. He does pay homage to Horace in the programmatic Satire 1, but in the ambiguous phrase *Venusina lucerna*, which hardly specifies what in Horace he admires. In the next paper, then, without denying that Juvenal thoroughly knew the *Sermones* and recognized their significant place in the tradition of the genre, I suggest that the most likely pattern for Juvenalian indignation in Horace can be found in the violently patriotic *Epodes* and *Odes*. Later, when Juvenal altered his manner toward that of Democritean laughter, from the period of Satire 10 and Book IV on, the relaxed, non-indignant manner of Horace's satirist functions as a more useful model.

In the next pair of papers, I deal with the function of imagery in the Satires of Horace, Persius, and Juvenal. Imagery not merely characterizes the speaker, as in Horace I, 9, but also conveys the essential qualities of the particular satiric vision of each of these three quite different poets. It is methodologically effective to contrast the tactics of Horace and Juvenal, and in "Imagery in the Satires of Horace and Juvenal" I distinguish what I call the "intellectual" quality of Horace's metaphors and similes from the "irrational" stress of Juvenal's. Horace obliges us to examine an assertion of likeness between a man and an animal, a man and an insect, or a man and an obvious human fool, then to formulate the essential differences that define man's unique intellectual and ethical nature. His Satires push us toward responsible fulfillment of our basic human nature. Juvenal, on the other hand, insists on our animal qualities, our loss of, or corruption of, the ethical aspects of our supposedly "higher nature." He portrays the world around him as degenerate, dehumanized, un-Roman; paradoxical assertions of likeness between men and beasts, men and tragic villains, contribute to his indignant vision. Whereas Horace, by pressing discrimination and intellectual awareness of man's special ethical position, propels us toward an optimistic view of our world, Juvenal, by stressing paradoxical likenesses and the replacement of reason by irrationality, of ethical responsibility by bestial corruption, contrives his powerfully pessimistic account of the Roman world a century later.

Persius' method of using imagery blends Horace's "intellectual" and Juvenal's "irrational" functions. He isolates a select group of saved Stoics who exhibit the ideal features of the intellectual and ethical humanity that we meet in Horace, and he starkly contrasts with them the corrupt mass of human beings who have lost or perverted their humanity, distorted it into subhuman or bestial or even inanimate states. In "Part versus Whole in Persius' Fifth Satire," I show how the dominant slave metaphor of the second part of the poem receives its preparation, how the opposite theme of moral freedom is established in the opening section.

There, in dramatic conversation with his idealized mentor Cornutus, the satirist chooses a responsible ethical style and reflects on his total acceptance of the liberating principles of Stoicism. In setting up this symbolic antagonism between the satirist's perfection and most people's corruption, Persius achieves an austerity and an alienation that differ strikingly from the tones of both Horace and Juvenal.

In "Persius and the Rejection of Society," I use the imagery and the characterization of the satirist to illustrate the unique social position adopted by Persius. Unlike Horace, who holds out hope for Roman society, and unlike Juvenal, who indignantly protests at the corruption of Roman mores, Persius' satirist expresses an absolute intolerance and contempt for the majority of people. Defining himself and his Stoic teachers as alone capable of dealing rationally with circumstances, he rejects without compunction all others as unredeemable.

Of the remaining six papers, which deal with Juvenal, the first two originated in my dissertation of 1954. The purpose of "Studies in Book I of Juvenal" and of "Juvenal 6: A Problem in Structure" is to analyze the compositional techniques of Book I (Satires 1-5) and of Book II (Satire 6 alone). We should not expect Juvenal to glide smoothly into his theme, probing it with ever greater depth, appealing to our ethical rationality, as Horace does. Juvenal has announced indignation as his mood, which prescribes an attitude of mainly irrational passion. It follows that his themes will be such as to sustain indignation and will not be subjected to careful, probing development. I suggest a general scheme that is applicable to Satires 1-6: a paradoxical basic theme, which is clarified and proved by a series of exemplary illustrations, but not appreciably altered over the course of the poem. Satire 6, which is over 600 lines long, introduces a slight modification of this scheme by pausing for a recapitulation halfway through and then shifting the emphasis from one to another corruption dominant among Roman women.

In "The Programs of Juvenal's Later Books," I argue that Juvenal not only changed his manner after Satire 6 but also used the initial Satires of each subsequent book—Satires 7, 10, and 13—to put forward his new "program." This paper constitutes a protest against those who uncritically declare that Juvenal was always indignant and those who note the change but attribute it to some psychological factors in Juvenal himself, most commonly to aging and mellowing with success. I prefer to account for these changes in terms of conscious poetic choices rather than autobiographical pressures. The most obvious assertion of a new mood occurs in Satire 13, where the satirist mocks the naive indignation of his companion and calls for a more sensible attitude toward everyday crimes. But indignation is also criticized and modified in Satire 10, when the satirist opts for the sardonic laughter of Democritus over the passionate involvement of Heraclitus. His elegant presentation of the Vanity of Human Wishes follows the Democritean model, ridiculing without indignation such prize fools as Sejanus, Alexander, Cicero, and Silius, all of whom earned death by their foolish ambitions. Thus, like Horace, who altered his methods from Book I to II, Juvenal devised new poetic techniques for satiric presentation over his thirty-year career.

The longer paper, "Anger in Juvenal and Seneca," discusses this change from indignant to Democritean satirist in greater detail and connects Juvenal's poetic decisions with ethical analysis and criticism of anger and indignation, of which two essays of Seneca form ideal examples. We may say that Juvenal planted numerous clues in Satires 1-6 to indicate that his angry satirist was riddled by tensions and inconsistencies, and hence we should not accept the indignant vision of Roman degradation as fully valid. Furthermore, a review of Senecan criticism of anger suggests that both Juvenal and his audience would have been familiar with, and would no doubt have accepted, the view that indignation was an inadequate ethical feeling. It becomes even more likely that Juvenal knew and recognized theories like Seneca's when we turn to Satire 10 and the poems grouped after it, for there we find the idealization of Democritus' laughing sanity and the contempt for irrational, womanish anger much as they stand in Seneca.

The next step in my interpretation of Juvenal's art comes in "*Lascivia* vs. *ira*: Martial and Juvenal." In order to clarify the integrity of Juvenal's poetic representation of anger and indignation, I contrast it with the playful methods of Martial, who frequently anticipated Juvenal's subject matter. Whatever may have been the historical relation between the older Martial and the younger satirist, it is evident that Juvenal was not just another witty version of Martial. Although he does employ wit, it is manifestly subordinate to the mood of indignation in the early Satires. Juvenal's indignant satirist is a caricature in his extremism. Just as we possess some control over him in the careful theories of Seneca, so we can postulate the reactions of Juvenal's audience by visualizing the circumstances of a recitation in the first decades of the second century. Like Archie Bunker, the celebrated bigot of American television during the late 1970s, Juvenal's satirist is an essentially comic dramatic type. When the comfortable Roman aristocrats attended a recitation by Juvenal, they were amused by the disparity between their circumstances and what the Satires denounced, and they enjoyed the satirist's indignation. Thus, Juvenal showed great poetic skill in creating an angry satirist, but he knew that his original audience could distinguish truth from exaggeration and would enjoy his extremist. Little did he anticipate that an age of Romanticism would wholeheartedly believe his satirist, that social historians would quarry him for details, and that literary critics would admire his indignation and seek its sources in some traumatic experiences.

Finally, in "Juvenal and Quintilian," I assess the art of Juvenal in connection with another older contemporary in order to give a positive reading of its often maligned rhetorical aspects. After reviewing the arguments on behalf of the theory that Juvenal actually studied under Quintilian and finding them unconvincing, I propose using the writings of the rhetorician in the *Institutio Oratoria* as representative of good rhetorical theory such as was commonly taught in Rome and was familiar to Juvenal. Thus, Quintilian says much about the utility of the mood of indignation or anger for a speaker when dealing with certain subjects, and we can find that Juvenal followed the decorum for indignation as he devised the speaker of his early Satires. His announced indignation and the simple compositional techniques he used help us to categorize Juvenal's works among the display pieces of the *genus demonstrativum*, which concentrate on praise or blame: the Satires obviously blame as they create a lurid portrait of decadent Rome, once the proudest city in the known world. When we extend this analysis to Juvenal's style, it is easy to perceive that, in openly flaunting his rhetorical devices, the satirist marks a sharp gap between himself and the colloquial, smiling Horace. Many of his highly visible tropes serve the purposes of strong passion and the grand style according to Quintilian. Others, however, resemble what the rhetorician, a stickler for decency, would have called "abuses." In particular, Juvenal's propensity for flagrantly obscene vocabulary, for drastic mixture of vocabulary levels (for example, poeticisms and vulgarisms), and for a variety of exaggerations suggests that he carefully forged his own satiric decorum: his violation of the "rules" implies that the indignation of his satirist *persona* cannot restrain itself; it rejects the rigidities of decorum and launches itself wildly against a world whose corruption surpasses the usual range of "correct" rhetoric. It is perhaps useful to think of Juvenal's satirist as a deliberate throwback to that archetypal defender of virtue, Cato the Elder, the first great *vituperator* and the creator of one of the most influential definitions of the ideal orator, *vir bonus dicendi peritus*. That definition admirably fits Juvenal's satirist.

Behind this work of two decades has been lurking a definition of satire itself. I can perhaps best summarize that definition by quoting from the first paragraph of an article that I wrote this year: "When we risk generalizations about satire and the satirist, we tend to describe satire as both shapeless and capable of assuming many shapes, in other words, as a highly unstable genre with an often inconsistent point of view and elusive theme; and we consider the satirist himself unstable, inconsistent, an unsettling fellow who mixes laughter with anger, who sometimes presents himself as an ordinary person of no special literary talent and at other times seems to rant away like a character straight out of grand poetry. It has obviously been a valuable strategy for satire and the satirist to be chameleon-like, multiform and multi-toned, because, for all its professed preoccupation with the ethical problems of its subjects—or should we call them targets or victims?—satire keeps turning towards its audience and playing up to its sense of humor, its delight with wit and literary finesse as well as to its moral perceptions." This range of satire first displays itself in the works of Horace, Persius, and Juvenal, who not only differ among themselves but also, as I have shown, alter their own methods in the course of the years and successive books of Satires.

Berkeley, California
June 1, 1981

ACKNOWLEDGMENTS

THE FOLLOWING is a list of the places and dates of the original publications of the essays in this volume, according to the present arrangement. I wish to express my gratitude to the various editors and presses for their prompt and courteous permission to reprint.

"Roman Satirists and Literary Criticism," *Bucknell Review* 12:3 (1964), 106-13. Reprinted by permission of Associated University Presses.

"The Roman Socrates: Horace and his Satires," *Critical Essays on Roman Literature, Vol. II: Satire*, edited by John P. Sullivan (London: Routledge and Kegan Paul Ltd., 1963), 1-37. Reprinted by permission of Routledge and Kegan Paul Ltd. and Harvard University Press.

"Autobiography and Art in Horace," *Perspectives of Roman Poetry: A Classics Symposium*, edited by G. Karl Galinsky (Austin: University of Texas Press, 1974), 35-56. Reprinted by permission of the University of Texas Press.

"The Form, Purpose, and Position of Horace's *Satire* I, 8," *American Journal of Philology* 93 (1972), 4-13. Reprinted by permission of the Johns Hopkins University Press.

"Horace, the Unwilling Warrior: *Satire* I, 9," *American Journal of Philology* 77 (1956), 148-66. Reprinted by permission of the Johns Hopkins University Press.

"*Venusina lucerna*: The Horatian Model for Juvenal," *Transactions of the American Philological Association* 52 (1961), 1-12. Reprinted by permission of the American Philological Association.

"Imagery in the Satires of Horace and Juvenal," *American Journal of Philology* 81 (1960), 225-60. Reprinted by permission of the Johns Hopkins University Press.

"Part versus Whole in Persius' Fifth Satire," *Philological Quarterly* 39 (1960), 66-81. Reprinted by permission of the University of Iowa Press.

"Persius and the Rejection of Society," *Wissenschaftliche Zeitschrift der Wilhelm-Pieck-Universität Rostock, Gesellschafts und Sprachwissenschaftliche Reihe* 15 (1966), H. 4/5, 409-16. Reprinted by permission of the University of Rostock.

"Studies in Book I of Juvenal," *Yale Classical Studies* 15 (1957), 33-90. Reprinted by permission of Yale University Press.

"Juvenal 6: A Problem in Structure," *Classical Philology* 51 (1956), 73-94. Reprinted by permission of the University of Chicago Press.

"The Programs of Juvenal's Later Books," *Classical Philology* 57 (1962), 145-60. Reprinted by permission of the University of Chicago Press.

"Anger in Juvenal and Seneca," *California Publications in Classical Philology* 19 (1964), 127-96. Reprinted by permission of the University of California Press.

"*Lascivia* vs. *ira*: Martial and Juvenal," *California Studies in Classical Antiquity* 3 (1970), 1-34. Reprinted by permission of the University of California Press.

"Juvenal and Quintilian," *Yale Classical Studies* 17 (1961), 1-91. Reprinted by permission of Yale University Press.

Essays on Roman Satire

ROMAN SATIRISTS AND LITERARY CRITICISM

O N APRIL 9, 1778, Boswell dined with Samuel Johnson at the home of Sir Joshua Reynolds, in the august company of such people as Bishop Shipley, the painter Allan Ramsay, and Edward Gibbon. With Johnson present, it was inevitable that any dinner would develop into a symposium and that the conversation would range over the widest spaces. On this occasion, the diners began to discuss Horace. I now quote Boswell: "The Bishop said, it appeared from Horace's writings that he was a cheerful contented man. Johnson: 'We have no reason to believe that, my Lord. Are we to think Pope was happy, because he says so in his writings? We see in his writings what he wished the state of his mind to appear.' "

Johnson rightly drew a distinction between the poet's state of mind and the attitude which he chose to present in the first person in any particular personal poem. Moreover, he chose for analogy Alexander Pope, that misshapen genius, whose body would seem to be the archetype for that of the so-called twisted satirist imagined by the romantic mind, whose poems, however, run the gamut of attitudes from Horatian wit to Juvenalian indignation. This kind of distinction, which is reflected today in the critical terminology adopted by students of English literature especially, in the much-used word *persona,* has unfortunately not percolated down to many readers of classical literature. One of the most patient sufferers from our ignorance is Roman poetic satire. Too many, it seems to me, ignore the fact that Lucilius, Horace, Persius, and Juvenal were poets first and foremost.

From the first satires written by Lucilius, it was conventional for the *persona* to disclaim poetic ability, especially in contrast to the writers of epic and tragedy, and instead to place his emphasis on the down-to-earth, truthful qualities of his material. Let us see how these ideas were expressed in the works of Lucilius,

3

Horace, Persius, and Juvenal, then how expert Latinists have dealt with them.

The voice cries out in Lucilius: "I utter spontaneously whatever comes into my head according to the promptings of my heart, according to the immediate occasion, whether it be my state of health, my passion or anger against my concubine, my partisan political feelings, or what have you. Secondly, I am no poet like Ennius. I dabble at verse for the entertainment of the uncritical. I prefer to call my products plays (*ludos*) or mere conversation-like prose (*sermonem*). I can write so freely that I dash off 200 verses an hour, indeed 200 verses after a good dinner."

A proper critic today might be on his guard against such claims; the average Latinist has not been. The latter seems to use the following reasoning. "These words are spoken by Lucilius and must be sincere confessions on his part. Now, since he denies to himself poetic ability, we may ignore all poetic considerations that would, of course, be relevant to a talented writer like Vergil, and instead we should concentrate our scholarship on what is after all more reliable factual material: namely, what the Satires of Lucilius tell us about his biography, the social practices, and historical situation of his day." As a result of such reasoning, much excellent matter has been deduced from the Satires, matter, however, that is peripheral to the purposes of the poet; and, on the other hand, many mistakes have been committed by those who pursue a biography of Lucilius in the behavior of the *persona*.

Thus, the scholarship on Lucilius is remarkably unbalanced. On the one hand, there are elaborate analyses of his political thought and his place in the party politics of the Second Century B.C. On the other, scholars have permitted the most uninformed generalizations on literary matters to escape their lips, as, for example, that Lucilius is prosaic in all but meter or that his poetry is formless. When they compound their error by making guesses about the poet from the words spoken by the *persona* in a specially designed dramatic context, they radically distort the true proportions of Lucilius' poetry. Lucilius is a libertine, says one eminent Italian, because his Satires talk so much about affairs with prostitutes. Lucilius exhibits the mentality of an old soldier, says another scholar, because he again and again discusses military matters. In the midst of this, nobody cares to grapple with the

4

problem of the poetic purpose of satire. It does not seem to cross the mind of serious scholars that, had Lucilius desired merely to express the socio-political ideas that interest modern critics, then he would have done so quite frankly in prose. Instead of identifying the *persona* with Lucilius, we should be studying the processes by which this *persona* is effectively created and the novelty that the poet achieved in producing the first extensive personal verse in Latin literature. The question to ask is not: What can we learn about the biography of Lucilius? The question to ask is: What does this speaker, this *persona,* with his wild invective, his frank eroticism, his witty anecdotes, and his serious moral judgments, accomplish for the poem? It is no accident, therefore, that some recent studies in Germany and Italy have demonstrated that, far from being a clumsy versifier, Lucilius was a sophisticated poet, closer to the polished Alexandrians than many a contemporary writer.

When we proceed to Horace, we find him deploying the same conventional argument in the mouth of his *persona.* "I have a compulsion," says that character, "to speak out, to tell the truth with a smile (*ridentem dicere verum*), at least in the intimate company of my confidential friends. On the other hand, I lack the talent to produce genuine poetry, epic or tragedy, so I play at this (*haec ego ludo*)." If all things were equal, we should expect critics to treat Horace in the same cavalier fashion which has marked their handling of Lucilius. Fortunately, a number of new factors introduce differences that avert the worst errors of Lucilian analysis. In the first place, a good biography of Horace has come down to us from Suetonius and rendered otiose much biographical conjecture. Second, Horace's Satires survive complete, whereas Lucilius' poems are entirely fragmentary and so seem to encourage extravagant hypotheses and reconstructions. Finally, there are other quite different poems of the same poet, iambic vituperation, lyrics of the most diverse tones, and literary epistles, to warn us that Horace could don almost any mask at will, in order to show us, as Johnson long ago noted, the attitude which he chose to manifest. I do not think that anyone has actually said it, but the fact is, that Horace's *persona* as satirist acts a great deal older and more serious morally than his *persona* as lyric lover, drinker, and advocate of *carpe diem;* and yet the external evidence unanimously proves that he wrote and published the Satires ten or more years before the lyric Odes!

I should say, then, that Horace is the most adequately appreciated verse satirist of Rome. Not that a few critics do not pursue the old will-o-the-wisps. Did Horace really take that trip to Brundisium? Did he really have that conversation with the bore? On the whole, though, knowing that Horace boasts a great reputation in lyric, they somewhat mystifiedly accept the fact that his Satires are poetry and talk very learnedly of his superiority to Lucilius. If here and there an incautious word escapes them and they call the contents of Serm. 1.5 (the trip to Brundisium) a versified diary and make of Serm. 1.7 a rather unnecessary anecdote, they nevertheless will fight anyone who denies Horace's rank as a poet. Almost no one would follow that misbegotten Crocean, Durand, who recently argued that, because not only the Satires but the Odes were earthbound, devoid of soaring lyric sentiments, Horace must not be called a "poet" at all—no one, that is, except the distinguished Italian academy that awarded one of its most coveted prizes to Durand. But despite such absurdities in Horace's homeland, Horace can defend himself. His successors are in a far worse plight.

Persius, as we might expect, uses the same conventional argument in his Program Satire. The *persona* says: "Like Midas' barber, I am bursting with the truth about mankind and must speak out. However, I am no high-flown poet, but a half-boor (*semipaganus*) in matters of art; I produce pretty modest stuff, a great deal of nothing (*tam nil*), boiled down (*decoctius*) and direct rather than ornate." Our external controls on this disarming confession do not help us so much here. Six short Satires of Persius have survived and nothing else but fourteen apparently prefatory lines; in addition, a good biography was produced within a few generations of his death. However, unlike the *persona* of Horace's Satires, who is pleasing and constitutes a good model of sound moral thinking, the *persona* of Persius offends many and is so radically inconsistent with his programmatic disclaimer that critics find vast difficulties with these Satires.

There are many who eagerly agree with Persius that he is no poet and so pursue the usual factual material offered by any literature. Their favorite interest is the Stoic substance of Persius's discourse. By proving the self-evident, that Persius uses Stoic ideas, they believe that they have contributed immensely to the understanding of the Satires. Then, there are those who chase the red herring of political allusions. Persius wrote, they say, under the monstrous Nero; it is inevitable that he would make some references to the emperor. And they can find them everywhere! Almost any innocent remark, political or otherwise, made by the earnest *persona* can be twisted into a sneer against Nero. The climax of such maunderings—at least, I hope it is—is the recent hypothesis by one of Belgium's most eminent Classicists that Nero had Persius poisoned!

Italy celebrated this past year the anniversary of Persius's death, with a typical Italian *festa* in Persius' home town, Volterra. On this august occasion, various dignitaries assembled to do honor in their own academic way to the distinguished citizen of the town. Among the lectures delivered to commemorate the poet's passing was one that has since been twice printed, apparently because the speaker, the noted Latinist Paratore, did not wish the world to miss his brilliant thesis. He develops an interesting twist on the biographical fallacy. The authoritative biography tells of a session where Persius apparently recited some of his works and the young Lucan, when his turn to recite came around, burst out with rapturous words of praise. But, notes Paratore, Satire 1 opens with a sharp attack on the institution of public readings (*recitationes*). We must conclude from Satire 1, then, that Persius loathed such sessions and would *never* stoop to reading his Satires in public, and consequently it is necessary to emend the biography by removing the offending passage. Thus, the *persona* forces the facts about the poet to conform!

Meanwhile, the literary problems connected with Persius languish. If critics could grasp the fact that his Stoic ideas are so superficial as to be negligible and his political ideas non-existent, they might realize that Persius' main claim to glory is his fascinatingly labored manner of expressing these commonplaces through a specially contrived *persona*. With him more than any other satirist in poetry, the gap between the disavowal of poetic ability and the vast effort made to produce poetic moralization is patent. Therefore, the task of the critic—that ideal critic who has not appeared for Persius in 1900 years—remains to interpret those poetic methods first, knowing quite well that the disclaiming of talent forms a conventional and always ambiguous aspect of the *persona,* that the producer of poetic satire would not have essayed the genre without fundamentally poetic purposes.

The last victim of distorted criticism is a far greater poet than Persius, but one would hardly learn this from reading some of the latest discussions. In the conventional manner, Juvenal lets his *persona* make the same statements in Satire 1 as were made in the satires of his predecessors: "It is difficult not to write satire, for I cannot endure the many vicious scoundrels of this corrupt city. I admit that I have little talent, but my spontaneous indignation makes my verse, such as it is." Once again, the critics face these programmatic statements, identify them with the feelings of Juvenal, and try to decide whether this vaunted indignation is as sincere as the speaker makes it out to be. Those who, like Gilbert Highet in his *Juvenal the Satirist,* feel the sincerity of this anger then pursue the source of it. Highet argues this way: "Something very strange and violent must have happened in the first part of Juvenal's life to produce such powerful repercussions in the second [that is, the indignant Satires]. . . . Satirists are peculiarly sensitive, and their sensitivity means suffering. They have come into personal conflict with stupidity and injustice, and their satires are the direct result." Accordingly, Highet constructs an ingenious biography for Juvenal. Juvenal's indignation in the early Satires, he argues, resulted directly from his hatred of the villainous emperor Domitian, who had exiled him in or about A.D. 93 to Egypt.

It is not impossible that Juvenal was in fact exiled, but the evidence is ambiguous. Highet goes wrong in generalizing erroneously about the suffering of satirists—Lucilius, Horace, and Persius had no such impetus to write that we can discover—and then searching for some traumatic experience to motivate Juvenal's indignation. Similarly, when he comes to Satire 6, Highet feels compelled to explain its violent attack on women through an imaginary chain of sad circumstances, a fictional marriage of Juvenal with a proud, selfish, and intolerable Roman lady. Granted, the indignation of the *persona* strikes the reader as something new and powerful in Roman satire. However, it is no more original than Horace's smiling irony or Persius's intolerant Stoicism, and it can be successfully explained on a poetic level without resort to biographical conjecture. Merely that we lack any good biography of Juvenal does not mean that we should allow our imaginations free rein.

It must be said in behalf of Highet that he likes Juvenal and uses his biographical methods to give the Satires a sympathetic interpretation. Opposed to him are those who deny the sincerity of Juvenal, who insist on a sharp dichotomy between what Juvenal says and what he does. According to one of the most vigorously antagonistic critics, De Decker, there is in the Satires a poet occasionally, but more frequently an orator who undermines the work of the poet by his patently false methods for displaying indignation. Juvenal is, then, predominantly a *declamator,* a declaimer for the audience. With the help of misunderstood Crocean ideas, the Italian Marmorale has refurbished the dichotomy. Since in his view Juvenal lacks sincerity and emotional depth and, on the other hand, manipulates the literary *topoi* dexterously, Marmorale denies to him the rank of poet and instead christens him a *"letterato,"* a professional writer, in the pejorative sense.

Light comes to the darkened minds of Classicists these days from their more sophisticated colleagues in English. In the past twenty or thirty years, English satire has become again a respectable field for scholarship, and some of the sharpest brains have concentrated their labors on Dryden, Pope, and Swift. Maynard Mack's delightful essay, "The Muse of Satire," starts from disagreement with Highet's biographical methods and proceeds to outline the conventional character of the *persona* in Pope. More recently, Alvin Kernan has discussed Jacobean satire in an important book, *The Cankered Muse.* Kernan has shown that the Jacobeans favored a violent *persona* like that of Juvenal, whereas the Augustans favored Horatian methods. Even more important, it seems to me, is Kernan's suggestion that, in the case of these violently indignant speakers, the poet has deliberately attributed to them objectionable and offensive ways, more or less as a warning to the audience to dissociate itself from their indignation. In other words, sometimes the *persona* created by the satiric poet is so distinct from the poet's biography that the two are opposites.

I suspect that Kernan's theories provide the solution to the critical dilemma over Juvenal: that Highet is right in a sense to

9

argue for sincerity and Marmorale right in a sense to belabor the insincerity. If, following Kernan, we maintain a distinction between Juvenal and the speaker he creates for the Satires, then we can call the speaker genuinely indignant; but we must also add that Juvenal has so portrayed him that his prejudices and exaggerations are unacceptable, and for sound poetic reasons. The *persona* is indignant, but wrong, in many cases, as, for example, in his universal denunciation of women, even the most upright; reading or listening to such ranting, the Roman audience recognized the untruth and re-interpreted the described situations, stimulated by the Satires, more accurately.

We are possibly, therefore, at the beginning of a new era in studies of Roman satire, lagging as usual a generation behind the critics of English literature. We are discovering the conventions of the genre and seeing some of the implications of the critical doctrine that separates poet from personal speaker in the poem. When, therefore, the speaker in satire tries to distract us from the art of the poet and forces us to attend to his so-called "truth," we are less willing to be deceived than formerly. Nor shall we be perturbed to find that, after all, Roman satire is poetry.

HORACE

THE ROMAN SOCRATES:
HORACE AND HIS SATIRES

THE Romans, according to the great rhetorician Quintilian, invented satire, and they generally agreed that the man who deserved the title of 'inventor' was Lucilius. Nevertheless, had not Lucilius been succeeded by Horace, who gave the rather amorphous poetry left by Lucilius an entirely new form, it is difficult to imagine how Roman satire would ever have developed a tradition and survived antiquity to exercise its marked influence on Renaissance literature. So important is Horace's place in the history of satire that one eminent scholar, G. L. Hendrickson, found reasons to describe Horace as the first to use the Latin word *satura* in a generic sense; that is, the first to give the modern literary meaning to *satura*. Although other scholars would date the literary use of the word earlier, Hendrickson correctly saw that Horace did revolutionize the whole field of satire. In what respects Horace was a revolutionary is the subject of this essay.

Lucilius, one of the last archaic poets, died just before the opening of the first century B.C. During the period of Horace's youth Lucilius' poetry was one of the most carefully studied bodies of verse available to budding poets. Not every reader caught the true spirit of Lucilian satire. Some thought that by imitating the savage invective with which the poet had assaulted eminent politicians of the Gracchan Age they were producing genuine 'satires'. We know of writers who lampooned the Triumvirs or who uttered polemic statements against personal foes; such writers, if they used verse, apparently claimed to follow the Lucilian model. However, the truly creative poets of the 60's and 50's, often called the Neoterics or New Poets, saw more clearly into the contribution of the older poet. His artfully stylized conversational manner, his ability to write verse with a strong personal stamp, his choice of ordinary subjects, his anti-heroic attitude, and finally his refusal to accept the political values of many aristocrats, all these made Lucilius' poetry one of the ideals of the New Poets.

Horace, born in 65, went to Rome as a boy to complete the education which he had commenced in his home town Venusia. Thanks to the advantages which his ambitious father secured for him, Horace would have studied Lucilius along with his school-mates, sons of prominent senators. By the time he was a young man, he would have sensed the poetic trend which was gradually going beyond the Neoterics and their models. Another poet several years his senior, Vergil, published his *Eclogues* in 39; this work showed how far Roman literature had advanced from the Neoteric stage. Horace himself, shortly after the Battle of Philippi, had begun to compose his satiric verse. His efforts to chisel out a style and manner cost him much time, and it was not until 35 or 34 B.C. that he finally published a small body of ten *Sermones*, barely 1,000 verses. However, these 1,000 verses immediately proclaimed to the Roman world that Lucilius was challenged, if not superseded. The second great poet of the Augustan Age had appeared.

I. *The Socratic Style*

In his *Art of Poetry*, written long after 35, Horace cites as an especially fine model of correct writing the Socratic 'pages', those discourses of Plato, Xenophon, and other moralists of the fourth century B.C. which either presented the character of Socrates in action or used the same dialectic methods as he had once used.

> scribendi recte sapere est et principium et fons:
> rem tibi Socraticae poterunt ostendere chartae,
> verbaque provisam rem non invita sequentur. (*A.P.* 309–11)

The beginning and source of good writing is understanding: the Socratic pages will be able to indicate to you your matter, and, once you have determined your subject, the words will follow without difficulty.

It was familiar ancient doctrine, dear to the old Censor Cato, that the matter of a poem or speech came before its words. We do not think in that way any more, and it is pretty safe to say that Horace did not write that way. The very act of choosing words determines the meaning of a poem, often in a way quite different from the first poetic inspiration. Today, we would say that the words and the material of a poem cannot be separated and one element be regarded as prior in time and importance. Matter and words, form and content are inextricably related. Therefore, when Horace advocates Socratic content, we would not be surprised to learn that the accompanying words are also 'Socratic'.

G. C. Fiske showed more than forty years ago that Lucilius had created his satiric style in accordance with Stoic rhetorical doctrines. His Plain Style, a poetic version of the conversational manner, proved to be one of Lucilius' most influential innovations, and it affected not only satire but also, as I have said, the entire course of poetry in the first century. Nevertheless, when Horace decided to write satire in the modern style, he found Lucilius' version of the Plain Style altogether out of date. Struggling to define his own purposes, Horace could find no better way than to conduct a running polemic against Lucilius and his admirers. To put it at its simplest, Horace argued that Lucilius lacked the prerequisite of good writing, that understanding (*sapere, sapientia*), that self-discipline and conscious artistry which produces good poetry rather than witty anecdote or exciting invective.

To make his case effective, Horace emphasized one phase only of the double Lucilian tradition in the first century. While he virtually ignored the inspiration which his predecessor had given to great poets like Catullus, Horace concentrated on the invective poetry which Lucilius had also inspired. Thus, he characterized Lucilius by the Latin word *libertas*, using a pejorative sense of the word. No one English term can render all the meanings of *libertas*. Indeed, it took Horace himself a full poem to explore his idea of it (*S.* 1.4). Behind the noun, an abstract, lies the adjective *liber*, 'free'. The noun possesses all the possible meanings which 'being free' could have; it can refer to a noble freedom or a selfish irresponsibility. A Roman citizen, being free, could exercise certain political and social rights: he is not a slave. When one class interfered with the rights of another or when an individual tried to dominate Roman politics, the victims described this behaviour as an invasion of liberty. The political propaganda of the first century makes of *libertas* a passionate slogan. A secondary meaning followed on the first: if one asserted one's freedom by launching an invective against political foes, especially those that seemed to threaten one's rights, that was *libertas*. But a Roman citizen might display his freedom outside politics, especially this second sense of freedom. In his social intercourse he might be 'free' among friends of the same station. A true friend would express himself frankly and honestly, even when such freedom meant that he had to criticize a close companion; similarly, in the company of those he liked he would feel complete freedom to expose his deepest feelings. Lucilius represented himself as just such an honest friend. But since such freedom often took place in the setting of a banquet and at times degenerated into sheer licence, licentious remarks about others and unwise self-revelations; since also the Romans called the god of wine *Liber*, Horace deliberately associated *libertas* with the undisciplined and belligerent speech of a man under the influence of wine:

> saepe tribus lectis videas cenare quaternos,
> e quibus unus amet quavis aspergere cunctos
> praeter eum qui praebet aquam; post hunc quoque potus,
> condita cum verax aperit praecordia *Liber*.
> hic tibi comis et urbanus *liberque* videtur. (*S.* 1.4.86–90)

Often you can see four men dining on each of three couches, of whom one may like to bespatter with any sort of insult all the others except the host who provides the water; later, having drunk, the guest will insult the host, too, when truthful Bacchus discloses the secrets of his heart. To you, such a man seems genial, witty, and frank.

If we have not ourselves been drunk, we have seen drunks, and we all recognize the fact that Horace's picture of *libertas* is both prejudicial and accurate. It was meant to be so. While Horace rejects such drunken 'freedom', he refers to a person (*tibi*) who mistakenly values such liberty as both witty and amiable. This person, it seems clear, is thinking of Lucilius in these laudatory terms. And the satirist means us to see that Lucilius, the frank table companion, adopted an inadequate type of freedom. Ideally, the basis of freedom is a sense of responsibility, self-discipline which prevents one from interfering with the liberty of others. This besotted babbler—a caricature of Lucilius, I hasten to add—

violated all the rules of good manners so irresponsibly that he maligned his own host.

I shall return later to the moral problems which arise from Lucilius' use of *libertas*. For the present, I wish to consider how freedom, in the somewhat exaggerated picture provided us by Horace, affected Lucilian style; then I shall describe how Horace reformed this style in accordance with Classical principles. The passage which I cited from the *Art of Poetry* will afford us the critical term to define the Horatian manner: *sapere* or *sapientia*, understanding and conscious art, is the basis from which the Horatian satirist works and from which he expresses his disapproval of Lucilian freedom.

The drunken man has the unfortunate habit of cursing and slandering any and all people he knows; he also makes himself obnoxious by his long and incoherent monologues. If we listened to Horace, we would judge Lucilius to have been one of the most long-winded, incoherent, and undisciplined poets ever to have gained popularity; indeed, we would be surprised that Lucilius had won such favour with men of literary acumen. Yet Horace, at the very beginning of *S.* 1.4, closely connects with Lucilius' famous freedom of moral and political invective other less honourable traits: Lucilius constructed his verses crudely and heavily; he and his poetry flowed along muddily, with much material that an intelligent man would want to remove; he was garrulous and refused to tolerate the hard task of writing well (*scribendi recte*). Note how that last phrase, first proclaimed here as part of Horace's creed, remained a central part of his beliefs and hence recurred in the very passage of the *Art of Poetry* quoted above. The most vivid portion of Horace's description of Lucilius is a rapid sketch, almost a cartoon of the man:

> in hora saepe ducentos,
> ut magnum, versus dictabat stans pede in uno. (*S.* 1.4.9–10)

In a single hour, as if it were a great thing, Lucilius would dictate two hundred verses, standing on one foot.

Returning to this picture of Lucilian negligence in still another poem, Horace describes him as follows:

> ac si quis pedibus quid claudere senis,
> hoc tantum contentus, amet scripsisse ducentos
> ante cibum versus, totidem cenatus. (*S.* 1.10.59–61)

one who, content to enclose anything within the six feet of the hexameter, likes to have written two hundred verses before dinner and the same number afterwards.

Now, in Lucilius' time it was no crime to be able to dash off verse, especially for a banquet. Cicero, a warm admirer of Lucilius, himself took pride in his skill at composing verse rapidly. However, during the youth of Horace, the New Poets had attacked extemporaneous poetry and the cult of such versifiers; they demanded of the ideal poet absolute dedication to art. The small poem best answered their desires and most clearly represented the ideal of brevity and pungency which they insistently espoused; they extolled the poet Cinna for toiling nine years over his little epyllion entitled *Zmyrna*. Horace accepted these Neoteric principles. Throughout his *Sermones*, he mocks the facile Lucilius and his modern counterparts, fools who challenge the horrified Horace to a contest at extemporaneous versifying, fools like the man in *S*. 1.9 who really believes that the satirist will respect a man for contriving more verses more quickly than anyone else. To reform the incoherent chatter of Lucilius, then, this new satiric poet affirms as one of his basic tenets: *est brevitate opus* (*S*. 1.10.9). A poet must practise brevity.

Brevity characterizes Horatian satire from the smallest to the largest elements. In order to be more clear as to what Horace achieved, we should attempt to describe Lucilius' garrulity. Lucilius, a child of his times and therefore not at all averse to the mellifluous sound of repeated words or accumulated synonyms, showed a typical penchant for pairs and triads of synonyms. He used pronouns and conjunctions which would not be required by a reader a century later. Thus, glancing through his fragments, one gets the impression of a padded style, not spare and compact, but desultory and relaxed. In fact, it was the ideal style for the tone and character which Lucilius chose: his satirist was to be an urbane raconteur whose proper environment was the banquet. Horace, however, discarded this tone and this character, and consequently he consciously altered the style of his satire.

I shall not here attempt a detailed analysis of a Horatian passage to demonstrate the qualities of *brevitas*. Horatian satire is compact. The poet chooses his words carefully, so that one word, skilfully selected and emphatically placed in the verse, does the work of a whole Lucilian line. He tends to avoid synonyms, especially in a merely repetitive or emphatic function. When he uses pronouns, they count. Otherwise, pronouns, conjunctions, prepositions, in fact, anything that does not serve his Classical purposes are eliminated. Reading Horatian satire, then, is work. There are no moments for relaxation. Even the transitions from sentence to sentence often escape the casual reader, who suddenly finds himself in new territory, totally unable to explain how he got there. Brevity in phrase and sentence thus means that Horace can put more into his individual poems more effectively.

We can illustrate this effect of *brevitas* on entire poems by comparing two Satires, one of Lucilius' describing a journey to Sicily and Horace's *S.* 1.5, an account of a trip to Brundisium in the early 30's. According to the scholiast Porphyrio, Horace wrote his poem in part to vie with his predecessor and thus to demonstrate the clear superiority of the new satire. Of Lucilius' poem, there have survived some fifty lines, fragments never longer than four lines. Anyone who tries to piece these bits together must follow the evidence as far as it takes him, but inevitably he will resort to imagination; and differing views of the connexion between fragments have led to many varying reconstructions of the poem. However, despite all the variations, I feel safe in affirming that Lucilius' poem was considerably longer than Horace's. I would guess that it was between two and three hundred lines long, at least twice the size of Horace's poem of 104 verses. Lucilius described a private trip and the new sights and adventures that he had from day to day; what remains of his account has the character of a diary, with special entries on the number of miles from place to place, the type of lodging and food, and so on. It was a poem which must have been pleasant to listen to, which invited the comfortable, well-fed audience to picture the poor satirist toiling over rough roads, up and down mountains, tossing on the sea off Naples, taken advantage of by innkeepers and local prostitutes. In the satirist's diverting adventures a sensitive hearer could perceive an application to himself and all men, for this trip was symbolically no less than the journey through life, full of unpredictable changes, which must be faced with the same intelligent irony as shown by Lucilius' satirist.

Horace recognized the poetic merit of this theme. What he did was to compress and enrich the whole. He may give the illusion of writing a diary, but only an unobservant critic would be so obtuse as to call his poem 'a mere diary'. H. J. Musurillo has even urged a strong case for viewing the trip as a fiction. I myself tend to think that the trip probably took place, but that Horace so selectively recounted it that it has become a 'poetic fiction'. By compressing the details about mileage, terrain, and the like, Horace managed to give the full impression of a journey, without burdening the poem. He enriched the contents by making the expedition a collective trip of friends, all of them well known to his readers as prominent politicians and writers of the day. Whereas Lucilius pictured himself travelling to Sicily to attend to his estates, Horace attached his poem to an important political occasion. Maecenas has set out, accompanied by Horace, Vergil, Plotius, and Varius, to negotiate on behalf of the Triumvir Octavian with the emissaries of Antony and to make it possible for the two 'friends' to become reconciled. Momentous political events, then, are taking place, and the threat of war is very much alive; this time Antony and Octavian patched up their dispute, but the break was inevitable, destined to be settled a few years later at Actium. If a politician had recorded these events in a diary and then compiled his memoirs, we would have something like history, not a poem. The political events would have occupied the foreground, and Horace, nothing but a minor companion of the distinguished Maecenas, might have been listed as present, or again he might well have been ignored. Horace represents the episode from an entirely different perspective. The political crisis dwindles into the background, and instead the satirist and his friends, men of culture and humanity, take the front.

> postera lux oritur multo gratissima; namque
> Plotius et Varius Sinuessae Vergiliusque
> occurrunt, animae qualis neque candidiores
> terra tulit neque quis me sit devinctior alter.
> o qui complexus et gaudia quanta fuerunt!
> nil ego contulerim iucundo sanus amico. (1.5.39–44)

The next day dawns and is by far the most delightful; for Plotius, Varius, and Vergil meet us at Sinuessa. Never has the earth born more upright souls, and no man could be more bound to them than I am. O what embraces, what tremendous joy there was! While I am in my senses, I would compare nothing with the pleasure of friendship.

A slight Lucretian note pervades the poem, as if to suggest the Epicurean insight into reality, that the simple pleasures of life take precedence over blind ambition and political vanity. This satirist's ironic comments also have symbolic import. But while Lucilius' trip vaguely represented the ups and down of any life, Horace's trip dramatically faces his reader with urgent problems of the day and suggests a profound moral understanding of the relative value of politics and friends.

Lucilian *libertas* permitted the earlier poet to include within his poetry many topics which Horace, influenced by Neoteric tastes and Classical decorum, could not accept in his satire. Not only did Lucilius resort to synonyms and redundant pronouns, he also inclined towards language that would perhaps remind us of Rabelais because of its obscenity, sheer bombast, and delightful inventiveness. Lucilius regularly borrowed formidable compounds from Latin epic or created ridiculous ones of his own; and he was famous for his free use of Greek words, taken directly from Greek literature or slightly Latinized. This language fitted the exuberant genius of the poet and the tastes of his age, and it proved entirely congenial to the mask of the satirist. His racy language belonged to a man of wit, cultivated, intelligent, penetrating, but essentially more interested in displaying his cleverness than in pressing far into any moral or poetic problems.

From Horace's point of view, this exuberant satirist and his unrestrained witticisms, so manifest in his licentious language, had to be disciplined. True son of his age, which emphasized Classical ideals of balance, order, and self-restraint, Horace urged two important doctrines against Lucilius. First, the modern poet must adhere faithfully to *Latinitas*. By *Latinitas* Horace and his friends meant a good Latin style appropriate to an educated Roman citizen. Such a style would be free of provincialisms, of alien elements, of both vulgarity and preciosity. It had to fit the proprieties that had gradually been established for good Latin. Second, the poet should seek *concinnitas*. Cicero had long established the merits of *concinnitas* in rhetoric; the word includes within its meanings neat construction of a phrase or periodic sentence, harmonious balancing of ideas, elegant blending of words. Its common synonym is *elegantia*, a word that speaks for itself. Horace develops a persuasive argument in *S.* 1.10.20 ff in connexion with these two ideas, and, to do so, he uses a straw figure of an *adversarius* who praises Lucilius awkwardly and provokes crushing programmatic comments from the younger poet.

> 'at magnum fecit quod verbis Graeca Latinis
> miscuit.' o seri studiorum! quine putetis
> difficile et mirum, Rhodio quod Pitholeonti
> contigit? 'at sermo lingua concinnus utraque
> suavior, ut Chio nota si commixta Falerni est.'
> cum versus facias, te ipsum percontor, an et cum
> dura tibi peragenda rei sit causa Petilli?

Advers.—Lucilius really did a great thing when he blended Greek and Latin words.

Satirist—O what retarded standards! How in the world can you consider difficult or marvellous what comes by nature to the Rhodian Pitholeon [i.e. a foreigner]?

Advers.—But speech that is a smooth blend of each language is sweeter; it is like mixing the Falernian brand with Chian wine.

Satirist—Now I ask you, would you really hold to such an idea when you composed verse or when you had to conduct the arduous defense of Petillius in court?

By the time that he has dismissed this *adversarius*, Horace has clearly banned from his work all merely witty language, all outrageous vocabulary that suggests provincialism (such as that of a bilingual inhabitant of Southern Italy), and any Greek terms that have not long been at home in the Latin speech. Those who have amassed comparative statistics on Hellenisms in the *Sermones* have been able to demonstrate that Horace did precisely what he said he would: namely, he avoided violent borrowing of new Greek words, never constructed a Latin-Greek hybrid, and never quoted Greek at all. If, as I like to think of him, Horace modelled his satiric mask on Socrates, he definitely fitted himself into the Latin world as a *Roman* Socrates.

These three terms, *brevitas*, *Latinitas*, and *concinnitas*, have broader applications; but except for *brevitas* I have deliberately confined my attention to their immediate stylistic import, that is, to the way they direct the poet's selection of vocabulary. Now, suppose that a young Classical poet decided to adopt the Horatian criteria for satire. He would be most careful to be brief and pungent, to give the appearance of talking respectable Latin, and to have a sense of harmony. But where would he go from there? For example, what general tone or level of speech would he adopt?

The epic and tragic poets of Horace's age also accepted the three guiding rules which we have defined. Nevertheless, no writer of poetic satire would be mistaken for a tragedian or epic poet. Whereas the latter used what is called the Grand Style, the satiric poet, following the model of Lucilius, adopted the Plain or Low Style.

In general conception, the Plain Style in rhetoric and poetry aimed at an impression of conversation. I have repeatedly described the character of the Lucilian satirist as a witty dinner guest, well fed and moderately inspired by Bacchus, who delights others by his uninhibited discourse, sparkling with wit, gossip, anecdote, obscenity, political scandal, etc. Lucilius used several words to describe his poetry, but one particularly modest term which appealed to Horace was *sermo*; this means conversation. Horace does not call his poetic satires *Saturae* by way of title; instead, he calls them *Sermones*, discussions. The word *sermo*, then, defines the tone and range of Horace's satiric poems. As we shall see, the Horatian satirist does not assume the Lucilian mask, and therefore his brand of conversation differs markedly from the loose dinner remarks of his predecessor. Lucilian *libertas* yielded to Horatian and Classical *sapientia*.

While I have been using these rhetorical terms and simultaneously describing the writer of satire as a *poet*, the reader may have wondered what connexion there is. How does a conversational style become poetry? The answer to that question is not easy; it obviously bothered Horace himself. And yet unless we can answer it, we shall not really reach the true import of Horace's achievement. Anyone, with a moderate amount of effort, could summarize the Horatian moral philosophy, the Horatian attitude towards life, the Horatian outlook. Having done so, he would discover nothing especially novel. Horace is not an original thinker in his *Sermones*, and he does not pretend to be. It is so easy to parody his Golden Mean, for instance, that a teacher often finds himself embarrassed in commenting seriously upon it. The conclusion should be that, as in the case of most poetry, the heart of the poem is not the material discussed (as it would be prosaically summarized), but the way in which it is constructed and presented.

Horace plunges into a serious discussion in S. 1.4.39 ff in order to determine the place of his verse in the scale of literary forms. By associating satire with the more familiar Comedy, he is able to describe one type of verse that uses a simple conversational manner and to contrast it with the formal genres, best represented in Latin by Ennius' great epic, the *Annals*. If he were really as interested in Comedy as he affects to be, we would expect him to use the normal opposite of Comedy, that is, Tragedy. Rome boasted eminent tragedians in Ennius, Pacuvius, and Accius. But by choosing Ennius and epic poetry as his concrete antitype, Horace selects what is most precisely opposed to satire: epic is hexameter poetry on heroic topics in a noble style, satire is hexameter verse on mundane matters in a plain, everyday style. Thus, the true reason for linking satire with Comedy is probably that nobody really doubted the right of comedy to be called poetry. No sane critic would have denied that Plautus, Terence, or Caecilius were poets; he might have criticized them, but he had to treat them as poets. Similarly, while Horace seems to be asking and answering the question whether, in fact, satire and comedy can rightfully be defined as poetry, he is really endeavouring to describe the special poetic nature of the satiric style.

> primum ego me illorum dederim quibus esse poetas
> excerpam numero; neque enim concludere versum
> dixeris esse satis; neque si qui scribat uti nos
> sermoni propiora, putes hunc esse poetam.
> ingenium cui sit, cui mens divinior atque os
> magna sonaturum, des nominis huius honorem. (*S.* 1.4.39–44)

In the first place, I shall exclude myself from the number of those who I have conceded are poets; for you would not call it adequate merely to contrive a hexameter verse, nor, if anyone should write things more appropriate to everyday speech, as we do, would you consider him a poet. But if a man should possess genius, a particularly inspired mind, and a mouth able to pronounce great things, you would award this honorable name to him.

On the surface, Horace is contrasting grand poetry with his own slight genre. Taking an extreme position, he affirms that he is no 'poet', not at least in an important respect; he is not a grand poet. And for the moment he is willing to grant the title of poet only to the representatives of epic and tragedy. As if to emphasize the difference between *sermo* and epic, Horace does unorthodox things with his verse. In the first line he pushes three pronouns together with such apparent awkwardness that he has to elide *ego* and *me* and distort good prose and indeed poetic word-order. An elision of a monosyllable (*me*) reminds one of comedy and Lucilius; a collection of redundant pronouns was, we said, generally avoided by Horace, but typical of Lucilius. Horace also, for no good reason, reverses the order of *dederim* and *quibus*, and the consequent lack of elegance almost proves the sheer poetic incompetence of this *sermo*.

Now, looked at from a different side, these lines exhibit the special poetic possibilities of satire. Although the writer deals with a subtle argument, he explains his thoughts in simple language. Certain effects, like the personal pronouns, suggest the relaxed manner of conversation; yet at the same time they serve to emphasize the argument. By eliding both *ego* and *me*, Horace obliges us to feel the effacement of the lesser versifier by those august poets (*illorum*). Although he reverses the order of verb and relative pronoun and regularly removes verbs from their predictable prose position, Horace makes sure that important words are assigned to the key structual points of the hexameter. At the beginning of the line, the caesura, and the end of the line, he places words that count. Lucilius did not write like this, and this passage, like so many Horatian passages, reveals how a talented poet can conduct a reasonable argument and get the most out of his verse. Thus, we might say that Horace here proves how different *sermo* is from epic, but he also subtly shows that his own *sermo*, because it does so much more than imitate conversation, deserves the title of poetry.

As I said, Lucilius did not write like this. Thus, the brevity and clarity of the Horatian discussion acts as a commentary on the 'muddy' Lucilian manner. The implication of the passage seems to be that neither the interlocutor nor the poet would be content with such minimal achievements as contriving a verse and copying everyday speech, but that Lucilius was. The phrase *concludere versum* is pejorative in this context. Literally it means to enclose, confine, finish off a verse; but Horace alludes to the struggle which a mediocre versifier has in finding six metrical feet for the hexameter. I have already cited a passage, *S.* 1.10.59–61 (cf. p. 5), in which Horace turns this apparently general criticism precisely against Lucilius: Lucilius was a facile poet who was content to enclose anything within the six feet of the hexameter. Knowing what Horace does later, I think we can understand what he is more subtly doing here: while affecting to depreciate all satiric poets, he alludes pointedly to the man whom many contemporaries honoured as *Lucilius poeta*.

Lucilius, we are told by Horace, did regard it as a great thing that he could dash off two hundred hexameters on the spur of the moment. If any verse at all makes a poet, then Lucilius was a poet. But if a poet must be a craftsman, acting with insight and understanding, toiling and rewriting to get exactly the right touch, then Lucilius was no poet. Horace puts it another way a few lines later in *S.* 1.4. If you should take away the rhythm and meter and adjust the word-order slightly, Lucilius' verse would not retain a vestige of poetic quality; on the other hand, if you tried the same test on Ennius' *Annals*, you would still discover the elements of poetry in the disjointed fragments: *disiecti membra poetae* (62). In other words, Lucilius' verse was so intrinsically prosaic that, without the hexameter and its slightly distorted word-order, it possessed none of the virtues which Horace demanded in poetry. It is true that Horace includes himself together with Lucilius in this class of prosaic versifiers, but that is merely irony. His own verse belies him; he is master both of word-order and the hexameter.

The *Art of Poetry* contains a famous passage which we may confidently call one of the guiding principles of Horatian poetry:

> in verbis etiam tenuis cautusque serendis
> dixeris egregie, notum si callida verbum
> reddiderit iunctura novum. (46–48)

Again, modest and careful in sowing your words, you will have spoken better than most if a clever arrangement has made a familiar word new.

Everywhere in the *Sermones* an observant reader will find a *callida iunctura*, evidence that the poet has subjected his genius to rational scrutiny and made his words count. The word-order accomplishes much, and chiefly it contributes to the purposes of proper emphasis, ironic commentary, and economy. If one thinks of all the phrases which we owe to Horace, it is easy to see that their success depends on the fact that Horace chose the right words and placed them in the right order, with an inimitable skill; thus, *disiecti membra poetae* in *S.* 1.4. It simply is not true that Horatian Satires could be converted into prose without damage; my own reasonably exact translations should amply prove that.

The intellect which has limited the range of vocabulary, which strives for brief, precise statement of ideas, captures these ideas in the most lucid, reasonable, and artful style ever achieved in Roman satire. This ability to write such modest and yet so novel phrases was described by Petronius in the memorable words *curiosa felicitas*: he meant what we all soon observe, that Horace's signal felicity of expression depends upon the care which the poet used in selecting and arranging ordinary words.

Lucilius was no contemptible metrician. Before he chose the hexameter, he mastered the difficulties of two other meters, experimented with them as vehicles for his poetry, and discarded them. He knew exactly what he was doing in adopting the hexameter, and Horace's decision to follow in Lucilius' footsteps proves the value of the hexameter. Nevertheless, since the time of Lucilius, many poets had worked with that meter, and innovations and improvements made Lucilian verse seem heavy, crude, and slipshod. I shall not elaborate the details of Horace's changes; I merely wish to call attention to a few facts. Horace increases the dactylic quality of the line in accordance with contemporary tastes. He cuts down elisions, in particular elision of monosyllables. Above all, he gives the verse greater flexibility and movement by the dexterity with which he manipulates the caesurae and enjambement. Whereas much of Lucilian verse was end-stopped, Horatian conversation keeps on from one line into another, and the reader is drawn ever on into the discussion.

In conclusion, from these details, I would like the reader to gain an impression of a thoughtful conversational style. While Horace chose to caricature Lucilius by *libertas* (in a pejorative sense), he meant us to picture himself in an entirely different light. Irresponsibility and lack of artistic discipline marred Lucilian verse; total artistic discipline makes the Horatian style the monument of Classical poetry that it is. Yet I do not want to imply that the style should be viewed and savoured by itself. Horace criticizes Lucilius' irresponsibility in general, and Lucilius' talkativeness and refusal to work on his language and verse are merely symptoms of a general failure, in Horace's judgement. By the same token, the reasoned style of Horace, with its conversational basis, should serve to give us an impression of an un-Lucilian satirist, one whose reasoned conversation seeks not the immediate advantages of *libertas*, but the more permanent goal of *sapientia*.

This Socratic satirist will be the subject of consideration in the next section.

II. *The Socratic Moralist: Book I*

I have been talking so far about Horace's stylistic doctrines. I do *not* want to discuss Horace's moral theories or Horace as a moralist. My reason is quite simple: we do not know enough about Horace the moralist. There are details in the *Sermones* which biographical scholars have long taken as facts, but which a sceptic might legitimately question, and which in any case have been inserted to produce a certain impression for the immediate context. Musurillo has shown the logical inconsistencies in *S.* 1.5, and he doubts that Horace ever went on a diplomatic mission to Brundisium. The portrait of Horace's father, a composite of loving tributes in *S.* 1.4 and 6, raises difficulties. In the first place, Horace seems to be imitating Bion, a Greek forebear in diatribe. Secondly, Horace stresses the frugal simplicity of his father in such a way that one has difficulty in perceiving that, in fact, the elder Horace had a comfortable income. Again, the exceptional emphasis on the father has caused some people to wonder why Horace never once mentioned his mother. Not only does the portrait of the speaker acquire useful colour from these details, but Horace also makes sure that distracting facts do not mar or blur the picture. For example, we know from other sources that Horace studied a year or two in Athens, an opportunity enjoyed by only the most favoured young Romans. Yet he allows no such fact to enter the *Sermones*, for it might hurt the character of the commonsense moralist which is presented. After those few years of university education, Horace followed Brutus during the Civil Wars of 43–42 B.C., commanded a legion as a tribune, and fought at Philippi against the victorious forces of Antony and Octavian. Fifteen years later, in the Ode to Pompeius, he was able to look back on that battle and his flight with ironic amusement; at the time that he was writing his *Sermones* he could not discuss his recent political convictions. Therefore, his speaker affects complete lack of interest in politics.

It is important that we grasp this central feature of Horatian and all Roman satire: the speaker makes his criticism in the first person, and he presents himself as the poet, whether it be Lucilius, Horace, or Juvenal. In fact, this speaker is not fully identical with

28

the poet, no more than the impassioned lover is entirely identical with the poet of elegy or lyric. In all personal poetry, the poet assumes a mask, plays a part, and the role he takes may or may not be very close to traits in his own personality. What we should demand of the speaker is dramatic consistency; it is quite indifferent how far he copies the poet's career and feelings, but it is absolutely essential that he should remain in character. When a few years later Horace composed his Odes, he felt enterprising enough to assume several quite different masks in different poems: in one he is the inspired bard, in another the wistful, ageing lover, in still another the moralistic preacher of intelligent enjoyment, again the fiery patriot, the religious devotee, or the warm-hearted friend. There are enough Odes so that these various characters or masks all become familiar after a while. We know that Horace published the nearly ninety poems of Books I–III in a group. On the other hand, when he wrote the longer Satires, he did not want any one of the ten poems in Book I to appear strikingly out of character with the others. Accordingly, although he was in his late twenties at the time of writing, although he certainly had suffered in the social, political, and economic crisis of the Civil Wars, and despite the fact that at that youthful age he must have sought much feminine consolation, nevertheless, he strikes us as a considerably older man, possessing the wisdom of experience, serenely above the materialistic pursuits of his fellow men, capable of a self-irony which only the profoundest self-restraint and self-analysis will permit. How much effort must have gone into the creation of that character by a young man not quite thirty, I leave to the reader's imagination. The main point is that Horace produced a Socratic satirist probably quite unrepresentative of himself; and this satirist, the speaker in his *Sermones*, is one of the greatest achievements of Horatian poetry.

I shall hereafter use the words 'the satirist' to refer to the speaker in the Satires, as distinguished from his dramatic creator, the satiric poet. In my usage, 'the satirist' will never be the real Horace, and 'the satirist's' words, ideas, and behaviour will never be assumed to be identical with those of Horace.

Horace did not invent this method of speaking through a mask in satiric poetry. As a little reflection should indicate, the satirist speaking in the first person is merely an extension of dramatic and rhetorical practices long known, according to which any actor or orator must assume the character appropriate to his speech. Rome produced the first elaborate personal poetry, and the first significant writer of personal poetry was Lucilius himself. Thus, Lucilius was the first to grapple with the problems of the mask in satire, and he showed the way to later poets in both elegy and satire. We have already discussed some of the more important aspects of Lucilius' satirist, particularly as they affected his style. All through the first century, during the time when Horace was acquiring his poetic tastes, his teachers and his fellow poets summarized the satirist in the single word *libertas*. While these critics felt no apparent need to distinguish Lucilius from his satirist, they did mentally draw the distinction. Varro used as a synonym for the licentious manner a significant phrase, *Lucilianus character*. The Latin *character*, based on the similar Greek word, does not yet possess all the connotations of our 'character', and I do not therefore mean that Varro's phrase precisely describes the *dramatic* role of the satirist. However, Varro did feel that Lucilius had stamped a certain personality upon his Satires and that that personality could be abstracted and discussed without reference to Lucilius' biography.

Today, we owe most of our impressions of Lucilius and his satirist to Horace. If we fail to differentiate Lucilius from his satirist, it is largely because Horace's polemic deliberately confuses the two. When, for example, Horace talks of Lucilius as garrulous or describes him writing two hundred verses on one foot or after a banquet, he is borrowing details from the Satires, spoken by or about the satirist, details which, in my opinion, are not fully applicable to Lucilius. One of the most sympathetic descriptions which Horace ever produces of Lucilius implicitly criticized the poet by confusing him with his satirist:

> me pedibus delectat claudere verba
> Lucili ritu, nostrum melioris utroque.
> ille velut fidis arcana sodalibus olim
> credebat libris, neque si male cesserat usquam
> decurrens alio, neque si bene; quo fit, ut omnis
> votiva pateat veluti descripta tabella
> vita senis. sequor hunc. (*S.* 2.1.28–34)

As for me, I take pleasure in (metrically) enclosing words according to the manner of Lucilius, the superior of us both. He once entrusted his secrets to his books as if to trustworthy companions, never running

30

off anywhere whether things had gone badly or well; as a result, the whole existence of the old man lies open like a painted votive tablet. I follow in his footsteps.

While on the surface this appears to be a generous tribute to the first satiric poet, especially with its admission that Lucilius was 'better' than Horace or his companion Trebatius, below the surface runs the same series of charges against the slipshod and undisciplined Lucilius that Horace explicitly makes in Book I of the *Sermones*. Now, however, Horace does not use such pejorative adjectives as *garrulus, lutulentus, incompositus*; instead, he lets the criticism emerge from the description itself. Most of us have written diaries at some stage in our careers, in our youth when going through the throes of juvenile love or possibly during a trip to strange lands. We would be ashamed to let others, even our closest friends, peruse our indiscreet comments, because half the attraction of a diary lies in its permissiveness. We *can* indulge ourselves without fear of reproval so long as the diary remains secret. Now, Lucilius' satirist may have abused *libertas* to the point of indiscretion, but it does not necessarily follow that Lucilius himself was totally involved. Nor is it likely that Lucilius would publish all the facts about his own failures and evil intentions— we all have them—as Horace asserts. The satirist produced this impression of total revelation upon the reader, but Lucilius planned it that way. Therefore, when Horace compares the effect of Lucilius' Satires to that of a painted votive tablet, we may well wonder how far we should pursue the hints in the simile.

I vividly remember a visit I made about ten years ago to a little church in Marseilles. Inside it, covering the walls around the altar were the modern counterparts of the Roman votive tablets. I saw pictures of ships sinking (the most common topic of the Roman votary), trains bearing menacingly down upon tiny automobiles, of children about to race in front of speeding cars, all in garish colours and grotesquely dramatic gestures which testified to the anguish of the moment from which the Virgin had rescued the pious. This is art at the lowest level. The simple believer has no money to pay for a beautiful painting and usually lacks the taste or understanding even to wish for anything else. In that respect, Horace implies the inartistic picture produced by Lucilius. But it was also patently clear to Horace and his readers, who could visit shrines littered with wretched religious art or who saw sailors on the street begging with the help of a melo-dramatic painting of a shipwreck, that the votive tablet did *not* correspond to reality. It was a poor version of life, distorted by the incompetence of the artist and by his desire to concentrate all attention upon a lurid, no doubt overemphasized tragedy. Now, ancient critics had long since compared painting and poetry; Horace uses this comparison as a prominent theme of his *Art of Poetry*, indeed grasps the whole topic in his excellent phrase: *ut pictura poesis*. Poetry is like painting, and poets should endeavour to resemble superior painters. Good painters, as Horace knew, reflected long on the way they would compose their picture and what colours they would use. Similarly, he required of a poet discretion and judgement, an ability to select and suppress, to hint at facts briefly. The more the poet reflected, it seemed, the better would be his rendering of the meaning of life. Thus, the votive tablet representing Lucilius' poetry indicates first of all the inartistry of that poet, but it also introduces the criterion by which the satiric poet must be judged. He should be an artist and, like a painter, depict an intelligible and coherent portrait, not a luridly incompetent adventure.

The prevailing impression which, through Horace, we gain of Lucilius is that of an excellent dinner companion. The great Scipio Aemilianus and Laelius valued Lucilius' company, we are told (*S.* 2.1.70 ff), and enjoyed gossiping and idly jesting with him on the occasion of a banquet:

>   atqui
> primores populi arripuit populumque tributim,
> scilicet uni aequus virtuti atque eius amicis.
> quin ubi se a vulgo et scaena in secreta remorant
> virtus Scipiadae et mitis sapientia Laeli,
> nugari cum illo et discincti ludere donec
> decoqueretur holus soliti. (*S.* 2.1.68–74)

And yet Lucilius ripped away at the most important men and at the people, tribe by tribe, of course fair to virtue alone and to virtue's friends. However, when virtuous Scipio and gentle, wise Laelius had retired from the mob and the public stage, they would regularly sport with him and uninhibitedly play until the cabbage was cooked.

Those damning two hundred verses always appear, in Horace's polemic, in the context of a *cena*; and when Horace alludes to Lucilian wit, he usually manages to imply that this wit was stimulated by wine. I infer from the near-uniformity of setting in which Horace conducts his polemic that Lucilius' satirist must have been typically presented either in a banquet scene or talking in a manner that was consistent with the *libertas* of the dinner table.

The virtues of such a satirist are relatively obvious: he seems friendly, amusing, frank, and confiding; he can talk seriously or lightly, but you yourself do not have to take him too seriously. Both Lucilius and Horace frequently employ the verb *ludere* and the noun *ludus* to define their methods, and we can profitably describe Lucilius' satirist as *lusor*, a playful individual. Horace treated the Lucilian satirist's virtues as negligible, or almost so, because in his opinion they were heavily outweighed by defects, all implicit in those words *lusor* and *libertas*. Balancing the slipshod style which Horace detected was a slipshod morality. At first reading, we might feel admiration for a satirist who never ran off to avoid describing both his good and evil (cf. the passage just cited). Second thoughts should suggest another interpretation. Take the verb *decurrens*: it can describe a person running, but it can also be used for a torrent running down a slope from the summit. Since Horace often uses the metaphor of the raging, muddy, uncontrolled torrent for Lucilius, this verb implies a typical Lucilian defect. He should have halted himself and not flowed on in the same heedless course regardless of content. For in Horace's opinion the satirist's *libertas* led him to impolitic and unethical comments.

Many people in Horace's youth reduced Lucilian *libertas* to mere invective. They recalled how the satirist had assailed a prominent triad of the late second century: Rutilius Lupus, Mucius Scaevola, and Metellus Macedonicus. I think it safe to say that Lucilius' satirist produced artistic and skilful political propaganda, but it also seems likely that it did impress readers as propaganda, written from the partisan perspective of the Scipionic Circle. That Horace disapproves of such attacks is more than obvious: he implies that the Lucilian satirist was half drunk when he assailed people. Sometimes, Lucilius' satirist took a more general position and attempted to reveal the contemptible and ridiculous behaviour of less distinguished people such as misers and spendthrifts (especially in the perspective of meals that they served) or foolish lovers. Having this intention, the satirist contented himself with a selection of pejorative details and epithets;

one of the most common adjectives in the surviving fragments is *improbus*, 'vicious', used as a label without adequate explanation. Again and again, the satirist branded a man of whom he disapproved as *improbus*, and the reader gains the impression that the attack on, and the exposure of, certain people entirely answered the satirist's purposes. For Horace, such a limited goal seemed merely one more defect of Lucilian *libertas*: the satirist of Horace, therefore, would not rest happy if he provoked laughter at the expense of some bitter victim. Finally, as *lusor*, the Lucilian satirist took a prominent, often dominant, part in certain amatory episodes. He was entirely in character when he described his attachment to Hymnis or Collyra and even when he adopted the role of *praeceptor amoris* and presumed to advise young lovers. However, Horace's satirist takes a more serious attitude towards life, and he refuses, except in *S.* 1.2, to entertain erotic ideas.

If one seeks a reasonably clear statement of the attitude of Horace's satirist, one does not have to read far in the opening Satire of Book I. Just after he has described the basic condition of human dissatisfaction, the satirist makes his transition as follows:

> praeterea ne sic, ut qui iocularia, ridens
> percurram—quamquam ridentem dicere verum
> quid vetat? ut pueris olim dant crustula blandi
> doctores, elementa velint ut discere prima;
> sed tamen amoto quaeramus seria ludo—
> ille gravem duro terram qui vertit aratro . . . (*S.* 1.1.23–8)

Furthermore, not to run over these matters laughingly, like a man running through his jests—although what prevents a man who laughs from telling the truth? Just as sometimes teachers give cookies to their young pupils as a bribe so that they will be willing to learn the alphabet; however, let us put aside our playing and seek the serious—that man who turns up the heavy earth with his hard plough . . .

Prepared as we are, we can read these lines with something like the background of the Roman audience and recognize the allusions to Lucilius. Horace's satirist discards *iocularia* and mere *ludus* as inadequate to his purpose, for he really begins his satiric development where the Lucilian satirist presumably left off. He intends to be serious, that is, morally serious. No doubt many people have heard that Horatian phrase *ridentem dicere verum* and thought of it as a summary of Horace's satirist. So long as we know the context in which the phrase originally appeared, we can use those words to summarize the satirist. However, if we should interpret those words apart from their context, we might be tempted to think that the laugh with which the satirist told the truth was a sardonic one, or we might guess that the 'truth' seen by the satirist was a partial, if not distorted, one. Then, the Horatian satirist would be no better than the Lucilian. But because we do have this context, we know that the Horatian satirist smilingly told a *serious moral* truth. Here is the principal distinction between the Lucilian and the Horatian manner: while the former is essentially *lusor*, the Horatian satirist is *doctor*. He is a teacher instructing puerile mankind in serious elementary moral truths, but willing to coax us by his laughing, ironic manner in order to impress his truths more effectively in our hearts.

Horace sets about depicting his satirist with the artistic skill that he apparently missed in Lucilius. Even in his arrangement of the poems in Book I, he tries to give a general impression of the satirist before letting the satirist speak about himself. The first three poems have the form of diatribes: the satirist discusses with an *adversarius* his conviction that avarice lies at the root of human dissatisfaction (*S.* 1.1), that our diverse sexual behaviour can be taken as the symbol of our moral self-punishment in general (*S.* 1.2), that self-indulgence and hypocrisy towards others undermine friendship (*S.* 1.3). Now, the diatribe had been created and much used by Greek popular philosophers, especially the Cynics and the Stoics, in the third century B.C. and thereafter. But it owed its origin to Socrates and the Socratic writers whom I cited at the beginning of this essay. In fact, as scholars have pointed out, diatribe is an approximate Greek equivalent of the Latin *sermo*, the title which Horace uses for his Satires. The Cynics and Stoics often took an overly righteous attitude and seemed to enjoy condemning the public in the harshest terms; we are familiar today with that method in the sermons of some revivalists, and Horace himself briefly describes, with ironic good humour, an arrogant Cynic at the end of *S.* 1.3. It becomes clear, however, that this satirist goes back beyond Lucilius and the Cynic-Stoics to Socrates himself for his model. He does not denounce; he does not unfairly ridicule; he does not triumph rhetorically over vice; he does not ignore his own failings. Like Socrates, he uses the disarming technique of discussion to force people to re-examine their consciences and to achieve a more rational attitude towards fundamental ethical problems.

Lucilius had devoted several poems to avarice and to amatory interests, and friendship served him as a constant sub-theme. Content to label the miser or lover as *improbus* and laughable, the Lucilian satirist made no explicit effort to instruct or to broaden his moral insights beyond the immediate problem. Therefore, to some readers, especially to those whom the satirist had picked out by name for ridicule, it seemed that Lucilian verse was *maledicus*, malicious and slanderous. Anyone reading Horace's first three poems would immediately catch the difference. This new satirist rarely fixes on a living person as an example, and never with animosity. He treats avarice carefully, trying to get at its basic implications. Then, he expands his argument and shows how avarice lies at the bottom of human unhappiness. Similarly, sex, which had been a playfully sensational topic in Lucilius, becomes in this satirist's hands a serious Epicurean problem bearing upon Man's predicament in life: he seeks *voluptas*, pleasure, irrationally and so inevitably incurs *dolor*, pain. Thus, the first three poems reveal a satirist who makes ethical inquiries into large, important human problems, discusses them calmly—with irony and not bluff ridicule—and makes them lead towards rational insights into ourselves and the moral order supporting the universe.

After these first three poems, in which we meet the satirist playing the role of the *doctor*, the Socratic inquirer using ordinary conversation to compel men to think about vital ethical questions, Horace placed three poems in which the satirist talks about himself and his personal convictions. *S.* 1.4, as we have seen, argues the new theory of *libertas*, responsible freedom and disciplined poetry. It ends with an appealing account of the satirist's father, who instructed the satirist in the use of moral examples and thus moulded his highly ethical use of specific people as illustrations. We have also seen how *S.* 1.5 provides the satirist an opportunity to contrast the meretricious goals of political ambition with the values of friendship and humane enjoyment. This attitude towards politics is explicitly proclaimed in *S.* 1.6: the satirist frankly admits his humble parentage—he is the son of a freed slave—and willingly relinquishes any right to engage in politics. Far more important to him are the friendship of Maecenas, the memory of an honest father, and the liberty of a disengaged life:

haec est

vita solutorum misera ambitione gravique;
his me consolor victurum suavius ac si
quaestor avus pater atque meus patruusque fuissent. (*S.* 1.6.128–31)

This is the life of men released from the wretched and heavy burden
of ambition. With such occupations I console myself, for I shall live
more pleasantly than if my grandfather, father, and uncle had all been
quaestors [i.e. attained political office whereby they automatically
became Senators].

S. 1.7 and 8 exhibit considerable wit, but the personality of the
satirist gains little from them. In *S.* 1.7, an anecdote of the Civil
War era is cleverly rendered; in *S.* 1.8, Priapus takes the place
of the satirist and gives a diverting tale of witches and how he
frightened them out of their senses. With the final two poems of
Book I, Horace takes up again the important themes of earlier
poems. As he was walking down the Sacred Way, recounts the
satirist in *S.* 1.9, a man came up to him and dogged his steps,
trying every method imaginable of gaining the satirist's favour
so as to secure an introduction to Maecenas, until fortuitously
another person appeared and snatched the first off to a law court
on some charge. In the encounter between satirist and the aggressive individual, Horace dramatizes the conflict between the prevalent view of political goals (and of Maecenas' friends) and the
satirist's genuine desire to devote himself to his friends and
poetry. *S.* 1.10 reverts to the polemic of 1.4; its criticism of
Lucilius is more specific, and the satirist now invokes the literary
authority of Maecenas and his circle to guarantee his poetic merits.
As far as the satirist is concerned, the moral issues of *libertas*
received ample comment in the other nine poems, and he devotes
this final poem to an explicit defence of the status of satire, particularly Horatian satire, as poetry.

When a Roman thought about Socrates, he instinctively
thought of intelligent conversation on moral topics; then, he
might recall that Socrates surrounded himself with talented
friends, both literary men and politicians; or he might remember
stories about the utter simplicity and healthful nature of Socrates'
life. To this extent, the Horatian satirist feels completely in character. However, if the satirist had lacked another primary trait of
the famous Athenian, none of his other qualities would have
helped him in the least. That essential trait of Socratic discourse,

irony, is likewise an essential feature of Horatian discourse, and this guarantees his Socratic character.

The Romans valued irony, for they recognized how difficult it is to achieve the finest type of irony. Some scholars believe that Lucilius intended to achieve an ironic tone, and here and there some of his Satires do in fact lend themselves to such an interpretation. However, all too often the Lucilian satirist let his *libertas* proceed too far, and consequently his laughter became sardonic and mordant or mere jesting. Irony is intellectual; it smiles and avoids uproarious laughter. It uses humour where the tragedian uses pathos, to expose human failures, but always with a tinge of optimism. If we can understand the workings of such faults as political ambition, avarice, or sexual indulgence, and if we can be amused at the folly of those who do plunge into such faults, possibly we ourselves will be able to exercise our reason and so avoid similar error. For in the end all irony fails unless it ultimately is directed at oneself. Once we have understood ourselves and laughed or at least smiled at our mistakes, then we are entitled to express our amusement at others' mistakes. Our awareness of our own fallibility will make us more indulgent of others, less interested in the useless sport of exposing them to merciless ridicule.

We noted that the Horatian satirist rejected from the outset mere jests and foolery (*iocularia, ludus*) and yet approved of telling truth with a laugh: *ridentem dicere verum*. It takes little effort to perceive that this famous phrase summarizes the methods of Socratic irony. If we watch the irony at work in *S.* 1.1 or in the two other diatribes, we note how gently the satirist treats his *adversarius*. When the miser claims as his model the provident ant (1.1.33), the satirist does not sneer at his hypocrisy, as we might. Instead, he cleverly elaborates the points of difference between miser and ant and implies what may be the truth, that the miser is not so much hypocritical as unable to understand himself and his genuine motives. Thanks to this irony, the satirist really probes the truth, really enables us to understand the self-deception of the miser. When in *S.* 1.2 the satirist turns his attention to the mentality of the amorous male, he again shows us ironically that the real cause of our sexual difficulties resides not in our sexual instincts, but rather in our inability to subject them to rational inspection and control. The silly lover, for example, who thinks of love as a game and takes pleasure only in the pursuit of reluctant females (103 ff) stirs our amusement and helps us to see how irrational most sensual indulgence can be.

> 'leporem venator ut alta
> in nive sectetur, positum sic tangere nolit'
> cantat, et apponit 'meus est amor huic similis; nam
> transvolat in medio posita et fugientia captat.'
> hiscine versiculis speras tibi posse dolores
> atque aestus curasque gravis e pectore pelli? (1.2.105–10)

Lover (lyrically)—The hunter pursues the hare through deep snow, but refuses to touch the animal if within reach. My love is like that: for it flits past the available females and seeks to capture those who flee.

Satirist—And with trivial verse like that you hope that your pains and passions and your heavy lover's anguish can be driven from your heart?

To put it simply, Horatian irony is constructive, humane.

While the first three poems do use some self-irony, we can gain a clearer impression of its value by studying such 'personal' poems as 1.4, 5, 6, or 9. When in *S.* 1.5 the satirist concentrates on the sheerly mundane problems and pleasures of the trip to Brundisium and utterly ignores the momentous political discussions which occasioned the expedition, he is a master of irony. At first, we might take him for a man of no imagination, as we listen to his comments on poor food, eye trouble, a faithless prostitute, and the like. But gradually we see that such mundane crises and equally ordinary pleasures do make up the important part of human experience. The satirist's ability to look back upon this wearisome journey with pleasure and amusement reveals him as one who practices the Socratic virtues in his own existence.

In *S.* 1.6 the self-irony focuses on the satirist's admission that he is the son of a former emancipated slave. Another man would have regarded such an admission as a confession of weakness, and the satirist permits us to believe for a while that he, too, has been humbled. However, before the poem has ended, he boasts of his father and ironically proves that his simple, non-political form of life releases him from all sorts of miseries so that he can enjoy what really counts, namely, books, poetry, mild exercise, and friends. In other words, what the foolish regard as a grave disability, obscure birth, turns out to be the source of great moral strength. *S.* 1.9, like 1.5, lets the satirist recount an experience real or imaginary and, by his ironic reflections, reveal to us how a man with proper ethical standards should behave. Part of the irony depends upon a mock-epic vein that runs cleverly through the poem: the satirist suggests that his encounter with the political opportunist was a duel between two epic heroes. Unwilling to fight this opponent, the satirist wittily dramatizes his aversion to political engagements. On another level, the satirist shows himself too kind and sensitive to this insensitive man's feelings, and consequently he never says the one thing that would free him of his tormentor: a brutally frank 'Go away!' Again, he describes how his companion tries to ingratiate himself by boasting of an ability to write more verses faster than any Roman alive!

> 'si bene me novi non Viscum pluris amicum,
> non Varium facies: nam quis me scribere pluris
> aut citius possit versus? quis membra movere
> mollius? invideat quod et Hermogenes ego canto.' (1.9.22–25)

If I know myself well, you will not put a higher value on the friendship of Viscus or Varius. For who could write more verses and more quickly than I? Who could dance more delicately? Why, I can sing what even Hermogenes would envy.

What more ironic way could there be to appeal to the meticulous satirist, who weighs every word, toils over each verse, and constantly compresses his poetry into the narrowest effective scope?

The ironic manner, then, is the crucial means of instruction used by this Socratic satirist. Whether he assumes the role of *doctor* in the three diatribes or practises his own teaching in the later poems, he does constitute a positive model of behaviour which we can oppose to the series of deluded individuals who embrace some error to their ultimate sorrow. Essentially, he shows the contentedness available to a man who conducts his affairs by reason. Since the truth which he perceives is a complex one, he does not proclaim himself the saviour of mankind, nor does he sneer at others less intelligent than himself. Reason is the common possession of all men. If other men will utilize this special power, then they, too, can escape the materialistic and sensual commitments that have marred their lives. Hope exists for all men, provided that they use their understanding and look deeply into themselves as the satirist has done.

Book I of the *Sermones* marks a crucial stage in the development of Roman satire and of Horatian poetry. After studying Lucilius' very successful Satires, Horace decided on a thorough renovation. I assume that his primary interest was a poetic one. He set about to reform the style of satire, its tone, manner, and material. In opposition to Lucilian *libertas* he introduced Socratic *sapientia*. Such Socratic understanding demanded complete disciplining of vocabulary, exact choice of words, a delicate touch in word-order, and improvement of the metre; but the final product was what I call a Socratic style: an intelligent use of all the poetic materials available to the writer of verse satire in order to create an intellectual poetry. Yet this style did not exist by and for itself. Horace fully integrated it with his material, so that it is quite impossible to say that the contents followed on the style; the two go hand in hand. Thus, the intellectual style enables Horace to create his intellectual satirist, a modest and genial teacher (*doctor*), who shuns the cruder methods of Lucilius' playful and superficial satirist (*lusor*). As he serenely converses with misers, lovers, or Stoics in the early diatribes, or as he recounts his own convictions, based upon personal experience, this satirist makes it his business to tell the truth with a smile. If we grasp the import of that ironic truth, then we can achieve a balanced existence also. For this satirist is one of the clearest exponents of the Classical ideals which would become so dear to the Augustan Age. Thus Horace the poet forged a new style in Book I of the *Sermones* and created an entirely new satirist, a poetic achievement which forever dimmed the fame of Lucilius.

III. *Book II and the* Doctor Ineptus

Shortly after the Battle of Actium, apparently in 30 B.C., Horace published a second book of *Sermones*. These eight poems strike the reader as a further development away from the course set by Lucilius, and scholars today do not agree on the merits of this development. Some, like Fraenkel, argue that Horace went too far and so lost some essential virtues of satire; others feel that this second book reaches a poetic height that entirely justifies all its innovations. Fraenkel has shown how skilfully Horace borrowed from Plato in certain poems, and I wish to pursue the path which Fraenkel has indicated. In my opinion, the poetic genius of this book lies in its Platonic features.

It does not take one long to realize that the methods of conversation in Book II differ radically from those in Book I. We became accustomed to listening to the satirist in Book I, whether he argued serenely with some fictitious *adversarius* or recounted his experiences or stated his convictions about satiric poetry. The word *sermo*, as I showed, refers to conversation and can be regarded as in part equivalent to the Greek word *diatribe*. However, when Horace wrote Book I, he chose to let the satirist dominate the stage, and so, even where discussion takes place, the *adversarius* has no opportunity to elaborate his ideas and is confuted with ease by the didactic satirist. Opening Book II, we find ourselves in a strange world. The satirist lets himself be crowded off the stage by various fools who proclaim their warped ideas on various subjects, while the poor satirist meekly listens to them, uttering no criticism, often himself the target of misplaced ethical attack. It is as if we have plunged into a convincingly dramatic atmosphere, where the truth is no longer told, but is implied and awaits our investigation. The satirist's eminently intelligent discussion has yielded to a vividly erroneous discussion by someone other than the satirist; *sermo* has acquired a new sense.

The Socratic writings referred to in the *Art of Poetry* include the works of Xenophon and Plato which employed Socrates as a main character of dramatic dialogue. Xenophon admired Socrates as a teacher and attributed to him a didactic strain that may have been more Xenophontic than Socratic; his Socrates, at any rate, controls discussion and positively instructs all and sundry. I would suggest that the Socratic satirist in Book I bears a close resemblance to Xenophon's Socrates. Plato, who was both philosopher and dramatic poet, caught the spirit of Socrates differently. He typically wrote dialogues in which Socrates would be represented as ironically seeking instruction from someone else, asking questions which seemed easy but often led the other speaker to statements of manifest absurdity. Such dialogues frequently end without drawing any specific conclusion; Socrates does not state the philosophic truth, and we are left to resolve the problem with our own understanding, on the basis of what has been said. As I read the artful dramatic dialogues of Horace's Book II, it seems to me that I am expected to do precisely what Plato asks of his readers, to criticize the foolish speaker with my own rational faculties and thus to reach a clearer comprehension of the moral truth than the speaker possesses. Plato has found a successor who is at least worthy of him in poetic capacity.

The first four poems of Book II illustrate progressive stages of the Platonic development. In *S.* 2.1, because he feels troubled by hostile reactions to his work, the satirist consults his friend Trebatius as to what should be done. Trebatius gives various bits of solemn advice, but finally agrees that writing moderate satire may be a permissible occupation. Now, while I have summarized the general argument of the poem, I have not given an adequate impression of the dramatic dialogue. To understand the full import of the discussion it is necessary to grasp the character of Trebatius as here portrayed. Trebatius enjoyed the reputation of a prominent lawyer and friend of Caesar (soon to be hailed as Augustus). When consulted, therefore, he immediately assumes the habits of an attorney and gives serious legal advice to this satirist-client of his. Since Trebatius starts from the basic assumption that satire is a trashy, dangerous, and illegal type of poetry, the satirist really fails to communicate with him at all. On the one hand, Trebatius urgently prescribes behaviour that will avoid trouble with the Law; on the other hand, the satirist describes his understanding of the 'laws' of satire and how he endeavours to write good poetry within the bounds set by these 'laws'.

> 'sed tamen ut monitus caveas, ne forte negoti
> incutiat tibi quid sanctarum inscitia legum:
> si mala condiderit in quem quis carmina, ius est
> iudiciumque.' esto, si quis mala; sed bona si quis
> iudice condiderit laudatus Caesare? (2.1.80–84)

Trebatius—Nevertheless, be warned and see to it that you don't get into trouble through ignorance of the ordained laws, to wit: 'If anyone composes evil CARMINA against another, he is subject to trial and judgment.'

Satirist—All right, *if* they are evil. But suppose someone composed good CARMINA and was praised by Caesar the judge? [Trebatius' evil CARMINA are malicious incantations; the satirist's good CARMINA are poems of high quality.]

Against the background of the legalistic Trebatius' obtuse remarks, the satirist's confident grasp of his genre wins our smiling respect.

While in *S.* 2.1 the satirist does not attack Trebatius' statements, nevertheless he does implicitly render Trebatius somewhat ridiculous. In *S.* 2.2, the advice comes from a character who does not differ entirely from the satirist; in fact, the satirist affects to repeat the doctrines of Ofellus, a man whom he respects. The early comments of the satirist, in which he disclaims personal responsibility for the doctrine, probably can be traced back to Plato's *Symposium*:

> nec meus hic sermo est, sed quae praecepit Ofellus
> rusticus, abnormis sapiens crassaque Minerva. (2.2.2–3)

And this is not my own discourse, but the precepts of Ofellus, the farmer, a homespun philosopher and man of rough intellect.

By denying responsibility for the following precepts and by describing Ofellus in this particular way, the satirist automatically sets up a conflict. For just as he could not follow the advice of the legalist Trebatius, it soon becomes apparent that neither he nor we can fully accept the harsh ways of Ofellus. This homespun philosopher sets out to harangue us on the merits of living modestly, and especially on the value of simple food. No sensible man would object to that purpose. However, in arguing his point Ofellus treats the gourmet with such contempt that we might, and should, feel his zeal excessive. Here, we could suspect, the satirist parts company with the man whose precepts he repeats. For in Book I the satirist adopted a more gentle attitude towards the mistaken, and he also described a less strenuous tenor of life on his part than Ofellus advocates. After all, our satirist is no self-taught farmer.

The satirist in *S.* 2.3 is sharply distinguished from Damasippus, the other character, who, in fact, dominates the conversation. To give the poem the fullest amount of dramatic irony, Horace sets the scene on the Saturnalia, which, like the old English Twelfth Night, was an occasion when fools played the master. The satirist has retired to his villa to avoid the riotous festivities and there, surrounded by his books (including Plato), he prepares to write his thoughtful poetry. Suddenly Damasippus bursts in, sneers at the slight merit of the satirist's poetic *sermo*, and proceeds to inflict upon the uncomfortable man a series of *praecepta* (34) that he has learned by heart from the wretched Stoic sage Stertinius. It seems that Damasippus had gone bankrupt in his antique business and, about to cast himself into the Tiber, was stopped by

Stertinius, who consoled him with the thought that not only Damasippus was crazy, but almost everyone else. Inspired by this dubiously profound thought and apparently forgetting that he himself is convicted of insanity, Damasippus launches into an interminable diatribe to demonstrate that all men tainted by avarice, ambition, luxury, or superstition are mad. The satirist asks one question: how does this apply to me? So Damasippus tries to convict the satirist of insanity, by the most extreme of charges, of which the last is that our mild little satirist feels passion for a thousand girls and a thousand boys! After all this ranting, the satirist makes his comment in a single verse:

o maior tandem parcas, insane, minori!

O you who are a greater mad man, spare at last a lesser one!

Stoic extremism and the virtual hypocrisy of Damasippus thus tend to make the precepts of Stertinius suspect; they are not totally wrong, but they have been misused. A mute figure of reproach to impractical moral fanaticism, the satirist suffers the unreason of another without trying to correct him.

The opening of *S.* 2.4 might remind an educated reader of Plato's *Phaedrus* by its dramatic setting. As the satirist is calmly walking along, he encounters Catius, who appears in a great hurry. Questioned, Catius says that he is indeed pressed for time, since he wants to write down precepts that surpass those of Pythagoras, Socrates, and Plato. Such an extreme assertion naturally stirs the satirist's curiosity, and he pretends great eagerness, in order to persuade Catius to talk. Reluctantly, then, and with a fine show of condescension, Catius says: 'I shall sing these very precepts from memory' (11). As we soon discover, these *praecepta* directly oppose those voiced by Ofellus and Damasippus, for Catius is a gourmet inspired with strains of Lucretian enthusiasm to 'sing' an epic poem on the art of preparing a tasty meal for the perfect epicure. Scholars have convincingly shown that the recipes and dishes recommended by this didactic 'philosopher' do not violate good taste: they are not extravagant or exotic. Indeed, the reasonable satirist would be likely himself to partake of such food. However, because Catius exaggerates the value of preparing the ideal dinner into the proportions of an ethical philosophy, he exposes himself to criticism. But unless we our-

45

selves have already determined the dramatic irony, the satirist's
final remarks are lost on us:

> at mihi cura
> non mediocris inest, fontis ut adire remotos
> atque haurire queam vitae praecepta beatae. (93–95)

'I am indeed most anxious to be able to approach those secret springs
and to drink the precepts of the happy life.'

In pretending to share Catius' 'philosophic' interests and in
parodying the Lucretian tone of Catius' inspired speech, the
satirist maintains the irony to the very end.

I cannot here discuss all the eight poems of this book, but I
hope that I have made the 'Platonic' trend more or less clear.
Horace abandons the satirist of Book I, who endeared himself to
us as a Socratic teacher. Instead, like Plato, Horace now constructs
a truly dramatic dialogue and pushes the satirist into the supporting role, until by S. 2.4 the satirist does not even make a clear
comment in opposition to Catius. In all four poems the satirist
and we are obliged to listen to a series of slightly distorted
precepts, whether they be Trebatius' irrelevant and learned dis-
quisitions on the Law or the harsh rantings of the zealots Ofellus
and Damasippus, each labelling as crazy all those who do not
blindly accept their fanaticism. For the most part, the moral
interpretation must come from our own poetic and rational insights, for even in S. 2.1, where the satirist presumably wants to
argue the merits of his satire, he does so in such an ironic way that
his best ideas usually escape the reader's attention. Perhaps we
can make the distinction between Books I and II by describing
the chief character (the man speaking to the virtually silent satirist)
as a *doctor ineptus*. He is a teacher who fails to grasp the implications of his own precepts and thus ends as a figure of fun.

We described the ethical position of the Socratic satirist in
Book I in terms of Classical balance: he did not condemn anyone
utterly, but, urging the need for rational inquiry, tried to guide
mistaken people from extreme error towards a modest happiness.
To do so, he used his role as teacher to point out the misery suffered by those pursuing money, sexual gratification, ambition,
and the like; or he described, by contrast, his own reasonable
existence as a model of that happiness which he recommended.
Now, except for one poem in Book II, the satirist has no oppor-

tunity to dominate the stage, and even that poem illustrates the different ethical method. Let us look briefly at *S.* 2.6.

As in *S.* 1.6, the satirist describes his happy life in contrast to the unfortunate pressures endured by the ambitious. But there is no argumentation, no effort to persuade us of a position. Instead, the whole poem works dramatically towards its end. We see the satirist in a moment of happiness on his Sabine farm. Next, he imagines himself plunged into the conflicts and tensions of Rome, where various people make unreasonable claims on him and envy him his close connexion with the influential Maecenas.

> per totum hoc tempus subiectior in diem et horam
> invidiae noster. ludos spectaverat una,
> luserat in campo: 'Fortunae filius!' omnes.
> frigidus a Rostris manat per compita rumor:
> quicumque obvius est me consulit: 'o bone, nam te
> scire, deos quoniam propius contingis, oportet,
> numquid de Dacis audisti?' nil equidem. 'ut tu
> semper eris derisor!' at omnes di exagitent me
> si quicquam. 'quid, militibus promissa Triquetra
> praedia Caesar an est Itala tellure daturus?'
> iurantem me scire nihil mirantur ut unum
> scilicet egregii mortalem altique silenti.
> perditur haec inter misero lux.

During this whole period, day by day, hour by hour, I have become increasingly exposed to envy. Suppose I watched the Games with Maecenas or played ball with him in the Campus Martius: everyone would call me a child of Fortune. Suppose a chill rumour seeps through the streets from the Rostra; then, whoever encounters me asks my advice. 'Good old Horace, you ought to know, since you practically touch the powers that be: what have you heard about the Dacians?' —Really nothing, I assure you.—'Oh, you will always joke, won't you?' —But I swear it; may all the gods drive me crazy if I have heard a word.—'Well, how about the land that Caesar promised to his veterans; is he going to allot it in Sicily or Italy?'—When I swear that I know nothing, they marvel at me as a unique specimen of extraordinary and profound taciturnity. This is the way I wretchedly waste my day.

Longing to escape from such misguided people, the satirist recalls with nostalgia the pleasant dinners which he would have in the country with his friends. At a typical banquet, Cervius might tell his fable of the Country and the City Mouse. It is with the satirist's version of Cervius' fable that the poem ends; and no final comment is permitted on the story. We may think of this fable as equivalent to the precepts of earlier speakers: it takes a moral stand, but we would be rash to identify the Country Mouse directly with our satirist. In fact, to make sure that we do not insist on absolute parallelism, the satirist describes the fable as a commentary on the anxious wealth of a certain Arellius (78). As I said before, the satirist is no farmer. He has retired to a small estate in the Sabine Hills which is worked by his servants; by contrast, the Country Mouse, like Ofellus, is a confirmed rustic, born and bred in the country and briefly lured to the city by his smooth-talking cousin. It remains for us to try to work out the relevance of the tale. According to my understanding of it, it serves as an ironic recommendation of rural contentment. The mouse fled from the Molossian hound and sought security in the country, resolved to accept its humble food as an inevitable consequence. The satirist longs for 'a delightful forgetfulness of the anxious life' (62), which cannot be achieved by flight alone, but primarily by an attitude of mind and heart. In itself, the country does not guarantee peace of mind; only after the satirist has controlled his acquisitive desires and his ambition does he find that charming oblivion that he associates with the rural landscape.

Thus, the poems of Book II demand a different response from our rational faculties, but they continue to demand rationality. No longer is our path marked out for us, as though all we had to do was to grasp the reasoning of the smiling Socratic teacher and follow his genial example. Now, between us and the 'truth' looms the opaque wall of dramatic irony. The *doctor ineptus*, whichever he may be, happily clings to his illusions and recites to the tolerant, but silent, satirist ideas which the speaker fondly believes to be glorious truth. However, as he launches enthusiastically into his 'precepts' the dramatic situation implies some inconsistency. This inconsistency, this dramatic irony is our means of breaking through to the truth. If we can see the difference between Damasippus' second-hand moral ideas and moral reality; if we can distinguish between true happiness and the culinary pleasures of Catius; then, perhaps, we may slowly work our ways towards that life of rational contentedness which the satirist still represents.

As I have indicated, many readers prefer the more direct appeal to reason that characterizes the Socratic satirist of Book I. I shall not attempt to prejudice the case by injecting my own preferences. Suffice it to say that the indirect manner of dramatic irony makes high demands on the poetic skill of Horace, who succeeds in assigning quite distinct characters to the various deluded 'teachers' in the eight poems. Moreover, Horace may come a little closer to the Classical spirit in Book II by leaving the truth undefined, dramatically indicated, and firmly believed, yet unstated. But regardless of each reader's special likings, the fact remains that Horace's *Sermones* stand as a magnificent and early monument of the ideas and poetic art which best characterizes the Augustan Age. When Persius and Juvenal decided to write poetic satire they knew all too well that they were competing with a great poet; for in their thinking it is amply clear that Horace replaced Lucilius as the standard against which all later satiric poets would measure themselves.

Autobiography and Art in Horace

One of the chief developments of Roman literature involved the creation of genres in which the writer spoke forth in the first person, most notably, poetic satire and love elegy. At the same time that some writers were creating these personal or subjective genres, others were also modifying the once-impersonal genres and producing epic with the subjective qualities of Vergil's *Aeneid* or of —in an even more marked fashion—Ovid's *Metamorphoses*. It is obvious that Romans of the first century B.C. found it very natural to talk of themselves and to hear others speak of themselves and that egoism was not a distressing factor. On the contrary, personal writings seemed to have the appeal of ingenuous confessions that reveal the common humanity of us all. Subjective poetry was not, however, exactly the same as subjective conversation, not even when the satirists claimed to be conversing informally and spontaneously or when the love elegists affected to be addressing themselves directly to the circumstances of their love. Between the poet and his honest effusions were meter, the conventions of his genre, and his own artistic goals, to mention but the most patent obstacles to direct communication. Moreover, the poet had to consider his audience: what did it expect, to what extent could he manipulate those expectations fruitfully? Here then, we have the two elements that form my subject: autobiography on the one hand, art on the other. I should like to explore the complicated interrelationships of these two in the work of the Roman poet who, beyond all others, has utilized a subjective manner and the subjective genres, who indeed has told us more about himself than any other Roman poet while achieving an art in those genres that no other Roman poet ever equalled. I refer, of course, to Horace.

We possess a reasonably good though brief biography of Horace that was compiled, on the basis of sound evidence, within about a century of his death.[1] It tells us a few things that Horace himself does not tell us, but the important thing is that it agrees very well with the scattered data provided by the poet in his various poems. What it ignores, we have learned to regard as particularly important, thanks to the discoveries of Freud and modern psychiatry: we would like to know a great deal more about Horace's childhood and formative years. For that kind of information, we are obliged to go to Horace's poetry. Here is part of a famous early passage in *Satire* 1.4 where he describes his father:

> . . . insuevit pater optimus hoc me,   105
> ut fugerem exemplis vitiorum quaeque notando.
> cum me hortaretur, parce, frugaliter, atque
> viverem uti contentus eo quod mi ipse parasset,
> "nonne vides Albi ut male vivat filius, utque
> Baius inops? magnum documentum ne patriam rem   110
> perdere quis velit": a turpi meretricis amore
> cum deterreret, "Scetani dissimilis sis":
> ne sequerer moechas concessa cum venere uti
> possem, "deprensi non bella est fama Treboni"
> aiebat: "sapiens, vitatu quidque petitu   115
> sit melius, causas reddet tibi: mi satis est si

[1] The biography of Horace was put together by Suetonius and included in his collection *De poetis* (ed. A. Rostagni, Turin: Biblioteca di Filologia Classica, 1964), a product of the first decade of the second century A.D. The most elegant analysis of this biography and the most readable discussion of additional details provided by Horace will be found in Eduard Fraenkel, *Horace* (Oxford: Clarendon Press, 1957), pp. 1–23.

traditum ab antiquis morem servare tuamque,
dum custodis eges, vitam famamque tueri
incolumem possum; simul ac duraverit aetas
membra animumque tuum, nabis sine cortice." sic me 120
formabat puerum dictis; (S. 1.4.105–121)

[My wonderful father used to pick out examples of faults and call them to my attention, so that I would avoid them. When he urged me to be thrifty, frugal, and content with what he provided me, he would say: "Don't you see how bad a life the son of Albius has, how Baius is bankrupt? That's strong evidence to prove that you shouldn't waste your father's money." When he would deter me from a debasing love affair with a prostitute, he would say: "Don't be like Scetanius." To prevent me from pursuing willing adulteresses, he would remark: "When Trebonius was caught in bed with someone's wife his reputation was damaged." And he added: "Someday the philosopher will explain to you better what you should avoid and what seek; I am satisfied if I can maintain the customs handed down by the past and keep your life and reputation undamaged so long as you need a guardian. As soon as years have hardened your body and your character, you will be on your own." It was with words like these that my father shaped me when I was young.]

In this era of permissive education, we may not quite comprehend a personality like that of Horace's father, but we have little difficulty in identifying it. He was an authoritarian parent. The important point to note here, though, is that Horace is paying tribute to the authoritarian aspect of his father and claiming that, in his own moral poetry, he has inherited the same propensity.[2]

---

[2] I use the term "authoritarian" loosely and as the antithesis of the term "permissive." Greco-Roman New Comedy had for several centuries suggested a dichotomy of father types: the father who was severe, domineering, rather frightening, and too often angry vs. the father who was indulgent and easygoing. Not all domineering fathers need be represented as angry, but New Comedy portrayed them this way in order to exploit their greatest dramatic and comic potentialities. Plautus's *Bacchides*, adapted from Menander, shows the standard pairing of *senex iratus* and *lepidus*, Nicobulus and Philoxenus; and Terence's plays, especially the Menandrian *Adelphoe* (about which I shall have more to say), frequently manipulate these two kinds of fathers. E. W. Leach ("Horace's *pater optimus* and Terence's Demea: Autobiographical Fiction and Comedy in *Sermo* I,4," *AJP* 92 [1971]: 616–632 makes the interesting suggestion that Horace deliberately constructs the details of this passage as "autobiographical

Before we consider this passage more fully, let me cite a passage of somewhat similar content:

When you kick out for yourself, Stephen—as I daresay you will one of these days—remember, whatever you do, to mix with gentlemen. When I was a young fellow I tell you I enjoyed myself. I mixed with fine decent fellows. Everyone of us could do something. One fellow had a good voice, another fellow was a good actor, another could sing a good comic song, another was a good oarsman or a good racket player, another could tell a good story and so on. We kept the ball rolling anyhow and enjoyed ourselves and saw a bit of life and we were none the worse for it either. But we were all gentlemen, Stephen—at least I hope we were—and bloody good honest Irishmen too. That's the kind of fellows I want you to associate with, fellows of the right kidney. I'm talking to you as a friend, Stephen. I don't believe a son should be afraid of his father.

As you probably have realized, this comes from Joyce's autobiographical novel, A *Portrait of the Artist as a Young Man*,[3] and the son reacts with disgust to his father's advice. The words Joyce puts into the mouth of the father of Stephen Dedalus are meant to mock the older man and help to indicate the new directions ahead of the sensitive young artist, who scorns gentlemen of his father's type, rejects the easy use of the adjective *good*, and detects in his father almost everything that is wrong with Ireland and the Irish. Joyce inherited a great deal from his father, but he consciously struggled against it all through his adolescent and adult years.

Of course, by any standards, James Joyce was an extraordinary person, and his reaction against his father went beyond that of most people. Nevertheless, as our own experience should tell us and as modern psychiatry has led us to believe, sons naturally react against fathers during childhood and adolescence, at certain periods more than others. And what especially provokes filial reaction is a preachy father. Was the relation between Horace and his father unusually amicable, or does Horace merely reconstruct it in that manner for artistic purposes? When we come down to it, Horace was quite as extraordinary a person in his achievements as James Joyce later was,

---

fiction" in a recognizable comic pattern in order to define his relationship to Lucilius. Although my interpretation uses the data differently, Leach's argument is very tempting.

[3] I have cited the text from *The Portable James Joyce* (New York: Viking Press, 1948), p. 341.

and we can hardly deny him the sensitivity of growing poetic awareness that Joyce had as a young man.

Someone might be tempted to object to the suggestion of a link
between Joyce and Horace on grounds that first-century Rome differed radically from twentieth-century Dublin, and Roman sons respected their fathers unquestioningly, while Irish sons were more
rebellious. Let me put Horace's autobiographical comments in a
clearer perspective by citing a passage from one of Terence's comedies, which was written more than a century before the satire. In
this passage a father, convinced of the efficacy of his methods of
bringing up his son, describes them with passionate enthusiasm to a
slave who, with barely concealed mockery, congratulates the old
man.

DE. Syre, praeceptorum plenust istorum ille. *SY.* phy!
domi habuit unde disceret. *DE.* fit sedulo:
nil praetermitto; consuefacio; denique
inspicere, tamquam in speculum, in vitas omnium   415
iubeo atque ex aliis sumere exemplum sibi:
"hoc facito." *SY.* recte sane. *DE.* "hoc fugito." *SY.* callide.
DE. "hoc laudist." *SY.* istaec res est. *DE.* "hoc vitio datur."
SY. probissime. *DE.* porro autem. *SY.* non hercle otiumst
nunc mi auscultandi. piscis ex sententia   420
nactus sum: î mihi ne corrumpantur cautiost. (*Adelphoe* 412–421)

[*Demea.* Yes, Syrus, my boy is full of good principles of that kind.
Syrus. Of course. He has someone like you at home to learn from.
Demea. And learn he does, all the time. I never miss a chance to teach
        him. I get him used to it. I tell him to look at everybody's lives
        as if they were mirrors, to take other people as examples. Like
        "do this . . ."
Syrus. That's really great.
Demea. "Don't do that . . ."
Syrus. Excellent.
Demea. "People approve of that."
Syrus. Right on.
Demea. "This, now, they disapprove . . ."
Syrus. Splendid.
Demea. And then I go on . . .
Syrus. I'm sorry, but I haven't time to hear any more now. I've bought
        some excellent fish, and I want to make sure *they* aren't ruined.]

The dramatic context of Terence's comedy leaves no doubt as to how we are to interpret the father's words. For all his genuine attempts to drill right principles into his son, this father has failed ridiculously. And the pathetic thing is that he does not know his failure and believes the slave when he uses flattery to deceive him. His son has in fact rejected the examples held up to him and has fallen in love with the first prostitute who pretended some interest in him. In Greco-Roman comedy, sons regularly go against their fathers' wishes. The stricter and more authoritarian a father is, in fact, the more likely it is that the son will rebel against him and that the playwright will manipulate our sympathies in favor of the son. But even when the father is lenient, the son will disappoint him, because the young men featured in these comedies are at the age when they will test their own strength and naturally try things that fathers have told them not to do.

There is, then, nothing unusual in the way Horace represents his father's using examples to deter him from harmful behavior and appealing to tradition: fathers do that. What is unusual is the totally acquiescent role that Horace assigns himself. I find it quite incredible. When he heard his father preaching to him, he surely must have felt the same restlessness and occasional resentment that any son has ever felt on such occasions, from the time of Terence to that of Joyce and right up to the present (as so many contemporary movies like *The Graduate* demonstrate). Two observations, I think, will confirm my argument. First, Horace did not fully imitate his father when he grew up. Although he maintained a moralistic strain throughout his poetry, he rejected the preachy, authoritarian manner. In place of the seemingly dead earnestness of the father, we find in Horace the smiling tolerance of one who knows that we all make mistakes, that an occasional love affair with a prostitute is normal, that sometimes overeating and drunkenness are appropriate. The fact that father and son choose to convey their ethical ideas differently suggests that a certain critical tension exists between them. Second, Horace seems to be using his father in *Satire* 1.4 to make a polemic point, not merely to provide autobiographical data. In order to convince his audience that his moral satire is designed not to wound but to instruct, Horace tells them that he has learned his methods from his father, who clearly used moral examples to educate his son. Thus, he cancels presuppositions that as a satirist he might resemble the caustic

Lucilius or any standard scandalmonger: he is like a concerned father. A charming image. But does it sound convincing, when we realize that Horace was a young man of thirty at most, an ambitious young poet eager for patronage? In my opinion, the "fatherly" Horace of *Satire* 1.4 reveals the interworking of art and autobiography.

It is generally assumed, on the basis of our meager evidence, that Horace's father exercised the major influence on his childhood and adolescence.[4] Of Horace's mother, we know nothing; he never mentions her, and he shows little interest in mothers in general.[5] Psychiatrists might make much of this unmentioned mother, perhaps by drawing interesting connections with Horace's failure to marry and have children and by trying to isolate some warped sexuality. I

[4] Cf. Fraenkel, *Horace*, p. 5: "The poet knows that he owes more to his father than to anyone else." Fraenkel carefully discusses the occupation of the elder Horace. Horace never tells us the origin of his *pater libertinus*, and most scholars assume, as I do, that his father was one of the numerous slaves imported from the Greek world. Recently, however, N. Terzaghi ("Il padre di Orazio," *Atene e Roma* 10 [1965]: 66–71) proposes the ingenious theory that Horace's father was an unusual case, the product of a union between a freeborn citizen, Horatius, and a slave woman. Under these circumstances, the child would legally be a slave. Terzaghi hypothesizes that the father immediately emancipated his son, so that for all practical purposes Horace's father lived as a free man, though under the stigma of ignoble birth. The evidence is by no means conclusive.

[5] W. H. Alexander ("The Enigma of Horace's Mother," *CP* 37 [1942]: 385–397) attempted to work out a theory about the unmentioned mother. Working primarily from *Serm.* 1.6, Alexander suggests that Horace's father was probably a Levantine Greek, that his mother (possibly alluded to in line 36 as *ignota matre*) might have been a Levantine Jew, and that Horace was ashamed to mention her in the face of the marked hostility to Jews in Rome. Again, the evidence is tenuous. By examining the contexts in which Horace uses the word *mater* and its adjective, one may arrive at the following conclusions: Horace uses *mater* mostly in conventional situations such as would be well defined by poetic and social traditions. Twice, he mentions the dominating mother type, in *C.* 3.6.39–40 (a patent allusion to the distant historical past of Italy) and *Epist.* 1.1.22 (reference to a free mother in an average free family); neither of these situations applies to himself, and Horace attaches no special emotion whatsoever to the mother. E. E. Best, Jr., in *CJ* 65 (1969–1970): 199–204, discusses the influence of certain mothers of prominent Roman families upon the careers of their sons. Educated mothers (*mater docta*) often inspired their sons to become great orators and politicians. However, Horace's situation is by no means similar. Nor is it like that of the poet Persius, whose twice-widowed mother presumably carefully planned the training that influenced his short career: she was a woman of good birth and considerable education and influence.

might remind those who wish to essay this Freudian theme that the biography provides us with one extraordinary fact, one that has perplexed and disturbed classicists for centuries. In his mature years, we are told, Horace placed mirrors all about his bedroom so that he could enjoy various perspectives of himself and his mistress when in sexual intercourse![6] But rather than work in a vacuum, I would prefer to concentrate on the father, about whom we know a few things. He was a slave of unknown origin, who had been freed by his master and later settled in Venusia, earning a modest income as collector of money for an auctioneer. Although this background hardly entitled him to large ambitions, Horace's father decided to take his son from Venusia and give him the best possible education in Rome.[7] Every day, he attended young Horace to school and served him more as a slave than as a father. What did he intend for his son? According to Horace, his father had no grandiose plans and would not have been ashamed if the son had followed him in the lowly role of collector for auctions.[8] I am not so sure of that.

When we try to produce a coherent sketch of Horace's father, using the evidence Horace gives us, our interpretation differs from the one Horace emphasizes. The man who insists on driving homespun morality into the heart of his son appeals to the ancestral customs of a culture to which he came as a slave. As soon as he has a little money, he transports himself and his son to the capital city and sacrifices all in order that his son may have the same educational opportunities as the sons of the most distinguished Roman families. Why? Because the Horatian pattern resembles the pattern of many immigrant families in nineteenth-century America, we tend to assume that Horace's father wanted his son to make good in terms of the Roman dream. All that education would enable Horace to become a rhetorician and politician, not a collector or ordinary businessman.[9] It may be true that the father's authoritarianism confined itself to moralistic admonitions, but I think it more likely that he also

---

[6] So Suetonius: "ad res Venerias intemperantior traditur; nam speculato cubiculo scorta dicitur habuisse disposita, ut quocumque respexisset ibi ei imago coitus referretur" (p. 119 Rostagni).

[7] These details are provided by Horace himself in *Serm.* 1.6.71–82.

[8]   nec timuit sibi ne vitio quis verteret olim
      si praeco parvas aut, ut fuit ipse, coactor
      mercedes sequerer; neque ego essem questus. (*S.* 1.6.85–87)

[9] Such a career was apparently planned for Vergil by his farmer-father, for

urged his son toward specific goals. Horace admired his father, respected him for all his sacrifices, and perhaps went along with the ambitions that were held out to him. But by 35 B.C., the date of our Satire, the immigrant dream had been exploded. Horace had failed to make a successful political start because he chose the losing side at the battle of Philippi, and about the same time his father lost his money and died. Without money and political support, Horace had no chance of success in ordinary ambitions.

Another early satire (1.6) tries to make Horace the model of unambitious integrity.[10] To accomplish this, the satirist most ingeniously exploits both his friendship with Maecenas, the second most powerful man in Rome, and his now-dead ex-slave father. His friendship with Maecenas has no political overtones, he claims, because he did not push himself on the great man, and Maecenas can distinguish between true friendship and political opportunism.[11] Indeed, Maecenas has freed himself of prejudices and does not let Horace's ignoble birth interfere with an honest recognition of his merits; and, from Horace's viewpoint, it is his ex-slave father who has given him the character that wins Maecenas's affection. Now Joyce might have said that his father made him an anti-Irish writer, and it would have been true in a certain sense. We know, however, that Joyce's father had no such designs for his eldest son. Similarly, we may doubt that Horace's father intended to make his son what he became. But Horace could later affirm that his poetic success and the creative friendship with Maecenas resulted[12] from the tension between his own sensitivity, his failures, and his father's driving purposes.

Once again, autobiography and art interact in this Satire. Horace affectionately credits his father for making him the happy man he is

---

Catullus and Ovid by their middle-class parents. In each case, however, the son exploited his Roman training in rhetoric to enhance his poetic talent.

[10] For an able analysis of the main themes of this poem, see Niall Rudd, *The Satires of Horace* (Cambridge: At the University Press, 1966), pp. 36–53.

[11] Horace gives his account of how the friendship developed in 49–64.

[12] I am offering a theory to account for what Horace says of himself, and it may be wrong. Not everyone in Augustan Rome would have accepted it. One can infer from what Horace says about the backbiting he suffered (S. 1.6.46–52) that some contemporaries regarded the poet as a typical climber. As they saw it, he had used his money while it lasted to buy himself a military command at Philippi; then, when the money was gone, Horace had tried to worm his way into friendship with powerful Maecenas in order to exploit the opening that the

at the time of writing; and he boasts of this ex-slave instead of apologizing for him. But had Horace's father been alive, one might have heard different ideas from him: he might have understood his son no better than those who attacked Horace's supposed ambitions.

I believe that we can infer the powerful influence of Horace's father on his childhood, but I doubt that this time in the poet's life was precisely as free of tension as Horace later implies. He credits his father with the hard-won results of his own personal development without ever expressly revealing the older man's purposes. In the authoritarian portrait he produces of the ex-slave, I find it difficult to detect a man who would readily acquiesce in his son's choice to be a struggling poet. It is probably also significant that Horace mentions his father only in these two early satires that I have so far discussed and in one late passage, which I shall discuss. If the father dominated the poet's youth as much as Horace claims, if Horace feels the affection for this father that he states he does, we might expect more references to the old man, at least in the form of straight autobiographical comments. The fact is, though, that none of the subjective confessions in Horace's poetry is straight autobiography. In his first published poems, Book I of the Satires, Horace purposely defined himself in terms of his father, to suggest paradoxically that he was identical with his excellent father in using homespun morality and pursuing the simplest of goals in life. Later, when he was successful and had a villa in the Sabine Hills and powerful friends in Rome, when he was reckoned among the foremost artists of Roman poetry, the chasm between simple father and sophisticated son was too obvious to bridge by ingenious art. And Horace's father disappears from the poetry. I do not mean that he disap-

---

friendship would give him to power and money. Such critics would have been disposed to dismiss Horace's words of filial affection as utter lies. For my part, I believe that Horace did honor his father and give him credit for the happy, if unanticipated, results that came from his father's concerned upbringing. But I daresay that Horace knew his poetic career would have surprised the old man. Those critics more expert in psychoanalysis may find that these data suggest another interpretation. My friend John Trimble has mentioned that he detects in Horace's behavior signs of what is called a "reaction-formation"; that is, Horace may neurotically have been covering up his difficulties with his father by honoring him greatly after his death. See Otto Fenichel, *The Psychoanalytic Theory of Neurosis* (New York: W. W. Norton and Co., 1945), pp. 151–153.

peared from Horace's affections and gratitude, only that art no longer needed that kind of autobiography.

I have suggested that the battle of Philippi proved to be a turning
point in Horace's life, because it caused him to discard most of the
goals that his father had encouraged him to aim at.[13] Horace does
not tell us about the difficulties he encountered in the years between
the military disaster and his successful meeting with Maecenas, who
became his friend and patron (a new kind of father). We know that
he held a civil service post in Rome, but it is not difficult to guess
that he merely performed his job while his mind was elsewhere.
Slowly he adjusted to the disaster, began to write poetry that won
him friends among the poets, and gradually from the failure of his
political ambitions emerged a new and more viable career as poet.
From the vantage point of success twenty years later, Horace no
longer interpreted Philippi as a personal disaster, but as a divine
blessing, the miraculous intervention of some benevolent force that
freed him for the happiness and sense of power that he now felt.
Once he may have regretted escaping with his life from the battle-
field. By the time he wrote *Ode* 2.7 (at least a decade after the early
satires), he could represent his survival as miraculous preservation.
Art collaborates with autobiography to produce a charming "myth."
As he now tells it, in the moment of rout, he had abandoned his
shield ignobly and was fleeing, when suddenly the god Mercury
lifted him up and transported him in thick mist away from danger
to safety.[14] Why did Mercury intervene? Horace is not so gauche as
to boast of his successful career, but he implies that Mercury, as

[13] It is interesting to observe that the Suetonian biography treats Horace as
though his life first became significant at Philippi: it offers no details about his
youth. In a recent article, K. Büchner ("Horace et Épicure," *Assoc. Guillaume
Budé, Actes du viii* Congrès* [1969], pp. 457–469) focuses on the trauma of
Philippi in a different fashion. He argues that one can detect in Book I of the
Satires a strenuous effort by Horace to cope with his loss of faith in Roman values by giving serious thought to the values offered by Epicureanism. The defeat
at Philippi was both a shock to his political ideals and a permanent blow to
possible political ambitions.

[14] Critics generally agree that Horace's self-conscious reference to the abandonment of his shield, while it no doubt could fit his actual behavior at Philippi,
was meant in this poem to align him with the celebrated Greek poets Archilochus and Alcaeus, who boasted of their unheroic flight in time of war. Thus,
the allusion to the Greek poets and the mythical account of escape form part of
a coherent whole.

messenger of the gods and inventor of the lyric instrument, has saved Horace from political ambitions so that he could develop his special divinely blessed talents as poet.

Horace likes to use this motif of miraculous preservation to define, usually with enough irony to take away the tone of boasting, his special vocation as poet. Such a motif is a feature of the Odes, but appears originally in S. 9 of the first book of Satires.[15] Once when Horace was struggling helplessly to escape a leachlike fellow whose ambitions were worse than his mere garrulity, Apollo, he claims, intervened and rescued him from certain extinction. Why? Because he was an innocent poet, both helpless and unfit for the ambitious world in which he was placed by the bore. Apollo's rescue, like Mercury's intervention in *Ode* 2.7, borrows from Homeric battle motifs and thus gives the scene exaggerated epic tones that enable us to smile with the poet at his escape. Perhaps the most obviously amusing of these Horatian myths is the famous *Ode* 1.22. Horace reports that he was singing a love poem he wrote in honor of his girl Lalage when along came a gigantic wolf. However, even though the wolf was huge and Horace unarmed, the wolf turned tail and fled. Why? Obviously not because Horace's voice was so terrible that it frightened the beast, but because a love poet bears a charmed life and passes unscathed through all dangers! Maybe Horace once did see a wolf for a second on his Sabine farm, but, if so, art has taken over autobiography from that point.

Another miraculous escape occurred when Horace was strolling on his property and a dead tree fell unexpectedly, barely missing the poet's unoffending head. Out of this personal experience the artist has created several interesting themes in different poems. The first time he refers to his escape, in *Ode* 2.13, Horace affects to have just gone through the soul-shaking episode. Naturally, then, he begins by cursing the tree. When he has spent his emotions on that motif, he reflects more reasonably on the problem of death, reaching the familiar conclusion that death is unavoidable and unforeseeable. As he ponders this theme, he speculates on what it would have been like to be dead, and in his imaginary picture of the dead Horace he implicitly explains why he was not killed. If he had died, he confidently declares, he would have gone to the special part of the

[15] See my article, "Horace the Unwilling Warrior: *Satire* I, 9," *AJP* 77 (1956): 148–166.

underworld set aside for the greatest poets, who by their songs are able to triumph over the miseries associated with death. Their eternal triumph over death is but a permanent version of Horace's temporary escape: he has been preserved to be a poet in his own world and, when finally he has completed his poetic mission on earth, to pass on to the immortality of his Greek models, Sappho and Alcaeus.

This special destiny of the poet, which explains on one level the miracle of Horace's life, impels the poet to use his miraculous escapes artistically to contrast with the more ordinary careers of others, whose destiny is bleak death that nevertheless cannot make them do something with the precious moments of the present. As Horace keeps observing in the Odes, we are not only not going to escape the finality of dying, but we are also so foolish in our preoccupations as to be enduring a living death. So Horace's happy escape of 2.13 is immediately contrasted in 2.14 with the inevitability of Postumus's miserable death following his miserable existence.[16] Twice Horace builds a single poem out of the contrast between his special providence as poet—proved by his escape from the damned tree—and Maecenas's unenviable distinction as statesman. In each of these poems, Horace credits a different divinity with his preservation. Although both deities suggest concern for the poet, their other associations explain why Horace has manipulated the autobiographical facts and as a result produced quite different poems. In *Ode* 2.17, the occasion is Maecenas's melancholy and hypochondriac presentiment of death. Horace jokes with his friend, asserts on the basis of comic manipulation of astrology and the zodiac that Maecenas will never die before himself, and then cites two incidents that supposedly prove the special destinies of each man. When Maecenas was seriously ill, he staged a miraculous recovery. Why? Obviously because the supreme god Jupiter acted to save such an important man. With a smile, Horace then adduces the incident of the dead tree as a humble parallel to Maecenas's noble escape. It was Faunus (the Roman equivalent of bucolic Pan) who intervened on Horace's behalf. As son of Mercury, Faunus watches over the favorites of Mercury. By giving the credit for his escape to Faunus, Horace deliberately portrays himself as a humble rustic and thus sets up an

[16] I have discussed the relationship between 2.13 and 14 more fully in "Two Odes of Horace's Book Two," *Calif. Studies in Classical Antiquity* 1 (1968): 59–61.

effective contrast between himself and the urban politician Maecenas; bucolic Faunus is opposed to Maecenas's Jupiter. Behind these contrasts, which maintain the illusion of Horace's humility, lurks a different contrast: Horace is happy and attuned to the realities of life, and he with his poetic insights must comfort the great, but greatly miserable, Maecenas.

In still another ode, 3.8, the autobiographical occasion is Horace's celebration of the anniversary of his escape, when he was almost "funeraled" (as he comically puts it with a word made for the poem, *funeratus*) by the blow of the tree. Here, for a very specific reason, he provides for us the date of the near tragedy and hence of the anniversary celebration: it was March first. March first in the Roman world had great public significance as the day when husbands sacrificed to Juno, goddess of marriage, and gave presents to their wives. Yet here is Horace, a notoriously unmarried type, conducting his private rites, sacrificing not to Juno but to Liber (or Bacchus)! A comic paradox to begin the poem with. We know that Bacchus could function at times as a patron of poets; Horace's Odes show that he recognized this motif.[17] However, as everyone knows, Bacchus mainly connotes wine and the pleasures to be gained from drinking. When he chose to credit Bacchus for his escape, Horace was planning the most effective contrast with Juno and the more sedate ceremonies proper to the commemoration of marriage. Then he goes from this initial humorous contrast to draw a more penetrating contrast between himself, the contented poet who has come to terms with life, and Maecenas, the anxious statesman who worries himself sick over the dangers that threaten Rome. Horace then advises Maecenas to drink, to seize the pleasures offered by the moment.[18]

In one of the great Roman Odes, Horace draws all his miraculous escapes together, explains them pointedly as the work of the Muses, and then goes on to demonstrate poetically that the quality that works in the poet and accounts for his greatness is also at work in the ideal statesman (though in somewhat different terms). He men-

---

[17] Steele Commager (*The Odes of Horace: A Critical Study* [New Haven: Yale University Press, 1962], pp. 337–341) ably analyzes the way Horace in *C.* 2.19 presents "Bacchus, the inspirer of poetry."

[18] This same contrast between statesman and poet is most fully elaborated in *C.* 3.29. There, in addition to the pleasures of drinking, Horace offers Maecenas the pastoral bliss of his Sabine villa.

tions the rout at Philippi, the nearly fatal incident involving the tree, and another occasion, apparently a near drowning, about which we have no other information.

> vester, Camenae, vester in arduos
> tollor Sabinos, seu mihi frigidum
>   Praeneste seu Tibur supinum
>   seu liquidae placuere Baiae.
> vestris amicum fontibus et choris
> non me Philippis versa acies retro,
>   devota non exstinxit arbos,
>   nec Sicula Palinurus unda. (*C.* 3.4.21–28)

[I belong to you, o Muses, I belong to you, whether I go up into the Sabine Hills or sloping Tivoli or whether my delight is the water of Baiae. Because I was a friend of your fountains I was not killed during the flight from Philippi nor when the damned tree fell on me nor by the seas off Sicily.]

Horace's experience with the ubiquitous benevolence of the Muses convinces him that his future will be secure, wherever he may be, in the flesh or in the spirit. His poems will survive him. The quality that Horace isolates to define his vocation as poet and the noble vocation of Augustus, the ideal statesman, is *pietas*. The poet, by dedicating himself selflessly to poetry, establishes a firm link with the divine realm through the Muses, deities themselves. Without the assistance of the Muses, he can accomplish nothing important. That same selfless devotion to divine purposes impels the ideal statesman, who chooses to end self-aggrandizing wars in order to work for the well-being of his people in peacetime. This is the poem in which Horace most clearly defines his concept of the poet, and here, though art is very prominent, we may catch the autobiographical passion that encourages Horace to set his métier on a level with that of Augustus. It was precisely this sense of personal integrity that enabled him to say no both to Maecenas and to Augustus when they tried to restrict his freedom as poet and use him for purposes that they considered valid.[19] Whether or not they were valid, Horace

[19] In *Epistle* 1.7 Horace advocates independence in the face of demands that might be made on him by his friend and patron Maecenas. However, we probably should not use this Epistle as a historical document to prove that Maecenas did in fact mistreat Horace. In *Epistle* 2.1 Horace exhibits independence in his relations with Augustus, which tends to substantiate the story told

knew that the life he needed and wanted depended on total commitment to the Muses, absolute *pietas*.

In this same magnificent ode Horace describes the only experience of his infancy that he or anyone else ever records. When I think of what Freud did with the sole infant experience reported by Leonardo da Vinci, I somewhat tremble for Horace, but I shall go ahead.[20] Here are Horace's words:

> me fabulosae Vulture in Apulo
> nutricis extra limen Apuliae   10
>   ludo fatigatumque somno
>   fronde nova puerum palumbes
> texere, mirum quod foret omnibus,
> quicumque celsae nidum Acherontiae
>   saltusque Bantinos et arvum   15
>   pingue tenent humilis Forenti,
> ut tuto ab atris corpore viperis
> dormirem et ursis, ut premerer sacra
>   lauroque collataque myrto,
>   non sine dis animosus infans (*C.* 3.4.9–20)   20

[When I was a baby, I crawled away from my nurse's house near Mt. Voltur in Apulia and, tired out from play, I fell asleep. As I lay there in the woods, miraculously, doves covered me up with fresh leaves, an absolute marvel to all who live in the region, how I slept on, safe from black vipers and bears, covered by sacred laurel and heaps of myrtle. For not without divine blessing was I, a mere baby, alive.]

I am prepared to believe that little Horace crawled away from his nurse once and that, after a long search, she found him asleep in a pile of leaves. The rest of the details, however, resemble artistic elaborations designed to give the incident special significance. After all, who could verify that doves could and did cover the baby with

---

by Suetonius that Augustus tried to make Horace his private secretary and was refused. See Fraenkel, *Horace*, pp. 17–20.

[20] See Freud's essay, *Leonardo da Vinci and a Memory of His Childhood* (1910), trans. A. A. Brill (New York: Random House, 1947). Leonardo reportedly remembered an odd childhood experience when a bird, apparently a kite, flew down while he was sleeping and struck him repeatedly on his lips with its tail. Freud detected many veiled sexual references in the details of this childhood memory.

leaves? Why should leaves protect the baby from vipers and bears, and who can say that they, in fact, did save him? This artistic embellishment of autobiographical fact in no way illuminates the nature of Horace. Instead, it serves to confirm his myth that from birth the Muses had consecrated Horace as their servant, and that he was destined to be the great poet he became. In this first incident of miraculous preservation we see the archetype of all the others.

The first three books of Odes, almost ninety poems, were composed over a ten-year period, and published together in 23 B.C. when Horace was forty-two. Although Horace continues to use the personal manner in his lyrics, the person we encounter in the Odes is not the same as the speaker in the Satires. Nor is it enough to observe that Horace was considerably older in the Odes than in the Satires. True, when we add a decade to age thirty, we radically change our nature, as most of us over forty regretfully admit. However, when we read the Odes, the age of the poet does not seem important. In fact, if one did not know the date of the Satires, I daresay that most readers would guess that the satirist was older than the lyric poet: the moralistic contents of the Satires suggest an older and wiser author, while the lighter contents of the erotic and drinking poems suggest that they were composed by a younger man. Generic conventions also account in large measure for the manner in which autobiographical detail is employed in the Satires and Odes. Inasmuch as a satirist is supposed to be a simple down-to-earth man, Horace can readily introduce his ex-slave father in the Satires to explain both his homespun ethics and his lack of ambition. He boasts of his father and at the same time denies himself the rank of poet in Satire 1.4. On the other hand, when the satirist turns into a lyric poet, those simple intimate facts about the elder Horace no longer serve his purpose. If there is one thing Horace wishes to emphasize in the lyrics, it is that he is a poet with a sacred vocation. Therefore, when the lyric poet looks into his past for relevant experiences, he no longer consciously recalls his father and all the sacrifices that started Horace on the practical road toward his career. Instead he colors an incident from his infancy in such a way as to exclude his father totally and introduce as his permanent guardians, the Muses. Earlier, Horace affectionately remembered how his father had sworn to protect his life and honor as long as he was a youth; the childhood episode cited in Ode 3.4 replaces Horace's father with the Muses. I think that as Horace wrote the Odes he realized that he had left his father's narrow world far behind, and that he could no longer satisfactorily account for the gulf that now separated him from his youth except in terms of the Muses. The events at Philippi may indeed have effected the change, but Horace now began to see in other events, even a half-remembered incident from his babyhood in Apulia, the mystique of a special destiny, miraculous preservation from danger, and a consecration as poet that supposedly determined his entire life.[21]

In keeping with this total dedication to the Muses, Horace throughout the Odes published in 23 B.C. impresses us as a man who has not only replaced ordinary political ambitions with his commitment to poetry, but also rejected riches for a modest existence and sublimated amatory passion in his cool poems about love. Being a poet compensates him richly for all the frenetic and disappointing preoccupations of most men. As he enters his forties, Horace finds that poetry will comfort him as he grows old. I see that motif in the famous and elusive poem that Horace wrote on the Fountain of Bandusia. If we knew precisely where this humble spring was located, we might be able to control the autobiographical detail better. As it is, some scholars place it in Apulia where Horace grew up, and others are equally certain that they still see the spring today spurting from the hillside above the Sabine farm that Maecenas gave the mature poet. Nevertheless, whether the fountain represents an allusion to Horace's youth or to his maturity, the poem suggests that Horace, by sacrificing a spirited young goat to the water, is symbolically consecrating his own youthful passions. As the cool waters are briefly dyed with the hot red blood of the kid and then run clear and cold again, as those same chill springs overcome weariness and piercingly hot weather, so, in a sense, when Horace honors that cool comfort, he gracefully yields his own hot passions to the soothing actions of the Muses, the source of his life's inspiration.[22] In short,

---

[21] Similarly, Horace briefly looks back at his early years and humble origin in *C.* 3.30, the final poem of his first collection of Odes. The phrase *ex humili potens / princeps* (12–13) suggests a dramatic political achievement, and only the words that follow prove that Horace is recording the miracle of his poetic success. The same ideas return in *C.* 4.3, written about 17 B.C.; Horace emphasizes the way the Muses pick out the future poet at the time of his birth.

[22] For other interpretations of the symbolism of this poem, see F. Gillen, "Symbolic Dimensions in Horace's Poetry," *CB* 37 (1961): 65–67; M. R. Lef-

during the rich years when Horace was composing his masterpieces, the Odes, art not only colored autobiography, but also became autobiography; for poetry was Horace's life.

In the fifteen years that followed before his death in 8 B.C., Horace, growing older and feeling his age, explored again his own existential purposes and redefined his relation to poetry. Instead of the passionate regrets for youth that make the poems of the older Yeats so exciting, we find in Horace a graceful resignation to age, an awareness of his limited powers that impels him to abandon lyric and the once-cherished themes of the Odes. Not that he gives up poetry. Far from it. In the opening poem of his next collection, published within three years of the Odes, Horace declares that he is henceforth putting aside verse and other light matters (*Epist.* 1.1.10), but since he utters this sentiment in a good hexameter line in the course of a carefully wrought poem, we know that he is not abandoning poetry. The hexameter, the subject matter, the express statement that the older poet does not feel the same as the younger lyric writer, and finally the more serious tone of these lines indicate that Horace is choosing a new genre to match his own new interests. At first sight, these new poems resemble the Satires in form, and we wonder why Horace has reverted to the poetry of his twenties. But when we look closer, we begin to note significant differences. The new works are Letters, ostensibly private communications addressed to friends, in which he shares personal moral concerns. In these letters Horace encourages young people to be serious about life, insists on the merit of life in the country away from the entanglements of the city, yet never calls attention to himself as poet, as confident critic of others.[23] And at the end of the collection he offers this miniature autobiography to his audience:

> me libertino natum patre et in tenui re   20
> maiores pennas nido extendisse loqueris,
> ut quantum generi demas virtutibus addas;

---

kowitz, "The Ilex in *o fons Bandusiae*," *CJ* 58 (1962): 63–67; and Commager, *Odes of Horace*, pp. 322–324.

[23] See M. J. McGann, *Studies in Horace's First Book of Epistles* (Brussels: Collection Latomus 100, 1969). In his discussion of the conclusion of *Epist.* 1.20, McGann supports my views: "The autobiographical sketch which ends the book is appropriately concerned with Horace as a person and in particular as a moral person rather than as a poet" (p. 86).

me primis Vrbis belli placuisse domique;
corporis exigui, praecanum, solibus aptum,
irasci celerem, tamen ut placabilis essem. (*Epist.* 1.20.20–25)   25

[You may say that I was born of an ex-slave father and in strait-
ened circumstances, but flew from my parental nest on broader
wings; so what you subtract from my family you should add to
my own good qualities. I have pleased the foremost men of the
city in war and peace. I am short, prematurely gray, addicted to
sunbathing, quick-tempered, but also easily calmed down.]

In this sole reference to his father since *Satire* 1.6, at least fifteen
years earlier, Horace uses his parent only to define his humble be-
ginnings. Neither the father nor the Muses are given credit for
Horace's success. The implicit suggestion is that he has done it himself. What does this self-portrait mean? It means, I think, that for
the purposes of the Epistles, where he talks of himself as a searcher
for the right way to live, Horace wishes to represent his past as a
personal achievement, one that promises success to his present
search. Notice that he does not even represent himself as a poet.

If the Epistles have introduced a new autobiographical manner,
in which Horace virtually ignores his father and seems to slight the
Muses and the variety of tutelary deities (Apollo, Mercury, Faunus,
Bacchus) that he associated with himself earlier, we may well ask
what has happened to the rich theme of personal salvation. Salvation
by the Muses alone is worse than irrelevant to the theme of the Epistles: it contradicts the point that Horace now emphasizes, that salvation is essentially ethical and is achieved by individual effort. Horace no longer uses the genial myth about the Muses because he no
longer feels the Muses so close and realizes that poetic creation results from a great deal of hard intellectual and moral effort. Writing
an epistle was a grueling job for a highly conscious artist. Uncon-
scious inspiration, that charming madness (*amabilis insania*) which
occasionally possessed him in the writing of the Odes, no longer
worked. Sternly rejecting such uncontrolled inspiration, such poetic
madness, Horace demanded of himself full rationality as he poetically worked out the vital ethical themes of the Epistles.

Thus, if the poet is to be saved, he must first relinquish his belief
in sheer inspiration: so Horace now urges. In three important places
in the Epistles, Horace describes playfully (but with serious intent)

the desperate state of the poet who insanely trusts to mere inspiration and will not be saved from his madness. There is an old Roman saying to the effect that saving someone who does not want to be rescued is the same as killing him. Horace ironically applies this saying to the possessed poet: since such a person clutches wildly to his delusions, coming to his senses is a traumatic experience, and perhaps it would be a mercy to let him stay mad. The first time this theme of trying to save the deluded poet occurs, Horace is, so to speak, arguing with himself. In the Epistle containing the autobiographical portrait which I cited above, Horace argues against a tendency in himself to seek publication and quick fame. His alter ego, the character with whom he is arguing, is represented as the Book, the collection of Epistles, which rushes out to display itself coquettishly in public. That popularizing attitude, Horace warns, will doom the Book to rapid oblivion, but why try to save someone who will not be saved?[24] The very form of this internal dialogue shows that Horace has indeed opted for a new kind of salvation.

Again, in the long Epistle to Florus, Horace describes the permanent struggle confronting the true poet and affects to feel too old to continue the battle. Ironically claiming that he would prefer to be a writer who is insane (*scriptor delirus*) and happy than one who is sane and miserable, he tells the story of a somewhat dotty old Greek who had a number of harmless aesthetic delusions that made him happy. Well, his family took the old man to a psychiatrist, who cured him. Instead of being grateful, the old man complained that his friends had not saved him, but killed him, for they had taken away his pleasant delusions.[25] And that story is supposed to prove the advantages of being insane. The recurrence of this same sequence in the *Ars poetica* in a context where Horace clearly chooses to be sane confirms the irony of this anecdote. As he says, the beginning, the very source of writing poetry properly, is the capacity to use one's reason: "scribendi recte sapere est et principium et fons" (*A.P.* 309). But the poet who trusts in inspiration is a madman for whom there is no help. Look at the poet-philosopher Empedocles. He wanted to be regarded as a god and threw himself into the molten crater of Mt. Etna. A hopeless case. You just have to let poets kill themselves,

---

[24] *Epistle* 1.20.16: *quis enim invitum servare laboret?*
[25] *Epistle* 2.2.138–139: *pol me occidistis, amici, / non servastis.*

because, if you save them against their will, it's the same as killing them.[26]

This new view of the poet's role treats harshly the pleasant autobiographical constructions of the Odes and the ingenuously appealing manipulations of Horace's father in the Satires. In his final autobiography, Horace made his life a steady progress toward truth and sharply curtailed the significance of poetry in it all:

Romae nutriri mihi contigit, atque doceri
iratus Grais quantum nocuisset Achilles.
adiecere bonae paulo plus artis Athenae,
scilicet ut vellem curvo dinoscere rectum,
atque inter silvas Academi quaerere verum.   45
dura sed emovere loco me tempora grato,
civilisque rudem belli tulit aestus in arma
Caesaris Augusti non responsura lacertis.
unde simul primum me dimisere Philippi,
decisis humilem pennis inopemque paterni   50
et laris et fundi, paupertas impulit audax
ut versus facerem: sed quod non desit habentem
quae poterunt umquam satis expurgare cicutae,
ni melius dormire putem quam scribere versus? (*Epist.* 2.2.41–54)

> [I happened to be raised in Rome, where I was taught from the *Iliad* how much the wrath of Achilles injured the Greeks. In noble Athens I then acquired a little more education, enough to want to distinguish the straight from the crooked and to seek the truth among the groves of Plato's Academy. However, hard times forced me to leave this pleasant place; the tide of civil war carried me off, an utter tyro, to join ranks that were not destined to match the might of Augustus's army. As soon as Philippi's defeat released me, humiliated, my wings clipped, deprived of my father's estate, I was driven by rash poverty to produce verse. But now that I have enough to live on, I would be incurably insane if I didn't prefer sleeping peacefully to writing verse.]

I do not mean to minimize the ironic notes in this passage; the artist is still shaping his autobiography. Thus, the assertion that poverty drove him to poetry (as though it were a means of profit) and the claim that, since his poetic efforts have insured him a guaranteed

---

[26] A.P. 466–467: *sit ius liceatque perire poetis, / invitum qui servat idem facit occidenti.*

income, he is now ready to retire from this painful and sordid occupation, must be viewed as gross exaggerations. But the total scheme for his life is unified: it is self-education, marked by a series of interruptions, leading toward his present commitment to ethical introspection. Therefore, when he refers to his education in Rome, he now talks of the ethical lessons he learned from books, and Greek books at that, not the role of his father in passing on homespun lore, not the self-sacrifice of the old man that gave him the opportunity to live in Rome in the first place. Again, it was his father who somehow scraped together the money to send Horace to Athens, but Horace disregards that point to discuss the philosophic enhancements of his training. Joining Brutus's army and fighting the disastrous battle of Philippi counts now as a hiatus in his ethical progress. We are not allowed to speculate on Horace's abortive military career as the last effect of his father's influence on the son to enter politics, nor does Horace try to read into his survival at Philippi the personal myth of salvation by the Muses. Writing poetry now becomes a stopgap, another enforced hiatus in his ethical progress. Horace has come a long way from *Satire* 1.4 where he professed uncritical admiration for his simple father and thereby defined the nature of his poetic effort.

I have been attempting to show the complex and changing interrelation of autobiography and art in the works of the most subjective of all Roman poets. Although it is tempting to doubt that some of the so-called personal experiences ever occurred, I believe that we can be satisfied for the time being that almost every episode, whether factual or not, has been shaped by the artist to fit the genre, to lend itself well to the particular kind of self-analysis of each period, and to make the most effective impression on the audience. When Horace, an unknown poet between twenty-five and thirty years of age, was writing the first book of Satires, he still felt the powerful influence of his recently dead father. In order to win favor for his kind of poetry, he used his father to define his own personality and purposes, quite consciously selecting only those details of his father's activities that fitted his needs. What is consistently unmentioned and what probably most distorts our perception of the father's influence is the exact career he had in mind for Horace. I strongly doubt that the father ever envisioned that all his sacrifices would result in a poet. In later years, Horace tended to deny his father by stressing how great he had become, how high he had soared from his humble beginning, whether through the intervention of the Muses ($C.$ 3.30.11–16) or by his own rational efforts (*Epist.* 2.2.41–54).

In the case of Horace, the complex interrelation of autobiography and art is particularly interesting because he is not merely trying to twist facts in order to make himself important. What he is doing is showing how the career of the artist, the responsibilities of the poet affect his own experiences at different times, even oblige him to reinterpret earlier experiences. The ambitious young poet, who thought he could reprove his readers in satire and do a better artistic job than Lucilius, eventually became convinced that his talent lay in writing lyric poetry. Horace viewed his success in this genre as that of a "friend of the Muses," a man saved from Philippi to write poetry in the tradition of distinguished Greek poets, such as Sappho and Alcaeus. So the Odes contained little myths about his personal salvation and accounted for his phenomenal creativity during that decade by presenting him more or less as a servant of the Muses. Then came a new stage, perhaps foreshadowed by such late Odes as that on the Fountain of Bandusia, in which the poet's advancing age increased his self-consciousness and made him no longer content with lyric or the ostensibly unthinking, almost impersonal response to the Muses. His art became cerebral again, resembling in that respect the art of the Satires, but the morality focused on the poet's personal development; he no longer pretended to know it all and criticize others from that superior perspective. He was trying to save his own soul, and his poetry described his efforts. When he was writing the Odes, art became autobiography because poetry was Horace's life. In this final stage of development, we must reverse the equation. Through the way Horace rejects or depreciates his earlier poetic concerns, we glimpse a new awareness: his autobiography is now poetry because his life is the only fitting poetic theme. For his older readers at least, this is the ultimate and most satisfactory integration of two uneasy factors, art and autobiography. Horace is constructing his own understanding of life as he produces his epistolary poetry. And after all, isn't this a most profound application of the Greek word *poiesis*?

THE FORM, PURPOSE, AND POSITION OF HORACE'S
SATIRE I, 8.

When a scholar has immersed himself for so many years in Roman history, archaeology, and literature, it is only appropriate to offer him an essay on some aspect of Rome. Inasmuch as Henry Rowell's studies have ranged widely from Naevius to Ammianus Marcellinus, there is still a wide choice of apt material. However, it seems to me that he has repeatedly returned to topics concerned with Augustan Rome: Vergil, Horace, and the Forum of Augustus. With that in mind, I have chosen to discuss the amusing, but usually ignored, Horatian *Satire* I, 8, a poem which records one of the first topographical changes that anticipate those of Augustan Rome and, I think, draws from that change significance that is typically Horatian.

haec verba qualiacumque ridens legat vir sapiens atque facetus.

According to the usual view of this Satire, it may be classified as a rather slight anecdote with some basis in facts known to Horace's more intimate friends.[1] Canidia, one of two leading characters, plays an important part in two Epodes as well as this Satire and receives incidental mention in *Epode* 3 and *Satires*, II, 1 and II, 8.[2] Whether or not the information of Porphyrio is correct, that Canidia is the Neapolitan Gratidia, it is generally agreed that Horace used Canidia as a symbolic figure.[3] The other leading character in this Satire, Priapus, was invented by Horace, but the invention was presumably inspired by an actual statue in the Gardens of Maecenas.[4] Finally,

---

[1] Cf. E. Fraenkel, *Horace* (Oxford, 1957), p. 124, and W. Ludwig, "Die Komposition der beiden Satirenbücher des Horaz," *Poetica*, II (1968), p. 318. N. Rudd, *The Satires of Horace* (Cambridge, 1966), p. 160, expresses skepticism about any effective links between *Satire* I, 9 and the previous two.

[2] On Canidia, see the able discussion of Fraenkel, pp. 62 ff., and V. Pöschl, *Entretiens Fondation Hardt*, II (1953), pp. 102-4; also C. E. Manning, *Mnemosyne*, XXIII (1970), pp. 393-401.

[3] Porphyrio repeats his statement, that Canidia is Gratidia, in his notes on *Epodes*, 3, 8 and 5, 43 and on *Sat.*, I, 8, 23.

[4] So Rudd, p. 72.

the scene of this little drama, the gardens which Maecenas had made for himself from terrain once used as *commune sepulchrum,* was well known and much frequented by Horace and other friends of Maecenas.[5] Despite these factual links, however, this Satire has not impressed its readers. Modern critics view it as peripheral to the main concerns of Book I of the *Satires,* and some go so far as to assume that Horace put it together from materials alien to the best of his *Satires,* more to get ten poems for the Book than to write an appropriate Satire.[6] Since both I, 7 and 9 may also be classified as " anecdotes," Horace has been conceded the credit of at least grouping his anecdotes, slight though they may be.[7] But that fact hardly improves the general impression of this poem.

The events of Horace's "anecdote" do not arouse much critical interest and can be rapidly summarized. Into Maecenas' garden, where a somewhat powerless talking statue of Priapus presides, come two witches, in order to exploit the former funereal associations of the place for their black magic. When they have proceeded quite far in their fiendish spells, Priapus produces a loud fart and frightens them off, then calls for our laughter (and applause). That four-letter Anglo-Saxon word which I have boldly used has traditionally embarrassed English-speaking critics into a variety of euphemisms, and similar circumlocutions have emerged from French, German, and Italian interpreters. For the same reason, I think, the commentators have not tried to deal with the poem in its own right, as a perhaps carefully composed Satire with qualities analogous to those of the other Satires in Book I. Instead, treating it as an anomaly, they tend to devote their attention to the elements in it which can be regarded as extraneous to the Satires. According to Fraenkel, then, the genesis of I, 8 would be as follows:

[5] Cf. Porphyrio's note on *Sat.*, I, 8, 7. Horace is proceeding towards Maecenas' Esquiline villa in the scene of *Sat.*, II, 6, 23 ff. (cf. 33). In *C.*, III, 29, 9 ff. he tries to lure Maecenas away from the same spot into the quieter country. On the significance of the *horti Maecenatiani* for the recovery and reflourishing of a large part of Rome, see G. Lugli, *I monumenti antichi di Roma e Suburbio,* III (Rome, 1938), pp. 456 ff.

[6] Cf. Fraenkel, pp. 112 and 124.

[7] E. g., by Ludwig (above, n. 1) and his predecessors.

Horace took certain conventional forms and slightly manipulated them in order to place them, with at least partial propriety, in a book of Satires.[8]

As Fraenkel observed, when Horace decided to make the statue of Priapus into the narrator, he was exploiting a tactic common to a variety of Greek epigrams. Statues bearing inscriptions are often represented as speaking in the inscription, just as funerary inscriptions frequently affect to give a voice to the dead.[9] Priapus resorts to the familiar contrast between *olim* and *nunc,* not only in relation to his own change from useless wood to god but also in commenting on the transformation of the common burial ground into Maecenas' charming garden. This, too, adheres to well-known inscriptional patterns. But a talking statue of Priapus owes something to a poetic form popular in Horace's own period, Priapean verse, of which somewhat more than eighty poems have survived from a collection assembled in the first century of our era. In these poems, Priapus presents himself less as *furum aviumque / maxima formido* (the claim he advances in *Satire* I, 8, 3-4) than as the terror and delight of handsome young boys and girls. The purpose of Priapean verse is to extract witty situations from the ithyphallic god.

It does not take much effort to see that the identification of epigrammatic and Priapean features in *Satire* I, 8, does not contribute much to its interpretation. The opposition of then and now in 1-3 serves merely as an opening motif and, as I shall show, does not operate independently but is subordinated to the major themes of the Satire. Horace's Priapus possesses all the requisite equipment to threaten obscene penalties in the conventional Priapean manner, but Horace chooses to represent him in quite a different fashion: this Priapus can do nothing with the witches, is himself terrified by their magic, and it is only by accident, when he loses control of himself from fear, that the unintentional fart causes the comic dénouement. Thus, the normally prominent *mentula* remains quite literally

[8] Fraenkel, p. 124.

[9] In *Iamboi* 7 and 9, Callimachus represented Herms as speaking, to provide a local aetiology. These are perhaps the closest Greek parallels to *Sat.*, I, 8.

inutile lignum throughout the poem,[10] and Horace's Priapus scares off the intruders paradoxically with a novel part of his anatomy.

The commentators then resort to another conventional aspect to help explain Horace's purpose in this poem: it is aetiological, they suggest. "When he was walking in Maecenas' gardens Horace may possibly have seen a wooden Priapus with an oddly shaped posterior."[11] Possibly. But since Horace does not use the standard methods of aetiology, for example those of Callimachus' *Iamboi* 7 and 9 or Propertius in IV, 2, such aetiology as is present in *Satire* I, 8 could be appreciated only by the private friends of Maecenas who frequented his gardens and recognized the veiled allusion to a particular statue. Another feature of the poem attracts commentary: the dramatization of magic rites. Lejay found this the most significant aspect of *Satire* I, 8, and he connected it with what seems to be a controversial view of magic in this period of the 30's B. C. Thus, he argued that Horace expressed through this drama his adherence to the position adopted by Octavian when he expelled sorcerers from Italy.[12] Rudd does not go that far, but he also believes that the magical element of the Satire has definite contemporary reference.[13]

This accumulation of material about epigrams, Priapea, aetiology, and magic does shed some illumination on *Satire* I, 8, but not so much as the commentators seem to think. They have not accounted for the essential form of the Satire; they have evaded the issue of its purpose by vaguely labeling it an anecdote; and they see only the slightest reasons for its inclusion in Book I of the *Satires* at this point. Accordingly, I consider it more important to read the poem for itself and as part of its book than to attempt to illuminate it by external data.

[10] The author of *Priap.*, 73 contrived an ingenious situation from *inutile lignum*, understood in this obscene sense.

[11] Rudd (above, n. 1), p. 72.

[12] P. Lejay, in his edition of the *Satires* (Paris, 1911), p. 220. Since the expulsion of sorcerers took place in 33 B. C., several years after the publication of *Sat.*, I, 8, Lejay assumes that the official antagonism to magic was manifested well in advance of the drastic action of 33 and that Horace, friend of Maecenas, knew and shared it.

[13] Rudd, pp. 72 ff.

Consider again the point made by Fraenkel: the talking Priapus uses the epigrammatic contrast of *olim* and *nunc*. The contrast is there, but it is not really helpful, I think, to label it epigrammatic, for Horace has constructed the entire poem on a series of contrasts, only one of which might be derived from epigram. As Priapus has changed from *inutile lignum* (1) to *deus* (3) and *maxima formido* (4), he is located in "new" gardens (*novis in hortis,* 7), and by mentioning this, he introduces the second antithesis. What once (*prius,* 8) was the common burying ground of paupers has now (*nunc,* 14) become a healthful and pleasant spot for a stroll. Is there a connection between these two interwoven contrasts? It seems likely, especially when one realizes that the main scene features a hostile encounter between Priapus and the witches Canidia and Sagana. The function of Priapus is to preserve the new pleasant garden-like qualities of the spot, whereas Canidia and her companion have invaded the garden in order to revive its former sinister aspects as a cemetery. As they proceed in their malevolent rituals, Priapus seems to grow weaker, when the sudden sound that he produces in weak terror terrifies in turn the witches and so once again gives him mastery over his little domain. Thus, an important theme of the entire Satire emerges in the contrast between once and now. The former times are associated with a useless piece of figwood, a paupers' graveyard, and evil witches; the present times offer instead a genial and well-behaved Priapus and a delightful garden which is in his care. The plot of the Satire focuses on this opposition, the threat to present values from former evils, and the miraculous defeat of this menace.

Horace devotes by far the largest single portion of the Satire to his lurid description of the rites practiced by Canidia and Sagana (22-44). With their fingernails, they scratch a hole in the earth, over which they kill a black lamb, rending it with their teeth. Setting up two mannikins, one of wool and one of wax, they proceed to invoke the evil powers of the Underworld. They have nearly completed the rite when the providential fart drives them off. All these minute details work, I think, to emphasize the sinister nature of Priapus' enemies. It is a cumulative effect; Horace does not single out for special emphasis parts of the total picture.

Since we are viewing these witches through the eyes of Priapus, it is important to note how he comments on them. First of all, he presents himself in a curious way, for he does not talk or behave like the usual Priapus. He seems devoid of the salty lust normally exhibited and boasted about by the god of the Priapea and familiar myths. Far from being a successful and frightening guard for the park, poor Priapus feels helpless before these witches, *carminibus quae versant atque venenis / humanos animos* (19-20). At the climax of the scene, he declares that he did not fail to avenge what he had witnessed (*non testis inultus,* 44), but surprises us by the main verb which follows in enjambement: *horruerim* (45): I shook with fear! Then he explains. Indirectly, his fear did wreak vengeance, for it caused the terrifying *peditum.* Whereupon the lurid scene dissolves into comic movement, as the witches rush back into the city dropping in their haste various essential parts of their horrid being.

On the one hand, then, *Satire* I, 8 dramatizes an encounter between the new and the old qualities of the Esquiline; on the other, and in more general terms, it shows how the inoffensive and fearful Priapus took vengeance on the women "who upset human minds by spells and poisons." Rudd briefly noted that *Satire* I, 8 "resembles 1.7 in being a tale of comic revenge" ; [14] but he did not pursue the point except to observe correctly that I, 8 handles its revenge more skilfully. I know of no scholar who has remarked on the more important link between the plots of I, 7 and 8, which can be recognized by matching the passages cited above from I, 8, 19-20 and 44-5 with the opening lines of I, 7:

> proscripti Regis Rupili pus *atque venenum*
> hybrida quo pacto sit Persius *ultus,* opinor
> omnibus et lippis notum et tonsoribus esse.

Persius gained revenge against the poison of Rex by resorting to a bad pun on Brutus the regicide that dissolved his fierce encounter with the foe into comedy. Now, we are bound to admit that the poison of Rex was metaphorical: it was venomous invective. I hope to show, however, that the distinction between

[14] Rudd, p. 67.

metaphorical and literal poison is less important here than the fact that Horace used the same key word for both, to work out a common dramatic situation, the comic punishment of the " poisoner."

In a recent article, Buchholz has probed the meaning of *Satire* I, 7 and shown how Horace has employed the comic dispute between Rupilius Rex and Persius in order to present, among other things, some of his own literary ideas in polemic.[15] When Persius cracks his pun and reduces Rex to the laughing-stock of the court, he effectively punishes Rex for his intemperate name-calling. In a certain sense, then, Horace is dramatizing a basic theme of his satiric disagreement with Lucilius, that simple laughter achieves more than spiteful invective. All the angry words of both Rex and Persius accomplish nothing, whereas the bad pun devised by Persius as a last resort achieves more than he anticipated: the audience laughs at his enemy. No doubt, the audience was laughing at both foes, and the main result is that the pun reduces the tensions of the bitter dispute. Nevertheless, according to the stated theme, we have been watching how poison was punished.

If the anecdotal *Satire* I, 7 exhibits, though with artful dissimulation, some of Horace's fundamental literary ideas, it is equally possible that *Satire* I, 8, anecdotal as it may be, works with basic Horatian themes. Priapus tells of his revenge upon the witches who upset men's minds with their charms and poisons (*carminibus atque venenis,* 19), and in fact he frightens them away while they are in the process of making their spells and concocting seemingly poisonous potions. Unlike Persius in *Satire* I, 7, Priapus is not the intended victim of the poison, and this fact helps to clarify the antithesis between the witches and himself. Although his notorious shape and the special personality given him by Horace make him superficially comic, Priapus also acquires associations from his connection with Maecenas. The witches, on the other hand, are prejudiced by their attempts to exploit the older features of the cemetery. Thus, the rather genial, inoffensive, easily shocked Priapus may suggest, in a humorous understated manner, some of the positive

[15] V. Buchheit, "Homerparodie und Literaturkritik in Horazens Sat. I 7 and I 9," *Gymnasium,* LXXV (1968), pp. 542 ff.

values of Maecenas' Circle, whereas the malevolent witches suggest the literary opponents who are too devoted to the dead, destructive past. It is not of course necessary to allegorize the antithesis into a strictly literary one, but on the other hand the literary allusions form part of the total complex. Thus, the "charms" and "poisons" of the witches remind us of the poisonous invective of lampoons and the Lucilian tradition.[16] The attitude towards the literary/ethical failing implied by poisonous language (*Satire* I, 7) and poisonous spells (I, 8) is a consistent one in Book I of the *Satires*: Horace and his friends reject it, ridicule it, and substitute for it the more genial manner of laughter: *ridiculum acri / fortius* (I, 10, 14-15). Everyone but Rex and Persius laughs at the comic animosity which these two "heroes" express. Similarly, Priapus invites us to laugh at the comic discomfiture of the witches: *cum magno risuque iocoque videres* (50). Their malevolence has dwindled to nothing. With the same playful ending, Horace concluded the report of his journey to Brundisium: *Gnatia . . . dedit risusque iocosque* (I, 5, 97-8): he laughed at trivial events and ignored the bitter political antagonisms that swirled around his head.

In the narrator-hero it employs, then, *Satire* I, 8 recapitulates many of the central themes of Book I, though in a patently comic form. Priapus announces his function as that of frightening away thieves and birds (*furum aviumque / maxima formido,* 3-4). In fact, he neither performs that role in this drama nor does he behave in the lusty, menacing way towards boys and girls that his counterparts in the *Priapea* constantly exhibit.[17] In a grotesquely accidental fashion, by means of his prodigious fart, he overcomes the evil witches and their ghoulish designs, thus preserving the creative, idyllic world of Maecenas' garden

[16] In *Sat.*, I, 4, 100-1 Horace represents the spiteful language of people (like Lucilius), which he avoids, in metaphorical terms as follows: *nigrae sucus lolliginis* and *aerugo mera.* Verdigris is poisonous. In *Sat.*, II, 1, 48 Horace playfully deals with the invective aspects of Roman satire and once again uses Canidia's poison as an analogy for the satirist's harsh language. And in II, 1, 82 he puns on *carmina* (poems or lampoons).

[17] It is perhaps relevant to point out here that Horace in *Sat.*, I, 4, 60 ff. expressly differentiates his satiric manner from the fearsome ways of Sulcius and Caprius, "detectives" whom he calls *magnus timor latronibus.*

from assault. Master of the scene after the hasty retreat of Canidia, he almost invites us, it seems to me, to view him as a humorously distorted image of Horatian satire itself. I shall not go so far as to call Priapus a comic version of Horace, although I would not reject such a suggestion. However, the first-person narrative of a "dangerous encounter" that ended paradoxically in victory for the weaker individual takes us easily from *Satire* I, 8 to *Satire* I, 9, where indeed Horace narrates his own experiences, where Horace "defends" Maecenas' home from attack, where Horace has all but succumbed to the belligerent pressures of his talkative, ambitious companion when a "miracle" occurs to rescue him and preserve Maecenas' world intact.[18]

I have attempted to describe the way Horace uses this Satire, to which he gave the ostensibly innocent form of an anecdote, to glance at some of the dominant themes of his Book: his admiration for Maecenas and the creative goals of political and literary development to which Octavian's adviser dedicated himself; his disagreement with the methods and results of Lucilius; his working hypothesis that laughter achieves more than venomous invective; his charming sense that one's own efforts are most subject to ironic observation. It remains only to suggest some of the good reasons Horace found for placing the Satire where he did in the Book.[19] Satires 5 and 6 both deal with Horace's view of politics as a way of life; he ends the latter poem by openly declaring for *otium* rather than the *onus* of political office. They also exhibit the satirist's view that invective accomplishes less than laughter, partly by laughing at those who use invective, partly by winning the audience through laughter to agreement with his moral argument. In Satires 7, 8, and 9 Horace avoids the tactic of preaching about himself and casts his poems in the form of anecdotes, only the last of

[18] See my article, "Horace, the Unwilling Warrior: *Satire* I, 9," *A. J. P.*, LXXVII (1956), pp. 148-66.

[19] The most important works on the arrangement of the *Satires* in recent years are those of Ludwig (above, n. 1) and C. A. van Rooy. Van Rooy has so far published articles on the order of I, 1-4, on I, 4 and 10, and on I, 5 and 6. See *Acta Classica*, XI (1968), pp. 37-82, XIII (1970), pp. 7-27 and 45-59. Another article on I, 7 will appear in *A. C.*, XIV (1971) and a final one on I, 8 and 9 in *A. C.*, XV (1972).

which records an experience of Horace himself. In 7, as some critics have noted, Horace makes of a trial an exchange of invective that produces general laughter, much as he did earlier in Satire 5 with the "battle" between Messius and Sarmentus (51 ff.). Inasmuch, however, as he describes the plot in terms of revenge upon infection and poison, he prepares a parallel with the plot of Satire 8. The energy and passion which Rex and Persius expend upon their mutual name-calling elicit laughter from the court and from the satirist, and indirectly they tend to confirm the value of the *otium* which the satirist has chosen in Satire 6.

In Satire 8, although the encounter between Priapus and the witches follows the general plot of Satire 7, new features appear. The satirist withdraws, and we enjoy the narration of a central character, Priapus himself. Instead of two relatively unimportant men, now perhaps dead, whose encounter took place nearly a decade ago far from Rome, we observe Priapus, Canidia, and Sagana in Maecenas' newly created gardens. The representative qualities of both Priapus and the witches seem so obvious that it is not difficult to view this encounter as a conflict between the malevolent forces of the past (including the Lucilian tradition) and the creative spirit of Maecenas and his friends. Priapus' revenge, totally accidental and the comic result of his own fear, once again emphasizes the surprising power of laughter. And now the way has been well prepared for Satire 9, in which Horace replaces Priapus as narrator, his defense of Maecenas' way of life becomes explicit, his adversary plainly encompasses the sins both of ambition and literary vulgarity, and the escape of Horace appears as dramatic as Priapus' theatrical fart, but less gross. Thus, Satire 8 plays an important part in the succession of three anecdotes, all of which should be read as more than mere anecdotes, for it picks up the plot of Satire 7 while introducing new motifs that in turn ready us for Satire 9.[20]

[20] In 9, 31 Horace may be alluding to the theme of poison of the previous two Satires: he repeats a prediction that he will not succumb to poison or other familiar dangers, but will perish because of something much worse, a *garrulus*.

HORACE, THE UNWILLING WARRIOR: *SATIRE* I, 9.

In his monumental study of the influence of Lucilius upon Horace, G. C. Fiske brought the question as close to a definite answer as the fragmentary nature of Lucilius would permit. Considering these few remnants and the well-known scruples of Horace against extended verbal imitation, one must admit that Fiske emerged with an impressive list of similar motifs and expressions between the two satirists.[1] To be sure, similarities in detail are not always an exact indication of the individual method of treatment,[2] and the latitude, which a poet might require, was never denied Horace.[3] When he came to consider *S.*, I, 9, Fiske inherited a theory first advanced by Iltgen,[4] but ignored by subsequent scholars,[5] that the Satire was largely influenced by an earlier work of Lucilius. Careful study of Horace and an imaginative reconstruction of the fragments of Book VI of Lucilius convinced Fiske that Horace was indebted, not merely for lines, but for the general plan of his poem. " We may conclude, therefore, that the sixth book of Lucilius contained a satire upon the bore, which was the direct model for Horace's ninth satire of the first book." [6]

Of approximately fifteen lines in Lucilius which confirmed Fiske in his opinion, perhaps those which are most generally accepted as influencing Horace's poem are 231-2 (Marx) :

---

[1] G. C. Fiske, *Lucilius and Horace: a Study in the Classical Theory of Imitation* (Madison, 1920).

[2] Vergil offers the best example of controlled imitation. In his important book, V. Pöschl, *Die Dichtkunst Virgils* (Wiesbaden, 1950), studies Vergil's use of Homeric similes and reaches striking conclusions about the former's methods of imitation.

[3] E. g., Fiske, pp. 46, 134.

[4] J. J. Iltgen, *De Horatio Lucilii Aemulo* (Montbauer, 1872), pp. 18 and 19.

[5] None of the following editions regard the influence of Lucilius upon *S.*, I, 9 as significant beyond lines 1 and 78: L. Mueller (Wien, 1891); J. Orellius, 4th ed. (Berlin, 1892); J. H. Kirkland (Boston, 1894); P. Lejay (Paris, 1911); E. P. Morris (New York, 1909); Kiessling-Heinze, 5th ed. (Berlin, 1921).

[6] *Op. cit.*, p. 335.

(nil) ut discrepat ac ‘ τὸν δὲ ἐξήρπαξεν ’Απόλλων ’
fiat.[7]

The Greek phrase resembles so closely Horace, I, 9, 78: *sic me
servavit Apollo*, that, even without the authority of Porphyrio,[8]
a connection between the two passages would ultimately have
been observed. The question next arises: In what sense and why
is Horace imitating Lucilius? The answers proposed fall into
three main groups:

1. Horace, like Lucilius, is referring to the ultimate source
of the allusion, Homer. He thus, like Lucilius, acquires the
advantages of epic parody and ends his description on a humorous note appropriate to the ironic character that he here most
successfully achieves.

2. Horace is implicitly criticizing Lucilius for citing the
original Greek.[9] He therefore carefully translates the Greek,
places the line in a significant position, and still has the advantages of parody.

3. Horace is implicitly criticizing Lucilius' uneconomic use of
the parody and demonstrating his own technical superiority. It
appears that Lucilius inserted the Greek phrase, as was frequently his custom, to serve as a witty contrast, as a neat, exaggerated reference to an incident entirely alien to his context.[10]
On the other hand, when Horace adopts this phrase as his conclusion, he cleverly makes it relevant to his dramatic development. Here, the focus of economy is *Apollo*. As the god who
watches over poets and concerns himself with principles of justice, Apollo can be regarded, on the supernatural level, as the
agent effecting Horace's release from the *garrulus*. In human
terms, the bore's legal opponent appeared when Horace was
desperate, dragged the fool off to justice, and thus left Horace

[7] *Op. cit.*, p. 335: "The closing line of the Horatian satire was
directly modelled on that of Lucilius, as is proved by Porphyrio's quotation of line 231."

[8] Porphyr.: "Hoc de illo sensu Homerico sumpsit, quem et Lucilius
in sexto Satirarum repraesentavit sic dicens. . . ."

[9] Cf. Horace's attacks on Lucilius' use of Greek words in *S.*, I, 10,
23 ff.

[10] Cf. the reconstruction of Lucilius' argument by Fiske, *op. cit.*, pp.
335 ff.

a free man. It is, however, the genius of Horace to transform this experience into an amusing drama, to picture Apollo as a *deus ex machina*, and to give the scene a finished form by recalling the opening reference to his poetic concerns (line 2).

It is evident that none of these explanations of 9, 78 is exclusively correct; in fact, the most adequate interpretation would—as Lejay did [11]—synthesize these apparent alternatives into a coherent whole. Accordingly, the understanding of Horace's conclusion generally agrees with the words of Ritter: "clam se inde discessisse poetice significavit," [12] where "poetice" is applied to the wealth of allusion which Lucilius' successor ingeniously develops from a line used by Lucilius in his typically witty and extravagant manner.

Synthesis of these three interpretations does not necessarily exhaust the potential allusions in Horace's line. Since economy is characteristic of Horace, it is tempting to speculate on other applications of his words, which would extend the scope of his poetic parody. Recently, E. T. Salmon, without denying the validity of the literary explanations hitherto advanced, has proposed an additional reference for *Apollo*. [13] He believes that the Satire has consistent topographical allusions indicating various stages in Horace's progress towards Caesar's Gardens, the destination announced in 18. As we are told in the first line, Horace was walking along the Via Sacra when he was accosted by the *garrulus*. Later, he mentions arriving at the Temple of Vesta (line 35). Apart from these two specific references to sites in the Forum, Horace gives no further direct indication of the scene of action. Salmon, assuming quite plausibly that there are indirect indications, has suggested an attractive solution to the difficulty usually sensed in *tricesima sabbata* (l. 69) [14] by interpreting the phrase as a subtle allusion to the Jewish Quarter

[11] *Op. cit.* in his excellent notes on line 78.

[12] F. Ritter, in his edition of the *Satires* (Leipzig, 1857), note on line 78.

[13] E. T. Salmon, "Horace's Ninth Satire in its Setting," *Studies in Honor of Gilbert Norwood* (Toronto, 1952), pp. 184-93.

[14] Cf. the efforts of interpretation in Orellius, *op. cit.*, and Lejay, *op. cit.* Because of the difficulty and the absence of any definite indications as to the significance of the phrase, Kiessling-Heinze, *op. cit.*, regard the words as devoid of factual application.

near the Forum Boarium. Horace, in this view, has moved out of the Forum Romanum, down the Vicus Tuscus, and into the Jewish residential area. Further, it was near here that the *garrulus* unexpectedly met his legal opponent. In the ensuing confusion, Horace escaped, to take refuge in the sanctuary of the patron of poets, as Salmon infers from the conclusion. *Apollo*, who signifies the god of justice and poetry, can also be considered topographically relevant, as applying to the Temple of Apollo Medicus, newly re-built by Sosius in the late Thirties B. C.[15] In this type of interpretation, there is an opportunity to check the theory against facts. For this reason, Salmon has been challenged by the Roman topographer F. Castagnoli, who denies the allusions suggested and attempts to return to the limited interpretations listed above. *Apollo*, in fact, he restricts to its Homeric relevance, while he seems to regard the Lucilian parallel as coincidental. Accordingly, he states: " L'acceno ad Apollo non ha bisogno di un riferimento topographico, ma, come commenta Porfirione, e semplicemente una reminiscenza omerica (*Il.* XX, 443) citata anche de Lucilio." [16] The present writer takes no position in this controversy; yet it is significant that the disagreement springs from the relevance or irrelevance of an admittedly allusive line.

Castagnoli's phrase " reminiscenza omerica " suggests still another method of interpreting *sic me servavit Apollo* and of defining the limits of Lucilius' influence upon this poem. In the first place, Horace translates Homer freely, whereas Lucilius cited him verbatim. When, then, Lucilius used the phrase, he was obliged to attach the Greek line to a Latin context; he was, we may say, aiming at the conflict between the Greek and Latin, between the epic and the satiric, the supernatural and the real. As if to mark the opposition clearly, Lucilius connected the Homeric words to his context in the form of a negative simile

---

[15] There is a potential difficulty in dating the Satire as late as the building of Sosius' Temple, since the date of construction is often assigned to the year of Sosius' consulship. Salmon argues plausibly that the temple was erected in 33 B. C., as Shipley had already suggested. If so, there is no necessary conflict, since Book II of the *Satires* was written in the years 33-30 B. C.

[16] F. Castagnoli, " Note di Topografia Romana," *Bull. Comm. Arch. Com.*, LXXIV (1952), p. 53.

(*nil ut discrepat ac*).[17] The effect is to imply the inapplicability
of the Homeric context to Lucilius' story, and, in my opinion,
Fiske rightly concludes that the satirist was humorously referring to a frivolous situation, quite possibly the unwelcome
presence of a bore.[18] Such an inference would be consistent
with what is known of Lucilius' treatment of Greek: his tendency to extravagance, but also his achievement of witty statements.[19] By contrast, Horace assimilates the line of Homer to
his context, makes himself the object instead of the non-per-
sonal τὸν, and alters ἐξήρπαξεν to the more emotional *servavit*.
These changes enable Horace to use *Apollo* more fully. In particular, the rejection of the simile as a method of using the
reminiscence frees Horace from the necessity of a mechanical
citation of Homer merely for purposes of witty contrast, permits
him instead to adapt Homer with subtlety to his dramatic
account.

The indirect method of citation, I suggest, makes Homer more
relevant to Horace than to Lucilius. It is, therefore, necessary
secondly to return to the context in Homer upon which Horace's
phrase is based, to see what possible bearing it can have upon
Horace's hypothetical experience with the bore.[20] At this point
in Book XX of the *Iliad*, the epic poet describes the brief encounter between Hector and Achilles. Hector's efforts to wound
Achilles are checked by Athena. As Achilles is rushing in for
the kill, Apollo intervenes and carries the Trojan off in a cloud
to safety. These details fit the traditional interpretation of
Horace previously mentioned, namely, that the intervention of

[17] The negative *nil*, not in Porphyrio, is added by Marx. Subsequent
editors, however, have accepted the emendation: so Warmington and
Terzaghi; and Fiske reads *nil*.

[18] Fiske, *op. cit.*, p. 335 rejects Marx's interpretation of the line.
Marx imagined a situation in which somebody is badly beaten up and
prays that he may be saved in the miraculous manner of Hector: " ita
enim pugnis et fustibus erat male mulcatus." I doubt that Lucilius'
use of Greek words was that subtle.

[19] On the use of Hellenisms in Lucilius, cf. W. C. Korfmacher,
"'Grecizing' in Lucilian Satire," *C. J.*, XXX (1935), pp. 453-62; also,
M. Puelma Piwonka, *Lucilius und Kallimachos: zur Geschichte einer
Gattung der hellenistisch-römische Poesie* (Frankfurt, 1949), pp. 13 ff.

[20] I agree with the majority of scholars, who regard this Satire as
based on an imaginary experience.

Apollo in the *Iliad* is humorously appropriate to his imagined rescue of the poet Horace. One factor, however, has been ignored: the original context is a battle scene. Apollo saves his favorite, who is a warrior, not a poet. On the surface, the basic martial context seems to have no bearing upon the drama here enacted, which plainly presents anything but warfare. But Horace has employed throughout *S.*, I, 9 a number of similar expressions, epic and martial, which can be related to the Homeric battle; when related, they assume form as a new level of meaning based on the significance of battle in this Satire, of Horace as a warrior. Further developed, this new pattern explains more specifically certain portions of the drama which have been viewed simply as humorous exaggerations. It can be shown, I believe, that Horace has treated the dramatic situation in a different manner from Lucilius, so as to utilize extensively the martial overtones of his Homeric original.

As Heinze noted, the first obvious statement of a military word occurs in 42-3, where Horace visualizes the bore as a conqueror (*victore*). If, however, this passage is patent, reinforced as it is by *contendere*, it is also anticipated at several earlier points, as Horace intimates his attitude towards his companion in terms applicable also to war. When the bore rushes up and seizes his hand, Horace implies that the act is an affront to him. The man does not sense the unfriendliness in Horace's over-polite reply to his own effusive greeting; he persists. Horace, therefore, determines to end the conversation immediately and bluntly says goodbye (6). The word suggesting bluntness, *occupo*, is more commonly employed in other senses. In its root meaning, it is a word of war: to seize, take possession of, and, by derivation, to begin the attack.[21] By itself, the word might be simply humorous. Supported in the context by *arrepta*, which regularly has violent associations,[22] it hints at a battle

[21] For *occupare* with a personal object in a martial context, cf. *Aen.*, X, 699: *Latagum saxo atque ingenti fragmine montis / occupat os faciemque adversam.* Horace uses this word in *Epist.*, I, 7, 66 to signify abrupt address, though without any suggestion of the military theme.

[22] There are four usages of *arripere* in Horace, all of them indicating violent activity. Three of them suggest the ferocity of animals. Cf. *A. P.*, 475, where *arripuit* is associated by simile with *ursus*. In *S.*, II, 1, 69 and 3, 224, the verb is characteristic of the satirist's invective.

theme which will gradually become clearer. In this sense, the opening lines could be visualized as the first stages of a personal combat between Horace and the bore. The man's attitude is aggressive (*arrepta*) and offensive to Horace, so, in desperation, Horace determines to fight (*occupo*). It is a strange type of battle. Longing only to escape, Horace tries every device he can invent to frighten or discourage the *garrulus*. No matter what he does or says, he is beaten; while, the *garrulus*, merely by forcing his company on the unfortunate poet, is regarded as an enemy in pursuit. In each passage of arms—an intolerable effusion from the *garrulus* followed by a desperate, though polite, reply from Horace—the bore emerges victorious, because he is completely obtuse to Horace's feelings and irresistibly persistent in his own crude designs. This nightmare battle,[23] perceived in the conflict of personalities, is fought by words. As the drama proceeds, it becomes more and more evident that the satirist treats the situation as a real combat between himself and his objectionable companion.

Part of the irony of the Satire depends upon the fact that the bore does not realize how offensive he is. When he praises himself as *doctus* (7), it is a painful wound (*misere*, 8) to a real poet. No longer willing to fight bravely face-to-face, Horace tries to break off the battle (*discedere*, 8).[24] The engagement becomes a running conflict, in which Horace periodically makes a futile gesture of resistance and attempts to discourage his pur-

Only *Epist.*, I, 7, 89 does not fit the metaphor. As for the phrase *arrepta manu*, it is quite possible that Horace is thinking of a line in Plautus and its violent associations: cf. *Curc.*, 597: *manum arripuit mordicus*. That the line is well-known is indicated by the fact that it is imitated by Turpilius (*Com.*, 108) and by Apuleius (*Met.*, VIII, 23). In short, the first view we have of the *garrulus* is carefully influenced by *arrepta*, so as to suggest his aggressiveness.

[23] I should like to have found support for my first impression, that the whole scene resembles Achilles' pursuit around the walls of Ilium in *Il.*, XXII; I do not now believe, however, that Horace justifies the connection.

[24] Horace uses *discedere* three times in this same military sense. Cf. *Epist.*, I, 7, 17: *victor violens discessit ab hoste*; also, *Epist.*, II, 2, 99, where he is describing the rivalry of critics, and *S.*, I, 7, 17, where he comments on the famous meeting of Glaucus and Diomedes in the *Iliad*. For the military meaning in general, cf. *T. L. L.*, *s. v.*, § C. It appears in Caesar, e. g., *B. C.*, III, 112, 7, and Livy, e. g., IX, 44, 8.

suer. First, he tries to outdistance the man (*ire ocius*, 9); then, he stops to fight, makes a stand (*consistere*).[25] The martial sense of *consistere* and the normally poetic connotations of *ocius* are then combined with the context implied by *sudor* (10). On the dramatic level, Horace's sweating is an amusing exaggeration; an unpleasant conversation does make one perspire, but one is hardly bathed in sweat. In the *Iliad*, however, men sweat (ἰδρώς) under the strain of combat when they are defeated and flee in terror, as Lycaon (XXI, 51); when they have been wounded;[26] and when they fight well, but against greater numbers.[27] The passage concerning Ajax and his battlesweat (XVI, 109) is a prototype for the description of Turnus, when he is hard-pressed within the encampment of the Trojans; and ἰδρώς is the basis of *sudor* in Vergil.[28] After this, other intolerable remarks from the *garrulus* provoke the unspoken thought in Horace: *o te, Bolane, cerebri / felicem* (11-12). Horace wishes that he were choleric, that his temper frightened company; his exaggerated emotion, however, continues the overtone of epic warfare. Frequently, the epic hero cries out in a moment of crisis, envying the fortune of another, particularly his happy death in battle.[29] Similarly, Horace envies Bolanus, because a bad temper has always permitted the latter to escape from such predicaments as that which the poet faces.

Even the obtuse bore eventually perceives that Horace is trying to get away (14). Rather than permit this, he blatantly insists on accompanying his victim. As he puts it, Horace is helpless (*nil agis*, 15); he, the bore, will hold on to his man (*usque tenebo*); he will continue his pursuit (*persequar*, 16) wherever Horace goes. The militant overtone of *persequar* is unmistakable, and it tinges the other verbs. Confident of capturing Horace, the bore boasts that he will pursue him indefinitely. Still, Horace tries some strategy. He invents a friend

[25] Cf. *Aen.*, IX, 789: *agmine denso / consistunt*. For the military meaning in general, cf. *T. L. L.*, *s. v.*, § I 2b. The word appears in Caesar, e. g., *B. G.*, II, 21, 6, and Livy, e. g., I, 27, 5.

[26] Cf. *Il.*, V, 796; XI, 811.

[27] Cf. *Il.*, XIII, 711; XVI, 109.

[28] *Aen.*, IX, 812.

[29] Cf. *Aen.*, XI, 159: *felix morte tua*. It is in a similar context that Aeneas voices his emotions: *o terque quaterque beati* . . . (I, 94).

far across the Tiber, a sick friend, whom he must visit (17-18). This ruse makes not the slightest impression on the dull wit of the fool. Instead of being discouraged by the prospective walk, he boasts of his energy and repeats his threat of constant pursuit: *non sum piger: usque sequar te* (19). The choice of *piger* is designed, for to be *piger* is to be unheroic.[30] When, however, the bore denies that he is *piger*, Horace is making him reveal his basic fault. A definite relation exists between his energetic eagerness and his offensiveness, to the extent that, concentrated on his own antipathetic purposes, the *garrulus* is blind to the reactions of others. With ill-concealed distaste, Horace resigns himself to the pursuit: he compares himself to an overburdened ass (20-1).[31] Then, his companion sets out to ingratiate himself with the poet. Naturally, he chooses the most offensive approach, comparing himself to Hermogenes, the most obnoxious of poetasters in Horace's opinion (22-5). The stage directions are suggestive: *incipit ille* (21). As a verb of speech, *incipere* is generally associated with epic.[32] Moreover, when the verb precedes its subject, the form resembles the emphatic technique of formal poetry. Implicitly, then, 22 ff. is introduced as an epic speech. At the end of 22, where it will receive stress, Horace has placed *amicum*, a word which is markedly ironic as applied to this person who antagonizes Horace with every word he speaks. Rather, the boasts uttered by this man render him *inimicum, hostem*. To me, there is a suggestion here of another aspect of battle. About to come to blows at last, our epic heroes praise themselves and threaten the enemy with reports of their fearsomeness. Horace interrupts the offensive chatter of the *garrulus* with his rejoinder (26-7). It is intended to use the sick friend as a threat. As it is put, though, the satirist seems to be reminding the bore of his fond relatives, warning him of the

[30] Cf. *Epist.*, II, 1, 124: *militiae quamquam piger et malus*. In fact, *piger* regularly denotes him who is unfit for military exploits. Cf. Cicero, *Fam.*, VII, 17, 1; Livy, XXI, 25, 6; Juvenal, 8, 248. By contrast, *impiger* connotes the zeal and energy necessary for war. Cf. *Carm.*, IV, 14, 22: *impiger hostium / vexare turmas*.

[31] Tempting though it may be, the simile should not be taken as analogous to the epic simile in *Il.*, XI, 558 ff., describing Ajax in terms of an ass.

[32] Cf. *Aen.*, VI, 103: *ut primum cessit furor et rabida ora quierunt, / incipit Aeneas heros*.

folly of attacking so mightly a hero as himself.[33] Thus, *salvo* (27) connotes not merely preservation from sickness, but safety in war.[34]

Unfortunately, the bore frustrates Horace's fearsome threat. He has buried all his family, and there are no relatives to worry about his health. Horace can only envy the dead as *felices* (28), people who have died and fortunately escaped the fate he is undergoing (cf. 12). Now at last the hero realizes that he is doomed. Fatalistically he enters combat, requesting a quick finish (*confice*, 29).[35] Then begins the oracle which, as others have noted, is an epic parody.[36] To describe a passage as epic parody, however, does not reach the heart of the question, as this paper is attempting to demonstrate; while implying the humorous effect, it does not explain the function of the parody in its context. From acquaintance with Horatian economy, it would be reasonable to assume that the poet has used epic parody here because it is thematically functional, not merely for its witty impression. It is accordingly necessary to determine the epic context specifically relevant to this Satire. We have seen that the satirist regards his unwelcome companion, to a certain extent, as an enemy and therefore pictures himself as a warrior fighting a losing battle with him. Now, a situation suggests itself in which the satirist describes himself as the hero who suddenly remembers the prophecy of his death in battle at the moment of fulfilment. There are analogues in Homer. Ritter pointed to the oracle which Polyphemus recalled after being blinded.[37] On the whole, the context is not so appropriate as the more common use of oracles in

[33] Cf. the speech of Achilles to Aeneas in *Il.*, XX, 196.

[34] In two other cases, Horace uses *salvus* to apply to circumstances of war: cf. *Epist.*, I, 2, 10 and 16, 27.

[35] It will be noticed that Horace is practicing ellipsis regularly and has here omitted the direct object of *confice*. The conventional object would probably have been something like *negotium*, as it is interpreted in *T. L. L.*, *s. v.* § I A 2b. However, the ellipsis permits a personal subject, specifically *me*. To fit such a construction, there is a sense of *conficere* related to killing: cf. *T. L. L.*, *s. v.*, § III E 1. Cf. Livy, VI, 13, 5: *iusta caede conficere hostem posset*.

[36] Cf. Orellius, Kirkland, Lejay, Morris, Fiske, Kiessling-Heinze, and others.

[37] *Od.*, IX, 507 ff.

the battle scenes of the *Iliad*. The phrase of introduction seems conclusive; yet, to my knowledge, no commentator has observed that the words *instat fatum me triste* (29) are a good translation of *Il.*, XXII, 303: νῦν αὖτέ με μοῖρα κιχάνει. The Greek acts as one of the formulaic phrases of Homer, in which any personal pronoun can be substituted, providing it is metrically equivalent.[38] Its context is always the death of a warrior. In the single instance where the personal pronoun is με and the parallel with the Latin is exact, Hector is the speaker. The hero realizes that he has been overcome by the gods and his own weakness; after speaking, he turns to face Achilles and meet the inevitable death. On the other hand, Hector does not mention a prophecy in his moment of realization; he is, so to speak, his own prophet. We must look to other portions of the *Iliad*, where the death of a warrior is foretold, but the formulaic phrase not used. For example, Polyidus foresaw the death of his own son;[39] Achilles hears his doom prophesied;[40] Aeneas is threatened with death by the supreme prophet, Apollo;[41] and Achilles acts the prophet.[42] Because of the negative manner of prophecy here exhibited and not illustrated in Homer, a different ancient analogue has been suggested.[43] Diogenes Laertius reports an epigram recited about Zeno the Stoic which has a similarly negative form.[44] Although the context of the epigram involves neither battle nor death, it is not impossible that Horace parodies the epigram as well as the epic. Curiously enough, Shakespeare provides the closest parallel of all in *Macbeth*. Deceived up to the last moment by the speciously convincing oracles, Macbeth sees one after the other fulfilled; finally, he meets Macduff and hears the nature of his enemy's birth. It is at this moment (Act V, Scene VII, line 59) that, certain of his death, he faces Macduff with those famous words: " Lay on, Macduff . . ." (cf. *confice*). Whatever may have been the exact source of

[38] Cf. *Il.*, XVII, 478 and 672; XXII, 436.

[39] *Il.*, XIII, 666.

[40] *Il.*, XIX, 409.

[41] *Il.*, XX, 332.

[42] *Il.*, XXI, 110.

[43] The credit for suggesting this new analogue, as Lejay notes, goes to Kiessling.

[44] *Lives*, VII, 27. The epigram is fully cited in Orellius, Kirkland, and Lejay.

Horace's passage—if there is a single source—epic gives the tone to the language. The circumstances in which the oracle was uttered (*cecinit*, 30) suggest epic grandeur. Moreover, the first line (31), containing the poetic *dira* and the archaic *hosticus* and concerned with the type of destiny associated with epic or tragedy, fits the mood of an oracle or formal, grand poetry. It is the irony of the prophecy to descend from tragic deaths, which it denies our hero, through more prosaic fates to the most ridiculous of all ends. Horace must perish ignobly at the hands of a *garrulus* (33). Still, suffering the fool's aggressiveness, while an ignominious fate, is significantly placed in the same context of hostility as a death in real battle would be. In fact, the anticlimactic end of the prophecy, with its mock-epic tmesis *quando . . . cumque* (33), reveals the weapon which, above all others, is deadly to Horace: meaningless verbosity. Accordingly, he criticizes Lucilius for talkativeness in *S.*, I, 4 and 10; he attacks Hermogenes for his lack of literary discipline in I, 2 and 3; and he sets up as his own great artistic ideal *brevitas*.[45] There is, then, no alternative: Horace is irrevocably doomed.

In terms of epic battle, the remainder of the Satire determines the fate of the doomed poet. Conquered now, he is granted his life and made a helpless prisoner. Possibilities of escape occur, are hopefully grasped, but as quickly forestalled by captor or fate. The first chance arises as a result of the lawsuit impending against the bore (33 ff.). On the basis of their mutual friendship, the fool asks Horace to stop a moment and give him support. Since this "friendship" (38) is viewed by the poet as enmity, he swears that he cannot and will not stop (*inteream*, 38). Villeneuve found problems in the traditional interpretation of the phrase *valeo stare* (39).[46] He rejected construing *stare* as equivalent to *adstare*[47] and, pointing to a common theory about Horace's delicate health, treated *stare* as a properly simple verb. According to this interpretation, Horace has not the strength to stand; there is no other implication. Limitations on the relevance of Horace's language, as 78 and the systematic connotations present in this Satire imply, generally result in the error which comes from eliminating important meanings.

---

[45] Cf. *S.*, I, 10, 9: *est brevitate opus.*

[46] F. Villeneuve, *Horace: Satires* (Paris, 1932), *loc. cit.*

[47] One might assume *adstare* on the basis of *ades* (36).

Quite probably, Horace has used the simple verb as a simple verb *and* for its compound.[48] Such usage would be consistent with economy, since the simple verb, not specifying the preposition in the compound, allows a moderate freedom of application. For instance, the legal context here suggests the prepositions *ad-* or *prae-*; but Horace's unhappy condition might well support *con-* or *prae-*, with their thematic relevance. The military metaphor, that is, cannot be totally disregarded. At any rate, Horace has no fight left; he certainly can no longer fight the presence of the bore. For a hopeful moment, the man hesitates as to whether to face his lost cause in court or retain Horace captive. The latter alternative seems preferable and, captor that he is, he leads off his victim (*praecedere*, 40). The poet cannot resist (*contendere*); he resigns himself and meekly follows the triumphant *garrulus* (*victore*, 41).

For the next fifteen lines, the dreadful predicament of the captive seems to be ignored. The two men converse about Maecenas, and the bore expresses his desire to be admitted into his select circle. If, however, the military theme is applied, it is not out of place. As Horace looks back upon this period, he compares it to supreme torture; he has been under the knife, he says (*sub cultro*, 74). With the poet in hand, the *garrulus* is considering a more valuable conquest, that of the great Maecenas himself. As an instrument of his campaign, he will employ Horace. Therefore, he keeps threatening the poet, in order to make him pliable to his designs. When the man reveals his plot upon Maecenas, he also discloses an aspect of his character which has so far only been implicit: he is not only antagonistic because of his chatter; he is also highly aggressive, in fact unscrupulous in the pursuit of his ambitions. These two qualities are complementary in his personality, to be sure, but aggressiveness does not necessarily follow from talkativeness. Impelled as he is by ambition, the fool makes the egregious error of

---

[48] The exact implication conveyed when a simple word is used for its compound varies according to the context. Frequently, abbreviation of this type has informal connotations and is congenial to satire. Cf. E. Wölfflin, " Bemerkungen über das Vulgärlatein," *Philol.*, XXXIV (1876), pp. 149 ff.; F. Ruckdeschel, *Archaismen und Vulgarismen in der Sprache des Horaz* (Diss. Munich, 1910), pp. 25 ff.; A. Engel, *De Q. Horati Flacci Sermone Metro Accomodato* (Diss. Breslau, 1914), pp. 68 ff.

attributing the same aggressive traits to Horace, and, under this illusion, he appeals to the poet by the crude motives influencing his own manner. Since Horace is a good friend of Maecenas, he assumes that Horace has consciously seized opportunities (*fortuna*, 45)[49] to pretend the sort of friendship which makes use of a powerful political figure. So begins Horace's torture. Fortune governs the military sphere as well as the political, at least when one is crudely ambitious. In as much, then, as the poet already has the advantages of Fortune, the *garrulus* devises a campaign which will depend on Horace's Fortune and will have as its object the capture of similar Fortune. To begin with, he speaks of himself as a potential *adiutor* (46) of Horace's ambition. The metaphor in *adiutor*, ambiguous in its clause, quickly acquires a precise meaning as a result of the definite stage metaphor in *ferre secundas*. Since, however, it precedes the specific dramatic image, it might also possess momentarily a valid military significance. If so, the *garrulus* first proposes himself as Horace's aide-de-camp,[50] then requests a supporting role in the play where Horace takes the lead. The plan of operations is simple: the poet will introduce the *garrulus* to Maecenas.[51] The word used for "introduce," *tradere* (47), is the equivalent of *commendare*.[52] It is not unlikely, however, that the word betrays the aggressive nature of the speaker by suggesting also a military overtone. By this interpretation, a scene could be imagined where, introduced into the fortified city, the enemy overcomes all resistance (*summosses*, 48)[53] and treacherously seizes power from within. At this point, thoroughly antagonized by such shameless effrontery, Horace protests at the schemer's misconceptions. There is no truth in the belief that Maecenas' circle has political importance; rather,

[49] I interpret the ellipsis, with most editors, as implying *te*, not *illo*.

[50] Cf. Livy, X, 26, 2: *adiutorem belli sociumque imperii darent.*

[51] Though it would be convenient for the image to have *hunc hominem* refer to Maecenas, one must interpret the phrase, following Porphyrio, as a familiar expression probably accompanied by a gesture, as the *garrulus* points to himself.

[52] Cf. *Epist.*, I, 18, 76-8, where Horace uses *commendare* and *tradere* in the same sense.

[53] Cf. Caesar, *B. G.*, I, 25: *victis ac summotis resisterent*; also, *B. G.*, VIII, 10.

it is opposed to unscrupulous climbing: *his aliena malis* (50).[54]
Just as the fool's ways arouse the antagonism of Horace, so his
ambition only earns the hostility of the artistic circle to which
the poet belongs.

Horace's protests only fire the man's desire to win the favor of
Maecenas. When the fool applies to himself the metaphor
accendis (53), Horace immediately construes it in its military
sense and completes the ellipsis mentally to read: "you fire my
courage." Carrying on in the same vein, the satirist now openly
uses the military metaphor as proper to his companion's manner.
As he ironically puts it, nothing could withstand the persistence
of such a person; the man will take Maecenas by storm (*expug-
nabis*, 55) in an easy victory (*vinci*). In this metaphorical
context, *virtus* (54) also reverts to its original meaning of
manliness, fitness for war. Once again, by its striking incongruity, the image stresses the moral significance of the Satire.
The bore is aggressive and offensive: that constitutes his *virtus*.
Because, however, his aggressiveness springs from crude personal
ambition, devoid of any trace of honor, his *virtus* must fall far
short of the epic ideal. Therefore, too, the military theme will
always be an ironic suggestion of the schemer's ignobility. With
this implication, Horace continues: there are strategic approaches (*aditus*, 56), he says, to Maecenas' city, but difficult
and well-guarded. Completely missing Horace's irony and taking
his cue from the military metaphor, the schemer openly parades
his methods and his scale of values: he will use bribery on the
guards (*corrumpam*, 57). If the gates are shut on him and,
like a lover, he is ignored (*exclusus*, 58), he will remain true
to his character: he will not give up. Awaiting his opportunity,
he will attack his man in the street (*occurram*, 59),[55] force a
meeting. He will impose himself on Maecenas as an escort; he
will, in other words, lead Maecenas captive just as he is now
leading Horace (*deducam*).[56] Then, as if to summarize his

[54] Lejay glosses *aliena*: "hostile, contraire." For the meaning "hostile," cf. *T. L. L.*, *s. v.*, § II A 2.

[55] For the use of *occurrere* in a military sense, cf. Lucretius, III, 524:
falsae rationi vera videtur / res occurrere et effugium praecludere; also,
Lucretius, VI, 32. In Caesar, cf. *B. C.*, I, 40 and III, 92: *ipsi immissis
telis occurrissent.* Cf. also *Aen.*, X, 734.

[56] Prof. H. T. Rowell has pointed out to me a second Horatian usage

energetic character, he recites the noble truism, which he has perverted to his own purposes:

nil sine magno
vita labore dedit mortalibus. (59-60)

As Heinze noted, the saying originated in the dignified Greek oracular proverb:

οὐδὲν ἄνευ καμάτου πέλει ἀνδράσιν εὐπετὲς ἔργον.

It is perhaps significant that the unscrupulous *garrulus* has perverted the neat hexameter unit as well as the moral basis of the original.

The greater offensive of the schemer has now been exposed; Horace remains in his predicament. At this juncture, Fuscus Aristius comes up—as Horace hopefully believes—to the attack (*occurrit*, 61; cf. 59). The warriors, prepared for battle, make a stand (*consistimus*, 62; cf. 9). By every means in his power, Horace tries to show his longing for rescue (*eriperet*, 65), gesticulating, nudging, going through a series of facial contortions. Aristius pretends obtuseness. Furious yet helpless, Horace describes his desperation in physical terms: *meum iecur urere bilis* (66). Though by no means an exact parallel, there is a possible reminiscence here, I suggest, of Homeric phrases used to denote deep feeling, such as χόλον θυμαλγέα.[57] When subtle methods bring no result, Horace is obliged to speak out. He reminds Aristius of an important message which requires privacy (67-8). It is amusing to tease, and Aristius refuses to co-operate, alleging a flimsy excuse (68-71). With a cry of frustration, the intensity of which suggests epic emotionality, the poor satirist curses his evil day: *solem / tam nigrum* (72-3). After Aristius has fled from battle with the bore (*fugit*, 73), he is doomed. The phrase *sub cultro*, according to Porphyrio, is a well-known proverb. Unfortunately, this proverb is used once in extant Latin literature, in this passage.[58] Most commentators

of *deducere* in this meaning of leading in triumph: *Carm.*, I, 37, 31: *scilicet invidens / privata deduci superbo / non humilis mulier triumpho.* For the general military sense, cf. *T. L. L., s. v.*, § I A 2f. With this significance, it is used in Caesar, e. g., *B. G.*, III, 38, and Livy, e. g., XXVIII, 32, 7.

[57] Cf. *Il.*, IX, 260.

[58] Cf. A. Otto, *Die Sprichwörter und sprichwörtlichen Redensarten der Römer* (Leipzig, 1890), p. 100; also, the article on *culter* in *T. L. L.*

99

gloss the phrase: " as a sacrificial victim." It seems likely that this interpretation should be accepted, for the *culter* was most commonly used as a sacrificial knife and victims were put under the knife.[59] In Ovid's time, though, the *culter* could be spoken of as a weapon also; and by 50 A. D. the short sword of the gladiator was sometimes called *culter*. There is, then, considerable justification for interpreting the victim under the knife as human and accepting Heinze's ingenious gloss: " wie ein wehrloses *Schlachtopfer*, bereit, den Todesstoss zu empfangen." [60] At this point, Horace's predicament seems desperate indeed.

Suddenly, another warrior (*adversarius*, 75) arrives on the scene, to contest the way (*obvius*, 74). As he recognizes his enemy, the newcomer hails the *garrulus* with a curse, takes the willing Horace as witness, and drags his man violently off to trial. In this final scene, the description is very allusive, and the poet uses his economic device of ellipsis to advantage (77-8). Although specifically he is depicting the uproar occasioned by the cursing *adversarius*, the resisting *garrulus*, and the crowd of spectators, he also succeeds in suggesting a scene of battle. Possibly, one might think of an episode such as that in the *Iliad*, when the Greeks and Trojans fight over the body of Patroclus. Wherever the battle is hottest, the most men are involved, and reinforcements are continually pouring in. The *garrulus*, by nature antagonistic, must be the center of battle, and when he is dragged off, his victim Horace, a naturally peaceful individual, is left in tranquillity. The uproar (*clamor utrimque*, 77) is similar to the thunder of battle in the *Iliad* (ὀρυμάγδος). When the curious onlookers run up (*concursus*, 78),[61] there is a general confusion like that of a violent engagement. Rescued from battle at last, free of the intolerable aggressiveness of the

---

[59] Cf. *Aen.*, VI, 248: *supponunt alii cultros tepidumque cruorem / suscipiunt pateris*; also *Georg.*, III, 492.

[60] Cf. *Trist.*, V, 7, 19: *dextera non segnis fixo dare vulnera cultro.* Seneca mentions the use of the *culter* by gladiators in *Epist.*, 87, 9. In his note on the passage, Heinze associates the phrase with the obvious military metaphor of 43, *victore*.

[61] For the military application of *concursus*, cf. *T. L. L.*, *s. v.*, § I 2. There is a curious parallel to *clamor utrimque, / undique concursus* in Cicero, *Tusc.*, II, 37: *quid? exercitatio legionum, quid? ille cursus, concursus, clamor, quanti laboris est?* Cf. also Livy, XXII, 19, 12: *pertinaci certamine et concursu.*

garrulus, Horace thinks of Apollo as his protector. Apollo has saved him, indeed, from a struggle as ominous for him as the hopeless conflict between Achilles and Hector. Unlike Hector, the satirist is not snatched away (ἐξήρπαξεν = *eriperet*, 65); instead, his enemy is carried off (*rapit*), and he himself remains safe.

None of this elaboration of the battle and war symbolism in I, 9 negates the validity of the factual interpretations or the perceptive comments made by previous scholars in regard to this poem. At most, it questions what should always be questioned in the criticism of poetry: dogmatic, absolute assertions of a single specific interpretation, limiting Horace at points where he appears to have been deliberately unspecific and suggestive. On the positive side, it serves to explain some of the intricacy of Horace's technique. The observation has long since been made, for instance, that the satirist frequently uses military metaphors.[62] In *S.*, I, 9, this practice can be explained as systematic and economic development of the moral insight of the poet. In an ordinary situation, a meeting between a typically contented, unambitious, sensitively artistic writer and an unwelcome, pushing poetaster, the satirist perceives, through his controlled irony, the elements of epic battle. The point of contact between the described event and the imagined overtones of war is the personality of the *garrulus*, which, being thoroughly objectionable, motivates the action of the drama. The man is *aggressive*; he make himself *offensive*; he arouses *antagonism* in Horace. These metaphorical terms epitomize the relation between drama and battle, the relation which Horace is subtly stressing in his account. At no time does it appear that the action is sacrificed to the symbol. Where the symbol pushes forward, as in the exaggerated descriptions of Horace's feelings (10, 12, 28, 66, 72), the oracle (29-34), or the unambiguous metaphors (42, 55, 73), it is always nicely blended in the attractive irony of the satirist. But humor in Horace is not usually uneconomical or un-moral. It is his genius to suggest much without asserting and without ever distorting his dramatic setting. In *S.*, I, 9, accordingly, he has expressed his insight into

---

[62] F. Bäker, *Die Metaphern in den Satiren des Horaz* (Stralsund, 1883), p. 20.

101

the character of a typical man by ironically identifying an aggressive personality with the heroic standards of epic. The incongruity is subtly controlled, maintained throughout the poem. To fit it neatly to his drama, the satirist depicts himself as the unfortunate warrior, fatally inferior to the aggressor, whose doom, long since prophesied, is now at last brought almost to fulfilment before our eyes. Only the providential intervention of Apollo saves him. It is perhaps doubtful that *Apollo* can be identified with a specific Roman monument of Apollo. It does, however, appear certain that Horace is speaking of the Apollo of mythology and literature, the god of poetry and justice, the character in Lucilius' clever, but limited, parody, and the deity whom Homer originally described as intervening to save Hector. Only Horace could devise a poem in which he subtly condemned Lucilius' use of Greek words and uneconomic parody by taking a specific line borrowed by his predecessor from Homer and using it more dexterously. The martial context of the *Iliad*, admirably adapted to the ordinary incident here dramatized, extends the significance of the Satire and reveals the maturity of Horace at this relatively early stage in his poetic career.

I. *Venusina lucerna*: The Horatian Model for Juvenal

Juvenal inherits a tradition in satire to which belong Lucilius, Horace and Persius; and like his predecessors he exploits a program poem in order to define his place in that tradition. Horace had thought it so important to establish his relation to Lucilius that he wrote three program satires. Persius did not challenge Horace and restricted his programmatic theories to *Satire* 1 and to the beginning of *Satire* 5. Therefore, when Juvenal cites first Lucilius, then Horace as models, it is natural to think that, just as he can only mean Lucilius the *inventor* of *satura*, so he must refer to Horace the writer of the *Sermones* and *Epistulae*. The scholiasts and such editors as Grangaeus, Britannicus, Lubinus, Calderinus, Macleane, Mayor, Wright and Duff all agree that *Venusina lucerna* (1.51) should be interpreted as Horace the satirist. However, in the comment of Duff one can see the implicit difficulty to which I shall address myself in this paper; Duff remarks: "The allusion is to Horace, a satirist of a very different kind."[1] It will be my purpose to question the general assumption and advance reasons for interpreting *Venusina lucerna* as an allusion, not to Horace the satirist, but to Horace the poet of fiery patriotic indignation.

[1] J. D. Duff, *D. Iunii Iuvenalis Saturae* xiv (Cambridge 1898) 122.

Let me begin by analyzing the verbal associations of this striking phrase *Venusina lucerna*. With the adjective, no commentator experiences any difficulty; it patently denotes Venusia, birthplace of Horace.[2] On the other hand, we find that *lucerna* evokes several interpretations. One early scholiast thought it necessary to understand the word in direct relation to the satiric tradition and accordingly commented: "'Lucerna' ideo dicit, quia satirici ad omnium vitia quasi lucernam admovent et vel adurunt vel ostendunt crimina, quae noverunt." Mayor developed this interpretation as follows: "There is also an allusion to the scorching heat of satire . . . and its fierce glare (cf. the lantern of Diogenes, *seeking a man*)."[3]

I think we can firmly reject this theory of the scholiast, as elaborated by Mayor. In the first place, satirists do not necessarily expose vices to the scorching heat and fierce glare of their verses, least of all Horace the satirist. While the scholiast may evoke the picture of Diogenes the Cynic, only Persius even vaguely approached the manner of Diogenes. Horace, who carefully represents himself in his very first *Satire* as the man who laughingly tells the truth, would be diametrically opposed to this classification of *satirici*. Of Lucilius, I need only say that he was read by the men of the first century B.C. as an urbane, elegant, witty and highly frank poet; such a complex impression does not fit the scholiast's simplification of the satirist. In the second place, *lucerna* does not connote to the Romans either scorching heat or fierce glare.[4] Although Diogenes did go around with his lantern looking for an honest man, *lucerna*, for a Roman, signifies first and foremost the ordinary illumination required at night. Horace, for example, uses the word six times, thrice in the *Sermones*, thrice in the *Odes*, and with no distinction of meaning appropriate to the different poetic form. Four times the *lucerna* graces banquets and suggests the pleasant protraction of convivial drinking far into the night.[5] Once a brothel and sexual intercourse are illuminated (*Serm.* 2.7.48), and once we hear of Natta

[2] Cf. the scholia: "'Venusina' autem ideo, quia haec fuit civitas Horatii."

[3] J. E. B. Mayor, *Thirteen Satires of Juvenal*[4] (London 1889) 1.109. I repeat his italics. "The scorching heat of satire" he documents by citing Ennius' famous fragment about his *versus flammeos* (Vahlen, *Sat.* 6–7).

[4] Nor, for that matter, do I believe that Ennius' phrase *versus flammeos* indicates scorching heat; rather, it seems to concentrate our attention on the flaming, brightly shining quality of his poetry.

[5] *Serm.* 2.1.25, *C.* 1.27.5, 3.8.14, 21.23.

stealing oil from lamps (*Serm.* 1.6.124). The one occurrence of *lucerna* in Persius adds nothing (cf. 5.181). Juvenal himself employs the word seven times. Of these, five agree with the usage of Horace, and two of the five appear direct variations of Horatian passages.[6] In short, *lucerna* itself does not evoke to the Roman mind burning, glaring satire; and even if it did, it would never fit the character of Horace the satirist.

Since the lamp functioned not only to illuminate banquets and prostitution, but also any activity of the dark hours, a derivative association of *lucerna* early appeared in Latin. While the scholiast ignored this second association completely, Mayor, it should be noted, regarded it as the dominant meaning of the word in this context. The *lucerna* could and did frequently evoke the "midnight lamp" and the "midnight oil" which we today still associate with studying. Most commentators urge this interpretation, and Mayor provides the reader with copious illustrations of its application in Latin. Indeed, the one remaining passage of Juvenal, which I did not cite above in connection with the connotation of mere illumination, produces the phrase *olfecisse lucernas* (7.225), to describe study in the early morning before dawn. From the context of 7.225 we also gather that both Horace and Vergil were school authors who demanded such extreme labor. Unique though Juvenal's phrase *Venusina lucerna* is because of its rhetorical compression, nevertheless Varro provides us a reasonably close analogue: *non solum ad Aristophanis lucernam sed etiam ad Cleanthis lucubravi.*[7]

Putting these associations together, we may conclude that Juvenal's phrase, "Venusine lamp," suggested the inspiration of studious Horace or the poetic example elicited from carefully studying Horace. Up to this point we can follow the commentators. However, when they proceed to specify the inspiration or the poetic example of the Venusine as the *Sermones*, we need not agree. It is not unreasonable to assume that one satirist, referring to another poet who among other things is renowned for his satires, would invoke those satires as his model. If, on the other hand, the satires of the first do not in the least resemble the putative model either in tone or in content, then we

[6] Cf. 6.131 with Hor. *Serm.* 2.7.48; 6.305 with Hor. *Serm.* 2.1.25. The other three occurrences of *lucerna* which agree with Horace are in 8.35, 10.339, and 12.92.

[7] Varro, *Ling. lat.* 5.9.

might well hesitate to obey our first instinct. As Duff automatically notes, and as all readers of Juvenal quickly sense, Juvenal does not write Horatian satire.[8] But not only should our immediate awareness of the peculiarly Juvenalian tone prepare us to question it when the commentators interpret the "Venusine lamp" as Horace the satirist; we can also inspect the phrase more closely and detect surer indications that it alludes to Horatian works quite other than the *Sermones* and *Epistulae*.

The poet who studied late was conventionally the epic or tragic poet; the speaker who worked far into the night on his oration was the thunderous successor of Cicero or Demosthenes; and even the scholar, like Varro, who pored over his texts by the light of the lamp was no ordinary pedant but a mighty intellect like Aristophanes of Byzantium or the celebrated Stoic Cleanthes. Lucretius invites us to visualize him staying up in the quiet hours of many nights as he seeks to find words and phrases appropriate to his vitally important poetic ideas.[9] This is quite different from the image which we have of Catullus, who spends his nights in love and feasting, his days in playful recollections. With Horace, the *persona* of the satirist differs sharply from that of the writer of formal odes, at least those which engage the emotions. Moreover, where he exploits the *topos* of *recusatio*, Horace brings out the obvious contrast between his slight ability and the magnitude of the epic subject,[10] between the intrinsic poetic quality of epic and the mere poetic trappings of satire.[11] Not only that, but the characteristic pose of the satirist is of a man who dabbles at verse, never toils at it, least of all into the late hours of night.[12] When Damasippus attacks Horace in *Serm.* 2.3.1 ff.,

[8] Cf. I. G. Scott (Ryberg), *The Grand Style in the Satires of Juvenal* (Northampton [Mass.] 1927), especially 112 ff. I suspect, too, that the scholiast's effort to generalize about *satirici* sprang from embarrassment with the facts of Horatian satire.

[9] *Rer. nat.* 1.140 ff. Cf. Propertius 2.3.7, *studiis vigilare severis*, where he opposes the conventions of epic to those of his elegy.

[10] Cf. *tenues grandia, C.* 1.6.9.

[11] Cf. the deliberate comparison of Ennian style with that of *sermo merus* in *Serm.* 1.4.39 ff.; also the implicit paradox of the phrase (influenced by Callimachus), *Musa pedestri* in *Serm.* 2.6.17.

[12] Cf. *cantamus vacui, C.* 1.6.19; *relictis iocis, C.* 2.1.37; *ubi quid datur oti | illudo chartis, Serm.* 1.4.138–39; the picture of Horatian leisure in *Serm.* 1.6.111 ff., especially 122–23: *post hanc vagor, aut ego lecto | aut scripto quod me tacitum iuvet unguor olivo*, and 128: *domesticus otior*; and finally, the direct opposition between the satirist and the epic poet in 1.10.36–37, concluded by: *haec ego ludo*. All the conventions of *sermo* and the plain style conflict with the studied skill of the grand poet.

he concentrates on precisely these features. Although Horace has brought along important poets to study, says the critic, he has failed to study them; instead, he has wasted his time drinking and sleeping: *vini somnique benignus/nil dignum sermone canas* (3–4). Part of the irony in Trebatius' remarks may also depend on this same theme. Consulted by Horace in *Serm.* 2.1 as to what he should do about adverse reactions to the *Sermones*, Trebatius tells the satirist to take a rest, that is, from poetry and from replying to the critics. To this, Horace rejoins that he would dearly like to take a rest but he would not be able to sleep (7). Well, says Trebatius, if you cannot sleep, you should try hard exercise in the form of swimming—unimaginable for Horace, the reader quickly sees—or you should write an epic poem about Augustus (10–12). That is, Horace should either overcome his insomnia or utilize it in the conventional manner.

According to the recognized convention, therefore, Horace and his fellow satirists belong among the writers of light verse, who compose slight poetry in a playful manner, in odd moments of idleness, and who would never waste a good night of banqueting and precious conversation among friends and lovers to labor over a poem.[13] A few years before Juvenal wrote his program satire, Martial composed a programmatic epigram, in which he exploited the same contrasting conventions. While the wretched epic and tragic poets work to midnight by the lantern, he plays (*ludere*), produces witty, light little material.[14] Juvenal's *Satire* 7 exhibits his awareness of the convention. With bitter amusement he describes the epic subject as *vigilata proelia* (27), battle scenes which have obliged the poet to work many sleepless nights. Twice he introduces Horace in this *Satire*, the only times he mentions him after 1.51; and in each case he associates Horace with Vergil. To depict the true poet, he cites the inspired Bacchic Horace of

---

[13] I stress this matter of convention, because behind the mask of the playful satirist existed a dedicated poet who worked as hard and as late on the *Sermones* as he did on the passionately serious formal poems. Cf. *Epist.* 2.1.111–13.

[14] Mayor cites this useful *Epigram* 8.3.17–20:
> scribant ista graves nimium nimiumque severi
> quos media miseros nocte *lucerna* videt.
> at tu Romano lepidos sale tinge libellos:
> adgnoscat mores vita legatque suos.

I have counted 21 occurrences of *lucerna* in Martial; almost all of them fit into scenes of banqueting and love. For the *topos* of late study applied to epic by an epic poet himself in Juvenal's time, cf. Statius *Theb.* 12.811.

C. 2.19 and Vergil deeply involved with the tragedy of Turnus (62 ff.). Similarly, when the lamps smell up the study as the students pore over Vergil and Horace, I am inclined to think that the grimy text of Horace was rather a collection of the *Odes* and *Epodes* than the *Sermones* (225–27). For, as Quintilian shows, the high and serious tone of grand poetry could immediately serve the interests of the budding orator.[15]

In itself, therefore, *Venusina lucerna,* a phrase which probably suggests both Horace's own meticulous labor over his poetry and the example which he sets to a careful student of his craft, does not connote the conventions of humble, playful satire; rather, it evokes the *persona* of the epic and tragic poet, the *vatis.* Further indications as to its significance are supplied by the word which, ignored thus far as the reader undoubtedly observed, belongs to the full phrase written by Juvenal. Angrily he asks in 1.51: May I not believe these details of moral enormity worthy of the Venusine lamp? (*haec ego non credam Venusina digna lucerna?*) The adjective *digna* requires two comments. First, one of its basic meanings involves a comparison between one thing or person and another, in which the first is said to possess the *dignitas* of the other.[16] Among the things frequently so compared are the subjects of poetry with the magnitude of the topic and the conventional idea of the genre, or one poet's work with another's. Lucretius, whom I mentioned above as exhibiting the *topos* of work by night, also speaks of poetry on which he has long toiled and contrived with sweet labor, which he desires to be worthy of his noble reader (*carmina digna,* 4.420). Even more relevant to our interest is that the poet who desires to write *carmina digna* usually looks up to the epic and tragic poets. Vergil, addressing Asinius Pollio, exalts his patron's tragedies in these terms: *sola Sophocleo tua carmina digna coturno.*[17] In refusing to produce an epic on Agrippa's exploits Horace asks how anyone could write worthily of Homer's topics.[18]

[15] The values which Quintilian anticipates from poetry assume concentration on grand poetry. Cf. *Inst. orat.* 10.1.27: *namque ab his* (i.e., poetis) *in rebus spiritus et in verbis sublimitas et in adfectibus motus omnis et in personis decor petitur.*

[16] Cf. *ThLL,* s.v. "*Dignus* i."

[17] *Ecl.* 8.10. Horace similarly refers to the *dignitas* of tragedy: cf. *Epist.* 2.1.164 and *AP* 91.

[18] *C.* 1.6.13 ff. For other uses of *dignus* in connection with the high style of epic, cf. Horace *C.* 4.8.28 and *AP* 138; Ovid, *Am.* 1.3.20 and *Met.* 5.345; and Statius, *Theb.* 3.102. The context of Juvenal's phrase, which we cited above (*vigilata proelia,*

In the second place, *digna* might well be connected with the preconceptions of *indignatio*. The basic idea behind rhetorical indignation is that the speaker, himself *dignus*, feels stirred by something *indignum*. Just before Juvenal proclaims his use of *indignatio*, he sardonically summarizes the moral plight of Rome as follows:

> aude aliquid brevibus Gyaris et carcere *dignum*,
> si vis esse aliquid. (73-74)

It is because Romans have destroyed the ethical conception of *dignitas* and attach honor now to crimes which merit serious punishments, that Juvenal feels impelled to vent his *indignatio*, he asserts. As we shall shortly see, certain works apart from the *Sermones* do exploit the devices of *indignatio*.[19] I would suggest, therefore, that *digna* indicates two aspects of Juvenal's material: that it rises to the level of the more exalted works of Horace and that it merits the same tone of patriotic indignation.

If now we momentarily turn away from our phrase and consider the entire program satire and the book for which it was written, we find several additional clues by which, I think, we can determine the Horatian poetry to which in fact Juvenal refers. One hardly needs to argue that Juvenal knew Horace's works well. Like the schoolboys he describes in *Satire* 7, Juvenal himself studied searchingly all the poems of the great poet.[20] Now were he using Horace's *Satires* as his model, we should expect to find some evidence of the *Sermones* and possibly the *Epistulae* in Book 1. However, of the comparative material collected by Schwartz and Highet, little of importance connects Book 1 with the satiric efforts of Horace; and the most compelling verbal echoes of the *Sermones* prove the utterly un-Horatian approach of Juvenal.[21] Highet correctly notes that, when composing his memorable phrase, *si natura negat, facit indignatio versum*, Juvenal could not have been unaware of Horace's programmatic comments in *Serm.* 1.10.56 ff.:

7.27), includes also *carmina sublimia* and *dignus hederis*: the epic poet must work late in order to be worthy of the Homeric crown.

[19] For a full discussion of the rhetorical conventions of *indignatio*, see my article, "Juvenal and Quintilian," *YClS* 17 (1961) 30 ff.

[20] Cf. P. Schwartz, *De Juvenale Horatii imitatore* (Diss. Halle 1882).

[21] G. Highet, "Juvenal's Bookcase," *AJP* 72 (1951) 388, lists the most striking imitations of Horace in Juvenal; his list is a sound reduction of Schwartz' exaggerations.

quid vetat et nosmet Lucili scripta legentis
quaerere, num illius, num rerum dura *negarit*
versiculos natura magis *factos* et euntis
mollius . . . ?

It is even more important for our argument to point out the difference in meaning which the two satirists develop with their parallel vocabulary. Horace criticizes the inartistic verses of Lucilius and suggests that we can legitimately ask whether Lucilius' natural ability (or the intractability of the material) be held responsible. Inasmuch as one of the dominant features of Lucilius' nature was the *libertas* which comes under consideration in *Serm.* 1.4 and 10, Horace insists on disciplining by art the instinct to blurt out exactly what one feels; and his superbly controlled satire provides the perfect example of classical order in the history of Roman satire. But Juvenal patently rejects discipline and classical order, explicitly here, implicitly throughout Book 1. I may be deficient in *natura*, he admits, but if so, indignation will write or justify my verse; for I am not interested in art, content to produce as ragged poetry as the works of the poetaster Cluvienus. In short, Juvenal turns away from the classical discipline of Horatian satire to the outspoken attacks characteristically attributed to Lucilius: *indignatio* comes before *ars*; he makes no attempt to compromise.

Juvenal also uses the themes of the program satire, first exploited by Lucilius and then made conventional through the adaptations of Horace. Besides modifying the conception of *libertas*, Horace had made quite clear that he did not attack people for the sheer pleasure of injury but to make of them moral *exempla*; that he regarded *satura* as stylistically quite distinct from epic and other types of grand poetry, without, however, impugning the values of epic; and that he utilized an artistic version of the plain style, of which one implicit definition comes in his familiar phrase, *ridentem dicere verum*, an appeal to the image of Socrates. What does Juvenal do with these themes? He attacks people who are (or recently were) utterly depraved, who do not serve as *exempla* for moral improvement, but as illustrations of the utter degeneracy of Rome. He holds himself in from assaulting the living only because it is dangerous, not from concern for another's feelings. He denies the validity of epic in his time, in order to raise *satura* up to the level of the grand style and so replace the counterfeit topics and emotions of epic and tragedy. On every count, then, Juvenal distances himself from Horace, writer of the *Sermones*.

Again, we may compare subjects attacked in Juvenal with those in Horace. Juvenal's *Satire* 2 concentrates on male perversions, something which Horace never mentioned in his *Sermones*. *Satire* 3 contrasts the city with the country, a topic also utilized in Horace, *Serm.* 2.6; but the two satirists can treat it in diametrically opposed manners. Horace does not hate Rome, nor does he restrict corruption to the city; he belongs both to the city and to the country, essentially interested in a manner of living rather than in outward circumstances. Juvenal makes of Rome a monster of tragic proportions, which one must forsake. *Satire* 4 has no analogue in Horace, and the mock-epic attack on Domitian belongs, as Juvenal himself consciously notes (cf. 4.34–36), to a style avoided by Horace.[22] Finally, *Satire* 5 depicts a *cena*, one of the favorite topics of Horace in Book 2 of the *Sermones*. No reader needs to be told that the urbanity of the *cena Nasidieni* (*Serm.* 2.8) differs utterly from the express indignation (cf. 5.120) suffusing Juvenal's picture; nor is it an accident that so much of Juvenal's high emotion depends for its conviction on his skillful use of epic allusion.

To return to *Satire* 1, we should review the vicious characters whom Juvenal presents in 22 ff., both before and after his outcry concerning Horace. Not one of them, I make bold to assert, reminds us of people in the *Sermones*. Horace could not have presented such imperial perversions as the female gladiator or the *delator*; but the political upstart, the unscrupulous trustee, the husband conniving at his wife's prostitution, the poisoner, and the like all existed in the first century B.C. Therefore, when after listing a group of such depraved men Juvenal asks whether such people and such vice do not merit the Venusine lamp, he looks elsewhere than to the Horatian works of specifically satiric form.

We seek a Horatian model for Juvenal which will possess the following qualities, as implied by *Venusina digna lucerna* as well as

[22] I regard *Serm.* 2.5 as an exception. Indeed, E. Fraenkel, *Horace* (Oxford 1957) 144–45, discusses its proximity to the Juvenalian tone and quotes W. Y. Sellar, *Horace and the Elegaic Poets*[2] (Oxford 1899) 70: "If Juvenal recognizes any affinity between his own invective and the 'Venusina lucerna,' it must have been with the spirit of this Satire that he found himself in sympathy." The critics, that is, find no Horatian Satire but 2.5 which even vaguely fits the manner of Juvenal.

by its context; it will be written in the grand style, close to that of epic and tragedy; it will involve urgent moral problems centering on the utter perversion of Rome; it will contain some of the topics specified by Juvenal in 1.22 ff.; and it will appropriate the rhetorical manner of *indignatio* or something closely akin to it. Since we have discarded the *Sermones* and *Epistulae*, we must look in the *Odes* and *Epodes*. However, many of the *Odes* and *Epodes* obviously do not fit our specifications, and we can remove them from consideration right away. When we pass over the erotic and convivial poems, we find ourselves left with a nucleus which includes among its most striking components the patriotic odes and epodes. Here we encounter Horace the *vatis*, the inspired poet, or, as he also calls himself, *Musarum sacerdos* (*C.* 3. 1.3); he thunders forth his denunciations of Roman degeneracy and his urgent demands for moral reform, while reform is possible. Aroused as he is, he perceives situations which evoke utter despair and the indignation which often erupts against triumphant vice.

The clearest prototypes of Juvenalian indignation in Horace appear in *Epodes* 4, 7, 16, the Roman *Odes* of Book 3, and also *C.* 3.24. As has often been noted, these poems strike the same notes as much of Sallust; Sallust's grim picture of Rome stirred echoes in Juvenal's day, most notably in Tacitus.[23] The entire setting of *Epode* 4 corresponds to the situation in Juvenal 1. A former slave, who has promoted himself to great riches and political prominence during the civil wars, parades haughtily down the Sacra Via in Rome; at the sight, native Romans cannot help but express their feelings of outrage, characterized by Horace in the significant words *liberrima indignatio* (10). Similarly Juvenal stands on the street-corner in Rome (1.63–64) and denounces upstarts like Crispinus the Egyptian (26 ff.) and the nameless ex-slave from Mesopotamia who now claims priority over tribunes on account of his wealth (102 ff.). *Epode* 7 voices the despair of the thirties in a highly rhetorical manner, implying that the rival camps, all *scelesti* (1), are bringing Rome to inevitable doom (16). Equally despairing, *Epode* 16 recommends the action which Umbricius takes in *Satire* 3: namely, to abandon Rome. In the pose of the *vatis* (66), afire with emotion, the speaker urges people to forsake corrupt Italy altogether and

[23] Cf. G. Schörner, *Sallust und Horaz über den Sittenverfall und die sittliche Erneuerung Roms* (Diss. Erlangen 1934).

112

sail to the mythical Isles of the Blest, where they may recapture the honesty and happiness of the Golden Age.

In the Roman *Odes*, Horace forces upon the reader an awareness of the grand style which he appropriates to render his patriotic emotions. While we never sense the total pessimism of Juvenalian satire, the poet does focus on crucial moral perversions and resort to the same illustrations and mood as we find later in Juvenal. Most obvious, in this respect, is the conclusion of *C.* 3.6: the inevitable degeneracy which Horace foretells has become a reality for Juvenal in 1.147:

> nil erit ulterius quod nostris moribus addat
> posteritas, eadem facient cupientque minores.

The same ode derives its harsh verdict from the utter pollution of the institution of marriage (17 ff.). Indeed, while it evokes common details with *Satire* 1, we might well recognize its proximity to the ideas of *Satire* 6. For our purposes, however, it suffices to note the scene in 25 ff., an admittedly conventional topic, but one never mentioned in the *Sermones*: the husband prostitutes his wife, pretending to be too drunk to notice. Juvenal exploits precisely the same scene in 1.55, portraying the husband as *doctus leno*, and with the same fury.[24] The effects of *avaritia* and *luxuria*, which pervade all of Book 1 of Juvenal's *Satires* and particularly attract the satirist's fury in 1.87 ff., constitute basic themes, as causes of Roman corruption, in the Roman *Odes*. Furthermore, just as Horace exalts the ideal of martial *virtus* in 3.2 and 5 and contrasts with the ignoble behavior of Crassus' soldiers the inflexible bravery of the ancient and legendary Regulus, so Juvenal represents the gap between the heroism of old Republican Rome and the unheroic, cowardly contemporary Rome, most vividly, of course, in the savage details of *Satire* 2. Juvenal differs from Horace in his complete absence of hope. Nothing in the *Satires* of Book 1 corresponds to the quasi-epic exaltation of *C.* 3.3 and 4. However, if Juvenal does think of a specific Horatian precedent for his indignant despair over Roman degeneracy, he could not have chosen better than from the *Epodes* and from the pessimistic *Odes* which frame Horace's visions of Augustan grandeur.

To conclude, I find it impossible to believe that Juvenal referred to Horace, the author of the *Sermones*, in the striking phrase

---

[24] Horace voices concern over the breakdown of marriage also in *C.* 3.24.17 ff.

Venusina lucerna. If my interpretation be correct, the phrase would connote a type of Horatian poetry akin to the grand style of epic and tragedy, automatically ruling out the *Sermones*, the model of the plain style. Furthermore, the details which Juvenal specifies as *haec* do not correspond with those found in the *Sermones*; they do, in part, find analogues in the *Epodes* and *Odes* devoted to patriotic issues: the upstart viewed with *liberrima indignatio*, the compulsion to flee from degenerate Rome, the husband conniving at his wife's prostitution, the lost military virtue of the country. I need not point out that Archilochus, inspiration behind the *Epodes*, also constituted one of the influences on Lucilian invective. But just as these *Epodes* parallel the outspoken patriotic fervor of Lucilius, Scipio's friend, so the Roman *Odes* develop themes common to the moralists, whether satirists, historians, or diatribists, living at the end of the Republic. Therefore, when Juvenal chose *indignatio* as his mood and a perverse Rome as his topic, when he selected from the Lucilian corpus only those poems which fitted the heroic type,[25] then he naturally turned from the *Sermones* of Horace to poems which he could also view as "satiric" in his restricted sense: namely, to the patriotic *Odes* and *Epodes*.

[25] Juvenal represents Lucilius in a manner quite different from his predecessors Horace and Persius. For Horace, he is many things, but most of all a delightful, outspoken type who belongs in the setting of a *convivium*. Persius in 1.114–15 emphasizes the invective in Lucilius' *Satires*. In doing so, however, he attributes no grandeur to the satirist, but develops an image of an animal biting people. When Juvenal describes Lucilius, he makes him into an epic hero, a portrayal which he can make only by ignoring those large portions of Lucilius' writings in which humorous confessions and good-natured jokes provide the dominant note. The chariot metaphor in 1.19–20 goes with an epic periphrasis, *magnus Auruncae alumnus*, which effectively exalts Lucilius into epic stature. Similarly, *Lucilius ardens* wearing armor and fighting his mighty battles against vice is a Lucilius created after Juvenal's image rather than a Lucilius corresponding to the great satirist of the second century B.C. (cf. 1.165 ff.).

114

IMAGERY IN THE SATIRES OF HORACE AND JUVENAL.

Some Greek and Latin poetry abounds in figurative passages and lends itself readily to the modern interpretative technique of analysis through imagery. In this respect, one immediately thinks of Aeschylus, Pindar, and of Vergil. There are other types of poetry where imagery plays a less obvious, though still important, role. I shall concern myself in this paper with the latter class of poetry and attempt to define the general nature of imagery as employed by Horace and Juvenal in their Satires. Studies of the metaphors and similes in Horace's works and of the metaphors in Juvenal do exist; which, however, mainly written some time ago, exhibit the particular interest of this period in classification rather than interpretation.[1] No effort

---

[1] For Horace, cf. F. Bäker, *Die Metaphern in den Satiren des Horaz* (Stralsund, 1883); D. Eberlein, *Poetische Personifikation in den Dichtungen des Horaz* (Diss. Erlangen, 1914); F. Schneider, *Gleichnisse und Bilder bei Horaz* (Diss. Nürnberg, 1914); also, the more recent and specialized articles of E. A. Hahn, "Horace's Use of Concrete Examples," *C. W.*, XXXIX (1945), pp. 82-6 and 90-4; and of E. G. Wilkins, "The Similes of Horace," *C. W.*, XXIX (1936), pp. 124-31. I cannot agree with the methods employed by M. Andrewes, "Horace's Use of Imagery in the Epodes and Odes," *G. & R.*, XIX (1950), pp. 106-15. For Juvenal, the only study devoted exclusively to metaphor is that of H. Jattkowski, *De Sermone in A. Persii Flacci et D. Junii Juvenalis satiris figurato* (Allenstein, 1886). But some useful remarks on metaphor will be found in L. O. Kiaer, *De Sermone Juvenalis* (Copenhagen, 1875), pp. 220 ff.; and in I. G. Scott (Ryberg), *The Grand Style in the Satires of Juvenal* (*Smith College Classical St.* VIII [Northampton, Mass., 1927]), pp. 31 ff. and 64 ff. Juvenal's similes have never aroused interest.

has been made to distinguish the special function of the metaphor in Roman satire, nor has any study shown how the treatment of imagery changes with the particular view of satire embraced by a writer. It seems to me that we can study with profit three aspects of Horatian and Juvenalian imagery: 1. the place of the image in the texture of its passage, or, how the image fits into its immediate context; 2. patterns of imagery and their relation to the meaning of the Satires; 3. the logical structure of the image, or, in what respect the satirist equates two different entities for poetic purposes. By studying these three aspects I propose to connect Horace's and Juvenal's techniques of using imagery with their general approach in satire, on the assumption that the image, while an important aspect of poetic meaning, forms a part only, a representative part, of the total significance of each Satire.

I. Horace

In order to be clear about the class of imagery which Horace adopts, let us briefly consider an example of dense figurative usage, the famous beginning of Book IV of the *Aeneid*:[2]

> at regina gravi iamdudum *saucia* cura
> *vulnus alit* venis et caeco *carpitur igni*.
> multa viri virtus animo multusque *recursat*
> gentis honos: *haerent infixi* pectore vultus
> verbaque, nec placidam membris dat cura quietem.

Vergil describes the psychological state of Dido passionately in love, but struggling to conceal and control that passion. We are not to think of the love as a pleasant or beneficent sentiment: it is not *amor* but *cura*, mental disturbance. Even before we have arrived at *cura*, with its special suggestivity, we encounter the first of many metaphors: *saucia*; that is, we know how to interpret the queen's state of mind before we learn what causes her troubles. Continuing in this general manner, avoiding any concrete details, the poet elaborates his metaphor in the first half of the second line and introduces a new one in the second half: Dido nurses a wound and her vitals are ravaged by

---

[2] For a thorough discussion of the imagery in this book, cf. F. L. Newton, "Recurrent Imagery in *Aeneid* IV," *T.A.P.A.*, LXXXVIII (1957), pp. 31-43.

fire. In short, the poet has stated the metaphors by which we should regard Dido's love, and he has given them priority over the facts of her love; the metaphors stand clearly out from the passages in which they are set. The poet in fact has here announced the dominant images of the whole book: the wound becomes more and more serious until finally it is transformed into the fatal physical wound of suicide; the fire burns its way on and on until ultimately it becomes the funeral pyre and the symbolic burning of Carthage in the final simile.[3] For the present—and I shall return to this passage—I call attention to the fact that the epic poet has used several metaphors to define and interpret Dido's feelings, has immediately re-stated the image of wounding (*haerent infixi*), and by the way in which he has introduced them, given the metaphors a strikingly significant function.

By way of contrast, let us take a number of passages where Horace states or at least anticipates an important metaphor at the beginning of a Satire.

> sunt quibus in satura videar nimis acer et ultra
> *legem* tendere opus. (II, 1, 1-2)
> unde et quo Catius? "non est mihi tempus, aventi
> ponere signa nova *praeceptis*, qualia *vincent*
> Pythagoran Anytique reum doctumque Platona."
>   (II, 4, 1-3)
> hoc quoque, Teresia, praeter narrata petenti
> responde, quibus amissas reparare queam res
> *artibus* et modis.   (II, 5, 1-3)
> "iamdudum ausculto et cupiens tibi dicere *servus*
> pauca reformido."   (II, 7, 1-2)

Those who are familiar with the four Satires involved[4] might well object to treating the italicized words as metaphors in at

---

[3] In addition, Vergil exploits an advantage of epic not available to Horace: he draws upon the associations of fire and wounds already established in earlier books. For instance, much of Book II links fire and wounds, as in the scene of Polites' death (especially II, 529). Cf. B. M. W. Knox, "The Serpent and the Flame," *A. J. P.*, LXXI (1950), pp. 379-400, and B. Fenik, "Parallelism of Theme and Imagery in *Aeneid* II and IV," *A. J. P.*, LXXX (1959), pp. 1-24.

[4] It will be observed that the four examples above come from Book II of the *Sermones*. I cite no instances from Book I simply because there are none; Horace employed a different technique of introducing theme

117

least three cases. This is a legitimate objection and points up a striking difference between the dense metaphorical presentation of Vergilian epic and Horace's treatment of imagery. Vergil's passage calls attention to the metaphor and constructs the tragedy of Dido upon the metaphorical framework, while Horace employs a word which, in its context, remains ambiguous or seems so conventional as to possess no immediate force. In *Serm.*, II, 1 we listen to a discussion between the idealized person of the satirist and a well-known Roman lawyer, Trebatius. The satirist begins and focuses his attention immediately on the problems of writing satire; he registers the conflicting opinions that seem to prevail about his earlier work. Incidentally, as an apparent synonym for *nimis acer*, he uses the phrase *ultra legem tendere opus*. As the commentators have shown, an ambiguity exists in *legem* that concentrates the significance of the whole Satire. On the one hand, it is probably to be taken as a metaphor (the "law" or convention of the literary form known as satire); on the other hand, the literal-minded legalist Trebatius seems to interpret it as relevant to his professional status, for he immediately begins to play the role of attorney. Thus, while Trebatius stolidly argues out the legal implications of satire, the satirist keeps returning to the metaphor and probing the underlying significance of satiric conventions. The metaphor never emerges in complete freedom, but remains tied to and qualified by the literal content of the conversation.[5] Here, then, we encounter a major technique of Horace in dealing with a key metaphor: he merges it with the dramatic framework of his Satire so skillfully that it possesses no immediate, but a cumulative, significance. It is only as we realize that the satirist and Trebatius converse on two entirely different levels that we sense the force of the legal metaphor.

There is no need to go deeply into the other passages cited. In *Serm.*, II, 4 Horace places an ambiguous metaphor in the

and metaphor in his earlier Satires, in keeping with his different method of development. As will be shown later in the discussion of *Serm.*, I, 1 and 6, the theme of the diatribal Satires tends to be so forceful that imagery recedes into the background, unobtrusively providing a cumulative insight into the deeper relevance of the theme.

[5] For a recent discussion of the legal metaphor in *Serm.*, II, 1, cf. J. S. C. Teijeiro, "Apostillas jurídicas a una sátira de Horacio," *Arbor*, XXXI (1955), pp. 65-75.

mouth of Catius. In itself, *praeceptis* possesses no special vigor and consequently blends easily into its context. However, Catius qualifies these precepts as superior (*vincent*) to the doctrines of three great Greek philosophers, and the very flippancy of his reference to Socrates by antonomasia might well prepare us for what comes. As Catius starts retailing his precepts, it becomes clear that he is treating culinary recipes as equivalent to philosophic principles. Accordingly, Horace exploits the confusion between the literal meaning of *praecepta* and the common ethical associations (which may be considered metaphorical) of the word. In *Serm.*, II, 5 Ulysses asks Tiresias by what arts he may recoup his financial losses in Ithaca. As in *Serm.*, II, 1 the word receives a weakening synonym, and we soon perceive that Ulysses refers merely to means, devices rather than to the mental and moral associations of *artes*. However, the ambiguity inherent in *artibus* [6] manifests itself throughout the Satire: the Homeric Ulysses, whose heroic values became defined through the high ethical goal implicit in his arts, has degenerated into the artful *captator*,[7] merely unscrupulous in his devices. Finally, Horace exploits the confusion between the literal and metaphorical meanings of slavery in *Serm.*, II, 7. The slave Davus begins the conversation, and accordingly *servus* must be taken literally on its first appearance. However, its position gives it potential significance, and, as we soon see, Davus can take advantage of the Saturnalia to ignore his usual servile relation to his master. In fact, he attempts to reduce Horace to the status of a slave by misusing the Stoic metaphor and paradox. Once again, the point of the Satire consists in exploring the apparent relation between the literal *servus* and the moral "slave," and once again Horace prevents the metaphor from being stated in a glaringly obvious manner.

[6] Horace has called attention to *artibus* by carefully separating the construction *quibus . . . artibus*, so that the reader remains in suspense while Ulysses explains his purpose of recouping his losses. Only then, in the emphatic position at the beginning of the next line, does the poet end the hyperbaton. As a result, Horace has succeeded in implying his whole ironic theme in that single phrase, that is, the degradation of *artes* for the service of *res*.

[7] Horace plays upon the similarity between *captator* and *captor* by constant ironic reference to the military prowess of Ulysses, so as to render the will-seeker into a soldier trying to capture an enemy.

The relative unobtrusiveness of Horace's metaphors involves at least two factors. First, the context in which the metaphor appears so envelops it in literal associations that one does not sense the significance of the image in the same affective manner as those so pointedly affirmed by Vergil in the second line of *Aeneid* IV. Second, the metaphor itself is so conventional as to lack direct force, and it fades imperceptibly into the literal context. Conventional metaphors of a similar type occur in Book I of the *Sermones*. For instance, the common image of "fighting" a law suit provides the metaphorical substance of *Serm.*, I, 7; "suffering" the consequences of error functions as the Epicurean criterion for rejecting avarice in *Serm.*, I, 1 and indiscriminate sexual indulgence in *Serm.*, I, 2; moral "freedom" in *Serm.*, I, 6 serves as the answer to those who estimate personal worth solely according to free, noble birth. Such metaphors as these achieve their effect not by forcing themselves strikingly on the imagination from their first occurrence, but by repetition and cumulative association.

A glance at Horace's technique of developing his theme in *Serm.*, I, 6 will illustrate the methods of cumulative association or metaphorical patterns. In this Satire Horace sets out to define the relation between birth and personal value. Most people, he notes, would deny the right of the emancipated slave's son, like himself, to any dignity or honor at all. Horace does not fight this prejudice at first, for he prefers to leave the impression that he lives "free" of ambition—I use the metaphor advisedly. Incidentally, though, he provides insight into the political world of "honor" by his metaphors: the populace would not have "bought" Laevinus for more than a single as; the masses act as "slaves" (16) to fame; he Horace should stay in his own "skin," not masquerade as a politician (22); Glory drags noble and ignoble alike "fettered to its glittering chariot" (23); the ambitious man is "mad" (27) or "sick" (30). As a result, politics emerges as a slave's existence: the mob both masters and serves the ambitious; the ambitious enslave themselves to the dubious goal of Gloria, the hope of becoming lords of Rome. Honor therefore becomes a highly relative quality, desirable to an intelligent man only under special circumstances, for instance, when he is a Servius Tullius or a Decius. As Horace implies, he and Maecenas have removed themselves from vulgar concepts (18); which amounts to saying that he understands the true concept of *libertas*.

Turning from the limited world of politics, the satirist defines an area of greater scope and importance, first friendship untinged by ambition, then the fundamental principles of the ideal life. It may be that the son of a freedman should not engage in politics, but no social stigma should taint him, to prevent him, if worthy, from enjoying the friendship of people like Maecenas. To describe the inception of his close relation to Maecenas, Horace does not resort to metaphor. Chance did not operate, but strict ethical principles, and any comparison, it seems, might weaken the force of such words as *optimus, pudor, quod eram, secernis honestum*. Ironically, then, the son of a freedman has reached a position next to the great which the common herd regards as political honor and resents, but which in fact bears no real resemblance to the false criteria of political success, since it is ambitionless and informed by the ethical purposes underlying true friendship.

Horace's irony does not stop there; he goes on to give his father, the emancipated slave, the entire credit for the moral character which he possesses and accordingly for that honor of Maecenas' friendship. Because of his father, he received a special education in Rome, worthy of sons of the nobility and those of inherited wealth; he escaped the plebeian training of the crude citizenry of Venusia. His father acted as his *custos* (a position usually assigned to an elderly and trusted household slave), but did so with a moral, not a servile, attitude. The former slave aimed at true honor (83) and paid no attention to what career his son would adopt, whether humble like his own or dignified, as in fact Horace's career came to be. Thanks to his father, Horace can express perfect contentment with his existence and would not exchange his humble parentage, which after all has accounted for his success, for any long pedigree. A family name, as he puts it, would amount to taking on a heavy burden (99); the metaphor alludes to the "slave" of ambition. Again, irony has altered the conventional perspective, to make the servile existence not that of the freedman's son, but that of the aristocrat's son or at least of the ambitious like Tillius. Horace lives a life of total freedom, goes where he wants, does what he likes and when he likes; and he implies this quality of *libertas* in words like *si libet* (105) and *libido* (111). His life guarantees him pleasure, absence of worry, no pressing responsibilities, no formalities to be observed: he is a man "free of painfully heavy ambition" (129). To conclude, the slave's life and the life of freedom, if one searches at all profoundly, are found to have their reality not in the world of literal legalism, but in that of metaphor, of moral truth.

At no time has Horace asserted that he is a morally "free" man, that, to understand him properly, one should regard him as *liber* rather than *libertino patre natus*. The metaphorical theme, therefore, remains implicit, suggested by the images applied to the world of ambition, by the careful elimination of imagery in describing the discriminating friendship of Maecenas, by the ironic portrait of his father as *custos*, and finally by the contrast between his own liberal tenor of life with the overburdened, slavish ways of the ambitious. The metaphors for ambition, likening it to slavery, indicate by opposition that the freedman's son who knows better than to involve himself in politics must be "free."

How does that other class of imagery, namely similes, fit into these unobtrusive patterns? To go back to our original comparison with *Aeneid* IV, we observed there at the beginning two dominant metaphors of wounding and burning. At key points in the action of Book IV, similes occur involving these two symbols: for instance, the burning wound of passion makes Dido like a wounded deer (66 ff.); the burning madness of the queen at the rumor of Aeneas' departure renders her like a Bacchante (300 ff.); and the symbolic effect of the fatal wound that Dido deals herself resembles the disastrous results of an enemy assault on, and the burning of, Carthage or ancient Tyre (665 ff.). Vergil, it seems legitimate to remark, integrates his similes precisely with his metaphorical themes to form one rich pattern of symbolism; and the similes receive full emphasis together with the metaphors, standing out pointedly, affectively in their contexts.

Horace uses similes of a different order. It is well known that, in accordance with the prosaic tradition of satire, he frequently employs animal similes; and in general the level of such imagery avoids the "poetic." Moreover, the satirist does not lavish rich evocative detail on similes or permit them to extend for more than a few lines, if that; he introduces similes with much less emphasis. Finally, he often substitutes for the simile the concrete example or analogy. Like metaphors, therefore, similes blend easily into the general texture, imperceptibly contributing to the general associations of the theme. In regard to patterns of imagery, similes in the conversational Satire function differently from those of the dramatic epic. The integration of simile with metaphor and general symbolic pattern exists, but in a looser form. Instead of forcing itself visually on the imagination as a part of the picturesque scheme of symbolism, the simile may well seem to contribute only a momentary effect, designed purely for its immediate context. But a subtle link with other imagery usually prevails. In *Serm.*, I, 6, whose metaphors I have discussed above, Horace inserts a brief simile (65 ff.) to describe his moral character: its faults are minor, like the scattered spots on an otherwise strikingly handsome body. Now, this appears at first sight to perform no general purpose, until one realizes the implications in the phrase *egregio corpore*. Without arousing any objections by his modest phrasing of the simile, Horace in fact suggests that his character, like the body, escapes the corruptions of the common slavish herd (*grex*).[8] This etymological use of *egregio* illustrates the general technique of Horatian simile: the simile will possess an allegorical rather than an immediately dramatic connection with the theme.

The Satires of Book II do not employ much simile, and one can see good reason for Horace's practice: he permits another to do most, if not all, of the speaking, and the subjects of the speeches do not call for comparisons, being advice to hosts or will-seekers, accounts of personal experiences, or parodies of Stoic sermons operating with *exempla* more easily than with simile. For the simile, in two cases, Horace substitutes the animal fable: in *Serm.*, II, 3, 314 ff. Damasippus uses what he calls an *imago* about a frog,[9] and *Serm.*, II, 6 exploits the story (*fabella* 78) of the country and the city mouse. In order to find a satisfactory illustration of similes integrated with total

[8] We can connect this simile with the metaphor in 22: *in propria non pelle quiessem*. There, Horace refers to the popular prejudice against political upstarts, and the metaphor of the animal ironically reveals how the common herd thinks of others.

[9] I discuss this *imago* extensively below, pp. 241-2.

symbolism, we must turn back to Book I. I have chosen one of the latest and most mature of the Satires, *Serm.*, I, 1.

In form this Satire is a diatribe which attempts to produce a true concept of *avaritia*. To do this, Horace engages in a fictive conversation with a typical materialist and forces him to defend his admitted goal of accumulating money. As his first excuse, the *avarus* claims that he intends to put aside the means whereby he can ultimately retire in leisure (31); then he tries to prejudice his argument by comparing himself to the industrious ant. At this point, Horace catches him in inaccuracy; spinning out the simile to its logical end, the satirist finds an essential difference between the *avarus* and the ant in the fact that the ant stops accumulating during the winter and utilizes its store of food, whereas the miser never pauses to enjoy his hoard. The simile, therefore, has served to expose the falsity of the miser's purpose, with the result that the ant's pile of food (*acervus* 34) can hereafter serve as an ironic metaphor (cf. 44 and 51) for the useless pile of things which the miser amasses. The satirist proposes a more accurate simile: the miser is like a slave carrying a pannier full of bread for a slave train, all destined to be sold; he benefits no more from his heavy load than the other slaves carrying nothing (46 ff.).

The above simile suggests the ironic point which Horace drives at in the Satire, that the miser's pile is a source of misery to him, not a means of pleasure (as he argues). With this insight, we can appreciate the excuse which immediately follows on the above simile: *"at suave est ex magno tollere acervo"* (51). We have seen the small amount of pleasure available to the miser, and we have watched the satirist analyze the inaccurate usage of the ant's pile. We are not surprised, therefore, when Horace moves on to examine a new aspect of the defense, namely, the pleasure derived from drawing on a *large* hoard. As a synonym for *tollere*, Horace uses *haurire* (52), proceeding immediately from that transitional metaphor to a new simile about drawing water to quench one's thirst. The obvious point is that it makes no difference to the thirst whether one secures water from a little spring (*fonticulus*) or a tremendous river (*magnum flumen*): the magnitude of the source does not make water wetter. However, again Horace analyzes his simile and ends by suggesting that the premium on size leads to disaster.

The largest river would logically be one swollen into a spring torrent, so we watch the fool approaching the turbid Aufidus, falling into the river, and swept away to his death, as the bank, hollowed by the action of the current, gives way beneath his weight. The pleasurable draught has resulted in drowning.[10]

Still another simile answers the excuse that one should pile up money so that one's family will take care of one in time of sickness. Obviously, says Horace, he who places money before family for the greater part of his life cannot expect to buy the love of his relatives in emergency, no more than he could expect to train an ass to run in harness (90-1). The pile of money has destroyed the love of the family and replaced it with hate, and similarly the ass will completely frustrate the expectations of his foolish trainer.[11] The image of training and driving an ass yields to the final simile of the Satire (114 ff.). The insatiate, always envious miser, hurrying to catch up to a richer man, resembles the driver of a chariot in a nightmarish race where there are always chariots ahead: he may pass some, but he keeps madly whipping the horses to catch up with the next ones. This little vignette of frenzied activity epitomizes the ceaseless anxiety of the *avarus*, an existence which stands in polar opposition to the Epicurean ideal of rational pleasure which Horace here espouses.[12]

[10] This simile is picked up again in a momentary allusion to the thirsty Tantalus and his futile effort to catch *fugientia flumina* (68).

[11] This simile has been the subject of recent controversy. Cf. E. B. Stevens, "Horace, *Satires* 1.1.86-91," *C. W.*, XLII (1948-9), pp. 104-6, and N. W. DeWitt, "Horace, *Satires* I.1.86-91; A Different View," *ibid.*, pp. 245-6. Stevens called attention to some proverbs which expose the folly of training an ass for war, to replace a horse in a glorious, but often fatal, role. DeWitt urged rather the Epicurean relevance of the simile and the stress on the trainer instead of the ass. I would only observe that both have ignored another aspect of the comparison, an aspect which is central to the Horatian simile. Horace does not merely introduce the comparison to describe futile effort; he also indicates the nature of the *avarus*, who does in fact think of his family as beasts of burden, donkeys to be beaten and trained to impossible tasks. It is because the miser cherishes this animal image of his family that human affection is impossible. Horace, as is observed below, refuses to see Man as an animal, but as a rational being.

[12] I said above that the chariot race was the last simile of the Satire. This is not quite true: it is the last simile describing the *avarus*, but

Now that we have considered five of the principal similes of *Serm.*, I, 1, we may summarize the Horatian handling of such imagery. Horace uses short comparisons, introducing them very casually. Sometimes, the brevity of a simile used by an interlocutor calls for further examination, and the satirist pushes it to its logical conclusion, at which point we find the interlocutor exposed. Sometimes, the simile starts from an unobtrusive metaphor; sometimes, it provides a metaphor for subsequent irony. Similes do not combine into a rich symbolic vision of avarice; there is no easy relation between the ant and the driver of the chariot such as subsists between Vergil's similes of the wounded deer and the burning city, both held together by the dominant metaphors. One perceives the connection only after thought.

I think it profitable to distinguish a special "intellectual" quality in the Horatian simile as against the Vergilian dramatic simile. By this, I mean that Horace uses the image to clarify his argument, whereas Vergil interprets psychological states or important actions through his type of simile. When the poet compares Dido to a wounded deer, he momentarily crystallizes the pitiful reversal in the once-proud queen; and it is vital to the total meaning of this simile that Dido should once have been compared to the huntress deity Diana, that love should have been defined explicitly as a wound. But when Horace describes the miser as a careening charioteer, chasing but never catching up with all the chariots ahead in an eternal race, the simile does not interact visually or emotionally with those that have preceded it. Rather, it sums up the futility of the miser's goal, an implicit aspect of previous similes which have concentrated primarily on subordinate qualities of avarice. To grasp the meaning of this simile, then, we abstract the allegorical significance, for the satirist urges us towards the abstract, the underlying truth, and only by combining the allegorical implications of the five similes do we grasp their interrelation. In short, as we might well expect, Horace responds to the exigencies of a careful analysis of a concept, in this case of *avaritia*, by taking different facets of the concept and illustrating them with different, superficially unrelated similes; Vergil responds to the

Horace introduces a brief comparison in 119 (*uti conviva satur*) to evoke the Epicurean ideal of rational pleasure. The satisfied banqueter provides an ideal antitype to the anxious charioteer.

requirements of dramatic epic and constantly shows the connection between the first and subsequent acts or passions of his characters, between feelings and their concrete results, between people and the natural order.

The above contrast between the "intellectual" quality of Horatian simile and the dramatic quality of Vergil's brings us to the final phase of our inquiry. To complete the discussion, we must take apart the metaphors and similes of Horace to determine their logic. It is conventional to analyze metaphor and simile into three components: the thing compared, the thing to which it is compared, and the link between the two. These components can be represented as three propositions, by which we come closer to the logical quality of the image. In the metaphor which we have discussed, *famae servit ineptus* (i. e., *populus*; *Serm.*, I, 6, 16), the propositions may be stated as follows: 1. The Roman populace possesses certain necessary qualities (including freedom). 2. Slaves do not possess freedom. 3. The Roman populace acts as a slave when it comes to *fama*. Now, the virtue of a metaphor or simile, as critics have defined it, inheres in the asserted connection between two different entities, whereby a tension is set up, the resemblance pulling one way, the differences another. In the next pages, I shall investigate this tension in Horace and Vergil, because it provides us with another aspect of the "intellectual" quality of Horatian imagery.

In the above metaphor of the slavish masses, Horace has created what appears to be a paradox. By definition, Romans are free, not slaves, so how can they be said to be slavish? The answer, of course, is that their moral nature belies the legal status of the Romans. However, the paradox does exist and constitutes the main effect of the metaphor: Horace, that is, overtly stresses the difference between the two compared terms at the same time that he asserts their likeness. A similar effect results from the Horatian simile. If we examine, for instance, the simile in *Serm.*, I, 1 about drawing water, we quickly grasp the common link between the avaricious and the thirsty man: both desire to satisfy a craving. But Horace does not leave it there. His point, which he carefully makes by discussing the comparison, is that the acquisitive miser differs radically from the thirsty man, for the physical need can be met by a moderate amount of water drawn from *any* pure source; whereas the miser

127

believes that he can satisfy his needs only from a large (unattainably large, as it turns out) accumulation of wealth and precious items. The needs are substantially the same, but the criteria of satisfaction so differ in the two cases that the miser rather resembles a fool who accidentally falls into a torrent while trying to satisfy his thirst. Such meticulous examination of comparisons to bring out both sides and especially to make clear fundamental and significant distinctions will account for the curiously ironic treatment of the ant simile in this same Satire. The *avarus* asserts a likeness between himself and the ant in terms of provident industry; Horace comments rather on the difference between ant and man in respect to the way they employ their hoarded stores.

Vergil again provides a useful contrast with Horace. To return to the passage in *Aeneid* IV already cited, we noted the striking metaphors by which the poet defined Dido's passion in terms of wound and fire. It is certainly true that the tension between likeness and difference operates in these metaphors, but Vergil's effect patently diverges from that of Horace. The common factor between passion and fire or wound is the destructive force inherent in all of them; and to make sure that we imagine destructive fire Vergil uses *carpitur*. The likeness is all explicit, overt; not so with the differences. We can point out that passion is a human feeling, fire is a physical force, and a wound results from a blow. Do the differences consist, then, in the opposition between human and inanimate (or inhuman)? Immediately, though, we plunge into a problem central to Vergilian psychology: are the passions human or subhuman? From the way the poet portrays the ruinous effects of Dido's love, of Juno's hatred, of Turnus' enmity, we can see the inhuman aspects of violent feeling. On the other hand, from the way our sympathies linger with Dido and Turnus and even with the blasphemer Mezentius, we might well argue that the supremely human quality for Vergil is passion. It is not my purpose to solve this problem, but to define it, for in this central ambiguity at the heart of Vergilian imagery—both metaphor and simile— we encounter the true distinction between Horace's and Vergil's approaches. Vergil does not argue out his similes nor does he present explicit paradoxes in his metaphors. On the surface of each comparison rests a broad mass of relevant, dramatically vivid likeness; underneath, never discussed, but always implicit, exists a profound tension, the veritable ambiguity of man's nature. We should always ask the question whether or not our passions render us merely into beasts or destructive forces (fire, wounds, storms, savage waves, etc.), but Vergil will not answer it for us.

Horace does provide us with a type of answer by appealing to reason. For the satirist, man must be defined as rational. The rational universe has its complexities which Horace never minimizes, but it implicitly possesses a coherence which man, using his intellect, can control. Therefore, the satirist forces us to examine the differences between two compared entities and thus re-inforces his argument. As a result, we observe that the components of comparisons in Horace have a persuasive appeal which is absent from those of Vergil. Our mind, not our emotions or imagination, is engaged.

Ancient rhetoric notes that in comparisons four classifications exist: living things may be substituted for others; inanimate things exchanged for inanimate; animate for inanimate; or inanimate for animate.[13] We might well subdivide the animate into the human and the animal; and, for Vergil, we might add the divine. Now, Vergil most characteristically compares humans to animals or inanimate things and vice-versa.[14] It is not common for the poet to compare one type of human being with another, and, when he does so, the tension is more obvious than otherwise. For instance, Vergil uses the verb *immolo* three times in the *Aeneid*, all three in connection with Pallas' death, two as metaphors. Shortly after he has captured eight Italians for *sacrifice* to the shade of Pallas (X, 519), Aeneas attacks a priest and butchers (*immolat* 541) him. Then, in the final act of the epic, he plunges his sword into the heart of Turnus crying out: "*Pallas te hoc vulnere, Pallas immolat*" (XII, 949). The metaphor makes of Aeneas a priest sacrificing a victim, and the

[13] Cf. Quintilian, VIII, 6, 9 ff.

[14] In a few dramatic instances, Vergil also compares humans with deities and vice-versa. Thus, the first simile of the poem (I, 148 ff.) compares Neptune to a venerable statesman; we first see Dido in terms of Diana (I, 498 ff.); Aeneas, about to ruin Dido, is the handsome Apollo (IV, 143 ff.); and Turnus, the ringleader of the hostility towards the Trojans, properly becomes Mars himself (XII, 331 ff.).

horror of it is that he is killing fellow humans, one a genuine priest. I do not doubt that we should in fact feel the sacramental aspect of these deaths or at least understand Aeneas' sentiments, but the dominant reaction in the reader would properly be to shrink away from a man who treats a fellow human like a dumb beast, while seeing himself in a priestly role. A simile of the same ironic type occurs in X, 803 ff., again focused on Aeneas. Just before killing Lausus, Aeneas is compared to a plowman: the destroyer appears as the creative worker! Such stark images, as I have said, are rare in Vergil. Usually, the surface seems smooth in a comparison between man and beast or between man and inanimate force.

When dealing with his primary subject, Man, Horace most regularly compares one sort of man with another, or a man with an animal; that is, using Quintilian's classification, he substitutes one living thing for another. If we review the similes in *Serm.*, I, 1, for instance, we find that four out of the five treated compare man with man, and the fifth inaccurately compares man with ant. The equal humanity of each member of the simile enables the reader to perceive the distinctions which constantly emerge in Horatian comparisons. In a Satire which I have discussed more fully in a previous issue of this Journal, *Serm.*, I, 9, Horace creates a pattern of military imagery to help interpret his encounter with the *garrulus*.[15] The "bore" turns out to be something more, namely, an eager, ambitious time-server, whose character is best defined by our metaphorically appropriate adjectives: aggressive and antagonistic. However, the point of the Satire does not consist in representing the *garrulus* dramatically, but rather in implying the correct values in a world of political antagonisms. Thus, Horace describes how he is trapped by the man, how the man applies his belligerent standards to the mild poet, and how the poet "defends" himself, by distinguishing moral from political values. In the end, Apollo enters to save the poet, as once before he had saved the warrior Hector. The analogy of the *garrulus* and the warrior has been appropriate, though the former lacks all heroic qualities; by contrast, the effort of the "bore" to apply his aggressive standards to Horace's serene world has, by its patent inappro-

[15] Cf. "Horace, the Unwilling Warrior—Satire I, 9," *A. J. P.*, LXXVII (1956), pp. 148-66.

priateness, brought into the open the moral doctrine of the Satire. Epic drama has become in the satirist's hands a means of rational inquiry, for, by comparing an ambitious man to a heroic warrior, the satirist has been able to probe into the ethical goals of mankind in general.

When Horace compares man and animal, he also brings differences to the fore. It should be observed, for example, that a large part of the animal imagery in the Satires applies ironically to the man who embodies the whole rational drive of the poems, namely, the satirist himself. The traditional apologia for satire which Horace inherited from Lucilius involved, among other things, coping with the popular image of the satirist as a malicious scandalmonger, or, in metaphorical terms, as a rabid dog.[16] Horace dismisses this image, vigorously denying that he is *mordax* and substituting for the animal the concept of an intelligent, morally responsible human being.[17] In other words, the animal imagery so frequently applied to Horace is either explicitly replaced or so patently inappropriate as to amuse the reader: e. g., the simile of the ill-tempered ass in I, 9, 20. Unlike Vergil, who represents inaccesible areas of human psychology by animal imagery, Horace constantly implies that man should never be comparable to a beast, that reason can and should operate permanently to direct a moral, not a purely physical, existence.

In conclusion, I should like to consider the implications of the *imago* connected with Horace by the fool Damasippus (*Serm.*, II, 3, 313 ff.). Damasippus tells how a calf stepped on and killed several young frogs, but one escaped to explain to the mother frog what had happened. Not knowing what a calf was, the baby frog could only say that a tremendous monster (*ingens belua*) had caused the disaster. The mother wanted to know how big, and started puffing herself up to approximate the size of this unknown monster. But the baby answers—and here Da-

---

[16] Cf. G. C. Fiske, "Lucilius and Persius," *T. A. P. A.*, XL (1909), pp. 121-50, and my discussion of this point in *C. Q.*, LII (1958), pp. 195-7.

[17] One of the reasons for introducing his father in *Serm.*, I, 4 lies in the value the old man has for the image of Horace as a highly rational, self-controlled human. The moral education which his father gave him seems to guarantee that Horace is anything but a "dog."

131

masippus makes his point—"You could not equal its size even if you burst." This little parable, which Damasippus thinks so apt to Horace's situation (320), receives no direct interpretation from the ironic satirist, and the reader is left with the problem of explaining it. As we might well infer from the effort to liken the satirist to a frog, the comparison leads the reader to observe the more significant differences and ultimately to attain a just understanding of Damasippus' diatribe. An immediate absurdity makes itself felt: the childless, peace-loving Horace is compared to a mother frog whose children have been crushed.[18] Moreover, the details of this frog tragedy, in fact irrelevant to the point of the comparison, act to weaken one's contemptuous attitude towards the puffing parent, for one tends to connect her senseless effort to equal the monster with her maternal concern for her babes so cruelly destroyed. Damasippus has told his parable clumsily, then. Beyond this, as we consider the story more carefully and ask ourselves what it illustrates, an even greater absurdity emerges. According to the introductory lines (312-13), Horace keeps trying to copy the lordly gestures of Maecenas. We have good reason to suspect Damasippus' allegation in any case, but the parable completely undermines it. When we start equating supposedly analogous members in the comparison, we find to our amusement that Damasippus has made Maecenas the *ingens belua* who has done such damage to Horace's (the mother frog's) household that consequently Horace emulates Maecenas not out of admiration, but from outrage. One comment suffices to expose the inanity of the comparison: the conversation between Horace and Damasippus takes place in the country house which that "formidable monster" Maecenas has given the poet and which functions as a permanent symbol of Horace's escape from ambition and worldly concerns.

[18] Damasippus tells the fable approximately as it appears in Babrius 28; Phaedrus 1, 24, followed by Martial X, 79, 9, gives a slightly different ending by making the mother burst. We have no example besides this passage of Horace where the whole tale is applied concretely. By recounting it all, instead of alluding to the ending as Martial, Damasippus encourages us unwittingly to inspect the details, to picture first of all the bereaved and vengeful mother. When we try to fit this to our concept of Horace, as the satirist plans, we find ourselves in disagreement with Damasippus even before we arrive at his main point.

In this section, I have attempted to make several points about Horatian imagery in his Satires and to focus these comments by reference to more familiar qualities of Vergilian imagery. Horace maintains a smooth argumentative or descriptive tone, and his metaphors and similes do not disturb the placid surface of discourse. Rather, because of their conventionality, their ambiguous statement in many cases, and the brevity with which they are devoloped, they tend to blend easily with the argument, not stand out against it as an overt means of interpretation. Analysis of typical Satires (*Serm.*, I, 1 and I, 6) shows that Horace does create a pattern of imagery, but that the pattern inheres in the allegorical or, as I have preferred to call it, the "intellectual" interaction of metaphors, similes, and theme. The intellectual quality of Horatian imagery, its essential difference from Vergilian imagery, manifests itself when we study the logic of the satiric image. The meaningful tension between likeness and difference becomes the target of the searching powers of human reason. Commonplace metaphors and similes are exposed to ridicule; moral metaphors are found to possess a reality that ironically reverses the literal meaning of words; and above all, man vindicates his claim to a special place in Nature because his reason defies animal comparison. In short, the intellectual imagery of Horace illustrates the dominant quality of Horatian satire, its rationality.[19]

II. Juvenal

Juvenal's Satires start from indignation, he affirms, and their general character differs accordingly from that of Horatian Satire. One would expect to find that Juvenal adopts themes capable of supporting a mood of indignation and that he constructs his Satires with the same purpose in mind. Similarly, Juvenal's imagery should, in order to fulfill its function, possess

[19] It should go without saying that I regard the rational appeal of Horace's imagery as an asset of his poetry. I do not agree with those who still argue that verse relying on reason and logic, stressing reflection and thought, even verse such as that of Horace, can never attain the lyrical heights, the passionate fire that define poetry. For such a depreciation of Horace, cf. F. Durand, *La poesia di Orazio* (Turin, 1957), a book which ironically was awarded a prize by the Accademia dei Lincei.

a quality totally different from that which in Horace we have isolated under the title of intellectual imagery.

The writers and poets of Juvenal's age all labor under the stigma of modern critics for excessive use of rhetoric. In fact, it has often been found to be illuminating to characterize Juvenal in terms of the principles espoused by the declaimers or the grand poets.[20] If one appreciates the literature of Silver Latin, one can find in the Satires some of the finest features of the period. Therefore, in order to determine the exact nature of Juvenal's imagery, we should also be aware of contemporary poetic practices, primarily those of epic. I have chosen to analyze herewith the imagery of Statius, a poet whose work Juvenal knew well and indeed may have heard during a public *recitatio* (cf. 7, 82 ff.), one of whose pieces seems to have inspired the satirist to a savage mock-epic.[21] Early in the *Thebais* occurs a passage which will start our inquiry into the function of the image in its immediate context:

> atque ea Cadmeo praeceps ubi culmine primum
> constitit adsuetaque *infecit* nube penatis,
> protinus attoniti fratrum sub pectore motus,
> gentilisque animos subiit furor *aegraque* laetis
> invidia atque *parens* odii metus; inde regendi
> saevus *amor*, *ruptaeque* vices iurisque secundi
> ambitus impatiens, et summo dulcius unum
> stare loco, sociisque *comes* discordia regnis.   (I, 123-30)

Like Allecto in *Aeneid* VII, Tisiphone has appeared to cause the conflict in Thebes which forms the subject of the epic. The above lines describe the effect of her efforts and are immediately followed by the first sustained simile of the poem, which exemplifies the futility of the shared kingship of Thebes as the impossible pairing of two untamed bullocks. In such a context, we might well expect Statius to exhibit his artistic technique most clearly, and indeed the italicized words do illustrate important features in Statius' metaphors. First of all, what may be called the texture of the passage is not smooth, and the

---

[20] Cf. J. De Decker, *Juvenalis declamans* (Ghent, 1913), and Scott (Ryberg).

[21] Cf. S. Reinach, " Juvénal et Stace," *R. Ph.*, XXXI (1907), pp. 45-50, and P. Ercole, " Stazio e Giovenale," *Riv. I. G. I.*, XV (1931), Fasc. I, pp. 43-50.

metaphors function patently as disturbing elements: one notices them. On the other hand, they do not stand out clearly against a purely blank background, for other words, non-metaphorical words, act in the same context to diffuse a general impression of lurid drama over the situation, and we cannot take in the metaphors apart from these other effects. One cannot help but notice, for instance, that Statius wrote: Tisiphone "infected" with her customary cloud the *Penates*; the household gods serve as a metonym for the palace and the royal brothers therein. Not that the metaphor conflicts with the metonymy, but the metonymy does reduce the immediate sharpness of the metaphor. If Statius had written, as Vergil would, that the infection worked directly on Eteocles and Polyneices, then we would not have been distracted from the metaphor. I do not here imply that Statius adopts a technique inferior to Vergil's, but I wish to define the difference. Accordingly, we find that the force of *aegra*, which continues the metaphor in *infecit*, competes for our attention with the word immediately juxtaposed, *laetis*: Statius has contrived an antithesis which deprives *aegra* of much separate effect. With the other metaphors similarly, the rhetorical phrase forms the unit of meaning which, as a whole, stands out in the texture, employing the metaphor as a portion of that total emphasis. The epigrammatic and paradoxical conceits, that fear is the "parent" of hate, that the brothers felt a bestially fierce "love" of ruling, that they decided upon a system of alternate rule which had as its inevitable "companion" discord, all these work strongly upon the reader's impressions and prepare him for the inevitable war; but the paradox rather than the metaphor is the effective rhetorical unit.

As an example of the texture in which Juvenal employs metaphors, we might aptly take the passage describing Statius' temporary success in Rome:

> curritur ad *vocem* iucundam et carmen *amicae*
> Thebaidos, *laetam* cum fecit Statius urbem
> promisitque diem: tanta dulcedine *captos*
> adficit ille animos, tantaque *libidine* volgi
> auditur; sed cum *fregit* subsellia versu,
> esurit, *intactam* Paridi nisi vendit Agaven. (7, 82-7)

While Juvenal's tone differs from that of epic, his use of metaphor does resemble Statius', in that he contrives rhetorical units that include metaphor but depend only in part upon the image for effect. To start with the texture of this passage, we observe that, despite the fact that many metaphors appear here, they stand out with less immediate clarity than those of Statius. We need only look at the first two to explain the muted quality of Juvenal's metaphors. Juvenal says that everybody rushed to hear the pleasant voice, the song of their friend (female), and, since he has finished the line, we can easily gather the verse into a complete scene devoid of metaphor; only then, with his regularly subtle enjambement, the satirist suddenly adds *Thebaidos*. For the first time, we realize that the "voice" and the "friend" refer metaphorically to the epic poem. As a result, when we finally grasp the image, we have already perceived other rhetorical qualities in the clause which create a totality of significance from which the metaphor should not properly be extricated: it is less the image than the surprising felicity of the sudden personification that strikes us. In a similar manner, Juvenal renders *laetam* metaphorical, but only after delaying the word which determines the image, *urbem*, to the end of the line. The metaphor in *captos* acts in the Statian manner, by paradox, inseparably bound up with *dulcedine*; and this suggestive collocation of words prepares us for the ironic sexual metaphor in *libidine*, sensed only as part of the phrase including *volgi*. Another surprise awaits us in the next line, where Juvenal tells us that the poet broke the seats, an act which one would normally take in a literal sense, then wittily adds the qualifying word *versu*. Now the phrase has become a typical conceit: Statius has provoked such enthusiasm that, as we might say, he brought the house down. Finally, the delayed revelation of metaphor renders the trite adjective by which poets claim originality (*intactam*) into a device of double-entendre, for suddenly the poet becomes a pander. In short, if this passage is, as I believe it is, representative of Juvenal's art,[22] we find that the

[22] For a similarly affective use of personification, cf. the description of the fall of Sejanus, especially how the statues of the great man, even the bronze or marble horses on which he sits, are made into pathetic victims, living victims, of fickle popular feeling (10, 56 ff.). Juvenal also exploits word-position when he makes the metaphor a means of epic parody. Scott (Ryberg), p. 65, cites as a case of parody 10, 218: *circumsilit agmine facto / morborum omne genus*. The epic phrase *agmine facto* receives considerable emphasis at the end of the line and

136

satirist exploits word position so that we cannot grasp his metaphors by themselves, but rather as elements in a whole striking attitude, often suddenly sprung upon us.[23]

Before going on with metaphor, it will be appropriate to pause briefly over the use of simile in epic poet and satirist. Statius inherits a rich tradition of similes, a standard element of epic from the beginning, through his great predecessors Vergil and Lucan.[24] In the many scenes of battle and emotional tension of the *Thebais*, Statius regularly summarizes the dramatic situation with such an extended image. It is unnecessary to observe that similes stand out in the texture of the epic, because obviously they interrupt the narrative to evoke a picture of varying extent designed to abstract the reader from the immediate action and to concentrate his attention on a different world which somehow implies the significance of the world to which it is compared. In the three hundred lines that focus on the final battle of Tydeus (VIII, 456 ff.), Statius uses ten similes of length varying from one line to six.[25] Just after he has killed the unwarlike Atys, Tydeus is described in an image which may serve to epitomize Statius' treatment of similes:

> sic ait, et belli maiora ad praemia mente
> ducitur: innumeris veluti leo forte potitus
> caedibus imbellis vitulos mollisque iuvencas

---

calls for a subject of heroic qualities. Instead, Juvenal takes advantage of the enjambement to raise our expectations, only to surprise us, for sicknesses of all sorts constitute the subject of the verb and the explicit point of the parody.

[23] The sudden force of metaphors makes itself felt especially when the image occurs by itself, often in a *sententia*, rather than in an extended, systematically developed pattern. For instance, in 6, 473, Juvenal describes the desperate efforts of women to improve their looks by expensive cosmetics and processes which amount to face-lifting, then comments on the results: *facies dicetur an ulcus?* The final position of *ulcus* and its radical difference from *facies* illustrate Juvenal's standard practice of rendering the metaphor a part of a larger rhetorical unit.

[24] Cf. B. Deipser, *De P. Papinio Statio Vergilii et Ovidii imitatore*, *Diss. Philologicae Argentoratenses*, V (1881), pp. 85 ff., and W. Michler, *De P. Papinio Statio M. Annaei Lucani imitatore* (Diss. Breslau, 1914), pp. 65 ff.

[25] Cf. VIII, 460-5, 474, 532-5, 544-7, 572-6, 593-6, 616-20, 675-6, 691-4, 749-50. These similes average slightly under four lines in length.

transmittit: magno furor est in sanguine mergi,
nec nisi regnantis cervice recumbere tauri. (592-6)

The point that can be made about Statius' similes, I believe, is
that the comparison often becomes involved in a striking conceit,
with the result that the details of the simile ignore reason for
effect. I do not mean that Statius wastes details. Here, for instance, *regnantis*, a key term in the comparison, artfully prepares
for the next scene in which we see Tydeus, in pursuit of King
Eteocles (663 ff.). But we seem to detect the function of the
simile in this: the lion must be personified with such human
qualities that it can be said to discriminate between "unwarlike"
calves and soft cows so as to lust for blood, but spurn all victims
except the most glorious, that of the "king" of the herd. The
pathetic fallacy emerges even more patently in other similes, as
for instance when, to describe two evenly matched warriors,
Statius employs two mountain torrents which descend into the
same valley but, though in fact merged, refuse to blend their
waters in their pride (VIII, 460 ff.); or when, to illustrate the
death of Prothous, crushed beneath the weight of his dying horse,
Statius adduces an elm tree falling and destroying a vine with
itself, the tree especially grieving for the innocent vine (544 ff.).
In short, the point of Statius' simile often makes a more pronounced impression than the image itself: our eye does not rest
on the whole scene, but we focus our attention on a single aspect
which is often patently personified. As a result, the texture of
similes presents the same phenomenon as the texture of passages
containing metaphors in Statius: there is a dual tension between
image and other verbal effects so as to render the image less
directly significant by itself.

Juvenal does not fall back on a tradition of simile in satire.
While the first book of Horace's Satires contains a fair proportion of skillfully employed similes, the second book, using a
less argumentative form of presentation, dispenses with the
intellectually analyzed comparison.[26] Persius, who follows the
ideas of the more mature Horace, also seems to have agreed
with the elimination of simile, for there are less than ten such
comparisons in his six hundred lines.[27] Therefore, Juvenal can

[26] See above, pp. 233 ff.
[27] In reading Persius I have found five definite similes, all short and

follow his own inclinations in this matter, either to use similes for argument and other poetic purposes or to treat them as a minor, inessential aspect of his poetry. To take, for example, a typical section of over three hundred lines, Satire 3 has a number of comparisons (47-8, 74, 90-1, 137), but no true similes. On the other hand, Satire 5 exploits a different technique of presentation and makes affective use of epic diction and allusions to qualify the banquet given by Virro. If Trebius dares to gape at the meat, he will be dragged out feet first just as the corpse of Cacus killed by Hercules (125); a mushroom is set before Virro like those delicacies which Claudius used to eat, of course before that fatal one given him by Agrippina (147-8); Virro partakes of apples like those which Phaeacia produced in its marvellous orchards, which might even have been stolen from the Hesperides (151-2). The savage point in all three of these momentary similes does not need to be elaborated, and it can safely be said that the point, the witty analogy, accounts for the main impression of the passages. Whereas Statius develops his similes in true epic manner, Juvenal moves directly to the effective portion of the comparison; rarely does the Juvenalian simile have the opportunity to expand into a complete picture. Normally, a line or two provides adequate scope for the striking comparison, and the satirist ties it closely to the grammar and sense of a larger sentence. As one might expect, then, Juvenal treats similes like metaphors: he makes them stand out sharply in their context for a line or two, but lets them contribute part only of the total rhetorical effect of their context. Virro enjoys apples like those of Phaeacia or an African paradise, yes, but the passage remains incomplete. Juvenal must insert between the apples and the qualifying simile a relative clause to enhance the total significance: Virro eats apples which Trebius enjoys only as a delightful scent wafted in front of his nose (150).

We have found that the texture of passages in which Statius uses imagery follows the general epic convention, the imagery being prominent; but we have also observed that various other verbal devices achieve concomitant prominence, so that the image forms but one of several elements, all contributing to the total

rather unimportant, namely, 1, 97; 3, 16; 31; 79; and 6, 62. In addition, it could be argued that the following serve as similes: 1, 66; 2, 70; 3, 42; and 5, 73.

rhetorical effect. In Juvenal, too, it became clear that, unlike Horace, his imagery achieves a sudden brilliance rather than a moderate, almost unobtrusive statement. One might be tempted to deduce from these observed facts a theory connected with our next area of inquiry, namely, the extent to which Juvenal elaborates his imagery as a continuous element of meaning in a whole Satire. We might suspect, for example, that Juvenal would restrict himself to brief but overt and affective patterns of imagery. But rather than indulge in conjecture, let us proceed directly to the material in the text.

Statius limits himself considerably by the way he presents his subject of the Seven aganst Thebes, but it seems relatively clear that he exploits those self-imposed limits. Of the major characters in the epic, not one appeals to our sympathies. The story proceeds on a level of unrelieved hopelessness, savagery, and, with the exception of a few scenes containing women, sheer inhumanity. As one reads the poem, again and again one meets the adjectives *ferus* and *saevus*, epithets applied indiscriminately to any man. Most of the similes concentrate on animals: lions, wolves, tigers, bulls, boars, etc. Such imagery fits most aptly the character of Tydeus, and indeed Statius lavishes animal symbolism on the man. Tydeus comes from Aetolia wearing a boar's hide that serves as an omen for Adrastus and as a symbol for us. He fights Polyneices on the first occasion that we see him, and he continues to exist only for war and killing until his last moment. Thus, our final vision of the man presents to us his bestial character as a whole: he dies gnawing on the head of the Theban who has given him his fatal wound.

If Tydeus seems the most signal example of bestiality in the *Thebaid*, the brothers Eteocles and Polyneices do not lag far behind. Returning to the passage cited from I, 123 ff., we find that the metaphors possess extensive relevance to the picture of fratricidal hatred. In the royal family where one might expect to find prosperity and health, sick envy exists; love of a brother has been perverted to love of his throne; parental qualities cannot be assigned to Oedipus, who has cursed his sons, but to that fear which causes the perverse hatred of brother; and finally, the result of sharing the rule has paradoxically been to destroy companionship and rather to make discord the constant companion of Eteocles and Polyneices. Just as the proper succession has been broken (*ruptae vices* 128), so all the normal fraternal bonds have shattered, so as to pervert the usual associations of family affection into terms properly applicable to the murderous ambitions of the two men. Polyneices receives less of our distaste, but he carries like Tydeus the symbol of his brute nature, in this case a lion's pelt. Eteocles can properly be compared to a snake (II, 411 ff.) as he meditates the ambush for Tydeus. And the lurid details of the final combat between the brothers combine into a striking portrait of savage beasts (XI, 497 ff.): the two fight like animals, with tooth, claw, and animal treachery, until fittingly they have killed each other. Even in death their bestial hatred persists. The symbolic scene in which the pyre of Eteocles repels the corpse of Polyneices exhibits, as Antigone states, the survival of savage feeling (*ferus* XII, 438; *saevos* 446). In short, Statius employs his imagery as part of a general symbolic pattern, metaphors and similes contributing to the dominant impression of the poem, that men have cast off their human feelings and willingly become the most savage of beasts.

Juvenal, as we saw, does not use extended similes, and his metaphors recede into a position of subordination. Moreover, the nature of his satire does not lend itself to symbolic scenes very readily, especially because he cannot fall back on the dramatic associations of earlier books or Satires. To many readers, therefore, a unified pattern of imagery in Juvenal would seem unlikely, precisely because imagery plays such an ancillary role and disunity constitutes such a central impression of the Satires. It might be easier, then, to start with two Satires in which Juvenal does exploit symbolic scenes and achieve a result similar to that of Statius. Satire 4, after a short introduction, consists entirely of a story (*res vera* 35) historically narrated about Domitian and a turbot. With few open metaphors and no operative similes,[28] Juvenal elaborates his tale, using as one of his most prominent thematic words *saevus* and its noun *saevitia*.[29] That this generally pejorative word "savagery" here possesses its original animal associations may be quickly shown.

[28] In a certain sense, the whole story functions as a comparison, demonstrating how much worse Domitian's banquets were than those of his extravagant courtier Crispinus: cf. *qualis . . . epulas* (28).

[29] Cf. my article, "Studies in Book I of Juvenal," *Y. C. S.*, XV (1957), pp. 71 ff.

Domitian is said to rend the world (*laceraret*: cf. 15,102 for proper connotations); flattery makes his crest rise (70). His savagery (85) can be associated with *clades* and *pestis* (84).[30] He inflicts a brutal death (95) on the younger Acilius, having already failed to get rid of him by exposing him to bears in the Alban arena. Domitian renders his courtiers savage if he does not kill them: Pompeius, who readily murders (109), and Fuscus, who plans destructive wars and will eventually, ironically, feed vultures himself (111). In the last words of the Satire, therefore, the monarch dripping with the blood of his victims seems to epitomize the quality of *saevitia* which marked his times (151). As Juvenal presents his picture of Domitian's court, the original associations of *saevus* recover their force, and the Emperor emerges as a beast. More than that, the exaggerated attitude towards the turbot serves to symbolize this bestiality. The monstrous fish awakens the animal appetites of the Emperor, and his menacing violence pervades the atmosphere from the moment the poor fisherman catches the turbot. I do not say that Juvenal's dominant theme is *saevitia*, but certainly the perversion of imperial augustness into bestiality constitutes a powerful element in the meaning of this Satire.

Juvenal's exploitation of savagery as a theme remained throughout his career, to make *saevus* one of his favorite persuasive epithets and to incline him in his last complete Satire to center his attention on the paradox of man become a savage beast. As in Satire 4, so in Satire 15 metaphors and similes play an unobtrusive role in the total symbolism. When the people of two neighboring villages in Egypt become involved in a riot over religious beliefs, one man is killed, torn apart, and eaten raw, bones and all. It is this case of cannibalism which acts as the symbolic heart of the poem, and Juvenal proceeds to reflect on the incident, steadily eliminating parallels and potential associations until the deed emerges nakedly as sheer savagery, worse than the actions of animals. In introducing the act, the

[30] It is not uncommon for *clades* and *pestis* to be associated in reference to a plague: so Lucretius, VI, 1125 and Ovid, *Met.*, VII, 562. On the other hand, *pestis* frequently applies to a human being as here or to a snake: so Vergil, *Georgics*, III, 419 and Statius, *Thebaid*, II, 282 (at least paired with Tisiphone's serpent). I note that the Lewis and Short Dictionary erroneously refers to Nero in conection with this occurrence of *pestis* in Satire 4.

satirist calls it *feritas* (32). By itself, the word might easily be ignored, if the animal allusion had not already been established. In fact, Juvenal concentrates our attention from the beginning on the religious connection between the Egyptians and animals which they worship as deities, that is, as morally their superiors. The Egyptians would, accordingly, never slaughter even a goat-kid, but they cherish no scruples about human flesh as edible meat (13). To emphasize the enormity of his tale in advance, Juvenal continues with an analogy to the incredible adventures of Odysseus. If Odysseus had tried to spin a yarn about man eating man, he would have provoked a roar of disbelief; as it was, his savage (*saeva* 17) Charybdis and cannibalistic Laestrygonians and Cyclops remained within the bounds of propriety only by being monstrous. By such persistent reference to animals and inhuman behavior, Juvenal prepares his reader to sense the original implication in *feritas*, namely, animal behavior. The scenes of savage fury (54) and bestial appetite (78 ff.) reinforce the prejudice, and the subsequent reflections (93 ff.) make Juvenal's theme patent: the Egyptians are the supreme example of bestiality, worse than the Vascones who rent (*lacerabant* 102) human limbs only after consuming all their animals and herbage; more bestial (*saevior* 115) than Diana who demanded human sacrifice; more rabidly savage (*hac saevit rabie* 126) than northern barbarians; finally, worse than the rabid tiger (*rabida* 163) and savage bears (*saevis* 164), inasmuch as the wildest of beasts at least spares its own kind.

Satires 4 and 15 show Juvenal dealing with a theme of savagery and working it out by metaphor, symbolic episode, and analogy. Other Satires operate less through a single episode than by means of numerous representative details, discontinuous incidents, or separate *exempla*. As a result, when we study the structure of such Satires, we usually look for the unifying theme and do not expect much immediate help from the imagery. Such "catalogue" Satires, as Highet has aptly called them,[31] state their subject at the start, imply the moral paradox with which they deal, and then proceed to illustrate the theme with example after example. Satire 6 serves as the most patent instance of this structural technique, but Satires 3, 7, 10, and

[31] Cf. G. Highet, *Juvenal the Satirist: a Study* (Oxford, 1954), pp. 158-9.

presumably 16 exhibit similar tendencies. Now what part do systematic patterns of imagery play in these Satires? As we have already cited a passage of imagery from Satire 7, we may properly begin with it.

The metaphors in 7, 82 ff. transform the inanimate epic of Statius into a very attractive female, whose allure resides entirely in her sex. On the surface, Juvenal describes the tremendous popularity earned by the poet at his *recitatio*; by metaphor he concentrates our attention on the poetic product, implying that the poem was not merely a female, but a prostitute, that the delight of the mob (*libidine* 85) consisted of sexual pleasure. Therefore, as Rigault noted,[32] the innocent phrase *promisitque diem* (84) acquires associations from the context and suggests the assignation of a prostitute with lover. As the passage continues, the personified adjectives *iucundam*, *amicae*, and *laetam* become more and more restricted in meaning, referring to sexual delights. Statius acts as a pander, now pleasing with amorous *Thebais* the general public, now prostituting virginal *Agave* to a wealthy taker, Paris; and Statius the *leno* would starve without Paris. In adding this significant metaphorical level to the passage Juvenal does not repeat a metaphorical pattern already established in the Satire, but does fit into it. To state the dominant image of Satire 7, we can do no better than cite the *inscriptio* appearing in many manuscripts at the beginning of the poem or after verse 16: DE STERILITATE STUDIORUM.[33] The unproductivity of the arts accounts for a series of images related to farming (e. g., 48, 98, 103, 112); for the constantly ironic use of *labor* and *merces*, whose primary associations with hard physical labor conflict with their usage here to refer to the efforts and rewards of intellectuals; and for allusions to the unspoiled natural beauties of Helicon (8, 60), the gardens of Lucan (79), the groves of Quintilian (186), and the like. According to his characteristic approach, Juvenal proceeds in Satire 7 to strip away from the arts their normally honorific associations and expose them in the lurid light of his reality: the arts have sunk

[32] I find this note mentioned, but not approved, in J. E. B. Mayor, *Thirteen Satires of Juvenal with a Commentary* (London, 1893²). Cf. R. Pichon, *De Sermone amatorio* (Paris, 1902), p. 6.

[33] For this *inscriptio*, cf. the recent edition of U. Knoche, *D. Iunius Juvenalis Saturae* (Munich, 1950).

to the level of physical labor, and even lower, because the intellectuals cannot even earn a living wage (*merces*). Thus, Statius has prostituted his Muse, lawyers are obliged to leave Rome for the provinces, and in general the scale of intellectual values has suffered complete reversal. To conclude, when writing a more elaborate poem than those founded on a single episode, Juvenal introduces subordinate images, as in 7, 82 ff., to illustrate his central theme. In order to earn a living (*merces*) by verse, the poet has to become a pander to popular tastes.

When one reads Juvenal's Satires, imagery does not make a pronounced impression, and consequently one does not sense a particularly vivid system of symbolism based on metaphor and simile. Still, imagery does play its part in the Satires, working together with other devices to promote the emotional effect of the unifying theme. In the three poems which we have briefly reviewed, it appears that we could in fact state Juvenal's theme by metaphor. The medieval scholars perceived this point in connection with Satire 7 and rightly called attention to the farming image; and Satires 4 and 15 both concentrate on the bestial aspects of Domitian's court and the Egyptians respectively. If we attempted to apply the theory to other poems, we could express the theme, for instance, of Satire 3 as the un-Roman nature of Rome, and of Satire 10 as the deadliness of ambition. The metaphorical possibilities of the theme permit Juvenal to allude intermittently to the dominant image and in certain Satires like 4 and 15 to dramatize it by a single long *fabula* or *exemplum*. Elsewhere and more commonly, the satirist introduces a series of concrete instances or brief *exempla*—the passage on Statius serves in this capacity—which can employ their own pattern of imagery, subordinate to the dominant image and coordinate with the imagery of other such *exempla* in the same Satire. Accordingly, the passage on Statius aptly uses a sexual metaphor to illustrate the plight of the poet; the brief discussion of the historian (7, 98 ff.), which immediately follows, employs the agricultural image; and the next section on the lawyer (105 ff.) uses a mock-heroic technique to point up the ignominy of that once dignified profession. Similarly, in Satire 10, the tower constitutes the image for political ambition, the torrent for eloquence, and beauty for military glory, all implying the mortality of ambition in general.

Having discussed the texture of Juvenal's imagery and its systematic usage, I come now to the final area of inquiry, namely, the logic of the image. We can take a metaphor or simile and analyze its structure into the three parts of which it consists: two separate entities and a conecting link. To discuss the logic of the image would involve examining the connecting link and determining its proportion of likeness and dissimilarity and the poetic consequences for the image. For example, we have discussed the animal imagery of Statius and shown how the characters of Tydeus, Eteocles, and Polyneices exhibit bestial qualities, which are epitomized in their final symbolic acts. Now, Statius could, as Vergil does, leave us with an ambiguous impression about this animal image: that is, he could give us other facets of his heroes' characters and he could make the picture of the animal sympathetic, so as to stress the human as much as the subhuman in passionate actions. But in fact Statius adopts a different technique by narrowing his scope and eliminating uncertainty, so as to concentrate on affirming the totally bestial nature of his central characters. As one reads the *Thebais*, one does not reflect on the personality of Tydeus or Eteocles, in search of human traits. The metaphor and the simile are statements of fact: Tydeus is *saevus* and *ferus* without qualification, and he entirely resembles whichever wild beast to which he may be compared. As a result, instead of the Vergilian glimmers of hope, the suggestions of human complexity that make of Man an imprecise blend of destructive passion, noble emotion, rational design, and mechanistic inhumanity, Statius plunges us ever deeper into a picture of unrelieved blackness, where the leading warriors become cannibals, outrageous blasphemers, and fratricides, where they achieve nothing but futile destruction.

I do not need to observe that the restricted application of Statian imagery possesses great dramatic power, especially when combined, as it is, with luridly affective symbolic scenes. Rather, I am concerned with its absolute poetic quality, by which I mean its implicit representation of the nature of reality. While the world which Statius creates within the limits of his epic is a consistent world and does nakedly exhibit its bestial character, our experience informs us of another area of reality and might well suggest, if Statius gave us a moment for meditation by a few qualifying comments, that his characters could be more fully explored. By giving us this partial view of Man, then, Statius appeals not so much to reason and experience as to emotion and produces what we might call a drama of horrors as distinguished from a tragedy.

Just as Statius represents a type of dramatic presentation opposed to that of Vergil (as exclusive to inclusive), so Juvenal exploits a style of imagery very different from that of Horace. Horace makes his imagery a part of his total appeal to reason by constantly emphasizing the degrees of difference between the two so-called similar entities in metaphor or simile. When he compares a man to an animal, Horace implicitly denies that the likeness is in any way desirable. Since Man by definition ranks above the animals, Horace always suggests the possibility of using Man's unique power of reason to negate the metaphorical relation. In the same way, he deals with the concept of slavery and freedom, as if true freedom has nothing to do with legal definitions, but with a certain moral attitude available to all classes of society. If he calls the Roman people slavish, he does so because he knows and urges that Man is born to a higher destiny. Horace, therefore, uses the image to suggest the fundamental nature of Man; one always senses the irony, the ethical direction in the metaphor or simile which depicts men through a lower order of reality.

The " intellectual " image does not exist in Juvenal. Whereas Horace can ironically compare himself to a mouse or a donkey and thereby suggest the rational and ethical goals of mankind, Juvenal says that Domitian is unqualifiedly a savage beast and the Egyptians worse than beasts. In this we may perceive one reason why Juvenal allowed the simile to decline in importance, for the Horatian simile, where we sense a certain hesitation about the comparison and an effort of the poet to examine in detail its relevance, does not answer Juvenal's need. He replaces simile with metaphor and changes the comparison into an outright assertion of fact, of total identity. Indeed, Juvenal's power inheres precisely in this: he asserts as unqualified facts the most outrageous paradoxes. Not that the satirist specifically denies the existence of that higher reality in human nature to which Horace continually appeals; he merely ignores it as irrelevant. He affirms that the world which he describes, whether it be Rome or Egypt or, as in Satire 10, the human race, is devoid of ethical values or, in its perverse way, has transvalued all that once was good.[34] The capacity of Man to conquer his lower nature by reason, to achieve that higher "freedom," no longer exists in Juvenal's world; in Satire 3 we hear that a horde of servile Greeks controls Rome and effectively destroys the opportunities of a free client like Umbricius, and in Satire 5 we watch the "free" Trebius transformed into a slave before our eyes. While Horace could evolve a new concept of *libertas* in connection with the artistic function of satire (*Serm.*, I, 4), Juvenal stresses the crushing of freedom in his Program Satire and the prostitution of poetry in the passage cited from Satire 7. Juvenal's imagery, then, operates within the confines of a hopelessly perverted world and serves to depict that world as a fact. When we plunge into Juvenal's scenes of horror—and in this he resembles Statius—we cease to follow our reason, for rationality no longer applies here. Instead, we rely upon our instincts; or, to put it more accurately, Juvenal creates an atmosphere in which instinctive indignation alone seems to act. The fact that a poet must prostitute his art comes to us suffused with the outrage of a Roman who knows, and expects us to know, of those glorious days when Horace and Vergil wrote freely, exempt from financial worries. The infinite freedom of rational Man belongs to a dead age, Juvenal implies by imagery and theme, and the present involves the inescapable fact of Roman and human perversion, irrationality, bestiality. Since Man has hopelessly identified himself with the lowest species, all we can do is express our abhorrence of this reality, reveal in a futile manner through *indignatio* our latent concept of what Rome originally represented. We cannot expect to restore to Man his humanity, and, if we ourselves are to keep free of shame, we must abandon that reality like Umbricius.

If I were to propose an adjective to define Juvenal's imagery, I would attempt to suggest his radical difference from Horace

---

[34] Juvenal also insists that he produces a truthful picture of this corrupt world. Cf. his affective use of *verum* in 2, 64; 4, 35; 6, 325; 7, 112; and 8, 125. Within the limits of Juvenal's carefully defined world, "truth" can only expose degeneracy, Man's identity with beasts; it never involves hope by suggesting higher values or a nobler status open to a rational, moral human being.

and, without perjorative implications, epitomize Juvenal's as "irrational" imagery. We have seen this "irrational" factor in the technique of asserting identity rather than logically examining likeness. Looking at the texture of the Satires again, we can see how the "irrational" affects the presentation of the image to the reader. Although Juvenal does not conceal images, he does not state them directly to our imagination, but rather integrates them with a larger affective rhetorical unit. Thus, the image, subordinated to a purpose of sharp antithesis, sardonic personification, or the like, becomes an element of assertion, not suggestion. One has only to compare the unobtrusive image that forms such an integral part of Horace's discursive reasoning, to see what Juvenal accomplishes.

Again, when we study symbolic patterns in Juvenal, we detect a persistent appeal to the irrational emotions. Juvenal takes extreme images rather than conventionally appropriate ones[35] and makes the shocking disparity seem valid by able use of dramatic rhetoric. In the passage about Statius, he fixes on a brilliant image and reinforces it by carefully contriving an antithesis: we see Statius in a moment of great popular success, then turn sharply to the starving poet forced to sell his mime to Paris. Juvenal has selected the details for this antithesis; a reading of the *Silvae*, for example, would produce an entirely different impression of Statius' career. Whereas in Horace the pattern of imagery is unobtrusive, connected allegorically rather than visually by passages of argument, Juvenal develops patterns of imagery, as with Statius, which depend essentially on dramatically powerful symbolic episodes. These episodes, assuming the form of historical events or *exempla*, dominate the Satires, and, just as their inner structure exhibits rhetorical distortion, so their interrelation depends less on logical sequence than on sheer juxtaposition and accumulation. So in Satire 7 Juvenal presents several intellectual occupations and repre-

[35] Cf. the shocking quality, the motivation to indignation, in such images as the prostitution of poetry (Sat. 7), the feminine nature of aristocratic names once associated with military exploits (Sat. 2), the enslavement of Rome (Sat. 3), the bestiality of a Roman Emperor and master of the civilized world (Sat. 4), or, in passages of less general extension, the picture of a wife as master, king of the household (6, 224), of her face as an *ulcus* (6, 473).

149

sents them in parallel systems of imagery.[36] By varying his *exempla* and their imagery he seems to build up an indictment, an indictment which in fact depends upon affective juxtaposition of highly theatrical episodes exploiting a rhetorical antithesis and a strikingly paradoxical image. We may well conclude that such imagery blocks off reasoning or the logical development of an argument and constitutes a necessary element in Juvenal's satiric poetry, where, if one thing is emphasized, it is that unreason dominates the world. No longer does the image imply the capacity of Man to separate himself from the animals by his reason, as in Horace; Juvenal portrays only the bestial perversions of irrationality and leaves us with the feeling that Man has lost his highest potentialities. In this sense, the image of the pander Statius is the image of Juvenal's distorted, corrupt world.

[36] I do not mean that Satire 7 has a haphazard organization of unrelated material, for it is clear that Juvenal has arranged the successive paragraphs on the intellectual disciplines with a clear sense of structure. Cf. the excellent remarks of Highet, p. 269, n. 1. I do mean, however, that in each instance we go over the ground already covered and do not try to proceed deeper into the problem of why the professions involve financial failure and what might be done about it. Juvenal concerns himself only with establishing the fact beyond possibility of denial that there is no hope for the intellectual. Hence, **parallelism of imagery.**

PERSIUS

Part versus Whole in Persius' Fifth Satire

In recent years two major German studies have attempted to reinterpret the verbal technique of Persius as a step towards removing the current prejudice against his Satires.[1] Concentrating on the structure of phrases, imitation, and transitions, they have succeeded in eliciting general principles according to which Persius seems to act even in his most outrageous verses. The problem next arises of relating the verbal technique to the general theme of each Satire, and here, I believe, the satirist's defender faces his most severe test; for Persius' excessive emphasis on verbal manipulation produces a conflict between part and whole, between phrase and argument, which in turn affects his compositional technique, and in two curiously related aspects.[2] In order to make his thematic point despite his confusing phrase, Persius resorts to a method of repetition most apparent in his accumulation of metaphors.[3] But this repetition, in its turn, often has the effect of over-emphasizing incidents and obscuring the central connection between paragraphs, and the reader finds himself almost obliged to allegorize these incidents to discover their thematic relevance. That is, if we state it as a paradox, Persius' effort for precision of phrase forces him to compensate with a series of explanatory comments that plunge him into thematic imprecision. Consequently, the argument of a Satire proceeds jerkily, clear in its main outlines because of the repetition, yet constantly startling the reader by its apparently abrupt tacks.

Perhaps the most patent example of such composition occurs in Satire 5, generally conceded to be the best of Persius' work.

---

[1] Cf. W. Kugler, *Des Persius Wille zu sprachlicher Gestaltung in seiner Wirkung auf Ausdruck und Composition* (Diss. Berlin, 1940), and D. Henss, "Die Imitationstechnik des Persius," *Philologus*, IC (1955), 277-294.

[2] Kugler, pp. 79 ff., has attempted to apply his findings to the structural problem in Satire 3. In opposition to Hendrickson, *CP*, XXIII (1928), 332-342, he detects a unifying thread throughout the Satire and rejects the theory of transposition and interpolation.

[3] E.g., 3. 20-24, where Persius, in successive clauses, applies to the same person metaphors of the public performer, leaking fluids, badly-made pots, and unformed clay, all to imply the folly of the boy; or 5. 10-13, where the satirist uses three successive and different metaphors to stress a single idea.

Thanks to the satirist's practice of repeating himself,[4] commentators have no difficulty in summarizing the contents of the 191 lines: Persius expresses his gratitude to Cornutus; then he launches into his central interest, the Stoic theme of human stupidity interpreted as slavery. The word *then* exposes the difficulty which emerges in full clarity after one has studied the various proposed schematizations of the Satire.[5] The praise of Cornutus can be limited to 1-51; the Stoic theme begins in 73; and the intervening lines (52-72) attempt to bridge the gap between these two disparate portions by what Villeneuve called a laborious transition.[6] In other words, Persius seems to have constructed this Satire according to a plan by which the long opening section contributes nothing to his essential theme, which, with almost no preparation, first appears at 73.[7]

In a loose manner, most critics would grant, the two sections possess interrelations which can be tightened by 52-72. The achievement of Cornutus in bringing Persius within the fold of Stoicism constitutes an implicitly positive ideal which stands in polar opposition to the slavish lives, described in 73 ff., of those devoid of philosophic principles. By observing no additional relevance, however, commentators reveal their own embarrassment with a Satire which, despite the most elaborate schematization, fails to convince the reader of its unity. Following the prevalent opinion, we would be inclined to be most severe to the introductory section

---

[4] The repetition is particularly obvious in 73 ff., where the satirist moves from one example of moral slavery to another; but Persius also employs it in the opening sections, for example in 41-51, when stressing the fact that he and Cornutus live on the basis of perfect equality.

[5] I. Casaubon, *Auli Persi Flacci saturarum liber* (London, 1647), distinguishes the two parts, 1-51 and 73 ff., and calls 52-72 a transition to the Stoic theme. A. Cartault, *Perse: Satires* (Paris, 1920), employs the same scheme. O. Jahn, *A. Persi Flacci saturarum liber* (Leipzig, 1843), merely points out the two principal sections. F. Villeneuve, *Essai sur Perse* (Paris, 1918), pp. 332 ff., elaborates somewhat on Casaubon's scheme, dividing what he calls the Stoic diatribe of 73 ff. into two portions: 73-131 and 132-88. Even more elaborate is the analysis of G. Némethy. *A. Persi Flacci saturae* (Budapest, 1903); he distinguishes an exordium (1-51), six separate parts (52-72, 73-90, 91-123, 124-56, 157-75, 175-88), and a conclusion (189-91). In general, most scholars follow Casaubon or introduce slight variations on his scheme. However, F. Ramorino, *Satire di Persio* (Turin, 1905) divides the Satire at 65 and assumes two parts, namely, 1-65 and 66 ff. The view of Nino Scivoletti, *Auli Persi Flacci Saturae* (Florence, 1956), is that "La composizione è divisa in due parti giustapposte tra le quali è taciuto ogni trapasso."

[6] Villeneuve, p. 332.

[7] Casaubon, p. 356, notes the lack of close relation between the divisions: "Sunt igitur satirae huius distinctae partes duae." He also feels obliged to comment on the abrupt transition at 73 (p. 402). B. L. Gildersleeve, *The Satires of A. Persius Flaccus* (New York, 1875), p. 154, states: "The introduction (i.e., 1-51) is not wrought into the poem."

(1-51). The long discussion as to whether or not Persius should praise Cornutus in fulsome epic terms (1-29) would strike us as quite irrelevant, an awkward means of introducing a more modest review of Cornutus' benefits (30-51), itself hardly relevant to the harsh denunciation of human slavery of 73 ff. If, on the other hand, we adopt the thesis which I have proposed, namely, that Persius' repetitive grouping of pointed phrases regularly obscures the genuine continuity of his thematic development, we still may not have a better opinion of his poetic genius, but we may change our minds about his intelligence. And to assume that he constructed Satire 5 on the basis of a puerile contrast between himself and the masses somehow seems an affront to Persius' intellect.

It is of course tempting to plead the traditional informal structural techniques of Roman satire and dismiss our problem as non-existent. As a cursory review of Persius' predecessors, Horace and Lucilius, reveals, the satirist's adoption of the conventions of *sermo* presupposes the relaxed, not necessarily unified, pace of conversation. Granted this, we still must inquire into the structural technique of Persius before adopting the easy explanation of informality. If Persius employed principles in his other Satires consistent with the alleged structure of Satire 5, we would be justified in treating the problems raised by 1-51 as a natural phenomenon of his satire. As it is, however, neither of the other longer Satires follows the system here defined of two loosely connected sections,[8] whereas they do, I believe, employ principles of thematic development parallel to those exhibited in Satire 5. Since, then, the satiric form does not provide an adequate explanation of Persius' poetic method, the problem, as we have defined it, must be approached differently. Consequently I shall consider 1-51 in relation to the rest of the Satire in order to show its basic thematic function.

To begin with, we may briefly summarize the contents of this

---

[8] Both Satire 1 and 3 may be divided into two portions, but they are closely related, as Persius makes entirely clear in the continuity of his imagery and symbolism. In Satire 1, Persius writes a program poem to explain his satiric principles in connection with current poetic practices. Immediately subjected to criticism, he turns and attacks the immoral assumptions of formal poets and their audience (1-106), then easily glides into discussion of his own moral purpose in satire (107-34). Satire 3 deals with the opportunity of philosophic study presented to youth and the consequences of neglect, interpreted in terms of the Stoic paradox: all but the *sapiens* are mad. There is a division at 62, all the more pronounced if, as many think, Persius discusses his own youth until then. In 63 ff., we are shown the sickness, metaphorically speaking, of the ignorant. Both Satires, therefore, depend upon a technique of contrast, good vs. bad, but the contrast is implicit in the metaphors throughout each poem.

controversial section. Persius himself speaks the opening lines (1-4), apparently launching forth on a turgid appeal to the Muses; but before he gets far—yet far enough to expose his folly—Cornutus interrupts to criticize the use of artificial verbiage (5-13). Cornutus conveys his prejudice against the grand style by comparing it successively to food and air. Then he continues (14-18) and recommends to Persius the simple, unadorned, and presumably earnest, style of the normal citizen. To this Persius replies (19-29) that he was speaking from his heart, but that he wished to express with what he considered proper emphasis, by means of epic language, his gratitude towards Cornutus. Nevertheless, in obedience to his master's suggestions, Persius goes on in a modified style, confessing his adolescent need for Cornutus (30-37) and then recounting the transformation produced in him by his tutor (37-44). Now the two have become so unified in purpose that Persius can claim an astrological influence of harmony upon their lives (45-51).

Except in the striking contrast between the mood and subject of 1-51 and 73 ff., there is no apparent connection between this summary and the portion of the Satire generally considered to be of essential importance. If Persius really relies on more than contrast, if he conceives of the Satire as a thematic entity, as I maintain, then it would seem necessary for him at least to allude to slavery and freedom. I need hardly remark that slavery and freedom function as metaphors for the foolish and philosophic life. Precisely because of this metaphorical nature, clear allusion to them becomes difficult in other than tropical terms. An indirect technique of allusion, however, is employed, and in adopting it Persius assumes a unique stylistic position among Roman satirists and poets. In 73 ff. Persius associates with his central symbol, slavery, a series of metaphors, symbolic situations, and thematic terms. Similarly, in 1-51 the apparently redundant metaphors in contorted phrases serve to give the context of Persius' friendship for Cornutus several important connotations. It is by this associative process that Persius achieves thematic unity, for the allusions in 1-51 parallel to a remarkable degree those which center on the Stoic ideas of freedom and slavery. For example, the satirist uses *nugis* (19) in a pejorative sense to refer to turgidly pretentious poetry, then employs *nugator* (127) and *nugaris* (169) in patent reference to the slavish mentality. Is it possible to connect poetic folly with the folly which Persius calls slavery? I believe it is, and our method of approach lies in relating these and other such terms which, it seems highly likely, Persius repeated because of their parallel associations.

The initial concern with questions of style (1-29) seems especially remote from slavery. When, however, we realize that Persius adopts a moral position in this discussion, the gap narrows. In fact, the satirist takes the same attitude as he did in Satire 1, where he frankly argued from the proverbial principle: "Le style c'est l'homme." Since Seneca accepts the same approach,[9] it appears that Persius is consistent with contemporary Stoicism at the beginning. But in what sense does this stylistic problem, by its connotations, introduce the ultimate theme of slavery? Allusions to the preparation, serving, and consumption of food form a striking portion, we observe, of Cornutus' speech in 5 ff.; he sneers at the grand style of epic or tragedy as *carminis offas* (5) and *olla Thyestae ... insulso cenanda Glyconi* (8-9). While Cornutus is the first frankly to use the metaphor, he does not snatch it from the blue. As frequently happens in Persius, the metaphor has been suggested by a phrase which potentially could evoke the scene of a waiter setting before a banqueter a hearty meal: *fabula seu maesto ponatur hianda tragoedo* (3). The myth that demands a gaping mouth of the tragic actor becomes, in Cornutus' patent imagery, the meal of Thyestes eaten by the actor Glyco. Parallel to their concern with food, the opening lines also lay emphasis on eating by the way they progressively qualify the familiar phrase *centum voces* (1). Persius unwittingly uses mouths and tongues as the equivalent of voices (*ora et linguas* 2), and these words, coupled with the *fabula hianda*, introduce Cornutus' contemptuous *centeno gutture* (6). The elderly philosopher has observed, it is implied, that poets take such exaggerated delight in the heightened style of epic and tragedy as to savor, like a gourmet, the mellifluous words they utter. Scorning the tragedian's *cena*, therefore, he recommends to his foolish young pupil modest meals, *plebeia prandia* (18), that is, a style commensurate with popular speech.

Obviously, there is no specific reference to slavery here. It would be far-fetched to urge that the poet, when compared to a cook or server of food, is potentially servile because, in Rome, slaves cooked the meals and waited on the tables. Rather, the connecting link is the common attitude of the formal poet, as suggested by the metaphor, and of the slavish fool when placed in analogous situa-

---

[9] Seneca, *Epist.* 114, starts from a Greek proverb meaning that style provides a key to a man's character.

tions. In the second part of the Satire, Persius frequently mentions food and its effect upon the slave.[10] The slave steals food; or, in his vulgar avarice, he slurps up mud, to grasp a lost penny; or his desire to acquire riches by trade is interpreted through the unpleasant *cena* which he must endure; or special diet conveys the servile quality of superstition. A man's attitude towards food can define his character, and the true slave fails to discern the essential values of life when he makes money or superstition the criterion according to which he will eat. Equally servile, the grand poet ignores the significance of his subject, debasing epic or tragedy to a banquet of tasty phrases. In short, Persius takes a general prejudicial metaphor from the introduction and applies it strictly to the slavish mentality in the second part, even employing verbal echoes, as though poet and slave could be identified.[11]

Cornutus has already spoken ironically of the mists of Helicon (7); but he effects a clear transition to the equally prejudicial idea of poetry as hot air by means of the ambivalent verb *coquitur* (10). The poet resembles the man operating the bellows at the forge to increase combustion,[12] or the raven with its lugubrious croakings,[13] or the child puffing out its cheeks and making a popping noise. When, later, Persius exposes human slavery, echoes of this description recur,[14] again starting from the joint inability of poet and slave to control themselves.

The poet cooking up his savory epic and the poet accumulating hot air within himself have servile potentialities because they lack full control over their material, and it runs away with them into simple inanity. In his positive recommendations (14-18) Cornutus draws a contrast which once more could prepare for the opposition between slave and free. Several valid interpretations exist for *verba togae* (14), but Cornutus refers, among other things, to the language of a *free* Roman. Accordingly, he recommends an ethical attack on vice with the manner of a freeborn citizen (*ingenuo*

---

[10] Allusions to food occur in 5, 6, 8, 9, 10, 17, 18, 77, 112, 115, 147, 150, 176, 177, and 182 ff.

[11] E.g., *hianda* 3 and 176; *ingeris* 6 and 177; *cenanda* 9 and 147.

[12] Persius probably varies, as Casaubon observes, Horace, *Serm.* I 4, 19-21: *usque laborantis dum ferrum molliat ignis.* Like Persius, Horace stressed the futile and thankless efforts of the poet. It is also true that slaves worked in the forge. Cf. Vergil's description of Vulcan's workers, *Aen.* VIII 424 ff.

[13] Persius' phrase *clauso murmure* might perhaps suggest a sound like that of the winds of Aeolus, whose *magno murmure* (*Aen.* I 55, 124) indicates need of control.

[14] Cf. *coquitur* 10 and *decoquit* 57; *premis* 11 and *presso* 109; *rumpere* 13 and *rupi* 158.

ludo 16),[15] and, reverting to the eating metaphor, concludes by advocating *plebeia prandia* (18). Certain other contrasts reinforce this allusion to freedom, understood as self-control. The unrestraint of the epic language opposes the moderation of satire; the gaping tale of tragedy conflicts with the nice concise phrases (*iunctura acri*) advised by Cornutus; and the essential crudity of epic matter (cf. 5) opposes the real problems challenging the ideal satirist. In addition, moderation and conscious art serve later as synonyms for liberty, once the theme receives a clear statement,[16] whereas the inartistic extravagance of the tragedian, an instance of the lack of self-control, can easily blend into the connotations of the failure of self-control in general: namely, slavery.[17]

When Persius responds to Cornutus' criticisms (19 ff.), he accepts the prejudice against epic style and its falsifications, but claims that his own genuine depth of feeling requires a lofty tone. Thus, he takes up the air metaphor (*turgescat, fumo* 20) and admits that such inane poetry deserves the title of trivia (*nugis* 19). As for his own emotions, though, they do not spring from the mouth, to make a superficial sensuous appeal to a vapid audience; they have established themselves permanently in his heart (*in pectore fixi* 27). Therefore, the revelation of his natural affection can be characterized as breaking the seal of a carefully written document (*resignent* 28), in contrast to the undisciplined bursting and popping of the poet's cheeks (13). Consistent with the technique already discussed, Persius employs verbal reminiscences of these lines at points where he leaves no doubts as to their implications.[18] The futility of grand poetry, for example, (*nugis*) involves the same lack of moral liberty as that implicit in the futile efforts of the slaves to folly (*nugator* 127, *nugaris* 169), while Cornutus, called *dulcis amice* (23), functions as the ideal free man later described as *dulcis amicis* (109).

Persius praises Cornutus by describing what his master did for him (30 ff.). Cornutus took him at an age when he enjoyed freedom

---

[15] As Villeneuve notes, Persius contrasts satiric freedom such as that exhibited by Horace with another regular connotation of *ludo*, namely, the gladiatorial contests. The word *ingenuus* is a strong motif of Horace *Serm.* I 6, and Horace frequently describes his work in terms of *ludus*. In the gladiatorial games, by contrast, one might recall that the contestants were regularly slaves.

[16] Cf. *modicus* 109 and *ars* 105.

[17] Persius establishes a vital contrast between the concept of rational control (*doctus* 16, *disce* 91, *ratio* 96, 119) and mental incompetence (*inepte* 12, 175; *nescius* 34, 101; *stultis* 93, 121; *inscitia* 99).

[18] Cf. *nugis* 19 and 127, 169; *dulcis amice* 23 and 109; *dinoscere* 24 and 105; *in pectore fixi* 27 and 117, 144.

159

of other controls and yet still lacked personal discipline, and by careful education made him a convinced Stoic, thus saving him. Any schoolboy would accept an analogy between education and slavery,[19] and the satirist exploits the situation to show the difference between true moral instruction and the vulgar concept of it. As he puts it, therefore, that period of adolescent freedom before Cornutus took him over gave him license, not liberty. His parents' control, implicit in *custos purpura* (30), ceased, and he wandered the city with impunity in boyish ignorance and curiosity.[20] The suggestive conjunction here of *impune* and *nescius error* looks forward to the specific use of the slave symbol. As Persius later points out, no man whose lack of self-control creates for him a number of masters in his passions can regard himself as a free man, safe from punishment (*impunitior* 130). The young Persius, we might say, was a slave to his own ignorance when Cornutus, by adopting (*suscipis* 36) him, made him a free man. Under the tutelage of his master, Persius slowly acquired knowledge and self-discipline, upon which all moral freedom depends. He submitted his mind to reason (*premitur* 39), toiled towards defeat of his lower nature (*vinci laborat*), and slowly molded his personality according to the design of Cornutus (40). After this period of mental apprenticeship, in which one detects a contrast with the slavish search of the poets for facile expressions, Persius emerged a totally free man, capable of sharing the liberal and positive delights of his tutor as an equal. Whereas a slave to his passions never escapes, Persius endured a temporary period of education—which fools might consider slavery —until his moral maturity fitted him for life as a responsible individual.

When the satirist describes the new life of "freedom," he adopts a series of expressions which recall by contrast the opening lines of the Satire, particularly the repeated *centum*. For this reason, I have postponed discussing *centum* until now, because it is important to consider this contrasting section simultaneously and, in fact, treat at length the significance of the number theme in relation to the dominant metaphor of slavery.[21] One has no difficulty in interpreting the hundred mouths, so damagingly qualified in 1-2,

---

[19] Cf. Persius' description of education in 3. 44 ff., where he also points out the unreasoning nature of the schoolboy.

[20] Seneca, *Epist.* 94. 55 joins the two ideas of *custos* and *error* also. All men, he states, need a guardian to help them avoid straying.

[21] I emphasize this point because, to my knowledge, commentators have not adequately interpreted what I consider to be a vital theme of the Satire in words of number.

as the sign of poetic falsification, for Persius proceeds no farther than his fulsome exordium before Cornutus brusquely interrupts him. And Cornutus makes his attack directly on those hundred mouths, now pejoratively rendered *centeno gutture* (6); for, instead of *centum ora,* he advocates moderacy of mouth (*modico ore* 15). In his response also, Persius admits the prejudice against poetic bombast (*centenas fauces* 26), and, in accordance with Cornutus' remarks (cf. *hinc trahe quae dicis* 17), claims that he evokes the deep sentiments of his heart to utter them in full honesty (*voce traham pura* 28). In short, as the indication of controlled, honest speech, Persius opposes to the hundred voices and mouths of the epic and tragic poets his pure voice and modest mouth. In our earlier discussion we observed that moderation (*modico* 15, 109) constitutes a basic element of freedom; can we now find reason to suggest that *centum* involves moral qualities metaphorically definable as slavery?

Throughout the section describing Stoic "freedom" (41-51), the words of Persius stress the fact that he and Cornutus have achieved complete equality and unity of purpose (*tecum, unum opus, ambo, aequali*) and act in concert (*disponimus, foedere certo, consentire, concordia fata, frangimus*). The certainty which has come to him (45, 51) represents the only valid goal of life (cf. 65), a goal which slavish ignorance fails to attain (cf. 100). As a consequence, he makes advantageous use of time, and in the metaphor *decerpere* (42), he prepares us to think of Cornutus as the good farmer (*cultor*) with prize fruit (*fruge Cleanthea* 63-64) and to contrast him with the unproductivity of the slavish (*steriles veri* 75). Persius now knows when to enjoy himself (*laxamus* 44), whereas the servile miser always represses his pleasures (cf. 110). The emphasis on long days of sunshine (*longos soles* 41) provides an environment exactly opposed to the gloomy days (*crassos dies* 60) of the undisciplined. The general context of 41-51, one may conclude, points to the interpretation of this much-stressed concept of unity and equality as a symbol of Stoicism, in fact, as a sign of personal freedom.[22] The completeness of the individual, his identification with the Stoic ideal, his rational control over his passions constitute values which Persius emphatically reiterates in his use of *unus, ambo,* etc. By contrast, Persius' earlier years suggest the symbol which would function as the antitype: two or more. Words like *iter am-*

---

[22] Seneca, *Epist.* 120. 22 provides a precise parallel to the concept of Persius: *praeter sapientem autem nemo unum agit, ceteri multiformes sumus.*

biguum (34), *nescius error* and *ramosa compita* (35) imply that imprecise alternatives of choice, moral uncertainty, confront the ignorant; and, because the individual really ceases to be free in dealing with them, he sinks into a state which can readily be likened to slavery.[23]

Accordingly, when we move from simple dualism to the gross plurality of *centum,* we may well feel that, in its context of potential slavery, this repeated term most clearly signifies the lack of personal liberty in literature. The poet serves a plethora of meaningless terms, unable to make a selection of the truly poetic; and the undisciplined man serves his several passions and conflicting desires, never able to concentrate on one because of his own uncertainty. For this reason, Persius immediately contrasts to the unity of his and Cornutus' life the thousand variegated (*mille, discolor* 52) goals of the non-Stoics. The fool wastes his days (66 ff.)[24] and, never able to attain his vain goal, may be compared to the rear axle, forever separated yet forever pursuing the front (*in axe secundo* 72). In fact, as the verb *sequi* becomes thematic, Persius stresses the ignorance of the fool as to what goal to follow (cf. 107) or which master to serve (155). In scorn, the satirist calls the fool a slave to many things (*tot subdite rebus* 124), a slave who cannot even remain faithful to one master (*ancipiti obsequio* 156). The vacillation of the man from one inferior purpose to another, we perceive, in marked contrast to the concerted Stoic drive for moral perfection, renders him a slave, whether he wavers between ambition and superstition (176 ff.), gropes among hundreds of empty poetic phrases, or shifts among thousands of futilely materialistic lives. A free man must be an individual, one and undivided (*totus et integer* 173 vs. *duplici in diversum scinderis hamo* 154).[25]

The opposition between unity and plurality continues throughout the Satire; in fact, with a not atypical use of irony, Persius ends on the same verbal note as he began, though with a sardonic twist. Three words evoke the number so much stressed in 1-2, namely,

---

[23] That *unus* can mean or imply self-possession, that singleness represents goodness should be clear from the above citation of Seneca. Cf., moreover, Vergil's use of *unus* in *Aen.* VI 47 and St. Matthew 6:23-3: "The light of the body is the eye: if therefore thine eye be *single,* thy whole body shall be full of light. But if thine eye be *evil,* thy whole body shall be full of darkness."

[24] In 68, Persius seems to oppose wasted time (*consumpsimus*) to his and Cornutus' careful use of the day (*consumere* 41).

[25] We may connect with this view of unity vs. division what Persius says in 122: *haec miscere nefas.* You cannot mix folly and reason, for this would only constitute disunity. Reason is pure and single, totally irreconcilable with the irrational.

centuriones, centum, and *centusse.* From one other reference to a centurion (cf. 3.77), it is possible to infer that Persius employed the soldier as a type for gross, stupid materialism. Because of the importance of the word *centum* in the Satire, moreover, *centuriones* also seems to function as a play on words, designed to exploit the number's connotations. Pulfennius guffaws and rudely rates all this doctrine as worth slightly less than a penny; or, as he puts it, a hundred such philosophers as our satirist—the centurion contemptuously labels them Greeks—might tempt him to put in a bid for them of a *centussis,* a coin, however, so badly clipped as not to be worth a hundred asses. Just as the poets pray for a hundred mouths by which to utter their grandiloquent nonsense, so now Pulfennius pretends to consider buying the doctrine of Persius if it also is multiplied and expressed by a hundred mouths. The distinction between Persius, who longed for *centum voces,* and Pulfennius, who now sneers at philosophy, depends upon the whole development of the Satire between introduction and conclusion. While Persius reveals that he can control himself and his style with a discipline that unifies all his actions under a single purpose, Pulfennius exposes his own folly, his inability to perceive moral truths when they are presented to him in any form. Pulfennius and the poets both stand convicted as slaves, both unable to recognize simple truth.

From what has been considered so far, the fact emerges, I believe, that Persius regarded his opening 51 lines not merely as a eulogy of Cornutus or an exordium, but as an integral part of the whole satiric theme, proclaiming the Stoic qualities which constitute moral liberty and tentatively announcing those ideas, in theme and image, which he will later clearly interpret as indicative of slavery. In what follows, I should like to discuss the relevance of the astrological phrase in 50, one of several alluding to the harmony of Cornutus and Persius:

Saturnumque gravem nostro Iove frangimus una.

In the terms of that eminent science, Persius avers that he and Cornutus, born each when Jupiter was in the ascendant, enjoy a favorable conjunction of planets, for, with Saturn in the descendant, they can expect a prosperous future together. Beyond the literal meaning, as several features of the phrase may indicate, the satirist may be indicating the basic theme of his Satire which he will soon expressly state. First, the other astrological allusions uniformly involve signs of the zodiac, such as Libra and Gemini, and carry no hint of opposition; while in 50 Persius is dealing with planets and with their symbolical opposition, good versus evil. Even more important, the words which he has selected, while appropriate to the jargon of astrology,[26] also combine effortlessly with the connotations of his satiric vocabulary.[27] Finally, Jupiter plays a relatively important, but ambiguous, part in later portions of the Satire (cf. 114, 139, 167) as the supreme god and/or a beneficent planetary influence. For these reasons, it seems legitimate to investigate any potential significance of 50, especially of Saturn, its symbol for evil.

Roman astrologers considered Saturn essentially malignant,[28] a baleful influence which could be counteracted only by a happy conjunction of planets.[29] Behind this attitude lay exact astronomical observations, e.g., that Saturn was the most remote of the known planets, that it therefore carried out its revolution more slowly than the others,[30] that it gave off a faint light because of its distance and so seemed dark, gloomy, and cold.[31] In myth, even more than in astrology, Saturn and Jupiter oppose each other. Romantic writers characterize Saturn's reign as one of great simplicity and contentment, free of commercial, political, and military conflicts.[32] On the other hand, realists sensed the disadvantages that go with a primitive period: Lucretius commented on the irrational quality of that

---

[26] For the best interpretation of the astrological allusion, cf. A. E. Housman in *CQ*, VII (1913), 18-21. Némethy and the scholia are also useful. The only word that might not seem technical, *frangimus*, can be seen in a similar context in Statius, *Silvae* I 3, 7.

[27] I mention particularly the thematic use of the concept of breaking in *frangere* and *rumpere* (13, 59—unless one reads with Clausen *fecerit*—158, 165, 185). Persius uses *frangimus* in 50 to convey his complete freedom from Saturn; he has utterly broken its evil influence. In other passages, he can use the verb ironically to show the inability of the fools to break free of their slavish faults.

[28] The most complete information on Saturn will be found in Wissowa's article *s.v.* ''Saturnus'' in Roscher, *Ausführliches Lexicon der griechischen und römischen Mythologie,* and in Thulin's article *s.v.* ''Saturnus'' in Pauly-Wissowa. As to the malignancy of Saturn, cf. Prop., IV 1, 83-4: *felicesque Iovis stellas . . . et grave Saturni sidus;* also, Manil., II 928 ff. and IV 501; Lucan, I 651 and X 204; and, above all, the passage which most influenced Persius' expression, Horace, *C.* II 17, 17-24.

[29] Frequently, as here, the conjunction depended upon the relative positions of Saturn and Jupiter. Cf. Cicero, *De Nat. Deor.* II 119, and Firmicus Maternus, V 3, VI 3, and VII 6. The last citation illustrates the belief of astrologers that the stars could influence the lives of slaves.

[30] Cf. Servius on *Georg.* III 93: ''Saturni stella tardissima est.''

[31] Cf. Vitruv., VI 1, and *Georg.* I 336. It is interesting to note that Seneca cites the latter passage in *Epist.* 88.14, only to ridicule anyone who trusts in astrology.

[32] E.g., Tibullus, I 3, 35 ff. It is generally thought that Vergil refers to the return of that period in *Ecl.* IV 6 and that the reign of Saturn serves as a constant frame of reference in the *Georgics.* Cf. *Georg.* I 125 ff.

existence, and Vergil hinted at a lack of restraint on the passions in his use of *Saturnia*.[33] Saturn, therefore, is not altogether beneficial even in the Golden Age. Eventually, when Jupiter overthrew Saturn, a myth which Stoics easily rationalized into the conquest of disorder by Reason,[34] a new world-order came into existence. Securely bound, Saturn ceased to control any part of the universe. Even in his statues, Macrobius says, the god appears in fetters.[35] The downfall of the great ruler is generally relevant to Persius' theme, most obviously because, as the symbol of irrational license reduced to chains, Saturn summarizes the course of such characters as Dama or Chaerestratus. Significantly, these slaves (non-Stoic fools) scorn Jupiter (cf. 139 and 167), the symbol of rationality and order, so as to demonstrate their difference from Persius and Cornutus. Freedom and the favor of Jupiter are synonymous (114).[36] Furthermore, while the Stoic friends together broke the evil influence of Saturn, the satirist exposes the essential slavishness of fools who are unable to break their bonds and escape conclusively. It seems as though fools enjoy the dubious favor of Saturn.[37]

Most important of all, the reference to Saturn in 50 tightens the relation between this Satire and the Satire of Horace which has so strongly influenced its conception, as if Persius, about to launch forth specifically upon his discussion of slavery, has clearly in mind Horace's use of Saturn under similar circumstances. Horace had exploited the paradox of the "free" slave in Satire II 7, with an irony, of course, that Persius could never accept. He placed the whole Stoic doctrine in the mouth of the ignorant slave Davus and, further to qualify his theme, he allowed Davus what he called the "freedom of December" (cf. 4). In short, Horace gave his Satire a dramatic setting directly relevant to its theme

---

[33] Cf. Servius on *Aen.* I 23 and IV 92; M. Taylor, "Progress and Primitivism in Lucretius," *AJP*, LXVIII (1947), 180-194, and "Primitivism in Vergil," *AJP*, LXXVI (1955), 261-278; and my article, "Juno and Saturn in the Aeneid," *SP*, LV (1958), 519-532.

[34] Cf. Cicero, *De Nat. Deor.* II 64.

[35] *Sat.* I 8, 5: Saturnus ipse in compedibus visatur. Cf. Statius, *Silv.* I 6, 4 and Martial, III 29. Lucian exploits the theme in *Saturn.* 7 and *Cronosol.* 10.

[36] Villeneuve comments usefully on *Iove dextro* in 114, connecting the phrase with the cult of Jupiter liberator. It is interesting to note that the deaths of two eminently "free" men under Nero, men very familiar to Persius himself, were sanctified by offerings to this Jupiter liberator. Cf. Tacitus on Seneca, *Ann.* XV 64, and on *Thrasea*, Ann. XVI 35.

[37] I might add two other associations of Saturn which are perhaps ironically reflected in Persius' phrase *heu steriles veri* (75). Saturn was a primitive agricultural deity before his amalgamation with the Greek Cronos, and Plutarch, *Quaest. Rom.* XI 12, calls him father of truth.

by staging it on the Saturnalia, when Saturn gave slaves temporary privileges in Rome. As though the satirist were slavish, Davus applied his foolish paradox to Horace himself, an ironical twist which may have suggested to Persius his own method of presentation in 1-51. He, too, suffers criticism for coveting the grandiloquence which, we later see, is definable as slavery, and he, too, acquits himself of the charge by exhibiting his moral freedom. We know that Persius was thinking of Horace in choosing his theme and that he had Horace in mind when he formed his astrological phrase in 50;[38] accordingly, it would not be unlikely that he has taken Horace's dramatic setting and altered it into a symbolic one. As Satire 5 progresses, Persius seems to contrive a psychological Saturnalia, where fools imagine themselves free and attempt to indulge in licentious activities, only to find themselves, after a short interval, slaves once again.

I would suggest that Saturn in 50 possesses connotations that unify the introduction and the specific discussion of moral slavery: Saturn, the lord of the age of irrational bliss, the prisoner of Jupiter, the patron of the Saturnalia (as exploited in Persius' Horatian model), and, of course, the malignant planet combines most of Persius' theme in his various associations.

It may seem that Persius does not really stress the conflict of Jupiter and Saturn, inasmuch as he mentions Saturn only here. There are, however, in the latter part of the Satire two other potential references to the god and his associations which I shall briefly consider. In 179 ff. Persius fixes upon the man enslaved to superstition and describes the un-Roman rites connected with the Jewish

---

[38] Casaubon, pp. 540 ff., remarks on the specific debt to Horace, *Serm.* II 7 and then analyzes Persius' general borrowing from various works of Horace in Satire 5. It is clear that our satirist knew Horace by heart and that anything could suggest to him a Horatian phrase. In 50, he draws expressly upon *C.* II 17, 17-24. Casaubon points out the more obvious borrowings from *Serm.* II 7: Persius 110: *iam nunc adstringas, iam nunc granaria laxes* and Horace 20: *iam contento, iam laxo fune laborat*; Persius 128: *nec quicquam extrinsecus intrat / quod nervos agitet* and Horace 82: *duceris ut nervis alienis mobile lignum;* and Persius 130: *qui tu impunitior exis* and Horace 105: *qui tu impunitior illa.* Further, while Persius borrows verbally from *Serm.* II 3, 262 in 172, Horace briefly depicts the *exclusus amator* in II 7, 89 ff. Other influences of the Satire of Horace upon Persius might be suggested: the free man in Hor. 86 is *in se ipso totus, teres atque rotundus*; in Persius 173 *totus et integer*: Horace uses the metaphor of the escaped animal in 70 as Persius does in 158 ff.: Horace makes food a criterion of slavery in 103 ff. Persius may reverse in 75 ff. what Horace says about the free man sinking to the status of a Dama (54); and the choice of the name Crispinus in 126 may depend on the fact that in *Serm.* II 7, 45 Davus admits the source of his doctrine as the doorkeeper of the ridiculous Stoic Crispinus. In short, as Casaubon observes, Persius seems to have set out in Satire 5 to imitate closely a particular Satire of Horace, something which he does in no other Satire.

sabbath, designated as *recutita sabbata* (184) and *Herodis dies* (180). So far as we know, the poet has invented the phrase about Herod as a means of prejudice, contemptuously substituting Herod for the Roman deity associated with Saturday. In fact, Saturn became, to a certain extent, associated with the sabbath by the time of Augustus, as Tibullus illustrates when he ironically refers to the sabbath and its superstitions, *Saturni sacram diem.*[39] If a legitimate connection, this would emphasize Saturn as the deity favoring a slavish foreign cult. The second possible reference to Saturn occurs in 190-91, where Persius concludes his Satire by attaching the theme of *centum* unmistakably to the slavish Pulfennius. With Pulfennius and his *curto centusse,* I would connect Lucilius 1172 (Marx), *Fanni centussis misellus,* and the remarks which Gellius makes in citing the fragment.[40] In the days of Lucilius, the Lex Fannia had established a limit to expenditures on the occasion of certain festivals and specified a miserable, as Lucilius felt, hundred asses for the Saturnalia. We know that Persius was inspired by Lucilius and freely imitated him. It is, therefore, not impossible that 5.190-91 is influenced by Fannius' Saturnalian *centussis misellus,* inasmuch as Pulfennius uses his clipped *centussis* in a way that obviously symbolizes his slavish illusion of freedom, his psychological Saturnalia. If so, Persius rounds off his Satire not only by making explicit the number theme, but also by alluding to the assumed background of his doctrine of slavery.

I have attempted to elaborate the inchoate unity of Satire 5 as I believe Persius conceived it. By over-emphasizing the question of style first, then his gratitude to Cornutus, he has obscured the central point, that the Stoic education which he has received has transformed him into a truly free man in the moral sense of the word *free*. However, in discussing the grand style Persius seems to have grasped the opportunity to introduce a number of thematic words, a fact which suggests that he regarded 1-29 as thematically consistent with the subsequently patent treatment of moral slavery in 73 ff. The formal poet demeans himself by his turgid language so as to resemble Dama in lack of self-control, of moderation and, by extension, of freedom. By contrast, Cornutus recommends the language of a free man to the boy Persius, whom he has made free. This equation of speech or style with moral character constitutes a

---

[39] Tib., I 3, 18.
[40] Gellius, II 24, 3.

basic tenet of Persius' doctrine, and he exploits it throughout Satire 1. After dismissing the grand style, Persius discusses his education by Cornutus (30 ff.). Education also tests the heart of man, as the satirist demonstrates in Satire 3, whether a man is a fool (therefore sick, insane, or servile) or whether he can claim Stoic wisdom. The satirist, accordingly, continues to prepare for the slave symbol by thematic words. As the most important thematic term of 1-51, we have concentrated on words of number, which Persius has stressed at the beginning and end of the Satire and at the point where he most forcefully depicts Stoic freedom (41-51); and we have concluded that one hundred opposes one to the same degree as slavery opposes freedom. As a secondary theme, Saturn and the atmosphere of the Saturnalia merited attention. In concept then, Satire 5 possesses unity; yet one might well argue that the satirist who adopted as his motto *verba togae* and here selected as his theme *libertas,* verbal and moral, has, in his very inability to establish an obvious connection between his two main sections, shown himself a slave to his own manneristic technique.

Persius and the Rejection of Society

Although to some it may seem that I have slightly overstated the case, my title, I feel quite sure, surprises nobody. Persius did turn his back on what we and the Romans think of as Society, and in so doing he abandoned part of the tradition passed down to him from Horace and Lucilius. When we imagine for ourselves Lucilius, we picture a man who sets himself in the center of Roman Society, who criticizes it because he belongs to it and appreciates both its values and its defects. To judge from the fragments of his poetry and from the selective comments of Horace, Lucilius found himself most characteristically in the setting of a banquet, a *cena*, where, often under the influence of that liberating god of wine, Liber, he poured out his scintillating, humorous, biting comments on people and events of Rome [1]. In Horace, though we encounter a man of different social status and personality, we still find a Roman and an apostle of *humanitas*, who looks hopefully upon human society and smilingly urges men to improvement by moderation and introspection. Persius is different: he denies any validity to Society. I think it may be worth our while to see in detail how he goes about his rejection of Society, for it throws some light not only on Persius himself but also on the very concept of satire that he held.

In the first place, Persius followed the pattern of his predecessors and made programmatic statements about his position as a satirist. To start with the choliambic lines, we observe that he established a sharp contrast between himself and the poets of such grand verse as Ennian epic; they are *vates,* but he is *semipaganus*. The unique word *semipaganus* might be pressed to yield several meanings. Plainly, it signifies that the satirist, a half-rustic, rejects the more dignified, artificial literary genres. It might also suggest that as a half-rustic he will concern himself with topics of real, everyday interest; that he will talk of them in a style appropriate to a half-rustic; and that he will argue, either implicitly or explicitly, for the values of his partially rural background. Persius seems to have invented a charmingly suggestive word in *semipaganus*. Before we can establish its meaning, however, he has twisted away from us; and consequently we are compelled to study certain Satires to clarify his half-rustic stance.

Leaving for later Satire 1, which may very well have been his last poem, we may pause over the beginning of Satire 5. There, once again, the satirist has produced the opposition between himself and the grand poets [2]. It is the custom of *vates* to cry out for a hundred voices, a hundred mouths, a hundred tongues to express the ineffable grandeur of their ridiculous subjects (1—4). The satirist understands the hyperbole of this epic posture, and he momentarily considers converting it to the use of satire, for he has a truth to express, a mighty truth about his real admiration for Cornutus. If he properly qualifies the appeal for a hundred mouths (using an "unpoetic" word *fauces* 26) for the more conventional *ora* or *voces)* and places himself in private communication with Cornutus, not in a public recitation among fellow littérateurs, if he insists on the truth of his utterance, possibly the hyperbole will have the force of overpowering fact. Cornutus, however, does not agree with this satiric strategy. He urges his pupil to forget such nonsense (14 ff.). "You are in the habit of pursuing words belonging to the toga *(verba togae sequeris)*, and you are clever at contriving the sharp, striking phrase *(iunctura callidus acri)*; you are polished and moderate of speech *(ore teres modico)*,

170

trained to scrape away on sickly pale behavior *(pallentis radere mores doctus)* and to fix down a fault with the playful manner of a native Roman *(et ingenuo culpam defigere ludo).* Get your diction from that source *(hinc trahe quae dicis);* leave to Mycenae its banquets with their heads and feet, and become acquainted with plebeian lunches *plebeiaque prandia noris)."*

In Satire 5, Persius does not pose as *semipaganus,* but he does pose as a young man who needs guidance from his teacher Cornutus. Continuing his hostility to Mount Helicon and all it represents, he clarifies his own position to the extent that he discusses poetic diction. Three phrases seem to characterize the satirist here: *verba togae sequeris, ingenuo culpam defigere ludo, plebeiaque prandia noris.* But do we really know what they mean? Take, for example, the first: *verba togae* looks like an elegant variation on the familiar satiric claim to speak *sermo merus* [3]). If so, then the handful of articles and dissertations on Persius' language should have been more useful than they actually are [4]). But no matter how hard scholars have tried, they simply have not been able to demonstrate that Persius produced *sermo vulgaris* or *sermo cotidianus.* No toga-wearing Roman ever spoke as this satirist does; not even Cornutus, despite the role that Persius here assigns him, as teacher of correct satiric diction, wrote in the way he seems to advocate. Horace did mean his audience to hear his hexameters as a poetic version of everyday speech, and most people feel that he was successful. We might suspect that Persius does not wish to be understood in the traditional manner, but he has done little to explain his position.

The second phrase also quickly loses its clarity when we stop to study it. What is meant by *culpam defigere?* The standard Latin-English dictionary of Lewis and Short admits defeat and classifies the usage of *defigere* as unique, offering the remotely derivative definition of "censure". Now, as we have seen in the case of *semi-*

paganus or the ingenious expression *verba togae*, Persius is not averse to inventing words or using them in a new sense. But, if Persius did use *defigere* in a new way, it is still up to us to elicit that meaning from the normal potentialities of the word. When the Romans used the verb, they were describing the act of fixing down; it might be the driving of a cross in the ground, or a weapon into a body; it might be the "fixing" or "fixation" which comes with shock, surprise, or bewitchment. Does Persius imply that he "nails down" a fault, that he "pierces it" as with a word, or that he "fixes it motionless and helpless" by the spell of his satire? Whatever the metaphor alluded to in *defigere*, Persius qualifies it by the phrase *ingenuo ludo*. It is most natural to interpret that phrase in Horatian terms, to assume, then, that Persius adopts the playful manner of a native Italian and of a typical satirist. After all, *ludus* is one of the most common descriptions of the satiric manner in Horace and Lucilius. Villeneuve proposed, on the other hand, to take *ludo* in a sense that would fit the martial metaphor perhaps utilized in *defigere* [5]). His interpretation might be paraphrased as follows: the satirist is trained to "spear down a fault in a gladiatorial combat that befits a freeborn Roman". I doubt that Villeneuve is right, but it must be admitted that he perceived a genuine difficulty in the whole passage. In the phrase *ingenuo ludo*, Persius suggests a mild, Horatian playfulness which does not accord with the violently expressive verb *defigere*. Either the satirist is playful, or he is vigorously transfixing faults: he cannot do both. Either the satirist is *ingenuus* or he is a man of violence.

Perhaps I can make more clear the obscurity of Persius' programmatic utterances if I compare for a moment what Juvenal did with the same basic situation [6]). In Satire 1, Juvenal professes to be very impatient with the conventional modes of poetry current in Rome. Like Persius here, he sneers at the trite topics of epic and tragedy. However, he does not protest particularly over epic style, for he is not concerned to develop an invidious contrast between epic and satiric diction. In ridiculing the familiar situations of grand poetry, he intends to bring out their artificiality so as to emphasize by contrast the pressing reality of his own topics drawn from everyday Rome. Contents opposed to contents, not style to style. Persius, I believe, thinks mainly of the opposition between styles. Rejecting the highflown manner of grand poetry, he seeks for terms which will emphasize his antagonism, and he quite naturally resorts to the conventional ideas of his predecessors in satire. But since he is not utilizing the everyday speech advocated by Horace nor the playful manner so brilliantly displayed by Horace, the Horatian allusions which he achieves in *verba togae, ingenuo ludo,* and several other phrases from this passage rather serve to confuse the picture of the satirist than to clarify it.

If Satire 1 was Persius' final poem, it proves beyond a doubt that Persius remained consistent throughout his career. Instead of firmly anchoring his position as satirist in Roman society, instead of rejecting grand poetic themes for subjects of immediate relevance, he continued to ridicule the style of other poets and by implication to recommend his own style. When he attacks the other poets this time, he uses a different strategy: he describes them during their recitations and cites their poems, doing his best to prejudice the picture with a series of metaphors. He is perhaps most telling in likening the whole art of poetry practiced by "others" to the process of eating and drinking. There is a liquid quality, a tastiness, a sensuous aspect in contemporary poetry which the satirist must entirely reject. What does he offer on his own? He calls it *aliquid decoctius* (125), something that has been more artfully boiled down. The emphasis falls on style, but it is possible to elicit from this metaphor an impression that is more accurate than the other programmatic statements of Persius. Precisely because here he does not depend upon tradition for his terminology, he does say something particulary about his own art. Although resorting to this culinary metaphor, Persius does not assert that he is cooking ordinary, plebeian fare (as if for ordinary people). He has a special meal to serve, and only trained palates will enjoy it, for his purpose has been to boil down ideas to their minimum, then to combine them in a meal that must prove indigestible to all but the elect.

To judge from Persius' programmatic professions, then, especially from the way he distorts traditional motifs, he has turned his back on Society to elaborate a style of great complexity and novelty, a style sharply opposed to Neronian diction. But why does he do this? What sort of a man does he claim to be? It was traditional for satirists to introduce themselves to their audience with great care, with highly selected details, so as to win confidence and make their Satires the satisfying kind of personal poetry that they normally are. We like Horace's Satires to a large degree because he made himself so appealing as the satirist; Lucilius, too, must have been a very engaging fellow in his poems, if the surviving fragments and ancient comments are an accurate indication. They, of course, posed as ordinary members of Society and so were quite right to support their pose with their poetical everyday speech or *sermo*. If Persius, however, has thrown over the tradition of *sermo* and chosen his uniquely individual diction, it is likely that he also has adopted a pose entirely different from that of his predecessors.

Near the end of Satire 1, Persius allows an adversarius to raise one of those questions which is traditional in programmatic Satires: "What is the use of scraping away on tender little ears with biting truth?" (*sed quid opus teneras mordaci radere vero auriculas:* 1.107—108). To this, Persius offers nothing but a sardonically sham answer, so that we are entitled to believe that he accepts the idea as more or less accurate: he will use biting truth to scrape at tender ears [7]. Compare Persius' attitude with that of Horace, who specifically argued against the charge that as satirist he was *mordax* [8]. The difference is clear: Horace does not wish to appear biting but congenial to people, whereas Persius adopts a pose of sharp antagonism to ordinary people and to those with whom he disagrees [9]. Behind the special way in which Persius casts the traditional question and the novel way in which he interprets it, lies a new metaphor. As a teacher, Horace would not want to appear *mordax*, for that sounds like animal behavior; Persius, however, converts the adjective *mordax* from animal to medical associations. He is a doctor dealing with very sick patients [10]. Thus, we have already seen him described by Cornutus in 5.15 as a man who knows how to scrape away at sickly pale behavior or character (*pallentis radere mores doctus*). What is being depicted in the phrase *teneras mordaci radere vero auriculas* is the common Roman practice of cleaning out the ears, in this case tender ears that definitely need medical attention, with a kind of mild acid, which of course is *mordax* and irritates. The ultimate purpose, however, is beneficial. For the reader with tender ears, then, Persius serves as a doctor who hurts, but helps. The ideal reader, on the other hand, already possesses the well-cleaned ear (*vaporata lector aure* 1.126), and he presumably can appreciate not only the truth of what the satirist says, but also the artful style in which this truth is conveyed.

In the context of Satire 1, the reference to tender and well cleaned ears is peculiarly relevant, for Persius there is studying the way audiences hear various kinds of contemporary poetry and the devices by which most Neronian poets work upon their auditory senses [11]. Whereas the satirist boldly asserts his indifference to the audience and dismisses with contempt the literary judgment of the general Roman throng (no more valid than the distorted criticism of Trojan women, *Troiades* 4, in the Iliad), most poets, he argues, are "gathering dainties for others' little ears" *(auriculis alienis colligis escas* 22). The somewhat curious idea of "feeding" the ears enables Persius to develop other scenes in which the fundamental metaphor is one of eating, drinking, or serving food. But he also intends to pursue the theme of "ears" in a special way. In line 8 he starts to ask a question (q u i s n o n ....), which he breaks off in a clever aposiopesis, as though it were wrong to continue. Later, he obliquely comments on the incompetent poets whose one ideal is to earn the praise of the public: an ordinary child might properly make at them the sign of the "white ears" *(manus auriculas imitari mobilis albas* 59). That sign, as any Roman knew, signified that a person was behaving like a donkey, in an asinine manner, for the long ears of the donkey are its most distinctive external possession. Poets are asses because they long to hear praise. But the general public is also asinine, for it wishes to listen to trivial, sentimental nonsense, not biting truth (107). Therefore, Persius returns to his unfinished question at the end of the Satire, having made clear his objections to most contemporary poetry: "Who does not have", he asks, "asses ears?" *(auriculas asini quis non habet?* 121), There is, then, for Satire 1 a critical distinction between the majority of "ears" both of poets and audiences and, on the other hand, the ideal "ears" which he desiderates; and he reinforces the point by repeating the contemptuous diminutive *auriculae* for the first group, but using the proper *auris* for the ideal reader.

"Feeding" the ears, as I mentioned above, is a curious notion. But to Persius it is entirely meaningful, and he ties it in neatly with the whole medical terminology which he adapts to the satirist. Through the food, as we all know, many of our diseases originate Overeating or the eating of improper food, therefore, was considered the cause of much illness. The aristocrat who became soft and overweight from too much rich food served as a common symbolic type for a man who has misplaced his values. Thus, in Satire 3, where the metaphors of eating and sickness function closely together, Persius uses an episode about an indulgent fool who has a stroke and dies in the act of eating and drinking as an allegory of the fool who neglects wisdom to seek the wrong things (18ff.). To live rightly, says the satirist, men should examine their state of "health" and cure themselves before their case is hopeless: *venienti occurrite morbo* (3, 64). The best general cure for vague ailments of the internal organs was a purge, a laxative, and the most common laxative for the ancients was hellebore. Again and again, in the various Satires, when Persius wishes to define the defective condition of "others", he talks of them as in need of hellebore or simply as „internally sick".

Why Persius appropriated these various metaphors and combined them in his Satires is reasonably obvious. He wished to suggest that the "sickness" of the mind or soul is caused by "eating" or "drinking in" through the ears of the wrong "food". "Health", on the other hand, is the precious possession of the wise man; it comes to one who eats the right kind of "philosophical food" and has his own ears clean, his internal organs wisely nourished. Possessing this special "health", the *sapiens* can then proceed to serve as "doctor" to the "ills" of mankind. When Persius describes the useful activities of his revered master Cornutus, he pictures him strangely busy with the ears of young men in the manner of both a surgeon and a fruit-grower: "cultivator of young men, you purge their ears and then graft them with the fruit of Cleanthes" *(cultor enim iuvenum purgatas inseris aures / fruge Cleanthea* 5.63—64). Not many lines later, he introduces another *sapiens* who refutes the foolish claims of a man confident in his perfect "freedom". To characterize this wise man, Persius writes a line which by itself is quite grotesque, but in the context of his known medical bias is entirely meaningful and intended to be approving: the wise man is "this Stoic whose ear has been washed with the biting vinegar" *(Stoicus hic aurem mordaci lotus aceto* 5.86). It is fair to say, I believe, that the satirist would accept this line as an apt description of his owen person.

The antithesis between doctor and patient constitutes one of the most effective metaphorical themes in Persius' Satires. However, it tells us nothing precise about the satirist in fact, except that this doctor seems more eager to point out sickness than to cure it. If we contrast the self-revelations of Horace and Lucilius, we can see that what Persius may be doing is concealing his true self, shielding it behind a metaphor; for after all, he is not a "doctor" except in a tropical sense. There are two or three passages where he does start to say something of himself, but they are curiously defeating also. What appears to be the most revelatory, in fact, turns out to be the most fictional. In Satire 3, as he shows the inadequate motivations to learning that immature young men can have, he affects to tell an anecdote of his own childhood: he pretended to be sick, he claims, in order to escape learning a memorable oration that he would have to declaim in the presence of his proud father (3.44 ff.). Unfortunately for the truth, it appears certain from the *Vita* that Persius' father was long dead at the time he would have been memorizing such speeches. No less evasive, however, is the beginning of Satire 5. Persius is talking to Cornutus, his revered tutor, eager to bear witness to his intense admiration for all that Cornutus has done for him. But instead of giving us details of their association, what they read, how Persius met Cornutus, where they talked, etc., Persius quickly flees from reality into a series of characteristic metaphors and literary reminiscences. He was sixteen, he says in his circuitous manner, unsure of himself and the freedom conceded to his adolescence, and so he put himself under the care of Cornutus (30 ff.)[12]. Cornutus "adopted" him with Socratic concern and proceeded to straighten out Persius' distorted character, mold his mind with reason, and give it an artistic form by his sculptural skill. Such are the metaphors by which Persius describes his long, important tutelage under Cornutus. He then goes on to borrow from a familiar Ode of Horace (Carm. 2.17), in which Horace declares his eternal link to Maecenas, and thereby Persius implies the similar union of souls between him and his Master.

I do not think that Persius committed a mistake in filtering out all strong personal references and particularized details about himself. He did so, it seems quite evident, because he saw the situation of the satirist differently from his predecessors. Instead of a personality with a full existence of amusing successes and failures, virtues and faults, his satirist is monochromatic, even monotonous (if you will). He is the steady incarnation of *sapientia.* Similarly, Cornutus lacks any clear personality, but he earns the same general metaphorical associations, because he, too, represents the same unchanging *sapientia.* Like Persius, he opposes the magniloquence of Helicon; like Persius, he concerns himself with purging ears. However, to add to his nobility, Persius says that Cornutus disposes of the "fruit of Cleanthes" *(fruge Cleanthea* 5.64) and welcomes his pupil to his "Socratic bosom" *(Socratico sinu* 5.37). In other words, Cornutus displays qualities associated with the great founders of philosophy, and particularly their uniform pursuit of wisdom. Accordingly, when Persius briefly evokes the spirit of Socrates in Satire 4, we should not be surprised to discover that his Socrates bears little resemblance to the figure of the Platonic dialogue to which he alludes. His Socrates is another Stoic type, whose ears have been well purged, who speaks the same series of metaphors and manifests the same antagonism towards the masses (*calida turba* 7, *popellus* 15) as our satirist does [13]).

If the satirist and his honored models all seem cut from the same pattern, the majority of mankind constituting the *stulti* is characterized by wide diversity. As Persius puts it in Satire 5, "There are a thousand kinds of men and practices of varying hues; each person pursues his own goal and no single aim controls lives":

> *mille hominum species et rerum discolor usus;*
> *velle suum cuique est nec voto vivitur uno* (52—53).

Such diversity is bad. In the ideal world that Persius seems to imagine, everybody would be without personality or individuality, all living according to that single aim of Stoicism which he has adopted for himself. To emphasize the badness of ordinary existence, Persius utilizes a series of metaphorical antitheses similar to those we have been studying. Not only are most men characterized by wide diversity and sickness, but they are also slaves, animals, leaky pots, crooked, undecided wanderers, devoid of all truth, the victims of idle passions, etc. All these metaphors, if one ponders them, bring out the irrational aspect of people, their incapacity to deal with the problems of life as men ideally should. Most men have lost somehow their most prized possession, their *ratio,* and so the satirist can rightly regard them as animals or defective things, objects acted upon rather than subjects acting consciously.

All the metaphors that contrast the satirist and his friends with average men stress, as we might expect, their total dedication to reason. As a doctor, the satirist understands others' sicknesses, himself healthy and immune to their ailments. As a farmer, he grafts productive branches from a fruit tree of Cleanthes' doctrines. As a judge, he can mete out penalties and discern guilt without bias, for he himself has no fault or temptation to crime. The satirist knows how to operate the scales and weigh exactly; he knows how to straighten the crooked; he can pick his way surely towards his destination. He alone is a free man; he alone possesses sanity; he alone is a true artist. To put it simply, the satirist and his friends are all-competent because of their *sapientia* and *ratio*, whereas others, the *stulti* are totally incompetent, not human at all in the proper sense of the word.

This absolute antithesis, which informs Persius' portrait of the satirist and the Society in which he finds himself, helps to explain why his Satires take the direction they do. The satirist logically cannot accommodate himself to Society, cannot take it or its self-contradictory aims seriously, cannot even desire to improve Society by some practical compromise. In his rigid terms, fools are absolute fools, and there is not one redeeming bit of right in them:

nullo ture litabis,
haereat in stultis brevis ut semiunci recti (5.120-121).

He has no reason to be indulgent, to smile tolerantly at the faults of others with the kindly moderation of one who knows that he, too, is not perfect. According to his special perspective, all those who are not with him are against him, and he constitutes himself their enemy. What can you do with your enemy, whom you sneer at as a crazy fool, an abject slave, a wild beast, a mechanical thing operated by passions? How can you improve those impossible defects?

In this absolutism of Persius' Satires, there is something both compelling and irritating, and Persius has, of course, both warm admirers and sardonic critics. We all recognize that we and Society fall far short of our express ideals; we admit, therefore, that in a sense we can be condemned as fools. Familiar as they were with the propaganda of all the philosophic schools, the Roman audience would have had no difficulty in appreciating the basis of Persius' rejection of the *stulti*. On the other hand, the voice of common sense cannot be stilled for long, and common sense, realistic thinking, practical living all insist that absolute dichotomies of this Cynic-Stoic kind falsify everyday existence. The option for either *sapientia* or *stultitia* is not a genuine choice for most people, who regularly find themselves in a situation where they can only be more wise than foolish. Thus, Seneca's Epistles seem to most readers a more sensible application of Stoicism than Persius' Satires. For Persius, it appears that financial problems were irrelevant, since he possessed a good income by inheritance; many fellow equestrians and people of the lower classes were not in the same fortunate station and were obliged to worry about material matters. Again, Persius lived in a period when political questions were uppermost in the minds of many good Romans, including such close acquaintances of his as Lucan, Seneca, and Paetus Thrasea. By the absolute criterion which Persius voices, these men were wrong to compromise with the immutable claims of *sapientia*, wrong to mix with Society and attempt to influence it.

Persius' Satires are so far removed from contemporary reality that there is no single verifiable allusion to events in Rome or the Empire during Persius' lifetime. All the nonsense which has been written and spoken by Latinists who have speculated on Persius' relations to Neronian politics and poetics cannot be judged as anything but romantic guessing. If they read Satire 1, such speculators find nothing important to comment on unless they assume that the uninformed scholiast was right and that the satirist not only parodied Nero's verses but also dared to mention the *rex* himself [14]). When they get to Satire 4, ignoring the fact that Persius quickly evades the political questions of the Platonic

dialogue and shifts to a standard, timeless, unreal
Stoic investigation of self-knowledge, they want to see
Nero in Alcibiades [15]). But to pursue such will-o'-the-
wisps is to reveal how badly one reads Persius, how
totally prejudiced one is in defining Roman satire.
As I have attempted to show, there is a logic behind
the attitude that negates Society in Persius' Satires.
Even though we dislike his narrow ridigity, we must
admit that it is consistent except where he repeats too
faithfully some of the conventional terms and catch-
words of a satiric tradition which he does not entirely
accept. But there is another point which is even more
important. Persius tends to refute the assumption that
Roman satire m u s t be concerned with Society, that
its definitive form is determined by what it says about
Roman Society.

In this august company which has assembled here
at Rostock, I perhaps labor the obvious. Professor
Knoche has rightly defined *satura* without reference to
its social ideas as a "poetic form of personal expression"
("poetische Form der persönlichen Äußerung") [16]) and
many of us have read the recent analysis of Persius
by R. G. M. Nisbet in which, among other good points,
he makes the following statement: "He [Persius] draws
less directly on life than could be wished, but there
is more than one way of writing poetry, and his
attitudes are serious, consistent, and authentic" [17]).
Nevertheless, I remind you of a book which has been
published at my own University and is regularly cited
with respect, J. W. Duff's "Roman Satire: Its Outlook
on Social Life", Berkeley, 1936. Duff quite evidently
believed that Roman satire was and should be a social
document: one studied it for its ideas, for its revelations about Roman Society. There may be many who,
hearing of a conference entitled "Roman Satire and
Roman Society" ("Römische Satire und römische Ge-
sellschaft"), would even nowadays leap to the assumption that the two words Satire and Society are somehow

essentially related, that there can be no Satire without emphatic social consciousness. It happens that Lucilius, Horace, and Juvenal all seem to support such an assumption. But since Persius rejects Society and insists on an isolated academic existence of pure *sapientia,* he presents an obvious problem which older critics could solve only by clinging to the shaky faith that Persius was a secret revolutionary against Nero.

The more we think about Persius in his own terms, however, the more we can perhaps realize that he helps us to grasp the truly fundamental essence of Roman satire, that *poetic* essence which Professor Knoche specifies. Then, we can see that Lucilius, Horace, and Juvenal were first and foremost poets, not social commentators. What they have to say about the different Roman worlds in which they found themselves is no more original than what Persius says about Stoic philosophy when ignoring Roman society; nor would it be considered very important as social commentary if we were better informed about those periods. It just happens that we have so few documents to throw light on the ancient world that we have naturally used whatever lies to hand; and in so doing we have abused Roman Satire. We have too often forgotten that Horace, for example, chose to write *satura* because it challenged his budding poetic talent and he saw many ways by which what Lucilius, a much admired poetic predecessor, had invented could be literarily improved. Poetry should have ideas, and Roman Satire should express its ideas very personally, but the ideas are secondary, the poetry primary. A good poet should be able to make poetry, competent satire out of ideas which reject Society and insist on the sole validity of abstract *sapientia,* just as good poets like Horace and Juvenal made excellent poetry out of their quite different views of Roman Society.

Now, earlier when I was studying certain phrases of

Persius, I tended to belittle them perhaps because they did not say altogether what Persius seemed to mean. He professes to be *semipaganus*, to be uttering *verba togae*, and yet nobody in his right mind would ever confuse the satirist for a half-rustic or imagine that what he heard in the Satires remotely resembled the language of a normal Roman in toga. But suppose the phrase is more important as a product of the imagination than as a literal statement? From the very line in which the highly original *verba togae* occurs, comes the phrase *iunctura callidus acri*. In this case, as so often, we can discern some of the processes by which the poet's imagination has worked, and Henss has done well to investigate these processes so searchingly [18]). All the commentators recognize the fact that Persius is reworking a passage of Horace, in which he says: "You will be extraordinarily successful in your diction if skillful combination (or phrasing) makes a new word out of a familiar one": *dixeris egregie notum si callida verbum / reddiderit iunctura novum* (A. P. 47—48). Wishing to exploit his audience's memory of Horace, but at the same time desiring to change Horace, Persius deliberately broke up the collocation *callida iunctura:* he used the personal adjective *callidus,* shifted *iunctura* to the ablative case, and gave the noun a new adjective *acri.* Not only does that change Horace's wording, but it also alters Horace's original meaning. Whereas Horace did not specify the rhetorical effect of the recommended *iunctura* except in declaring that it renewed the sense of a familiar word, Persius seems, by introducing *acri,* to assert the importance of "sharp" or "striking" phrasing. In altering the phrase, then, Persius has altered the whole artistic direction of his predecessor, for Horace clearly did not mean by "renewing a word" that the good poet should make it outlandish. For all his *callidae iuncturae* in the Satires and Odes, Horace remains in character as a congenial conversationalist (except in the intermittent

185

patriotic Odes). Persius, by contrast, seems to visualize the poetic process in two stages: 1) choosing vocabulary (but not language) appropriate to the ordinary Roman (*verba togae sequeris*, the first half of 5.14); 2) cleverly fusing these ordinary words into shockingly extra-ordinary phrases (*iunctura callidus acri*, the second hemistich of 5.14). The phrase dominates the voca-bulary, and the poet recognizes no obligation to assume a character consistent with his *verba togae*.

It is no accident that Persius has here revised the Horatian passage to say what is un-Horatian and express approval of *acres iuncturae*. In Satire I, speak-ing of contemporary poetry with great distaste, he particularly comments on the *iunctura* which is so smooth that the severest critic would miss the con-nection (1.64—65) [19]). That mellifluous flow of senti-mental banality, which other poets achieved by smoothness of meter and phrasing, Persius rejects outright as bad poetry. He wants to shock, to upset, to antagonize our expectations. When we read the Satires, especially the first time, we quickly notice that much of the poetry inheres in these *iuncturae*, many of which are so striking that we cannot help remembering them. Persius likes the forceful verb, the noun or adjective which rasps upon our ears, the sudden image which evokes something unpleasant. As he builds up the sentences, he regularly mixes his metaphors and deliberately flouts the rules of "correct" rhetoricians. Catachresis is one of his favorite devices. Instead of following the trend set in motion by Ovid with his fast-moving hexameters, the satirist does his best to avoid all *mollitia* of meter. Jerky assertions, angry elliptical comments, sardonic questions that break the line in half or thirds, crude enjambement that defies the normal rules of proper stylists, all these are quite conscious achievements of Persius' poetics. The effect? The satirist appears to us nasty, intolerant, and offensive. He breathes into his style, that is, the

186

contemptuous aloofness of his Cynic-Stoic creed; his style gives life to that attitude which we have been discussing: his rejection of Society.

Consider, for example, a three-line passage like the following:

> *fur es' ait Pedio. Pedius quid? crimina rasis*
> *librat in antithetis, doctas posuisse figuras*
> *laudatur: 'bellum hoc.' hoc bellum? an, Romule,*
> > *ceves?* (1.85—87)

Abruptly the satirist starts with two blunt monosyllabic words: "You're a thief". Then he reveals that somebody is speaking this charge *(ait)*, but he is moving too fast to care about the speaker; it might be anybody. It makes no difference who speaks, but it is important that he addresses Pedius, and *Pedio* defines the first hemistich. The next clause consists of an elliptical question of two pungent words, and it takes us only to the bucolic diaeresis. Having called attention to Pedius by his construction of the opening sentence, Persius now begins the question with Pedius' name, then merely adds the ugly monosyllabic *quid.* Even if we cannot be sure what verb to supply in the ellipsis, it takes no great clairvoyance to sense the sardonic tone of the satirist's question. Normally, should someone call a Roman "thief to his face, he would instantaneously leap to defense, if not to the attack. By interrupting the scene and even raising the question of Pedius' reactions the satirist warns us that this Pedius is not the normal Roman. Two complete thoughts have been dealt with in separate, bluntly worded sentences, all in four metrical feet of the first line. At the bucolic diaeresis, then, the satirist starts enjambement which will take him to the penthemimeral caesura of the following line: *crimina rasis / librat in antithetis.* The first word is fine: *crimina* refers back to the charge of thievery made at the beginning of the line. The second word is mysterious, however: *rasis,* whether dative or ablative, refers to something "shaved", but what that something might be, we have no way to guess. Thus the line ends "ineptly", "incorrectly" in terms of contemporary Neronian poetry, and we are pulled without stop, without time to savor any part of this jerky, interrupted first line, into the second.

The first word of the second line, *librat*, provides a verb and defines the function of *crimina* as object. But since the verb is metaphorical, it is intended to evoke a picture and so help interpret the attitude of Pedius. By itself, the verb-object construction *crimina librat* seems quite clear: Pedius balances the charges, his defense is a work of self-control and artistry. The satirist, however, does not allow the verb-object construction to appear isolated; he creates one of his *acres iuncturae* by inserting between the two grammatically related words the mysterious *rasis*, which not only interrupts the grammar but also disturbs the sense by its second, discordant metaphor. What can "shaved things" possibly have to do with the practice of "balancing"? The juxtaposed metaphors, at end and beginning of lines, thus make the enjambement an abrupt, shocking movement. Not even when Persius reaches the central caesura and reveals the entire grammar of his clause does he simplify his picture. "Pedius balances the charges in shaved or polished antitheses", a perfectly translatable notion, but an action that is easier to imagine than to analyze in words. Yet is not that exactly what we desire in a poet, an appeal to our imagination that somehow goes beyond the merely literal range of language? Thanks to this ingenious phrase, Persius conveys the trivial mentality of Pedius, who feels it more important to be rhetorically successful than to answer a charge that blackens his character. Without the uniquely used *rasis* and the resultant *iunctura,* the picture would be negligible.

From the caesura, the satirist proceeds with his

188

sentence, which spills over grammatically into the third line. The second hemistich of the line displays a phrase that seems perfectly regular: *doctas posuisse figuras*. Even the transferred epithet *doctas* has been common in that usage since at least Augustan times, and there is no need even to consider Scaliger's proposed emendation that would alter it to the nominative *doctus*. The satirist has chosen the epithet carefully, however, and he intends us to see and feel the artificial quality of Pedius' figures of speech. As we move into the third line, we are expecting a verb of weak quality like *dicitur* or *videtur* for the infinitive. Playing upon that expectation, Persius produces another shock in his first word, a highly meaningful verb, *laudatur*, one that radically abuses normal grammar. And then he comes to a full stop. Praise, then, stands sharply out in the line and exposes the true motives of this fool Pedius. Rather than refute the charges or defend his honor, he would like to earn applause with his frivolous eloquence, a mere show of style devoid of relevance. Persius jerks us harshly to the penthemimeral caesura with a two-word quotation of the "praise" awarded to the orator: *bellum* hoc. By repeating the two words in chiastic order and changing the assertion to an angry question, he violently undermines the insipid, conventional eulogy. But the question is really a double one, and so with another ugly jerk he asks the alternative: *an, Romule, ceves?* To call Pedius *Romulus* is no bit of flattery, for he has already been exposed as one who does not deserve the name of "Roman", let alone of the founder of Rome. The final violently vulgar verb, *ceves*, establishes the satirist's prejudice beyond question, for in the behavior of Pedius, as in that of the reciting poets of 1.15 ff. and those whose elegant *iunctura* is praised in 1.92 ff., he sees the signs of homosexual corruption.

I do not think that I can be accused of selecting an atypical passage of Persius. Indeed, we can all recall other contexts where the satirist outdoes himself. However, as we review the effects that Persius has achieved and the means by which he did so, few of us should doubt that we are face to face with a highly original poetic talent. There is nothing pretty about these lines, nothing that I would even call enjoyable, but the abruptness, the ellipsis, the deliberate effort to shatter the line's unity, the catachresis, the abuse of "proper" grammar, the chiasmus, rhetorical questions, and carefully placed vulgarity, all manifest the *callidus poeta* as Persius seems to have intended him. For my part, I believe that Persius valued style far above contents, but I also believe that this unique style, the product of his poetic rather than his Stoic purposes, provides a surprisingly successful diction for the Stoic speaker. As he utters his *aliquid decoctius*, the satirist summarizes all the hostility to normal Roman society which the most rigid, intolerant Cynic-Stoic could express.

Summary

Persius rejects Roman society because for a Stoic of his type nothing that is popular or plebean can be valuable. We all recognize this attitude of Persius. The purpose of this paper therefore is not to explain t h a t he is intolerant this way, but w h y he is. First, one can study the parts of the Satires where he speaks in a programmatic fashion. When he says that he is s e m i p a g a n u s and pursues v e r b a t o g a e, what does he mean? Not what might seem most obvious: that like Horace he speaks s e r m o m e r u s. Rejecting society, Persius also spurns its manner of speech. In fact, he is less s e m i p a g a n u s than s e m i v a t e s ; less rustic than m e d i c u s, i u d e x, v i r s a n u s, a g r i c o l a, v i a t o r c e r t u s, etc.; that is, he presents himself not in a personal, but in a metaphorical manner. In the Satires, he is almost devoid of personality because he is s a p i e n s, another Cornutus,

190

Cleanthes, Zeno, even another Socrates, always, speaking in the same style. It is this style which gives Persius' Satires a clear personality, which bears out the clever interpretation of Prof. Knoche, that Persius' Satires are "a poetic form of personal expression" Without this unique style, the Satires would be senseless; with this style, they are poetic and interesting. Indeed, more than a Stoic, Persius is a poet—or what he grotesquely names: S t o i c u s   h i c   a u r e m m o r d a c i   l o t u s   a c e t o.

---

1) See Horace Serm. 1.4.86 ff., which I take to be an allusion to Lucilius because of the repetition of the key phrase *comis et urbanus in* 1.10.65; also the mention of Lucilius' facile versification *ante cibum* and then *cenatus* in 1.10.60–61. The anecdote in 2.1.71 ff. evokes a similar scene.

2) I have analyzed the contents of this passage in greater detail in my article "Part versus Whole in Persius' Fifth Satire", Philological Quarterly 39, 1960, 66–81.

3) Horace Serm. 1. 4. 48.

4) On Persius' style or language, the bibliography is extensive. See, for example, A. C. White, De A. Persi Flacci genere dicendi, Diss. Ithaca, N. Y. 1887; J. Šorn, Die Sprache des Satirikers Persius, Laibach 1890; H. Küster, De A. Persi Flacci elocutione quaestiones, Löbau 1894, 1896, 1897; V. Gérard, Le latin vulgaire et le langage familier, M u s B 1, 1897, 81–103; M. Schönbach, De Persi in saturis sermone et arte, Weyda 1910; J. van Wageningen, Auli Persi Flacci satura, Groningen 1911, pp. xxv ff.; F. Villeneuve, Essai sur Perse, Paris 1918, pp. 364 ff.; V. D'Agostino, De A. Persi Flacci sermone, R i v I G I 12-14, 1928-30: T. Ciresola, La formazione del linguaggio poetico di Persio, Rovereto 1953; G. Faranda, Caratteristiche dello stile e del linguaggio poetico di Persio, RIL 88, 1955, 512–538.

5) I refer, of course, to Villeneuve's edition and commentary of Persius.

6) For fuller discussion, see my article, "Studies in Book I of Juvenal", Yale Classical Studies 15, 1957. pp. 34 ff., and E. J. Kenney, The First Satire of Juvenal, Proc. Cambr. Philol. Soc. 188, 1962, 29–40.

7) See my note on this passage, "Persius 1.107–10", CQ 52, 1958, 195–197.

[8]) Serm. 1. 4. 93.

[9]) Persius' attitude towards the *plebs* and *populus* is consistently hostile. In Satire 1, he sneers at *turbida Roma* (5, playing on *turba*), *os populi* (42), and *populi sermo* (63). In 3.86 he describes the populace laughing in agreement with the stupid centurion's mockery of philosophy. In Satire 4 he talks of *plebecula* (6) and *blando popello* (15). Satire 5 mentions *ri.ranti populo* (178), and Satire 6 summarizes the attitude of total isolation from the masses: *paulum a turba seductior audi* (42).

[10]) The basic study of medical terminology in Persius remains that of H. Lackenbacher, "Persius und Heilkunde", WS 55, 1937, 130—141.

[11]) This theme has been analyzed recently by K. J. Reckford, "Studies in Persius", Hermes 90, 1962, pp. 476 ff.

[12]) The *Vita* of course states this in absolutely lucid language: *cum esset annorum xvi, amicitia coepit uti Annaei Cornuti, ita ut nusquam ab eo discederet; inductus aliquatenus in philosophiam est.*

[13]) It is a general rule that in all the Satires of Persius the speakers who represent the ideal of Cynic-Stoicism speak in a uniform manner, whether they are identified as Socrates in Satire 4, Cornutus in the beginning of Satire 5, Persius in the remainder of Satire 5 and in Satires 1, 2, and 6 or the anonymous voice of criticism in Satire 3 (whom Housman and many since his time would identify with the better instincts of Persius himself, at war with his lower desires). All these speakers use the same series of prejudicial metaphors, advocate Cynic-Stoic astringency and sneer at the masses. The desire to force all into a single mold is particularly distorting in the anachronistic portrait of Socrates.

[14]) I myself do not think it profitable to speculate on the possible hostility of Persius to Nero, but the question has been much discussed. For an attempt to balace the issues, I refer the reader to W. C. Korfmacher, "A Résumé of the Persius-Nero Question", TAPA 69, 1938, p. xlii. More recently, there are a number of articles by Herrmann, "Les premières oeuvres de Perse", L a t o m u s 11, 1952, 199—201, and "Néron et la mort de Perse", L a t o m u s 22, 1963, 236—239. See also I. K. Horváth, "Perse et Néron", Stud. Clas. 3, 1961, 337—343.

[15]) E. V. Marmorale discusses this old question in his "Persio", Florence 1956[2], pp. 273 ff.

[16]) See U. Knoche, Die römische Satire, Göttingen 1957[2],. p. 16.

17) See Nisbet, "Persius", Critical Essays on Roman Literature: Satire, ed. J. P. Sullivan, London 1963, p. 70.

18) See D. Henss, „Die Imitationstechnik des Persius", Philologus 99, 1955, 272–294. Of considerable value in this connection is also W. Kugler, Des Persius Wille zu sprachlicher Gestaltung in seiner Wirkung auf Ausdruck und Composition, Diss. Berlin 1940.

19) Also in 1.92 Persius sneers at those who so stupidly defend contemporary poetry by protesting: *sed numeris decor est et iunctura addita crudis.*

JUVENAL

STUDIES IN BOOK I OF JUVENAL

SCHOLARS have long recognized that one of the principal difficulties in Juvenal springs from his methods of composition, but they have expressed various discordant attitudes toward these methods. Some have condemned them outright; others have sought their causes, while also spurning them; still others, and particularly in more recent times, have attempted to understand Juvenal's technique as a whole, in which compositional principles play a positive part and contribute to Juvenal's success, such as it is. We cannot honestly blink these difficulties, that is certain; yet we can, perhaps, along with those striving to understand Juvenal's composition, define his methods in a way that promotes the proper interpretation of his Satires.

Several factors, in traditional studies, bear upon the satirist's construction: his indignation; his rhetoric; his lack of control in parts, which amounts to planlessness in the whole, his use of symmetry; and his adoption of rhetorical or diatribal themes. For the purposes of this study, we may dismiss the first two as incidental or derivative characteristics and concentrate on primary qualities. Juvenal adopts indignation as his explicit mood and develops a style to fit it, so that indignation cannot account for the structural difficulty which is, in part, inability to convey a convincing indignation. Similarly, rhetoric constitutes an effect, not a cause. Juvenal appropriates a rhetorical technique to suggest his mood and to carry out his poetic purposes, and, as a tool, rhetoric responds to the guidance of the satirist, not creating, but exposing, his difficulties. We come back, then, to what scholars have traditionally perceived in Juvenal's specific methods, a certain disproportion and disunity, a certain symmetry, and preference for a limited theme. Nothing compels us to identify Juvenal's themes with rhetorical *controversiae* or with diatribes, but the general recognition that the satirist selects uncomplex themes—which has led to the connection with the simple *controversia* or diatribe—points to a definite aspect of his composition: construction of his Satires around a restricted idea.

To these traditional ways of approaching Juvenal, we should add others which, rarely or never employed, can today enhance our understanding of the Satires and, in some cases, transform the derogatory associations of disproportion and simple themes into positive qualities. I refer to the value from thematic words and metaphors, to the significance of repeated contrasts, and the semantic importance of allusions and dramatic scenes; I refer also to an observable technique of gradually exposing the theme, and a regular procedure of introduction and conclusion. When we consider the variety of techniques employed by Juvenal, all contributing to his particular structural scheme, we may well reverse our opinion of his work, or at least guard ourselves from viewing him with the preconceptions of the student of Horace or Vergil.

In his Book I, Juvenal achieved his greatest success, employing his structural principles with such skill as to create a masterpiece like Satire 3. Even in Book I, however, and even in Satire 3, we can detect instances of what is usually called disproportion, and Satires 2 and 4 provide scholars with what must be permanent difficulty because of apparent disunity. The purpose of this study, then, is to approach Juvenal's earliest work from these added aspects and to reconsider the traditional interpretations and problems of the Satires, in the hope that we may perceive a technique common to all five Satires and glimpse the essential merits of Juvenal's composition and, through them, attain a profounder grasp of his artistic goal.[1]

SATIRE 1

From the time of Lucilius, the satirist regularly felt obliged to explain his concept of his genre in a Program Satire which, in the writings of Horace and Persius, followed the pattern set by Lucilius.[2] Juvenal, too, faces the same problem, and he answers the potential questions of his readers in Satire 1 by covering the traditional themes: (1) the superiority of epic and the other genres of great poetry to satire; (2) the style appropriate to satire; (3) the moral responsibility of the satirist.[3] Where, how-

[1] The following study is based upon a portion of my dissertation, " The Rhetoric of Juvenal," presented to the faculty of the Graduate School of Yale University, in candidacy for the Ph. D. degree in June, 1954.

[2] Cf. G. C. Fiske, " Lucilius: the Ars Poetica of Horace and Persius," *HSCP*, 24 (1913), 1-36, and A. Hartmann, *De Inventione Juvenalis* (Basel, 1908), pp. 6 ff.

[3] Fiske seems to have worked independently of Hartmann, who did not ex-

ever, Horace carefully distinguishes these issues, Juvenal fuses them in his central theme, the nature of indignation. Indignation determines the answer to these traditional concerns, because, to a certain extent, Juvenal characterizes his satire solely by this violent passion. Throughout the Satire, in appropriate rhythm, he asserts the anger which motivates him, both directly in statements like *difficile est saturam non scribere* (30) and indirectly by choice of prejudicial words to qualify the characters and scenes in his vignettes. Anger sweeps away for him, he intimates, all objections as to his justification.

The satirist's first words express a violently overemphasized impatience with the literary dabblers of contemporary Rome. We do not know the precise cause of such wrath, but, as we gradually learn, Juvenal's stimulus is to be interpreted as his puritanic uprightness raging at the general concern with trivial things and the complete obliviousness that Rome is being destroyed by its own immorality. However, in the immediate context, the anger serves the rhythmic and semantic purpose objectively, allowing Juvenal to begin in a passionate tone, a characteristic, as we shall see, of his style. Whenever he writes satire, he fulminates against concrete abuses, which provoke him in exactly this manner. Here, he exaggerates his passion almost into bathos; by attaching it, however, to the literary themes of his day, he reduces them to insignificance. The opening, then, parodies the florid rhetoric of the schools, and, when the satirist discards his slightly counterfeit passion, he also contemptuously discards the whole literary scene which provoked it. He therefore modulates his tone, so that by the end of 21 he may reasonably ask for calm, rational appreciation of his satiric motivation.

si vacat ac placidi rationem admittitis, edam.

In these opening lines, Juvenal reveals his attitude toward grand poetry and thus satisfies one of the traditional themes of the Program Satire. As he contrives it, the inane contents of most poems excite his anger and thus expose to his readers the total antagonism between conventional poetry and satire. As far as he is concerned, no literary question exists to affect him. Where he pours out the passions of his inmost soul, epic manufactures emotions, and he denies it any value at all, sneering at its themes and piling up pejorative expressions around them,

tend his thematic research backward beyond Horace. On the other hand, Fiske did not apply his observations to Juvenal, so that Fiske and Hartmann complement each other.

using diminutives or a contemptuously indifferent *alius* to refer to a well-known hero (1–11). Epic, become the refuge of the dilettantes from the reality of the present, now concerns itself with the imaginary, a heroic past of legendary miracles and superhuman people. This artificial society of amateur poets has dignified itself with the name of bard, the height of absurdity.

> stulta est clementia, cum tot ubique
> vatibus occurras, periturae parcere chartae.   (17–18)

Juvenal uses grand poetry as a symbol of artificiality of theme, of complete unreality, to which he juxtaposes the urgent reality of contemporary immorality, one of his typically powerful thematic contrasts.

The new section (22–80) starts off from the quiet tone which Juvenal has reached in 21. Within a few lines, the temperature rises and steadily develops towards the final assertion in 79–80:

> si natura negat, facit indignatio versum,
> qualemcumque potest, quales ego vel Cluvienus.

As if standing on the street corner watching crowds parade before his vigilant gaze, the satirist reviews the types of moral degradation prevalent in Rome, selecting concrete details and attaching them tellingly to definite people.[4] In all this we should not fail to see the tacit contrast between epic and satire, fiction and fact, idle fancy and pressing reality. Juvenal, who started off with a burst of fury at literature in general, through which he revealed its vapidity, now builds up his fury again, but gradually, step by step, as he sees more and more examples of living vice. This time, he makes his indignation genuine, as it bursts out only under the pressure of outraged sensibility. The latent contrast between "poetry" and satire becomes explicit midway through this section, when Juvenal pauses to punctuate his series of examples with an impatient outburst. We observe him prejudicing epic themes so as to give them associations of inanity and, simultaneously, enhancing satiric themes by careful selection of details, so as to suffuse them with his own indignation.

> haec ego non agitem? sed quid magis? Heracleas
> aut Diomedeas aut mugitum labyrinthi
> et mare percussum puero fabrumque volantem,

---

[4] Cf. Hartmann and W. C. Helmbold, "The Structure of Juvenal I," *CPCP*, 14 (1951), 50, and G. Highet, *Juvenal the Satirist: a Study* (Oxford, 1954), p. 50.

> cum leno accipiat moechi bona, si capiendi
> ius nullum uxori, doctus spectare lacunar,
> doctus et ad calicem vigilanti stertere naso?   (52–7)

The Labors of Hercules, the martial deeds of Diomedes, the stories of Theseus and the Minotaur or of Daedalus and Icarus— none of these or their like can compare in reality and significance with the vicious greed of a husband who prostitutes his wife. The ironic *doctus* demonstrates how Juvenal examines the Roman scene and hints at the cause of its degradation. As one of his crucial methods throughout this section, he indicates the total overthrow of Roman *virtus* by transferring terms of moral approval to the description of immorality, by which he implies the transvaluation which has occurred among most Romans. This paradoxical use of traditionally moral terms [5] symbolizes the extent of Rome's degeneracy and justifies the satirist's uncompromising condemnation in 73:

> aude aliquid brevibus Gyaris et carcere dignum,
> si vis esse aliquid. probitas laudatur et alget.

While *dignum* illustrates the transvaluation indirectly, the epigram puts it with acid directness: honesty shivers. Men pay lip service to the old Roman standards, but the ideals of contemporary Rome attach value to the antithesis of *virtus*.

Has Juvenal arranged the vignettes in 22 ff.? Hartmann and Stegemann assumed so.[6] But their arrangement contributes formal order alone, while Juvenal's disorder suggests the effect of random observations.[7] At any point in the crowd the satirist can see degeneracy, the cumulative effect of which amply justifies his wrath. This section, then, with its absence of special order, indicates a potential answer to other remarks about Juvenal's disorganization. It is the immediate, uncritical reaction to specific instances of vice, not the rational explanation of the emotion, which is important in Juvenal. On the other hand, we would be wrong to emphasize the emotion so far as to identify it with the actual feelings of the satirist.[8] The satirist does not create his fury out of nothing, by imagining himself watching a

---

[5] E. g. *merentur* (37), *optima* etc. (38), *lautum atque beatum* (67), *melior Lucusta* (71).

[6] Hartmann, pp. 10 ff.; W. Stegemann, *De Juvenalis dispositione* (Weyda, 1913), pp. 12 ff.

[7] Cf. Highet, p. 50: "The satirist is not showing us a procession, but plunging us into a mob."

[8] Cf. Helmbold, p. 53: "It may be that Juvenal's emotions overcame him so

crowd of people. Juvenal has complete control of his emotions, but the character which he has assumed expresses anger. Hence, the artistic construction which, otherwise, would conflict with direct indignation. The section starts from the contrast between epic and satire and gradually adds a new contrast, between the traditional values and contemporary standards. In these contrasts, the satirist takes the conservative side against the present and explodes into a passion that is by no means irresponsible, for he perceives the significance of this degradation. Indignation sweeps away all concerns for matters of form and artistic ideals; not, however, from sheer irrationality. The moral insight justifies the emotion, and not vice versa, as Juvenal implies when he places his moral summary (73) several lines before his definitive statement about the motivation of his satire (79). Indignation applies only to questions of artistic form; it has no relevance in determining his moral criteria or influencing his perceptions. Indirectly, then Juvenal answers the potential objection of the second traditional theme in the Program Satire: the proper style of his Satires will be whatever his indignation dictates. In other words, stylistic and literary concerns have no importance for him; indignation will provide for his poetic technique, such as it is.[9]

Juvenal has so far developed two of the great themes of the Program Satire and hinted at the third. Epic he rejects indignantly as empty of meaning for his day. Developing that original indignation, he reaches the conclusion in 80, that formal style is also an inane concern, smacking of literary artificiality. At the same time, he has justified his indignation on moral grounds, so that he cannot possibly be attacked as a malicious gossip-

that he shouted aloud from the street corner, ' Commit a crime if you want to get on in the world! If you stay within the law, you'll starve on a good reputation.' "

[9] Undoubtedly, ambiguity exists in 79-80, but it seems to me that we must restrict their implications to matters of style. Indignation does not make the satirist's observations. Rather, as he puts it, the observation of conditions in Rome causes indignation, and, as a result, he may be unable in his emotional state to discipline his verse technique. The difficulty frequently exhibited in comments on this passage has stemmed from the fact that scholars have not distinguished between the actual sensation of personal revulsion and the incorporation of this sentiment into a poem. Failing to make this essential distinction, they have been distracted by the irrelevant concern of "sincerity," raising what is to them a serious question: how can indignation " make " verse? It would be wiser to recognize the self-conscious modesty of Juvenal in choosing the word *versum* and his humorous comparison of his ability with that of Cluvienus.

monger. His vignettes have expanded the scope of his Satire and cast the shadow of Rome, conceived of as a moral ideal, over every aspect of this section. Juvenal is tragic, in the sense that he depicts the downfall not of the whole human race but of the once-great Rome, the symbol of his country.

The humorous tag, *quales ego vel Cluvienus*, alters the tone of the Satire and punctuates the section 22–80. The following section, by its imprecise relation to the thematic structure, constitutes the greatest difficulty of the poem. It starts off from the reduced tone of 80, adopting an epic subject, Pyrrha and Deucalion, and the melodious technique of epic construction. Juvenal does not present the details of the Flood seriously; for a moment, the epic tone expands the horizon and lifts the mood away from anger to the more romantic sentiments evoked by the irrelevant, fictitious myth of long ago. Then the parody is impatiently dismissed, broken in upon by the harsh note of common speech and the angry, jerky language of indignation.

After his general opening to the new section, the satirist quickly concentrates on his object, detailing the subject material of his Satires. Helmbold would delete 85–6, on the grounds that Juvenal suggests too general a subject, whereas he actually concerns himself only with the negative member of each set of values.[10] However, Juvenal uses these lines to narrow the gap between the epic parody (81–4) and his specific, angry attack on prevalent immorality (87 ff.). The direct transition from the irony of 81–4 to the ferocity of 87 ff., without some intervening element, does not seem characteristic. On the other hand, the asyndeton of 85–6 suggests strong emotion that prepares for the violence of 87 ff., and the lines exhibit a verbal technique and a self-deprecation that we have already seen in the writer of this Satire.

The theme of 87–146 appears to be money.[11] The satirist con-

---

[10] Helmbold, p. 54, cites with approval the proposal of E. Harrison, *CR*, 51 (1937) 55-6. No manuscript authority for this deletion exists.

[11] Cf. Helmbold, p. 55. Hartmann, p. 16, and Stegemann, p. 21, designated the theme as *avaritia*. It would, however, take a liberal interpretation of *avaritia* to account for the relevance of the degrading insults to the *Troiugenae* (100 ff.) or the extravagant and self-indulgent meal of the *patronus* (135 ff.). Highet, p. 53, has suggested in an attractive manner that Juvenal here analyzes the subject "money" into the two correlative vices, greed and extravagance, in order to explain to his reader his basic topics. On the whole, I think that we must question his view, inasmuch as Juvenal makes both Satire 2 and Satire 3 of broader application; furthermore, the people he chooses to arraign in this Satire have committed crimes and vices which have but a remote connection with greed or extravagance.

centrates on a particular aspect of the general degeneracy, to demonstrate his methods and extend his critique. To portray the importance of money and the materialism of the day, he focuses on the scene of the *sportula* (95–126), where he represents several types of people as justification for his wrath: the indigent client (96) who depends on the *sportula* for his subsistence (119); the down-at-heels Roman nobility, the *Troiugenae* and the political officials (100); and the upstart foreigner who has acquired a position of prestige by unscrupulous economic practices (102). Dealing with these three groups are those who dispense the *sportula*, the servants of the master, of whom Juvenal specifically mentions the *praeco* (101), and the *patronus* himself (stylized as *ille* in 97). In the interrelation of these people, money is the common element. The client and the nobility represent the traditional Roman stock, with whom the master customarily dealt once on familiar terms. Once *patroni* themselves, the *Troiugenae* have now declined to the humble status of clients, and their noble name rings hollow. Indeed, the preference given to the anonymous freedman (102) symbolizes the complete degeneracy of the native Roman nobility. For the master, real wealth possesses more importance than noble birth. The old standards of social behavior have disappeared, and men now employ new criteria by which to judge fellow men and regulate the traditional relationship between client and patron. Money reigns supreme, able to confer social prestige on anyone that possesses it; without it, a man is nothing but an ignored client. In fact, money has become the goddess Pecunia, encroaching on the Roman pantheon.

> expectent ergo tribuni,
> vincant divitiae, sacro ne cedat honori
> nuper in hanc urbem pedibus qui venerat albis,
> quandoquidem inter nos sanctissima divitiarum
> maiestas: etsi, funesta Pecunia, templo
> nondum habitas, nullas Nummorum ereximus aras,
> ut colitur Pax atque Fides Victoria Virtus
> quaeque salutato crepitat Concordia nido.   (109–16)

Good birth clothes one with sacred honor, but the grandeur of wealth possesses a sanctity far beyond the degree of mere inherited nobility. Though the goddess has not yet been assigned a temple, she receives more reverence than the traditional Roman values which do have temples. In fact, in his details, Juvenal suggests that temple worship entails relegation to the sterility of religious rites and total neglect in other respects. *Fides* and *Virtus* cannot exist in a city where such depravity as is described in 22–80 receives the honor of positive moral attributes. *Concordia's* temple has been neglected, and, instead of the sound of ceremonies, the visitor is greeted by the flapping of birds flying out from the deserted eaves. If these three, the moral fiber of the Roman people, mean nothing, then *Pax* and *Victoria*, the achievements of the traditional Roman character, cannot exist. The neglect of this great moral heritage signifies the ultimate destruction of the imperial qualities.

In 127, Juvenal begins to describe the typical day. However, something has occurred between 131 and 132 which seems to require assumption of a lacuna.[12] Various people appear in 127-31; in 132, the satirist is suddenly describing the disappointed clients who apparently miss their share of the *sportula* and go home to their hunger, while the *patronus* gorges himself on a huge banquet alone. But retribution catches up with him in the end, as he eats too much and has a stroke in the bath after his meal. His loyal clients accompany the funeral cortege, but they cannot conceal their satisfaction at the death of a man who did nothing to maintain the relation once extant under the aegis of *Concordia*.

> ducitur iratis plaudendum funus amicis. (146)

This epigrammatic statement punctuates this section decisively. Hartmann, however, criticized this line; he claimed that introducing the theme of justice upon the immoral and gloating over a dead enemy weakened the indignant mood.[13] To a certain extent, Juvenal does reduce his indignation. He reaches the end of a section, and, to mark it off from what will succeed it, he lowers his tone and punctuates it with a clever epigram. On the other hand, he does not completely destroy his indignation. In describing the banquet of the rich man, he uses the third person

---

[12] A. E. Houseman, *D. Iunii Iuvenalis saturae, editorum in usum edidit* (London, 1905), was the first to propose the lacuna. In his more recent edition U. Knoche, *D. Iunius Juvenalis saturae* (Munich, 1950), has also assumed a lacuna, and I accept his view. Hartmann, pp. 26 ff., presents a case for an orderly sequence of thought without a lacuna. Juvenal, he argued, employs chiastic order so as to talk first about the *Troiugenae* in 127-31, then about the clients in 132 ff. In the lines immediately preceding 127, the satirist discusses the *Troiugenae*, and before that, the clients. Chiastic arrangement does not, however, really explain the problem, and the gap between 131 and 132 is large even for Juvenal, whose methods of asyndeton do not exhibit such audacity, striking though they undoubtedly are.

[13] *Op. cit*, p. 28.

singular. But when Nemesis strikes, he suddenly addresses the *patronus* with a direct, passionate *tu*, which does affect the account of the death, even though the final epigram brings the wrath under control. In general, Juvenal has given 81–146 a loose structure, which starts from a broad definition of the subject matter of satire and quickly comes to focus on the materialism of Rome. Where 22–80 presented a series of vignettes justifying the choice of genre, 81–146 show the satirist in action, concentrating on a single representative vice and criticizing Rome through details interpreted emotionally.

Once he has shown the reader his methods in practice, Juvenal returns to the thematic concerns of the Program Satire. He opens this final section (147 ff.) with a violent outburst similar in tone to that of 1–14 and parading a series of rhetorical clichés which alter the seriousness of his indignation to parody. It is as if the satirist deliberately works himself into a fury and self-consciously, melodramatically, tells himself to emote.[14] In the parody of rhetorical emotionality, Juvenal implies that even indignation is ridiculous when expended without control. At this point he introduces his interlocutor, in order to develop the final theme in dialogue. Instead of accusing the satirist of maliciousness, though, the interlocutor warns him of the danger he might incur by aggravating influential people. Uncontrolled indignation can jeopardize one's safety. In varying the traditional theme, Juvenal makes of satire a noble cause which requires complete self-dedication. Once again, he draws epic in for purpose of contrast (162). Now, he ironically calls epic themes preferable to satiric, because they are so safe, being devoid of relevance to the present. Satiric themes affect personal feelings directly and stir emotional reactions in the people they touch. Still, Juvenal infinitely prefers indignation to the sterile emotions of epic; real themes dealing with real people possess a patent superiority to the silly tales of Hylas and Heracles or even the more serious stories of Achilles and Aeneas. In the end, though, Juvenal's friend has made his point, too, for, with a surprising change, the satirist slips away from the world of the present into the world of the dead past.

> experiar quid concedatur in illos
> quorum Flaminia tegitur cinis atque Latina. (170-1)

---

[14] L. Friedländer, *D. Junii Juvenalis saturarum libri V mit erklärenden Anmerkungen* (Leipzig, 1895), *ad loc.*, commented on the hackneyed expressions *utere velis, totos pande sinus,* and the pessimistic commonplace about the abysmal degeneracy of the present.

The dead will be Juvenal's targets, so that he may live. At first sight, this seems a pusillanimous attitude, especially after the brave assertion of 79–80, for indignation cannot be very strong when so calculating. What does Juvenal imply by *illos*? Some critics have interpreted it to mean that Juvenal makes his subject matter only the Rome of Domitian, since Domitian was buried along the Flaminian Way and his favorite Paris along the Latin Way.[15] By contrast with this narrow interpretation, the other extreme makes the dead symbolic for the living. " He (i. e., Juvenal) will employ a cunning device: though he may seem to be dealing in stock figures, his intent will be precisely the same as that of Lucilius. He means in fact that he is about to attack *you*, ungentle reader." [16] Neither of these views corresponds with the facts; neither of them answers the more important question concerning Juvenal's apparent pusillanimity. Juvenal's world is broader than the Rome of Domitian, but it is narrower than the ample horizon of his reader.[17] In Book I, to which the Program Satire specifically applies, he makes his subject Rome. Rome, however, does not resemble a human being who dies and then cannot be affected by praise or blame. Rome persists even after the tyranny of Domitian, yet shows the scars of all the people who have ever lived in it. Thus, the city of the satirist's day results directly from the various currents prevalent in the city of Domitian's time. For Juvenal, the people symbolize the city that they inhabit; their faults can be generalized to include the whole area of Rome, then of the Empire. Therefore, by *illos* he refers to the dead of the recent past, the villains of the Flavian Era. In attacking the dead by name, however, the satirist exposes the vices which now dominate Rome. What he describes, though localized in the past, has influenced the present and threatens the future. Because the vice of the past has contemporary repercussions, Juvenal can still be angry, sensing that his native Rome is foundering. The scenes he saw on the street exhibit the direct result of the degeneracy he ascribes to the times of Domitian. Indignant at contemporary manifestations of vice, Juvenal can also be justly indignant at

[15] Cf. C. F. Heinrich, *Juvenalis saturae* (Bonn, 1839) and Friedländer, *ad loc.*
[16] Helmbold, p. 57.
[17] The people mentioned by name in Book I fall into three classes: (1) well-known figures from the era of Domitian and Nero in particular, now dead; (2) politically insignificant characters who are still alive; and (3) completely fictitious people. We may also include in this latter category those who are anonymous. For the latest discussion of proper names in Juvenal, cf. Highet, pp. 289 ff.

their sources in the past.[18] Finally, by selecting scenes from the past, the satirist implies that, in the interim between their occurrence and the present, these events have acquired an objectivity which checks any potential irrationality in his indignation.

The construction of Satire 1 provides a typical illustration of Juvenal's compositional methods. He selects a simple theme, to justify the characteristic attitude of indignation, showing it in operation on its typical victims. At the same time, the satirist justifies his genre to win the support of his reader. Indignation, seen under several different circumstances, has two normal stimuli: artificial literature and flagrant vice. Juvenal skillfully maintains a consistent contrast between these two motivations of *indignatio* and the quality of *indignatio* associated with each, the exaggerated rage at artifice as against the real fury over vice. He makes the characteristic of artifice vivid by repeated reminiscences of epic, dramatic themes, and rhetorical commonplaces, the details of which serve as a focus for his indignation. Similarly, the specific description of vice in the crowded streets and the scene of the *sportula* give immediacy to its insidious significance. Thus the convincing emotions evoked by contemporary immorality gain importance by contrast with the clearly defined falsehoods of myth. As a means of emphasizing his thesis, Juvenal employs a symmetrical reminiscence of the introduction at the end of the Satire. As the satirist faces the punishment of the amphitheater for his dangerous outspokenness, we may recall the significantly repeated *inpune* of 3–4, when Juvenal prays for retribution upon the poetasters, and see that he has now won his point, that the reality of his passions entitles him to assume the tragic manner. Satire, in fact, has become a tragic genre, replacing the empty artificialities of grand poetry. However, even the real *indignatio* must be qualified. In the first half of the Satire, the excessive emotion directed at literary dabblers justifies itself, when trained on factual situations. It receives its extreme statement in 79: *facit indignatio versum.* Then, in the second half of the Satire, Juvenal analyzes and ultimately justifies this audacious assertion as applicable only to the artistic aspect of his satire, not to his insights. Indignation acts upon the materialism of Roman society, and, in his criti-

---

[18] Highet, p. 57, is the first to have proposed a satisfactory explanation of Juvenal's " cowardice ": " Juvenal saw the empire as one long continuous process of degeneration." To his suggestion that the past represents the source of contemporary evils, I have added a second point, that the past, to a certain extent, promises objectivity on the part of the satirist.

cisms, the satirist shows himself perceptive, undistracted by his emotions. To obviate all objections, however, he guarantees objectivity by abandoning the living and accepting the dead as his targets. Indignation, unless controlled, can be partial. It can actually create a poem, but a completely wrong poem. If, however, its material has been placed in the proper perspective by time, *indignatio* can still exist and be legitimate. Accordingly, in the course of the Satire, Juvenal consistently modifies the source of his violence, but *indignatio* itself remains unchanged, dignified by the end with the proper connotations.

SATIRE 2

fugerunt trepidi vera ac manifesta canentem
Stoicidae. quid enim falsi Laronia? sed quid
non facient alii, cum tu multicia sumas,
Cretice, et hanc vestem populo mirante perores
in Proculas et Pollittas? (64–8)

The crux of the problem in Satire 2 has been the transition in 65 ff. Up to this point, Juvenal apparently attacks the hypocritical moralists, those who deliver fiery sermons on the degeneracy of their day and yet indulge in degrading perversions themselves when not under observation. The lines cited above mark the change, as the satirist transfers his attack to a type of immorality not apparently consistent with his theme: in 65–148, he exposes, not the hypocrite, but the flagrant pervert. It has, therefore, been the endeavor of commentators to explain the relevance of this new subject to the theme announced at the beginning:

qui Curios simulant et Bacchanalia vivunt. (3)

The traditional explanation can be credited to C. F. Heinrich and G. A. Ruperti.[19] According to this interpretation, Juvenal probably wrote Satire 2, his earliest surviving work,[20] either under the regime of Domitian or immediately after his death and gave it continuity in repeated references, direct and indirect, to the acts of Domitian and conditions under his rule. The chief thematic word, *censor*, first mentioned in 30,[21] alludes to the

[19] Heinrich, Intro. to Satire 2; G. A. Ruperti, *Juvenalis saturae* (2d ed. Leipzig, 1819), Intro. to Satire 2. Both Friedländer and Stegemann follow them.
[20] P. Ercole, *Studi Giovenaliani*, ed. E. Paratore (Lanciano, 1935) regarded Satire 2 as Juvenal's earliest poem. Highet, p. 250, regards it as early.
[21] This passage has attracted special comments from Heinrich, Ruperti,

notorious censorship of Domitian, in which, because of his incestuous relations with his niece, he felt obliged to reverse his stringent edicts against immorality. Subsequent references to this theme in 40, 62, and 121 touch Domitian only indirectly, but the first detailed statement in 30 influences the attitude toward all the others. Since this theme spans both sections of the Satire, the unity of the work consists in the historical importance of Domitian. The first section, then, deals with those who followed the pattern of the emperor's hypocrisy, inveighing with censorial rigidity against the morals of the time and, like him, indulging themselves in secret. By his transition in 65, the satirist transfers his attention to a different, but related, segment of the population under Domitian, and the second section deals with those who followed the censor less logically but whose activity was immediately conditioned by his behavior. Domitian eventually relaxed his censorial laws in order to enjoy his perversions freely, and these nobles followed his relaxed attitude. They neither philosophize nor try to hide their degeneracy. The satirist concentrates on them, because, in the end, they possess more significance than the hypocrites. The upper classes control the political and moral standards of the city, and, living in the debased manner they do, these nobles make Rome what it is, a place where a perverted tyrant can indulge his most deranged fancies.

The censorship theme provides the main support for the historical interpretation. Ruperti also suggested that the upper classes tacitly affect the first section.[22] In 23 Juvenal refers to Sextus who, according to the Scholia, is a senator. Moreover, Creticus first appears as a moralist in 67–8, before the satirist concentrates on his effeminate attire. Stegemann, also an adherent of the historical interpretation, pointed out that in the interests of symmetry much of the detailed description in 65 ff. serves to illustrate the general criticisms of Laronia's speech in 36 ff.[23] She mentions effeminate dress (40), homosexual relations (49), and the perverted interest in female activities such as sewing (54), all of which affront us in specific detail later, as applicable to the openly immoral.

Still, the historical interpretation, I believe, can only partially explain the unity of this Satire, for, while it appealingly

Friedländer, and Stegemann; also from P. de Labriolle and F. Villeneuve, *Juvénal, Satires*, 2d ed. Paris, 1932.
[22] *Op. cit.*, Vol. 1, pp. 17 ff.
[23] *Op. cit.*, p. 21.

elucidates the theme of censorship, exclusively pursued, it restricts the operation of other more central themes. To be sure, the transitional elements in Laronia's speech exist; the ambivalent role of Creticus as both moralist and flagrant pervert exists. But, by limiting the applicability of these transitional devices to a historical context, commentators have warped the rhetorical construction.[24]

In the transitional lines cited above, Juvenal states a theme in metaphor, a theme which, to my knowledge, has escaped general notice; for he describes the immediate reaction to Laronia's speech in terms of terrified flight (*fugerunt trepidi*). In general, Juvenal does not force thematic metaphors on the attention, and this, if such a metaphor, must be supported by an explicit theme. The image of battle in *fugerunt* receives some stress from the poetic *trepidi* and the epic tinges of the context. But, more important, this military image has a prototype in Laronia's speech, when she praises a hypocrite with ironic overstatement:

> felicia tempora, quae te
moribus opponunt! (38-9)

The suggestion of battle in *opponunt* becomes specific in the sardonic metaphor applied to the homosexuality of the false Stoics.

> sed illos
defendit numerus iunctaeque umbone phalanges. (45-6)

Even the scholiast remarks on this as a military metaphor. Laronia exploits it to emphasize the unmilitary character of the hypocrites. While the false moralist assumes the pose of a hero manfully resisting the degradation of his day, his martial appearance serves only to disguise his effeminate characteristics. Put to the test in battle with a woman, he is utterly routed.

In employing this military image, Juvenal achieves several economic comments on the immorality of the hypocrites. The defeat of the sham moralist is due to his cowardice, physical and moral, and his cowardice results from effeminacy. Masquerading as Stoic virility, effeminacy comes to battle with the natural sexual desires of genuine women. The rout of effeminacy, then, implies that women like Laronia, inasmuch as they yield to their natural propensities, are morally superior to men whose lusts express themselves in an unnatural form. Military language as

[24] Highet, p. 59, states clearly that the Satire takes as its subject homosexuality, with which I agree. However, he does not seem to regard the structure as a particular problem. Cf. p. 250, note 2.

211

applied to effeminates is self-contradictory, and the satirist makes use of this implicit contradiction to focus attention on his meaning, the perversion of the hypocrites.

Laronia's speech employs the military metaphor consistently, in a way that is partially parody, partially allegory. In the second half of the Satire, Juvenal develops the image and the contradiction it represents.

> en habitum quo te leges ac iura ferentem
> vulneribus crudis populus modo victor et illud
> montanum positis audiret vulgus aratris! (72–4)

Now, the image has become a theme, a means of contrast, and Creticus, whose exotic costume symbolizes his perversion, affronts the sturdy military classes who come from the country districts outside Rome. From its negative function, then, exposing the degradation of the hypocrites, the military theme gradually becomes a positive concept. No longer incorporated paradoxically and ironically in the description of immorality, it stands as a value which now places effeminacy in the proper perspective. But, to give the positive side strength, Juvenal associates the military theme here with rural values. As yet, it cannot stand by itself.

Military standards underlie the epic parody of 99 ff., which uses reminiscences from the martial contexts of the *Aeneid* to comment on the unheroic behavior of the Emperor Otho.[25]

> ille tenet speculum, pathici gestamen Othonis,
> Actoris Aurunci spolium, quo se ille videbat
> armatum, cum iam tolli vexilla iuberet.

The mirror receives the attributes which, in the *Aeneid*, were given to the armor of important warriors. By drawing on the famous epic, Juvenal introduces a new set of values by which to assess the degeneracy of his day. The mythical past provides romantic visions of invincible warriors, fighting on tirelessly for grand purposes. When these glorious associations concentrate on a real scene of battle, where a womanish emperor weakly faces defeat without a contest, they point up the prosaic, inglorious character of Otho, the gap between his actions and the mythical ideal.

In 149 ff. Juvenal stimulates the imagination to picture the

[25] For *pathici gestamen Othonis*, cf. *Aen.* 3.286, *magni gestamen Abantis*; and for *Actoris Aurunci spolium*, cf. *Aen.* 12.94, from which Juvenal cites directly.

scene in Hades when the effeminate meets the heroes of the
Roman past.

> Curius quid sentit et ambo
> Scipiadae, quid Fabricius manesque Camilli,
> quid Cremerae legio et Cannis consumpta iuventus,
> tot bellorum animae, quotiens hinc talis ad illos
> umbra venit?

Though a hypothetical situation, the satirist presents it with
convincing emotion, drawing upon the real heroes of Roman
history, the men who made Rome what it was. He produces a
formidable list and contrasts it with the single *umbra*, the heroes
who possess vitality even in death as against the effeminate who
is merely the shadow of a man even while alive. Moreover,
Curius picks up *Curios* in 3; *Scipiadae* recalls *Stoicidae* in 65,
both in the same metrical position, and together these reminiscences indicate the progression of the theme. In 3, *Curios* connoted correct moral behavior; here, it implies a specific attribute,
military grandeur. In short, the apparent theme of the opening
section, true morality against hypocrisy, has been simplified to
the more emotionally vigorous issue of martial glory against
effeminacy, where Roman history gives the final perspective to
the military symbol. The people of his day, the satirist says,
have abandoned their heritage, the martial exploits of their fore-
fathers, the consistent militarism that made Rome so powerful,
not merely for luxury but for perversions which even reject the
ideal of manliness.

The persistence of this symbol in both sections of the Satire
requires some interpretation, for it appears to have a unifying
function potentially stronger and more significant than the
censorship theme. Moreover, just as in Satire 1 the word *inpune*
at the beginning and the danger of the arena facing the satirist
at the end possess a certain thematic relation, so in Satire 2 the
opening sentence first suggests the military metaphor, while the
final paragraph explicitly interprets it.

> ultra Sauromatas *fugere* hinc libet et glacialem
> Oceanum, quotiens aliquid de moribus audent
> qui Curios simulant et Bacchanalia vivunt. (1–3)

> illic heu miseri traducimur! arma quidem ultra
> litora Iuvernae promovimus et modo captas
> Orcadas ac minima contentos nocte Britannos;
> sed quae nunc populi fiunt victoris in urbe,
> non faciunt illi quos vicimus. (159–63)

213

A relation exists between these passages, apparent in the use of *ultra*; the same expansive movement away from concentration on the scene at Rome to include the Empire and then the barbarian areas beyond helps to present the military theme. Structurally, these passages broaden the scope of the Satire, to create a convenient frame for the particular action in Rome. Thematically, they represent the first tentative suggestion of the military symbol and the subsequent clear affirmation of martial values. In the first words of the Satire, Juvenal introduces his theme: he, a morally upright person, is so overwhelmed by the power of degeneracy, that flight provides his only means of safety, flight beyond the boundaries of the Roman Empire. The second passage continues from the imaginary scene in Hades, from which Juvenal makes his transition by extending the application of *umbra* (157), the typical Roman effeminate, to every Roman through *traducimur*. Metaphorically, the word signifies that the Romans march as captives in a triumphal parade, a scene which, in transition, applies to Hades and to what follows. In reference to Hades, the image assesses the present Roman as a miserable specimen by contrast with the heroes of the past; on another level, in reference to actual existence, it asserts that Romans have become captives of their defeated foes because of their moral inferiority, that they do in fact descend to the underworld as part of a triumphal procession.

In the main body of the Satire, Juvenal has built up a series of associations around a military theme, all of them an immediate comment by parody or contrast upon the effeminate practices of Rome. By using the first person plural now in *traducimur* he draws himself and the reader for the first time into direct relation with the issue. It has become, he implies, a matter of formidable proportions, broader than the mere degeneracy of the Roman nobility, affecting the Roman Empire as a whole. The effeminacy of the city taints all Romans. In what follows, Juvenal pursues the explicit theme of militarism. He reviews some of the distant conquests of Roman imperialism, to show that victory has not been kept pure, that Rome has lost its glory. Having dealt with the northern area of the Empire in 160-1, he now selects a character from the eastern frontier, in order to make his implications as general as possible. Zalaces comes to Rome as a hostage, a defeated enemy; at Rome, he becomes the favorite of a certain tribune, loses his own native practices under this new culture, and returns to Armenia a Roman in habit.

> mittentur bracae cultelli frena flagellum:
> sic praetextatos referunt Artaxata mores. (169–70)

He abandons the uncouth-sounding weapons of Armenia for the degenerate customs of Rome. In this mutual conquest, Zalaces has the superior position, for, though he has let himself be seduced by a tribune, his seduction is tantamount to victory. Hence, the implications in *referunt*, the military metaphor which evokes the picture of a victorious warrior carrying home the booty he has won in battle.

While the military symbol pervades the Satire as the chief thematic device of the satirist, it does not deny the validity of the historical explanation, but enlarges it. Latent in the opening lines, the theme begins to develop in Laronia's speech, acquires associations from the ideas surrounding the sturdy yeomen of the Italian countryside, the epic warriors of the *Aeneid*, and the heroes of Roman history; and finally, in the last lines, Juvenal explains what he meant in *fugere hinc libet* (1). The impersonal verb applies as generally as the precise *traducimur*. The heart of Roman history beats in the military exploits which continue throughout Roman expansion and stop only when the Empire recognizes the limits of its powers. Juvenal uses the victorious past as the symbol best suited to reduce the present to its ignoble proportions. In parody, he shows the utter unworthiness of the present nobility; by contrast, he sets forth their degeneracy from the ideals of Roman training. Rome has lost its essential character, for, without the military values, she can no longer support her existence. She has become the captive of luxury, effeminacy, and the other vices of her conquered enemies. In conquering, she has taken in plunder their faults and aggravated them; she has let the manly virtues be plundered by her enemies. Therefore, the true Roman must flee beyond Rome's reach, in order to recover the conditions necessary for the preservation of the traditional standards.

If thematic, the symbol also provides structural unity. Suggested in the first lines, it does not receive precise statement until Laronia's speech. Hence, Juvenal prevents it from acquiring associations with the introductory section concerning hypocrite philosophers and relates it directly to effeminacy. Laronia places her emphasis on the perverted habits of men, whereas the opening lines were concerned with perversions only as a sign of hypocrisy. The Satire, then, tends toward a fuller explanation of the meaning of effeminacy and, intrinsically related to this, a fuller exposition of the military symbolism. Although the transition from hypocrisy to flagrant acts does not correspond to the presumed subject of the Satire, the treatment of effeminacy remains consistent and effects a permissible connection. Hypocrisy is not difficult to detect. When people do detect it, they naturally reject the criteria which the hypocrites have falsely espoused. The reaction to the speech of Laronia, therefore, establishes the transition to flagrant vice. In 1–64, Juvenal restricts himself to exposing the evil of effeminacy in contemporary Rome, as concealed by hypocrites beneath a martial disguise. Laronia's exposure of the hypocrisy routs the martial bearing, strips away the moral veneer, and frees effeminacy from any restraint. The hypocrite flees in terror, and in his place comes the open pervert. Triumphantly perversion sweeps through the city, destroying the true triumphs of war.

The orderly procedure of Juvenal's thought, supported by this symbol, has been disregarded by commentators, and, assuming 1–3 as the announced program of the Satire, they have been unable to explain the transition in 65. Like the medieval scribes, who entitled this Satire in the manuscripts " De Fictis Moribus Institutis," they have treated it as merely a variation on a rhetorical theme.[26] But the poem does not concern itself with pretence; it shows the significance of perverted manhood. When Juvenal opens the piece with an outburst of fury, he aims not primarily at the hypocrisy but at the vice which it conceals. Viewed in this way, the Satire presents a comprehensible sequence of thought and a sound structure. Juvenal strips the mask from effeminacy and comes to focus on it in its most flagrant manifestations in the city of Rome. He starts from the farthest boundaries of the Empire and works his way back to the city, the symbol of Roman values good and bad. Having exposed the significance of effeminacy from various angles, and especially through the antithesis with the military symbol, he moves away from the city out to the frontiers again, making clear the point he implied in the opening lines, that he must flee.

Interpretation in the light of a single symbol, even so dominant a one as the military in this Satire, runs the danger of isolating the significance of the work in one aspect, in as partisan a manner as the historical or diatribal approach. Other complementary thematic units bring the picture into greater artistic balance, as, for example, the antithesis between *tristis* and *turpis*, together with their respective synonyms. To state the antithesis most strikingly, Juvenal uses the form of paradox.

[26] For the titles, cf. Knoche.

> quis enim non vicus abundat
> tristibus obscenis? (8-9)

In those " severe-looking perverts " the satirist expresses a moral issue with the economy which best conveys his indignation. Once Laronia has removed the mask from the sham moralists, these words, no longer associated in self-contradiction, become polar qualities. Therefore, in Laronia's peroration, *tristis*, now better defined than in 9, appears again (62), when she attacks the sham propriety of the effeminates. As a moral term, it qualifies both the judgment and the judge; it becomes tainted when used by perverts to utter severe strictures on feminine immorality. While *tristis* acquires a positive symbolic value, the complete liberty permitted unnatural desires represents the other term in the antithesis. In the transitional lines, Creticus, who poses as a moralist, is quickly stripped of his disguise and described as degenerate.

> nudus agas: minus est insania turpis. (71)

The dichotomy between *turpis* and *tristis* becomes even wider as the Satire proceeds. In his rhetorical development, Juvenal makes the domain of *turpis* the whole world, while its polar opposite can find only implicit expression in the mythical world of epic (99 ff.), the dead world of the past (125 ff.), and the dubious realm of Hades (149 ff.).

Juvenal concentrates on the truly feminine character also, for his thematic contrasts. If, on one side, the military symbol provides a criterion by which to understand the degradation of Roman manhood, on the other side the natural womanly values provide a perspective on the unnatural effeminacy of the pervert. This antithesis first appears in paradox. The hypocrite pretends to be antifeminine, by adopting a superficially masculine pose and railing against the vices of women; in secret, he is an effeminate. But the antithesis extends in several directions. For valid moral reasons, the real moralist rails against women; the effeminate denounces women for reasons that exist in his unnatural perversion. It is as though he regarded the female as his rival and wished to supplant her. At first, then, Juvenal emphasizes the antithesis between pretended masculinity and active effeminacy (e. g. Sextus vs. Varillus 21). He turns next to expose the difference between the effeminate and the female, the unnatural and the natural, as if the hypocrisy merely furnished a means of introducing the more important antithesis. Laronia symbolizes the natural, who, while immoral and condemned as such, is at least female. She assumes the role of exposing the effeminate behavior of the homosexual, who invades the area of feminine activity, to enjoy her dress, sexual relations with men, and pleasure in weaving. A natural hostility exists between the pervert and the female.

> dives erit magno quae dormit tertia lecto. (60)
> dat veniam corvis, vexat censura columbas. (63)

As the Scholia point out, the proverbial difference between the raven and the dove involves sexual behavior. The effeminate cannot be classed as a female or a male; his is an intermediate sex which tries to render the female *tertia*. Laronia's speech exposes the facts of perversion and destroys the possibility of simulation. Therefore, in the second section of the Satire, the meaning of homosexuality to the Roman standards bursts into the open. Laronia routed the hypocrites by her sibylline revelations (*vera ac manifesta canentem* 64), and, in their place, come the frankly vicious. The military symbol points out the growing discrepancy between the traditional Rome of military grandeur and the contemporary seat of degeneracy; simultaneously, the feminine theme serves to stress the unnatural aspect of the same vice, for the female is almost driven from her normal area of activity, as rampant homosexuality strives to encroach upon all the feminine pursuits.

> exagitata procul non intrat femina limen:
> solis ara deae maribus patet. " ite profanae! " (88–9)

Men adopt the dress of women and take over their rites. When such pathics try to make war, they resemble Otho, whose weapon is a mirror. To emphasize his point, Juvenal unites his themes of women and war, using the martial qualities of Semiramis and the supremely feminine Cleopatra to make Otho and his ilk even more despicable (108–9). Women are superior to effeminates in an activity reserved for men, because such men have abandoned their sex. Instead, these perverts do everything in their power to become women, driving the true women from the Satire except as an implicit standard of reference. They hold marriage ceremonies and actually think of themselves as performing the woman's part.

> signatae tabulae, dictum " feliciter," ingens
> cena sedet, gremio iacuit nova nupta mariti. (119–20)

They even go so far as to desire to bear children, says the satirist, but here Nature refuses to indulge their unnatural fancies, and they die sterile (137 ff.).

In Satire 2, a series of themes and symbols combine to interpret the significance of homosexuality to a traditionally virile Rome. The historical relevance of the Satire has some bearing upon the interpretation; but the poem far more concerns effeminacy than Domitian. Juvenal first mentions the moral standards that he invokes to give his theme its tragic perspective as used by the hypocrites. He ironically applies the military metaphor to these effeminates; establishes their counterfeit Stoic pose as a paradox of severe moral judgment and immoral behavior; and, for the moment, upholds an antifeminine attitude. From this complex, paradoxical view of effeminacy, he proceeds through several stages of simplification toward a clear contrast, as the paradox resolves into an antithesis. Laronia's speech separates the paradoxical terms, and they emerge in 64 ff. as polar opposites. Interpreted in its full symbolic significance, her speech solves the problem of transition and unity. Homosexuality is the dominant theme. At first, it has no significance except as seen in terms of the paradox of metaphor and theme. By parody and contrast, however, Juvenal uses a series of details to sharpen the focus and clarify the potential ambiguity. In the end, the paradoxes have disappeared, and the metaphor has become a specific *exemplum*, the story of Zalaces. With a typical twist, Juvenal rounds off the Satire by linking the fleeing Roman of 1-3 with the half-civilized barbarian plundering the city of its virile qualities. Hypocrisy has been exposed and the vice that it conceals defined as a basic element of the Roman tragedy.

SATIRE 3

ergo vale nostri memor, et quotiens te
Roma tuo refici properantem reddet Aquino,
me quoque ad Helvinam Cererem vestramque Dianam
converte a Cumis. saturarum ego, ni pudet illas,
auditor gelidos veniam caligatus in agros. (318–22)

Satire 3 has not occasioned commentators much difficulty. It has justly been praised as the finest work of Juvenal, and the most extreme form of eulogy has been to call it nonrhetorical.[27]

[27] Friedländer, p. 189: " Nirgends ist hier Phrase oder ein bloss rhetorisches Pathos."

To be sure, De Decker could criticize its declamatory methods, its obvious transitions, and its disproportion, but he constitutes an exception.[28] In the manuscripts, the Satire acquired the title " De urbis incommodis et de digressu Umbricii," [29] which closely resembles the conventional modern view of the structure: "Meaning to describe the vexations and inconveniences of a town life, Juvenal supposes his friend Umbricius leaving Rome in disgust to retire to Cumae; and while the carriage is being packed Umbricius breaks out and tells his reasons for leaving his native place. No honest man can thrive there, he says." [30] Macleane goes on, in his schematization, to arrange each paragraph in order. He predicates the unity on the "inconveniences of a town life"; where that is difficult to follow, the direct speech of Umbricius provides the link.[31] Friedländer made the theme more specific, namely, " die Schattenseiten des Lebens in Rom für den unbemittelten und zugleich ehrenhaften Mann ";[32] but for him, too, the unity inhered in the kaleidoscopic effect of these " dark sides." Highet has articulated the theme in two different, but related, manners: " the power and the vileness of the big city " and " ' Why no one can live well in the City.' " [33] So stated, his theme approaches the traditional exposition. In my opinion, however, these interpretations represent a misunderstanding of Juvenal's true purpose and of the structure of this Satire. Apparently listing the " inconveniences " of Rome, Juvenal actually produces a composite picture of Rome and its degeneracy, a picture which complements that of Satire 2. Samuel Johnson came far closer to interpreting Satire 3 correctly when, in adapting it to the English scene, he entitled it *London*.[34]

The misconception of commentators may be illustrated in connection with the above citation of 318–22. For them, the problem has been to interpret *caligatus*. One favorite version has been to allegorize the word into a military picture: Juvenal, supported by his worthy friend, advancing to do battle with the

---

[28] J. De Decker, *Juvenalis declamans* (Ghent, 1913), pp. 37, 73, 92, 129.

[29] Knoche shows that four manuscripts have this title and five others a variant. Another, but less common, title appears: " Quare Umbricius urbem deserat."

[30] A. J. Macleane, *Decii Junii Juvenalis et A. Persii Flacci saturae* (London, 1857), p. 42.

[31] Cf. also Friedländer, p. 189: " Das Ganze den Eindruck einer zwanglosen Plauderei macht und machen soll."

[32] *Ibid.*

[33] Highet, pp. 65, 68.

[34] Johnson published his work first in 1738.

vices of the world.[35] Friedländer regarded such an interpretation as impossible, because Juvenal's military days are long since past.[36] For him, *caligatus* referred directly to the farmer's dress. No commentator has suggested the thematic relevance of *caligatus* or of this whole passage.[37] Yet, since it ends Umbricius' speech and the Satire, I contend that it must be more important than it has generally been considered to be. Because the construction of the Satire has been viewed basically as a list of instances, the central theme, the relation between these instances, has not been sufficiently stressed.

Umbricius has used the major portion of his speech to explain his reasons for leaving Rome, but at this point he alters his subject. As if assuming that his friend must share his views, Umbricius talks about the satirist's withdrawal, too, from Rome. The terms he uses to describe the withdrawal serve to prejudice his picture: *refici, properantem, reddet*. The satirist will be hurrying away from Rome; he will be seeking restoration, recovery. Around Aquinum, Umbricius weaves a series of attractive associations: he speaks of the divinities connected with the place; he pictures himself striding in his farmer's attire (*caligatus*) across the frozen fields; he implies the close friendship that would draw him from Cumae to Aquinum. On the other hand, *Roma* has no attributes; it stands starkly, stripped of connotations, in the midst of these alluring details applied to the country. Implicitly, everything reflects negatively on Rome. In the course of the Satire, as we shall see, Juvenal has had Umbricius point out one fault after another in Rome, the degeneracy from one Roman virtue after another. At the end, Rome possesses no connotations of its own. Its traditional values have abandoned it, and it remains an empty shell, a glittering façade which conceals its total rejection of the past, its complete subjection to foreign and debased practices. Therefore, this passage represents the climax of Juvenal's exposition, his final statement about Rome.

The construction of Satire 3, probably Juvenal's finest, depends upon a series of contrasts, all of them closely interrelated and contributing to the final imposing effect. With impression-

[35] Cf. Macleane, *ad loc.*

[36] *Ad loc.* Friedländer's exclusive interest in a historical interpretation has led him into error here. Juvenal's military career and the imaginary existence of Umbricius have no necessary connection.

[37] Highet cites the passage in full, p. 75, and discusses *auditor*, p. 256. note 23, but does not stress the thematic significance of the final lines.

istic methods, the satirist produces a picture of Rome as it really strikes him. Umbricius' speech dominates all but the first 20 lines, and, as he voices his reasons for abandoning Rome, he indirectly exposes the city's significance. His justification, then, constitutes the city's condemnation. As the play of light gives meaning to an impressionistic painting, so Rome articulates the composition of Satire 3. Each time he names the city, Umbricius denies any possible relation between its present standards and his.

> quid Romae faciam? mentiri nescio; librum,
> si malus est, nequeo laudare et poscere . . . (41–2)

>   me prior ille
> signabit fultusque toro meliore recumbet,
> advectus Romam quo pruna et cottona vento? (81–3)

> non est Romano cuiquam locus hic, ubi regnat
> Protogenes aliquis vel Diphilus aut Hermarchus. (119–20)

> da testem Romae tam sanctum quam fuit hospes
> numinis Idaei, procedat vel Numa vel qui
> servavit trepidam flagranti ex aede Minervam:
> protinus ad censum, de moribus ultima fiet
> quaestio. (137–41)

> haut facile emergunt quorum virtutibus opstat
> res angusta domi, sed Romae durior illis
> conatus. (164–6)

> commune id vitium est, hic vivimus ambitiosa
> paupertate omnes. quid te moror? omnia Romae
> cum pretio. (182–4)

> felices proavorum atavos, felicia dicas
> saecula, quae quondam sub regibus atque tribunis
> viderunt uno contentam carcere Romam. (312–4)

Rome, as the heart of the Satire, provides the self-contradiction on which all the series of contrasts hang. Over the years she has acquired a wealth of symbolism. Juvenal, therefore, steadily strips away her connotations, pointing up her adherence to standards entirely antithetical to the traditional ones. The living antitype to contemporary Rome is Umbricius, and the satirist depicts him sympathetically in terms of the antique Roman values. When he departs, he has made it clear that no Roman values survive in the city to identify it as Rome. The Roman standards must be sought far away from the metropolis.

In the conventional Satire, the satirist must express his own personality in such a way as to become an acceptable authority for his criticisms. He must assume the role of the honorable man (*vir bonus*).[38] Juvenal regularly conceals his personality: Satire 1 stresses only his emotional relation to the contemporary situation, and that emotion replaces any image of his character, appearance, environment, or past; he is to be visualized only in terms of a sweeping, righteous indignation. In Satire 3, Juvenal allows himself the first 20 lines as introduction, but interprets the scene at Rome entirely through the personality of Umbricius.[39] Therefore, he makes Umbricius the man required by his theme: *vir bonus atque Romanus*. He starts with a Rome full of rich associations and an unknown man, his friend. The exposition wins us more and more to the side of Umbricius and separates us from Rome; this Juvenal effects by identifying Umbricius progressively with all the traditional qualities of Rome, while steadily denying to the present city these very values. In the end, he has created a completely sympathetic, because completely Roman, Umbricius, and he has made a completely unsympathetic, because totally un-Roman, city.

As his personal preface to Umbricius' speech, Juvenal adopts a hyperbolic manner, to establish certain key thematic terms with striking emphasis.

> ianua Baiarum est et gratum litus amoeni
> secessus; ego vel Prochytam praepono Suburae.
> nam quid tam miserum, tam solum vidimus, ut non
> deterius credas horrere incendia, lapsus
> tectorum adsiduos ac mille pericula saevae
> urbis et Augusto recitantis mense poetas? (4-9)

It has been observed that, with the exception of the final sardonic detail about the *recitationes*, the satirist has here announced the main subjects of Umbricius' speech.[40] We should, however, note the thematic function of the other details. In broad strokes, Juvenal sketches the charm of Cumae, to which he immediately contrasts the city, as symbolized in *Suburae*. Moreover, he weights the comparison by associating with the Subura the infamous island of Prochyta. In establishing this initial antithesis, Juvenal employs hyperbole, partially to exaggerate his indignation, partially to clarify his structure. After

---

[38] Cf. M. Mack, "The Muse of Satire," *Yale Review*, 41 (1951), note 12.

[39] Cf. Hartmann, p. 33: "honestissimus ergo inducit (i. e. Juvenalis) hominem.

[40] Cf. Stegemann, p. 9.

20 he drops from the picture, and Umbricius, who, in contrast with the violence of the satirist, wins us by his self-control as well as by his Roman *virtus*, takes over. The introductory hyperbole extends to rhetorical questions; then, the vignettes by which Juvenal implies the degradation of the city end on a light note, poets reciting in August. With this levity he undercuts his false indignation and ends his initial thematic presentation, and in muted tone he now lays the scene for Umbricius.

Hyperbolic this introduction has been, but, in addition, it has served a valuable rhetorical purpose in establishing the contrast between Cumae and Rome. In defending the choice of Cumae, Juvenal introduces an important theme, when he pretends to apply to Cumae the adjectives *miserum* and *solum*, as if retreat from the city connoted wretched solitude (6). He suggests that Rome is worse (*deterius*), but his specific details only suggest what he will achieve in his subsequent exposition. In the course of his speech, Umbricius gradually separates the two adjectives: *miserum* comes to apply exclusively to the scene at Rome and the poor Roman trapped in it; *solum* acquires positive connotations in polarity to *miserum*.

> Romae durior illis
> conatus: magno hospitium miserabile, magno
> servorum ventres, et frugi cenula magno. (165–7)

> ergo optes votumque feras miserabile tecum,
> ut sint contentae patulas defundere pelves. (276–7)

> me, quem luna solet deducere vel breve lumen
> candelae, cuius dispenso et tempero filum,
> contemnit. miserae cognosce prooemia rixae,
> si rixa est, ubi tu pulsas, ego vapulo tantum. (286–9)

These, the only uses of *miserum* and its cognates after 6, indicate that Rome qualifies as the wretched place far more than Cumae. Moreover, the cumulative effect of Umbricius' detailed complaint symbolizes the misery of life in Rome, especially in the second part of the Satire, where he elaborates the subjects suggested in 7 ff. So Juvenal's exaggeration gains support from the facts presented in Umbricius' speech: Rome is more wretched (*deterius*) than any distant town.

The symbolism around *solum* is more complex, and, in transforming its prejudicial connotation, Juvenal adopts two methods of approach. First, at several points, he introduces alluring country scenes, where he specifically denies solitude: a rural festival, with its throngs of happy people (172 ff.); an agricultural vignette in appealing detail (223 ff.); and friendship among country folk (318 ff.). On the other hand, he portrays Umbricius in the city as a lonely figure who speaks of himself as though he were struggling single-handed against intolerable conditions: *quid Romae faciam?* In effect, the environment of Rome seems to be engulfing the individual and reducing him to an indistinguishable element of the masses. This denial of individuality emerges superbly in the brilliant portrait of urban confusion (239 ff.), where the metaphors used to describe the crowd, *unda* and *agmen*, reduce the individual to a drop in the ocean, a mere soldier in the military machine. Hartmann remarked on the skillful rhetorical development of 243–8.[41] The detailed enumeration of various parts of the body, of various instruments of injury, and of various agents all produces a kaleidoscopic impression of a bewildering series of blows and jostlings. But this passage also ties in with the thematic development. The individual, struck from all sides and completely defenseless, leads to Juvenal's symbolic scene interpreting the situation as indiscriminate reduction of personality, namely, the disaster which befalls the crowd. The wagons lumbering along the streets contain various materials for the construction of stately villas. When the axle breaks and the load is jettisoned on the crowd, the *agmen* metaphor of 244 recurs (258). Now the army is not on the offensive, and the lonely individual disappears in its mass. In the crushing of the army by the mountain of building materials Juvenal symbolizes the crushing of the populace by the degenerate standards of Rome. Like a Juggernaut, the wagon has moved along, with inhuman indifference, and, in the disaster, it is impossible to separate the multilated bodies. In Rome, the individual has no significance in himself; to acquire distinction he must have the accidental attributes of wealth. By contrast, therefore, with the poor man's arduous progress through the crowd, Umbricius describes the easy passage of the rich man, floating over the heads of the masses in his comfortable litter (239–42).

Umbricius stands opposed to the total submersion of individuality in Rome, as the implicit advocate of the particular against the general, and Juvenal further supports the positive value of *solum* by special stress on *unus*.

> quamvis digressu veteris confusus amici
> laudo tamen, vacuis quod sedem figere Cumis
> destinet atque unum civem donare Sibyllae. (1–3)

---

[41] *Op. cit.*, p. 52.

sed dum tota domus raeda componitur una,
substitit ad veteres arcus madidamque Capenam. (10–11)
est aliquid, quocumque loco, quocumque recessu,
unius sese dominum fecisse lacertae. (230–1)

uno contentam carcere Romam. (314)

The special significance of *unus* serves to distinguish the unique from the general. But, in 3, it is uncertain whether Juvenal conveys a positive concept or whether he implies rather deprecatingly " at least one." Before the introduction ends, *unus* has acquired a clearly sympathetic connotation, in relation to Umbricius' poverty. In the later instances, *unus* implies simplicity, righteousness, and individuality. To be the master of a single lizard is preferable to being the slave of the masses. Among the old Roman ideals, that of *libertas*, the freedom to act within the limits of social responsibility, permitted a Roman to rise by his own merits, to be assessed by his political and moral achievements, not by his possessions. This ideal reacted against incorporation into a system or machine. Hence, the contemptuous attitude toward the *vulgus* as a monster, easily manipulated by its appetites and emotions. The true Roman is an upright individual. Juvenal, then, represents Umbricius as the single Roman facing the leveling process of the big city who ultimately recognizes that the force of mass standards has defeated him and leaves Rome. Once content with a single prison, Rome now requires many. The movement from a negative concept of *solum* as loneliness to a positive definition as individual independence is thus gradually effected by the use of *unus* and the implications of Umbricius' words.

We have seen that the introduction establishes a number of important contrasts. One more remains to be discussed; it occurs in the lines after the hyperbolic opening, when Juvenal lowers his tone and sets the scene for the speech of Umbricius. His description suggests another aspect of the vulgarizing influence of the city.

in vallem Egeriae descendimus et speluncas
dissimiles veris: quanto praesentius esset
numen aquae, viridi si margine cluderet undam
herba, nec ingenuum violarent marmora tofum! (17–20)

Artificial theories of beautification have violated the natural beauty of the fountain, and Juvenal stresses the picture, as if to impress upon us the characteristic of the environment which

Umbricius is forsaking. The region to which the emigrant goes has already been described as an ideal spot of natural beauty (4 ff.). In Rome, men violate Nature; in Cumae, she constitutes the only immediate attraction. The contrast between the vale of Egeria and the delightful bay of Cumae serves as the basis for the antithetical use of idyllic rural scenes which periodically interrupt the narrative of conditions at Rome (168 ff., 223 ff.). The natural state of things possesses a freshness, an innocence, that can exist only in the country; in Rome, innocence can only be violated, so that the cheap decoration of the fountain symbolizes the whole scale of tawdry values of the city. As the Satire proceeds, the innocence of Nature comes to represent the original Roman character, and, in the charm of the country, Juvenal sets former Roman customs, Roman clothes, and Roman values now discarded in Rome itself. Since the country really constitutes the last stronghold of the Roman character, Umbricius must withdraw to Cumae, because there alone a true Roman will find satisfaction.

Violation of innocence has many aspects. The antitype to rural serenity and comfort is the Rome of confusion, of fires, street brawls, and all the other indignities that oppress the poor man.

> quis timet aut timuit gelida Praeneste ruinam
> aut positis nemorosa inter iuga Volsiniis aut
> simplicibus Gabiis aut proni Tiburis arce?
> nos urbem colimus tenui tibicine fultam
> magne parte sui; nam sic labentibus obstat
> vilicus et, veteris rimae cum texit hiatum,
> securos pendente iubet dormire ruina. (190–6)

Umbricius pointedly compares the remote country, with its associations of primitiveness, to the city. Simplicity, however, has a certain integrity and security which the makeshift character of the New Rome cannot replace.

The new Rome has also violated the innocence of the past, as Juvenal implies in his description of the vale of Egeria. Once an idyllic spot associated with the romantic myth of Numa, it has been destroyed by the present tastes, rented out to foreigners for their petty trading activities. The past acts as the point of reference for the degeneracy of the present, since in the past are locked the traditions by which Rome acquired its greatness and which the present has rejected. Except for one specific allusion to trustworthy ancestors (137 ff.), however, Juvenal avoids references to early Romans, presumably because they

227

would detract from the exclusive value of Umbricius. As a living, vital survival of the pristine Rome, he stands as the criterion and his words and actions constitute the sole standard according to which the present Rome must be judged. Therefore, the past remains implicit in all that he says, pulsing through every attack, without undermining his solitary significance.

In his maladjustment to modern Rome, Umbricius makes a damning indictment of its standards (41 ff.). As if admitting his incompetence, he recites a list of occupations which a more adaptable and unscrupulous person could turn to good use. These occupations represent the standards by which Rome now lives, and Umbricius cannot fit into such a scheme. Behind Umbricius, however, rise the traditional criteria of *virtus* and *honestas* and *honor*. The present falsity and viciousness of human behavior denies everything that the past has taught.

In his introduction, Juvenal objects to the fact that the Jews have occupied the vale of Egeria and now have converted the grove of the Camenae into their marketplace. As he works out his contrasts in specific detail during the course of Umbricius' speech, he comes back to this insinuation against aliens and uses the complete success of the foreigner to establish himself in the city as an illustration of the general corruption. Umbricius opens his speech by showing that he, a true Roman, is completely unable to face the new conditions (21–57). From admitting his own incapacity, he immediately switches to an attack on the cleverness of the foreigner which has defeated him (58–125). He makes his general point at the beginning of the paragraph, then proceeds to illustrate it by numerous examples.

> non possum ferre, Quirites,
> Graecam urbem—quamvis quota portio faecis Achaei?
> iam pridem Syrus in Tiberim defluxit Orontes
> et linguam et mores et cum tibicine chordas
> obliquas nec non gentilia tympana secum
> vexit et ad circum iussas prostare puellas. (60–5)

Rome is no longer a place for him, precisely because he retains his Roman character; it has become a Greek city, or, even worse, an Oriental city which offers all its opportunities to the adaptable foreigners. Umbricius now reviews the list of crimes and machinations which lay beyond his ability and demonstrates that the elastic character of the Greek can accomplish anything (73 ff.). Where he angrily rejected pretense, the foreigners are different.

In the first place, they possess a native versatility which enables them to cope with any problem.

> ingenium velox, audacia perdita, sermo
> promptus et Isaeo torrentior: ede quid illum
> esse putes. quemvis hominem secum attulit ad nos. (73–5)

In the second place, they thrive on every form of deceit, being a nation of actors: *natio comoeda est* (100). The Greek city signifies a degenerate city, because it has accepted non-Roman standards of behavior. If Rome has become a Greek city, then the true Roman, in order to continue to be such, must leave her.

The alien element has corrupted the morality of the city, and most obviously in the development of luxurious tastes, the new materialistic standard of existence; for luxury is the sign of the foreigner. In the next section (126–89), Juvenal isolates the degeneracy, which has come into the city with the Oriental, in the artificial valuation placed on wealth. As a result of the materialistic standard, the poor man has become a social pariah, since wealth, the basis of luxurious existence, constitutes the prerequisite for social prestige. Umbricius, then, speaks of this artificial monetary standard as entrenched in Rome, as though no longer a foreign element at all. In fact, as the Greek city makes the Roman an alien in his own Rome, so the false estimate of money makes the traditional Roman ideal of simplicity disgraceful. The Greek entrepreneur has become a man of importance and, in effect, ostracized the Roman poor man who, caught up in the race for wealth and in the adulation of money, has no chance against his more important rivals (126–30).

From this point, Umbricius explores the poor man's claim (*pauperis hic meritum* 127), and we recall that limited resources and a simple existence once defined the Roman. The *pauper* is a sympathetic person, but he cannot exist in the present Rome as the noble person he once was. Rather, he provides a standard by which we can judge the extent of contemporary degeneracy. He himself has declined from his original position of eminence, as he has suffered the taint of luxurious Rome. The rich man despises his poorer fellow citizen and reduces him to a cipher; but the *pauper* shows that he shares the same materialistic estimate of life, because he envies the rich man (182). Therefore, the traditional value of *pauper* as a positive term has no significance in Rome, and it can recover its meaning only when the poor man abandons the city and its artificial standard of luxury.

> quantum quisque sua nummorum servat in arca,
> tantum habet et fidei. iures licet et Samothracum

et nostrorum aras, contemnere fulmina pauper
creditur atque deos dis ignoscentibus ipsis. (143–6)

The nice juxtaposition of *deos* and *dis* emphasizes the alienation of the poor man even from religion. The debased values of
the city have even affected the gods, raising Samothracian
deities above the members of the Roman pantheon, and such
gods would presumably share this non-Roman contempt for the
pauper.

> nil habet infelix paupertas durius in se,
> quam quod ridiculos homines facit. (152–3)

Men are no longer assessed for what they are, but for what they
have. The poor man yields to the sons of the most unscrupulous
of entrepreneurs, the brothel keepers, the auctioneers, and the
like (154 ff.). He does not even possess the old freedom to make
his way into prominence, for, when he tries to lift himself up, he
finds himself hampered by lack of funds (160 ff.). Roman simplicity has become, in the minds of this generation, *infelix
paupertas*.

To balance this picture of social inequality, cleavage between
the rich and the poor, the transvaluation of simplicity, Umbricius invokes one of his idyllic descriptions of rural Italy
(168 ff.). From its attractive associations, he returns to Rome
with a series of indignant phrases in anaphora.

> hic ultra vires habitus nitor, hic aliquid plus
> quam satis est interdum aliena sumitur arca.
> commune id vitium est: hic vivimus ambitiosa
> paupertate omnes. (180–3)

Every inhabitant of Rome is then involved in this materialistic
system and can escape it only by escaping the city. Rome has
degraded her ideals into vices and exalted the un-Roman standards that she once despised and censored to the position
vacated by her ideals. Rome has violated her own nature and
created a city of fires, noise, crowds, and crime which Umbricius
so tellingly describes as the conclusive argument for his departure (190–314). From that essential paradox have come the
series of interrelated contrasts illustrating the unbridgeable gap
between the traditions of the city and its present vicious conditions.

The simplification of the paradox into an antithesis between
the Roman standards and the non-Roman city may be seen

epitomized in the changed attitude expressed by Umbricius toward Daedalus.

> hic tunc Umbricius: ' quando artibus ' inquit ' honestis
> nullus in urbe locus, nulla emolumenta laborum,
> res hodie minor est here quam fuit atque eadem cras
> deteret exiguis aliquid, proponimus illuc
> ire, fatigatas ubi Daedalus exuit alas,
> dum nova canities, dum prima et recta senectus,
> dum superest Lachesi quod torqueat et pedibus me
> porto meis nullo dextram subeunte bacillo. (21–8)

> in summa non Maurus erat neque Sarmata nec Thrax
> qui sumpsit pennas, mediis set natus Athenis. (79–80)

Daedalus first appears as a representative of escape, another person like Umbricius, whom Juvenal describes on his arrival at Cumae, weary from his disastrous trip over the sea. The hypallage *fatigatas* emphasizes his weariness and seems to endow it with sympathetic epic connotations: In the second passage the very fact that Umbricius does not name Daedalus adds significance to his name, obvious as it is through the circumlocution. He now represents Greek ingenuity, capable of any crime, and significantly Juvenal describes him at the beginning of his audacious trip. For the dignified *alas*, he substitutes the contemptuous synecdoche *pennas* and contrasts the sound and rhythm of *Thrax* and *Athenis*, to emphasize Daedalus' foreign, non-Roman character. Now Daedalus has lost all his sympathetic associations, as if his arrival at Cumae commenced the series of Greek invasions which ultimately have made of Rome a Greek city. In going to Cumae, then, Umbricius takes refuge in the one place available to him, the beachhead of the Greeks, whence they swarmed over the city of Rome. Daedalus, potentially sympathetic in 25, has been stripped of his complex associations and in 80 symbolizes that infiltrating corruption which ultimately destroys contemporary Rome.

Daedalus can summarize the Satire, for its fundamental theme, a similar paradox, employs a similar form of exposition. Rome automatically possesses rich associations. Juvenal progressively strips them away, so that the city no longer remains the Rome of the past, but the Rome of Daedalus and other base foreigners. On the other hand, Cumae, which Juvenal originally views as wretched and solitary, acquires sympathetic associations, as the satirist takes those concepts of misery and loneliness and applies

231

them more appropriately to the environment of Rome. The first main section (21–190) explores *solum*, and, by gradually exposing Rome as non-Roman and Umbricius as the ideal Roman, by showing his total incompatibility with the city, it makes loneliness a valid criticism of the crowded metropolis. The sole Roman cannot find anyone to understand his concepts; he cannot discover an honest means of existence; and he is slowly crowded out by the foreign elements. The second main section (190–314) explores *miserum* primarily and, by depicting in detail the dangers and discomforts of the city, shows that wretchedness is a valid criticism of the luxurious city. Rome is, therefore, lonely and wretched because it has ceased to be Roman. The complex view of the city as good *and* bad, the moderate view of Horace, appears potentially in the opening paradox, but Juvenal quickly simplifies his self-contradictory phrase to a direct, emotional antithesis. Rome is totally bad, because totally un-Roman.

SATIRE 4

ecce iterum Crispinus, et est mihi saepe vocandus
ad partes, monstrum nulla virtute redemptum
a vitiis, aegrae solaque libidine fortes
deliciae: viduas tantum spernatur adulter. (1–4)

The fundamental problem of Satire 4 centers in explaining the relation of the opening section (1–36) to what follows (37 ff.). Juvenal has suffered severe criticism for his failure to establish a lucid connection and so unify the poem clearly. " The poem is certainly ill-constructed." [42] " Juvénal s'est trop longtemps attardé au cas de Crispinus, ce qui rend l'introduction disproportionnée et ce qui a fait croire—erronément, sans aucun doute —à la juxtaposition de deux fragments satiriques distincts." [43] De Decker here has accused the satirist of failing to maintain the requisite proportions. Those who, as he notes, posit the juxtaposition of two separate fragments have done so in order to preserve Juvenal's artistic reputation, yet have acted upon the same assumption, namely, that 1–36 disrupts the proportions of the rest of the Satire.[44] A compromise view also exists, according to which only a tenuous relation subsists between the two

[42] J. D. Duff, *D. Iunii Iuvenalis saturae XIV* (Cambridge, 1898), p. 173.
[43] De Decker, p. 74.
[44] Cf. Friedländer, Intro. to Satire 4.

parts; but the informal aspect of the genre provides a sufficient explanation of this disorder.[45]

Until recently, the most sympathetic treatment of the structure of Satire 4 came from W. Stegemann.[46] Instead of attacking the Satire for disproportion, Stegemann attempted to detect the unifying thread between 1–36 and 37 ff. According to his interpretation, several features of 1–36 serve a positive rhetorical function as introduction. In the first place, Juvenal announces his theme of *luxuria* when he attacks Crispinus as the typical example of extravagant dissoluteness in the imperial court. From him, the satirist effects his transition to Domitian by the rhetorical device of *gradatio*.[47] He describes Crispinus' outrageous expense on his *mullus* (15 ff.). Then, in the course of his preface, he insinuates the gluttony of the emperor (28–9); and finally he depicts in detail, in 37 ff., the ridiculous warcouncil over the proper culinary treatment of a *rhombus*. But despite the thematic relevance of the opening section, a problem still remains: the importance of Crispinus in 1–36 does not square with his relative insignificance in the second part (108–9). It is at this point that Stegemann made what I believe is his particular contribution to the understanding of the Satire and Juvenal's rhetorical technique in general. As he acutely observed, a significant difference in tone prevails between a mock epic and a direct attack through invective. Though not quite impersonal, mock epic is a genial form of satire, concealing its attacks behind a mask of fair words, where the artistry of the parody implies mild and well-controlled sentiments. But the biting attacks motivated by *indignatio* deliberately rip any artistic mask and express undisciplined fury. As the introduction to the mock-epic section, Stegemann suggested, 1–36 provide the satirist with a specific person to attack directly. By contrast with the immediate violence of indignation in 1–36, the more urbane tone of the mock epic has greater impact. This technique of passionate, hyperbolic openings, to provide a valuable contrast with the saner development of the main body of a Satire, has already been noted in our study of Satires 1 and 3. Here, the specific details invoked against a specific person lend the opening section vividness and make the indignation credible. Therefore, we can legitimately regard 1–36 as an introduction, since it exhibits thematic consistency with the mock epic in regard to *luxuria*,

[45] Cf. de Labriolle and Villeneuve, p. 37.
[46] *Op. cit.*, pp. 30 ff.
[47] For De Decker, p. 112, this *gradatio* is excessively clumsy.

and it provides a nice rhetorical contrast with the epic parody of 37 ff. Moreover, symmetry suggests a definite connection between the two sections of the Satire: " primum igitur de sceleri-bus Crispini locutus adiungit (i. e. Juvenalis) facta leviora v. 11 sqq.; his opponit nugas (cf. v. 150) imperatoris et in fine rursus ad scelera ascendit. Haec symmetria symmetriae quam in secunda satura invenimus . . . similis, certe consilio poetae tribuenda est." [48] Stegemann concludes, therefore: " Sic saturae integritate defensa . . ." as though the question of disproportion possesses no further validity.

As the only constructive approach until recently to the prob-lems of Satire 4, Stegemann's explanation deserves full credit, for it pointed the way to the excellent work of Helmbold and O'Neil.[49] As Stegemann indicated, Crispinus parallels Domitian, the central figure of the mock epic; and Helmbold and O'Neil have demonstrated a similarity between the two men in three primary respects: their overconcern with a fish; their frivolous perversions, and their vicious characters.[50] Crispinus, then, serves to isolate the central themes of the mock epic because of his relatively simple personality; yet, as the dramatic metaphor of 1 clearly implies, Crispinus in 1-27 merely masquerades as Domitian, the leading actor.[51] Furthermore, by selecting Crispi-nus, Juvenal effectively mocked his model, for Crispinus' " lurid unimportance " [52] qualifies Domitian and also explains the petty role Crispinus plays in the anecdote after the introduction.

It may seem captious to criticize so useful a theory; and, in fact, criticism must confine itself to the omissions, for what Helmbold and O'Neil have proposed seems eminently reasonable. Since, however, we are attempting to define Juvenal's structural methods, we should note several questions still remaining. First, we should emphasize the consequences of parallelism, the sharp transition between 27 and 34 which does not attempt to glide smoothly from Crispinus to Domitian. In fact, Juvenal seems to avoid smoothness and seek out the striking effect of comparing the emperor directly with the parasite of the Palatine. We may suggest, then, that the radical juxtaposition, so seriously criti-cized by earlier commentators, forms part of Juvenal's rhetorical technique of emphasis. Second, we should consider carefully Ste-

---

[48] Stegemann, p. 33.
[49] W. C. Helmbold and E. N. O'Neil, " The Structure of Juvenal IV," *AJP*, 77 (1956), 68-73. Their criticism of Highet seems just.
[50] *Ibid.*, p. 70.
[51] *Ibid.*, p. 71.
[52] *Ibid.*, p. 73.

gemann's proposal, that Juvenal's rhetorical purpose of personal attack required a direct statement of the problem in an out-spoken onslaught on Crispinus before he could embark upon the less obvious criticisms of his mock epic. That is, we lack an explanation for the change in poetic tone as well as for the transition from Crispinus to Domitian. Third, we have not clearly isolated a theme, and we should perhaps consider whether Juvenal has selected a subject analogous in form to those of Satire 1–3 and presented it as a gradually simplified paradox. It is primarily with this third question that this study will concern itself.

Let us begin, then, by returning to Stegemann's theory of sym-metry. As an ideal of formal composition, particularly for Juve-nal's time, symmetry possesses dubious value and can justify itself only by a rhetorical function linking related themes.[53] Stegemann indicated the relation as follows: *scelera: nugae:: nugae: scelera*; but he failed to note the important difference in degree between the *scelera*, a difference which directly affects Juvenal's thematic exposition. Crispinus' crimes, presented in vague generalizations (2–4), then gradually specified (4–10), consist mostly of immoral relations with women and fondness for display. Hence, they easily shade off into the theme of *luxuria*. In the counterpart to 1–10, Juvenal introduces Domi-tian's *scelera* in a different manner.

> atque utinam his potius nugis tota illa dedisset
> tempora saevitiae, claras quibus abstulit urbi
> inlustresque animas inpune et vindice nullo!
> sed periit postquam Cerdonibus esse timendus
> coeperat: hoc nocuit Lamiarum caede madenti. (150–4)

The treatment of the *rhombus* episode has involved epic parody and the rich associations of imperial war councils and inter-national crises. When, therefore, Juvenal makes his transition back to crimes, he does it gradually and maintains the grandness of tone. The outrages of Domitian, far from being petty matters of sexual indulgence and sheer display, aim at ruthless destruc-tion of the nobility and a tyrannical rule that could be checked only by his own brutal hirelings. The symmetry, then, does not represent an artificial achievement of form, dictated by a desire

---

[53] Stegemann referred to his study of symmetry in Satire 2. Neither there (p. 21) nor in Satire 4 (p. 33) does he note the rhetorical function of sym-metry, apparently because he regarded the very existence of symmetry sufficient evidence of an artistic purpose, e. g. " certe consilio poetae tribuenda est."

for proportion; rather, it serves as an artistic device for pointing out the latent implications of a theme. Where once *scelera* were manifested in sensual corruption (*deliciae*), they now have acquired the simpler and more emotional connotations of savagery (*saevitia*).

The thematic relevance of the symmetry and the characteristic application of simplification to *scelera* suggest that the subject of the Satire might be more adequately interpreted in conformance with those of Satire 1–3. The opening lines, in fact, introduce more than the mere theme of *luxuria*. The key words occur in 3–4, where Juvenal has placed *fortes* in an emphatic metrical position, at the end of its line, in enjambment with the word it modifies. He thus contrives in *libidine fortes / deliciae* a phrase of oxymoron, for luxurious indulgence connotes softness and effeminacy, not strength. Accordingly, *fortes* provides a contrasting quality to the general atmosphere of sensuousness; it suggests manliness, which, associated with *deliciae*, creates a contradiction in terms, indeed, the tentative, paradoxical announcement of a theme which appears again in the introduction.

> qualis tunc epulas ipsum gluttisse putamus
> induperatorem, cum tot sestertia, partem
> exiguam et modicae sumptam de margine cenae,
> purpureus magni ructarit scurra Palati
> iam princeps equitum, magna qui voce solebat
> vendere municipes fracta de merce siluros? (28–33)

Juvenal has used irony throughout this passage, especially in the phrase: *gluttisse putamus induperatorem*, where *induperatorem*, both archaic and epic, clashes sharply not only with *gluttisse*, but with the whole context. The same clash occurs in *purpureus scurra*, *princeps equitum*. At the beginning, we observed an implicit paradox in *fortes deliciae*; in this passage, the paradox becomes explicit. The satirist is working from a self-contradiction between luxury and manliness to a precise antithesis between sensual indulgence and the military values associated with Roman government. Thus the venerable *induperatorem* introduces a value which Domitian cannot legitimately claim, not when he can also be characterized with the term *gluttisse*. Slowly, now, Juvenal transforms *fortes* into a positive concept, a polar opposite to *deliciae*. But *induperatorem* fulfills a further function: to prepare a transition to the second section (37 ff.). Here, Juvenal uses a tentative epic parody in the single ironic archaism; subsequently, he will employ a consistent parody,

236

where the whole context, rhythm, and vocabulary largely connote epic.

Having suggested the paradox of imperial qualities and gluttony, the satirist makes his transition, explaining the quality of epic which is to follow.

> incipe, Calliope. licet et considere: non est
> cantandum, res vera agitur. narrate, puellae
> Pierides: prosit mihi vos dixisse puellas! (34-6)

This passage represents a careful preparation for the parody in mock epic. Epic exploits the fabulous, when its fiction has to be made interesting by artificial adornments; but truth has sufficient impact in itself. This Juvenal says, then immediately jumps into epic. Logically, such a procedure raises questions, but rhetorically it serves as *praesumptio*, to emphasize the incongruity of Juvenal's subject and prepare the reader to view the scene with appropriate antipathy. Having denied the relevance of epic to this theme, the satirist can expect his audience to realize the absurdity of the situation, yet sense the second implication of epic. As used in 37 ff., epic connotes the ridiculous and the grand simultaneously, and Juvenal exploits this ambivalence. Although epic employs imaginary situations, it does present standards of heroism and patriotic self-sacrifice which implicitly comment on the court of Domitian. By definition, then, epic reinforces the military theme and gives it grandeur and definite polarity to the situation in Rome. Applied to the episode of the *rhombus*, epic shows up the disparity between the fish and the urgent affairs which should concern men of state. In 37 ff., accordingly, Juvenal continues the contrast between *deliciae* and *fortes*, gradually separating them off as antithetical terms, as the epic frame makes a new and more salient comment on each of these concepts.

So the epic, clearly undermined as mock epic, begins to clarify the paradox of the introduction.

> cum iam semianimum laceraret Flavius orbem
> ultimus et calvo serviret Roma Neroni,
> incidit Adriaci spatium admirabile rhombi
> ante domum Veneris, quam Dorica sustinet Ancon,
> implevitque sinus; nec enim minor haeserat illis
> quos operit glacies Maeotica ruptaque tandem
> solibus effundit torrentis ad ostia Ponti
> desidia tardos et longo frigore pingues. (37-44)

The clarification starts immediately in 37–8 with *laceraret* and *serviret*. These words do not belong in the ordinary Roman epic, where a Roman emperor would never be exalted as the scourge of the world, and Rome would never be said to serve anyone. Juvenal is expanding his theme. For the present, he has assumed as the standard of valuation the manliness which won the Roman empire and made the city great. When manliness is forgotten, men tend to forget their responsibilities and enjoy the products of the imperial power, debasing themselves in its materialistic advantage. Manliness disintegrates and servitude becomes possible. In the other direction, though, and, paradoxically, concomitant with the effeminate concerns of *luxuria*, comes the development of the despotic temperament. So *virtus* becomes exaggerated into *saevitia*, an insane violence for the mere thrill of it. The epic section of this Satire explores the breakdown of *virtus* into these correlative extremes, epic and its connotations functioning as the implicit criterion of judgment.

Juvenal does not, however, employ a continuous epic, but interrupts the noble epic flow intermittently with angry questions or a sardonic epigram. This technique has suffered severe criticism as merely a declamatory practice.[54] However, we may apply Stegemann's suggestion as to the rhetorical function of the introduction to such interruptions, too. To qualify the impersonal, distant attitude of epic, we may suggest, Juvenal repeatedly punctuates his parody with rhetorical questions and epigrams, in order to voice a direct, angry reaction toward a situation which is potentially only humorous. Then, returning to his epic, he again exploits the alteration in tone. At any rate, the interruptions consistently demonstrate the pursuit of contrast. In the above citation the satirist sets the scene in magniloquent terms, describing the capture of a colossal turbot near Ancona. He continues:

> destinat hoc monstrum cumbae linique magister
> pontifici summo. quis enim proponere talem
> aut emere auderet, cum plena et litora multo
> delatore forent? (45–8)

As soon as he has stated the purpose of the fisherman to give his catch to Domitian, the satirist makes his direct comment, an interruption of considerable extent (46–56), which starts pointedly with a rhetorical question, at the central caesura, after a highly colored epic phrase, *pontifici summo*. Epic and direct

---

[54] Cf. De Decker, pp. 182, 186.

comment thus come into a violent clash, and Juvenal uses the emotional epic phrase as the stimulus for his angry question and acid comment on the despotic character of the Empire. He then returns to epic after an angry *sententia*.

> si quid Palfurio, si credimus Armillato,
> quidquid conspicuum pulchrumque est aequore toto,
> res fisci est, ubicumque natat: donabitur ergo,
> ne pereat. (53–6)

The satirist's immediate interpretation halts at the trihemimeral caesura, where the epic takes over, in a skillfully contrived clash, with a rich description in anaphora. The interlude, in addition to its emotional implications, has also functioned to clarify the theme, and this final comment expresses the relation between the correlative aspects of degeneracy, the luxury of Domitian and his tyrannic temper, which appropriates whatever appeals to his jaded tastes.

The intimidated fisherman brings his gigantic *rhombus* to Domitian; in the next epic portion, Juvenal further exposes the contrast between epic and the directly satiric.

> itur ad Atriden. tum Picens ' accipe ' dixit
> ' privatis maiora focis. genialis agatur
> iste dies; propera stomachum laxare sagina
> et tua servatum consume in saecula rhombum:
> ipse capi voluit.' quid apertius? et tamen illi
> surgebant cristae; nihil est quod credere de se
> non possit cum laudatur dis aequa potestas. (65–71)

Again, the break between the two styles (69) occurs at the central caesura, emphasized by the irate rhetorical question, as the inconsequence of the servile address in the mock epic dissolves into indignation.[55] Once again, the parallel concepts of *luxuria* and *saevitia* impregnate the context, for the obsequious tone of the fisherman and his epic grace both emphasize the despotic attitude of Domitian, who has terrorized even his humblest subjects. Furthermore, the military symbol, suggested again in *capi*, eases the transition to the next section of epic, preparing a context for the council of war over the captive fish.

---

[55] Duff, *ad loc.*, aptly suggested that *animum laxare*, a common epic phrase, is being parodied in *stomachum laxare*. He failed, however, to observe that Juvenal creates a consistent tone of epic in certain sections. Thus he criticized *saecula* as a word employed only for metrical reasons, whereas the poetic plural, in my opinion, functions appropriately to maintain the epic mood.

The summoning of the council of war, to decide how to serve the turbot (72 ff.), serves as the occasion for Juvenal to sketch in salient detail the personalities of the important courtiers of Domitian's time. In accordance with his theme, he concentrates on two traits, *luxuria* and *saevitia*. First comes Pegasus, the pretorian prefect, but no better than a *vilicus*, since he is utterly subject to the will of his master Domitian.

> anne aliud tum praefecti? quorum optimus atque
> interpres legum sanctissimus omnia, quamquam
> temporibus diris, tractanda putabat inermi
> iustitia.   (78–81)

The military symbol provides the standard by which Juvenal criticizes the behavior of Pegasus. Domitian's rule really constitutes a time of war (*temporibus diris*); yet Justice, which would be administered by the prefect, is without arms, defenseless. The emperor can work his savage will, while those who should be defending Justice spend their time anxiously determining the fate of a turbot.

Next comes old Crispus, who is equally timid and equally interested in his own safety before anything else.

> maria ac terras populosque regenti
> quis comes utilior, si clade et pesta sub illa
> saevitiam damnare et honestum adferre liceret
> concilium? sed quid violentius aure tyranni? (83–6)
>
> sic multas hiemes atque octogensima vidit
> solstitia, his armis illa quoque tutus in aula. (92–3)

The war image becomes more specific this time, as Juvenal removes the uncertainty of the enemy referred to in *temporibus diris* and *inermi*. It is Domitian who acts as the foe; in fact, he represents a military disaster (*clade*) threatening the courtiers and the Empire. Juvenal characterizes the servile manners of Crispus as a means of defense against ruin (*his armis*), for, at the court of the tyrant, military values have been so degraded that they can function as a symbol for flattery. On another level, though, they describe accurately the rule of Domitian, as Juvenal interprets its effect upon Rome.

In 107 ff. Juvenal swiftly reviews several of the courtiers, having already made his general point in the detailed sketches of Pegasus, Crispus, and the Acilii (94–103).

> Montani quoque venter adest abdomine tardus,
> et matutino sudans Crispinus amomo

> quantum vix redolent duo funera: saevior illo
> Pompeius tenui iugulos aperire susurro,
> et qui vulturibus servabat viscera Dacis,
> Fuscus, marmorea meditatus proelia villa,
> et cum mortifero prudens Veiiento Catullo. (107–13)

The details emphasize respectively *luxuria* and *saevitia*, but *saevitia* now in the courtiers themselves. Juvenal depicts Montanus, Crispinus, and Veiiento each in terms of one salient trait connoting luxury: gluttony, a fondness for perfumes, and cautious servility. On the other hand, he describes Pompeius as a cutthroat, Fuscus as a combination of luxury and militarism, and Catullus as murderous. The portraits bring into focus what the satirist implies about the reign of Domitian: that the courtiers directly reflect their master. Manliness, degraded into effeminacy or vicious brutality, has disappeared.

When the council gathers and its members realize the imperial crisis, they begin to give their opinions as to the wisest policy. Inspired ironically by Bellona, Veiiento prophesies as if the *rhombus* portended military conquest. That the obsequious, cautious Veiiento should have any relation to the goddess of war is patently incongruous, and Juvenal exposes the complete absence of martial spirit by selecting him as the mouthpiece for the prophecy. However, Montanus makes the cleverest proposal.

> argillam atque rotam citius properate! sed ex hoc
> tempore iam, Caesar, figuli tua castra sequantur.
> vicit digna viro sententia. (134–6)

The martial metaphor occurs twice here, to emphasize the glaring inconsistency between the subject of this council and the true purpose of Empire. Potters represent an incongruity as vital elements in the military train, and, in *vicit*, the military standard has again been debased to the uses of luxury. To stress the significance of this *sententia*, Juvenal describes the frivolous tastes of Montanus in detail (136–43). Then he makes the importance of this council obvious by contrasting it with what would ordinarily be the function of such a gathering.

> surgitur et misso proceres exire iubentur
> consilio, quos Albanam dux magnus in arcem
> traxerat attonitos et festinare coactos,
> tamquam de Chattis aliquid torvisque Sygambris

> dicturus, tamquam diversis partibus orbis
> anxia praecipiti venisset epistula pinna. (144–9)

This has been a military council, it is clear; words like *dux* and *arcem* cannot be interpreted otherwise. But, where a vigorous and manly council would have been concerned with the invasions of the German barbarians, this group of degenerates has expended its effort on a fish.

The turbot can be interpreted as a symbol not merely of luxury but of the Empire and what Domitian has done to it by his despotism, as we may infer from Juvenal's ambivalent use of words. In 45, he describes the fish as *monstrum*; this same word he applies to Crispinus in 2 and to Veiiento in 115. The relation between the courtiers and the fish may be defined as follows: Domitian has made his confidants something unnatural; the extraordinary turbot belongs to him because the tyrant appropriates anything unusual. The physical enormity of the *rhombus*, then, ideally symbolizes the sensual and moral enormity of the court, for both suffer the violence of Domitian, and the court is a microcosm of the Empire.

Moreover, we may indicate a significant interrelation between the following three passages.

> cum iam semianimum laceraret Flavius orbem (37)

> quidnam igitur censes? conciditur? (130)

> > testa alta paretur,
> quae tenui muro spatiosum colligat orbem. (131–2)

In 37 *orbem* designates the imperial world; in 132, in the same metrical position, it refers to the shape of the fish. In 37, *laceraret* describes Domitian's tyranny, as though he were tearing to pieces the world; in 130, *conciditur* denotes one of the alternative proposals of the emperor as to the serving of the turbot. Moreover, the crisis of the fish has demanded the consideration of an imperial war council, and Juvenal can comment that the fate of the Empire possesses less significance than that of the *rhombus*. In part the military metaphor has been so developed as to imply an actual state of war, war between the emperor and his court, between the emperor and the Empire. Against this imminent disaster, people are completely defenseless, and they react as servilely as the fish, which wanted to be captured. Thus just as Domitian exploits the world to gratify his savagery and sensuousness, just as he has perverted his courtiers into servile panderers to and representatives of his degraded *virtus*, so the turbot becomes the object of his debased appetite, to be cut up and enjoyed. Interpreted this way, the *rhombus* epitomizes the three main themes of the poem: *virtus, saevitia,* and *luxuria.* As the object of the war-council's deliberations, it points up the traditional martial values and the way they have been perverted to the service of a vicious glutton. The Empire no longer represents a goal to be won by patriotic sacrifice, to be guarded with vigor, and to be maintained in prosperous security; it now exists only for the exploitation of the tyrant of Rome. The essential quality of Roman manhood, *virtus,* has perished and in its place has arisen a monster, a compound of luxurious effeminacy and vicious savagery, exaggerations in either direction from the ideal mean of manliness, both illustrative of the self-gratification which would prompt an emperor to make a fish a matter of imperial urgency.

While the emphasis of Crispinus in 1–36 creates serious difficulties, the opening lines do serve a definite thematic function as introduction. In Crispinus we meet a monster whose typical qualities may be described as powerful sensuality (*libidine fortes deliciae*). The paradox of these words announces the theme of the Satire, which will concern itself with clarification. Moreover, by using Crispinus, Juvenal takes advantage of the antagonism evoked by a real person when prejudicially treated. Thus, he starts his Satire on a hyperbolic note of indignation, so that, by contrast, the mock epic of the main section seems calm and convincing. In his transition (28–36), the satirist begins to distinguish luxury and manliness, preparing for subsequent simplification of terms.

The mock epic concerns itself with a monster, too—a gigantic turbot. As Crispinus serves to present the theme through paradox, so the fish draws to itself and clarifies the two debased forms of *virtus: luxuria* and *saevitia;* and the mock epic form serves as an implicit standard of ironical reference, the representative of the now mythical Roman courage. Moreover, to make his standard explicit, Juvenal repeatedly interrupts his epic with indignant remarks. He elaborates *luxuria* and *saevitia* together as concomitant evidence of degeneracy and thus divides the courtiers between those traits. Domitian possesses both vices to a supreme degree. As the crucial question of the council, the tyrant demands advice on dealing with the *rhombus:* how can he best enjoy it, by cutting it up or by cooking it whole? In the end, luxury determines the decision. Because, however, savagery remains more typical of Domitian, Juvenal adds a final comment on the tyrant's death. Thus the episode concerning the turbot takes the vague terms of Crispinus' description and simplifies them into black-and-white clarity, while its mock-epic form ennobles the original tone and supports the transition to the tragic summary of the final lines. As the focus of the imperial savagery and luxuriousness, the *rhombus* symbolizes the Empire. It is because Domitian exhibits his characteristic *luxuria* and *saevitia* even on a fish—it is because, in fact, the fish possesses more importance for him than the Empire—that his ultimate murder can be regarded as a fitting end to this Satire. As in Satire 1–3, Juvenal has brilliantly elucidated his paradox between the limits represented by the symmetry of Crispinus' and Domitian's *scelera*.

SATIRE 5

> si te propositi nondum pudet atque eadem est mens,
> ut bona summa putes aliena vivere quadra,
> si potes illa pati quae nec Sarmentus iniquas
> Caesaris ad mensas, nec vilis Gabba tulisset,
> quamvis iurato metuam tibi credere testi. (1–5)

Satire 5 is not an obscure poem, and commentators have, for the most part, observed its principal themes.[56] Juvenal adopts a straightforward method of presentation, using Trebius as an imaginary interlocutor and constantly repeating the limited point he is interested in making. He represents Trebius as a poor client who places high value on the possession of money and the sensuous pleasures of the table which it makes possible. In order to parody the ignoble standards of Trebius, Juvenal starts out with the language of ethical discussions (*propositi, mens, bona summa*). Even an Epicurean would hardly identify his moral goal with a banquet, so that Trebius' servility exposes him as a man of superficial values.

> tantine iniuria cenae,
> tam ieiuna fames, cum possit honestius illic
> et tremere et sordes farris mordere canini? (9–11).

Not only are his values superficial, however; they are implicitly slavish. If he endured the ignominy of the rich man's banquet, he would be inferior to the ignoble Sarmentus and Gabba. But the satirist pretends to believe that Trebius would never submit to such indignities and, at the start, clearly distinguishes him from

[56] Highet, pp. 83 ff., has treated Satire 5 excellently.

the buffoons. Even the freedom of a beggar, he suggests, would be more honorable (*honestius*) than the slavery of a client, even the food of a dog better than being the pawn of a rich man. With the emphatic *canini*, Juvenal ends the opening paragraph, since he has announced his theme in his typical manner. At the beginning, as a client, deserving much yet content with the contemptuous treatment of the last-minute invitation (17), Trebius possesses several qualities which render him the object of a paradox. As his structural plan, Juvenal will gradually strip away the traditional associations of clientship and leave only the ignoble ones imposed by Virro and accepted by Trebius.

In the rest of the Satire, Juvenal attempts to prove the life of a neglected client worse than a dog's, worse even than a real slave's. As we might expect, the final paragraph summarizes his theme.

> forsitan inpensae Virronem parcere credas?
> hoc agit, ut doleas; nam quae comoedia, mimus
> quis melior plorante gula?

> tu tibi liber homo et regis conviva videris:
> captum te nidore suae putat ille culinae,
> nec male coniectat.

> ille sapit qui te sic utitur: omnia ferre
> si potes, et debes. pulsandum vertice raso
> praebebis quandoque caput nec dura timebis
> flagra pati, his epulis et tali dignus amico. (156–73)

With his reference to *comoedia* (157) and *pati* (173), Juvenal recalls the comparison at the beginning between Trebius and the buffoons Sarmentus and Gabba. Trebius has now stooped to the role of a fool amusing his master at the table, but suffering indignities that the court buffoons would never have endured. Gone is the honor of the client. He may still entertain the grandiose illusion that he is dining with a king; but he consumes his wretched meal, not in the position of honored guest, as he fondly thinks, but in that of a captive. He has become, worse than a fool, a slave deserving the buffets and arbitrary ill treatment which a slave suffers. His roseate views of himself as a free man, as a royal guest, show that he still cannot perceive the truth of the situation; but the fact of his servility is undeniable. The complex character of the eager banqueter has been simplified to a single salient trait.

Between the paradoxical stating of the theme and the con-

cluding simplification, the main section of the Satire concentrates
on the antithesis of slave and king, as noted by commentators.
Juvenal repeatedly refers to the rich man as *rex* or *dominus* (14,
71, 81, 130, 137, 161). Trebius himself thinks of Virro as a king
(161), but ironically he believes that the correlative term for
himself should be *liber homo*. Juvenal, however, makes the point
that it is tantamount to confessing one's own slavery to regard
a rich man as king. After the opening paragraph, he leaves the
slave theme unstated, but implicit in the whole detailed description of the banquet. To add to the poignancy of Trebius'
self-delusion, a slave thinking of himself as a royal guest freely
accepting a gracious invitation, Juvenal recalls the clientship of
many years. In 19 ff. he describes that period of loyal service
indirectly; in 76 ff. he puts the description in the mouth of Trebius, who complains in bitter bewilderment at the treatment he
is receiving, on the grounds that a client deserves better consideration from his *patronus*. As a client, though, who sets more
store by wealth than freedom, he deserves what he actually
receives; for he is, in effect, denying his own independence.
However, Juvenal does not leave the rich man untouched, and, in
two digressions which interrupt the general course of the Satire,
he introduces some considerations on the responsibility of wealth
(107 ff. and 132 ff.). In 107 ff. he compares the stingy ways of
Virro with the munificence of men like Seneca and Piso and
climaxes this with one simple request: *solum poscimus ut cenes
civiliter* (111–12). Just as Trebius has sunk below his Roman
birthright as a free citizen, so Virro, by exalting himself above
the level of his fellow-citizen, has ceased to be a Roman. He has
become an Oriental despot. Trebius and Virro, slave and king,
represent the cleavage that has occurred among the Roman
citizenry as a result of the materialism of the present, to which
both Virro and Trebius have subjected themselves.

> quadringenta tibi si quis deus aut similis dis
> et melior fatis donaret homuncio, quantus
> ex nihilo, quantus fieres Virronis amicus!
> ' da Trebio, pone ad Trebium! vis, frater, ab ipsis
> ilibus? ' o nummi! vobis hunc praestat honorem,
> vos estis fratres! (132–7)

The only thing that can establish a firm relation between two
people is money. In fact, as Juvenal puts it, money itself counts
as a brother; money has acquired the connotations of family
affections. Virro cherishes standards no different from those of

his plaything Trebius, but he possesses the money to gratify his sensuality.

Not all commentators have accepted these digressions as integral portions of the Satire. Some praise the construction highly, as Heinrich did. " Carmen est ex pulcherrimis, locuplete rerum descriptione pariter ad delectandum et ad docendum aptissimum." [57] On the other hand, Friedländer severely attacked it. " Während es nun das Natürlichste gewesen wäre, die durch die Reihenfolge der Gange gegebene Ordnung durchweg festzuhalten, hat Juvenal sich auch hier nicht enthalten konnen, sie durch ungehörige Abschweifungen und Einschaltungen wiederholt zu unterbrechen und so den Zusammenhang zu zerstören." [58] In accordance with this judgment, Friedländer regarded 137–45 as a particularly purposeless interruption.[59]

> dominus tamen et domini rex
> si vis tunc fieri, nullus tibi parvolus aula
> luserit Aeneas nec filia dulcior illo.
> sed tua nunc Micale pariat licet et pueros tres
> in gremium patris fundat semel: ipse loquaci
> gaudebit nido, viridem thoraca iubebit
> adferri minimasque nuces assemque rogatum,
> ad mensam quotiens parasitus venerit infans.

Juvenal indulges his quixotic humor perhaps, but without digressing from his point. In his selection of details, he illustrates the dominant role that money plays even in the family relationship. Virro, the king, acts subservient to the same materialistic standards as Trebius. The satirist, therefore, imagines the case where Trebius suddenly becomes wealthy and takes a concubine who cannot give him legitimate children. Under such conditions, Trebius would become a king, and Virro would humble himself to court the favor of Trebius as a *captator*.[60] Materialism is supreme.

The thematic continuity of the poem remains obvious, as it is worked out in the manner typical of Juvenal, by clarification of a paradox. However, except for the key word *rex* and interruptions like the above, most of the specific articulation of the theme resides in the symmetric portions of beginning and end. The

[57] *Op. cit.*, Intro. to Satire 5.

[58] *Op. cit.*, p. 256.

[59] *Ad loc.*: " Eine selbst bei J. durch ihre Ungehörigkeit auffallende Einschaltung."

[60] For a different interpretation of this passage, cf. Highet, p. 145.

central section of the Satire (24–155), according to the general theory, functions as an illustration of the slave-king antithesis.[61] However, commentators have consistently ignored Juvenal's rhetorical methods, in order to localize the antithesis specifically in the particular items of food served. It has apparently occurred to few scholars what a *tour de force* Juvenal has contrived in providing the reader with contrasting menus, the first to reveal the fine food served Virro, the other to show up the contrastingly foul dishes set before his client Trebius. Nothing could be more inherently unpoetic. If, however, the food itself were the important aspect of the exposition and nothing else, Juvenal would not require the poetic framework, the extensive verbiage in which he wraps each item. Yet it is in such unpoetic terms that the construction of this main section is visualized. Juvenal's methods demand a fuller exposition, for the expansion of a mere menu into a thematic illustration depends upon his rhetorical handling of the contrasting items of the two menus.

> Virro sibi et reliquis Virronibus illa iubebit
> poma dari, quorum solo pascaris odore,
> qualia perpetuus Phaeacum autumnus habebat,
> credere quae possis subrepta sororibus Afris:
> tu scabie frueris mali, quod in aggere rodit,
> qui tegitur parma et galea metuensque flagelli
> discit ab hirsuta iaculum torquere capella. (149–55)

As the description of a menu, this would be a verbose means of stating the difference between two apples. However, Juvenal shows less concern with the objective entity of the menu than with a purpose of provoking an emotional response towards each item on the list. Therefore, he does not present the food as a mere bill of fare; therefore, too, he interrupts the straightforward development of the meal with digressions or long qualification, in order to destroy the impression of a mere menu. The contrast between *poma* and *mali* inheres in the relative clauses attached to each apple. Juvenal associates Virro's apple with the rich orchards of Phaeacia and the Garden of the Hesperides; Trebius' with the wizened apple which a miserable recruit would gnaw; and through these qualifying terms he influences the reaction toward the whole meal. Merely to state a theme is not enough. Juvenal proves his point stated in the opening lines; he convinces the reader of his assessment of Trebius by exploiting the contrast of dishes in the fullest rhetorical manner. By a pro-

---

[61] E. g. Macleane and Friedländer, intros.

gression of emotionally tinged antitheses, he gives the food of Virro the most attractive connotations, while surrounding the fare of Trebius with the most disgusting. Thus the meal illustrates Trebius' slavery, and its emotional impact prepares us to accept the exclusive definition of the poor client at the end of the poem: Trebius is a mere slave.

Juvenal exposes the richness of the food set before Virro in a series of descriptive phrases qualifying the particular items of his banquet. His wine connotes the distant past, when consuls wore beards, and the freedom-loving era, when Thrasea and Helvidius toasted the tyrannicides on their birthdays (30 ff.). His jeweled cup acquires the epic associations of Aeneas, in the romantic context of the hero's sojourn in Carthage (48 ff.). His slaves, the flower of Asia, are viewed from the perspective of early regal Rome (56 ff.). An exotic aura surrounds his mullet, as derived from the allusions to distant spots, Corsica and Taormina, and poetic phrases about Charybdis (92 ff.).

> Virroni muraena datur, quae maxima venit
> gurgite de Siculo; nam dum se continet Auster,
> dum sedet et siccat madidas in carcere pinnas,
> contemnunt mediam temeraria lina Charybdim. (99–102)

The boar set before Virro receives the epic associations attached to Meleager. The mushrooms he eats resemble those that once graced the imperial table of Claudius (147). All these varied associations inspire more or less detailed imaginary pictures of the scenes mentioned in sketchy outline, and, in their cumulative effect, give the banquet of Virro the romantic quality of epic, the stirring note of Roman history, and the allure of distance. Virro actually becomes a king through this rhetorical construction, and in this way Juvenal confirms the prejudice of his reader.

Around the meal of Trebius accumulate an antithetic series of connotations. His wine is described in terms of the drunken brawls of the Corybantes (25 ff.), and he must fight a war with his table companions. The broken cup from which he drinks once belonged to a wretched tailor of Beneventum (46 ff.). The slave that serves him provokes the picture of a lonely spot at night and the fear of a highwayman (54 ff.). The oil with which he garnishes his food introduces squalid Africa, the skiff from Micipsae, and the uncouth-sounding name of Bocchar (86 ff.). With difficulty he consumes an eel which has loathsome associations with the Cloaca Maxima (103 ff.). Moreover, any indelicate behavior on his part is threatened with the same summary severity which Hercules displayed toward Cacus (125 ff.). Except for this last vignette, all the associations attached to Trebius avoid epic, and, even in this epic allusion, he does not assume the glorious role of Hercules; rather, he tries to avoid being dragged ignobly from the banquet like Cacus. Juvenal allows nothing attractive, romantic, or glorious to color the meal of Trebius, whose food, appropriate to the man, consistently evokes the mean, ignoble, and worthless.

Of a menu, Juvenal has made poetry. His shrewd rhetorical handling has, in effect, made each particular meal the symbol of the man. Virro consumes a lordly meal, and the associations with epic and the romantic past symbolize his qualities of kingship. In fact, they so overstress his position that he emerges from these connotations a king, but a king who is humbled by the people with whom he has been matched. His kingship constitutes a travesty of the true heroic monarchy; his is a fictitious regality based on the possession of money, the ability to manipulate individuals through their appetites and reverence for his wealth. Similarly, by attaching entirely different associations to the meal of Trebius, Juvenal has created an increasingly convincing picture of servility. By manipulation of details, he has transformed a bare theme and a prosaic subject into something that stirs definite emotional reactions from his readers. A series of antithetic dishes, enhanced by appropriate associations, have formed the heart of the Satire, confirming the fundamental theme of slave and king.

CONCLUSION

We have now considered the first five Satires of Juvenal and may attempt a conclusion applicable to the principles of composition in the satirist's most consistently successful work, Book I.[62] To a certain extent, our generalizations may have validity for later books, but we cannot affirm their relevance prior to more detailed study.

If we treat the subject matter as the basic structural unit in a Satire, we conclude, as might be expected, that the traditional description of Juvenal's themes as simple statements has correctly stated the facts. On the other hand, we cannot support the inferences of those who have defined these themes in terms

[62] For Book II—that is, Satire 6—cf. my study, " Juvenal 6: A Problem in Structure," *CP*, 51 (1956), 73-94, especially p. 74 on the general question of structure.

of diatribes or rhetorical theses.[63] Such definitions have regularly led to an avoidance of the main issue, namely how Juvenal exploits a simple theme for satiric purposes that vary strikingly from the goals of both the diatribe and the thesis. It seems best, therefore, to discard misleading categorizations in terms of alien genres and return to our original point of agreement: Juvenal exploits a simple theme. From here, we can advance to a more exact definition of this simplicity, by direct reference to the contents of Satires 1–5.

As we have isolated them in Book I, Juvenal's themes assume a fairly predictable form. By doing some violence to them we can reduce them to a single radical assertion, e. g. satire is the truly tragic genre (Satire 1); or, a tolerant guest like Trebius is really a slave (Satire 5). To put it more specifically, Juvenal selects in Book I a theme which depends upon a self-contradiction or, as we have frequently put it, upon a paradox. In Satire 1, for instance, Juvenal claims that satire can replace tragedy, epic, and all grand poetry as though, indeed, satire were grand poetry and his indignation attacked actual conditions of tragedy in Rome. Strictly speaking, however, satire never can exalt itself into the confines of another genre, although the stylistic changes of Juvenal do bring it closer to grand poetry than it ever came before him.[64] However, this thematic self-contradiction between satire and grand poetry does motivate Juvenal's structural technique in Satire 1.

A paradox should not be examined too carefully, as any close reader of St. Paul would admit, for its significance depends upon its shattering irrationality. Juvenal, too, does not attempt to argue his point logically, to develop one aspect after another until the whole case unites to prove his insight true. Such a method of development would preclude indignation and require the moderation of Horace; it might even bar his characteristic themes, the truth of which becomes increasingly questionable with repeated reading. On the contrary, Juvenal has selected a paradox because of its capacity for indignation, and he conse-

---

[63] Friedländer, p. 52, designated Satires 5, 8, 10, and 14 as rhetorical theses. F. Gauger, *Zeitschilderung und Topik bei Juvenal* (Bottrop, 1936), pp. 91 ff., divides the Satires among three categories: (1) Theses: Satires 1, 2, 3, 5, 6, 8, 10, 13, and 14; (2) Diatribes: Satires 11, 12, 15; (3). Satires: Satires 4, 7, 9, 16. O. Weinreich, *Römische Satiren* (Zürich, 1949), p. lxii, employs the same categorization.

[64] Cf. I. G. Scott (Ryberg), *The Grand Style in the Satires of Juvenal*, Smith College Classical Studies, 8, Northampton, Mass., 1927.

quently rejects classical theories of development for a more conducive technique of presentation.

Let us consider, for instance, the supreme success of Satire 3, whose theme we may state as follows: Rome is no longer Rome. This paradox provides Juvenal with his approach and fully supports the emotion with which Umbricius condemns his native city. He takes the Rome of traditional associations—its majesty, justice, wealth, beauty, and honesty—and exposes its self-contradiction. Thus he comments on various conditions, the lack of opportunity, the aliens, the fires, the thieves, etc., all of which signify the loss of the traditional Roman qualities and cumulate in a totally negative picture of an uninhabitable city. When he leaves, then, Umbricius symbolizes in his act what he has been saying, that Roman characteristics no longer fit the city, for he is the last Roman.

We may say, then, that the thematic self-contradiction suggests to the satirist a technique of exposition by which he progressively strips away the potential connotations of a concept and ultimately leaves it with a single glaring significance that, by its enormity, justifies his indignation. For this process, we have used the word clarification, because the explosive theme exists from the beginning but awaits proper emphasis. The satirist fixes furiously upon a concrete situation at the beginning—e. g. the hypocrisy of certain homosexuals in Satire 2— and then proceeds to explain his attitude. Censorial severity in an effeminate demands attack, and an attack which consists in driving a wedge between the contradictory terms and demonstrating the irreconcilable opposition between Roman ideals of manliness and the actual effeminates. Opposition or contrast constitutes the essential method of Juvenal's presentation, and it extends its influence into the area of word choice. As we have observed, the thematic contrast frequently expresses itself through the medium of thematic words and metaphors as well as through antithetical situations. And if we pursued the matter further, we would discover that Juvenal's whole rhetorical manipulation of words depends upon an implicit reaction to a thematic opposition: e. g. his ironic use of moral terms to refer to vices in Satire 1 signifies the general transvaluation in Rome. By a pattern of antithesis, that is, Juvenal carries out his plan of clarification, attacking one representative situation after another until he feels his radical conclusion safe. As he moves from one outrageous incident to another, always with the same indignant antagonism, his theme steadily impresses itself more and more forcefully.

Now, while the technique of progressive simplification possesses obvious advantages, it contains within itself factors which do conflict with classical methods of composition. Juvenal starts and ends with the same idea, having devoted the poem to its exposition; whereas Horace gradually develops a simple attitude into a complex, balanced principle by considering relevant factors with an attempt at comprehension. Since Juvenal does not alter his theme, the scenes which he dwells upon must perform a parallel function of illustration, and an accumulation of such illustration ultimately forces the desired conclusion. For this reason, we could focus on a specific incident or detail, as, for instance, Umbricius in the crowd, and treat it as a microcosm of the whole Satire. For the same reason, we regularly find a close semantic connection between the introduction and the conclusion of a Satire, as Juvenal repeats key terms or situations. But a thematic connection differs from a developmental connection. Between parallel illustrations, accordingly, Juvenal does not always establish a close relation, nor does any thematic necessity obligate him to do so. For example, that Laronia successfully attacks the effeminates and that Creticus moralizes in effeminate attire before a rustic assemblage have no intrinsic relation, de-spite their juxtaposition in Satire 2; but each vignette promotes the simplification of Juvenal's paradox between Roman effemi-nates and what Romans once were. In Satire 2, at least, Juvenal subsumes many such illustrations under a fairly patent heading, but in Satire 4 he reduces the process of parallelism to its abso-lute limit. To be sure, as has been shown, the thematic contents of 1–36 and 37 ff. cover the same ground. Still, Juvenal has used only two extensive illustrative situations, varied their tone markedly, and in general so separated the introduction from the mock epic that he here gives us his most glaring example of the consequences of his compositional principles. We may claim that Satire 4 lacks unity, yet it employs essentially the same technique as Satire 3, except that Satire 3 accumulates more instances in a more evidently integrated context, namely Rome. Not that lack of unity achieves nothing. On the contrary, the striking cleavage between Crispinus and Domitian, apparently emphasized by the change to mock epic, seems effective in stress-ing the difference between courtier and emperor, masquerader and model. Whether the price Juvenal pays for his effect is excessive remains another question. We can here only insist that he has pursued his customary methods in Satire 4 with but slight differences.

In the end, a set paradoxical theme presented by means of

accumulated illustrations suggests a method of emphasis, not of unity or proportionality. We have seen the positive rhetorical effect of such a technique in Satire 1, 22–80, where the unordered series of vignettes supports the very point Juvenal stresses: that his indignant gaze can detect vice *anywhere* he looks. If one chose to analyze Satire 3 closely, he would see the same principle in operation. For Juvenal, emphasis is everything, and, if his Satires lack unity, we might better regard this as part of his emphasis than as failure in his art. Just as his simple theme necessitates an irrationally extreme attitude toward a situation, so the structure through which the theme emerges coheres with the pervasive passionate tone, as if to imply that the Roman world itself, the cause of the satirist's emotions, lacks all proportions in its degeneracy. Ultimately, we may feel that such extremism limits the achievement of Juvenal; but we should first realize that he has largely accomplished what he set out to do in Book I: to integrate structure, theme, and indignant mood in a portrait of a totally corrupt, chaotic, and disintegrating Rome.

JUVENAL 6: A PROBLEM IN STRUCTURE

THE central problem of Juvenal's *Satire* 6 is the relation of structure to contents.[1] Scholars have been divided in their proposed solutions: the brave have assumed a coherent organization; the prudent have abandoned what seemed a thankless and futile effort, denying any structural unity.[2] Failure, however, to attain a positive goal should be an inspiration to further efforts. Hence, in the latest study of Juvenal, Professor Highet is to be commended for defying the negative view and positing a definite pattern of organization.[3] In Highet's view, this is a "satire on marriage";[4] its structure can be reduced to four large sections[5]: (1) 1–132:[6] The unchastity of wives. (2) 136–285: The impossibility of love in marriage. (3) 286–351: The luxurious habits of Roman women. (4) 352–661:[7] The various follies and crimes of women which make marriage impossible. As he points out, these four sections are constructed to produce a climax[8]: (1) Wives cheat their husbands. (2) Wives tyrannize their husbands. (3) Wives ignore their husbands. (4) Wives kill their husbands. Although he takes the constructive view, Highet is not blind to the difficulties in this satire. Even in regard to his own pattern, he admits: "It is impossible to fit in two sections,

184–99 and 242–67."[9] Unfortunately, he fails to define the difficulties and attempts rather to explain them by bringing in the satiric "tradition of incoherence" and the irrational emotion expected of a poet.[10] Moreover, he adds another doubtful excuse, claiming that *Satire* 6 "clearly took Juvenal many years to mature and compose."[11] If the scope of Highet's study had been less broad, perhaps he might have been able to support his analysis in detail. As it is, we are never informed of the reasoning which led him to his optimistic view; nor do we understand how he conquered the precise problems presented by this satire.

The structural difficulties may be listed in the form of five questions: (1) Why does Juvenal drop Postumus halfway through the satire? (2) Why does Juvenal apparently repeat himself, presenting, for instance, the wife in the theater at 60 ff. and at 379 ff.? (3) Is the Oxford Fragment a relevant part of the satire? (4) What is the function of the pause in presentation, 286–300? (5) In short, what is the subject of the satire? It will be my project in this paper to face these questions and attempt an answer.

The first constructive attempt to define the structure, that of Nägelsbach,

255

is the key to our approach.[12] If anything is clear, it is that *Satire* 6 has a beginning, a middle, and an end. The middle consists of 286–300. Nägelsbach treated these lines as a dividing mark between the two great halves of the satire: the first half dealing with the impossibility of marriage, the second with the corruption of women. If, however, such an organization is assumed, the question immediately arises, What is the connection between the two halves? So, while potentially Nägelsbach's proposal answers some of our difficulties, it raises another. Neither Nägelsbach nor Stegemann nor Highet has convincingly solved the problem. The courageous scholars have ultimately failed because their pattern seems arbitrarily imposed rather than naturally perceived in the satire itself.

Generally speaking, the structural techniques of Juvenal have remained unexplained.[13] Some points, however, are relatively apparent. Juvenal frequently creates what I might call a "frame" within which to present his satire. This frame consists of an introductory sentence or paragraph and a concluding sentence, which are regularly distinct in tone. The introduction (or prologue), often hyperbolical, often very brief, announces the theme of the satire, but in a manner which seems to offer several methods of presentation. The satire proper is then an exploration of the theme, a gradual simplification of the subject matter into a polar antithesis of good and bad (e.g., Umbricius, the true Roman vs. the degenerate, Greek-infested, dissolute, luxurious Rome of his day). It cannot properly be said that Juvenal "develops" his theme. The clarified, simplified antithesis is potentially there in the opening lines (cf. *S.* 2 or 4). Juvenal's method of presentation is to move from scene to scene, pointing out one salient feature after another. Through the interrelation of his striking details, Juvenal contrives a cumulative impression of antithesis between good and bad. The skill of Juvenal consists in the selection of his exempla and their arrangement so that the details do not merely say the same thing, that Rome is intolerable (*S.* 3) or that marriage is impossible, but supplement each other. Then, in the conclusion (or epilogue), often hyperbolic, often, too, deprecatingly humorous, the satirist rounds off the structure by reverting to some of the ideas of the prologue as clarified in the heart of the satire. Juvenal's usual structural pattern, we might say, is a proof by examples of a theme stated at the beginning of the satire.[14]

Embarking on a more ambitious scheme in *Satire* 6, Juvenal still employed the general structural technique of Book 1. There is however one chief difference. Halfway through the satire, he changes the direction of his proof. To prepare us for this change, he introduces a second prologue (286–300). The change is not so radical as to render 300 ff. a second satire, nor is it totally unexpected. In fact, the second prologue is an economical device of transition; for it also functions as the epilogue to the first half of the satire. In turn, the second half has its epilogue at 643 ff. As in the satires of Book 1, the theme of each section is suggested in the respective prologues. It is my opinion also that the theme of the whole work is implied in the opening lines. This then is the immediately perceptible structure: a prologue, an interlude (which I have called transitional), and an epilogue. As to the thematic consistency, only a close analysis of the satire can establish the essential relation between structure and contents.

Prologue (1–20)

This prologue immediately invites comparison with those of Book 1. They were violent with exclamations and rhetorical questions; this is serene, approaching epic grandeur in its general breadth. Almost impersonal, it offers no point of attack, no specific, emotional subject. And the key word is the personified quality, the goddess Pudicitia. The tone, so shrewdly contrasted with the violence of 21 ff., helps to create one half the frame for *Satire* 6. Pudicitia should be an important element of the presentation.

Pudicitia is effectively presented as the evanescent touch of grace and beauty vouchsafed the brutal inhabitants of the uncivilized world. The words used to describe her presence, *moratam, visamque diu, multa vestigia.* emphasize her essential opposition to the earth; she has no place with mortals. The only relation that she can maintain with men depends on their state of civilization; for, as they progress away from the barbarous condition of aboriginal man, they also lose their contact with her. The quality which forced Pudicitia to abandon earth is represented in the characters of Cynthia and Lesbia. The latter, described in a contemptuous circumlocution (7–8), is the antitype of the *montana...uxor*, the cavewoman who was at least congenial to Pudicitia (5). In the tears which she sheds for her pet sparrow, Lesbia symbolizes an as yet unspecified quality which was clearly alien to Pudicitia. Thus, Juvenal represents Man's degeneracy through a double withdrawal: that of mankind from direct relation with Nature, that of the goddess Pudicitia from the earth.

The opening paragraph uses as its key word the abstract quality of Pudicitia. This word is echoed in the adjective *pudicus* and noun *pudor*, as applied directly to the actions and ethical attitude of women. Since these terms are concentrated in the first half, it is likely that Juvenal is concerned with the concrete actualization of Pudicitia primarily in Part I (21–285). He has deliberately avoided words describing Pudicitia; she is an abstract quality of which apparently nothing can be predicated. So the words applied to her merely serve to emphasize the tenuous hold that the earth has on her. However, there is an implicit relation between Pudicitia and *montana...uxor*, just as there is an implicit relation between Cynthia and the quality she actualizes. As long as men were uncivilized, as long as women were of the hardy mountain breed, mortals were permitted to enjoy the favor of Pudicitia, the one attractive feature of their otherwise crude existence. In the attributes of the *montana uxor*, then, it is natural to infer the conditions necessary for *pudor*, for retaining the favor of Pudicitia. First, the poverty of the habitation is stressed *frigida spelunca, parvas domos, communi umbra.* Then the crude furnishings are depicted in colored terms: *silvestrem torum, frondibus et culmo vicinarumque ferarum/pellibus*. Part I will use the *montana uxor* as its point of reference in exploring the loss of *pudor*, thus bringing into specific terms the symbolic separation of Pudicitia and mankind. It must be noted, however, that the cavewoman is described in an ambivalent manner (9–10). Her fertility is of importance; but her savage, disheveled aspect is not at all alluring. At this point, the interruption of the modern world and its idealized Cynthia and Lesbia make the uncouthness, the physical grossness of the aboriginal woman, all the more disgusting. Such a contrast raises doubts in the reader's mind. He approaches Part I sensing ambiguity in the satirist's viewpoint, not quite convinced that the world of the past is so desirable as that of the present.

Part I

(21–37) From the calm, controlled prologue, Juvenal makes an abrupt transition to the violent tone we should expect of him. Sweeping away the dim past, he focuses on the present, on a specific situation. His very first words, *anticum et vetus*, occasion doubt as to the intrinsic merit of the past. The occasion of the satirist's indignation is the intention of Postumus to enter the state of matrimony. After a relatively placid generalization on the adulterous habits of all men (21–22), Juvenal bursts into ferocious hyperbole to convey his reaction to Postumus' plans. Why, it is sheer madness to marry! (28–29) Death would be better than subjection to a wife; even pederasty is preferable! (30–37) Accordingly the matrimonial designs of Postumus introduce a new element into the thematic framework already established in the prologue. As opposed to the tranquil retrospective attitude toward the Golden Age, the hyperbole of the second paragraph is striking. Usually, Juvenal opens his satires with hyperbole. The separation here of prologue and hyperbolic address to Postumus implies that the themes of the prologue are central, that the dialogue form and the matrimonial theme are not the basic thematic and structural elements of the satire. The prologue is only incidentally interested in the relation between husband and wife; its focus is on the wife as a woman, as the concrete realization of the value of Pudicitia. But matrimony and Postumus' folly serve as the specific motivation for Juvenal's indignation

as well as the ideal context for presenting the theme of Part I. In the wife's relation to her husband and home, the satirist is best able to demonstrate the disappearance of Pudicitia.

(38–59) The hyperbole of insanity and folly is continued, as Juvenal now begins to focus on his theme with the key word *pudici* (49). Ursidius (Postumus) is a stupid beast (43), a madman needing medical attention (46–47), if he expects a wife of the old style. The past is forever gone; besides it was a dubious guarantee of chastity (cf. 21 to 22). Using *dignae* (50) as a general synonym for his thematic *pudicus*, Juvenal goes on to mock Postumus by ironically introducing details of the marriage rites (51–52). Hiberina hardly matches their sacred character (53–54). Then from the unchaste wife of the city, Juvenal goes to the country, to consider a rumored case of absolute purity (55–57). Among the attributes of the aboriginal woman was her primitive existence in the mountains and forests (*montana, silvestrem*). Now these attributes are stripped away from *pudor*. The country does not automatically confer *pudor*; it is not essentially virtuous (58–59). By emphasizing the verb *vivo* (56–57), the satirist throws doubt on the rumor; simultaneously he affirms the necessity, not of the environment, but of the life led in it.

(60–81) The role that a husband plays in contemporary marriage is that of a mere ox or fool. On the other hand, the wife's part becomes less and less feminine; she becomes more and more dominating. To begin with, however, Juvenal reveals the basic sexual irresponsibility of wives. Hence, the metaphor *imperat* (64) shows Tuccia unable to master herself. Meanwhile, Thymele, unprotected by her rustic background, is easily corrupted by the sensuous sights of the pantomime (66). So the theater exhibits the wife's unchastity; and again Juvenal recalls with irony the religious context of marriage, on the occasion of the birth of an illegitimate child (78–81).

(82–113) Worse than temporary affairs with actors, however, is the vicious liaison formed with a gladiator. For the sake of Sergius, Eppia abandons without a second thought her home and family (85–87). In this respect, she is implicitly contrasted with the *montana uxor*, whose whole existence was wrapped up in the menial domestic tasks required of her. Moreover, Eppia was brought up in all the material comfort that could be desired (88–91). While her moral fiber was thus softened, the miserable cave existence of the aboriginal woman seems to have contributed directly to her stern moral standards. With Sergius, however, Eppia's character exhibits an ironical transformation. Her flagrant self-indulgence at the cost of home, husband, and children is described in positive moral terms, words with connotations of bravery, heroism (*pertulit, constanti, fortem,* 92–97). Eppia is courageous; she has strength of character for the immoral deeds she commits (100). And the paradox is pushed home in 103–10. Eppia has been brought up in luxury, in circumstances directly opposed to those of the *montana uxor*; and she has taken exactly the opposite course with her domestic responsibilities. The extent of her perversion is illustrated in her complete loss of perspective. Not only has she lost a sense of responsibility befitting her station; she has also lost the aesthetic standards appropriate to her material environment. Therefore, her perversion takes the form of reversion toward the aboriginal state. She endures the discomforts of a rough voyage with the courage of a man. She chooses her paramour for the virility he exhibits, not for his handsome figure. In the physical ugliness of Sergius, there is a reminiscence of the physical loathsomeness of the caveman and his wife. Whereas there, however, uncouthness was a symbol of innocence and *pudor*, here it is a symbol of *impudicitia*. The primeval life is not intrinsically good because of its environmental conditions; it cannot be recaptured by imitating its brutality. Rather, any attempt to recover the past is mere reversion to bestiality. Pudicitia is gone.

(114–35) The exemplum of Eppia is immediately followed by that of Messalina, who symbolizes even more clearly the perverted effort to recapture the simplicity of the past, a simplicity of sensuality rather than of moral standards. Juvenal stresses his paradox in the juxtaposition *Palatino tegetem* (117). The vicious immorality of the empress is displayed in the shocking choice that she made. Nothing could illustrate the perversion of the age more succinctly than the cataclysmic behavior of *meretrix Augusta* (118). Therefore, Juvenal indulges in an unusually specific description of her sexual pleasures. Her pleasure is not merely the adultery of a noble Eppia; it is not predicated on lust for a particular person or body; it is the totally vicious and indiscriminate desire for the physical sensation of degradation. The reversion is utter.

(136–60) For a moment, the satirist pauses to answer two potential objections to his sweeping denunciation of all wives and the whole institution of matrimony. Some husbands are witnesses to their wives' virtue (*pudicam,* 137). Yes, but they themselves are not trustworthy; they have been bribed. As Juvenal goes on to say, exploiting the elegiac symbols, the arrows of

Cupid came from the dowry (138–39). In fact, the testimony of the husband merely proves the complete alienation of husband and wife. They live by a business arrangement. The wife has bought her husband; he must play the subservient part befitting his economic dependence. In effect, she is a widow (141), free to indulge herself with any man she so desires. Based on the possession of wealth rather than genuine moral standards, the wife's *pudor* is counterfeit. Some men, however, really possess the elegiac passion; they burn for their wives (142–43). Yes, but not for the person, only for the body. Therefore, the wife prostitutes herself to her husband for the material benefits that can be derived from marriage. She holds him by a contractual arrangement similar to that between Caesennia and her husband, except that it is she that is bought. Juvenal is now making his transition away from the wife regarded simply as a sexual being. At first, he dealt with women who allowed their passion its natural expression, like Tuccia. Then came wives who titillated their senses with physical degradation, complete violation of their background, of whom Messalina was the supreme example. Caesennia has bought her husband, to preserve the appearance of respectability. Though still unchaste, she is farther removed from an uninhibited expression of her natural desires. With Bibula, the satirist is moving almost out of the area of sexual pleasures. She is a counterpart to Messalina, who posed as a prostitute for the sensation. Bibula *is* a prostitute for the jewelry and clothes which she can extort from her passionate husband. The husband means as little to her as to Caesennia. She controls him with her body, in order to gratify her materialistic desires; Caesennia controls her husband with her money, in order to gratify her lust and still retain her reputation. So the virtual prostitute reigns over the household (*regnat*, 149), she uses her sex as an instrument to acquire something which she considers more important than bodily pleasure. Juvenal is presenting a more complex woman.

(161–83) Now, instead of filtering out unchastity as the essence of *impudicitia*, Juvenal singles out other faults which, for him, exemplify *impudicitia* equally well. For instance, he concedes what are traditionally regarded as the essential characteristics of *pudor*, asserting that they are all vitiated by *superbia* (161 to 66). His exempla make clear his meaning. Cornelia, *mater Gracchorum*, is immediately placed in the desired perspective by the epithet. All her family pride, all her own personal virtue resulted in the Gracchi, the representatives, for the Romans, of corrupting power. There was no intrinsic moral core in her *superbia* to orient all her variegated virtues to a purposeful end. On the other hand, Niobe is nothing but a sow (177), a symbol of fecundity. She, too, is reminiscent of the cavewoman, except that the maternal instincts of the latter were controlled and useful. The children of the Golden Age were not the expression of the mother's egotism, but human beings to be nursed and raised to maturity. Domestic virtues mean nothing without the moral direction which a genuine understanding of herself would provide a wife. Cornelia and Niobe misuse their virtues by lording it over husband and neighbor. Pride is not Pudicitia, but its sterile aftereffect.

(184–99) Even minor faults can warp a wife's personality and corrupt good qualities. The affectation of Greek ways is so reprehensible because it involves such perversion of the self. Greece is the symbol of moral corruption. Therefore, Juvenal exploits the juxtaposition *Tusca Graecula* (186), using the diminutive to prejudice his meaning. In the Roman matron, *superbia* did not destroy the good qualities she possessed; it revealed their inadequate basis. When, however, a wife affects Greek speech, she opens the way to the insidious encroachment of Greek vices. Her concept of beauty becomes tainted by the artificial criteria of Greece (186); soon she loses the Roman values on which *superbia* could be based. Moral restraint is abandoned (191). And, says Juvenal, the affectation has even been adopted by octogenarians (192), a sardonic, hyperbolic dig at a habit which destroys *pudor* (*pudicus*, 193). This paragraph is not disturbing, but, as Highet observed, it is not very closely related to the context either. Still, the affectation can be viewed as a counterpart to the *superbia* of the preceding paragraph. The wife who is not rendered one-sided by her sexual desires is regarded as one-sided in her more complex personality. She still does not possess the *pudor* to control her purposes.

(200–30) Juvenal then goes back more directly to the relation between husband and wife. He presents his interlocutor with a dilemma (200–8). Obviously, since one cannot find love in marriage, it is folly to marry. The animal metaphor is repeated (207–8); as in line 43, the husband is a stupid ox. More important than the metaphor is the ambiguous phrase *simplicitas uxoria*. In itself, this could apply either to wife or husband. A wife is *simplex* when she is uncorrupted by the veneer of civilization, when she follows the basic function of her sex.[15] A husband would be *simplex* if he followed the function of the male sex. The adjective *uxoria* taints *simplicitas* with an inter-

mediate significance; the husband is *simplex* in terms of a woman's role. Normally, the woman is the subordinate member of the menage. When the husband becomes uxorious, he accepts the subordinate status and permits the wife to use him as she wills. The abasement of the man is brought out in the rest of the paragraph. He is compared to the lowest elements of the population and found inferior. They, at least, have a modicum of *libertas*; he lacks even that (216ff.). The house is the woman's kingdom (*regna*, 224). She holds an absolute right over the lives of her slaves (219ff.). She can issue her royal edict to her husband (*voluntas*, 223). Where the man has lost his freedom, the woman has acquired the royal license to do whatever she wills. Like a queen, she is completely arbitrary in her decisions, lacking even elemental discrimination. To her, a servant is not human (222). Since, however, she treats her husband as a beast of burden, a slave to her desires, she is tacitly affirming that he is not human (212–18). Moreover, *demens* (222) recalls the original hyperbole about marriage (28). Postumus was insane to dream of matrimony; here the wife treats her husband as mad, because he does not share her own warped standards. Juvenal is driving toward a complete reversal of the traditional roles of husband and wife. He has progressed a long distance from the prologue and the idealized world where the wife was a domestic drudge.

(231–45) In the preceding paragraph, Juvenal used the metaphor *spoliis* to signify the tyrannical exploitation of the husband (210). Now he repeats the metaphor (232) and supports it with the ironic implications of *concordia* (231). There is an actual war between husband and wife, in which the wife emerges victorious, stripping the body of her enemy. The pair of words, *rude* and *simplex* (234), recall the cave existence of aboriginal mankind; they also recall the closer *simplicitas* (206). Women are no longer simple organisms. They have escaped subjection to their sexual desires; they are rational creatures, able to capitalize on instruction (*docet*, an ironic anaphora, 232–33), to carry on shrewd intrigues (234 ff.). Such valuable knowledge comes from the sage advice of the mother. And the whole calculating character of wives, as inculcated by their mothers, is symbolized in the next vignette. They can engage in lawsuits and conduct them with a skill that belies their sex (242–43). While men are becoming gradually more uxorious, wives are abandoning their primary function as part of the home, subordinate to the will of the husband, and have begun to invade the spheres normally reserved for males. Juvenal emphasizes the incongruity by placing *femina* in juxtaposition to *litem*, a word to which it is traditionally antipathetic.

(246–67) The invasion of the male sphere is even more apparent in the gladiatorial exercises of some wives. Juvenal recalls his theme of propriety with the ironic superlative *dignissima* (249). No woman who wears a helmet can possibly possess *pudor* (*pudorem*, 252). No woman who invades a man's world can still claim the moral qualities of a female. *Pudor* necessarily implies a strict observation of the limitations of one's own nature. By dabbling in gladiatorial habits wives are abandoning their sex and their *pudor* (253). To love violence is automatically to ally oneself with the male character. However, the wife refuses to become a man (254). She prefers the advantages of both sexes. In the marital relation, she has taken over the man's supreme role; but she asserts the irresponsible privileges of a woman, *voluptas* (254). In the context of the gladiatorial games and with the verbs of 248 ff. and 259 ff., Juvenal proves that the woman is mannish (*cavat, lacessit, sudant, perferat, curvetur, gemat*). She has developed the male propensities, ignored her femininity.[16]

(268–85) The final paragraph of Part I brings the theme of *pudor* to a conclusion. In her gladiatorial interests, the wife was almost masculine. Now, she is described as counterfeiting feminine emotions; she only pretends to be a woman. She moans as if outraged by some fault of her husband, all the while aware of her own vices, deliberately distracting her husband from what she wants to conceal. Her emotionality is neatly compared to the fury of a bereaved tigress (270). The wife is devoid of sexual characteristics, except for those which she counterfeits. Therefore, she is *orba*, in the sense that she is sterile. Another word, *uberibus* (273), has ironic feminine connotations; it implies the fertility which she clearly rejects. The rejection of femininity is inherent in the pretence; moreover, it is rhetorically symbolized by the military metaphor (274). With military discipline, she has drilled her emotions in a way atypical of women; like sentries, they stand, awaiting her slightest order. Hence, the woman is able to turn her tears on and off, in order to extort the advantages due the weaker sex. Meanwhile, she actually is the stronger partner in the ménage. She treats her husband as her slave, and her slave as her husband (279). With utter effrontery she argues her case. Where Quintilian could find no defense, she prepares a beautiful reply, the epitome of specious logic (280–84). Her conclusion, *homo sum*, is the conclusion of Part I. The wife means that her existence as a human being entitles her to complete moral freedom. But *homo* is a thematic word. Once, the wife denied that a slave was human (*homo*, 222). Now, she makes her humanity the excuse for indulging herself with a slave. She has twisted the doctrine of humanity to apply to immorality, not to the essential responsibility entailed in moral freedom. Warped as her understanding and actions are, she is ultimately isolating herself as human, nothing else. She has no *pudor* any more, since she has no sex.

Part I of *Satire* 6 has explored the role of woman as wife, within the perspective of the aboriginal existence. In the ambiguity of the prologue, Juvenal linked Pudicitia and *montana uxor*. To the latter he attached a number of attributes allied with the simplicity of her existence. There was an implicit venerability in the past; but the attitude toward the aboriginal woman was ambivalent. She was morally upright, physically uncouth. Taking the occasion of Postumus' approaching marriage, Juvenal proceeded to consider the importance of *pudor*, the virtue he had personified in the prologue as Pudicitia. While interested in the home environment, at least enough to clarify his attitude about the accidental qualities and the essence of *pudor*, he was specifically concerned with *pudor* as it affected a woman *qua* wife. He used the cave themes to show how far women degenerated from their simple life, how much they were softened by the pampering of luxurious surroundings; the cave themes gave import to the reversions of Eppia and Messalina. In Part I, however, the cave is basically a symbol of a proper domestic relation, not of simplicity. The wife should be subordinate to her husband, working in the home, bringing up his children, sharing his hardships. This domestic quality is one aspect, the most common aspect, of her feminine character, her *pudor*. Part I studies the breakdown of the marital relation, where the wife is ideally subordinate. Juvenal begins with sexual enormities, in their various stages from adultery to perversion. Then he studies the qualities which gradually inhibit sexual proclivities, the growing calculation of the wife, her increasing domination of her husband, her encroachment on the world of men, the law court and the arena. With the final assertion *homo sum*, the woman has destroyed the marriage relation. She no longer needs a husband, because she implicitly rejects the function of a wife. Pudicitia is absolutely routed. At this point, too, the dialogue form of presentation, between Juvenal and Postumus, can be dropped, since Postumus and the marriage theme are no longer relevant. Whatever follows Part I will be based on the assumption that the consideration of the marital question is closed. A new theme must be adopted.[17]

Epilogue and Prologue (286–300)

The transition to Part II, functioning as epilogue and prologue, recalls the original themes and transmutes them into a new subject for subsequent exploration. Juvenal's attitude toward the aboriginal woman was ambiguous, approving of her standards, ironical toward her physical attractions. During Part I, however, she was the standard of reference, because the emphasis was not so much on her material and physical attributes as on the immaterial relation between herself and her husband. This relationship was expressed by the cavewoman in terms of domestic action, drudgery, and complete subordination to her husband's and the family's needs. In the course of Part I, the ambiguity

263

was incidentally clarified; it became apparent that Juvenal was driving at the moral basis of existence, not the material circumstances. Now, however, he sets up a new point of reference free from ambiguity. By moving the domestic ideal forward from the time of the Golden Age, which was mythical and half ridiculous, to a definite period in Roman history, that of the Hannibalic Wars, he establishes his standard on a firm foundation. The themes of the first lines are deliberately recalled (287–91). There is the same domestic interest, the same close and sympathetic relation to the husband. But circumstances have changed. Instead of being uncouth, the wife is attractive. Civilization has advanced; the wife no longer is stripping skins from wild beasts, but is occupied with weaving; she is no longer explicitly and disgustingly crude, but implicitly modest and humble.[18] As an epilogue to Part I, this passage takes up its themes and gives them a new, unambiguous context in which to operate.

It is through his concern for the environment of *pudor* that Juvenal makes his transition to Part II of the satire. He clears up any possibility of ambiguity, then pushes the matter farther. Part I concerns wives; it proves that Pudicitia is gone from the earth. Wives no longer possess the *pudor* befitting their sex, they have encroached upon the sphere of men until they are men in all but minor physical considerations. The question of wives and Pudicitia is accordingly settled. Part I was not concerned with an explanation of the phenomenon, except in terms of personal moral standards. In the epilogue, the satirist reviews the themes and suggests an explanation for the loss of *pudor*. *Luxuria* is the cause (293). The environmental conditions, after all,

did qualify the morality of wives. By using *paupertas* (295) as the positive quality opposed to *luxuria*, Juvenal is subtly substituting a new theme for the old one of *pudicitia*. At the moment that he has finished with *pudicitia*, the satirist makes his transition by suggesting that *luxuria* is the condition behind the degeneracy of the marital relation. Therefore, the transition is a symbolic replacement of the positive concept of Pudicitia (which is no longer possible, as Juvenal has shown in Part I) with the negative concept of Luxuria (which will be the theme of Part II). In describing Luxuria, Juvenal uses military metaphors (292–93). This recalls the very feminine impression made by Pudicitia in the opening lines and the significant metaphor *fugere* (20). It is now clear that Pudicitia and Luxuria are polar opposites, that Luxuria is the belligerent force which caused the flight of Pudicitia. The unnamed tutelary deity of Cynthia and Lesbia has at last been identified.

Part II

The structure of Part II has two main problems. One of these is the Oxford Fragment, which will be treated later. The second can be discussed tentatively at this point, since it is related to the transition. Juvenal has been criticized for his repetitious use of exempla.[19] He describes the sexually perverted woman twice, the martinet twice, and in general Part II seems to be rendered superfluous by the treatment in Part I. There is, however, a distinction between the general theme of the satirist and the details selected to present it. The repetitions are there; but repetition is not automatically inartistic. The defense of those who have striven to preserve the reputation of Juvenal has been to point out the subtle difference between the similar passages. Because, however, they treated each situation separately, not as an element of the whole theme, the defenders failed. The answer to the problem, I believe, lies in the change from Part I to Part II. In dealing with similar contexts, the satirist is constantly, consistently aware of the different themes he is impressing on them. The breakdown of *pudor*, the rout of Pudicitia were exemplified in Part I. From his exempla and descriptions Juvenal distilled the theme of *pudor*. Ultimately there was nothing but a void left where once *pudor* thrived. Into that void he puts Luxuria. In Part I, where the marital relation and *pudor*, the quality essential to any right marriage relation, were the dominant themes, Luxuria would have been a disturbing element. It would have distracted the attention from the demonstration. Once Pudicitia is gone, Luxuria can be permitted to take her place as the central theme. With this new theme, Juvenal can travel back over the same circumstances and situations, this time emphasizing the effect of Luxuria. But this structural device does not merely produce a variation on a theme already played before. Part I was a progressive proof, by a series of carefully chosen and arranged exempla, of the idea implicit in the prologue, that female *pudor* had vanished. In Part II, the same purpose impels the satirist to select his details. When he reaches the final epilogue (643 ff.), he has a theme of tragic proportions, justifying the appropriation of a Sophoclean style. His emotional reaction to the tragedy he perceives, in fact the tragedy itself, can be foreseen in the themes implicit in 286–300 and 1–20; it is prepared by the new thematic content of his exempla.

(301–49) The symbol of Part II is proclaimed in 300, *Venus ebria*. This phrase can be considered as a reference to the goddess, but also as metonymy for those who thrive under her besotted aegis, the Cynthias, the Lesbias, the Tullias, and the Mauras. However, it is the nature of this drunken Venus which is stressed by the satirist: she is totally irresponsible. So, too, her followers cannot make even elemental distinctions (301–2). Besotted themselves, they cannot see straight (303–5) nor control themselves (306–13). Their obscene irreverence toward the altar of Pudicitia symbolizes their debasement and the complete irrelevance of *pudor* to the contemporary situation.[20] Already, then, the emphasis has changed. It is not the marital status of these women which is important.[21] Rather, Juvenal is stressing the effect of Luxuria, specifically of a banquet, on the moral standards and behavior of women. The key word is therefore no longer *pudor*,[22] but the vicious implications of carelessness (300), lack of discrimination (301), and perverted pleasure (*gaudium*, 365, 379, 420, 602).

The perverted delights of a Maura, a woman of the lower elements, are repeated on a larger scale in the public rites of the matrons of Rome. The stress is on lust (329 ff.), on the aspect of the female which is basic (*simplex*, 327). So long as the matrons can satisfy their instincts, they do not distinguish between *adulter* and *asellus* (329–34). The contest between the Roman matron Saufeiia and the common prostitutes is made by Juvenal into a vicious parody of an athletic event (320–23). The *virtus* of the matrons is triumphant. Moving to another scene, Juvenal describes the notorious violation by Clodius of the rites of Bona Dea (335–45). Into the center of his vignette the satirist inserts a comparison with the reverent past (342 ff.). Like Part I, Part II has started from the basic sexual nature of women. The point of reference, however, is no longer home and husband, but traditional Roman religious rites. Unchastity is as inconsistent with Roman piety as it is with marriage. Accordingly, Juvenal is now intent on the effect of Luxuria on Rome (cf. 292–95). The choice of Clodius, moreover, for his exemplum was not without purpose. As the brother of Catullus' Lesbia (Clodia),[23] he recalls the contemptuously described lyric heroine of the Prologue. Lesbia and her history form a clear antithesis to the Roman ideal of 286ff., also a clear pattern for Juvenal's analysis in Part II. As women become more complex, they will be treated more and more as symbols of a greater issue, the general decadence of Roman civilization.

(350–65) The next scene (350ff.), of the woman in the amphitheater, is reminiscent of Eppia and Sergius.[24] But here the extravagance of the woman is stressed, not the utter rejection of husband and home for the gratification of a perverted desire. By asyndeton, Juvenal forces the details of Ogulnia's extravagance upon the reader's attention (352–54). Moreover, he uses *pudorem* (357) in such a way as to fix its new meaning. The enjambement causes one momentarily to expect some qualification as in Part I relating to marriage. With the alliterative *paupertatis*, the satirist once more indicates the change in his presentation (cf. 295). Luxuria and the materialistic estimate require a new type of *pudor*. But a woman, unlike her provident husband, heedlessly spends on her inane pleasures (*gaudia* 365).

* * *

Oxford Fragment (O 1–34)

There are three ways of approaching the problem presented by the Oxford Fragment.[25] The first is concerned with the textual tradition and the explanation of the fragment's appearance in one manuscript alone. The second, a literary approach, determines whether the passage is consistent, logical, and typical of Juvenal. The third, also literary, deals with the relation of the passage to the general theme of the satire. All three of these attacks have been used with varying results since the discovery of the Fragment in 1899.[26]

Textual criteria cannot determine the genuineness of the Fragment without the support of literary and rhetorical evidence. However, the Fragment seems most vulnerable to the textual critic. Since the ingenious, but unacceptable, proposal of Winterfeld, there have been a series of tentative explanations of the omission of these lines from every codex but that of Oxford.[27] Some are based on a theoretical pagination of the archetype; the copyist missed a page or two, as often has happened.[28] Some assume a deliberate excision from the text for reasons of purity.[29] Leo's theory of a "doppelte Recension" suggests that Juvenal might have written both the Fragment and the three lines 346–48, but at different periods of his life and for different editions.[30] His interpretation of the scholia would support his theory. At 347, remarks in the oldest scholia reveal that at least two lines of the Fragment, O 32–33, were known before the time of the Nicaeus edition. However, Jachmann and Knoche have evolved a more credible theory of interpolation on the basis of the scholia.[31] According to them, it is foolish to father off on Juvenal the clumsy work of an inept interpolator who lived between the time of Juvenal's death and the first scholarly edition. However, no theory has adequately explained how the thirty-four lines survived in a single manuscript down to the day when they were copied into O, and O alone. I propose a more complex explanation, which, however, seems to meet the situation and the known evidence more satisfactorily. First, I assume that the Fragment is not the work of Juvenal. I agree, too, with the theory of Jachmann and Knoche, but only as far as the evidence supports it. The scholiast was aware of the final five lines of the Fragment, as they existed in one of his texts at about 347ff.[32] However, I see no reason for assuming that the other twenty-nine lines were also known to the scholiast.[33] In my opinion, he knew a three-line and a five-line version of the same passage. The editor of the Nicaeus text knew these versions too, but nothing larger. On standards of style, perhaps, too, on criteria furnished by his manuscript, the editor chose the three-line version. Axelson has shown to my satisfaction that the shorter version is clearer, more economical, and far more satirically pungent than the diffuse and repetitive five-line version.[34] Therefore, I believe that the original three lines of Juvenal suffered expansion from the hands of an interpolator in the period after his death and before the Nicaeus edition. That leaves twenty-nine lines to explain. I assume that the five-line version survived nowhere but in the scholia. In browsing through these, probably along the margin of the manuscript he was copying, the scribe of O came upon this variant. Taking off from *lascivae*, he let his mind wander and produced this not very creditable piece of literature. The length is entirely irrelevant and cannot be used to imagine an original pagination; these twenty-nine lines are a tour de force of no merit, and could have gone on indefinitely. Thus, just prior to the copying of O, I suggest, these twenty-nine lines were composed, prefixed to the five extant in the scholia, the whole thirty-four being inserted after 365 in O.

The second problem of the Fragment is its inner consistency, another vulnerable point of attack.[35] Unfortunately, scholarly judgment has largely been affected by preconceptions rather than the evidence of the text. Buecheler rejected it almost solely on the basis of a clumsy hiatus observed in 2.[36] Others have noted unique usages of words and damned the Fragment.[37] On the other hand, the number of commentaries evoked by the Fragment, the recondite explanations of its obscenity and difficulties, and the desperate attempt to prove its inner coherence reveal the weakness of the defenders' position. Knoche has raised against the Fragment nearly thirty counts, all based on its total confusion.[38] Despite some overstatement of his case, he has presented a great number of valid arguments which require answers from those favoring the genuineness of the piece. He points out that the opening lines appear to refer to an effeminate, the companion of the husband. At O 3 the writer made a clumsy transition by means of *similes* to a different type who could be the companion of the wife, a point that arouses some logical doubts. The long digression of 6–10 does nothing for the picture except increase the confusion, for the point of comparison is obscure. After that, according to Knoche, the text proceeds with relatively little confusion until 27. There is the minor logical point of *uxor* in 14, which seems to render *nubunt* in 17 self-contradictory. As, however, the writer drew to a close, total confusion descended on his composition. I admit my inadequacy; Knoche asserts his inadequacy; and the defenders prove their inadequacy to explain what is happening in 27–29.[39] Speakers change with a kaleidoscopic speed. By 30, a transition has been made to a dialogue form of development; but the connection between 26 and 30 is, for me, a mystery. I cannot explain the confusion; I can propose an explanation of the cause of the confusion. The incompetent writer was obliged to go through tortuous maneuvers to force his style and content into a form consistent with the content of the already existing 30–34. In my opinion, then, the text must be rejected as incoherent and totally unworthy of Juvenal. It says almost nothing; what it does say, it says so confusingly as to render it worse than nothing. The obvious efforts of the writer to effect a transition to 30 ff. convince me that he was motivated by the five lines (30–34), not that he wrote them himself.

The third and final problem concerns the relevance of the Fragment to the general context of the satire. Ercole[40] and R. Clauss[41] have attempted to defend its genuineness on this basis. Clauss used a dubious argument, that Juvenal frequently loses track of his theme, that the confusion here is accordingly eminently typical of his rhetorical artistry. I prefer to distinguish this text from the rest of Juvenal's work. Because it is confusing and inconsistent, it is difficult to determine what point it is making. Whatever the point, however, it does not bear an essential relation to the context. The theme of Part II is Luxuria, the corrupting effect of material environment on the materialistic standards of women. As one of the thematic words, *gaudium* signifies the pastimes of women of leisure. In Part II Juvenal tends to ignore the husband.[42] He has developed the theme of the marital relation between husband and wife in Part I;

he has shown that the husband is no longer important. But this Fragment, if it has any theme, seems to be related to the domestic theme of Part I, not to the broader ideas of Part II. The description does not emphasize the materialistic explanation at all; on the other hand, the role of the husband is important to the writer. In the confused transition of 27–29, he even has the man speak one of the parts. It is the violation of the marriage that receives the stress rather than the debased mind of the woman. In the Fragment, the woman is very much of a wife; for the other women of Part II being a wife is of little moment. Again, I suggest that the writer of this Fragment was inspired by *lascivae*, the remnant of the five-line variant in the scholia. He observed that the next paragraph would deal with the perverted sexual relation between eunuchs and women; so he inserted an intermediate stage in the process of degeneracy, the relation between women and pretended effeminates. But, whereas the other paragraphs use the sexual details to emphasize the theme of Luxuria and its particular aspect of *gaudium*, the writer of this Fragment developed his account in the more usual way, to depict the destruction of the marital union. On all three counts, then, I am convinced that the Oxford Fragment stands condemned as spurious.

* * *

(366–78) Some women prefer the safe embraces of a eunuch to the lusty ability of a Clodius. In Part I, the sexual impetus was at first direct, then perverted, then gradually calculated and controlled, and finally diverted into other activities. Part II has a similar course. Now the sexual relation is completely sterile, merely a sensation. Ju-

268

venal uses a variant for the concept of *gaudium* (*delectent*, 367); pleasure is becoming a desperate search for titillation. In this paragraph, too, the satirist uses *domina* twice (376–77). The woman *qua* wife is no longer important. In Part I, *uxor* occurred nine times and *domina* once; in Part II, *uxor* is used three times, *domina* five. So *domina* and words of a similar type are being substituted for *uxor* to stress a different aspect of the female function.

(379–97) Now the woman takes to dabbling in the musical world, though with an obvious sexual motivation. She lavishes kisses on the musical instrument of one of her favorites (384), in a way reminiscent of *oscula* in 367. Her bejewelled hands sparkle on another's lyre (381). However, the standard of reference is not her domestic function. Her home is mentioned incidentally; but far more in evidence are the ancestral rites, the religious practices of Rome. Luxuria has corrupted both the women and the religion they practice (385 ff.). It is this double corruption, of women and of divinities, that provokes the angry apostrophe to *Iane pater* (394). To the indignant satirist, the gods must live in complete idleness, if they have time to pay attention to the debased prayers of the society matrons: *magna otia caeli*. The state of indifferent relaxation in heaven, symbolic of moral laxness, is the counterpart of the Luxuria prevalent in Rome.

(398–412) The next vignette describes a Roman matron whose sole object in life is to collect and retail succulent bits of gossip. Juvenal deliberately emphasizes her abandonment of her proper role as mother with *siccis mamillis* (401). With complete effrontery, she talks with generals about their campaigns, not because she has the interest of the patriot, of the woman, for instance,

whose husband was standing guard on the battlements of Rome (291); her only motive is to enjoy the gossip, the scandal, the importance which comes from being the first to hear the latest rumor. Some of her best stories concern the sexual vagaries of other women; these she can describe in full detail, achieving a perverse satisfaction in the account of another's immorality (405–6). What gives this paragraph point, however, is the triviality of a Roman matron's life. Luxuria causes triviality, because it makes existence so easy, time so free, and pleasure so complicated.

(413–18) The jaded attitude toward the more simple pleasures caused by prolonged Luxuria is represented in the temperament of the woman: she becomes irritable, assertive, domineering. She forsakes the conventional pleasures of women, those which revolve around the family and home; but she can find no purpose toward which to direct her emotions or energies. The slightest irritation becomes magnified into an invasion of her most sacred rights. She has a neighbor beaten for the yapping of his dog, because her deep sleep, probably the sleep of drunkenness, has been troubled (416–17). Now the woman can be described as *gravis*. In Part I *gravitas* was one of the conventional virtues (178). Now, the adjective (418) signifies the failure to distract the idle mind, the disillusionment which etches its misery on the temperament and the face, producing the hardened beauty of unhappiness.

(419–33) The dominating type of female is also described at one of her soirées, a context which recalls the functions normally associated with the Roman matron (287 ff.). Now she has no concern for home or social responsibilities. Juvenal's description brings out the physical grossness (*gravi* 421) of the woman, a consequence of her self-indulgence; and he emphasizes it by his ironic use of the military metaphor (419). Because of her expensive existence and gluttonous ways, the matron has become fleshy, a prey to the grosser pleasures of overeating and overdrinking. Even more gross is the pleasure her fat flesh takes in a massage (421 ff.). Her life is debased, as the shrewd juxtaposition *summum dominae femur* implies. Unable to control her appetite, she makes a vulgar spectacle of herself in her own home (425 ff.).

(434–56) The musical pleasures of matrons were tinged with sexual fascination. In their literary dabblings, they have no conscious sexual motivation. They arrogate to themselves the pose of the most objective critics. With careful deliberation, they weigh the value of Homer and Vergil (435 ff.). But Juvenal insinuates the true subjectivity of women: Dido's unhappy love affair with Aeneas makes them lose their perspective completely. They can pardon her (435), because they do not understand the dangers which luxurious Carthage and an irresponsible love affair possessed. The great Roman theme which Vergil developed is lost on them. Similarly, they pose as moralists (444) or rhetorical specialists (450). And the woman becomes even more objectionable (*gravior*). She forces her opinions on others, criticizes her friends and husband for slight grammatical errors (455–56); and yet her attitude is nothing but a perverse form of pleasure. She is so intolerable because she has no perspective, no discrimination (*nec curanda* 455), by which to distinguish a useful from the useless purpose to which she puts her knowledge.

(457–73) In his transition (457–59), Juvenal shows the direction of his thought. The relation between a wealthy woman, or a woman subject to the corruption of Luxuria, and the traditional moral standards is progressively strained to the breaking point. Sexual aberrations are no longer exciting for her. They are an immediate assertion of the simple being, and she has destroyed that already. When the woman restrains her sexual instincts, she tries to find a secondary expression for her emotions. She begins to throw herself into the various evanescent attractions of the materialistic religion. Clothes and cosmetics become her ideal. As her debased life has made her hopelessly ugly, Juvenal can mock her desperate efforts at beautification and ask with a sardonic sneer, *facies dicetur an ulcus* (473)?

(474–507) The transition of 474–75 appears to promise that the satirist will deal with the daily routine of a Roman matron's existence. Instead, though, he incidentally mentions what a woman might do in the morning, then passes on to other matters not arranged in any temporal sequence. Viewed as irony, the transition has rhetorical justification. Juvenal makes one of his sweeping generalizations on the basis of a detail and implies that the whole day is represented in the vapidly cruel pursuits of the morning. Undoubtedly, though, this explanation does not completely remove the difficulty.[43] In his description, the satirist picks up two separate themes, stated in previous scenes, and joins them. He has spoken of the woman's petulance (413 ff.); he has spoken of her exaggerated concern with cosmetics (461 ff.). These themes were tentatively joined in the summary description of the woman as *gravis occursu, taeterrima vultu* (418). Now, the interrelation is clarified. It is because of her desperate efforts to adorn herself, generally in order to meet some lover (488–89), that the woman is so irritable and tyrannic. Juvenal exploits the ironic metaphor of the law court (e.g., *praefectura* 486). And the negative *non mitior* (486) is synonymous with *gravior*. Whereas *gravitas* is a Roman virtue, denoting a severity controlled by reason, the woman's *gravitas* is the cruelty of someone seeking satisfaction in another's misery. The satirist points this perversion up by his sympathetic description of Psecas (490–91); her nudity and disheveled state sharply emphasize her employer's self-concern and lack of interest in her slaves. Moreover, the legal metaphor recalls from Part I the interest of women in legal matters (242–45). The mannishness of the activity is here interpreted not as a violation of the marital relation, but as a stage in the degeneracy of pleasurable pursuits. A concern with beauty, which is predominantly feminine, and a savage temper that exults in the cries of one's slaves are inherently self-contradictory. Luxuria permits no goal in life but *gaudium*; but it taints *gaudium* from the beginning. It destroys discrimination; so petty tyranny assumes the role of justice. Physical attraction becomes a necessity which the very dissipations and disillusionments of Luxuria render impossible. The point is repeated, this time with a metaphor taken from the political or military council (498–501). An existence, undirected by any goal except the pursuit of pleasure, makes pleasure itself impossible. In the course of the vain pursuit, the woman tries every resource of her own sex, then violates her sexual limitations and seeks satisfaction in masculine activities. But the inhibition of her essential nature must destroy any possibility of pleasure. Here, the female interests and the male temperament come into explicit conflict. Hence, any threat to her appearance can be regarded as a *discrimen*, as dangerous as those menacing reputation or life (500). In that Luxuria has replaced Pudicitia, there can be nothing but tainted happiness for women; the life of Andromache is beyond recall (503).

(508–68) Juvenal suggested that the woman was perhaps preparing herself for the priest of Isis (*Isiacae...lenae* 489). In this vignette, he elaborates the point, depicting the woman as a prey to oriental superstitions. There is Bellona, whose eunuch band easily imposes on the foolish woman (517–21). There is no understanding of true danger any more. Peril is now associated with social gossip (500) or with petty omens (520). Superstition is a direct consequence of the moral confusion of the woman. One woman sets absolute standards for every minute ethical question (444 ff.). Her rigidity and the pliability of the superstitious woman are two sides of the same coin: neither woman has any genuine moral standards, because Luxuria has destroyed the possibility of morality. Unable to find any moral authority in herself or the traditions of Rome, the woman desperately adopts the most abject slavishness to foreign cults. Their authoritarianism makes her a miserable parody of herself, the tyrant in the home (510–11). She becomes a slave for Isis (522 ff.), an abject consultant of the most despicable series of diviners and astrologers (542 ff.). She even does penance for being a proper wife (535–36). At the beginning of Part II, Juvenal described the defilement of the altar of Pudicitia (308 ff.), then the debasement of the traditional rites of Bona Dea (314 ff.). He implied, in addition to the obvious corruption of

271

religion by Luxuria, that a new religion was replacing the old. Now, having explored the total breakdown of morality, the complete inanity of libertarian ethics, the lack of direction in any hedonistic life, the satirist makes the implication of the earlier scenes explicit. The new religion is under the aegis of Luxuria. As the supreme deity, she has made the environment receptive to foreign superstitions. Therefore, reflecting Luxuria, the moral codes of the new cults are relativistic; they have no standard but the promotion of the superstition or pandering to the secretly observed desires of the cult-adherents (565–68). In the apparent authority of these religions, women find justification for their aimless search of sensations.

(569–91) Superstition reaches its nadir when, not content with inquiring about and propitiating the future, a woman accepts the absolute rule of the horoscope, a predetermined course of existence. The moral vacuum has expanded into a totally irrational void. The woman cannot even make a decision. The Roman matron would have gone to Egypt to find some water for the cult of Isis (527); but she will not accompany her husband on his official functions if the revered numbers of Petosiris are against it (576). The absence of discrimination and perspective is illustrated by the transitional sentence (569–71). Dominated by superstition, women cannot even foresee happiness (in terms of Venus) or unhappiness, let alone direct their lives according to their desires. Oriental religion has encroached so far that Saturn and Venus have become only unimportant stars, not even relevant to astrology, no longer gods who dictate the proper behavior of mortals.[44]

(592–609) The lower classes were also caught up in the train of superstition (582ff.). At least, though, a common woman performs the function of motherhood (592–94). Society matrons will not undertake that role. In fact, should she become pregnant, a woman will do anything to have an abortion, to become sterile (595ff.). The degeneracy from properly female activities continues. Anubis could pass judgment on the legitimacy of marriage; now a woman can avoid childbirth. The thematic word *discrimen* is again subject to misuse. Once, *labores*, whether in childbirth or in the household, had a positive moral connotation (289). Now Luxuria spurns any work at all; murder is preferable (596). Still, there are easy ways of producing children for an eager husband. After all, pleasure is a relative thing All that matters is to deceive the husband. Pleasure has become warped into paradoxical emotions, satisfaction in the sterility of marriage (*gaude* 597), disillusion in the birth of a child (*gaudia* 602) From illegitimate relations come the officials of Rome, the pontifex and the Salian brotherhood. It is Fortuna now who plays with the destiny of Rome, *Fortuna improba* (605). She is the goddess of nondiscrimination, of moral relativism. Under her aegis, a wife could plead the case for her immorality by saying: *homo sum*! Under her motherly care—and the metaphor of *fovet* and *alumnos* (606ff.) is carefully selected—bastards are dignified with patrician names.

(610–42) The satirist condemned abortion as murder (595–97). Women also use potions to make a husband insane or subject to their personal whims; in fact, potions are employed to kill husband and stepchildren. Claudius, who was cuckolded by Messalina, was murdered by Agrippina. Clodia was also suspected of poisoning her husband Metellus. Beyond this, a woman cannot go. She has exhausted the perverted delights which are within the limits of the law; and the pleasures of crime are drained dry by a Pontia. When Juvenal expressed his horror at the prospect of Postumus' marriage, his hyperbole made his friend insane, marriage worse than death. Now, the hyperbole becomes a fact. A man is insane to marry, for his wife will undermine his sanity with her potions. He is undergoing a fate worse than death, because, as the coup de grâce after her other torments, his wife will poison him and his children. The moral scale has suffered a complete reversal (628). The arbitrary decisions of the tyrannous matron could be spoken of in terms that ironically contrasted her attitude with the impartial justice of the law court (486). Now, moral degradation has perverted the meaning of *fas*; murder is morally right. The full implications of *gravis* and *saevior armis luxuria* are revealed. As Luxuria has corroded the foundations of Roman morality, it has given impetus to license. At first, licentious behavior could find satisfaction in sexual sensationalism. However, the corrosion etched its way deeper, and sex was not enough. The disintegration affected the mind of the woman; her lack of moral discrimination led to an objectless oscillation between vapid rationality and total irrationality. She arrogated to herself the right of discrimination, when she had no principles on which to base her judgment. But she considered herself the soul of morality. Then her shift to the unstable authoritarianism of foreign cults and astrology reflected her irrationality. And now, her diseased imagination can regard the murder of her stepchildren as morally right. She plans her crimes calmly, with full calculation of means and the results she expects to achieve. The very sanity which is predicated of the murderess (652) symbolizes the extent of her moral insanity. Luxuria is *saevior armis*, it is *gravis*, because it causes the moral breakdown which is the condition for the savage sanity of a Pontia.

By the time that he has reached the final paragraph of the satire, Juvenal has transmuted his theme of Luxuria into something grander. In Part I, the more general theme of Luxuria was implicit in the treatment of Pudicitia. The more general concept of tragedy is implicit in the treatment of Luxuria in Part II. Luxuria is tantamount to the moral breakdown which makes existence a random search for pleasure. As the satire has proceeded, the vista has repeatedly expanded, especially through the use of Roman religion and justice as standards of reference for the contemporary collapse. Women have rejected more than their own proper sexual function; they have rejected the full series of Roman values as represented in Roman religion, Roman justice, and a firm reverence for Sapientia against Fortuna. In the rejection of Roman values, in the decline from the traditional restraint of those glorious days when Rome rose single-handed and defeated Hannibal, Juvenal sees the great tragedy of women. And it is a tragedy not only of women, but of all Romans. Hence, the ironical significance of the proud boast: *homo sum*!

Juvenal's Book 1 was devoted to exposing the various aspects of the Roman ideal, the simple individual, and the military hero. *Satire* 6 (Book 2) is designed as a counterpart. As the general decadence of Rome was seen in the particular perversions of men, so, here, the decadence is portrayed in the perversions of women. *Satire* 2 revealed the effeminacy of men against the background of Roman military ideals.

Part I of *Satire* 6 reveals the masculine characteristics of women against the background of *pudor*, the wife's proper function at home. *Satire* 4 showed the degradation of *virtus* to the extremes of *saevitia* and *deliciae*, using an epic framework. Femininity, in *Satire* 6, becomes a composite of *gaudium* and *saevitia*. *Satire* 3 explored the death of *paupertas Romana*; *Satire* 5 exposed *luxuria* at banquets. As its explanation for the disappearance of Pudicitia, *Satire* 6 uses these themes in Part II. Thus, in Book 2, the actions of the woman are generalized into the Roman tragedy.

Tragedy requires special diction and special subject matter. Accordingly, in 634–37, Juvenal specifically suggests that his style is tragic, Sophoclean; he goes on to state that a Pontia justifies his apparent violation of genre limits. What is apparently a stylistic defense serves actually to present another viewpoint, by which the moral situation can be judged. The ideas of Greek tragedy can be brought into the picture and placed as a relevant standard against the habits of contemporary women. So, in the final lines of Part II, Juvenal expands his horizon to embrace the eternal concepts of tragedy; once again, he suggests themes from Part I and Part II, this time giving them their final form as indicative of the Roman tragedy.

Epilogue (642–61)

Juvenal uses myth to emphasize by contrast the reality of his subject matter.[45] In the Epilogue, he uses the tragic themes to sharpen the portrait of contemporary wickedness. So the present has all the evil of tragedy, but none of the dramatic illusion. Women are passionless and calculating in their crimes (645, 652); their prototypes at least were motivated by feelings of vengeance, feelings which had justification because of their very irrationality (646–50). In 286, the satirist condemned the breakdown of the marital relation as *monstra*. Now, *monstra* (645) refers to the ultimate stage in the moral breakdown due to the corrosive effect of Luxuria. Alcestis is a vanished ideal (653); Clytemnestra is the new model for women (656 ff.). In fact, if the lot of Alcestis were ever offered to a modern woman, she would rather save her puppy than her husband (654). Thus, having analyzed the modern tragedy Juvenal recalls, at the end, the ideas of the Prologue. The crude, but loyal, wife of the Golden Age has in effect been replaced by Lesbia, who is so feminine as to find the sword a crude weapon for murder (657–59), who can waste such emotion on a sparrow or a puppy, who, in short, has emancipated herself from Pudicitia and become a slave of Luxuria.[46]

Is this, then, as Highet states, a "satire on marriage"? As a means to an answer, Juvenal's usage of the key word *maritus* is helpful. A form of *maritus* occurs eighteen times in *Satire* 6, about equally divided between Parts I and II.[47] Moreover, both because of its difficult scansion and its importance, Juvenal alway places it in the significant final position. To support *maritus*, he also uses *vir*.[48] Obviously, the husband is an important element throughout the satire. I maintain, however, that marriage is not the central element of structure. A woman's life must be judged by some external standard, the ideal according to which she should live. For the Romans, this was Pudicitia. Because most women ultimately marry, concrete manifestations of Pudicitia are most common among married women; similarly with examples of *impudicitia*. However, while including marriage, Pudicitia has a broader scope, as the Prologue shows. Therefore, if Juvenal had been writing a satire on marriage, he would not have used the Prologue, which would have suggested too much, but begun at 21, continued until 285, and ended with a brief, sardonic comment. In Part I, it does seem that the subject is marriage, but because of the Prologue and the transition in 286 ff. to something different, the conclusion is inescapable that marriage is being used to demonstrate a larger theme. In the Prologue, Juvenal said that Pudicitia was gone. In Part I, he proves it by showing that there is no *pudor* left in marriage, the institution in which Pudicitia is especially important. In using *maritus*, Juvenal places it in close relation to *uxor* or *illa*; the wife's treatment of her husband, to whom she should be subordinate, is good evidence for the extent of her *pudor*. The disappearance of Pudicitia is convincing; its significance, however, is only hinted at in Part I (e.g., 118, 265). Accordingly, the satirist proceeds to assign a reason for her flight. Instead of choosing the antithetic quality, *impudicitia* or *libido*, a choice rendered unnecessary by his negative presentation of Part I, he makes a transition, via the ideal Roman wife of the Hannibalic wars, to the materialistic concept of Luxuria. Luxuria is the condition of *libido*; *paupertas Romana* is the condition of *pudor*.[49] Part II, then, proves the materialistic explanation, that *saeva luxuria* dominates women, Roman women; for *Romana* is an in-

dication of the ultimate purpose of the satirist. Most women are married; therefore a husband can be assumed. Because, however, the theme is not marriage, the husband is presented in a different manner. It is as a passive symbol of a woman's proper role that *maritus* is used. The perversion of religion by sexual orgies (301–48) has no bearing on marriage; therefore, the husband is an incidental victim (312, 346). Again, the desperate search for pleasure has little bearing on marriage. While *maritus* is used in nearly every paragraph from 400 ff., his role is that of the spectator. Finally, when the woman has exhausted the resources of pleasure, she turns against the symbol of her ideal function and destroys it. The murder of her husband is the proof of her moral irresponsibility, of the triumph of Luxuria. In 284, she ended Part I and the marriage relation by declaring: *homo sum!* Now, she ends Part II and her search for diversion by murdering her husband. The deed is correlative to the assertion, because, as 286–300 showed, the flight of Pudicitia meant the victory of Luxuria. The structure of *Satire* 6 is conclusively against an interpretation of the central theme as that of marriage. The subject of the satire is Woman, Roman Woman, and her tragedy. She has lost her womanhood (*pudor*, 21–285); in its place, she has adopted viciousness (*saeva luxuria*, 301–643). Clodia, the unchaste wife, has become Clodia, the poisoner of her husband.

NOTES

1. The following article is based upon a portion of my dissertation, "The Rhetoric of Juvenal," presented to the faculty of the Graduate School of Yale University in candidacy for the Ph.D. degree in June, 1954.

2. Among the brave, I would list C. F. Nägelsbach, "Ueber die composition der vierten und sechsten satire Juvenals," *Philol.*, III (1848), 469–82; W. Stegemann, *De Juvenalis dispositione* (Weyda, 1913), pp. 36 ff.; T. Birt,

"Der Aufbau der sechsten und vierten Satire Juvenals," *Rh. Mus.*, LXX (1915), 524–50; and P. Ercole, *Studi Giovenaliani* (ed. E. Paratore, Lanciano, 1935), pp. 185 ff. The prudent would include G. A. Ruperti, *Juvenalis saturae¹* (Leipzig, 1819), p. 92; L. Friedländer, *D. Junii Juvenalis saturarum libri V mit erklärenden Anmerkungen* (Leipzig, 1895), p. 278; and P. de Labriolle, *Les Satires de Juvénal: étude et analyse* (Paris, 1932), p. 124.

3. G. Highet, *Juvenal the Satirist: A Study* (Oxford, 1954); hereafter referred to as H.

4. H., p. 91.

5. H., p. 267, n. 8. He also refers to the work of Vianello, with which I personally have no acquaintance. V.'s scheme ranks him among the brave.

6. H. transposes 133–35 to 626.

7. This section includes the Oxford Fragment, which H. accepts as genuine.

8. H., p. 101.

9. H. p. 267, n. 8.

10. H., p. 97.

11. H., p. 103.

12. *Loc. cit.* For the structure, cf. H., p. 267, n. 8.

13. Cf. the explanations in H., pp. 93 ff. and 170 ff. The works of Stegemann, *op. cit.*; A. Hartmann, *De inventione Iuvenalis* (Basle, 1908); and J. de Decker, *Iuvenalis declamans* (Ghent, 1913) are, though unsatisfactory, still basic.

14. This is not to be interpreted to mean that Juvenal merely uses rhetorical theses in his satires. Juvenal adapts rhetorical techniques to his satire; he does not subject himself to a set pattern taken from the schools. Cf. the doctrine of De Decker, *op. cit.*

15. Cf. the ironic use of *simplex* in 327.

16. This is one of the sections which H. finds it impossible to fit. If my understanding of the thematic presentation is correct, the theme of *pudor* degenerated is well represented in this scene. On the other hand, as I shall attempt to show, there is a different theme for 300 ff. Therefore, there is good reason for the disposition of this section here.

17. Cf. De Decker, *op. cit.*, p. 92. He criticizes the degeneration of the dialogue form of exposition, assuming that dialogue is a basic element of satire. Even after 200, he says, Postumus is merely a person to be addressed. One difficulty to my theory remains. In 377, Postumus is addressed for the last time by name. However, it might just as well be another Postumus, since the satirist introduces him only to make an ironic point. By addressing a specific person, he makes his remark more vivid. This Postumus, however, has no further function than to make the remark vivid. Also, he seems different from the original Postumus, *moechorum notissimus* (42). The stylistic habit of breaking away to make a direct address is common in Juvenal. Cf. 8. 181. Juvenal uses a fictitious interlocutor much in 300 ff., as is his regular practice, but one never feels that the man contemplating marriage by the name of Postumus exists. I suggest, therefore, that the treatment of Postumus in 377 is different from that of the early Postumus, as a stylistic asset rather than a vital character in the thematic presentation of Part II.

18. Cf. H., p. 268, n. 11: "Notice the implied identification of the noble, simple Golden Age of myth with the great days of the Roman republic."

19. Cf. Friedländer, *op. cit.*, p. 278: "Wiederholt ist Zusammengehöriges auseinander gerissen." See also Ruperti, *op. cit.*, p. 92.

20. The symbol is reinforced by a verbal echo from 14.

21. In Part II, many of the women described are not married or marriageable, as, for instance, Maura the prostitute. And *uxor* is replaced by *domina*; cf. p. 87 above.

22. Juvenal uses *pudor* in a new manner in 357, *q. v.*

23. Lesbia represents the effect of luxury on Roman women. She is forever tainted by her former lover Catullus as incestuous, by her former lover Caelius as the murderer of her husband. She probably connived in the escapade of her beloved Clodius. Cf. n. 46 below.

24. H., p. 101, calls 351 ff. a "catalogue of the vices." I believe that there is some sequence to the various scenes.

25. Cf. H., p. 336, n. 19. His division is similar to mine, though he reaches a different conclusion.

26. The bibliography is extensive. For the period up to 1930, it is cited in Ercole, *op. cit.*, p. 224, n. 6. H.,

p. 336, n. 19, gives a selection of notable treatments up to 1954. To be added are R. Helm, *Burs. Jahresb.*, CCXXVIII (1943), 15 ff. and J. Colin, "Juvénal, les baladins et les rétiaires d'après le manuscrit d'Oxford," *Att. Acc. Sci. Tor.*, LXXXVII (1952–53), 315–86.

27. P. von Winterfeld, "Zu den Oxforder Juvenalversen," *Berl. phil. Woch.*, XIX (1899), 793–94, and a review in *Gött. gel. Anz.*, CLXI (1899), 895 ff.

28. F. Nougaret, "Juvénal: Omission du fragment Winstedt," *Mélanges E. Chatelaïn* (Paris, 1910), pp. 255–67; L. Herrmann, "Sur la disposition de l'original de Juvénal," *Latomus*, XI (1952), 334–36; R. Verdière, "Juvenalianum," *Latomus*, XI (1952), 25–26.

29. E. g., A. E. Housman, "The New Fragment of Juvenal," *CR*, XV (1901), 263–66; J. P. Postgate, "On the New Fragments of Juvenal," *CR*, XIII (1899), 206–8.

30. F. Leo, "Doppelfassungen bei Juvenal," *Hermes*, XLIV (1909), 600–17.

31. G. Jachmann, "Studien zu Juvenal," *Gött. Nachrichten* (1946), 321 ff.; U. Knoche, "Handschriftliche Grundlagen des Juvenaltextes," *Philol.*, Suppl. XXXIII : I (1940), 68 ff.

32. The scholia comment on the phrase *cauta est et ab illis incipit uxor* as follows: "qui nunc lascivae furta puellae / hac mercede silent: crimen commune tacetur," (Ò 32–33).

33. Cf. Ercole, *op. cit.*, p. 249: "Le parole delle *scol...* attestano in modo non dubbio che, pur dopo l'omissione del frammento A nel testo tradizionale, non se n'era del tutto perduta la memoria, ma esso s'era continuato a leggere—e non negli ultimi 5 versi soltanto, *ma per intero*—in qualche antico manoscritto perdutosi."

34. B. Axelson, "A Problem of Genuineness in Juvenal," Δράγμα *Martino P. Nilsson* (Lund, 1939), pp. 41–55.

35. Hence the many immediate attempts at exegesis. Cf. the bibliography.

36. F. Buecheler, "Der echte oder der unechte Juvenal ?" *Rh. Mus.*, LIV (1899), 484–88.

37. U. Knoche, "Ein Wort zur Echtheitskritik," *Philol.*, XCIII (1938), 196–217. Cf. the third point of Highet's analysis (p. 336).

38. *Ibid.* His vehemence is criticized by Axelson, *loc. cit.*

39. Cf. H., p. 336, n. 19: "I myself believe it is Juvenal's work because I cannot think of any other poet who could have written it, esp. such lines as O 14–16 and O 25–29, and remained unknown to fame."

40. *Op. cit.*, pp. 243 ff.

41. *Quaestiones criticae Juvenalianae* (Leipzig, 1912).

42. Cf. p. 92 above.

43. Friedländer, *op. cit.*, p. 50, considered this a typical example of "Abweichungen von dem vorgezeichneten Plan."

44. It was under the rule of Saturn that Pudicitia lived on earth (1). Venus, too, has become besotted by 300, so that the happiness of love is impossible.

45. Cf. the attack on myth which opens *S.* 1 and the device in 15. 13 ff.

46. I do not insist on the importance of Lesbia (Clodia), but the mention of her in the Prologue and the similarity of her history to the conclusion is, to me, suggestive. Also, cf. the references to Clodia: Cic. *Pro Cael.* 8. 18, *hanc Palatinam Medeam*; Quint. *Inst. or.* 8. 6. 53, *quadrantariam Clytemestram*, quoting a familiar sneer of Caelius. Clodia was compared by her contemporaries to the tragic heroines who murdered their husbands.

47. The word *maritus* occurs in 10 (the Prologue), 100, 136, 149, 184, 211, 229, 232 (Part I), 291 (Transition), 400, 432, 456, 463, 475, 509, 611, 619 (Part II), and 652 (Epilogue).

48. The word *vir* is used for *maritus* in 112, 116, 224, 270, 389, 508, 575, 654.

49. Val. Max. 9. 1 is entitled *De luxuria et libidine*. In his introduction, the author insists on the interrelation between the two moral faults: *iungatur illi* (*luxuriae*) *libido, quoniam ex isdem vitiorum principiis oritur.*

THE PROGRAMS OF JUVENAL'S LATER BOOKS

IT IS conventional to describe Juvenal's First Satire as a "program poem," and for good reasons. Not only does the satirist explain his attitude toward his genre, but he does so according to the traditional methods of his predecessors, Lucilius, Horace, and Persius. However, not all students remember the chronological order of the poems, and consequently one will meet again and again statements about Juvenal's satires in general, which spring from the tacit assumption that the program of Satire 1 applies with equal validity to the poems of the later books. For example, Scaliger's phrase about *saeva indignatio* was apparently written, and is always cited, to characterize the mood of every satire, or at least the attitude which we should associate with the satirist. Again, scholars will write about Juvenal's hatred of Domitian and insist on detecting marked evidence of it as late as Book 3. It was a twisted application of such an assumption that prompted the outrageous thesis of Ribbeck's *Der echte und der unechte Juvenal*, almost a hundred years ago. Because he failed to find in the satires of Books 4 and 5 the techniques which belong to the indignant Juvenal, Ribbeck felt free to label Satires 10, 12, 13, 14, and 15 as the work of an interpolator.[1]

Although nobody today would go so far as Ribbeck, it is of the utmost importance to stress the fact that Satire 1 was written at the time of Book 1 and for Book 1 only. Not that an observant student need fall into error; for the reaction against Ribbeck necessitated vindicating the later Juvenal by admitting the changed emphasis, but insisting that the style remained substantially the same. And Highet's recent study shows how much can be elicited from the satires, if they are viewed in chronological order, that is, as capable of an altered attitude.[2] However, more can still be said about the changing attitude of the satirist, especially if we free ourselves from a biographical approach to the question and recognize the distinction between Juvenal and the speaker in the satires (whom I shall hereafter call "the satirist"). This paper will seek to define the basic terminology appropriate to *indignatio*, then demonstrate how the satirist steadily disowns the indignation which supposedly makes his verse in Book 1. Finally, I shall propose the theory that the initial satire in *every* book, while less obviously than Satire 1, serves a programmatic purpose in its particular book.

I shall not trouble the reader with an exhaustive analysis of Satire 1, since it is a familiar poem and has been frequently discussed; but it might be well to run over the principal aspects of Juvenal's program as there set forth.[3] They may be summarized in four propositions: (1) The satirist has swept aside epic and tragedy and replaced them by his epical, tragic satire. (2) He is justified in so doing, because he takes as his subject a theme worthy of epic, particularly the counter epic of the Silver Age: namely, the utter ignominy, the total degeneracy of Rome. (3) Reacting as he does to Roman corruption, the satirist proclaims as his characteristic mood *indignatio*. (4) In order to express indignation appropriately, in accordance with rhetorical theories, the satirist adopts the Grand Style, the first time that a satirist has dared to do so since Horace established the doctrine of the Plain Style as alone fitting for satire. In short, the satirist announces a perfectly coherent program, in which the moral insight justifies the style and the impatience with the artificial topics of epic and tragedy; or, if you prefer, in which the style and the rhetoric of indignation determine the moral comments. Whichever one chooses to place first, style or ethical attitude, the fact remains that the satirist summarizes his own program so perfectly that most commentators are content to cite his words: *facit indignatio versum*.

While Satire 1 states the creed that indignation makes the verse of the poems in Book 1, it also represents this indignation at work, both through selected rhetorical devices and through self-conscious description of the satirist's emotions. I shall not discuss the techniques appropriate to indignation, for example, such devices as rhetorical questions, exclamations, apostrophes, and ellipsis,[4] but shall concentrate instead on the language by which the satirist explicitly indicates his passion. Indignation typically "erupts," "blazes," or "burns the vitals," when one rages against evil seen or experienced. The evil is *indignum*, something on the order of *vitium, crimen, scelus, iniuria, monstrum*. Thus, to begin the poem, the satirist expresses his fury over the *iniuria* which he constantly suffers from the grand poets, and he cries for punishment (*reponam* 1, *inpune* 2, 3). While his rage seems exaggerated, it effectively introduces a new section in which he proceeds to set forth a catalogue of typical Roman vices, this time a more adequate excuse for indignation. Punctuating the list of evils here and there, the satirist implies his *indignatio* for the Roman reader long before he openly uses the word in l. 79. First, after describing the married eunuch, the unsexed Mevia, and Crispinus (22–29), he states: "It is difficult not to write satire." Why? Because who could be so tolerant of a corrupt city, who so ironhearted, as to hold himself in check when he saw the informers and a whole new series of scoundrels (30–31)? In the satirist's angry rhetorical question, he gives us a complete description of indignation: he faces an evil city (*iniquae urbis*) and cannot endure or suffer it (*patiens*), cannot put irons on his emotions (*ferreus*) so as to restrain himself (*teneat se*). The fact that indignation erupts and blazes forth presupposes another fact: that a good man cannot endure evil, cannot control the surge of righteous wrath that wells up in him at sight of vice. Accordingly, one of the basic themes of indignation in Juvenal's satires is the word "endure": *ferre, pati, tolerare*. When the satirist introduces a scene provoking his fury, he often asks as in l. 30: "Who could endure this?" Or he may assert, as in 3. 60: "I cannot endure a Greek city."[5]

The satirist punctuates his catalogue a second time at 1. 45, and, as before, he effects his transition to additional evils by a rhetorical question which again defines his indignation: "quid referam quanta siccum iecur ardeat ira, cum . . . ?" For the purposes of rhetoric, anger and indignation were considered to be substantially similar.[6] But for the satirist, it was especially convenient to make the identification, because the physiological symptoms of wrath had long been a favorite *topos*, adapted to rhetoric and poetry from the popularizing medical treatises. As we have seen, indignation "burns"; the verb *ardere* and its compounds frequently appear in descriptions of this emotion. However, in 1. 45 the "burning" of wrath becomes an actual physical sensation caused by the dry liver; and when the satirist chooses to be more specific, instead of referring to the liver, he names the bile, the liquid secreted by the liver and considered intrinsically related to anger.[7]

Two more rhetorical questions, interrupting the parade of villainy, lead us inevitably to the explicit appeal to *indignatio*. First, the satirist asks:

haec ego non credam Venusina digna lucerna ?
haec ego non agitem ? sed quid magis ? He-
	racleas
aut Diomedeas aut mugitum labyrinthi . . .
	[51–53] ?

I have argued elsewhere that the satirist refers to Horace the grand poet, composer of the Epodes and Roman Odes, not to Horace of the *Sermones*. My argument is borne out, I believe, by the immediate allusion, by way of contrast, to the hackneyed topics of tragedy, utterly worthless in comparison with the patriotic themes of Horace. So the satirist's wrath and the villains whom he intends to portray entitle him to rise to the heights of Horatian emotion. I call attention also to the thematic *digna* in 1. 51: the word is sardonic here, in 73, and often elsewhere. It stresses what is in fact *indignum*, supreme villainy that is not "worthy" at all, but rather "deserves" the harshest attack, the severest punishment. Later, in 63, the satirist cries out: "nonne libet medio ceras inplere capaces quadrivio, cum iam . . . ?" The passage implies that this satire feeds on reality, is utterly true, and secondly that the satirist speaks or feels impelled to speak out frankly in public. The word *libet*, as *liberet* in 152, should remind the reader of the dominant trait of Lucilian satire, its *libertas*.

The satirist's fury sweeps over the whole history of mankind, he claims, from the moment that men first returned after the Flood; ever since Pyrrha and Deucalion, that is, ever since the Age of Iron and its legendary corruption, material has existed to stir a moralist's despair. (81 ff.). Using the Flood or the end of Saturn's reign, both symbolizing the same thing, as the starting point of sin and hence of indignation is a common *topos* of other satires.

At the end of Satire 1 (147 ff.), the satirist takes up several *topoi* from the traditional Program Satire. He opens the paragraph by once again asserting his anguish over Roman corruption and calling for the magniloquent diction of the Grand Style in order to express his passion: "utere velis, totos pande sinus" (148–50). Does he possess the necessary *ingenium*, though, he imagines his interlocutor asking. And, since *ingenium* in this context automatically reminds one of the powerful lines of Lucilius, the question continues: How could you ever equal the directness and honesty of the first satirist ?

	unde illa priorum
scribendi quodcumque animo flagrante liberet
simplicitas [151–53] ?

279

The words used here to describe the manner of Lucilius, soon supported by the picture of *Lucilius ardens* (165), with drawn sword, roaring down upon his victims, make of him the ideal prototype of Juvenal's satirist. As Juvenal's satirist burns with fury to speak out immediately against Roman corruption, so Lucilius, according to this version, did voice his fiery feelings with utter frankness. To be sure, in this later age Lucilius' successor cannot practice the same *libertas* and hope to live; but Juvenal's satirist insists on a complete identification between his *indignatio* and the flaming passion with which Lucilius is supposed to have written.

That the mood announced by this Program Satire does pervade the poems of Book 1 is a fact that few would deny. Thoroughly imbued as he is with rhetorical techniques, Juvenal does not confine himself to a single method of voicing indignation. Accordingly, while Satire 2 as a whole abounds in angry questions, apostrophes, and carefully selected details that represent the jaundiced mood of the satirist, Juvenal also attributes to Laronia, the woman who contrasts the natural honesty of her sex with the perversions of men, an indignant speech; he introduces it with the typical phrase: "non tulit ex illis torvum Laronia quendam / clamantem" (36–37). Laronia's refusal to endure such vice becomes, in Satire 3, Umbricius' long denunciation of Rome, where he appropriates the role of the indignant satirist. In Satire 4, *indignatio* expresses itself by means of a savage mock epic. It is, however, Satire 5 which especially uses the terminology of indignation that we have discerned in the Program Satire.

To put the theme of Satire 5 in terms relevant to our argument, we may say that the indignant satirist tries to rouse the indignation of an abject client Trebius, to the point where Trebius will proudly reject a humiliating invitation from Virro to what would be a cruelly demeaning dinner. Will Trebius tolerate Virro's insults ? If so, then he will have debased himself to such an extent that he will be no free guest, but a buffoon owned and abused by the sadistic Virro. Nowhere else but in Satire 5 does Juvenal use the word *indignatio*, to match its appearance in Satire 1.[8] Nowhere else in Book 1 does he show such interest in the psychology of anger. Thus, the introduction prepares us for the later scene when Trebius slavishly endures without protest what the satirist calls *iniuria cenae* (cf. 9):

si te propositi nondum *pudet* atque eadem est mens,
ut bona summa putes aliena vivere quadra,
si potes illa *pati* quae nec Sarmentus *iniquas*
Caesaris ad mensas nec *vilis* Gabba *tulisset* [1–4].

The main portion of Satire 5 (12–155) portrays the dinner of Virro and focuses indignantly on the vicious discrimination by patron against client. Then, in his conclusion, the satirist returns to the vocabulary of indignation, to press home the ideas announced in 1–4. Trebius lamely suggests that Virro is saving money (156). "Nonsense," retorts the satirist, "Virro enjoys torturing you to see how much humiliation you can stand; he hopes to provoke your indignation and see you torn between your appetite and your just wrath." Since tears and anger go together—the tears suggesting the helplessness of the wrath—the satirist summarizes the nasty scheme of Virro as follows:

hoc agit, ut *doleas*; nam quae comoedia, mimus
quis melior *plorante* gula ? ergo omnia fiunt,
si nescis, ut *per lacrimas effundere bilem*
cogaris pressoque diu stridere molari [157–60].

While *dolor* can apply to any unhappy emotion, here, as often in Juvenal's satires, it is adapted to a context of indignation and therefore serves as a synonym for anger. I have mentioned the importance of *bilis* as a technical term for indignation, in connection with 1.45. The tears and clenched teeth constitute other natural characteristics of the same passion.

If the reference to *comoedia* and *mimus* in 157 fails to remind the reader of the buffoons Sarmentus and Gabba in 3–4, then the final four lines will do so; for what the satirist implies as a possibility in the introduction (that Trebius will sink below the level of court jesters) turns into a fact which he can predict without fail in the conclusion.

ille sapit, qui te sic utitur. omnia *ferre*
si potes, et debes. *pulsandum* vertice raso
praebebis quandoque caput nec dura timebis
flagra *pati*, his epulis et tali *dignus* amico.

Thus, Book 1 ends by strongly reasserting the importance of *indignatio*, not only as the dominant mood of these five satires, but as the birthright of a free Roman, to be relinquished only at the price of his entire independence.

Before discussing the intermediate Books 2, 3, and 4, I shall proceed directly to Satire 13, the opening poem of Book 5, to indicate how differently the satirist now talks, with respect to the terminology of indignation.[9] If we confine our attention to the satirist and indignation, we may safely summarize Satire 13 as follows: the satirist urbanely ridicules the naive indignation of Calvinus, who has suffered considerable financial loss when a friend reneged on a loan, and then ironically "consoles" him for the "tragedy." Quite different from the attitude of Book 1, where, as I have pointed out, the satirist attributes to Laronia and Umbricius a righteous wrath with which he

fully agrees, here the satirist's urbanity acts in total contrast with the fury of Calvinus; and the fury suffers by comparison. Let us look at some of the terms used to render Calvinus' emotions in the introduction:

ponamus nimios *gemitus. flagrantior aequo*
non debet *dolor* esse viri nec volnere maior.
tu quamvis levium minimam exiguamque
    malorum
particulam vix *ferre* potes *spumantibus ardens
visceribus*, sacrum tibi quod non reddat ami-
    cus
depositum? *stupet* haec qui... [11–16]?

Here are depicted the same emotions, in the same terminology, as in Book 1, with the striking difference that now, instead of appropriating them to himself to render dramatically sympathetic his patriotic fury, the satirist ridicules them in someone else, insisting that they exceed reality and the limits set by reason. He no longer burns at inequity (cf. *inaequus* 1. 30 and 5. 3).

As in Satire 1, the satirist punctuates his discussion with quick references to indignation, this time, however, to the indignation of Calvinus, from which he laughingly dissociates himself. Whereas an Umbricius achieved grandeur by exclaiming over the Greek city's unbearable corruption and whereas Trebius' craven endurance of insults merited our contempt, now the satirist calmly urges the necessity of tolerating life's misfortunes: *ferre incommoda vitae* (21). Not to bear evil tranquilly becomes now the sign of immaturity, childishness.[10] As a man of sixty, Calvinus should know better.

dic, senior bulla *dignissime, nescis*
quas habeat veneres aliena pecunia? *nescis*
quem tua *simplicitas* risum vulgo moveat...
    [33–35]?

As if to increase the contrast with Satire 1 and the preconceptions of *indignatio*, the satirist patronizes the "wor-

281

thy" Calvinus and treats the older man's wrath as infantile rage; he refuses to consider here the serious breach of friendship which has provoked Calvinus' ire. In the same way, he now mocks *simplicitas*, once a synonym for the noble *libertas* of Lucilius (cf. 1. 153): anyone would laugh at Calvinus, even the lowest members of Roman society.[11]

When in Satire 1 he had established the basis of *indignatio*, the satirist proceeded to affirm the universal perversion by referring to the times of Pyrrha and Deucalion. Ever since then, corruption has prevailed, he asserted, but never worse than now. The altered manner in Satire 13 embraces this motif also: instead of provoking the satirist's despairing fury, however, the universal degradation serves as a sobering fact which we all should frankly and rationally face. Accordingly, after laughing at the *simplicitas* of Calvinus, the satirist immediately embarks on a fanciful and ironic portrait of the Age of Saturn (38 ff.), in which he seems to project his conception of *simplicitas* so slyly that the mythical virtues of that age appear altogether incredible, incredibly naive. Let us be frank, he concludes. An honest man today is like those legendary characters: a *monstrum*, a portent, like the omen associated with Aeneas' arrival in Italy (68–69), like the trite *adynata* of the poet. Once again, the terminology has changed its implications, for in Book 1 the satirist treated the corruption as *monstrum*, from which his indignation took its cue; now he plays with the same word.

While the satirist never showed much piety in Book 1, he did exploit apostrophe to the gods and descriptions which, by showing the neglect of the temples or the invasion of new, un-Roman cults, revealed the extent of Roman degeneracy. And as we shall see, he continues to use the gods as a stimulus for indignation in Book 2. Therefore, the reader should recall such strident apostrophes as those of 2. 126 ff. and 6. 393 ff. when he comes to 13. 112 ff. Calvinus' appeals to Jupiter, couched in terms remarkably similar to the language of 6. 393 ff., must be interpreted now as ludicrous:

tu *miser exclamas*, ut Stentora vincere possis,
vel potius quantum Gradivus Homericus,
"audis,
Iuppiter, haec nec labra moves..."

In 2. 128 the satirist fiercely invoked Gradivus against the effeminates, in vain of course; now Gradivus merely reminds us of Homer's bellowing bully. All through Satire 3, Umbricius extracted sympathy by his use of *miser*; now the word contains the note of contempt which consistently characterizes the satirist's attitude toward indignation in this satire.

Playing the role of the calm rationalist, the satirist instructs foolish Calvinus in the way to bear evil, never entirely seriously, always ready to poke fun at childish fury or to make ironic concessions to it. The consolation which he professes to give (120 ff.) belongs to the stock material of rhetoric; the arguments can be watched in the formal *consolationes* of Seneca, and, in the role of diatribist, Seneca uses them in his essays *De ira* and *De tranquillitate animi*. However, the familiar arguments permit the satirist to introduce a new consideration, which renders Calvinus' indignation not only infantile, but suspect. For if Calvinus feels such exaggerated fury over the loss of a little money, he reveals his own inadequate values; his crass materialism blocks his progress to *sapientia*. To make this prejudicial point from the beginning, the satirist compares the *dolor* and *gemitus*—the same terms as he used in 11–12 —occasioned by a death in the family with the grief provoked by financial losses. Nowadays, the first is a counterfeit emotion, paraded before the public; the second springs from the heart, or, as he says, "ploratur lacrimis amissa pecunia veris" (134).

The first argument of the *consolatio* uses the familiar *topos*, associated with death, but also with wrath, that this event is common and really not so serious as the sufferings of others: "rem *pateris* modicam et mediocri *bile ferendam*" (143). Look at all the crimes which come daily before the prefect Gallicus, says the satirist, with a calm reasonableness which utterly breaks with the satirist of Book 1, who gained such momentum for his indignation from a catalogue of similar crimes. As he continues, he seems to concentrate increasingly on the standard themes about anger. The wrathful Calvinus demands vengeance: *quid plus velit ira* (176)? To this, the retort comes that vengeance does not repair the loss, nor should it characterize an intelligent man: vindictiveness belongs to the ignorant and to women: "nempe hoc indocti, quorum *praecordia* nullis / interdum aut levibus videas *flagrantia* causis" (181–82). Finally, Calvinus hears that conscience tortures the criminal more than any legal punishment, and that, in any case, the habit of crime will eventually bring the wretch to his merited end. And with a last sneer the satirist pictures Calvinus exulting in the harsh penalty (247) inflicted on his former "friend" and now delightedly confessing his belief in divine justice.

Here, then, the satirist contemptuously rejects *indignatio* as unreal, excessive, childish, and motivated by corrupt traits in Calvinus' soul. Does this not sound like some of the typical attacks by critics on "Juvenal's sincerity"? However, it is not my purpose to examine the merits of indignation or urbanity. Rather, we should now ask whether the attitude evinced in Satire 13 holds sufficiently true for the other satires of Book 5 to serve as a programmatic statement. Our answer is a qualified, Yes. In Satire 14, the satirist acts as an instructor, eager to urge a positive doctrine of education. Although in the course of his discussion he becomes overwrought against *avaritia*, still he follows the ideas of diatribists so closely that we have no trouble identifying him with the speaker of Satire 13. Satire 15 goes even farther in its open hostility to vice, but, while we may call the satirist indignant again, we should recognize the difference between the speakers in Satires 1 and 15. In Satire 15 the satirist chooses an extraordinary instance of vice, the result of bestial *ira*[12] patently labeled as unusual and alien, then exposes its incredible vileness from the perspective of Stoic humanitarianism; and he regards this *humanitas* as a valid and practicable ideal. In other words, while he utterly condemns Egypt, he preaches a positive creed that he expects to win favorable hearing among his Roman audience, exempt from such vice.

Satire 16, mutilated as it is, does not permit us to define its attitude exactly. I agree with Highet that it could potentially end in a sardonic indictment of the path by which such generals as Trajan and Hadrian gained the throne.[13] However, we lack that crucial ending. All we can say is that the satirist speaks in an urbane manner about the inequitable discrimination between soldier and civilian. While the subject could be dangerous, still the satirist presents to us a smiling mask in the sixty lines that survive. To conclude, Book 5 does not exhibit the single manner of Book 1, but it does uniformly reject the *indig-*

natio that Satire 1 proclaims; and the four satires present a satirist who is far more consistent with the speaker of Satire 13 than with the indignant orator of Book 1.

Between Books 1 and 5 Juvenal wrote seven satires, which he organized as three books. Satire 6, which reached sufficient length to be treated as a book in itself, seems to have been composed shortly after the publication of Book 1, at any rate in the reign of Trajan. It is a companion piece to Book 1, designed to extend to Roman women the indictment which the satirist had heretofore concentrated upon Roman men.[14] It is not surprising, therefore, that it shows no appreciable change in manner. We find the same savage implications in the adjective *dignus*; the theme of endurance serves regularly as a means of transition from one female vice to another, for the satirist himself cannot stand a corrupt woman, and he constantly asks how any man could tolerate a wife of any sort, even the most virtuous.[15] A man should be angry over the behavior of women, just as Laronia refused to tolerate the hypocrisy of the effeminates in Satire 2. Thus, in one scene, the satirist describes a husband's disgust at the vulgar appetite of his wife: "ergo maritus / nauseat atque oculis *bilem* substringit opertis" (432–33).

Juvenal begins Satire 6 with a passage that might be regarded as a new programmatic statement, and he ends it with lines that scholars always cite in connection with the program announced in Satire 1. In the introduction, the satirist returns to the same starting point as in 1. 81 ff. or, as we have seen, in 13. 38 ff.: namely, the legendary collapse of the Golden Age and the consequent triumph of vice. However, whereas in Satire 1 he selected from the amplitude of human concerns only *avaritia* to at-

tack, in Satire 6 he renders the Golden Age and its downfall in terms only of *pudicitia*. With the loss of *pudicitia*, the way lay open to the manifold perversions which Roman women now embrace, the major portion of which can be subsumed under the heading *libido et luxuria*. The same pessimism, the same extreme antagonism to his victims, the same strident rhetoric characterize the satirist from the moment that he abandons the Golden Age.

The conclusion begins at 634. As if aware of objections in his audience, the satirist checks himself and says:

fingimus haec altum satura sumente coturnum
scilicet, et finem egressi legemque priorum
grande Sophocleo carmen bacchamur hiatu
montibus ignotum Rutulis caeloque Latino.
nos utinam vani [634–38].

Then he goes on to demonstrate his right to a tragic style, inasmuch as once unique tragic villainesses, he claims, have become such common everyday figures that every village boasts its Clytemnestra.[16] Essentially, he makes the same proclamation as in Satire 1, that he totally replaces tragedy and epic with his lurid portrait of contemporary monsters; and I think it valid to argue that Juvenal relies on familiarity with the program of Book 1. We might, however, sense one slight, but significant, difference. While the satirist of Book 1 generalizes his denunciation of Roman corruption in a patently extreme manner, he never once admits exaggeration or seems to contemplate the possibility that people might object to his accuracy. Now, the satirist self-consciously calls attention to his violations of the Horatian tradition. Granted, in this particular context, the assumed objection merely serves as foil for a vigorous reassertion of his satiric vision; but it may well indicate a restlessness with this indignant satirist that requires a new manner in the future.

The opening poem of Book 3, Satire 7, has troubled scholars for centuries. I do not claim to solve all the numerous problems of its introduction, but I would propose a different way of treating those difficult lines; namely, as a new programmatic announcement. I disagree with the most recent interpretation of Satire 7, an ingenious attempt to revive a thesis popular seventy years ago, to the effect that the poem attacks Domitian and that the introduction sets the tone of sardonic antagonism to that much maligned emperor.[17] If we can be confident of anything in the poem, it is that the tone of the introduction differs radically from that which the satirist used in his savage assaults on Domitian's memory in Book 1. Who the Caesar and the *dux* is, whether Trajan or Hadrian, does not make any special difference to this argument, although I personally would prefer Hadrian. What we are meant to feel is that a fresh atmosphere, epitomized in those opening words, *spes et ratio*, pervades Rome; and that could hardly apply to Domitian's era.

Before treating the introduction, I should point out some general facts about the satire which tend to support my theories. First, the satirist chooses a topic which does not admit of indignation to the same extent as the subjects of Satires 1 to 6. It is not so easy to stir feelings over the plight of literature as it is over the vicious ways of the Roman nobility and the Greek interlopers. Secondly, the satirist of this poem does not employ the vocabulary of indignation. Apart from the introduction, it is impossible to find any thematic use of *dignus* or of the various words for endurance; nor is there any self-conscious description of anger.

Thirdly, whereas the satirist of Book 1 sneered at the writers of epic and tragedy and pushed his satire forward in their stead, this satirist of Book 3 expresses so much sympathy for the formal poets that in one instance he even identifies himself with them (48–49). Thus, the Statius whom he parodied in Satire 4 becomes the neglected Statius for whom he feels patent affection (82 ff.).[18]

While we may concede these changes in tone, the question remains why Juvenal wrote this introduction, then plunged into a bleak picture of contemporary literature. If, as many scholars believe, the main portion of the poem depicts the present state of literature and the introduction expresses hope for the future, apparently because of the accession of a new ruler whose interest in literature has long been demonstrated, the greater emphasis on the unhappy present tends to efface the impression of hope. Nevertheless, it has been characteristic of Satires 1–6 to draw contrasts between the present and other times, as a means of darkening the mood toward contemporary Rome and denying all hope. To use the same technique, but optimistically to compare present with the future, indicates not so much a new constructional method as a startlingly new attitude on the part of the satirist. Instead of gloomily urging the inevitable corruption of our posterity as in 1. 147 ff., the satirist proclaims a new era, when the infuriating circumstances surrounding literature will change: "nemo tamen studiis *indignum ferre laborem* / cogetur posthac" (17–18).

The passage just cited provides the sole examples in this satire of the terminology which we have come to associate with indignation. However, the satirist does not here speak with anger, for he describes with pleasure the end

285

of an evil situation: no longer need the writer endure his plight. Caesar will be a patron of the arts, in sharp contrast to the Roman nobility who have long neglected all branches of literature. At this point, arguments employed by other poets, satirists, lyricists, and elegiac writers in connection with patrons, especially with the royal patron, come to mind. Therefore, this introduction will be described in terms of the artful rhetorical technique familiarly known as the *recusatio*.

In the standard *recusatio*, of which we find numerous examples in Augustan poetry,[19] the writer of a nonepic form contemplates the possibility of producing an epic in honor of the ruler or of his powerful supporters, then reluctantly abandons the idea, all too aware of his inadequacy. Many variations can be played on this theme, as, for example, when Propertius exalts Cynthia to the status of an epic heroine, a veritable Helen, with the result that his elegy seems to be a worthy substitute for patriotic epic. Sometimes, the refusing poet consoles himself and his patron with the thought that a better man will sing those heroic exploits, a Varius or a Vergil. Regardless of the variation, the tensions of the *recusatio* provide the poet the opportunity for delicate tributes to the patron, while at the same time he can imply the independent validity of his chosen form.

In Satire 7 the speaker avoids speaking about himself, and yet a certain impression of his person penetrates the introduction. He has long watched the neglect of the arts, presumably suffered with other poets the insults of the nobility, and now he feels old like the wretched writers that he describes: "taedia tunc subeunt animos, tunc seque suamque / Terpsichoren odit facunda et nuda senectus" (34–35). Therefore, while he

responds to the bright possibilities of the new regime, he knows that he cannot so alter his style and his long-practiced form as to write a heroic epic. He turns instead to address the young poets, whose future lies before them and who can vibrate with the excitement of the new Caesar. They are the ones to write the epic: "hoc agite, o iuvenes. circumspicit et stimulat vos / materiamque sibi ducis indulgentia quaerit" (20–21). Youth must produce the epic; the older writers will plod along in their familiar ways, the satirist still composing satires , except that now his theme will be *spes et ratio*, the motto of the new Caesar's reign. The satirist does not specify the subjects of the Caesarian epic, but reference to *ducis*, the strong word *stimulat*, and the later comment on *vigilata proelia* (27) probably point to a martial topic.[20]

Although the impersonal manner of the introduction in Satire 7 does not agree with the usual subjectivity of the *recusatio*, yet, viewed in this way, the whole satire can make sense. At the start, we glance over past, present, and future, for a turning point has arrived with the accession of a new Caesar. Caesar and the younger poets belong together to that glorious future, while the old regime and the satirist have become inextricably united. Accordingly, after welcoming the future, the satirist, too bruised by the past to be able to escape it, turns back. "Listen [he says] to the present situation of literature as inherited from the past; this is my subject, for this gloomy world which Caesar now closes forms a significant part of my nature."

Whether or not the introduction to Satire 7 be a *recusatio*, implying why the satirist must write satire, it does announce a new mood of *spes et ratio*. Can we find echoes of this optimistic attitude, so different from the indignation of Books 1 and 2, in Satires 8 and 9? I think we can. Satire 8 contains two new features closely fitting a different satirist—that of Satire 7. First, the poem uses for the first time the more sedate manner of the Epistle, with a dedication to an unknown Ponticus and discussion of a principle presumably dear to that august-sounding name. Secondly, for the first time the satirist treats a positive doctrine: he advocates the true meaning of *nobilitas*, and his attacks on the decadent aristocracy form part of the generally hopeful mood of the poem. He sweeps back sixty years to seek his most vivid examples from the reign of Nero, the last of the Julio-Claudians: "haec opera atque hae sunt generosi principis artes" (224). Is this possibly a much more enthusiastic greeting for Hadrian, the second of the adoptive monarchs, in accord with Satire 7? Does the satirist advocate the very virtues of innate worth which are presupposed by the accession of the new ruler? In any case, indignation has nothing to do with this poem.

We do encounter indignation in Satire 9, but significantly in a way that looks forward to the methods of Satire 13. While the satirist continues to voice the serene good sense which we met in Satire 8, Naevolus the pervert exhibits the character of the indignant man. It helps, therefore, to consider this poem not only in the perspective of Satire 2—the topic is the same—but also in that of Satire 3. Naevolus can be viewed as a decadent Umbricius, for he describes himself as a client who has not been rewarded for indubitable services. Juvenal lets Naevolus attack Virro and his type with the rhetoric of indignation—such devices as rhetorical questions, angry exclamations, savage apostrophes, and epithets. The word *mon-*

strum, which the satirist has not used since Satire 6, occurs now in Naevolus' mouth (cf. 38). The satirist specifically comments on these angry remarks with words which the reader quickly perceives are ironic: "iusta doloris / Naevole, causa tui" (90–91). Even the danger of speaking the truth (93ff.) might remind us of the perils of *libertas* mentioned in Satire 1. Still, all this indignation is suspect, for Naevolus' clientship differs radically from that of Umbricius, despite his proud language. Hence, the ironic use of the word *spes* (cf. 125, 134, and 147): Naevolus' hopes depend upon what the satirist mockingly calls his *propositum*. The important voice of the poem remains that of the satirist, who retains his tranquillity and good humor even in the face of this paradoxical creature, an indignant pervert.

The rational, hopeful satirist, who in my opinion announces himself in the introduction to Satire 7, especially through the words *spes et ratio*, provides the dominant mood in Book 3. Perhaps he lapses here and there, as in the pessimistic picture of the present state of literature or in the protracted attack on the Neronian nobility and their vicious master (8. 146 ff.). However, even when he lapses, he does so against the circumstances which the new regime has ended or promises to end. When he wrote Book 4, Juvenal continued to emphasize *ratio*, and he made his hopeful satirist into an appealing figure who reminds many readers of Horace. Satire 10, the first of the book, reveals its program in a careful discussion of Democritus and Heraclitus, archetypes of two different satiric manners.

The satirist's eye sweeps over the whole known world from farthest Spain to India, as earlier his imagination took him back over the range of time to the end of Saturn's reign. Now, however, he does not concern himself with Roman vices provoking Roman rage, but with human failures arising from lack of *ratio*: the satirist supplies the *ratio*. In Satire 1, after proclaiming his indignation, the satirist immediately applied it to *avaritia*; in Satire 10, the satirist proceeds from his general thematic statement to discuss the dangerous consequences of *avaritia*. Gone is the anger now, nor does the reader feel himself confined to a corrupt Rome. The satirist expresses ideas that fit a man who himself feels no bitterness over poverty, who has controlled such idle desires by his reason. And right at this point, he refers to the two satirical attitudes represented by Democritus and Heraclitus (28ff.).

Eichholz has recently commented on the importance of Democritus for the mood of Satire 10; Lawall has shown that Heraclitus serves a purpose also, for the satirist proceeds easily from a mocking attitude to one of pathos in his brilliant series of exempla.[21] However, I should like to combine with their ideas the points made by Hendrickson and Lutz, so as to treat Democritus as the symbol of the satirist's manner in this poem and as the most prominent exponent of the program of Book 4. Neither Heraclitus nor Democritus represents the indignant type. Heraclitus, who weeps over life as a tragedy for mankind, comes closer to the angry, despairing satirist of Books 1 and 2 than Democritus does; but Heraclitus differs from the tragic satirist of 6. 634–36, who fulminates against vicious women and would never dream of passively deploring their ways. Juvenal introduces Heraclitus principally as foil to Democritus, his satirist's new model, for Democritus and Heraclitus have long been used to define two comple-

mentary visions of life.[22] However, as the emphasis in the passage indicates, it is Democritus who provides the best comment on vain ambitions in conformance with the satirist's ideas.

The hallmark of Democritus is harsh laughter, *rigidi censura cachinni* (31). The satirist plucks him from his village of Abdera and imaginatively transports him to contemporary Rome, there to voice his sardonic amusement at the empty political parade that attracts so many. We hear now no details about *delatores* or vicious hangers-on of rulers (like the associates of Domitian in Book 1), nothing to provoke wrath; instead, the satirist concentrates on the vain trappings of political office: "praetextae, trabeae, fasces, lectica, tribunal" (35). So it is all ridiculous, part of the human comedy which Democritus supposedly affirmed in his day five centuries earlier:

tum quoque materiam risus invenit ad omnis
  occursus hominum, cuius prudentia monstrat
  summos posse viros et magna exempla daturos
vervecum in patria crassoque sub aere nasci
  [47–50].

Consider how different this attitude is from that in Satire 1. There, the satirist raged over the innumerable examples of depravity that passed him as he stood on the street corner, that kept coming before his eyes (cf. 1. 63ff. and *occurrit* 69). Here, while placing Democritus and himself in the same station, merely by altering the details a little, he totally reverses the mood of the poem and transforms the material of indignation into that of laughter. Moreover, he summarizes the Democritean insight in words which constitute a direct denial of the program of Book 1. Nobody needs to be reminded of the famous catalogue of human interests from which the satirist launched his attack on *avaritia*: "quidquid agunt homines, votum, timor, ira, voluptas, / gaudia, discursus, nostri farrago libelli est" (1. 85–86). However, I suggest that we should recall it as we read 10. 51–52: "ridebat curas nec non et gaudia volgi, / interdum et lacrimas." In *curas* Juvenal summarizes the emotions of 1. 85, which now are laughable, not infuriating. Moreover, the men chosen to exemplify the satirist's topic in Satire 10 portray all the traits cited in 1. 85–86. Describing the folly of *vota* (cf. 10. 23), the vain *voluptas* imagined in prolonged life or physical beauty, the satirist demonstrates how briefly endure the *gaudia* for those who gain their wishes, how rapidly follow *timor* and destruction, often caused by the *ira* of a jealous or anxious ruler.

The *ratio* which governs the insights of the satirist, like the *prudentia* (48) which defines Democritus' character and justifies his laughter, is restated in the conclusion to Satire 10, where also the satirist returns to the *curas et gaudia volgi*. He lists a series of valid *vota* which correspond and are arranged according to the order of 1. 85: *timor, ira, voluptas*: [23]

fortem posce animum mortis *terrore* carentem,
qui spatium vitae extremum inter munera
    ponat
naturae, qui *ferre queat* quoscumque labores
    (dolores ?), [24]
nesciat *irasci*, cupiat nihil et potiores
Herculis aerumnas credat saevosque labores
et venere et cenis et pluma Sardanapalli
    [357–62].

It is especially significant that the satirist now at last expresses himself in opposition to *ira*; for, although it had been one of the errors to which he implicitly took exception in the catalogue of 1. 84–85, yet he also identified it with his own *indignatio* (cf. 1. 45) and therefore could not attack it in Book 1. Now,

however, he visualizes an ideal man who does not know how to become angry, who can endure any difficulties (if not infuriating personal pains, *dolores*). And as he discards anger and indignation, he reminds the reader of his Democritean model: "nullum numen habes si sit prudentia" (365).

That Democritus can serve as a valid symbol for the satirist of Book 4 is amply demonstrated by Satires 11 and 12. Satire 11, often called the most Horatian of Juvenal's works, [25] presents to us a Socratic speaker, like Horace, who invites a close friend, not altogether unlike Maecenas, to a simple dinner. Satire 12 goes even more deeply into the values of friendship, when it describes the satirist's pleasure and the sacrificial gifts which he makes on the occasion of Catullus' miraculous preservation from the perils of the sea. In both poems, the satirist clearly speaks with the voice of *ratio*, commenting on the ridiculous extravagance of some dinners or on the foolish behavior of *captatores*; but his antipathy to indignation is particularly prominent in Satire 11. In the first place, he has adopted a subject which in Satire 5 provided him ample material for anger, but which here, by careful alteration of the emphasis, changes into a vehicle for Horatian irony or, to be more accurate, for Democritean *cachinnus* (cf. 2, 55, 171). Secondly and more significant, he explicitly treats as inappropriate to his serene dinner the same distressful happenings which once he seized upon with enthusiasm: namely, financial problems, an adulteress-wife, domestic crises of any sort, or even ungrateful friends (185ff.). "Abandon your cares" (*dilatis curis* 183), he says. "Don't let your wife's behavior rouse your wrath" ("nec...tacito bilem tibi contrahat uxor" 187). And to epitomize his aversion to anger, he says: "protinus ante meum quidquid dolet exue limen" (190). It is no accident that the poem ends on the note of *voluptates* (208).

To conclude, the creed which the satirist proclaims in Satire 1, *facit indignatio versum*, holds good for Book 1, is adopted and publicly reaffirmed for Book 2, but ceases to serve at that point. I have deliberately drawn the contrast as sharply as possibly by confronting the program of Satire 1 with the satirist's attitude in Satire 13; nothing could make clearer how differently *indignatio* can be regarded. I might have used Satire 10, which consciously adopts Democritus as a satiric model; and, though with less ease, I could have argued from Satire 7, both from its opening words (*et spes et ratio*) and from its lack of the familiar terminology of indignation and hence its avoidance of pronounced wrath. However, the farther he gets from Satire 1, the more outspoken does the satirist grow against

his once cherished *indignatio*. The silent rejection of anger for *spes et ratio* in Satire 7 progresses to the open adoption of Democritean laughter in Satire 10, until finally in Satire 13 the satirist explicitly abjures indignation as both infantile and suspiciously hypocritical.

A second important conclusion emerges from this analysis. I did not arbitrarily choose Satires 7, 10, and 13 to exemplify my thesis; they alone contain the remarkable self-examination, implicit or explicit, which belongs to the programmatic poem. And therefore I suggest that the initial position which Juvenal assigned them in their respective books indicates a conscious plan: in *each* book the satirist unfolds his program in the initial satire. If we read Satires 7, 10, and 13 correctly, we would never extend to their respective books the program of *indignatio* announced in Satire 1.

1. Cf. O. Ribbeck (Berlin, 1865), chap. i.

2. G. Highet, *Juvenal the Satirist* (Oxford, 1954), pp. 44–46, 89–90, 104–5, 122–24, and 138–39.

3. For a more detailed discussion of Satire 1 and its program, see my "Studies in Book 1 of Juvenal," *YCS*, XV (1957), 34 ff.

4. I have studied the rhetoric of indignation in "Juvenal and Quintilian," *YCS*, XVII (1961), 30 ff.

5. In his edition of Juvenal, J. D. Duff (Cambridge, 1957) comments at 6. 651 on the formulaic nature of *tulerim*, but fails to connect the word with the satirist's announced indignation.

6. Cf. Sen. *De ira* 2. 7, where he feels perfectly free to interchange *ira* and *indignatio*; or Quint. *Inst. or.* 6. 2. 26 and 11. 3. 61 for a close association of the two passions.

7. Cf. 5. 159, 11. 187, and 13. 143. Behind the Roman use of the word *bilis* stood the Greek use of their word χόλος, as we probably can infer from Plaut. *Bacch.* 537. Horace characteristically described anger or outright insanity with *bilis*, and at least four times he uses the word in a playful manner of his own *persona*: cf. *Epod.* 11. 16, *Serm.* 1. 9. 66, *C.* 1. 13. 4, and *Epist.* 1. 19. 20.

8. Cf. 120, *indignatur* 64, and *dignus* 62, 115, and 173.

9. From l. 17, we know that Satire 13 could not have been written prior to A.D. 127, and 15. 27 suggests that Juvenal was writing several years later. In other words, some twenty years have passed since the publication of Book 1, enough time to allow Juvenal to reconsider the manner of his satirist. Horace developed new satiric tech-

niques in the short period of five years between Books 1 and 2 of the *Sermones*.

10. Cf. the use of *ferre* in 13. 9, 14, 21, and 143.

11. I interpret the adverb *vulgo* in this free manner: cf. 11. 2–3.

12. The basic motive of the Egyptians is *inmortale odium* (34; cf. 51), for which the satirist uses as synonyms the following words: *furor* (36), *rabies* (126), and *ira* (131, 169). This rage "burns" in the same way that the satirist's did in Book 1; cf. 35 and 52.

13. Highet (above, n. 2), p. 159.

14. Cf. my "Juvenal 6: A Problem in Structure," *CP*, LI (1956), 91–92.

15. Cf. the thematic *dignus* in 6.50, 61, 161, and 230; the thematic *ferre*, *pati*, *odi*, and the like in 30, 116, 166, 184, 208, 399, 413, 451, 613, and 651.

16. Note that the indignant satirist naturally finds more appealing the women who act in anger, "when fury ignites the liver," than those who commit their crimes in cold blood; cf. 6. 646 ff.

17. Cf. W. C. Helmbold and E. N. O'Neil, "The Form and Purpose of Juvenal's Seventh *Satire*," *CP*, LIV (1959), 100–108. The authors draw their strongest arguments in support of their thesis from their interpretation of 7. 20–21 and say: "The language of the verses shows clearly this derogatory intention" (p. 101). Careful study convinces me that the language shows no such thing. Here are the words which they find produce this derogatory impression: (1) *hoc agite*; (2) *circumspicit*; (3) *stimulat*; (4) *ducis*; (5) *indulgentia*,

(6) *sibi quaerit*. To be fair to the authors, I think that I, too, should examine these words one by one, to determine whether they individually or as a group convey the necessary prejudice. (1) The authors use only Stat. *Silv*. 5. 2. 125, *ergo age iam*, which occurs in the same context as the phrase *ducis indulgentia*. Because they regard *ducis indulgentia* in 7. 21 as "a sarcastic reference to Statius," they assume that *agite* bears the same relation to Statius' *age*. The fact is, as Mayor's notes abundantly prove, that *hoc agite* is a ritual phrase; and the nearest parallel to 7. 21 is provided not by Statius, but by Sen. *Ben*. 3. 36. 2: *hoc agite, optimi iuvenes*. The words can then be used to describe the efforts of the formal poet, to judge from Juvenal's own practice: cf. *hoc agimus* (7. 48) and the similar *haec agitem* (1. 52). The derogatory intention is therefore most doubtful. (2) For *circumspicit*, the authors cite only Juv. 8. 95, which is no parallel at all. The word almost never has a derogatory sense. It is used again and again by Cicero to refer to careful consideration; it frequently describes the cautious ways of a general and his troops (e.g., Caes. *BG* 5. 31; Livy 7. 14. 6 and 9. 28. 5); and its past participle, *circumspectus*, serves as the ideal epithet in the writings of Juvenal's contemporary, Suetonius, to define the ruler's foresight (cf. Suet. *Tib*. 21, *Claud*. 15). Again, no derogation in Satire 7 can be demonstrated. (3) For *stimulat*, the authors cite only Juvenal 14. 84, which is hardly parallel, and argue that the word is unusually strong. The word, in fact, can be strong, but that proves nothing here. Statius shows how the verb can be effectively employed and, I believe, how Juvenal probably expected to be understood. When the epic hero is stirred to some important act, then the poet naturally resorts to *stimulare*; Statius uses it repeatedly in the *Thebaid*. Statius also employs it in a way that is remarkably close to this context: he says in *Silv*. 5. 3. 235 that his father inspired and encouraged him to write his epic: *cantus stimulare meos*. Instead of sneering here, the poet is properly describing the interest which a new Caesar takes in a martial epic. (4) The authors cite Juvenal's use of *dux* and point out that the word is sometimes sardonic and once refers to Domitian (4. 145). However, they concede the fact that *dux* may sometimes carry no such association in Juvenal. We may point out that readers of Satire 7 would probably have thought of a more contemporary general, either Trajan, whom Pliny in his *Panegyricus* (cf. 10 and 12–16) repeatedly exalts as the perfect *dux*, or Hadrian, another great general in his own time. (5) The strongest argument for identifying the *dux* with Domitian is the passage from Statius *Silv*. 5. 2. 125, for Statius uses the phrase *ducis indulgentia* in precisely the same metrical position, and in reference to Domitian. To the authors' assumption that therefore Juvenal sarcastically alludes to Statius in 7. 21, we can reply on several levels. First, Statius' context is not the same as Juvenal's. Statius writes his poem for young Crispinus, who contemplates the first stages of a military career; and accordingly *ducis indulgentia* means the benevolence of Domitian as commander-in-chief of the Roman army. Crispinus will be advanced in rank, thanks to this *dux*. Helmbold and O'Neil understand *ducis* in Juvenal to mean simply the "emperor" (a travesty of the ideal *dux*), and, since they detect a bad sense in *indulgentia*, they feel justified in viewing the entire phrase as parody of Statius. But while the satirist is now speaking of the emperor as a patron of literature, and not as the general who will influence the young officer's career, still *ducis* by itself and in this context retains its military associations. The emperor as *dux* looks for heroic martial poetry. Secondly, *indulgentia* is a virtue of the Roman aristocracy which became one of the prime imperial qualities. Statius uses the word in the conventional sense. Tac. *Dial*. 9. 5, which the authors cite to illustrate the bad sense of the word, in fact represents the conventional usage. Tacitus refers to Vespasian. Tacitus' and Juvenal's contemporary, Pliny, feels the term the single most appropriate word for Trajan's imperial kindness: *indulgentia* appears again and

again in the *Panegyricus*, and it fills the correspondence with Trajan (at least twenty occurrences). Thirdly, Suetonius, still another contemporary, writes of Julius Caesar's great prestige among the troops; only in the Civil Wars and for a brief time did the soldiers mutiny, and even then he overcame them more by his authority than by concessions ("nec tam indulgentia ducis quam auctoritate," *Iul*. 69). That Suetonius can use the phrase *indulgentia ducis* of the greatest general that Rome ever produced proves, in my opinion, that Statius did not invent the phrase—it was entirely conventional—and that Juvenal in no way referred to Statius. Rather, like Statius and Suetonius, he addresses the emperor in a perfectly conventional manner, as the commander-in-chief and as the source of all benefits, especially, in this particular instance, patronage for epic poets. (6) The authors note that *sibi quaerit* is used sarcastically in 9. 92; but they would be the first to admit, I am sure, that *sibi quaerit* (disposed in different metrical positions from 7. 21) themselves carry no special prejudice apart from their context. Thus, Ter. *Heaut*. 315 uses verb and reflexive with *laudem*; Cic. *Clu*. 27 uses the same construction with *remedium*. In short, on all six counts, it seems to me that Helmbold and O'Neil did not possess adequate evidence and that the evidence of the usage of Juvenal and other Latin writers, especially Juvenal's contemporaries, points overwhelmingly to a different interpretation. Far from being derogatory, 7. 20–21 are conventional lines, precisely the type of verse that an imperial poet of Juvenal's time would address to any emperor.

18. In general, we should expect the satirist to display the same vitriolic hatred of Domitian as in Book 1, if this satire really develops an attack upon Domitian. But where-as no doubt arises concerning the satirist's indignation in Satires 2 and 4, it takes considerable imagination, if not actual distortion of the language, to interpret the *dux* of 7. 21 as the same person as the *dux* of 4. 145. Admittedly, Quintilian causes some problems, because his promotion was due to Flavian influence. However, a careful reading of the passage (7. 186ff.) shows that the satirist did not take advantage of his opportunity to attack Domitian. Instead of attributing Quintilian's success to a vicious emperor or to *indulgentia* (or some other imperial quality), the satirist assigns the entire credit to Fortuna. In other words, Quintilian, like Statius, represents the unpredictable situation of literature prior to this new Caesar: one man here or there might manage to live by the arts, deservedly or undeservedly, if he were lucky; but there was no considered policy. At no time since the Augustan period did the nobility promote literature. The satirist does not pick out Quintilian as an example of Domitianic villainy—after all, Vespasian first gave the rhetorician his post, and Domitian merely continued his father's policy—but as illustration of the quixotic nature of imperial patronage before now. Thanks to the new Caesar, such glaring exceptions will now cease to be the rule, and general encouragement of the arts will prevail.

19. For the most recent discussion of this convention, cf. W. Wimmel, *Kallimachos in Rom: Die Nachfolge seines apologetischen Dichtens in der Augusteerzeit, Hermes*, Einzelschriften, Heft 6 (1960).

20. As pointed out in n. 17, *stimulat* is a natural epic word, and was regularly used by Statius in the *Thebaid*; also, *circumspicit* often refers to a general's careful inspection of the scene of battle. The reader will have observed that *vigilata proelia*, in the satirist's mouth, seems to be ironic. The satirist contrasts the typical themes of traditional epic, that is, legendary battles like those of a *Gigantomachy*, an *Argonautica*, or a *Thebaid*, which are wasted effort, with the real Roman wars of the present, a glorious and rewarding topic for the younger poets. I have also toyed with the idea that we might use Juvenal's somewhat tentative language as a new criterion for determining the *Caesar*, Trajan or Hadrian; but I feel no confidence here. It might

be significant that, instead of specifying Trajan's known successes in Dacia and his ambitions to war on Parthia, the satirist leaves the whole subject vague. Possibly, he has already seen that Hadrian does not intend to prosecute his predecessor's campaigns and therefore speaks with caution.

21. Cf. D. E. Eichholz, "The Art of Juvenal and his Tenth Satire," *Greece and Rome*, III, 2d ser. (1956), 61–69; G. Lawall, "*Exempla* and Theme in Juvenal's Tenth Satire," *TAPA*, LXXXIX (1958), 25–31.

22. Cf. G. L. Hendrickson, "Satura tota nostra est," *CP*, XXII (1927), 52 ff., and C. Lutz, "Democritus and Heraclitus," *CJ*, IL (1953–54), 309–14.

23. As noted by E. N. O'Neil, "Juvenal 10. 358," *CP*, XLVII (1952), 233–34, the primary reason for the arrangement of these valid wishes is the corresponsion to the vain desires cited in the body of the satire.

24. Two of the good manuscripts, G and U, and several more recent manuscripts read *dolores* instead of *labores*. No editor accepts *dolores*. However, the error sprang from the natural association in the mind of a good Latinist between the process of enduring mental and physical pains and the conquest of anger. I have already cited 7. 17, where *ferre laborem*, used with *indignum*, obviously fits the vocabulary of indignation also.

25. Cf. A. Widal, *Juvénal et ses Satires: Études littéraires et morales* (Paris, 1869) p. 247; J. A. Gylling, *De argumenti dispositione in saturis IX–XVI Iuvenalis* (Diss., Lund, 1889), p. 63; and Highet, *op. cit.* p. 123.

ANGER IN JUVENAL AND SENECA

INTRODUCTION

IN A RECENT BOOK entitled *The Cankered Muse: Satire of the English Renaissance,* Professor Kernan has developed the most elaborate, all-inclusive, and accurate theory of satire which is known to me.[1] The most useful portion of his theory for the Classicist would probably be his discussion of the satirist. By "the satirist," Kernan means not the writer of satire, but the voice speaking in the satires; by careful use of this term he skillfully avoids the error into which we all tend to plunge, namely that of attributing to the writer every idea expressed by the speaker, the writer's creation. All satirists, Kernan argues, exhibit what may be called a public character and a private character. To take the public character first, "very simply, the satirist always presents himself as a blunt, honest man with no nonsense about him."[2] The private character is more complex, and Kernan makes a great contribution by concentrating on the series of tensions that define this character. As he demonstrates, the typical satirist experiences or exhibits internal conflicts on at least five levels: (1) he is a plain, blunt, simple artless speaker who yet makes the most skillful use of rhetoric; (2) he proclaims the truth of what he says, while he wilfully distorts facts for emphasis; (3) although he loathes vice, he displays a marked love of sensationalism; (4) despite his moral concerns, the satirist can take sadistic delight in attacking his victims; (5) sober and rational as he may claim to be, he frequently adopts the most shockingly irrational attitudes.

To those who are familiar with scholarly opinions on Juvenal, it should be obvious that Kernan's theory of "the satirist" conflicts sharply with the prevalent view. Most critics have not been able to distinguish the voice of the speaker in Juvenal's Satires—and hereafter I shall adopt Kernan's term of "the satirist"—from that of Juvenal himself. In some cases, the failure to draw this necessary distinction has led the critics to elaborate theories about Juvenal's exile, his poverty, or his attitude toward sex. In other cases, critics have concentrated on the private personality of the satirist and held up to scorn the very tensions which, as Kernan defines them, are exhibited in common by all satirists to a greater or lesser degree. For example, the tension between the blunt speaker and the rhetorical artist has attracted the attention of De Decker, Marmorale, and Serafini, to name but a few; all have, in one way or another, treated this tension as a grave artistic and moral

---

[1] A. Kernan, *The Cankered Muse* (New Haven, 1959).
[2] Kernan, p. 16.

inconsistency in Juvenal, one that bars him from the rank of poet as well as of honest man.[3]

Again, scholars will often dispute whether Juvenal tells the truth or exaggerates the facts of Roman degeneration, without realizing that they are debating over the satirist, a dramatic personality, whose exaggerations and appeals to truth make him the forebear of John Marston's "satyric hero" in Renaissance England, who is the heir of Persius' and Lucilius' satirists as well as of Horace's. Editors of Juvenal have long been perturbed over Satires 2, 6, and 9, and the unhappy reader must frequently suffer from the Victorian tastes of commentators who deplore the satirist's obscenity as though it were a sign of Juvenal's poor breeding. Even in the time of Lucilius, the writer of satire faced savage criticism as a sadist who hypocritically masqueraded as a moralist. Accordingly, Lucilius wrote the first Program Satire to explain the satirist's attitude, and his successors down to the time of Juvenal felt obligated to account for their *libertas*.

Finally, more than one critic has commented adversely on the irrationality of Juvenal's analysis of Roman decline, especially as applied to the happy eras of Trajan and Hadrian when many a Roman like Pliny lived contentedly, and when the whole Roman world enjoyed marked prosperity. In short, scholars have repeatedly observed these five tensions which Juvenal's satirist shares with other satirists, regarded them as the unique paradoxes of Juvenal's personality, and developed elaborate arguments from them by which to convict Juvenal of moral and artistic failure.

Once he has defined these tensions in the satirist of the English Renaissance, Kernan goes on to show how poets and dramatists used their satirists' tensions as a means of exploring reality more deeply than the "warped" satirists themselves did. In poetic satire, the satirist is made to discredit himself to a certain extent by confessing his diseased imagination and his pleasure in delivering painful blows to others. However, it is the Jacobean dramatists who employ the satirist with the greatest effect. In varying degrees, all show the satirist in the company of people, only some of whom he can legitimately mock: others prove themselves distinctly superior to this mocker, able to face the human comedy and live useful lives, or, in the tragedies, prepared to meet death with human dignity. Indeed, as Kernan demonstrates, the logical extension of the satirist's inconsistencies is the presentation of the satirist as a villian, a perverse wretch who plots to create a diseased social order in conformity with his vile conception of life.

[3] J. De Decker, *Juvenalis declamans* (Ghent, 1913); E. V. Marmorale, *Giovenale* (Bari, 1950[2]); A Serafini, *Studio sulla satira di Giovenale* (Florence, 1957).

Kernan has raised some questions and suggested answers which might profitably be applied to the original satirists. In particular, the "cankered Muse" of the English Renaissance resembles the angry satirist of Juvenal, for the obvious reason that Juvenal, more than any other Roman writer, influenced the English theories of satire in that period.[4] But while it may be true that the English satirist is the son of Juvenal's satirist, possessing many marked traits of his father, it would be wrong to attribute to the father all the characteristics of the child. Thus, as the reader must already have realized, the Roman satirist does not suffer the same ultimate condemnation as the English satiric villian. That reservation made, I may quickly point out that Juvenal, on the other hand, does oblige us to question the adequacy of his satirist's conception of life. The innumerable comments on Juvenal's hypocrisy, his rhetorical dishonesty, his unscrupulous exaggerations—comments which, of course, should rather be applied to Juvenal's satirist—attest to the fact that readers do not accept the satirist's words as the entire truth. Therefore, it seems worth the effort to investigate Juvenal's satirist with particular attention to the tensions which exist in his *persona* and which have provoked harsh criticism.

From the start, I draw a sharp distinction between the earlier and the later Satires, for, although Ribbeck gravely erred in attributing the later poems to some clumsy declaimer, he was quite correct in defining their different manner. I shall treat as "earlier" Satires 1 to 6, and for the purposes of this paper, it will suffice to ignore Book III—its transitional features include a transitional satirist—and use Satires 10 to 16 as the "later." In the earlier Satires, Juvenal creates an indignant satirist, as he openly announces in the Program Poem written for Book I, and as he seems to announce again in the course of Satire 6. For reasons which we can never entirely determine, Juvenal then abandoned that satirist, tentatively in Book III, and conclusively in Book IV, where he proclaimed as his model the laughing Democritus. This laughing satirist, who has never been adequately discussed, stands at the opposite pole from the indignant satirist; indeed, he serves as the severest critic of the indignation exhibited in the earlier poems.

Accordingly, the problem set in this paper is to determine the extent to which Juvenal showed awareness of the difficulties into which his indignant satirist plunged. This analysis may be performed in two ways, both of which I intend to utilize. First and foremost, I shall use the text of Juvenal's Satires, to discover where in the early poems the tensions in his satirist come to the surface and where in the later poems

---

[4] See Kernan's discussion of "Juvenal, Prince of Satirists," p. 64 ff.

the smiling manner constitutes an implicit criticism of the earlier indignation. Secondly, I intend to use for the first time, as a means of defining more clearly the moral ambiguity of indignation, two treatises of Seneca: *De ira* and *De tranquillitate animi.* Elsewhere, I have shown that the rhetoricians prized, and therefore recommended, the artful display of indignation.[5] Seneca's treatises will demonstrate that the moralists disagreed over the value of this emotion and that good Romans, for example Seneca himself, firmly condemned anger. In other words, the tensions which readers discover in Juvenal's Satires were already long familiar to the literary public and, it would appear, they form a necessary part of the portrayal of indignation.

[5] See my article, "Juvenal and Quintilian," *YCS* 17 (1961), 1–93.

I. TENSIONS IN SATIRES 1-6

BLUNT SPEAKER VS. RHETORICAL ARTIST

DE DECKER WROTE a stimulating book entitled *Juvenalis declamans;* Marmorale christened Juvenal *"un letterato."* Each critic acted upon the assumption that Juvenal's marked proficiency in rhetoric vitiated any appeal to indignation. In an earlier study, I have used one method of arguing against such criticism: I cited the rhetorical presuppositions of *indignatio* and tried to show that Juvenal faithfully adhered to them where he could, or adapted them in other cases to meet the special needs of his satire.[1] In other words, Juvenal's treatment of indignation, while particularly notable, should be viewed without antagonism as a conventional treatment, one that would awaken no special protest among the rhetorically adept Romans. Much of the rhetoric put in the mouth of the satirist, according to my view, serves to characterize the indignation within predictable conventions rather than to expose the artful dissimulation of the speaker. However, the satirist himself calls attention to his oratorical ability and thus obliges us to seek additional answers to the criticisms of De Decker and Marmorale.

All readers of Juvenal remember the famous assertion:

si natura negat, facit indignatio versum.
(1.79)

Essentially, this memorable thematic statement differs little from the conventional appeal of the orator, who seeks the favor of his audience by insisting simultaneously on the strength of his convictions—innocence, outrage, patriotism, and the like—and on his lack of skill in speaking. If the satirist restricted himself to such professions, he would not especially disturb the normal reader. But when he openly proclaims his acquaintance with declamations and flagrantly brandishes the tritest commonplaces, the reader may legitimately ask whether indeed this satirist is innocent.

Satire 1 opens with a violent outburst by the satirist against the formal poets, to whose dreary legends, reworked from Greek mythology for the millionth time, he has been impatiently listening at *recitationes.* Such an openly literary background, such a strong appeal to readers who know poetry well, seems almost to project us into a *recitatio* ourselves. Now, instead of enduring the poetastry of others, the satirist regales his audience with a display of rhetoric. As if to insist on this

---

[1] See "Juvenal and Quintilian," 30 ff.

"literary" context, the satirist proceeds to state his claim to the title of rhetorical poet:

> et nos ergo manum ferulae subduximus, et nos
> consilium dedimus Sullae, privatus ut altum
> dormiret.
>
> (15–17)

Trained by rhetoricians as rigorously as the formal poets, skilled in the typical *suasoriae*, like that on the question of whether or not Sulla should retire from his dictatorship, the satirist demands an equal hearing.

The opening paragraph of Juvenal's Program Satire insists on the fact that the satirist has been trained and feels adept in rhetoric; the second paragraph closes (79–80) with a ringing appeal to naïve indignation. The indignant speaker is apparently unaffected by any natural skill in versification, let alone the acquired skill derived from long practice and many canings in the school of some *rhetor*. What are we to make of such pronounced inconsistency? Look again at another passage:

> omne in praecipiti vitium stetit. utere velis,
> totos pande sinus.
>
> (149–150)

Returning to his Program after a prolonged description of *avaritia Romana* (87 ff.), the satirist declares that criminal vice has reached its extreme point in Rome. It is only natural that, from such a strident outcry, he should immediately proceed to reaffirm his basic indignation. What is far from natural is the manner in which he does so. "Spread your sails," he says to himself, "spread them as wide as possible." Any Roman reader would have heard this trite metaphor hundreds of times a year; it crops up again and again in ironically self-conscious passages of Ovid. Instead of displaying his indignation, the satirist has once again called attention—and here, because of the juxtaposition, we are forcefully exposed to it—to the artful manner in which he controls his mood. If he can so consciously, in such commonplace terms, invoke the indignation of the rhetorical schools, then presumably, for all his vaunted honest anger, he can lay aside his fury at will—whenever, that is, he stops haranguing his audience.

While Satire 1 most clearly reveals this particular tension in the satirist—his untutored honesty and his highly trained rhetorical ability—the same inconsistency affects other Satires also. For example, Satire 3, after a brief introduction by the satirist, is a speech delivered by Umbricius, a simple native Roman (21 ff.). Umbricius emphasizes his naïve honesty almost in his first words (*artibus* ... *honestis:* 21), and he soon insists upon his forthright ways:

> quid Romae faciam? mentiri nescio; librum,
> si malus est, nequeo laudare et poscere.
>
> (41–42)

Later, he sneers at the Greeks, as though he did not understand their language (see 63), for their general versatility and particularly for their verbal dexterity: *sermo / promptus et Isaeo torrentior* (73–74). The Greeks and the Hellenized Orientals, as Umbricius describes them, are a people expert in adulation, a nation of actors: *adulandi gens prudentissima* (86); *natio comoeda est* (100). On the other hand, poor Umbricius feels himself so deficient in the art of deception that he does not even bother trying: he would not be believed (see 92–93).

I need hardly remark that Umbricious serves Juvenal as the spokesman of indignation and that he therefore displays the same bag of rhetorical tricks as the satirist in the other early Satires. However, at one point at least the inconsistency comes to the surface, within plain sight. As he nears the end of his general introduction, Umbricius begins to lose his concentration on the satirist, his only companion and therefore the sole member of his audience. The single path to success in Rome, he say, obliges one to become an accomplice in serious crimes (49 ff.) But all the gold in the Tagus is not worth the loss of sleep and the danger that one consequently undergoes. Now, apart from the fact that this moralization ill accords with the simple, undidactic nature of Umbricius, it is also significant that he uses the generalizing second person singular (*tibi, careas, sumas, timearis:* 54 ff.): he could be haranguing the satirist, but, since he apparently knows him too well to make such a mistaken assumption about the satirist's greed, it is more likely that he invokes an impersonal interlocutor for the first, but not the last, time in this speech. I note these momentary lapses of the honest man's mask by way of introduction to the following lines:

> quae nunc divitibus gens acceptissima nostris,
> et quos praecipue fugiam, properabo fateri,
> nec pudor obstabit. non possum ferre, Quirites,
> Graecam urbem.
>
> (58–61)

As I have already said, the dramatic frame of the Satire has set the stage for an intimate conversation between the satirist and Umbricius; except for the muleteer, who will eventually signal to Umbricius from the distance (see 317–318), no other actor is present. Long before then (58 ff.), Umbricius stops and begins a speech as if from the platform to his fellow citizens (*Quirites*), and moves toward an apostrophe to Romulus (*Quirine:* 67). Not only does his rhetorical impetus make him oblivious of his lone companion; but he also effects his transition to this new topic by utterly transparent means. In effect, he says: "And now I am going to deliver a speech on the people who do succeed in gaining the favor of the rich." One might pass over a sharp but swiftly transitional *accipe* or *respice,* but two and a half lines of introduction strike me as so self-conscious that the typical phrase of the indignant man, *non possum ferre,* loses a large amount of its acerbity by juxtaposition.

Here, then, occurs a basic tension in the satirist, and I should go so far as to claim that Juvenal created this tension. As I shall argue, the tensions in the satirist render him a dramatic character who is not only quite distinct from the poet, but sufficiently alien to Roman readers, so that it is incorrect to sympathize entirely with his passions and prejudices.

Before I proceed to another of the five tensions defined by Kernan, let me mention a variation on this first one. As Satire 3 illustrates, sometimes the satirist can contain himself quietly while someone else assumes his role. Satire 2 presents Laronia in a brief paragraph; as Umbricius rails at un-Roman ways, so she attacks the vice which most seriously affronts her nature. Like the satirist in 1.30–31, like Umbricius in 3.60, Laronia is impatient, and her speech is introduced with one of the thematic words announcing indignation: *non tulit* (36).[2] Despite her impatience and despite the fact that she replaces the satirist in condemning the homosexual hypocrites, Laronia does not erupt in fury; instead, she uses a sardonic manner (*ita subridens:* 38). Mockery is not in accord with indignation, because it presupposes reflection and self-control, precisely those qualities which indignation so clamorously lacks. Therefore, the mock-epic employed in Satire 4 places the satirist at a considerable distance from his victims, Domitian and his advisers, who are regarded with the reflective eye of a poet-rhetorician.

The honest speaker, impelled by his righteous wrath to speak out immediately, should not be characterized by urbanity, and, by the same token, he should not exhibit humor in his comments. The few people who have studied humor in Juvenal's Satires have not reached much agreement on its extent.[3] Saint-Denis and Mason, however, do suggest,

[2] Concerning the thematic terms defining indignation, see my article, "The Programs of Juvenal's Later Books," *CP* 57 (1962), 145–160.

[3] See J. Jessen, "Witz und Humor bei Juvenal," *Philologus* 47 (1889), 321–327; F. S. Dunn, "Juvenal as a Humorist," *CW* 4 (1911), 50–54; E. de Saint-Denis, "L'humeur de Juvénal," *Inform. Litt.* 4 (1952), 8–14. H. A. Mason, "Is Juvenal A Classic? An Introductory Essay," *Arion* 1:1 (1962), 8–44, 2:39–79, lays great stress on wit, closely patterned on Martial's, as the "key to Juvenal's art."

I think correctly, that there is much more humor than people have been led to believe. I note at this point that introductions to Satires often exhibit marked traces of irony. For example, the satirist speaks comically of exercising *clementia* in sparing the doomed paper (1.17–18); then, shortly after, he insists that the reader listen quietly to his words of sound reason (*placidi rationem admittitis:* 21). Both passages suggest that the satirist or the poet is amusing himself with elaborate overstatements. Far from calmly and rationally discussing his purposes, the satirist bursts into irrational rage within a few lines of this passage. Similarly, in Satire 3, the satirist seethes with apparent fury at the vicious city (*saevae / urbis:* 8–9) and lists some of its frightful aspects. Although it is true that the list does to a certain extent correspond to the contents of Umbricius' tirade, nevertheless the satirist concludes the list on an anticlimactic note; one detail he mentions as the apparent worst, a detail which Umbricius never discusses later on:

> nam quid tam miserum, tam solum vidimus, ut non
> deterius credas horrere incendia, lapsus
> tectorum adsiduos ac mille pericula saevae
> urbis *et Augusto recitantes mense poetas?*
>
> (3.6–9)

Finally, few people, reading the opening of Satire 6, could feel convinced that the satirist's apparent praise of the cavewoman is entirely serious, for the details that he has chosen to emphasize make of the woman a freak; for a moment, indeed, the satirist sounds remarkably like the urbane and cultivated Ovid.

TRUTH VS. EXAGGERATION

From the fact that the satirist erupts spontaneously in indignation, it would follow that he speaks the simple truth; on the other hand, if the satirist so prominently displays his irony and humor, let alone his rhetorical pyrotechnics, exaggeration goes hand-in-hand with truth. Long before Juvenal wrote, his predecessors had made it a tradition for the satirist to insist on his *libertas,* his simple, direct honesty and concern for the truth. Accordingly, in Juvenal's Program Satire, the satirist emphasizes his preoccupation with facts and contrasts invidiously the trite mythological materials which are the themes of the epic and tragic poets. He claims several times that he is the spiritual descendant of Lucilius, whom he pictures as the truly grand poet: *Lucilius ardens* (165) striking with his verse as with a sword. Before the poem ends, however, the satirist has backed down and frankly

admitted that his words will not correspond to actuality. His interlocutor has asked him an embarrassing question:

> unde illa priorum
> scribendi quodcumque animo flagrante liberet
> simplicitas?
>
> (151–153)

While *Lucilius ardens* brandishing his sword and the ancients (including Lucilius), their passions fired, speaking out with *libertas* and
simplicitas, perfectly fit the usual conception of indignation, the satirist
who avoids attacking the living and concentrates on the dead (170–171)
sounds like a devious coward, a man who calculates every word he
utters.

Truth is a powerful theme in the early Satires. I have already cited
the passage in which Umbricius asserts that he does not know how to
lie (3.41). When Laronia completes her sardonic attack on the perverts,
the satirist says:

> fugerunt trepidi vera ac manifesta canentem
> Stoicidae; quid enim falsi Laronia?
>
> (2.64–65)

In Satire 4, he appeals to the Muse to begin her epic denunciation of
Domitian:

> incipe, Calliope. licet et considere: non est
> cantandum, res vera agitur.
>
> (34–35)

In this mock-epic, the Muse supposedly does not sing her truth, whereas
Laronia's sardonic speech becomes an epic song in the satirist's view.
Arguing with Trebius in Satire 5, the satirist keeps urging the wretched
client to stop fooling himself, to open his eyes and see the truth of his
abasement. Thus, the satirist affects complete disbelief in Trebius' desire to attend Virro's banquet: he would doubt Trebius' word even if
accompanied by an oath (5); again, when Trebius lamely suggests that
Virro may be discriminating against him to save money (156), the
satirist directly contradicts him.

The most celebrated assertion of the satirist's truthfulness illustrates
how self-consciously he teeters on the verge of exaggeration:

> fingimus haec altum satura sumente coturnum
> scilicet, et finem egressi legemque priorum
> grande Sophocleo carmen bacchamur hiatu
> montibus ignotum Rutilis caeloque Latino.
> nos utinam vani.
>
> (6.634–638)

Anticipating objections from his audience to the fact that he goes far beyond the *simplicitas* of Lucilius and the Plain Style of Horace in order to produce a tragic satire utterly unknown to the tradition, the satirist asserts that he does not write falsely, dearly though he would love to. Immediately he points to Pontia, who has poisoned her two sons and proudly admits it, indeed wishes that there had been seven to kill. The satirist concludes that the tragedians spoke the truth also: *credamus tragicis* (643); for how can one doubt the possibility of a Medea or a Procne when everywhere you may see Danaides and Eriphyles today, when every village boasts its Clytemnestra (655–656)?

This passage has long served as a proof-text to demonstrate the satirist's attitude toward indignation and truth. I need hardly point out, however, that its self-conscious discussion of truth and its dubious reasoning, while pleasing the lover of rhetoric like myself, should also raise some questions in the reader's mind about "satiric truth." Nowhere in Book I does the satirist suggest any doubts in himself, any hesitation in regard to his audience. Here, at the end of Satire 6 (as if to balance the playful introduction to his attack on women in 6.1–20), the satirist comments on his own truthfulness, then flies off in a series of wild and comic exaggerations. He does not expect people to believe in the truth of tragedy: he hardly imagines that we will credit his tale that any wife would rather save a pet puppy than her husband (652–654); and the contrived picture of the husband (called by antonomasia *Atrides*) who has wisely immunized himself to poison after the example of Mithridates (identified by periphrasis only as the thrice-conquered Pontic king) strikes me as an hilarious way to end the poem.

The satirist insists on his truthfulness, but by Satire 6, he openly calls attention to the exaggerations that condition our attitude toward his "truth." That passage should invite us to inspect with healthy scepticism his use of exclusive terms like *omnis* and *nullus*. One recalls a rhetorical question in 6.345: *sed nunc ad quas non Clodius aras?* The logic of the entire early portion of Satire 6 consists in implying that *no* woman in the whole world, least of all in Rome, could be found worthy to be the wife of even the most notorious adulterer. Suppose we let ourselves go along with the satirist in this assertion, ignoring the fact, of course, that he had a mother and that we can hardly destroy the institution of marriage; but suddenly the unknown interlocutor asks the obvious question: *'nullane de tantis gregibus tibi digna videtur?'* (6.161) How does the satirist answer? He goes one step farther in humorous distortion. For, instead of coming right out with it and declaring that no woman satisfies him, the satirist turns around and rails at the ideal woman, the *rara avis* (165):

quis feret uxorem cui constant omnia ? malo,
malo Venustinam quam te, Cornelia, mater
Gracchorum, si cum magnis virtutibus adfers
grande supercilium et numeras in dote triumphos.
(166–169)

It makes no difference whether she is supremely virtuous and chaste
or otherwise: the satirist affects abhorrence of every woman in the world.
Perhaps, instead of using these exaggerations to support conjectures
that Juvenal has suffered a tragic marriage and now is about to turn
for consolation to pederasty, readers should appreciate the importance
in this poem of the conventional elements, of the exaggerations, and
realize that once again Juvenal has created a satirist whose wild attacks
cannot entirely be accepted as truth.

There are many signs in Satire 6 that the mask of indignation was
wearing thin and that Juvenal did not mind exposing his satirist to
critical inspection. However, even earlier the satirist's truthfulness appears inconsistent. It may be picayune to observe that the celebrated
Concilium of Satire 4 is no *res vera;* but the fact is that it abounds in
anachronistic details, that it makes of Domitian a tyrant some ten years
before his suspicious temper actually gained the upper hand; and most
important of all, it develops a conventional scene of the tyrant's banquet
and of his wretched "friends." Again, Umbricius, who could not lie,
labels Rome a "Greek city" (3.61) or, to be more accurate, an Oriental
city; he intends to leave it and settle down in solitary Cumae as its sole
citizen (*see* 3–4). Any Roman, living under Trajan, would have known
that Rome was as much a Spanish and Gallic city as Oriental; and any
Roman, travelling down the new road put through to Cumae by
Domitian, would have been aware that the countryside was at least
moderately populous. The point is not to pick holes in the false assertions of the satirist; but to see his insistent claim of truth and his
almost simultaneous distortions of that truth, whether by exaggeration or by suppression of redeeming details, as a vital part of his character. Rhetorically, this sort of emotional appeal is to be expected;
morally, especially when the satirist calls attention to it, it is bound to
alienate readers from the satirist and make him what he is, a dramatic
character subject to criticism.

Let me illustrate this tension between truth and distortion by one
more Juvenalian passage. At the end of Satire 2, the satirist once again
brings up the matter of *veritas*. Laronia, it will be remembered, had
denounced the perverts in ironic, but plain, language, and the satirist
in wild, but mistaken, enthusiasm had exalted her words as those of the

Muse herself (*vera . . . canentem:* 64). Now, he begins a new emotional development in this manner: first he declares that nobody would believe in personal survival within some mythical subterranean kingdom of Pluto, not even children, unless they were too young to have the slightest understanding; then he addresses the reader: *sed tu vera puta* (153); and he continues by bringing the *umbra* of an effeminate face-to-face with the shades of Rome's mightiest conquerors of the past. Under the circumstances, how can the reader take seriously the satirist who has frankly exposed the fiction even before embarking on his rhetorical flight? While the audience should and does enjoy this fanciful construction and admit its success, I would maintain that its pleasure depends to a considerable degree on the fact that it can follow Juvenal's broad hint and distinguish between the satirist's "truth" and truth itself.

SAINT VS. SENSATIONALIST

Kernan defined another tension in the satirist who typically insists that he loathes vice, yet exhibits a disturbing propensity to seek sensational details. Anyone who has read Victorian discussions of Juvenal or tried to secure an annotated edition of all the Satires knows how embarrassed the commentators feel in connection with Satires 2, 6, and 9. At best, the typical editor deplores Juvenal's lack of good taste in dealing with sex; at worst, he may attempt any number of autobiographical interpretations to explain these three on the whole skillfully composed poems. For my part, I see no reason to restrict the conception of sensationalism to matters of sex; the satirist typically chose sensational instances, whether he described sexual vagaries, avarice, gluttony, or the miseries of Rome.

That Juvenal's satirist abhors vice hardly needs to be argued. After all by definition *indignatio* means righteous fury over something *indignum;* and the indignant speaker characteristically describes himself or is described as afire, impatient, erupting, quite unable to endure the crimes which he denounces. In Juvenal's Satires appears a common metaphor, developed as the dramatic motivation of Satire 3, namely that of flight. The satirist professes a passionate desire to flee beyond the bounds of the Roman Empire at the beginning of Satire 2. Umbricius does flee to Cumae. And Pudicitia in Satire 6, fleeing from the corrupt world (20), left mankind, especially the Romans, to the horrors of their unchastity. However, it is no mere chance that the satirist, for all his voiced hatred of Rome, for all his apparent desire to flee and his frank admiration for Umbricius' decisive action, still remains. Juvenal has from the beginning revealed the complex nature of his satirist's abhorrence and so made the *persona* dramatically more interesting: the satirist hates *and loves* the city, abhors and yet is fascinated by its vices, longs to flee and simultaneously feels himself trapped, unable to move, a lonely prophet in the corrupt city.

No doubt each reader has his own list of sensational, highly memorable descriptions in the Satires. Of those devoted to sexual perversions, I naturally think of the vivid details used to enliven the *secreta orgia* of the homosexuals in 2.83 ff. and of the unforgettable handling of Gracchus' marriage with a Greek, a man, a trumpet-player (2.117 ff.); then, of course, of Messalina and her insatiable lust (6.114 ff.), of the vile behavior of Maura and Tullia (6.306 ff.), and of the "contest" that marks the ultimate stage in the libidinous celebrations for Bona Dea (6.314 ff.). On the whole, the satirist's sensationalism stops well before the point to which the English satirists permitted themselves to go: he avoids shocking language based on the excretory functions and limits the number of sordid details he uses. Filth and excrement, standard topics of Renaissance satire, have not yet broken their way through the restrictions of *decorum*. Nevertheless, the satirist attains enough power within his confines to horrify many a prudish critic.

Rhetorically speaking, this sensationalism is designed to represent the truly awful state of Roman immorality; dramatically speaking, it serves to define the by no means simple character of the satirist. A careful reader will observe, for example, that the satirist familiarly describes what are specifically *secreta orgia:* in Satire 2, a travesty on the female rites for Bona Dea; in Satire 6, the perversions which supposedly go on when the women, freed from the observations of all men, actually celebrate this goddess. It might well be asked how the satirist learned these secrets. Was he among the transvestites too? Did he sneak into the company of the women, as Clodius once did? Again, the reader might wonder about the manner in which the satirist constructs his picture. One homosexual, it seems, holds a mirror, an heirloom passed on by the effeminate Otho (2.99 ff.). To put this fact in a desirable perspective, the satirist is made to parody Vergil, to allude to the recent work of Tacitus, then to introduce comparisons with those celebrated viragoes, Semiramis and Cleopatra. Such literary *amplificatio* inevitably raises questions about the satirist's abhorrence. A little later, having depicted the essential facts of Gracchus' "marriage," the satirist apostrophizes Mars (2.126 ff.). Although the tone affects indignation, the actual picture of Mars should remind many a reader of the playful Ovidian portraits in the *Fasti;* and the allusion to Mars' complaint to his father

306

evokes the famous Homeric scene in which the bully Ares goes bellowing off the field of battle to complain to Zeus.[4]

I detect no lapses in the superb sensationalism on Messalina. However, the reader should feel the cleverness in the satirist's rendering of the rites devoted to Bona Dea. Note, for instance, the insistence on truth, so often a warning that the satirist is about to leap into fantasy:

> nil ibi per ludum simulabitur, omnia fient
> ad verum, quibus incendi iam frigidus aevo
> Laomedontiades et Nestoris hirnea possit.
> (6:324–326)

Together with the typical *omnia* and the hyperbolic appeal to *verum,* the satirist makes an amusing allusion to aged Priam and Nestor; to Priam under the cover of antonomasia and by a word that mockingly occupies the first hemistich of 326; to Nestor with the typical epic circumlocution, except that instead of an expected reference to virtue, the heart, or the soul, the satirist naughtily uses *hirnea.* He goes on, and soon displays a rhetorical climax. For want of an *adulter,* the women will resort to a *iuvenis;* if he fails them, they will try the slaves; after the slaves, there remains the *aquarius;* and finally, when the supply of men is exhausted, the women will without compunction use a donkey (329 ff.). We have hardly had time to swallow this magnificent lie before the satirist tries again to shock us with his sardonic constructions:

> atque utinam ritus veteres et publica saltem
> his intacta malis agerentur sacra; sed omnes
> noverunt Mauri atque Indi quae psaltria penem
> maiorem quam sunt duo Caesaris Anticatones
> illuc, testiculi sibi conscius unde fugit mus,
> intulerit, ubi velari pictura iubetur
> quaecumque alterius sexus imitata figuras.
> (335–341)

Starting off with the predictable *omnes,* the satirist insists that the whole world, from North Africa to distant India, knows about Clodius, even under the allusive form in which he is here presented. The naughty discussion of the size of the singer's *membrum,* enhanced not only by the esoteric allusion to Caesar's verbose attack upon Cato, but by the significant contrast between the pentasyllabic ending of 338 and the monosyllabic ending of 339, produces such a mixed impression of the scene that the reader cannot possibly let himself naïvely believe that pure, untainted indignation produces this effect.

Take another passage in a Satire that has nothing to do with sex. In

---

[4] In Satire 13, where the speaker rejects the mood of anger, he mockingly compares angry Calvinus to Homer's bellowing, complaining Ares (cf. 112 ff.).

3.197 ff. the indignant Umbricius begins to describe the terrible dangers from fires that constantly threaten himself and other poor people.

> iam poscit aquam, iam frivola transfert
> Ucalegon, tabulata tibi iam tertia fumant:
> tu nescis; nam si gradibus trepidatur ab imis,
> ultimus ardebit quem tegula sola tuetur
> a pluvia, molles ubi reddunt ova columbae.
>
> (3.198–202)

The basic situation is not entirely unbelievable: a fire has started apparently downstairs in a Roman apartment house, and the panic gradually communicates itself over the whole building until it finally reaches even the garret where the poor interlocutor, as Umbricius imagines it, lives, among the nests of the pigeons. However, the situation has been carefully chosen. Now, how does the satirist (Umbricius) emphasize the plight of the victim? He resorts to epic, in order to gain a meretricious pathos. Every Roman child knew by heart the story of the Burning of Troy in *Aeneid* 2; every child no doubt was familiar with the rhetoricians' adverse comments on Vergil's bold metonymy: *iam proximus ardet / Ucalegon (Aen.* 2.311).[5] Juvenal has Umbricius playfully vary the Vergilian passage so as to avoid the "improper" figure, while maintaining the rhythm and the essential words; *ardebit* in 201 returns to the Vergilian language. Into the epic context, Umbricius sets the everyday word *frivola,* to produce a clash of associations. The alliteration in 199 is no accident; *trepidatur* in the impersonal evokes the panics of war and epic; and the extended description that introduces the pigeons brings the whole passage to a serene, but mocking, end. But where has Umbricius left "you"? Right in the middle of the fire, apparently doomed to perish. Without another word, Umbricius turns from this sensational fire to an artful contrast between the menage of Cordus and his dwarf wife and that of the wealthy, old, childless Persicus. In short, Umbricius here, like the satirist in dealing with sexual perversions, constructs episodes, which in themselves constitute extreme instances, in a patently literary, not to say humorous, manner so as to force us to dissociate ourselves from his vaunted indignation and rather to enjoy the dramatic creation.

OBJECTIVE MORALIST VS. JAUNDICED FAILURE

The Renaissance satirist typically expresses a passionate moral concern, yet frankly admits that he enjoys flailing his victims. Such inconsistency has its prototypes in Roman satire. From the time of Lucilius, one of

---

[5] For criticism of the Vergilian passage, cf. Quintilian, *Inst.* 8.6.25.

the principal themes of the Program Satire was whether or not the satirist took pleasure in hurting others; an interlocutor would charge *laedere gaudes,* and the satirist would defend himself. No Roman satirist ever claimed that he did delight in injuring others' reputations; still, in the case of Lucilius, the violence of attacks on Mucius Scaevola, Metellus Macedonicus, and Lupus may have justified the charge. Juvenal's satirist pointedly states at the end of the Program Satire that he does not attack the living, so that he, more than any other satirist, seems exempt from this particular tension.

However, another type of inconsistency occurs in Juvenal's satirist, one which has some affinities with the manner of the immoral moralist of the Renaissance. He frequently exhibits an attitude which is less pleasure in hurting others than sheer self-indulgence, childish self-assertion before and against a world that ignores one's merits. In some cases the satirist himself, but more often those who speak for him explode in an indignation which, because of their character, impresses the reader as of limited validity. I can illustrate this most easily by referring to Laronia. From the manner in which her speech is introduced (*see* 2.34–35), it seems necessary to assume that she represents the lustful women who have violated the *lex Iulia;* she personifies *vitia ultima,* biting back at the hypocritical perverts who attack them. Although it is true that women who indulge their passions naturally, even outside the marriage bed, seem greatly superior to men who give free rein to unnatural vices, nevertheless the reader is permitted to ask whether Laronia makes her charges from impatience or whether she tries to obscure the fact of her own corruption by pointing to the perversion of others.

One often hears the charge that Juvenal's true motivation in attacking contemporary Rome came from his personal failure. Highet has developed this point most precisely in his reconstruction of Juvenal's biography. After commenting on one of the primary themes of the early Satires, fear, Highet goes on to discuss a second, disappointment: "The disappointment appears as a profound and bitter sense of social injustice. Yet it is not the purest hatred of injustice as such. Juvenal is not really sorry for the very poor, or for the working class. He is sorry for middle-class men like himself who cannot get advancement."[6] Later, discussing Satire 1 and the parade of vicious characters who provoke the famous assertion about *indignatio* in lines 79–80, Highet remarks: "If we analyse his [i.e., Juvenal's] complaints we soon see that his chief objection to these people is that they are rich while he is not. True, he

---

[6] Gilbert Highet, *Juvenal the Satirist* (Oxford, 1954), p. 37.

would not commit their crimes for all their wealth. But we feel that he would not be nearly so indignant about them if he were not poor. Since he is poor—or has been impoverished—he cannot stop thinking about money; the final source of his gnawing and sleepless indignation is the formula: wealth = crime, *or* vice, *or* corruption.'" I quote Highet so extensively because he interprets the tone of the Satires almost precisely as Juvenal set it; and, had he made the distinction between Juvenal and his satirist instead of leaping to biographical conclusions, he would have realized where Juvenal was leading the reader. It is quite true that the satirist seems unnaturally preoccupied with the poverty of himself and his friends and, on the other hand, the lavish style of life possible for the renegade nobility and the upstart freedmen. However, this propensity in the satirist tells nothing about Juvenal's character or biography; instead, it shows once more the complexity of the satirist, his inner tensions which constantly oblige readers to dissociate themselves from his jaundiced assertions and to discover reality for themselves.

Like the satirist's indignation over his impoverishment and others' prosperity, so his fury against Roman women stirs doubts. The biographically-minded, as I indicated above, have leapt upon Satire 6 and developed a fantastic tale of a tragic marriage which soured Juvenal against women and turned him into a homosexual. None of that exists in the Satire or anywhere but in the perfervid imaginations of romantic critics. Nevertheless, the satirist does leave a mixed impression that tends to alienate readers from his ferocious denunciation of women. In the first place, twenty arguments against marriage, if one chooses to schematize Satire 6 in that way, prove no more convincing than Lucretius' twenty-odd arguments against the survival of the spirit. Few men would utterly spurn the fairer sex, for few men can achieve a satisfactory existence without women. Thus, to rail at women for more than six hundred lines would make a stirring *recitatio,* but it should strike any audience as utter fantasy, divorced from reality and distorted beyond measure. Like a child, the satirist has struck out against society, and his is a child's pleasure.

Secondly, the satirist frequently adds details about the husband, who supposedly suffers so severely from his wife's unfaithfulness and wild extravagances; and it is not always easy to feel much sympathy for this *maritus.* For example, Ursidius decides to take a wife and earnestly searches for a woman bred according to old Roman customs. What sort of man is Ursidius? The satirist calls him *moechorum notissimus* (42). The reader might also think that the senator who allowed Eppia to act

⁷ Highet, p. 51.

so fastidiously is a pretty contemptible specimen of manhood (see 95 ff.); and most Romans were conditioned to despise Claudius as a fool, especially because he permitted Messalina so much freedom, whether as the *meretrix Augusta* (118) here described, or as the power behind so many unjust condemnations. Caesennia's husband has been bought (136 ff.); Sertorius is the sort of husband that we nowadays associate with Hollywood: he loves his wife's looks and will divorce her as soon as her beauty fades or palls on him, or if he sees another pretty girl (142 ff.). We later hear that Postumus, the prospective husband to whom the satirist addresses his tirade, has a catamite named Bromius (377–378). All in all, there is not a single husband in Satire 6 who awakens much sympathy, and some of them seem contemptible, far more vicious than their wives, certainly far less interesting. As I said in discussing 6.314 ff., the reader might well ask himself how the satirist acquired his information about the secret rites of Bona Dea. Is there any reason to conclude that the satirist here acts like a disappointed husband rather than an expert *moechus?* One thing is certain: there are more inconsistencies in the satirist's indignation in this poem than in any Satire of Book I.

I suggest, then, that Juvenal has carefully delineated the character of his satirist first by placing him in situations where his extreme anger and his limited perspective tend to render his motives suspect, and then by attributing to him assertions which at times border on the pathological, and at other times seem remarkably close to self-irony. From Laronia, an adulteress herself, who sneers at male homosexuals, to Umbricius, who pours hatred upon the Greeks because they have pushed him aside and made a profitable living in Rome, and who therefore retires from the city less from noble motives than from a sense of defeat and inadequacy, is a short step. And the satirist, who sees so indignantly what is vicious in others' *avaritia,* shows definite signs of being tainted with the same fault, though unsuccessful in satisfying his desires. Similarly, when the satirist voices his passionate hatred of Roman women, when he makes the *maritus* such a silly fool, not to say a corrupt scoundrel, the reader senses the fantastic nature of the denunciation and rightly wonders about the satirist's morality. Is he not ranting away for the sheer pleasure of denouncing others and ignoring his own faults? Rarely does the indignation of Juvenal's satirist operate unequivocally.

RATIONALIST vs. IRRATIONALIST

The Renaissance satirist often proclaimed his sober rationality, while irrationality pervaded his outbursts against society. This tension between rationality and irrationality does characterize certain Roman satirists, namely those of Lucilius and Persius; but both Horace and Juvenal freed their respective satirists, for the most part, from this difficulty. Horace used his two Program Satires in Book I to circumscribe the image of Lucilius and so make amply clear his satirist's position as a man of common sense, who viewed the world as fundamentally intelligible and inclined toward rational order: I find it useful to describe the resultant satirist as a Roman Socrates. Juvenal adopted an entirely different position, but one which is similarly consistent: he created a satirist who thundered out against the basic disorder and irrationality of the universe, or at least of the Roman environment in which he found himself.

When Juvenal's satirist asserts that indignation makes his verse, he implies that he ignores the value of poetic discipline so regularly stressed by Horace. When he deigns to notice the critics who protest against his exaggerations and his invasion of the area set aside for tragedy, he retorts that exaggeration seems the only accurate means to describe the facts, for Roman ethics have become monstrously, tragically perverse. The brilliant rhetoric of indignation is perfectly adapted to such an extreme vision. And true to character, the satirist acts with great dramatic verisimilitude as though he lived in a chaotically degenerate world, the very reverse of the structured, ironically perceived Horatian environment—a travesty of Augustan Rome.

There is, however, one passage in Satire 1 which might suggest another insight into the Juvenalian world; and it comes before the satirist is permitted to declare his indignation. After lashing hyperbolically against the other poets, the satirist decides that *clementia* (in saving paper that poetasters would waste anyway) is senseless and so prepares to write satire. Aware, however, that the reader might ask why he chooses satire instead of a more dignified poetic form, the satirist politely calls for the reader's calm attention to his explanation:

si vacat ac placidi rationem admittitis, edam.

(21)

As I have remarked, the contents of the ensuing lines are anything but *ratio,* anything but an appeal to placidity. Why, apart from the desire to punctuate the first paragraph and set it off from what follows, did Juvenal assign to his satirist such flagrantly inconsistent words?

To put it in the simplest form, I would answer in this way: Juvenal expects his Roman readers, especially since they have long been trained in the art of *dissimulatio* as applicable to the portrayal of indignation

312

and of other useful rhetorical emotions, to remain rational throughout the satirist's tirades, to distinguish reality from the satirist's distorted version of reality. Let the satirist decry a world out of joint; people have to live as though life had some sense, and so they cannot accept the satirist's implicit picture of life as nonsense. In the early Satires, *ratio* is one of the words most inappropriate for the satirist. Nevertheless, although the satirist forfeits his right to reason, although the drama that we witness shrieks out against the irrationality of contemporary Rome, we readers should not therefore suppress our rational faculties. It is a shallow poet who insists that the world is fundamentally disordered; and I do not believe that Juvenal, any more than Euripides, should be used to bolster the pathetic cult of irrationality today. He knew as well as Pliny and Tacitus did that the Empire was there to stay and that a useful existence could be led under Trajan, not to mention Domitian. He knew that dwelling upon the mythical virtues of 300 B.C., of Republican Rome seen through rosy glasses, was as irrational and impractical as possible. Therefore, when he created a satirist to embody such a set of fantastic ideas, he could legitimately expect that the reader would recognize the fantastic satirist for what he was, a dramatic character by no means identical with Juvenal's ideals and equally alien to the reader's preconceptions.

In my opinion, the reader today should start as the Roman audience did nineteen hundred years ago, with a clear realization that the poet is a rhetorical artist and that what he allows to be said in his poems, whether in the first or the third person, does not correspond exactly to his own psychological state: the poet dons a mask or creates an objective character. However, even if the reader of Juvenal does not start off today with that ability to draw such a distinction between Juvenal and his satirist, the problems into which he plunges by identifying Juvenal and satirist should ultimately oblige him to reject his initial instinct as invalid. De Decker's and Marmorale's protests over Juvenal's sly rhetorical insincerity illustrate one typical error that results from identification; and Serafini's anxiously argued chapters about Juvenal's "truth," while more sympathetic to Juvenal, seem to my mind needless effort. The clearest example of another typical error is Highet's ingenious reconstruction of Juvenal's biography: again and again, Highet applies what the satirist says or seems to say directly, without the slightest qualification, to the personality of Juvenal. How far such readers are from understanding the art of the ancient poet, let alone of all poets!

By contrast, I would contend that Juvenal has provided ample reasons for disassociating him from the attitudes expressed by his satirist. In the first place, he depicts this satirist as torn by serious tensions that tend to disqualify the satirist's reliability as a social observer; and secondly, he assigns to the satirist moral ideas that we could not possibly share, not so long as we have our wits about us. The satirist proclaims his honest indignation, yet he manifests the self-consciousness of the orator and even plays with his supposed passion. While he makes a powerful theme of *verum,* his "truth" demands constant distortion, exclusive allegations about evils which no sane person would believe, and no truthful person would utter. Demonstrating his opposition to every facet of contemporary Rome, constantly reiterating the desirability of "flight," the satirist stays on, trapped by the very fascination of evil, convicted by his own prurient sensationalism. For all his vaunted moral concern, the satirist's tirades against *avaritia* expose him to the same charge, his denunciations of women raise questions about his own *pudor;* in short, his indignation often originates not in what is truly and objectively *indignum,* but what his angry failures make him believe is an outrage. Finally, the satirist's irrationality, lightened here and there by a trace of irony, humor, and incredible hyperbole, should not rob the reader of his senses. And this is perhaps the most ironic fact about many Juvenalian scholars: they either accept the satirist's irrationality as a mirror of Roman society in A.D. 90–130, or abuse Juvenal for being limited in his range and blind to the facts of Trajanic and Hadrianic Rome.

I would also contend that Juvenal's dramatization of the indignant satirist is a masterpiece; the poet has fully realized the possibilities of the role and created a complex character that engages our feelings while at the same time offending our moral and rational sensibilities. No reader is wrong for preferring the early Satires to the later. The early Satires are better, not because Juvenal is younger and more passionate, not because we admire his fearless denunciation of Rome, but because Juvenal has produced so masterful a characterization of his satirist and faced us with an intricate combination of attractive and repellent traits. To grasp the truth about this satirist perhaps requires more effort than is usually assigned to Juvenal's Satires, but the rewards repay the labor.

II. SENECA'S DISCUSSION OF ANGER

KERNAN CONVINCINGLY DEMONSTRATED the Renaissance satirist's essentially dramatic nature by reference to documents, prose and poetry, that have survived to this day. Thus he showed that English writers of the late 1500's and early 1600's described the satirist in nearly identical terms; that the most wretched versifiers copied the satirists that able poets like Marston had successfully devised; in short, that the critic can legitimately isolate in English literature what can properly be described as "the Renaissance satirist." For lack of such documents, those who study Juvenal are obliged to adopt a somewhat different attack. Of the few contemporary satirists in Juvenal's era whose names are known, such as Turnus, nothing has survived. No contemporary theory of satire or discussion of the satirist exists; Quintilian's famous passage obviously is irrelevant in this matter. Although we could profitably draw conclusions from the "satiric" epigrams of Martial and the "satiric" manner of Tacitus, and although the rhetorical preconceptions of *indignatio* throw much light upon Juvenal's art, in this section, it seems to me, more is to be gained from using a document which Juvenal probably knew well, Seneca's essay for Claudius, *De ira.*

Seneca feels no compulsion in this discursive essay to create a perfectly proportioned analysis of anger; the reader should not demand it of him. However, rather than follow Seneca's pleasantly repetitive course, I shall make a careful selection of his main arguments. For, after all, Seneca's essay concerns us here only insofar as it casts light on Juvenal's art.

True to the principles of diatribe and moral discussion, Seneca creates an interlocutor or *adversarius,* to represent the views about anger which Seneca desires to confute. Accordingly, it is possible to distinguish in this essay two sets of attitudes toward *ira:* the erroneous ones of the *adversarius,* briefly and schematically stated, and the elaborate retorts of Seneca, who persuasively develops a "correct" interpretation. In the dramatic dialogue that Seneca has contrived, his disagreements with his *adversarius* correspond at numerous points to the tensions—what I might call the internal dialogue—between the honestly indignant satirist and his distorted self, and indicate that Juvenal, familiar with such ideas, artfully contrived a character whose moral position had to be suspect.

To prevent any misunderstandings, let me say from the beginning that, while *ira* is not the same emotion as *indignatio,* in Latin any more than in English, the Roman rhetoricians and moralists used them synonymously. Valerius Maximus may serve as a good example of the average, uncritical usage of these terms. In his discussion entitled *De ira aut odio,* Maximus employs two characteristic synonyms for *ira:* namely, *doloris impotentia* (9.3.3) and *indignatio* (9.3.8). When he uses the latter term, he cites for his *exemplum* Sulla, no particular favorite of any Roman, who, in a paroxysm of fury (*ardens indignatione*), had a stroke and died. Quintilian thinks and writes of anger and indignation as virtually identical.[1] Juvenal's contemporary, Tacitus, describes men and women who are indignant, using the synonyms *dolor* and *ira.*[2] Juvenal himself permits his satirist to describe his mood as *ira* (1.45) before insisting on his *indignatio* (1.79). Thus, when Seneca interchanges *ira* with *indignatio,* he violates no linguistic rules; and consequently it is legitimate to apply his criticisms of *ira* to that special form of anger found in Juvenal's Satires, *indignatio.* For while Seneca knows many prejudicial words for *ira,* such as *furor, rabies, feritas, infirmitas,* it is quite clear that he considers *indignatio* an accurate synonym, one that carries no implication for good or bad.[3]

The anger which Seneca discusses involves angry acts, not angry words. Consequently, I shall not re-use the same organizational scheme as in my treatment of the satirist's tensions, for several of those tensions (e.g., honest speaker vs. orator, truth vs. distortion, abhorrence of vice vs. sensationalism) presupposed an indignant speaker. Instead, I propose to introduce a new scheme of inquiry, which is primarily applicable to Seneca's treatise, but which can be extended to cover the satirist's indignation. I shall analyze anger under four headings, as suggested by the interests of the moralist: the causes which stimulate *ira;* the character of *ira;* the character of the angry man (*iratus*); and the purpose of *ira.*

THE CAUSES WHICH STIMULATE IRA

Anger originates as the result of *iniuria,* whether directly inflicted upon the person or indirectly, whether already suffered or still feared. Seneca and other Roman writers feel free to describe this injury as *dolor,* a grief suffered, but as I have already said, *dolor* can mean *indignatio,* inasmuch as grief suffered leads to grief felt and the passion which one naturally feels against the cause of grief. The ambiguous nature of

---

[1] See "Juvenal and Quintilian," 31 ff.

[2] See such phrases as *liberi doloris* (*Ann.* 2.34.2); *dolor ira* (2.82.2); cf. 1.41.5, 2.19.2, *ira et questus* (4.72.5). In the declamations falsely ascribed to Quintilian, we find the same associations: e.g., *dolor ... iniuria ... indignatio nulla possit tolerare patienter* (*Decl.* 246); *dolor ... ira* (246, p. 14); *dolor ... indignatio* (280, p. 143).

[3] See Seneca's use of *indignatio* as a synonym for *ira* in *De ira* 2.28.1, 3.5.7, and 3.16.1; also his use of the verb *indignari* as virtually equivalent to *irasci.*

dolor is demonstrated by the definition of anger which Seneca attributes to Aristotle: *ait enim iram esse cupiditatem doloris reponendi* (1.3). While *dolor* describes the emotion aroused by a personal affront, *ira* or *indignatio* seems to apply more particularly to either personal or public *nequitia* (*see* 2.7.1; 12.1; 28.1).

Although theoretically one might grow angry if an enemy retaliated for some insult or injury, this type of *iniuria* would raise so many questions and might reflect so adversely on the angry man that it is not worth considering in a short treatise. Seneca assumes that *iniuria* is a gratuitous, unmerited, and unexpected act of evil:

duo sunt, ut dixi, quae iracundiam concitent: primum, si iniuriam videmur accepisse, ..., deinde si inique accepisse .... iniqua quaedam iudicant homines, quia pati non debuerint, quaedam, quia non speraverint. indigna putamus quae inopinata sunt. itaque maxime commovent quae contra spem exspectationemque evenerunt. (2.31.1)

Convinced that they have suffered or seen something *indignum,* people burn with *indignatio* or *ira.* There are many degrees of such *iniuriae.* At one extreme occur verbal insults: *maledicta, contumeliae.* A slave or a child may answer his master disrespectfully. At a banquet, under the influence of too much wine and the *libertas* which generally prevailed at ancient *convivia,* a guest might hurt one's feelings (3.37). Seneca cites a long list of historical *exempla* illustrating *maledicta* and the way great men could suffer them calmly (3.22 ff.): Antigonus overhears some soldiers airing typical soldiers' complaints against their general, presumably in the typically foul language of the troops; Philip of Macedon appeals in a friendly fashion to the Athenian ambassadors, and Demochares tells him to go hang himself; Augustus lets Timagenes insult him in historical writings.

Closely related in degree of importance are the slight insults also known as *contumeliae,* injury to one's pride rather than a permanent hurt. Seneca cites two cases of exemplary behavior on the occasion of such *contumeliae:* as Diogenes delivered a diatribe against anger, a brash young man spat in his face, presumably to test him; the Catilinarian Lentulus similarly spat with all his force in the face of Cato, as the latter was arguing a case (3.38.2).

At the far extreme, where the *adversarius* places himself when justifying anger, are grave and permanent outrages to oneself and one's family. Eager to make his case as strong as possible, he chooses two extreme examples: *quid ergo? vir bonus non irascetur, si caedi patrem suum viderit, si rapi matrem?* (1.12.1). Although the *adversarius* gives no details about these outrages, Seneca elaborates upon several of a similar horror. These involve the behavior of tyrants against helpless subjects and the firm endurance of the subjects, even though the tyrant malevolently tried every ingeniously sadistic device to provoke an angry outburst. For example, Astyages invited Harpagus to a banquet and served the father his own sons (3.15). When he turns from Herodotus, Seneca can tell in loving detail a story from his own experience, of how Caligula invited the knight Pastor to dinner on the very day that he had executed Pastor's son and of how Pastor endured Caligula's sadism so as to protect another son: *non lacrimam emisit, non dolorem aliquo signo erumpere passus est* (2.33.4).

Besides the personal injuries occasioned by slander, trivial insults, stolen goods, bodily abuse of daughter, wife, or mother, and finally murder, Seneca and his *adversarius* discuss the public outrage caused by the very existence of *nequitia,* the prevalence of evil, the general success of the wrongdoer. As the *adversarius* puts it, anger and evil are concomitant phenomena of nature, anger being the natural result of evil: *nequitia de rerum natura tollenda est, si velis iram tollere* (2.12.1). Seneca himself pictures the degenerate state of the world, especially of Rome, in words that anticipate the pessimism of Juvenal's satirist:

quod enim momentum erit quo non improbanda videat [sc. *sapiens*]? quotiens processerit domo, per sceleratos illi avarosque et prodigos et impudentis, et ob ista felices, incedendum erit; nusquam oculi eius flectentur, ut non quod indignentur inveniant. deficiet, si totiens a se iram quotiens causa poscet exegerit. haec tot milia ad forum prima luce properantia, quam turpes lites, quanto turpiores advocatos habent! alius iudicia patris accusat, quae vereri satius fuit; alius cum matre consistit; alius delator venit eius criminis, cuius manifestior reus est; et iudex damnaturus quae fecit eligitur; et corona pro mala causa proclamat, bona patroni voce corrupta. (2.7.2-3)

Together with the above passage, which hurries the vicious before the eyes of the wise man, somewhere near the Forum, in a way and with examples that should remind the reader of the catalogue of criminal types observed by Juvenal's satirist from his vantage-point on the street corner (1.23 ff.), I cite extensively another passage that voices the same indictment of human degeneracy as the satirist does in 1.147 ff.:

omnia sceleribus ac vitiis plena sunt; plus committitur quam quod possit coercitione sanari; certatur ingenti quidem nequitiae certamine; maior cottidie peccandi cupiditas, minor verecundia est; expulso melioris aequiorisque respectu, quocumque visum est libido se impingit; nec furtiva iam scelera sunt, praeter oculos eunt; adeoque in publicum missa nequitia est et in omnium pectoribus evaluit, ut innocentia non rara, sed nulla sit. numquid enim singuli aut pauci rupere legem? undique, velut signo dato, ad fas nefasque miscendum coorti sunt. (2.9.1-2)

As I have mentioned, Seneca himself, in his own person, mentions many of these details: all the elaborate *exempla* from Books II and III

318

are his, and the passage on general *nequitia* just quoted is but a small portion of what he says on the subject. In other words, Seneca makes no effort to deny the facts. Personal affronts and injuries do occur, and evil stares one in the face wherever one looks in Rome. The *adversarius* may choose an extreme case in crying out about a murdered father or a raped mother, but the moralist does not attack him on this count. What Seneca does, while admitting the *iniuria,* is to question whether it constitutes an immediate and sufficient cause of anger.

iram quin species oblata iniuriae moveat non est dubium; sed utrum speciem ipsam statim sequatur et non accedente animo excurrat, an illo adsentiente moveatur quaerimus. (2.1.3)

If, as Seneca insists, the mind does assent to anger, then the mind must entertain some fancies about the value and purpose of anger; and these fancies must be studied and discussed before the moralist can reach any decisive conclusions about how to deal with anger. Therefore, although I have entitled this section "The Causes Which Stimulate *ira,*" it should be recognized from the beginning that no *maledictum, contumelia, iniuria, scelus, nequitia,* or *indignitas* directly produces anger or indignation: they "stimulate," but they do not "cause" *ira.* Once the moralist has inserted that reservation, it becomes necessary to turn away from what we assumed, with the *adversarius,* to be "causes" and to consider the role of the mind in assenting to anger. What do people think of *ira?*

THE CHARACTER OF IRA

Just as Juvenal's satirist in the early poems describes *indignatio* as an honest and noble emotion, so the *adversarius* thinks of *ira* as the habit of a morally upright Roman, the *vir bonus.* Not only does he firmly believe that the proper Roman should be angry, especially when his father has been murdered or his mother raped, but the *adversarius* can also quote Theophrastus in support of his opinion: *non potest, inquit Theophrastus, fieri ut bonus vir non irascatur malis* (1.14). It is not far from this uncritical opinion to the conviction that *ira* and *virtus* are closely allied, and soon he declares: *virtus, ut honestis rebus propitia est, ita turpibus irata esse debet* (2.6.1). Once he assumes that *virtus* can be angry, then the *adversarius* can describe anger as a virtue, one appropriate to the finest ideals of Roman manhood. Thus anger is a natural attribute of courage; anger and direct, spontaneous honesty belong together; anger befits the desire for, and expression of, freedom; and finally anger possesses a certain nobility, a grandeur that the *adversarius* considers most desirable. I shall treat these ideas in detail to see how the Senecan moralist demonstrates, to the contrary, that anger is a grave fault which no intelligent, hence moral, being should embrace.

In arguing that anger is a virtue, the *adversarius* rests his case on two quite diverse points: (1) the average man, untrained in philosophy, instinctively feels that anger can be justified under many circumstances and that it would be unmanly to check anger over personal outrages; (2) some moral philosophers, and particularly the Peripatetics, regarded moderate anger as a virtue existing midway between irascibility and mean-spiritedness. Had the *adversarius* the necessary intelligence to understand Aristotle and Theophrastus, it might be worth while reviewing more fully the Peripatetic theory of anger. However, the *adversarius* shows no grasp of the doctrine and merely quotes a few catch phrases that he considers useful; never is he permitted to elaborate on Aristotle or to define the philosophic theory adequately. When one compares, for example, the thorough and persuasive discussion of ὀργή in the *Nicomachean Ethics* (4.11) with the seemingly silly statements that the *adversarius* mouths, it is easy to realize that Seneca had no intention of tilting seriously against Aristotle.

The *adversarius* appeals to, or Seneca rejects, the authority of Aristotle on three separate occasions, but always in connection with the same argument, namely, that anger and courage are mutually beneficial.

ira, inquit Aristoteles, necessaria est; nec quicquam sine illa expugnari potest, nisi illa implet animum et spiritum accendit. utendum autem illa est, non ut duce, sed ut milite. (1.9.2)
Aristoteles ait affectus quosdam, si quis illis bene utatur, pro armis esse. (1.17.1)
stat Aristotles defensor irae et vetat illam nobis exsecari. calcar ait esse virtutis; hac erepta, inermem animum et ad conatus magnos pigrum inertemque fieri. (3.3.1)[4]

The commentators note that Seneca has attributed to Aristotle in the first passage a statement that is otherwise unknown, one which cannot be found in the extant Aristotelian writings. However, it does not seriously conflict with what Aristotle did say and may be regarded as at least a Peripatetic idea. That Seneca thoroughly disapproves of any attempt to connect anger with courage and military exploits is of especial relevance to Juvenal, because Juvenal's satirist draws this very connection in his ennobling portrait of Lucilius, who both drives an epic chariot (1.20) and, afire with militant fury, brandishes his sword against his foe (1.165).

---

[4] Cf. the words attributed to the *adversarius* in 1.7.1: "*extollit animos* [sc. *ira*] *et incitat; nec quicquam sine illa magnificum in bello fortitudo gerit, nisi hinc flamma subdita est et hic stimulus peragitavit misitque in pericula audaces.*"

Seneca makes a slight effort to dismiss the Peripatetic theory in 2.6, in answer to the seemingly foolish claim that *virtus* can, and should, be qualified by the attribute *irata*. Essentially, he asserts that moderate anger, a *modus* between fury and tameness, can never be achieved because it is a contradiction in terms. And he faces his opponent with a dilemma: either a man will be unfair, if he is equally angry at unequal crimes; or he will be too angry, if he seethes with wrath as often as evils merit it. To rebut the more emotional appeal to anger as a militant virtue, Seneca carefully takes up the images stated in 1.9 and 17. Anger is by definition—Seneca's definition, to which I shall come—*contumacia*, or recalcitrance, repugnance to authority. Just as a general would never knowingly rely on rebellious troops, so reason should never employ wild, undisciplined passions like wrath. As for the comparison of anger with weapons, Seneca's answer should be quoted in full:

quod verum foret, si velut bellica instrumenta sumi deponique possent induentis arbitrio. haec arma, quae Aristoteles virtuti dat, ipsa per se pugnant, non exspectant manum, et habent, non habentur. nil aliis instrumentis opus est, satis nos instruxit ratione natura. (1.17.1–2)

In short, anger and *virtus* are mutually opposed.

The *adversarius* thinks of anger as basic honesty, a direct and spontaneous response to *iniuria;* and he applies to this honesty the honorary term which occurs also in Juvenal's Program Satire, namely *simplicitas: simplicissimi omnium habentur iracundi* (2.16.3). Seneca comments in Book III:

non vis admoneam, quo diligentior quisque sit et ipse se circumspiciat, alia animi mala ad pessimos quosque pertinere, iracundiam etiam eruditis hominibus et in alia sanis inrepere; adeo ut quidam *simplicitatis indicium iracundiam* dicant et vulgo credatur facillimus quisque huic obnoxius? (3.4.5)

The moralist wastes no time on this point. As far as he is concerned, the *adversarius* is quibbling over terms, and what the *adversarius* considers simple frankness, the moralist contemptuously rejects as folly. No intelligent man, in other words, should naïvely resort to anger.

If anger cannot be defined as *simplicitas*, neither can it be logically regarded as a desirable form of *libertas*. Says the *adversarius: ut scias iram habere in se generosi aliquid, liberas videbis gentes, quae iracundissimae sunt, ut Germanos et Scythas* (2.15.1). For the Greeks, the noble savage was ideally the Scythian, as readers of Herodotus know; similarly, the Romans found their model of nobility among the Germans. While Tacitus' *Germania* provides the best example of the Roman tendency to idealize the savage, Tacitus' contemporary Juvenal exploits the same commonplace. Satire 2 begins and ends on this motif: the satirist longs to flee from corrupt Rome, at the beginning, to go north to the Sarmatian tribes; at the end, he describes how a Parthian hostage, from the eastern borders of the Empire, has been corrupted by his stay at Rome.[5] Among the Sarmatians, it is to be presumed, Juvenal's satirist would find a congenial environment for his *libertas*.

Seneca spurns this form of *libertas*, because it reflects an absence of culture and mental discipline, not any positive virtue. By nature the Germans and Scythians are brave and love freedom; that is good. But unless they learn to control their natural instincts and to discipline their propensity to anger, bravery degenerates into sheer rashness. Putting this *libertas* in the most unattractive light, Seneca concludes his attack as follows:

deinde omnes istae feritate liberae gentes leonum luporumque ritu ut servire non possunt, ita nec imperare. non enim humani vim ingenii, sed feri et intractabilis habent; nemo autem regere potest, nisi que et regi. (2.15.4)

Later, in 3.2 the moralist returns to these savage people, now called simply barbarians, and he describes one of the familiar scenes of Roman experience: how the wild tribesmen, lashed by vain fury, hurl themselves suicidally upon the Roman legions and die by the thousands.

The *adversarius* sees both freedom and nobility in the hot temper of the Germans; elsewhere also he asserts that anger is a fitting attribute of a great spirit: *animalia generosissima habentur, quibus multum inest irae* (2.16.1); *languidus animus est, qui ira caret* (2.17.2); *minus contemnemur, si vindicaverimus iniuriam* (2.33.1). Juvenal's satirist assumes the same prejudice in the early poems. The Grand Style which he appropriates from epic and tragedy is in theory adapted to the fiery emotions of the noble Roman who fulminates against national degradation. While the satirist treats Umbricius as a hero, he makes Trebius appear to be an obsequious slave, one who deserves every indignity that he receives; and the compliant husband of Satire 6, who fails to voice the proper spirit of indignation against his vicious wife, is a contemptible fool. Even an angry woman has something heroic about her (*see* 6.646 ff.).

Seneca disagrees strongly, and he devotes a long chapter to proving that anger does not befit nobility of soul; on the contrary, anger is the attribute of a weak, infirm mind. Seneca's argument forms the climax of Book I. First, he calls anger a kind of sickness: *tumor, morbus, pesti-*

---

[5] The Sarmatians seem to have been vaguely equivalent to the Scythians. Tacitus *Germ.* 1.1 and 46.1 locates them on the northeastern frontier of the area defined as Germania, that is, approximately in the region allotted to the Scythians by Herodotus.

lens abundantia (1.20). Then, using another metaphor, he proceeds to attack what some people name "lofty" anger. If to go beyond the limits set by reason is sublime, then anger is lofty. In fact, however, wrath resembles a poorly constructed building which lacks a secure foundation: inevitably it will collapse. So anger betrays a sick and unhappy soul, not magnanimity:

multum, inquam, interest inter sublimem animum et superbum, iracundia nihil amplum decorumque molitur; contra mihi videtur, veternosi et *infelicis animi, imbecillitatis sibi conscii*, saepe indolescere, ut exulcerata et aegra corpora quae ad tactus levissimos gemunt. ita ira muliebre maxime et puerile vitium est. (1.20.3)

There are some stirring remarks attributed to villains in tragedy or heard from tyrants, that the ignorant often mistakenly believe to be "noble." For example, Seneca cites that much-repeated phrase, *oderint, dum metuant*, once uttered by Atreus in Accius' play, but more familiar to his reader as a favorite saying of Caligula.[6] And he comments: *nec enim magnitudo ista est, sed immanitas*. Apparently, his phrase put Seneca to thinking about Caligula, for he soon describes an absurd scene to illustrate the supposed eloquence of noble anger: angry because a lightning bolt had disturbed a showing of pantomimes, the megalomaniac ruler challenged Jupiter to a duel to death. One can only agree with the moralist: *quanta dementia fuit!* (1.20.9) Thus, neither angry words nor angry actions can rightly be considered noble. Seneca concludes the argument and the Book in this manner:

nihil ergo in ira, ne cum videtur quidem vehemens et deos hominesque despiciens, magnum, nihil nobile est ... sola sublimis et excelsa virtus est: nec quicquam magnum est, nisi quod simul placidum. (1.21.1–4)

If, then, anger cannot be considered a virtue, if it is wrongly associated with the martial spirit, with *simplicitas, libertas,* and *magnitudo,* how should men describe it? Seneca's comment on Caligula is, in fact, his definition of anger: *dementia*. He quotes with approval in his very first chapter the common assertion, similar to that of Horace's *Epist.* 1.2.62, that anger is temporary insanity:

quidam itaque e sapientibus viris iram dixerunt brevem insaniam; aeque enim impotens sui est, decoris oblita, necessitudinum immemor, in quod coepit pertinax et intenta, rationi consiliisque praeclusa, vanis agitata causis, ad dispectum aequi verique inhabilis, ruinis simillima quae super id quod oppressere franguntur. ut scias autem non esse sanos quos ira possedit, ipsum illorum habitum intuere. (1.1.2–3)

Holding to this definition of *ira,* Seneca obviously cannot admit any

6 See Suetonius, *Caligula* 30.

compromise. Whereas the Peripatetics could conceive of a moderate and useful wrath, Seneca's definition renders the very idea of moderate wrath absurd, a paradox. How could anger, defined as irrational, ever be moderated? How could a fault ever become a virtue, no matter how slight?

If in refuting the *adversarius* so far, Seneca has delivered an implicit challenge to any figure like the angry, indignant satirist, his definition of *ira* or *indignatio* constitutes direct and open disapproval of a Juvenalian satirist. Seventy years later Juvenal's audience, undoubtedly familiar with Seneca's treatise or similar ideas, would have been bound to question the ethical propriety of *indignatio* and hence of the satirist's angry picture of the Roman world. What better comment on the theory of the Program Satire could one seek than this:

adde nunc ... circumscriptiones, furta, fraudes, infitiationes, quibus trina non sufficiunt fora. si tantum irasci vis sapientem quantum scelerum *indignitas* exigit, non irascendum illi, sed insaniendum est. (2.9.4)

Consider, too, how Seneca has glossed this brief insanity in 1.1 and what terminology he thinks fit to apply to it. Anger has no power over itself (*impotens sui*). That means, as he urges again and again, that it cannot endure or suffer injuries of any sort. However, what Seneca clearly regards as a serious fault, Juvenal's satirist, repeatedly admits, or rather boasts of as a definite virtue: *non possum ferre!* Anger ignores propriety (*decoris oblita*); Juvenal's satirist knows no propriety in either subject or language. Anger blocks its ears to reason and advice (*rationi consiliisque praeclusa*); Juvenal's satirist is an irrationalist in what he fondly asserts is an irrational environment. Anger is provoked by vain reasons (*vanis agitata causis*); how often this seems true in Juvenal's Satires! Anger cannot distinguish justice and truth (*ad dispectum aequi verique inhabilis*); irrational as it is, Juvenalian indignation insists on a distorted truth, part of its distorted vision of Rome.

The synonyms and metaphors Seneca employs to vary the description of *ira* deserve consideration here, for two reasons: first, they support the Senecan conception of anger as insane; and second, much the same language appears in the Satires of Juvenal to describe the satirist. As I have said, *indignatio* often stands for *ira* and is entirely neutral in sense. For a series of prejudicial synonyms, the following passage is useful:

quantum est effugere maximum malum, iram, et cum illa rabiem, saevitiam, crudelitatem, furorem, alios comites eius affectus! (2.12.6)

To this list, I add *contumacia* (1.9.2), *infirmitas* (1.12.4), *feritas* (2.15.4), *inhumanitas* (see 2.32.1), and *iniquitas* (3.29.2). Such synonyms betray the writer's antipathy to anger, not only rendering the emotion a form of insanity, but also depicting it as inhuman, indeed bestial. None of these synonyms occur in Juvenal's early Satires; the satirist is not so foolish as to cut off from himself all possibility of sympathy. The most that he will do is equate *indignatio* with *ira* and *dolor,* another neutral term. Not until the satirist himself changes do these prejudicial ideas of indignation make their appearance.

The most common metaphors which Seneca uses to describe anger are those of fire, wild animals, and eruption. A partial list of the fire-metaphors, with their first appearance cited, follows: *effervescit* (1.1.5), *exarsit* and *ardore* (1.2.3–4), *fervidi* (2.19.1), *flamma lumina ardentia* (2.35.5), *fervore* (2.36.4), *flagrantis* (3.4.3). Some of these metaphors occur repeatedly in Juvenal's Satires. Here are some of the animal-metaphors: *rabidum* (1.1.1), *saevierunt* (1.3.8), *ferum* (1.5.3), *effrenatam indomitamque* (1.9.3). These are so prejudicial that the satirist is *never* described by such words; and therefore the phrase *saeva indignatio,* Scaliger's conception of the satirist's mood, automatically condemns indignation. The metaphors for eruption are nearly all verbs: *rabida vocis eruptio, impetus rupturus se nisi eruperit* (2.35.3), *prorumpit* (3.5.6). Other metaphorical verbs make of anger a violent force, an avalanche or sometimes a storm (the opposite of *tranquillitas*): *tempestas* (3.1.1), *se ipsa rapiens violentia* (3.1.3), *praecipitat* (3.1.4), *impetu turbidus* (3.6.2).

Juvenal's satirist describes his *dolor,* often in terms of the physical discomfort and burning sensation caused by the bile, the seat of anger. Seneca once refers to the bile (2.26.3). On the other hand, Seneca gains considerable effect from picturing the angry man, as in a portrait:

flagrant ac micant oculi, multus ore toto rubor exaestuante ab imis praecordiis sanguine, labra quatiuntur, dentes comprimuntur, horrent ac surriguntur capilli, spiritus coactus ac stridens, articulorum se ipsos torquentium sonus, gemitus mugitusque et parum explanatis vocibus sermo praeruptus et complosae saepius manus et pulsata humus pedibus et totum concitum corpus magnasque irae minas agens, foeda visu et horrenda facies depravantium se atque intumescentium. nescias utrum magis detestabile vitium sit an deforme. (1.1.4)

The blood seething from the depths of the bowels resembles the effect of the burning bile (cf. Juvenal 1.45 and 13.14–15); the clenched teeth (or the compressed lips) serve as a defining characteristic of the indignant man in Juvenal 1.160 and 5.160; the groaning and jerky speech (*sermo praeruptus*) give an exact description of the style of Juvenal's satirist. Yet Seneca rejects as disgusting or inhumanly ugly what the satirist in the early Satires advances as presumed virtues.

Whereas Juvenal's satirist implies the righteous nobility of his anger, Seneca admits no justification at all for wrath or indignation. Anger, for him, is a vice, a vicious failing of human rationality, a disease, and, at its lowest mark, utter insanity. To get along in this world, a man cannot hope to cherish or act upon anger, for anger is suicidal. Thus, the Senecan portrait of anger and its congener, indignation, constitutes a familiar and well-established answer to the vaunted *indignatio* of Juvenal's satirist. Most Romans in the audience, having studied the rhetorical and moral theories on the subject, should have been prepared not only to recognize the mask of indignation, but to hold it up to criticism. Similarly, they would have been quite capable, unlike some modern critics, of perceiving the weaknesses in the satirist's character, precisely because he was angry.

THE CHARACTER OF THE ANGRY MAN

In this era when "The Angry Young Man" has become a stock figure on the stage, dramatists like Osborne have regularly given this type salient faults which tend to qualify and, in some instances, to nullify his vitriolic denunciations of people and society. Juvenal, too, possessed a good dramatic sense, and he shows, in his creation of the indignant satirist, that he had thoroughly grasped the ideas of such works as Seneca's *De ira*. His satirist, torn by a series of tensions that cumulatively invite us to suspect the man, is a typically angry man. Before Juvenal, Seneca had emphatically argued that anyone who embraced the insane vice of anger was himself both insane and vicious.

The *adversarius*, I showed, praised the angry man as *vir bonus*, on the grounds that anger itself was a virtue. It is not necessary to review Seneca's refutation; he successfully demonstrates that anger and virtue are irreconcilable, whether one uses the Peripatetic argument for a controlled wrath or whether one resorts to the everyday opinion of anger as equivalent to nobility. It follows from this that, to Seneca, the angry man cannot be *vir bonus*. If a good Roman suffers an injury unjustly, even one of those fantastic crimes chosen as examples by the *adversarius* (murder of father, rape of mother), he should not indulge his anger, but rationally set about the punishment or the ending of the crime. Anger contributes nothing to this goal. Therefore, using the words from which the term *indignatio* is derived, Seneca carefully re-defines the attitude of the *vir bonus:*

officia sua vir bonus exsequetur inconfusus, intrepidus; et sic bono viro *digna* faciet ut nihil faciat viro *indignum*. (1.12.2)

326

It is because the irate man is confused and beyond physical as well as mental self-control that Seneca particularly opposes anger. Although the *adversarius* can emotionally cloud the issue and paint a lurid picture of his angry one as righteous, naïvely indignant, magnanimous, and outspoken, the moralist replies by concentrating on the faults of which anger is symptomatic. The fundamental irrationality of *ira*, then, negates all supposed virtues, and Seneca's biting criticisms change them into a series of vices. For example, to compare the irate with the barbarian and talk mistily about their common nobility and love of freedom involves the *adversarius* in manifest illogic; and Seneca easily corrects him by calling the angry man a barbarian, but with no laudatory implications. When the *adversarius* describes his hero as *potens*, like those tyrants and tyrannous natures that display their fury for the purpose of asserting their importance, Seneca alters the emphasis and makes this "hero" into a captive of his own fury: *irae suae captivus* (3.4.4).[7]

One specious argument on behalf of *ira* can be made: *orator iratus aliquando melior est* (2.17.1). Inasmuch as Juvenal's satirist declares himself *orator iratus,* we are particularly interested in Seneca's rebuttal. Most readers would agree that the satirist of Juvenal's Books I and II achieves greater success, makes a much better case, than the satirist of the later books; and indeed I believe that the source of this success is *indignatio.* However, as I have earlier shown, this *indignatio* is a dramatic creation, and it fully coheres with the conventions established for it among the rhetoricians; and now Seneca repeats the same point in his rejoinder to the *adversarius.* True, the "angry orator" achieves greater success than his calm confrere; but the key to his success lies not in being angry, but in skillfully imitating wrath. Just as actors on the comic and tragic stage assume the ferocious mien of some choleric father or outraged hero and their acting wins the applause of the audience, so the orator before judge and jury must be prepared to simulate convincingly many emotions, among them anger. By so doing, he can provoke sympathetic anger while himself retaining all his faculties, ready to resort to a different emotion at need.

To put it bluntly, the *adversarius* has no case; under no circumstances can an angry man be thought a hero. He is not virtuous, simple, noble, vigorous; and even when his anger would seem to determine the success of a speech, it proves, upon examination, to be an artfully contrived anger, entirely under the rational control of the dexterous orator. Now that Seneca has routed the *adversarius,* he refuses to rest content with

[7] Cf. 1.1.2: *impotens sui.*

327

merely disproving the fool's allegations. For not only must it be shown that the character of the angry man is devoid of virtue; it must also appear manifest that the *iratus* is a mass of vices.

An angry man is a monster (*see* 3.3), and his monstrous character springs from the fact that, insane, undisciplined, hypocritical, and womanish, not to say bestial, he cuts himself off from the essential qualities of Man. Of these faults, the gravest are hypocrisy and inhumanity. First, the hypocrisy of indignation often blinds its victim to his own evils; he behaves like a judge without first examining his own actions and conscience, to the extent that he fails to see that sometimes he himself has contributed to the *iniuria* by a prior misdeed. Even where he has not specifically exasperated the criminal, still the indignant man could easily discover in his own character and behavior instances of the same or similar crimes.

non est autem prudentis errantes ödisse, alioqui ipse sibi odio erit. cogitet quam multa contra bonum morem faciat, quam multa ex is quae egit veniam desiderent; iam irascetur etiam sibi. neque enim aequus iudex aliam de sua, aliam de aliena causa sententiam fert. nemo, inquam, invenietur qui se possit absolvere, et innocentem quisque se dicit, respiciens testem, non conscientiam. (1.14.2–3)

Seneca repeatedly comes back to this point: we are all sinners. We cannot be fair judges if our minds are blinded by passion and if indignation prevents us from seeing ourselves and our troubles in the right perspective. Although we also have erred, our anger tends to make us believe in our innocence, to think too highly of ourselves and at the same time to react too harshly against those who have made us suffer.

si volumus aequi rerum omnium iudices esse, hoc primum nobis persuadeamus, neminem nostrum esse sine culpa. hinc enim maxima indignatio oritur: "nihil peccavi" et "nihil feci." immo nihil fateris. indignamur aliqua admonitione aut coercitione nos castigatos, cum illo ipso tempore peccemus, quod adicimus malefactis arrogantiam et contumaciam. (2.28.1)

Arrogant as we are, we grow indignant and think ourselves noble-spirited, when in fact we are mean and petty: *cum indignatio eius a nimio sui suspectu veniat et animosa videatur, pusilla est et angusta* (3.5.7).

Intent on correcting what he considers a vice, Seneca dramatizes a situation in which an *adversarius* declares himself stirred to wrath. Says the fool, in words that closely resemble those of Juvenal's indignant satirist: *non possum pati; grave est iniuriam sustinere* (3.26.1). And again: *quid ergo? impune illi erit?* To such passion the moralist has a lengthy answer, which in part repeats what he has said before, but adds to and summarizes his whole argument:

deinde ad condicionem rerum humanarum respiciendum est, ut omnium accidentium aequi iudices simus .... omnes inconsulti et improvidi sumus, omnes incerti, queruli, ambitiosi, quid lenioribus verbis ulcus publicum abscondo? omnes mali sumus. quidquid itaque in alio reprehenditur, id unusquisque in sinu suo inveniet .... mali inter malos vivimus. (3.26.3–4)

The final sentence places Seneca in direct opposition to Juvenal's satirist, who rants as though he were a voice crying in the wilderness: e.g., *vir bonus inter malos vivo.*

Because the indignant man fails to consider the human condition as a whole and to include himself among the culpable, Seneca labels him inhuman. Inhumanity involves several faults. For example, I showed that the *iratus* is pejoratively treated as a barbarian on account of his undisciplined character (2.15). Similarly, when the *adversarius* invokes spirited beasts such as lions to exemplify the nobility of wrath, Seneca lets him convict himself. Lions and wolves do possess *feritas* and *rabies* that can be considered analogous to *ira,* but only because *ira* itself debases Man to the level of the beasts. Animals live an instinctive existence, but Man has substituted reason for instinct; reason must control the instinct to anger, or a man negates his essential humanity (2.16).

The theme of humanity runs throughout Seneca's treatise. One of his first characterizations of the *iratus* runs as follows: *armorum, sanguinis, suppliciorum minime humana furens cupiditate* (1.1.1). And the last two sentences of the work urge upon his reader the need to live up to the human ideal:

interim, dum trahimus, dum inter homines sumus, colamus humanitatem; non timori cuiquam, non periculo simus; detrimenta, iniurias, convicia, vellicationes contemnamus, et magno animo brevia feramus incommoda. dum respicimus, quod aiunt, versamusque nos, iam mortalitas aderit. (3.43.5)

Unlike the indignant satirist, who can only shout that he, a righteous man, is trapped among a mass of criminals and perverts, the Senecan moralist admits to himself his own failures and, thinking practically and humanly, knows that, while he lives, he will continue to be with his fellow men. Therefore Seneca insists upon an intelligent facing of facts: we must be humane and endure, accepting the inevitable truth that all men err. In the perspective of our mortality, we waste our brief time on this earth raging over petty discomforts.

Indignation negates the human ideal most plainly in that it seethes with a bestial desire for vengeance. If someone cherishes hatred or vents his dislike upon another, a train of discord is started which not only destroys the ideal relationship between two human beings, but threatens

329

to engulf a larger portion of society. Elsewhere, in language typical of Roman moralists, Seneca defines anger as a womanish or childish fault (1.20). In Book II, where he tries to develop a positive doctrine for correcting irascibility, he strikes right to the heart of the issue with an appeal to basic humanity:

fert humana natura insidiosos animos, fert ingratos, fert cupidos, fert impios. cum de unius moribus iudicabis, de publicis cogita .... illud ante omnia cogita, foedam esse et execrabilem vim nocendi et alienissimam homini, cuius beneficio etiam saeva mansuescunt .... ut omnia inter se membra consentiunt, quia singula servari totius interest, ita homines singulis parcent, quia ad coetum geniti sumus; salva autem esse societas nisi custodia et amore partium non potest ..... inhumanum verbum est et quidem pro iusto receptum, ultio. (2.31.5–32.1)

In discussing 3.26 above, I mentioned that the *adversarius* sounded very much like Juvenal's satirist, when he claimed that he could not endure an injury and rhetorically asked whether the criminal should go unpunished. Indeed, the indignant man characteristically refuses to, and cannot endure (*ferre, pati, tolerare, sustinere,* etc.) evil. He is, as Seneca describes him, *impotens sui* (1.1.2). Furiously yielding to the first instinct, he tries to retaliate against his enemy as harshly as possible, like a beast. Satirists also are often charged with the desire to harm, often called sadists; and the charge is admitted by the Renaissance satirists. Not by the Roman satirists, least of all Juvenal's, who insists that he fixes his gaze on the past, on an era whose criminals have escaped the possibility of harm. However, upon closer inspection this satirist's intolerance convicts him of the very inhumanity that Seneca condemns. Indeed, *indignatio* necessarily dooms itself to condemnation because, while it achieves great dramatic force, it voices an hysterical impatience that alienates any cool thinker.

Juvenal's satirist implicitly desires the harm of the evildoer, not (as Horace's satirist would want) his correction. Thus, he gloats over the death of the stingy rich glutton in 1.135 ff. after first exclaiming over the man's intolerable vice (*quis ferat:* 139). He takes as his model a bellicose Lucilius (1.165 ff.). Furthermore, he regularly brings the evil of the present into irreconcilable opposition with the good of the ancient Republic, producing an impasse. He confronts the perverted nobles in 2.153 ff. with the militant heroes of Roman history; or he contrasts the single prison of early Rome with his contemporary, criminal-infested Rome (3.312 ff.). In other words, he admits nothing good or endurable in the present. Thus, together with his implicit death-wish for the criminals and his pleasure in recording Domitian's murder (4.153–154), goes a professed desire to flee from Rome and its corrupt society. Unwilling to accept the fallible humanity of his fellow Romans, refusing to exist among them as an admitted sinner, the satirist announces his longing to take flight beyond the boundaries of the Roman Empire, in the opening of Satire 2; and he enthusiastically projects himself into the plans of Umbricius, in Satire 3. On a slightly different note, he proclaims that Pudicitia has long ago fled from the world, in Satire 6.19–20, and then goes on to reject with horror the very thought of marriage. Far from accepting the Senecan ideal of *patientia,* he utterly despises poor Trebius, who is willing to bear insults in order to be a guest of the vicious Virro (5.156 ff.).

In short, Juvenal's satirist rejects his fellow human beings, and himself borders on inhumanity: His pessimistic portrait of contemporary Rome leaves no room for hope, and the motif of flight merely emphasizes his hatred of others. As we have seen, repeated materialistic comments indicate that the satirist himself has not freed his own character of the prevailing faults of Roman society, and they seriously weaken his implicit claim to be *vir bonus.* Thus, like all misanthropes, the satirist would be more practical and humane if he recognized his failures and lived sensibly, *malus inter malos.* Yet, in saying this, I do not intend to criticize Juvenal for inartistry. Rather, I mean to call attention once more to the fact that Juvenal's satirist possesses the interesting complexity that is required in all successful dramatic characters: his *indignatio* contains the germs of self-contradiction, as Seneca has indicated, which should prepare readers to listen to his criticisms, but to penetrate more deeply into the human situation they deplore. For Seneca argues that indignation has no valid purpose, whereas sensible patience enables men to live through troubles and achieve a rational existence.

THE PURPOSE OF ANGER

Until some *iniuria* has occurred to fire indignation, that passion can have no purpose. Then its announced purpose is to act upon the *iniuria,* with an eye to the future, whether to punish or execute the malefactor or to display such wrath that no other person will ever again be tempted to such crime. Of course, Seneca denied that *iniuria* was in fact the entire cause of *ira;* instead, he demonstrated that the mind assented to the emotion by abdicating its essential responsibilities. It follows, then, that anger has no valid cause among human beings. Similarly, he proves that it lacks a cogent purpose.

The Peripatetics, who argued that the *vir bonus* must respond with anger to injury, also claimed that anger has a definite and justifiable end: it is both necessary and useful. Its usefulness consists in the fact that it enables men to act more spiritedly, in a more courageous and manly way, they argued; and it prompts men to punish crimes, thus insuring that there shall be no recurrence. With great disapproval, Seneca cites Aristotle: *stat Aristoteles defensor irae et vetat illam nobis exsecari. calcar ait esse virtutis; hac erepta, inermem animum et ad conatus magnos pigrum inertemque fieri* (3.3.1). This conception of anger as *calcar virtutis* influences the thinking of the *adversarius* throughout Book I, where again and again he reverts to the image of the angry man as a soldier or general (cf 1.9). In fact, he insists that no soldier can act with extreme bravery unless fired by patriotic fury:

numquid, quamvis non sit naturalis ira, adsumenda est, quia utilis saepe fuit? "extollit animos et incitat; nec quicquam sine illa magnificum in bello fortitudo gerit, nisi hinc flamma subdita est et hic stimulus peragitavit misitque in pericula audaces." (1.7.1)

Although the Peripatetics were probably responding to the feeling of the average man in defining anger in this way, nevertheless they did insist that human psychology justified average opinion. Anger, to their way of thinking, stood midway between outright fury and outright pusillanimity. Without it, all the good qualities of the soul would be attenuated: *sine quo languebit actio et vis ac vigor animi resolvetur* (1.7.1). The picture comes to the mind—and it probably occurred to Aristotle—of the general haranguing his troops before battle. Any Greek of Aristotle's time or any educated Roman was familiar with the *topoi* of the general's speech, for Homer, Herodotus, and Thucydides all elaborate upon the main points, and the Sophists had no doubt thoroughly commented on the subject. No speaker would have questioned the purpose of the general's harangue: it served to fire the courage of the soldiers with hatred of the enemy and a desperate desire to protect home, loved ones, and fatherland. Therefore, the historians introduce important battles by writing set speeches for the generals.

The trouble with Aristotle's definition and with the commonplace rhetoric of battle-speeches lies in the omissions. If anger is really somehow synonymous with courage, good; if, however, the Peripatetics ignore the primacy of the reason in order to support the uncritical opinions of ordinary people, then they are guilty of serious error. In the battle-scene, do readers really place themselves in the position of the gullible crowd, or do they not rather sit back and enjoy the skill with which the general manipulates the undisciplined passions of his troops? Hearing the expected arguments, men take delight in the individual stamp imprinted on the topic by speaker or writer. In other words, the reader would not knowingly be among the mob stampeded by the orator; if he had his choice, he would be the orator himself. The Senecan moralist argued similarly. He insisted that reason, not passion, produced and inspired courage. Just as the general exerts complete control over his feelings in his speech and during the battle, able to distinguish between a foolhardy, suicidal rush and a calculated risk or a certain attack on a weak point in the enemy line, so in the same way courage, the basic attribute of manhood (vir*tus*), depends on the direction of reason, the essential and defining quality of Man. Before the general can expect much success from his harangue, he must be able to count on his troops to respond immediately to his orders. The disciplined Greeks of Homer, the rationally directed hoplites at Marathon or Thermopylae, the superbly trained men of the Macedonian phalanx, the experienced Roman trooper—in every case the soldiers act with courage and win their victories primarily because of their training and discipline, not because of a last-minute evocation of their wives and homeland. Thus, as Seneca would point out, the uncritical argumentation of the Peripatetics leads to idealization of the German barbarian, who rashly charges upon the spears of the Roman troops, to die senselessly. The true spur of courage is not anger; it is reason.

If, then, wrath is not really useful as the motivation of heroic acts in war—Homer's Achilles had long ago demonstrated this fact—nor in other activities where courage is required, what purpose does it have? The *adversarius* argues that it insures us against contempt, saves us from the undesirable reputation of mean-spiritedness: *utilis est ira, quia contemptum effugit, quia malos terret* (2.11.1).[8] If people scorn us, they will take advantage of us; whereas, if we flare up with anger at the slightest *iniuria*, they will respect and fear us, and consequently avoid the risk of stirring us up.

Seneca cuts right through this specious argument by sharply distinguishing respect from fear, contempt from injury. Just as Umbricius, for all his fury, achieves no prestige in his native Rome, but is elbowed aside by foreigners; just as the satirist rages, but frightens no one, so the angry man in general accomplishes little. And because he and his wrath are so powerless, he ironically exposes himself to contempt. In fact anger, not passive tolerance, provokes public scorn. Even where it arouses fear, anger cannot be respected. Like a foul sickness that all men loathe and fear, anger is fearful only because it is so ugly and brutal.

---

[8] Cf. the assertion of the *adversarius* in 2.33.1: *minus contemnemur, si vindicaverimus iniuriam.*

quid？ non timetur febris, podagra, ulcus malum？ numquid ideo quicquam in istis boni est？ an contra omnia despecta foedaque et turpia, ipsoque eo timentur？ sic ira per se deformis est et minime metuenda, at timetur a pluribus, sicut deformis persona ab infantibus. (2.11.2)

In short, far from achieving any useful purpose, anger deceives itself and thereby defeats itself. Seeking respect, it earns contempt; seeking to frighten, it often merely offends. The satirist might meet an even worse fate, which Seneca also notes: he might appear ridiculous: *si vero sine viribus* [sc. *ira*] *est, magis exposita contemptui est et derisum non effugit* (2.11.1).

The *adversarius* employs still another argument by misconstruing the basic definition of *ira*. Seneca defines anger unprejudicially as *cupiditas poenae exigendae* (1.3.2). Well, if anger is by definition so inextricably connected with punishment, says the *adversarius*, it follows that, inasmuch as punishing crimes is undeniably valid, anger must be valid and useful. Or, to make his case even stronger, he insists that anger is the prerequisite to adequate punishment: *iracundia opus est ad puniendum* (1.16.6).

Throughout the *De ira*, which some scholars think addressed to Claudius shortly after his accession, Seneca concentrates especially on the application of anger in the political world; and, above all, he focuses on precisely this question: whether or not anger is commensurate with the role of ruler and judge. Since the satirist does not possess legal prerogatives, it is not necessary here to place as much emphasis on the question as Seneca did. Far from being Emperor of the Roman world, the satirist rages impotently, and indeed that very impotence makes him tolerable. Were he to control the police and the courts in his native city, people would flee from his savagery.

Seneca makes two points which are relevant to an inquiry into the satirist's psychology. (1) Although anger is by definition the desire of exacting punishment, just punishment is not, and never can be, the fulfillment of that twisted desire. (2) The angry man is not *aequus iudex;* he cannot understand and practice what justice requires of him. I have already discussed the second point above, in studying the character of the *iratus*. But Seneca argues in both cases from the implications of *cupiditas:* to desire to punish in no way entails the justice of the punishment or even the execution of the punishment. Far from being necessary to punishment, therefore, anger should as much as possible be routed from the mind of judge and executioner. If not, the judge may commit the most outrageous injustice in the name of righteous wrath; and, stubborn in his anger, he will refuse to bend before criticism. Irrational as it is, *ira* lacks perspective, distorts facts, and plunges wildly into error, over-emphasizing one thing while ignoring something else equally bad or worse:

in totum inaequalis est: modo ultra quam oportet excurrit, modo citerius debito resistit. sibi enim indulget, et ex libidine iudicat et audire non vult et patrocinio non relinquit locum et ea tenet quae invasit et eripi sibi iudicium suum, etiam si pravum est, non sinit. (1.17.7)

We may fairly conclude with Seneca that anger lacks any valid objective purpose: that is, the angry man can achieve nothing good by means of his wrath. He is not a braver soldier nor more spirited for any endeavor when irate; he has merely thrown aside the reasonable faculties upon which all ultimately courageous acts depend. He does not earn respect in his fury; if not laughable, he is contemptible. His basic longing to punish distorts his ability to discern the truth and, where it does not frustrate, it at least invalidates the penalty inflicted. However, the *adversarius* still grasps one argument. Granted that anger has no valid objective purpose, it can be justified on subjective grounds: it satisfies the soul. *at enim ira habet aliquam voluptatem* (2.32.1).

Both the *adversarius* and Seneca are discussing a particular type of pleasure, namely, that derived from vengeance; and they both assume at this point that, like the Emperor Claudius, the *iratus* can actually satisfy his desire for punishment. I see no need of pursuing this *voluptas* very far, for it immediately condemns itself in our judgment. However, there is another type of *voluptas* available to the angry man, and Seneca, while not devoting specific paragraphs to it, shows awareness of it throughout his treatise. I refer to the implicit pleasure indicated in the passage from 1.17.7 which I cited above: *sibi indulget.*

Like other passions, anger, when men yield to it, is sheer self-indulgence. Seneca and his fellow-Romans thought of women and children as those most likely to indulge in wrath; and we today would automatically associate with *ira* the child's tantrum and the woman's instinctive and unpredictable moods. Not that men are exempt from anger. But Seneca's conception of this passion, and ours, indicates a deeplingering feeling that anger is childishness, that anyone who yields to anger is unconsciously letting himself revert to that world of unreality and license, childhood. Angry people slip the traces of self-discipline, escape from the necessities of rational control, and explode in fury. Anyone who has roared at a dog, at his own child, or even at a wretched student knows the guilty pleasure of the act. One hears frequently of eminent teachers, paragons of wisdom, who hurl chalk, tear up papers, or stalk pettishly out of the classroom. The momentary fit over, the father returns to his evening paper, the distinguished professor proceeds to the library and notable research. He has plunged into irrationality, become a child again, and now he reverts to his ideal: *homo sapiens*. So long as men can halt careering wrath, they remain human, self-indulgent human beings. Once, however, anger becomes permanent, beyond control, then they have disappeared indefinitely into that make-believe world of childish indulgence; they have become literally mad, and their anger is what Seneca by preference calls it: *insania*.

I have suggested that the dialogue which Seneca constructs on the topic of anger, while weighted on one side, can illustrate some of the basic conflicts of the Juvenalian satirist. Let me summarize what can be gathered so far from this study of Seneca. On the one hand, the *adversarius* voices opinions in favor of anger or its virtual equivalent, indignation; in reply, the Senecan moralist exposes the specious and emotional reasoning behind such opinions and on every count denies anger any justification, purpose, or merit. Thus, the *adversarius* insists that he is immediately moved to anger, as any honorable man would be, by the crimes committed on his person or by vice in general. Seneca retorts that the immediacy of the emotion indicates that reason has abdicated its proper role; whereas it should stand between crime and passionate indignation, it has weakly assented to the irrational rule of the emotions. Therefore, instead of labeling indignation virtuous, noble, magnanimous, liberal, or simply honest, he calls it insane. It follows from this that the indignant man, not a *vir bonus*, is much rather a person who has lost his essential humanity and sunk to the level of the beasts; if not hypocritically blind to his own errors and seeing *iniuriae* completely out of proportion, then acting inhumanely in his lust for purposeless vengeance. For in the end, just as it let itself be irrationally motivated, so anger has irrational purposes, or more accurately put, no real purposes at all. Indignation shrivels down into a childish *voluptas*, petty self-indulgence (though, in the case of a Caligula, it can be blown up into megalomaniac tyranny).

How can this be applied more precisely to the five tensions that I have defined in Juvenal's satirist? First, we saw that Juvenal dramatized his satirist as a simple, honest speaker (*vir bonus*), who yet displayed remarkable rhetorical skill. On this point, Seneca has several things to say. He denies any positive value to the vaunted *simplicitas* of the angry man; to Seneca it is little more than willful stupidity. Then, he questions the ability of an indignant man to discern the truth, deprived as he would be of his rational faculties. Then, he describes

336

with contempt the *praeruptus sermo* of the irate man. Because of the jerky violence of his speech, such a person is usually incoherent, often ridiculous. When the *adversarius* tries to establish a connection between persuasive rhetoric and the high emotion of indignation, Seneca retorts, as any rhetorician would, that indignant rhetoric presupposes a speaker who is simulating his passion, while holding himself entirely in check. So the dialogue between Seneca and his opponent comments on the tension in Juvenal's satirist: either the satirist is an irrational, incoherent fool or he is simulating his fury as a means of persuading us.

A second great tension in the Juvenalian satirist springs from his passionate insistence on the truth of what he says; for the audience sooner or later senses the wild distortions that underlie so many of his statements. Because of the nature of Seneca's essay, which is concentrated on indignant acts rather than words, he provides little precisely relevant to this point. Nevertheless, Seneca always insists that anger distorts. Under its influence, nobody can see himself in honest perspective, nor can he grasp the true proportions of any particular crime. Writing for Claudius, as he seems to, the moralist urges the ideal of the *iudex aequus,* an ideal which cannot be achieved by the indignant ruler. Thus, while he says nothing about the truthful *words* of the irate, Seneca affirms again and again that anger is inconsistent with truthful *judgment.*

Juvenal's satirist becomes enmeshed in a third tension by insisting that he abhors vice, yet suspiciously concentrating on the sensational: some readers feel that he behaves like a hypocrite, a prurient Puritan, and some detect a note of humor or self-ridicule in his overstatements. Seneca comments on the ridiculous aspect of indignation when he argues that, contrary to expectation, the angry man earns derision instead of respect. Caligula challenging Jupiter to a duel illustrates the fantastic and comic side of this emotion. More serious in Seneca's judgment is the tendency of anger to blind men to their own faults and to the true nature of reality. The *adversarius* appeals to extreme instances: a father's murder, rape of his mother. Seneca faces these crimes and worse with tranquillity, for he sees them in the perspective of fallible humanity. Even the tyrant's sadism can be overcome if the victim behaves with patience and self-control; anger is suicidal, neither heroic nor useful. Against the background of everyday life, the setting for our own and the satirist's existence, Seneca reasons that anger is unrealistic and hypocritical. Indignation springs from too high an opinion of one's own virtues (*a nimio sui suspectu*) and consequently creates an irrational, disproportioned view of others' faults. The intelligent motto for

337

us, according to Seneca, would be: *mali inter malos vivimus*. Holding to such a modest self-opinion, men would realize that they cannot rail against wives when they themselves lust for every other man's wife; they would not foolishly pose as Stoic defenders of *pudicitia*, while at the same time indulging in homosexual perversions; fathers would not disinherit sons for *luxuria*, themselves being even more extravagant. I have quoted some of Seneca's examples of hypocrisy (2.28); but readers of Juvenal might see their applicability. Because of his exaggerated opinion of himself and his self-righteous manner of shrinking, piously "fleeing" from the vices of Rome—while apparently fascinated with vice—the satirist renders his indignation suspect.

Juvenal's satirist parried the old criticism, *laedere gaudes*, by claiming no interest in the living. Since he could hardly injure the dead, he seemed exempt from the traditional charge. However, I suggested that the criticism could in a sense still be sustained, inasmuch as indignation, with its hypocrisy and self-assertion, often becomes mere self-indulgence. The unsuccessful Roman solaces his sense of failure by raging against the corruption of the invading Greeks; the disappointed lover or adulterer inveighs against the unchastity of Roman matrons; the *pauper* denounces the wealthy nobles. So, too, Seneca strips away from the *adversarius* all protection for, all justification of, indignation except the contemptible plea of *voluptas*. The angry judge childishly enjoys taking vengeance on some criminal; and, even where the angry man lacks the power to carry through his vengeful designs, he still indulges himself in the desire (*cupiditas*) for punishment and self-expression. There is a certain satisfaction in exploding futilely. Indeed, part of the delight in Juvenal's Satires, I suspect, arises from readers' vicarious pleasure when the satirist uncompromisingly denounces society. We, too, enjoy speaking like that sometimes, and we would dearly like to indulge ourselves as much as this satirist, were it not for the limits which reason sets us.

Reason as opposed to un-reason constitutes the fifth tension in Juvenal's satirist. For Seneca, this is by far the most important aspect of his treatise: to establish beyond doubt that anger and indignation have nothing to do with rationality, and hence must be condemned. His *adversarius*, who rages vainly against vice in general, is a prototype of the indignant satirist. Seneca insists that even rage against personal injuries fails to achieve its end; and outrage against the corruptions of Rome is impractical and insane. We shall always have evil with us, and primarily because we ourselves are partly evil. Therefore, the question is not so much how to punish others' crimes as how to live sane lives in the midst of sin. Instead of attacking the disordered world in a paroxysm of irrationality, says Seneca, we should start with ourselves. If we make sure that we ourselves employ our reason and subdue the impetus to anger; if we do not demand too much of our fellow-men, but a little more of ourselves, then we can hope to lead a calm existence of modest expectations and quiet pleasures. This is Seneca's answer to his *adversarius* and the ultimate reply to Juvenal's angry satirist: no sane man should seek the insanity of indignation, but should take as his goal something commensurate with the highest nature of man, *tranquillitas animi*. Juvenal himself recognized this and in his later Satires created a new satirist in close conformity with the Senecan ideal.

III. JUVENAL'S DEMOCRITEAN SATIRIST

I DOUBT THAT SENECA, in condemning anger and indignation, says anything which would not also have been said by Musonius and Epictetus to their respective listeners; and Juvenal's contemporary Plutarch knows the same arguments and illustrations as Seneca.[1] Moreover, as I have shown elsewhere, the rhetorical doctrines on *indignatio,* as well as the skillful manipulation of this passion in literature, reveal that there were common conventions affecting the use of indignation long before Juvenal. Thus, it makes no difference whether or not Juvenal had read

---

[1] See Plutarch, *De cohibenda ira* 9–10, *De liberis educandis* 10, and Seneca, *De ira* 3.12. Similar examples will be found in Cicero, *Tusc.* 4.78; Valerius Maximus 4.1 ext. 1–2; and Lactantius, *De ira Dei* 17. Like the illustrations, the arguments against *ira* became conventional. (Cf. Horace's brief discussion in *Epist.* 1.2.59 ff.)

Ultimately, as Seneca clearly indicates, anyone arguing about *ira* had to make some reference, sooner or later, to Aristotle, for the long tradition of essays on anger and its cure began with Aristotle. The Stoics Zeno and Chrysippus soon grappled with his theories, distorted them for polemical purposes, and then created the sharp dispute between the Peripatetics (who somewhat uncritically defended their Master) and the Stoics, as to whether or not *ira* was a defensible emotion. Cicero, *ad Quint. fr.* 1.1.37 ff., informs us that, in his day, many writings on anger existed; and Cicero's own discussions in *Tusc.* 3.11 ff. and 4.47 ff. reveal his familiarity with the topic. However, Philodemus' essay περὶ ὀργῆς is the earliest surviving work entirely devoted to anger. While Philodemus exerted no great influence on subsequent theories of anger, his contemporary Posidonius partially revived the Aristotlian conception of wrath, gave it its most intelligent exegesis, and compelled later writers like Seneca to answer his ideas. Behind Seneca, then, stand Aristotle, Zeno, Chrysippus, Philodemus, Posidonius, Cicero, Sotion, and a host of nameless contributors to the theory of anger. Many attempts have been made to sort out Seneca's sources: e.g., W. Allers, *De L. A. Senecae librorum de ira fontibus* (Diss. Göttingen, 1881); R. Pfennig, *De librorum quos scripsit Seneca de ira compositione et origine* (Diss. Greifswald, 1887); H. W. Müller, *De L. Annaei Senecae librorum de ira compositione* (Diss. Leipzig, 1912); H. Ringeltaube, *Quaestiones ad veterum philosophorum de affectibus doctrinam pertinentes* (Diss. Göttingen, 1913); P. Rabbow, *Antike Schriften über Seelenheilung und Seelenleitung auf ihre Quellen untersucht: I Die Therapie des Zorns* (Leipzig, 1914). Connected with these studies of Seneca's sources are those that have pursued the sources of Cicero's discussions concerning emotions in the *Tusculans* and the sources of Plutarch's various essays on the same subject. Cf. M. Pohlenz, "Das dritte und vierte Buch der Tusculanen," *Hermes* 41 (1906), 321–355; "Ueber Plutarchs Schrift ΠΕΡΙ ΑΟΡΓΗΣΙΑΣ," *Hermes* 31 (1896), 321–338; "Plutarchs Schrift ΠΕΡΙ ΕΥΘΥΜΙΑΣ," *Hermes* 40 (1905), 275–300; A. Schlemm, "Ueber die Quellen der plutarchischen Schrift ΠΕΡΙ ΑΟΡΓΗΣΙΑΣ," *Hermes* 38 (1903), 587–607.

In hunting the sources of Seneca's essay, scholars discovered problems connected with the composition of the *De ira.* Was it all written at one time, or did Seneca use different sources in Book 3 and write it many years after the first two? The question does not seriously affect my argument, but I shall register my opinion here that Book 3 does logically belong with Books 1–2. Hence, I agree with the recent conclusions of M. Coccia, *I problemi del De ira di Seneca alla luce dell' analisi stilistica* (Rome, 1958), who dates Books 1–3 all before Seneca's exile.

Moralists continued to talk and write about *ira* long after Seneca. Musonius and Plutarch were discussing anger in Juvenal's youth and mature years. Lactantius, Libanius, and Gregory Nazianzenus show that interest in the subject survived well into the 5th century. Indeed, we may safely conclude that this conventional topic appealed to rhetoricians, moralists, and clerics. Many of the commonplaces concerning *ira* have been usefully collected by Ringeltaube, pp..83 ff.

Seneca's treatise: the important point to establish is that popular treatises on anger were available in Juvenal's early years, that students would learn as a matter of course the moral ambiguity of indignation.

However, judging from the success that Seneca gained among the younger generation, Juvenal's generation, it is to be expected that Juvenal had read widely and carefully studied the revolutionary stylist of the Neronian Age. Schneider feels no hesitation, after comparison of the two writers, in affirming that Juvenal consciously imitated Seneca, his diatribe style, moral theories, and his very words.[2] Of course, Juvenal studied and imitated many Latin writers, as Highet clearly demonstrates: Vergil, Horace, Ovid, Lucan, and Persius among the hexameter poets were regularly used throughout the Satires.[3] Juvenal knew and appreciated the merits of the rhetoricians and historians. Not only had he read the old masters, Cicero and Livy, but he had undoubtedly studied Quintilian's ideas and eagerly followed the publications of his contemporary Tacitus.[4] Under these circumstances, I feel somewhat distrustful of any evidence which tends to show that Seneca exercised a decisive influence upon the creation of Juvenal's later satirist. I should much prefer to argue, as did Kernan, that these theories circulated freely in the First and Second Centuries and that no single source for Juvenal's new practices can or should be isolated. However, let me lay the evidence before the reader, with this cautionary remark, that we should be interested in Seneca less as a source than as a possible indication of and analogue for the new developments in Juvenal's Satires. This paper concerns itself primarily with critical insights into the Satires.

Throughout the *De ira,* the arguments in favor of anger as a noble and useful emotion run up against, and are ignominiously confuted by, elaborate counter-arguments based on Man's essential quality of rationality. In opposition to the sketchy figure of the *adversarius,* an angry and illogical type, stands the moralist, a man of reason. This moralist not only denies the merits of anger; but he also attempts to instruct his reader in the methods of overcoming anger and clearly proclaims the ideal toward which all men should be striving: *tranquillitas animi.* Mental serenity may be found in many men, and Seneca

---

[2] C. Schneider, *Juvenal und Seneca* (Diss. Würzburg, 1930). He points out some thematic and verbal resemblances between the Satires and the two Senecan essays which I have selected, but he does not try to apply Seneca's doctrines to the characterization of Juvenal's satirist.

[3] See G. Highet, Juvenal's Bookcase," *AJP* 72 (1951), 369–394. Ovid's *Metamorphoses* mockingly depicts many indignant deities, especially goddesses like Juno, Minerva, Diana.

[4] See H. F. Rebert, "The Literary Influence of Cicero on Juvenal," *TAPA* 57 (1926), 181–194; and my "Juvenal and Quintilian."

takes pains to cite for the presumed benefit of Claudius specific examples of calm self-restraint on the part of great rulers: Antigonus, Philip of Macedon, Augustus (3.22 ff.). However, to characterize *tranquillitas* in general, applicable to all stations and all circumstances, Seneca resorts to the semi-legendary figure of Democritus. In a passage which reminds most commentators of Juvenal 10.28 ff., Seneca draws a contrast between the supposed attitudes of Heraclitus and Democritus, with pronounced preference for the Democritean manner:

Heraclitus quotiens prodierat et tantum circa se male viventium, immo male pereuntium viderat, flebat, miserebatur omnium qui sibi laeti felicesque occurrebant, miti animo, sed nimis imbecillo; et ipse inter deplorandos erat. Democritum contra aiunt numquam sine risu in publico fuisse; adeo nihil illi videbatur serium eorum quae serio gerebantur. (2.10.5)

Seneca disapproves of Heraclitus because he involved himself in the petty tragedies of mankind and so felt moved to tears; whereas Democritus serenely removed himself from the trivial things which most men think so serious, and consequently, from his vantage-point above the storm of human folly, could laugh at the seemingly serious. The polar opposition between these two philosophers is imaginary and symbolic, and became an especially popular topic, so far as we can determine, during Seneca's lifetime, quite possibly because of the effective use which Seneca himself made of it in several of his treatises.[5] The mythical representation of Democritus arose, it seems, from the biographical interpretation of his treatise περὶ εὐθυμίας: that is, because Democritus convincingly argued the case for peace of mind, people supposed that he himself exemplified the ideal in his own life. Seneca knows of this treatise and refers to one of its precepts in order to amplify his own teachings on the means of achieving, and the value of striving for, *tranquillitas.*

eodem modo [i.e., like the serenity of the upper air, above storms and lightning] sublimis animus, quietus semper et in statione tranquilla conlocatus, omnia infra se premens quibus ira contrahitur, modestus et venerabilis est et dispositus; quorum nihil invenies in irato. quis enim traditus dolori et furens non primam reiecit verecundiam? ... quis linguae temperavit? quis ullam partem corporis tenuit? quis se regere potuit immissum? proderit nobis illud Democriti salutare praeceptum, quo monstratur tranquillitas, si neque privatim neque publice multa aut maiora viribus nostris egerimus. (3.6.1–3)

[5] C. Lutz, "Democritus and Heraclitus," *CJ* 49 (1953–54), 309–314, has studied the history of the comparison between the two philosophers. She finds that the first extant contrast is to be credited to Seneca's teacher Sotion (see Stobaeus *Flor.* 20.53). However, it was probably Seneca who made this a literary convention. Plutarch, *De tranquillitate animi* 465C, cites Democritus; but, because he misunderstands the passage, Plutarch spurns the Democritean model.

The *De ira* can be dated with some confidence to A.D. 41, before Seneca's exile. Many years later, toward the close of his life, Seneca returned to its theme. As he wrote the *De tranquillitate animi,* he seemed to hesitate over the world of politics; and Lana infers that the murder of Agrippina had just occurred, to place Seneca in a most equivocal position before the world as Nero's adviser.[6] Gone now are the regal examples of serenity; to replace them, Seneca invokes several Stoic types: Cato and Canus Julius; the moralists Bion and Diogenes; and, on three separate occasions, Democritus. It is important to make as clear as possible what Democritus represented to Seneca, and so I cite all three passages.

The first is another reference to Democritus' treatise. Seneca claims that by *tranquillitas* he is rendering as faithfully as possible the Greek term used by Democritus:

hanc stabilem animi sedem Graeci εὐθυμίαν vocant, de qua Democriti volumen egregium est; ego *tranquillitatem* voco: nec enim imitari et transferre verba ad illorum formam necesse est; res ipsa, de qua agitur, aliquo signanda nomine est, quod appellationis Graecae vim debet habere, non faciem. (*Tr. an.* 2.3)

In the second passage, Seneca again refers to the same precept that he cited in *De ira* 3.6. I give the context of the remark, because this time Seneca describes the vain pursuits of the Roman populace in a way that reminds one of both Satire 1.94 ff. and Satire 10.34 ff.:

unumquemque ex his qui ad augendam turbam exeunt inanes et leves causae per urbem circumducunt, nihilque habentem in quod laboret lux orta expellit, et cum, multorum frustra liminibus illisus, nomenclatores persalutavit, a multis exclusus, neminem ex omnibus difficilius domi quam se convenit .... hoc secutum puto Democritum ita coepisse: "qui tranquille volet vivere nec privatim agat multa nec publice," ad supervacua scilicet referentem. (*Tr. an.* 12.6–13.1)

The last passage elaborates the opposition between Heraclitus and Democritus again. This time, Seneca does not limit himself to calling Heraclitus weak-minded; the tearful attitude is nothing short of stupidity:

in hoc [i.e., in our reaction to the success of the evil] itaque flectendi sumus, ut omnia vulgi vitia non invisa nobis, sed ridicula videantur, et Democritum potius imitemur quam Heraclitum. hic enim, quotiens in publicum processerat, flebat, ille ridebat. huic omnia quae agimus, miseriae, illi ineptiae videbantur. elevanda ergo omnia et facili animo ferenda: humanius est deridere vitam quam deplorare. adice quod de humano quoque genere melius meretur qui ridet illud quam qui luget. ille ei spei bonae aliquid relinquit, hic autem stulte deflet quae corrigi posse desperat; et universa contemplanti maioris animi est qui risum non tenet quam qui lacrimas, quando lenissimum affectum animi movet et nihil magnum, nihil severum, ne miserum quidem ex tanto paratu putat. (*Tr. an.* 15.2–3)

---

[6] See I. Lana, *Lucio Annaeo Seneca* (Turin, 1955), p. 247 ff.

If we conflate the ideas embodied in these five passages from the *De ira* and the *De tranquillitate animi,* a carefully schematized portrait of Democritus emerges. He wrote a volume on the subject of the well-balanced attitude toward life (rendered by Seneca as *tranquillitas*), but Seneca considers one passage alone important enough to cite on two quite different occasions. No man desiring a serene life, according to Democritus, should involve himself excessively in his own private pursuits or in public affairs. This alone Seneca tells us about Democritus' ideas: that men can achieve *tranquillitas* by disengagement. However, this single idea agrees perfectly with the dramatic picture of the philosopher living among his fellow men, a picture which Seneca may have been the first to use so effectively. Democritus, he records, never walked in public but that he found ridiculous the pursuits of mankind. In case men fail to see how the philosopher's laughter represents the ideal of calmness, Seneca's commentary on the last passage brings out several key points. First, men should make light of human folly and endure it easily. Next, it is more humane to laugh at than to bewail the problems of life. Furthermore, when men laugh, they presumably entertain some hope for humanity, whereas tears would indicate total pessimism. And finally, he who laughs over the world is really nobler-minded than he who weeps, inasmuch as he involves so small a part of his emotions in what is, after all, of slight relative moment.

This Democritus of Seneca is the prototype of the satirist in the later poems of Juvenal, namely Satires 10 through 16. In order to adopt a satirist of this nature, Juvenal had to introduce some radical changes into his works, not only changing the tone and manner of the speaker, but also altering the very material which he chose to discuss. I regard the three poems of Book III as transitional, tending away from the *indignatio* of Satires 1–6 toward the laughter of Satires 10–16; but I do not think that the satirist's manner appears unambiguously enough to make it worth while discussing them in this particular context. Therefore, I take as my starting point Satire 10, the poem in which the satirist specifically appeals to the example of Democritus, exalts the value of *tranquillitas,* and adopts a subject which approximates the interests of Seneca's *De tranquillitate animi;* in short a poem in which a new Juvenalian satirist emerges.

Satire 1 had proclaimed *indignatio* as the characteristic mood of Book I: it had used contemporary Rome as its topic; and it had presented a satirist who as *vir bonus atque Romanus* erupted in fury over the indignities suffered by himself and his Rome. Thus, the satirist's appeal to *ratio* and a calm audience (1.21) changed in a few lines to a strident demand for anger. The satirist of Satire 10 is entirely different.

From his opening words, one quickly perceives that he embraces a larger world extending from the Atlantic to the Ganges in the far East; he does not restrict himself to time, and, as we soon see, he can move with equal freedom in the era of Xerxes or in that of Sejanus and Silius. This breadth of vision and disengagement from the immediate present depends upon a pervasive conviction, reflected throughout the Satire, that a man should live by *ratio* alone. Dedicated to reason, the satirist looks upon his fellow men and describes their irrational desires for private wealth, beauty, and longevity; for public recognition of themselves as politicians, orators, or soldiers. As he does so, he reveals the thread of irony which is woven in all unwise wishes and their quixotic fulfilment. Where men expect to gain true *bona,* they discover that their engagement with inferior goals has been suicidal and plunged them inevitably toward misery and death.

The satirist quickly describes the most common desire of men, to become enormously wealthy, and the fatal consequences of riches (12 ff.). To put it at its starkest, he contrasts the fearful traveller, anxiously proceeding through the darkness clutching his few little silver vases, with a *vacuus viator* who sings even when faced by a highwayman (20–22). Before he goes on to depict other common follies, the satirist pauses to introduce the antithesis of Heraclitus and Democritus (28 ff.). Without naming them, he describes two wise men (*sapientibus* : 28), one who laughed whenever he left his home, one who wept. Then he proceeds to comment on their diverse attitudes:

> sed facilis cuivis rigidi censura cachinni:
> mirandum est unde ille oculis suffecerit umor.
>
> (31–32)

Rhetorically, these lines serve as a dismissal of Heraclitus, who is never named and who now disappears entirely from sight. It is also interesting to observe that this satirist finds laughter easy and natural, but expresses amazement—not admiration—that tears could come to any man's eyes at the sight of such manifest folly. This satirist rejects any emotional engagement with the stupidities of other men, whether it be the weeping of a Heraclitus or, as we shall see, the indignation of a different satirist. His ideal is Democritus.

The Democritus of Satire 10 is as schematically pictured as Seneca's Democritus. Thus, having dismissed Heraclitus, the satirist continues:

> perpetuo risu pulmonem agitare solebat
> Democritus, quamquam non essent urbibus illis
> praetextae, trabeae, fasces, lectica, tribunal.
> quid si vidisset praetorem ...?
>
> (33–36)

Wherever he went in his little city of Abdera, the philosopher found food for laughter. The satirist, who finds in Rome and the Empire even ampler material for ridicule, presents himself as a second Democritus by asking the rhetorical question: what would Democritus have done today? So, after applying the Democritean critique to the vain pomp of praetor, consul, and zealous clients, the satirist once more turns back to his model:

> tum quoque materiam risus invenit ad omnis
> occursus hominum, cuius prudentia monstrat
> summos posse viros et magna exempla daturos
> vervecum in patria crassoque sub aere nasci.
> ridebat curas nec non et gaudia volgi,
> interdum et lacrimas, cum Fortunae ipse minaci
> mandaret laqueum mediumque ostenderet unguem.
> ergo supervacua aut quae perniciosa petuntur?
>
> (47–54)

Democritus, he says, constitutes one of the positive examples for our lives: he mocked the anxieties and the pleasures of the foolish herd, and he audaciously defied Fortune.[7] Immediately, on the basis of what he has just said, the satirist asks rhetorically if then these vain and ruinous things are being sought. Editors deal with 54 and 55 in various ways. Because 54 lacks a syllable (supplied here by *quae*, Buecheler's emendation), Leo and Knoche deleted 54 and 55. Clausen accepts them as genuine, but like other editors, prints them as a separate paragraph. I would urge that they belong in close connection with 53, if genuine, and that no new paragraph should be permitted. In support of my theory, let me remind the reader of the passage in *Tr. an.* 12–13, cited above. Seneca quotes Democritus' familiar doctrine to the effect that he who would live serenely should avoid excessive private or public attachments; and then comes the comment: *ad supervacua scilicet referentem.* Just as the *vacuus viator* perfectly represents the detached attitude, so *supervacua* denotes, in Democritus' view, the things of this world from which we should disengage ourselves. In asking the question in 54, therefore, the satirist refers precisely to all the material which he has covered so far, and particularly to the ideas of his model, the "great example," Democritus.

Seneca's essay on *tranquillitas* contains both positive and negative criticisms: like Democritus, Seneca sees hope of attaining serenity if

---

[7] Democritus was especially famous for abandoning all his money; and Seneca himself cites this tradition: cf. *Provid.* 6, *Vita beata* 27. This well known attitude towards wealth may account for the position which Juvenal assigned to Democritus in the argument.

men will realize their folly and rationally direct themselves toward their goal. Men should correctly gauge their own capacities, then assess intelligently the tasks which they undertake (6). Certain ends can be either good or bad, as, for example, having friends (7), possessing great wealth (8), plunging into research and scholarship (9). Therefore, before men commit themselves totally to them, they must make sure that reason controls the decision. Otherwise, they find themselves among corrupt companions, anxiously guarding wealth or wretchedly seeking more, or they discover that all their erudition merely amounts to *studiosa luxuria*.[8]

It may be, continues Seneca, that we have been placed in a situation where all our efforts, no matter how violent, can effect no appreciable change. This is due to Fortuna (10). The correct way to face troubles is not to grown indignant at them, but to suffer them: *non indignari illa, sed pati*. We are all bound to Fortune, and hence we can correctly describe all life, in a sense, as mere slavery. But *ratio* can combat Fortune: *adhibe rationem difficultatibus* (10.4). If tempted to envy those in a high position, we need but remember how dramatically such people plunge to their destruction: *quae excelsa videbantur praerupta sunt*.[9] The wise man will encounter Fortune boldly and make no concessions to her, utter no weak complaints (11). When death summons him, he will accept it bravely and serenely, knowing that Fortune may be playing one of her typical jests, but also knowing that he cannot live forever. After all, any observation of his fellow men should convince him that life is subject to every sort of change: *scito ergo omnem condicionem versabilem esse et quicquid in ullum incurrit posse in te quoque incurrere*. Take three characteristic situations of happiness, says Seneca: wealth, honor, and power. The rich Pompeius was reduced to poverty by Caligula; Sejanus arrived at the pinnacle of political honor, yet was torn to pieces by the mob; great kings like Croesus and Jugurtha were humbled at the end.[10]

Although Seneca has cited these examples to illustrate the change-

---

[8] Lana (cited above, n. 6) believes that Seneca selected the very faults of which he himself was guilty to criticize so severely. He had sought friends in the imperial family, and now as a result he was implicated in the murder of Agrippina. He had gained wealth through his connections at court, and many like Suillius criticized him as unscrupulous and hypocritical. He published much on scientific, philosophic, and poetic topics, but he was not a committed philosopher or scientist; hence, he was liable to the charge of merely seeking to display his talents so as to gain praise.

[9] 10.5 Cf. the imagery used by Juvenal to interpret the precariousness of political power: *numerosa excelsae turris tabulata* (10.105–06).

[10] Seneca is the first writer known to me, and this essay of his is the first work, to make use of Sejanus as an example. I suggest, therefore, that Seneca was the original inspiration of Juvenal's quite different and inimitable *exemplum*.

ability of human lives in a different context from that of Satire 10, it seems to me significant that he immediately proceeds to link with them the very ideas which do serve as the fundamental themes of Juvenal's poem:

proximum ab his erit, ne aut in supervacuis aut ex supervacuo laboremus, id est, ne quae aut non possumus consequi concupiscamus aut adepti vanitatem cupiditatum nostrarum sero post multum pudorem intellegamus, id est, ne aut labor inritus sit sine effectu aut effectus labore indignus. (12.1)

And shortly after, in this same section, Seneca makes his transition to Democritus, an ideal model for his listener. The passage, with its repetition of *supervacuis,* I have already cited and discussed.

If, then, we do not involve ourselves with the shoddy values of this world and if we can avoid becoming entangled in the misfortunes of others, we have a negative basis for *tranquillitas.* We have freed ourselves of the trivial (*supervacua*). To picture this uncommitted existence in an attractive manner, Seneca devotes the last chapter of his essay to positive recommendations. First, we should cultivate an honest simplicity of life: *at illa quantum habet voluptatis sincera et per se inornata simplicitas* (17.2). Second, we should make it a regular practice to withdraw from the crowd and commune with ourselves alone: *multum et in se recedendum est* (17.3). However, we should not always maintain a sober, astringent severity, for that would be false to our human nature, a combination after all of gravely rational and pleasure-loving faculties. If we keep it within its proper limits, we should intermittently pursue a calm *voluptas: nec in eadem intentione aequaliter retinenda mens est, sed ad iocos devocanda ... danda est animis remissio ... indulgendum est animo* (17.4–8).

The Democritus of Satire 10 possesses the same schematic character as the Democritus of Seneca: he represents an ironic withdrawal from the passions of mankind, scornfully described as *supervacua.* Furthermore, the negative theme of Satire 10 demands no indignation, but is practically identical with the ideas cited from *Tr. an.* 12 (*vanitatem cupiditatum*) and handled with proper Democritean irony. Juvenal's most powerful *exemplum,* that of Sejanus, may well have been inspired by Seneca's brief discussion. It remains to be seen how far the satirist incorporates the positive recommendations of Seneca in his brief, positive conclusion.

orandum est ut sit mens sana in corpore sano.
fortem posce animum mortis terrore carentem,
qui spatium vitae extremum inter munera ponat
naturae, qui ferre queat quoscumque labores,

nesciat irasci, cupiat nihil et potiores
Herculis aerumnas credat saevosque labores
et venere et cenis et pluma Sardanapalli.
monstro quod ipse tibi possis dare; semita certe
tranquillae per virtutem patet unica *vitae.*
nullum numen habes si sit prudentia: nos te,
nos facimus, Fortuna, deam caeloque locamus.
(10.356–66)

As line 364 indicates, the satirist accepts as the goal of life (and the underlying purpose of Satire 10) the Democritean εὐθυμία Seneca's *tranquillitas animi.* To attain this goal, the satirist points to individual *virtus* as the means. But he has already spelled out the components of this virtue in 356 ff. Above all, men must have a sound mind, a strong spirit. If they have that requisite *animus,* then they can ignore the meretricious pleasures of life, securely endure the necessary ills, know no anger, and desire nothing. Only by implication does the satirist here subscribe to *simplicitas;* and the apparent exclusion of all desires might make one wonder whether this satirist would permit himself the same self-indulgence advocated by Seneca. As I shall point out in Satires 11 and 12, he does. Nevertheless, Satire 10 does adopt the model of Democritus and his *tranquillitas* and faithfully apply it to a theme which the indignant satirist of Books I and II would have spurned. Hence, it is highly significant that this different satirist of Book IV pointedly rejects the mood of *ira: nesciat irasci* (360).

Satires 11 and 12 exhibit the Democritean satirist in new situations. Satire 11 combines the themes of *simplicitas* and *remissio animi.* The satirist, who can reject the ridiculous extravagance of his contemporaries and their empty excitement over the victory of the Green faction in the Circus, invites a dear friend to a simple, private meal with him. While the rest of Rome hurls itself frenetically into the Megalesian festivities, the satirist and his friend enjoy a quiet bath, a little sun, and their peaceful dinner.[11] In Satire 12, we again encounter the modest satirist, who celebrates a private festival, lives modestly, values friendship intelligently, and indulges in ironic rather than indignant description of others. His commitment to a simple life (10), his honest profession of friendship for Catullus, and his good-humored rejection of the *captatores* and their folly—all make him a copy of Democritus. Thus, Book IV consistently maintains as its speaker and its ideal a Democri-

---

[11] It is easy to see how greatly this satirist differs from the indignant one by comparing the treatment in Satires 5 and 11. Both Satires have a dinner as their basis, and both make use of the technique of contrast between dishes served, slaves waiting on the table, and the like. But in Satire 5, the contrast is handled with indignation, whereas in Satire 11 the distinction is viewed with good-natured Democritean irony.

tean satirist. Whereas in Book I readers are expected to view with distrust the indignant satirist and his irrational frenzy, in Book IV the saner attitude of the ironic satirist is ethically acceptable (if less effective in a poetic sense).

Satire 13 opens Book V. I have argued elsewhere that it should be regarded as a new Program Poem, largely accepting the ideas first proclaimed in Satire 10, but expressing much more specifically the new satirist's entire rejection of *indignatio*.[12] Moreover, the satirist's attitude and words closely resemble those used in Seneca's *De ira*.

Calvinus, who has deposited a hundred thousand sesterces with a friend, has been defrauded of the sum: the friend has denied the deposit and apparently carried off the crime with impunity. As a result, Calvinus is seething with fury and proclaiming the injustice of his lot to everyone he meets. When the satirist hears about the grief which Calvinus has suffered, he contrives an ironic *consolatio*. Exploiting the same arguments which one would use in the case of a death, this ironic satirist quickly reveals the discrepancy in the two situations: Calvinus is, in fact, showing more sorrow for his relatively slight loss of money than he would over the death of his own child. Moreover, the fury, the indignation which this man feels and expresses at the enormity of the crime betray his irrational, almost infantile folly. And in the case of Calvinus, a man past sixty, such naïveté stirs the satirist to laughter. The satirist, therefore, makes one obvious point and implicitly suggests a more profound interpretation of the incident. The obvious point is, that Calvinus' indignation is puerile and his longing to punish the criminal cannot in the least alter the fact of his loss. Less obviously but more significantly, the satirist shows that this unreflecting anger has arisen from a generally irrational code of values. Calvinus has committed himself to materialism, has trapped himself in *supervacua*, and therefore he has entirely lost his moral perspective.

Democritus, we remember, had announced as the basis of *tranquillitas* one precise axiom: men should avoid excessive commitment to public or private affairs. Seneca clearly explains the sense of Democritus' axiom in *De ira* 3.6.3–4:

numquam tam feliciter in multa discurrenti negotia dies transit, ut non aut ex homine aut ex re offensa nascatur, quae animum in iras paret.... alius spem nostram fefellit, alius distulit, alius intercepit.

As the satirist puts it, it is *intercepta decem sestertia* (13.71) that arouse Calvinus' anger.

---

[12] See my paper "The Programs of Juvenal's Later Books," pp. 149 ff.

There are, of course, innumerable *supervacua* in which foolish men can become enmeshed. While Seneca mentions several of these, especially for their potential application to an emperor like Claudius, he takes time also to devote a special chapter to the false goal of *pecunia*. Some of his remarks seem peculiarly applicable to Calvinus, this old man who yet has gained no understanding from his experiences: *senior bulla dignissime* (33).

circa pecuniam plurimum vociferationis est; haec fora defatigat, patres liberosque committit, venena miscet; ... haec est sanguine nostro delibuta; propter hanc uxorum maritorumque noctes strepunt litibus et tribunalia magistratuum premit turba ... libet intueri fiscos in angulo iacentis. hi sunt, propter quos oculi clamore exprimantur, fremitu iudiciorum basilicae resonent, evocati ex longinquis regionibus iudices sedeant, iudicaturi utrius iustior avaritia sit. quid si ne propter fiscum quidem, sed pugnum aeris aut imputatum a servo denarium, senex sine herede moriturus stomacho dirumpitur? ... quanto risu prosequenda sunt quae nobis lacrimas educunt! (*De ira* 3.33.1–4)

Seneca feels a Democritean urge to laugh at the tears of indignation which foolish *avaritia* causes; he concentrates with particular force on the anomaly of a childless old man who bursts with fury over a paltry sum of money. Essentially, this is the situation and the mocking manner which Juvenal has chosen for his satirist in this poem. Consider some of the satirist's early remarks to the furious Calvinus:

> ponamus nimios gemitus. flagrantior aequo
> non debet dolor esse viri nec volnere maior.
> tu quamvis levium minimam exiguamque malorum
> particulam vix ferre potes spumantibus ardens
> visceribus, sacrum tibi quod non reddat amicus
> depositum? stupet haec qui iam post terga reliquit
> sexaginta annos Fonteio consule natus?
> (13.11–17)

Here is another foolish old man for whom the satirist feels not the slightest sympathy. Sixty years old, Calvinus understands nothing about himself or life, and hence does not realize how ridiculous he is to the satirist and the more practical common masses: *nescis/ quem tua simplicitas risum vulgo moveat* (34–35).

This Satire 13 not only continues the Democritean manner of Book IV and seems to announce it for Book V; it also proves important for its clearly stated attitude on indignation, an attitude diametrically opposed to that of Book I. Whereas in Satire 10 the satirist merely asserted that the strong mind would not know how to be angry, here he portrays a situation in which a weak-minded individual explodes with wrath. With some slight changes of detail and emphasis, indeed, the basic plot could have been treated as a legitimate source of indignation in Book I; the language used to describe Calvinus' indignation is virtually identical with that found appropriate for the angry satirist earlier. The satirist in Satires 1–6, as did Seneca's *adversarius,* made a virtue of his *simplicitas,* that spontaneous impulse to anger. In Satire 13, on the other hand, the satirist interprets this *simplicitas* in accord with Seneca: it is both irrational and ridiculous. Had Juvenal desired to present Calvinus in a sympathetic light, he could have given him some of the traits found in Umbricius in Satire 3: Calvinus could have been a native Roman, steeped in and faithful to the old traditions, a simple *cliens* who had entrusted all the money he possessed in the world to an unscrupulous *patronus,* who had been defrauded of this precious sum through the machinations of some Oriental. Under such circumstances, especially if he were depicted leaving Rome in disillusionment, Calvinus could serve as Umbricius did in Satire 3, as a substitute for the indignant satirist.

However, Juvenal has changed his satirist; the anger which Umbricius expressed over the financial successes of the unscrupulous invaders of Rome has become discredited. By slightly altering the situation and by stripping from the indignant Calvinus all sympathetic qualities, and furthermore by creating an ironic satirist to comment adversely on this indignation, Juvenal produces an entirely different Satire. Instead of joining Calvinus, therefore, and denouncing the crime—an undeniable crime, we must remember—the satirist dissociates himself entirely from both victim and criminal and comments amusedly on their foolish commitment to meretricious values.

The ironic *consolatio* is the satirist's answer to Calvinus' anger. Although a *consolatio* might embrace various situations with its conventional arguments, it is safe to say that no writer would ever seriously essay a consolatory poem or speech on the occasion of some financial fraud. Indeed, Juvenal obliges readers to be aware of the conflict created by this abuse of the convention, for he has his satirist draw an explicit contrast between the grief uttered for the loss of a close relative and for the loss of coins:

> si nullum in terris tam detestabile factum
> ostendis, taceo, nec pugnis caedere pectus
> te veto nec plana faciem contundere palma,
> quandoquidem accepto claudenda est ianua damno,
> et maiore domus gemitu, maiore tumultu
> planguntur nummi quam funera; nemo dolorem

fingit in hoc casu, vestem diducere summam
contentus, vexare oculos umore coacto:
ploratur lacrimis amissa pecunia veris.

(126–134)

But while the satirist plays with the arguments which a friend conventionally utilizes on the death of another's wife or child, nevertheless he also develops themes which Seneca employs to condemn anger. In the first place, just as death must come to all men, it can be said that fraud exists everywhere among men. Every Forum, claims the satirist along with Seneca, is filled with the same complaint as that of Calvinus (135). Not only that, but Calvinus had probably suffered slightly in comparison with others:

rem pateris modicam et mediocri bile ferendam,
si flectas oculos maiora ad crimina.

(143–144)

Look at all the crimes which daily come before Roman judges. How can you be sorry for yourself, Calvinus, if you really perceive the misery of others around you? After all, among the Alpine peoples the goiter is nothing surprising, nor huge babies in Egypt, nor blue eyes and braided red hair among the Germans (163–165).

To help men overcome anger, Seneca exploits closely similar arguments; to the outraged man who claims that he cannot endure the *iniuria,* who angrily asks whether the criminal is to escape without punishment (*impune*), the moralist replies:

deinde ad condicionem rerum humanarum respiciendum est, ut omnium accedentium aequi iudices simus; iniquus autem est qui commune vitium singulis obiecit. non est Aethiopis inter suos insignitus color; nec rufus crinis et coactus in nodum apud Germanos virum dedecet: nihil in uno iudicabis notabile aut foedum quod genti suae publicum est. (3.26.3)

If we can distinguish between the truly exceptional and the commonly evil, then we can be more sure of our judgment. For, just as the Fora are full of similar cases for fraud, so the world abounds in evil, an evil that even embraces our own tarnished souls: *omnes mali sumus.*

All right, says the still unappeased Calvinus; even if fraud is a common crime, can I not at least demand that the criminal be punished? (174–175). The satirist then proposes a hypothetical situation: let the culprit be put in chains and executed at Calvinus' bidding. Could anger desire more? But regardless of the punishment, the loss will remain, and, if so, that makes the punishment seem ridiculous. When prodded to this extent, Calvinus exposes his vindictive nature. He has not in the least considered the legal and ethical basis of punishment; all he wants is petty vengeance:

> 'at vindicta bonum vita iucundius ipsa.'
> (180)

The satirist immediately attacks Calvinus for uttering such an ignorant (*indocti:* 181) idea:

> quippe minuti
> semper et infirmi est animi exiguique voluptas
> ultio. continuo sic collige, quod vindicta
> nemo magis gaudet quam femina.
> (189–192)

As we have already seen, Seneca uttered similar ideas about vengeance: he considered it womanish, the mark of a weak spirit, a sign of inhumanity.[13] The logical extension of indignation and anger, although not openly admitted by the satirist of Books I and II, is this vengefulness which appears so unattractive in Calvinus.

Juvenal's satirist completes his consolation by considering the situation of criminals like this perjurer, who have escaped the law's clutches. He argues that one of several things usually happens: the perjurer must deal with his own conscience; he becomes terrified at the thought of divine punishment; or he has steeped himself so thoroughly in crime that he inevitably commits another and another until ultimately caught. So in the end Calvinus' enemy will be exiled or executed and dragged forth to the Gemonian Stairs by the hook (244–247). Knowing Calvinus' lust for vengeance, the satirist can then ironically comment:

> poena gaudebis amara
> nominis invisi tandemque fatebere laetus
> nec surdum nec Teresian quemquam esse deorum.
> (247–249)

As throughout his consolation, so here the satirist distinguishes his own feelings sharply from those of Calvinus. He himself spurns revenge, but he knows that the weak spirit of his companion will seize upon the death of the criminal with ecstasy and at last be convinced that the gods do attend to human indignation.[14]

---

[13] See above p. 169.

[14] Highet's identification of the satirist and Juvenal leads him astray in interpreting this passage: "Juvenal consoles his friend by pointing out that the embezzler will surely commit another crime and suffer execution or exile, and then Calvinus can rejoice in his overthrow. This from the man who has just delivered a warning against the petty pleasures of revenge! Yet it is of a piece with Juvenal's character. He was vindictive and hateful himself, as we can see from the venom with which he pursues his dead enemies; and his character had been so twisted or crippled that he often praises the second-best and enjoys the less admirable pleasures." (*Juvenal the Satirist*, p. 143)

Seneca, too, takes time to discuss the principles of punishment, but more from the standpoint of a judge—as was appropriate for Claudius—than of a victim. In a few words, however, he covers much the same arguments as the satirist at the end of Satire 13:

bonus vir est qui iniuriam fecit? noli credere. malus? noli mirari; dabit poenas alteri quas debet tibi; et iam sibi dedit qui peccavit. (*De ira* 2.30.2)

That should be enough to satisfy any rational human being. The trouble with Calvinus is that he has learned nothing from his experiences over sixty years. He does not need formal philosophy to tell him of his error; a little common sense should reveal to him the folly of his anger.

> magna quidem, sacris quae dat praecepta libellis,
> victrix fortunae sapientia, ducimus autem
> hos quoque felices, qui ferre incommoda vitae
> nec iactare iugum vita didicere magistra.
>
> (19–22)

Democritus wrote a book on *tranquillitas,* on the conquest of *Fortuna* by reason, but ordinary people like the satirist are not excluded from *sapientia,* provided that they face their various trials with some practical intelligence. Seneca wrote for such ordinary people, not for the philosophers; he clearly regarded the Democritean attitude as applicable to the lives of all sane men. It is not surprising, then, to find at the conclusion of the *De ira* insistence like that of the Democritean satirist on the value of practical wisdom:

sive de ultimis suppliciis cogitas, sive de levioribus, quantulum est temporis quo aut ille poena sua torqueatur aut tu malum gaudium ex aliena percipias! iam istum spiritum exspuemus. interim, dum trahimus, dum inter homines sumus, colamus humanitatem; non timori cuiquam, non periculo simus; detrimenta, iniurias, convicia, vellicationes contemnamus, et magno animo brevia feramus incommoda. dum respicimus, quod aiunt, versamusque nos, iam mortalitas aderit. (3.43.4–5)

In Satire 13, then, the new Democritean satirist expressly condemns anger and indignation as illegitimate means of dealing with evil. Calvinus, the victim of a perjurer, emerges before our eyes a fool, a hypocrite, and a vindictive, inhuman monster; and by the same token the indignant satirist of Books I and II is implicitly condemned as inadequate to face this fallible world of ours. Neither the satirist in Satires 1–6 nor Calvinus here gains anything but emotional relief from his explosions of anger. But if Calvinus had adopted the attitude of the Democritean satirist, he would have lost his money without too great surprise; and, not being a slave to his possessions or vindictive, he would quite possibly have been able to laugh at himself and the unhappy, conscience-stricken perjurer. That would be the practical path from futile *ira* to rational *tranquillitas*.

The three other Satires of Book V all seem to contain a measure of the *tranquillitas* advocated by Seneca and the Democritean satirist of 13. Although Satire 14 troubles readers because of its structural enormities, it adopts themes which are entirely consistent with the rough ridicule of Democritus. That children imitate their parents is a commonplace; that parents go into paroxysms of fury when they finally notice their own faults in their sons had been a favorite theme of Greek and Roman comedy: the *senex iratus* became a stock figure. Plutarch, in his essay on training children, cautions fathers against such irrational anger.[15] And Seneca uses the foolishly angry parent as a natural example of the hypocrisy underlying much anger:

aliena vitia in oculis habemus; a tergo nostra sunt. inde est quod tempestiva filii convivia pater deterior filio castigat, et nihil alienae luxuriae ignoscit qui nihil suae negavit. (2.28.8)

Thus, when the Democritean satirist criticizes the father for raging at his son and heir, a perfect copy of the parental model (14.50 ff.), he stands on firm ground with Seneca.

A second portion of Satire 14 concentrates on a particular vice learned from parents, namely, that of avarice. Democritus, according to legend, had freed himself of all his money. The Democritean satirist also regards money as the primary obstacle to peace of mind, and so he tends in this part of the Satire to comment on the vice rather than on the parental example. He finds amusement in the fact that the son often murders his father, having learned all too well the lust for money and therefore desiring his father's property. But this amused attitude is best illustrated in the following passage:

> monstro voluptatem egregiam, cui nulla theatra,
> nulla aequare queas praetoris pulpita lauti,
> si spectes quanto capitis discrimine constent
> incrementa domus, aerata multus in arca
> fiscus et ad vigilem ponendi Castora nummi ...
> tanto maiores humana negotia ludi.
>
> (256–60; 264)

Unlike the satirist of Books I and II, who liked to identify his picture of Rome with tragedy, this Democritean satirist thinks of comedy; and his chief source of pleasure or humor is the human comedy. Men who

---

[15] Plutarch, *De liberis educandis* 20. Although the *senex iratus* was a stock figure of comedy, Caecilius Statius earned the reputation of having most successfully dramatized this type: see Cicero, *Pro Caelio* 37.

would find peace engage in *supervacua negotia*. What could be more appropriate than to describe such avaricious and restless spirits in the typical plight of the trader, caught symbolically in a storm and about to sink with his overloaded vessels? It is not surprising, then, that the satirist reverts to the same conclusion as in Satire 10:

> nullum numen habes, si sit prudentia: nos te,
> nos facimus, Fortuna, deam.
>
> (14.315–16; cf. 10.365–66)

Calvinus in Satire 13 lacked *prudentia* and therefore fondly believed that the gods would support his indignation over money; but the Democritean satirist found Calvinus ridiculous and here in Satire 14 treats the avaricious as but one more example of the human comedy.

Satire 15 expresses sharp scorn and disgust for the Egyptians, and there are places where the satirist presses beyond ridicule almost toward indignation again. However, what the satirist attacks is *ira*, a savage, bestial anger which could not be satiated until one tribe had committed an act of cannibalism on a member of another tribe. When he introduces his topic, he calls it a special crime, unlike the notorious crimes committed in tragedy, inasmuch as it affected an entire people (15.29–31). A reader of Seneca might recall that he, too, expressly singled out anger because of its peculiar power to provoke entire nations (3.2.2: *hic unus adfectus est qui interdum publice concipitur*). Probably the most famous passage in the Satire and one of the frequently quoted portions of Juvenal is the conclusion, in which the satirist eloquently affirms man's basic humanity and his special position in the universe as a rational and social creature. Like Seneca, who urged the same point (cf. 2.31.7: *ad coetum geniti sunt* ... etc.), this satirist demonstrates that the savage Egyptian anger violated the standards of humanity.

Satire 16 is a tantalizing fragment, but there can be no doubt about its basically ironic tone. In the sixty lines that we possess, the satirist affects a humorous interest in the "advantages" of the military life. Instead, however, of extolling the glories of fighting for the fatherland, of crushing the barbarians, of winning fame and fortune by attacking wealthy enemy cities, the satirist describes the pecuniary and judicial privileges enjoyed by soldiers. According to his portrait, soldiers possess more benefits in the civilian world than ordinary citizens, and these are the true advantages of the military life. This is a Democritean insight, the comic realization that soldiers join the army and risk their lives so that they can have special civilian *commoda:* fools who do not realize that all such material advantages are *supervacua*.

357

All readers have noted a difference in tone between the early and late Books of Juvenal's Satires. Indeed, Ribbeck felt the difference so strongly that he refused to believe in one and the same author for Books I–III and Books IV–V. The early books adopt a manner announced in Satire 1 and are best characterized by the satirists's words: *facit indignatio versum.* Starting with Satire 7, however, Juvenal began to alter the mask of his satirist. By the time that he wrote Satire 10, he had· entirely rejected the indignant satirist and created a new speaker, one who relied on reason, looked at the world more calmly and sanely, and discerned the ridiculous rather than the outrageous as the fundamental note of human endeavor. In Satire 10 this satirist announces an ideal which includes, among other things, the strength of mind capable of ignoring angry impulses (*nesciat irasci*). A few years later, when he wrote Book V, Juvenal chose topics which permitted his satirist to reject indignation even more explicitly. Satires 13 and 15 prove beyond question that the new satirist of Book IV is a conscious creation and that he cannot be defined in terms of the Program Satire of Book I.

The fact that the satirist's manner changes or, to put it more precisely, that there are two quite different satirists created by Juvenal, has led to various hypotheses. Unfortunately, these hypotheses have all started from the assumption that the speaker in the Satires—whom I call "the satirist"—is more or less identical with Juvenal. When commentators begin this way, they have but one avenue to follow, namely, a biographical interpretation of this fact. In order to produce a different satirist in Books IV and V, they argue, Juvenal himself must have become different. He grew older; he achieved recognition and financial ease; he turned Epicurean; he forgot his exile suffered under Domitian. Such are the biographical inferences growing out of an assumption which I would maintain is quite erroneous. On the contrary, both the indignant and the calm satirists are dramatic creations along recognizably conventional lines; they provide no reliable evidence about Juvenal except as a versatile poet. By studying Seneca's treatises *De ira* and *De tranquillitate animi,* it is possible to discern some of the central ancient conventions on anger.

Seneca unhesitatingly condemns anger and indignation. He permits an interlocutor, the *adversarius,* to state arguments justifying anger; then he crushingly refutes the arguments. As the *adversarius* presents his pathetic points one by one, precise verbal similarities occur between this inadequate exponent of *indignatio* and the eloquent satirist of Juvenal. Both insist that they are *viri boni* spurred by *virtus* and *magnanimitas* to challenge the evil that they have themselves suffered or seen perpetrated. Nevertheless, Seneca's insights easily prevail; and he totally annihilates all arguments on behalf of anger or the angry man. From the correct ethical perspective, anger must be viewed as insanity, a definite vice based upon irrationality and completely untrue to human nature. Similarly, the angry or indignant man is by definition denying his humanity and sinking to the level of irrational children and beasts, because he indulges himself in the spiteful, infantile pleasure of a tantrum, because he seeks vengeance.

Since Seneca has not invented his thesis against anger, since the same doctrines prevailed among the Romans from the time of Cicero and earlier until the period when Lactantius wrote his *De ira Dei*, it follows that the angry satirist was not only a poetic creation modelled on recognized rhetorical conventions, but that he was, by definition, morally suspect. A Roman who read Juvenal's early Satires would automatically fall back upon the moral doctrines concerning anger and therefore refuse to identify himself with the indignant satirist. He would see the dramatic tensions in the character of the speaker and recognize them as typical, as signs warning him against this *persona*. Modern critics will continue to draw the wrong conclusions about Juvenal's Satires until they, too, read them as Romans would have, for Juvenal's poetic genius produced a highly complex form of satire, the first of its type. A reader must not only forget biographical considerations in Books I and II, but he must come to realize that the heart of Juvenal's indignant Satires lies precisely in those tensions created by *indignatio*. Even if the *iratus* rejects reason and plunges into an inhuman interpretation of life around him, the reader should not blindly follow him or invent specious excuses for his folly; rather, the reader must exercise his own reason and discover and affirm a truth about life which the very existence of the indignant satirist negates.

To replace the erroneous opinions of his *adversarius*, Seneca advocates in the *De ira* a mode of life dedicated to serenity; and in a later essay, *De tranquillitate animi*, he explores the advantages of this existence and the means of achieving it. As he himself admits, he has borrowed his ideal from Democritus, whose term εὐθυμία he has rendered as *tranquillitas*. And Democritus provides one of the clearest patterns of this goal toward which he urges people. In the first place, Democritus had expounded his views on the balanced life and placed his emphasis on disengagement, avoidance of *supervacua negotia,* whether public or private. Then he had tried to live up to his ideal and, after his death, became a legend. He was reputed to have given away all his money so as to free himself from the fear of Fortuna; and his fellow-citizens thought him insane. He was said to have laughed whenever he walked among his fellow-men, apparently struck with the folly of their pursuits. Thus, Seneca, who also commends disengagement from material and political desires, who permits us to enjoy temperate *voluptas* and cherish some practical hopes in life, quotes Democritus and dramatizes the attitude of the philosopher in a striking contrast between his laughter and Heraclitus' tears.

It is difficult, if not impossible, to ascertain the extent of Senecan influence upon Juvenal. I find it significant, however, that Juvenal invented an indignant satirist with the failings detectible in Seneca's *adversarius;* then invented a new, rationally balanced satirist who is virtually identical with the ideal proposed by Seneca and best represented by Seneca's semi-historical Democritus. Indeed, in Satire 10, the new satirist proposes as his model the Senecan Democritus, while dismissing the lachrymose attitude of Heraclitus; he is, so to speak, a modern Democritus, applying the mocking insights of a Greek to the Roman scene. And when he chooses a theme for Satire 10, which is often entitled "The Vanity of Human Wishes," he closely follows the Democritean manner and a *topos* discussed by Seneca himself (*vanitas cupiditatum*). The other Satires of Books IV and V all reveal a new satirist consistent with this modern Democritus: he enjoys a simple life, cultivates a few friends, avoids the crowd and public folly, and, above all, declares anger ridiculous, infantile, and inhuman. Thus, whether or not Juvenal used Seneca to create this new satirist, it is undeniable that the speaker of Satires 10–16 belongs in a conventional category. We may most easily avoid the error of biographical interpretation by naming this new character "the Democritean satirist."

Just as for Seneca *tranquillitas* is the answer to *ira,* so the Democritean satirist answers to the indignant satirist. Whereas the indignant satirist views Rome angrily and irrationally, the Democritean satirist can discuss some of the same problems and emerge with a sane, relatively hopeful view. To judge from Seneca, this speaker of Books IV and V advocates a tenable attitude, morally sound and consistent with the best ideas of antiquity. However, he has never been a favorite, and Ribbeck describes him in the most antagonistic terms. The reason for such antagonism, I venture to say, is that this Democritean satirist lacks the dramatic power and conviction of the indignant satirist. Moreover, he fails to exhibit that saving grace of self-irony which makes Horace's satirist such an intriguing character. No reader is wrong for preferring the early Satires to the later or for finding the complex self-contradicting angry satirist more exciting than the seemingly content, somewhat self-satisfied character of Books IV and V. Still, the sharp diversity of these two satirists attests to Juvenal's poetic skill: sensitive to the rhetorical and ethical conventions of Rome, he was the first to create an indignant satirist and the first to suggest, in his own poetry, the answer to the angry man's view of life.

Lascivia vs. *ira*: Martial and Juvenal

Sandwiched between two lighthearted epigrams on the dubious physical attractions of a Galla and a Chloe, there appear in Martial's Third Book the following four elegiac lines:

> empta domus fuerat tibi, Tongiliane, ducentis:
> abstulit hanc nimium casus in urbe frequens.
> conlatum est deciens. rogo, non potes ipse videri
> incendisse tuam, Tongiliane, domum? (3.52)

Martial has so contrived his development that each line begins with a crucial verb, each marking an important stage in the total situation, and the final one driving home the witty point. The first couplet establishes the situation in general terms: the cost of the house, then its total destruction (cause unspecified). To correct the impression of disaster, however, to make sure that we grasp Martial's attitude and correctly view the character of Tongilianus, the second couplet reports the huge profit made from the fire because of public contributions (again, cause undefined), then ever so politely raises the question of arson. What might have been mistaken for sympathy in the first couplet has changed to ridicule, while Tongilianus has been transformed from a pitiable victim to a criminal.[1] The careful placing of *domus* closé to the start of line 1 and *domum* at the end of line 4; the alliterative use of personal pronoun *tibi* and possessive *tuam* with vocative *Tongiliane*

---

[1] Legally speaking, arson was a capital crime. In Juvenal's time, it was punishable by deportation; under the Severans it merited execution. See *Dig.* 48.8.3.5.

respectively in 1 and 4; the variation between the structure of the first couplet (one clause in each line) and of the second (one clause in a half-line, the next expanding to a line and a half); the use of three verbs to express the various nuances of Martial's suspicions in 3 and 4—these are some of the principal artistic devices employed to enhance this witty epigram. The incident with which it plays was no doubt one of the common scandals of the day, somewhat analogous to cases of arson today when a man sets fire to his house or factory in order to collect fraudulently on insurance. And Martial has treated this arson with the naughty laughter which is so typical of him.

Twenty to twenty-five years after the appearance of Martial's epigram, Juvenal published Satire 3, in which there occurs a sequence remarkably like that of those four elegiac lines.

> si magna Asturici cecidit domus, horrida mater,
> pullati proceres, differt vadimonia praetor.
> tum gemimus casus urbis, tunc odimus ignem.
> ardet adhuc, et iam accurrit qui marmora donet,   215
> conferat impensas; hic nuda et candida signa,
> hic aliquid praeclarum Euphranoris et Polycliti,
> haec Asianorum vetera ornamenta deorum,
> hic libros dabit et forulos mediamque Minervam,
> hic modium argenti. meliora ac plura reponit   220
> Persicus orborum lautissimus et merito iam
> suspectus tamquam ipse suas incenderit aedes.
>
> (3. 212–222)

Juvenal has devoted eleven lines to his development, which he presents as a number of related scenes leading up to the same point as Martial's. Instead of talking to the arsonist, the speaker addresses the audience. Thus, he does not inquire or report the price of the mansion, but focuses on the disaster to the building and the immediate public outcry that it provokes. The first three lines, it might be said, represent an elaboration of the single line in which Martial recorded and affected to deplore the total destruction of Tongilianus' house. Martial's equally terse and generalized report of contributions is also amplified here by a list of six contributors and donations, five of which are organized by means of anaphora with the initial demonstrative. After devoting a full line in 217, 218, and 219 to three contributors, Juvenal rapidly closes the list after the first half of 220. Then he starts to develop his point on the arson. First of all, what may have been somewhat puzzling in Martial, namely, why people should contribute so heavily to a victim of fire, receives explanation from Juvenal: his arsonist Persicus is one of the richest men in Rome and has no immediate heirs; hence, people are contributing so as to earn a profitable place in his will. Then, with the conjunction *et* followed by *merito* and a monosyllable, Juvenal deliberately creates a harsh ending to the hexameter of 221 and a jerky beginning of the enjambement into 222. Instead of the mockingly polite construction of three verbs employed by Martial, Juvenal cleverly exploits the line division to hold us in suspense as to what Persicus has "deservedly" accomplished, before placing *suspectus* in its prominent position at the beginning of 222. Martial's naughty question becomes a statement, and the satirist voices a decisive bias about the popular scandal: it has a likely basis in fact.

Martial and Juvenal have worked with the same kind of scandalous incident and built towards the same witty point, though Juvenal has gone at the situation with greater amplitude than Martial. Taken in isolation, too, this Juvenalian scene might appear to be using its wit in the same amused and amusing way as that of the epigram. Suppose we knew Juvenal's poetry only through this excerpt, found in some anthology of the tenth century: could we accurately assess its tone? Might we not be tempted to believe, especially after seeing the parallel in Martial, that the speaker of these lines was not seriously engaged with the criminal behavior of Persicus, but, like Martial, intent on the manipulation of words and details so as to extract from the well-told anecdote the maximum amount of wit for the audience's pleasure? The problem which I have set myself forms part of the larger traditional problem involving Martial and Juvenal. For years, scholars have inquired into the connections between epigrammatist and satirist, in an attempt not only to define but also to explain them. I shall briefly review this scholarship, then proceed to the particular problem involving Martial and Juvenal which seems to have the most contemporary importance for us. I may put it this way: to what extent does Juvenal accept, along with the material, the basic method of Martial; to what extent is his wit a clever variation on Martial's? In terms of my title, to what extent can we regard Juvenal's announced mood of *indignatio* and *ira* as an instrument of a dominant wit that closely parallels the integrated witty mood of *lascivia* proclaimed by Martial?

In reviewing the main facts about the relationship of Juvenal and Martial and the theories erected on these facts, we may classify the facts as biographical and literary. Evidence can be drawn from the life and times of the two poets and (as has been done at the beginning of this paper) from common material in their poetry. To begin in conventional manner with the biographical facts of the older poet, Martial, born in Spain about A.D. 40, came to Rome in the early sixties, hoping perhaps to gain advancement through the other Spaniards who had acquired influence at the court of Nero, for example, Seneca and the family of Lucan.[2] Although the Pisonian Conspiracy ended that particular hope, Martial remained in Rome nearly thirty-five years, at first forced to struggle for survival, then gradually establishing himself as a clever poet who merited patronage, whose epigrams deserved not only to be recited in Rome but also to be published and read all over the empire. He produced a slight volume to mark the inauguration of the Colosseum in 80, when Titus ruled; his major works, however, twelve books of Epigrams, appeared more or less year by year after 85, all but the last during the reign of Domitian.[3] Success came to him, then, when he was about 45. Having been conditioned by early years in Spain, by the chaos of Nero's last years, and by the decade of Vespasian's sound rule, Martial flourished under the Flavian brothers, as Rome somewhat relaxed from the necessarily austere ways of their father.

Juvenal arrived in Rome during those years when Martial first began to enjoy fame. Born about 60 and raised, it appears, in the Italian town of Aquinum, he proceeded to Rome at approximately the same period as his contemporaries Tacitus and Pliny, though with entirely different hopes.[4] They immediately entered upon the political

[2] The standard biography of Martial still rests upon the researches of L. Friedlaender in his edition (Leipzig 1886). See R. Helm's article in *RE*, M. Valerius Martialis.

[3] What we now possess as Books X and XI constitutes a revised edition of poems many of which were written between 94 and 96; this second edition adds poems that refer flatteringly to Nerva and the first years of Trajan.

[4] For the fullest recent treatment of Juvenal's biography, Gilbert Highet's *Juvenal the Satirist* (Oxford 1954) is very valuable if used with discretion. See especially his chapters I through V. Two recent articles challenge the reliability of the evidence on which the biography conventionally depends. G. Brugnoli, "Vita Iuvenalis," *Studi urbinati* 37 (1963) 5–14, dates the transmitted *Vita* no earlier than the fourth century and argues that its standardized categories of information make the detail suspect. E. Flores, "Origini e ceto di Giovenale e loro riflessi nella problematica sociale delle satire," *Annali fac. Lett. & filos. Napoli*

career to which their background and influence entitled them; both progressed steadily and had reached high positions during the reign of Domitian while Juvenal remained insignificant.[5] Since we hear nothing of Juvenal's political career, indeed virtually nothing at all of his experience, we assume that his background and influence (not his innate talent) were negligible.[6] He apparently settled for a literary career, first perhaps as a teacher of rhetoric, then later as a more or less independent poet under the patronage of various men of wealth. Martial counted Juvenal as a friend by 92, for in Book 7 published that year, he mentioned him twice (7.24 and 91). Exactly when Juvenal began to develop his satiric talents and write the Satires we now possess, is uncertain. Most of the earliest poems, it is generally agreed, were written during the reign of Trajan; and Book I does not seem to have been published before 110.[7] Since Martial had by then been dead five years and since Juvenal avoids giving specific details about himself and his friends, we should not be surprised to find no reference to Martial by name in the Satires. Assuming that Juvenal, like Martial, remained in Rome during the eighties and nineties—I find the evidence for Juvenal's exile at this time or any time unconvincing—we may conclude that both were involved contemporaneously, if not alike, for about fifteen years in the literary activities of the city, Juvenal as a tyro, Martial as an established figure. Martial left Rome in 98 and returned to his native Spain, from which he addressed to Juvenal a last epigram (12.18). Juvenal's success, which came under Trajan and Hadrian, sprang from conditions considerably different from Martial's.

Though twenty years younger than Martial, then, Juvenal did know him during the nineties and shared the literary scene in Rome with him at a significant period of his own poetic development. So much for the biographical facts linking the two. Now for the facts

10 (1962–1963) 51–80, sees reasons to assign the now-lost inscription of Aquinum to another, earlier Juvenal and to argue that the satirist did not own property in that area.

5 See the chapters in R. Syme, *Tacitus* (Oxford 1958) 59ff on the early careers of Pliny and Tacitus under Domitian.

6 The fact that Juvenal, Pliny, and Tacitus all agree in denigrating Domitian after the emperor's death can hardly be used as special evidence for Juvenal's sufferings from Domitian. Otherwise, we would be obliged to infer that Pliny and Tacitus had themselves suffered to a similar extent; and we know that to be untrue.

7 See the prudent comments of Highet, pp. 11–12. For a less likely view, see the ingenious article of A. Michel, "La date des *Satires:* Juvénal, Héliodore et le tribun d'Arménie," *REL* 41 (1963) 315–327. He dates Book I after the accession of Hadrian in 118.

provided by the poems. In Juvenal's earliest Book of Five Satires, four out of five have basic themes that appear frequently as the material of Martial's epigrams;[8] and the single exception, Satire 4, uses as the partial occasion of its drama an oversize turbot (*rhombus*), which is also a topos in Martial.[9] Satire 6, large enough to qualify by itself as Book II, surveys women's sexual proclivities; nobody needs to be reminded that Martial and his audience enjoyed the same subject. Book III, consisting of three Satires, was published probably early in the reign of Hadrian, some twenty years after Juvenal had last seen Martial. Nevertheless, Satire 7 describes the plight of poets and other practitioners of verbal arts in Rome, and Satire 9 toys with the world of male homosexuals: both topics occur over and over again in Martial. Finally, Satires 11 and 12 and the description of old age in Satire 10, all from Book IV, and to a lesser extent parts of Satires 13 and 14 in Book V show continued preoccupation with material common to Martial. In short, there can be little doubt that between A.D. 110 and 130 Juvenal used topics and themes which had earlier won wide favor in the epigrams published by Martial between 85 and 101. It is a significant exercise to go systematically through Juvenal's Satires, especially the earlier ones, and point out line by line, passage by passage, what he shared with the epigrams of his Spanish friend.[10]

We have a combination of biographical and literary facts: the two poets were both in Rome and knew each other fairly well, and after Martial's death Juvenal wrote poems which repeatedly parallel in 'significant detail the epigrams of Martial. How can we interpret these facts so as to illuminate the relationship between the two? Modern preoccupation with this problem received major stimulus from an article published in 1888 by Henry Nettleship, who, while assessing Juvenal's achievement in general, took time to put forth a

[8] In Satire 1, many of the vignettes of adulterers and adulteresses, gigolos, women who poison their husbands, women gladiators, etc., can be paralleled in Martial. Satire 2 deals with the crypto-homosexual who poses as a severe moralist and with his secret orgies. Parallels in Martial are common; see infra, pp. 24ff. I use Satire 3 throughout this article because of the many points it shares with Martial. Satire 5 scornfully portrays the *cliens* who, for a humiliating meal, allows himself to be "enslaved" and lose his *libertas* to an insulting *patronus*. Cf. Martial 4.40, 5.22, 5.44, 6.88, 9.100, 10.56.

[9] Cf. Martial 3.45.5 and especially 13.81.

[10] See the series of articles, based on his dissertation, by R. E. Colton in *CB* 39 (1963) 49–52 [on Satire 7 and Martial], 40 (1963) 1–4 [Sat. 4 and Martial], 41 (1964) 26–27 [Sat. 14], 41 (1965) 39, 41–45 [Sat. 11], *CJ* 61 (1965) 68–71 [Sat. 2], and *Traditio* 22 (1966) 403–419 [Sat. 3].

provocative explanation for the links between Martial and Juvenal, Epigrams and Satires.[11] According to him, Martial and Juvenal worked side by side in Rome during the nineties, but independently of each other, each drawing upon a common store of literary material then available in the city. And to make his thesis more plausible, Nettleship argued that the major portions of the Satires of Book I were composed, like the Epigrams, in the nineties.

Most scholars have rejected Nettleship's dating of the early Satires as well as his view of Juvenal's originality or independence. Thus, J. D. Duff, in the commentary which was first published in 1898, wrote: "The resemblance [between the two poets' themes] will not seem more than can be accounted for, if we believe that Juvenal, having already a thorough knowledge of Martial's epigrams, began to direct his satires against the same period and persons whom Martial had already riddled with his lighter artillery."[12] That same year, Harry Wilson printed his significant paper, which he had read in 1897 to the American Philological Association, on "The Literary Influence of Martial upon Juvenal." The title alone indicates that he stood with Duff against Nettleship on the question of independence.[13] Studying the mechanics of Martial's influence rigorously, Wilson argued that Juvenal used the typical techniques of *imitatio* normal for Latin poets; he knew Martial by heart, but did not simply copy him word for word. He either reused Martial's ideas in different words or used Martial's words in an altered context, to create Satires that were substantially different from the Epigrams.

The meticulous argument of Wilson and the general likelihood of his and Duff's assumptions that the older, successful poet influenced, but did not totally dominate, the younger have continued to prevail. There are, however, some questions which they did not face. Duff, for example, in stating that Juvenal dealt with the same period and persons as Martial, did not go on to explain the effect intended or achieved. What did the people and events of the eighties and nineties mean to Juvenal and his audience twenty to thirty years later? What

[11] "The Life and Poems of Juvenal," *JP* 16 (1888) 41–66, reprinted in his *Lectures and Essays* (Oxford 1895) 117–144.

[12] Duff. *D. Iunii Iuvenalis Saturae XIV*, p. xxii.

[13] Wilson, *AJP* 19 (1898) 193–209. Of less significance is the almost contemporary article of G. Boissier, "Relations de Juvénal et de Martial," *Rev. Cours et Conferences* 7 (1899) 2.443–451. Boissier commented rather generally on similarities and differences between the two poets.

was the point of being indignant over the dead past when Martial had treated it with his charming *lascivia*? By substituting heavy artillery for light (to keep Duff's image), was Juvenal moving farther away from reality or closer to the feelings of his audience? Wilson, too, left unexplained the fundamental literary connection between Juvenal's artful variations on Martial's wording and what he regarded as the evident difference between their respective styles and poetic purposes. If, as he wrote, "the high moral purpose and seriousness of the former [Juvenal] stand in sharp antithesis to the mocking triviality of the latter [Martial]," [14] one wonders about the range of Juvenal's *imitatio*. Assuming that we can distinguish the "high moral purpose" in the account of Persicus' arson from the "mocking triviality" of Tongilianus' arson in Martial, can we also say that this is a function of *imitatio*? Was Juvenal doing anything like Horace who used Lucretian language to comment on epic enthusiasm and on Epicurean exaggerations? That is, did Juvenal allude to the whole context of Martial and subtly differentiate his own attitude on all levels, or was he merely playing with Martial's words and, from quite another perspective, aiming at a moral purpose and seriousness to which the borrowings from Martial had no relevance?

Granted, then, that Juvenal did make use of Martial, both his words and his epigrammatic situations, the question remains: what was the extent of this use; what was its effect with the audience? It is not really an adequate answer to respond that Martial was a kind of satirist and so Juvenal drew from him what was naturally "satiric," for satire is so amorphous in form and manner (even without Martial) that turning Martial, for the purposes of argument, into a satirist says very little about how he might be utilized by Juvenal.[15] In theory it would be possible to argue that, because Juvenal regards Roman society with the dissatisfied eye of a wretched client and the literary situation in Rome with the unhappiness of a poet struggling for recognition, and because Martial earlier exhibited similar attitudes, Juvenal adopted his attitude from Martial. In fact, the shared viewpoints

[14] Wilson, p. 193.

[15] C. W. Mendell, "Martial and the Satiric Epigram," *CP* 17 (1922) 1–20 points out that, between the time of Catullus and Martial, the epigram came under the influence of satire and so can in certain cases be called "satiric." J. W. Duff, *Roman Satire* (Berkeley 1936) 126ff devotes an entire chapter to Martial. See now also H. Szelest, "Martials satirische Epigramme und Horaz," *Das Altertum* 9 (1963) 27–37. .

serve scholars rather to document the relative continuity of Roman conditions and the basis of the two poets' friendship: Juvenal is supposed to have felt the situation as personally as Martial.[16]

In more recent years, two scholars have offered more comprehensive answers to the problem of this relationship, directing attention as much to *how* the borrowings were made as to *what* was borrowed. Gilbert Highet, while discussing the broad tradition from which Juvenal drew, commented on Martial's part in it as follows: "So many of Juvenal's jokes and satiric ideas and proper names and turns of phrase are adapted from Martial that the epigrams of Martial were clearly one of the chief influences that trained him to be a satirist. What he did was to take Martial's keen perception, his disillusioned but witty sense of contrast, his trick of epigram, and his peculiar blend of suave poetry and vulgar colloquialism, to clean them up, to give them a moral purpose, and to build them into poems of major length."[17] This seems promising, especially because it does not exploit the invidious contrast between Martial's "triviality" and Juvenal's "high seriousness," but gives full credit to the artistry of the Epigrams. Highet represents Juvenal as a skillful poet who engages himself creatively with the art of Martial at every level and extracts from it material to which he can give new shape and life. Unfortunately, in his analysis of the individual Satires, Highet did not attempt to work out this view of a Juvenal trained by Martial. His emphasis upon the satirist as an unhappy, hypersensitive person who has experienced profound personal suffering and upon the passionate personal truth of the Satires obscures any concern with the creative poet who saw merits in and exploited Martial's obvious assets.

It was in patent disagreement with Highet's emphasis that in 1962 H. A. Mason published his influential essay entitled: "Is Juvenal a Classic?"[18] In order to deny the crucial assumption of Highet and other biographical critics that Juvenal's Satires tell us the

---

[16] Boissier (supra n. 13) commented on this in 1899. For more recent observations, see R. Marache, "Le revendication sociale chez Martial et Juvénal," *RCCM* 3 (1961) 30–67, and N. I. Barbu, "Les esclaves chez Martial et Juvénal," *Acta antiqua philippopolitana* (Sofia 1963) 67–74.

[17] Highet, p. 173.

[18] Mason, *Arion* 1:1 (1962) 8–44; 2 (1962) 39–79. This article is reprinted in *Essays on Roman Literature: Satire*, edited by Sullivan (London 1963) 93–176. Since that volume is more accessible and its numbering is easier to use, I shall consistently refer to its pagination.

truth about himself and his period, Mason resorted to Martial. As he explained this tactic, "the key to Juvenal's art lies in the study of Martial. The two poets appeal to the same taste and presuppose the same habits in their listening and reading public."[19] Later, by way of conclusion, he imaginatively elaborated what he believed Juvenal presupposed in his public, wording it cleverly as if the satirist were making prefatory remarks to an edition of the Satires:

> Dear readers, you have enjoyed Martial; now come and see whether I cannot give extra point to his favorite topics by setting them, as it were, to a different tune: the declaimer's mode. But I assume you understand what Martial was doing when he confined his poems to the conventional jokes of polite society. You will know then that to enjoy us you must both suspend and apply your critical and moral sense. We are not called on in our art to give you *all* the facts (you know them as well as we) or to assume all the moral attitudes (we are not moral censors) but to take those that allow the maximum witty play of the mind. Prepare yourselves, therefore, dear readers, to find in my poems all the butts of Martial's epigrams, and in particular, the comically obscene situations you enjoy so much in the mime. You will see from my rewritings of Martial that I have my own notes, particularly the sarcastic and the mock-tragic and epic, and that by fitting my sections together I can exhibit more attitudes to the same episode than you will find in any one of his epigrams.[20]

Mason offers the most detailed literary explanation of Martial's influence known to me, and he extends the range of this influence farther than any other interpreter: not only has Juvenal used

[19] P. 96.

[20] P. 165. It is of course an exaggeration to claim that Juvenal treated *all* Martial's butts or to imply that *only* Martial's butts appear in the Satires. Where in Juvenal are the mocking portraits of writers who are jealous of or plagiarize him? Where are jokes on physical deformities and malfunctions as common as in Martial? It is equally strained to liken Juvenal's use of obscenity to Martial's. How frequently does one hear of pederasty in the Satires? Consider some of Martial's all too common terms like *cunnilingus, fellator, tribas, ficosus, masturbare:* one would have trouble locating more than a single Juvenalian reference to each of these five sexual interests. As I shall try to show, Juvenal was not dependent upon obscenity to the same extent as Martial and did not use it as Martial had done.

his predecessor with great creativity but he also agrees with the basic attitude of Martial. In both poets wit is the main device for achieving effects: the essential manner of both is witty. So the answer to the question in Mason's title would be: Juvenal is a classic of wit.[21] Accordingly, "he was more interested in literature than social conditions and ... he lacks any consistent standpoint or moral coherence. Indeed his whole art consists in opportunism and the surprise effects obtainable from deliberate inconsistency."[22] Whereas earlier commentators plunged into problems because they insisted on the basic difference in attitude and technique of Juvenal even when he was using Martial, Mason has eliminated that problem by insisting on the identity of the two poets' subjects, witty manners, and audiences. Juvenal has become Martial set to a slightly different tune.

There can be no question that Mason has at last properly emphasized one of the most important elements of Juvenal's art and most cleverly employed Martial to demonstrate his thesis. Wit *is* important in the Satires. However, in order to win his argument, he has claimed too much. He has, I believe, tended to overstress wit at the expense of other important factors of Juvenalian art and to force Juvenal too harshly into the mould of Martial. Aside from the fact that Juvenal himself had different origins from Martial and a personality of his own, it is evident that the eras of Trajan and Hadrian differed markedly from that of Domitian, and it seems dubious to posit an audience for Juvenal equipped with the "same taste" as Martial's. To limit one's attention, as Mason does, to verbal opportunism or manipulation of the Latin language is risky. To defend these limits by asserting that there is no sustained theme of significance in Juvenal's Satires, no engagement with genuine moral issues is to provoke a protest from those who read Juvenal otherwise. Martial may provide "the key to Juvenal's art" in a way quite different from what Mason believes: his work happens to be the most conveniently available to show how much Juvenal re-shaped his literary heritage to fit his own purposes. In the remainder of this paper, I shall criticize Mason's thesis more fully, particularly by reference to Satire 3 and other Satires of Book I, in the hope of estimating more satisfactorily the function of Juvenalian wit and of defining its relation to the announced mood of indignation that characterizes the earlier Satires.

21 See p. 107.
22 *Ibid.*

Now that I have sketched out the lines of controversy, I return to the passage of Satire 3 with which I began. I had posed the problem of the tone behind Juvenal's wit and suggested that, taken in isolation, the passage about the arsonist-profiteer might possibly be interpreted like the parallel epigram of Martial, as a cleverly reported joke of Roman society. That would be Mason's view of the passage and the entire Satire; he would add only that Juvenal's tune differed and that the satirist was able to accumulate more attitudes around the episode by reason of his broader scope. Nevertheless, according to Mason, Juvenal's audience responded here, as they were meant, primarily to the joke; all other effects in the passage are subordinate to that.

When we study this arson narrative in relation to its context, I believe, it becomes evident that Juvenal has drastically altered Martial (assuming that he did work here under some influence of Martial). Above all, he has shaped what was supposed to be only a joke so that it no longer is an end in itself, but has become subordinate to what must be called larger thematic purposes. First of all, take the matter of names. Martial called his arsonist Tongilianus. We can be sure that the name did not identify anyone, because Martial has fabricated this odd name.[23] Since the name possesses no automatic connotations, the narrative determines the identity of the arsonist. Probably Martial's audience was expected to substitute for this fantastic name the name of a real Roman or wealthy alien resident to whom scandal attributed arson. Calling him Tongilianus, Martial caught the alliteration and supported the lighthearted purposes of his wit. Juvenal, on the other hand, offers two names: Asturicus (212) and Persicus (221).[24] These names are meaningful in themselves: we are to think of remote Asturia in Spain and of Persia in the East, and then we imagine the nobility and wealth that could be won by Romans in these exotic spots.[25] We are not expected to play drawing-room games

[23] The name occurs only here and in 12.88.
[24] There is disagreement as to whether we are dealing with one person or two here. Some scholars believe that Persicus owned *domus Asturici*, Asturicus either being a previous owner, perhaps builder of the house, or an ancestor. Others believe that Juvenal refers to two unrelated cases of arson, the hypothetical one involving Asturicus' house and a second one from which Persicus profited. See the next note.
[25] J. E. B. Mayor, *Thirteen Satires of Juvenal* (London 1889)[4], in his note on 3.212, says of Asturicus and Persicus: "names of conquering families." The two relevant entries in *RE* illustrate the disagreement mentioned in n. 24: on Asturicus, P. von Rohden

and guess the identity of Juvenal's arsonists: the names identify them as Romans from distinguished families.

Second, Juvenal has totally altered the narrative occasion and thereby changed our attitude toward the arsonist. Martial pictures himself, the irreverent Spaniard, striking up a conversation with Tongilianus, affecting to be sympathetic as the latter reports on his fire, then naughtily raising the question of arson at the end. In Satire 3, the speaker who recounts the episode is Umbricius, a character especially created by Juvenal for the poem.[26] He is not talking with the arsonist but with us, and he could never affect sympathy or amusement over this arson. Thus, the narrative has no real surprise, as Martial's does; it builds steadily toward its climax. For Umbricius, Asturicus and Persicus represent villains to whom he points with anger as he addresses each of us in the second person singular. The reasons for this anger, which are obvious from the fuller context (soon to be discussed) may be summarized in this way: he is a victim of the Rome which allows a distinguished Roman like Persicus to profit, not be executed, as a result of his criminal arson. The altered point of view and altered form of dialogue in turn decisively shape the wit here deployed.

Finally, Martial's totally independent joke, told for itself, has been subordinated by Juvenal to a larger context and thematic purposes. This case of arson is introduced in 212 in a conditional clause, to produce an antithesis to an actual instance of accidental fire, when the apartment of a poor man named Cordus was burned and all its miserable contents consumed (203–211). The list of people who react with horror at Asturicus' plight corresponds ironically to a heavily emphasized nobody (*nemo* in anaphora 211) who answered Cordus' need. The list of precious things contributed by "friends" to Asturicus corresponds to the list of diminutive, pathetically cherished possessions of Cordus which the fire destroyed (203–207). Whereas Umbricius

wrote: "Beiname eines vornehmen Römers, Iuv. 3,212. Wohl willkürlich gewählt." On the other hand, Groag, after an extensive discussion of P. Fabius Persicus [Fabius # 120], consul A.D. 34, used this passage of Juvenal to justify a hypothetical Fabius Persicus Asturicus [Fabius # 121]. We know for sure of no Asturicus, but Persicus is well attested. Juvenal addresses a Persicus, presumably a quite different man and a friend, in 11.57.

26 Umbricius is a rare name, too, but attested in Tacitus *Hist.* 1.27 and Pliny *N.H.* 10.19 as a noted *haruspex* in A.D. 69. See also *RE* s.v. Recently, Motto and Clark, *TAPA* 96 (1965) 275, have argued that "Umbricius is no historical figure contemporary to Juvenal," but that the name is chosen to refer to *umbra*: he therefore represents the shade of the deceased Rome.

summarizes Persicus' situation by saying that he recovered more and better things than he had before his planned fire, his pathetic summary of Cordus' plight dwells on the "nothing" he really possessed to begin with, all of which paltry "nothing" was lost without chance of replacement (*nil* rhetorically repeated 208–209). The antithesis rather than the verbal manipulation of the arson anecdote determines the ultimate effect of Juvenal's wit here. Cordus, the innocent, pathetic victim of a fire over which he had no control, decisively qualifies our attitude toward Persicus, profiteer from his act of arson. We can now conclude that Juvenal did not amplify Martial's anecdote with his lists of people sympathetic to Asturicus and of donors and donations merely to enhance his narrative with vivid details and so increase the final point. The expansions serve the antithesis, which in turn functions to express a pervasive theme about the injustice and un-Roman degeneracy controlling Rome. I think I can safely claim Martial never portrays a poor man as genuinely pathetic, never allows his audience to engage its emotions with problems of Roman justice.

Juvenal places the two contrasting stories about Cordus and the arsonists in a larger context that begins with Umbricius' question in 190:

quis timet aut timuit gelida Praeneste ruinam?

Beside Praeneste, Umbricius names three other charming towns or Latium or Southern Etruria, which implicitly offer pleasant, secure if humble homes in contrast with the Roman apartments that constantly threaten collapse. The contrast is worked out by a description of us (*nos urbem colimus* 193ff) fearfully sleeping when *ruina* is imminent (196). Then, the subject turns to fires, another aspect of urban residential danger, and "your" plight, anyone of "you" in the audience, as Umbricius suggests that outside Rome no fires occur at night, no sudden scares (197–198). He pictures "you" trapped on the top floor of a highly combustible apartment as fire races up the flimsy structure: "you" are doomed, it appears, when he suddenly abandons the desperate scene to describe Cordus' troubles (198–202). Plainly, though, "you" and Cordus are alike victims of fire in contrast with the arsonists, except that "you" will not survive, whereas Cordus did escape with nothing and became a beggar. Having closed the antithesis with what now we would call savage wit about profitable arson, Umbricius returns to "you." He offers "you" a fine home—a place of safety from that menacing fire—for the price you now pay annually for your dark Roman garret, away from Rome in three typical towns of Latium (223ff). These three towns obviously balance the four names in 190ff. And the paragraph closes with an elaboration of the attractions of rusticity, both charming and witty, as "you" are invited to entertain the vision of a small plot of land which you yourself work, at last the master of something you can count on, if only a lone lizard. "You" seem to have a choice between death in Rome and secure life in the country, between losing your few possessions in Rome (where arsonists profit) or enjoying them undisturbed elsewhere, between victimization in Rome and honorable rustic independence. How can "you" hesitate? Umbricius, the angry speaker, is now about to abandon this corrupt city, and the whole trend of this paragraph is to persuade "you" to follow his example.

Juvenal, then, has re-worked the naughty wit of Martial's light epigram to voice anger and serve the needs of a thematic antithesis. And this revised joke about arson is not the only wit in the passage to be so shaped. Umbricius starts with hyperbole: *nos urbem colimus tenui tibicine fultam* (193); note the alliteration used to enhance the wit. The closest analogy to this—and not very close at that—Mayor found in witty Ovid, who described a modest farm house "standing by means of a prop" (*stantem tibicine villam, Fast.* 4.695). To give substance to his exaggeration, Umbricius goes on to describe how the agents of apartment owners criminally conceal the structural faults in a building, then "urge renters to sleep soundly in the face of imminent collapse" (*securos pendente iubet dormire ruina* 196). Sound sleep, used paradoxically here, might well remind Juvenal's audience of the way Horace idealized the condition of the simple countryman in terms of easy, peaceful slumber.[27] When the fire starts in "your" apartment, "you" learn of it by the shouts and bustle of "your" downstairs neighbor Ucalegon (199). In this instance, the wit inheres in the phrasing of the Latin and the choice of the name, which echo a passage from *Aeneid* 2.[28] Aeneas had a next-door neighbor in Troy, whose house was already afire when Aeneas awoke from his last sleep in his home, then rushed out to fight. The modern Ucalegon is an impoverished

27 Cf. Horace *C.* 2.16.6 and 3.1.21, also *S.* 1.1.9–10.
28 Juvenal's metrical unit *iam frivola transfert | Ucalegon* parodies *Aeneid* 2.311: *iam proximus ardet | Ucalegon.*

376

"son of Troy," and his neighbor, the modern Aeneas, is "you" in your garret, about to be burned unheroically to a cinder. Martial commonly uses metonymy with names of mythical heroes, but you would never find him using the trope in this thematic manner, to underline the degeneracy of Rome from the noble ideals of the *Aeneid*.

Umbricius shifts to Cordus, characterizing his few possessions by diminutives. "Cordus owned a bed that was too short for little Procula" (who was apparently a dwarf, 203). An old bookcase contained his tiny Greek texts (206); illiterate mice gnawed on the divine poetry of Greece (207):[29] *et divina opici rodebant carmina mures*. With this witty hexameter, shaped as a Golden Line, Juvenal concludes his detailed list of Cordus belongings. The mice and poetry, illiteracy and divinity, all linked by the pungent verb, establish the clever paradox, which contains both pathos and humor. While Cordus loses his precious diminutive library, Asturicus will be gaining one, expensive tomes plus bookshelves and ornamental busts. Umbricius then epitomizes Cordus' condition with a witty sequence on the word *nil* / *nihil*. Nothing was what Cordus really owned, and yet he lost all that nothing: the key word begins and ends the sentence (208–209). To make sure we react here in a way different from Martial's audience, Juvenal adds the adjective *infelix* and makes Cordus "poor, pathetic." He does what Vergil and Ovid frequently did to direct sympathy. Martial uses *infelix* to characterize people who *cause* unhappiness, not suffer it. Thus, in the Epigrams, only an ungenerous patron, an unfaithful wife, and a lion that has killed two children can be called *infelix*.[30]

After reworking Martial's epigram on arson, Umbricius returns nastily to "you" and starts: "If you can tear yourself away from the Circus" (*si potes avelli circensibus* 223), then goes on to offer "you" a pleasant home in a country town. The implication here, as on the other occasions when Juvenal uses this common motif, is that most Romans let themselves be lulled by the exciting spectacles of the Circus and Colosseum into quiescence about the indignities they were suffering.[31] Umbricius' attitude suggests a man of moral integrity: we find it exhibited by Cicero earlier and near Juvenal's time by Pliny.[32] Martial, on the other hand, wrote epigrams expressing in witty terms

29 Mason comments on this passage, p. 130.
30 See Martial 2.46.9, 2.75.7, and 11.7.7.
31 Juvenal alludes to the same point in 6.87, 10.81, and 11.53 and 197.
32 See Cicero *Ad fam.* 7.1 and Pliny *Epist.* 9.6.

marvel and delight with the shows in the Colosseum. Umbricius resorts to wit to give a prejudiced picture of the garret "you" rent in Rome: *tenebras conducis* (225). Martial, as commentators note, describes an ill-lit public bath in terms of *tenebrae*, without, however, aiming at or achieving this typical Juvenalian pathos.[33] In the country, "you" can raise vegetables in your little garden, an idyllic scene which Umbricius punctuates wittily with a relative clause neatly worked into a complete hexameter: *unde epulum possis centum dare Pythagoreis* (229). Again, we are dealing with a joke that does not belong to Martial's repertoire and is not employed in Martial's manner. Juvenal also attaches pathos to the same joke in 15.173. Horace and Ovid handle differently the familiar jibe at the Pythagoreans and their foolish beans.[34] Finally, Umbricius brings the paragraph to a close on the hyperbolical note of "becoming master of a lone lizard" (321). Commentators cite analogues in both Martial and Pliny for this figure of speech, but I dare say that a formula existed, learned in school, for this kind of expression.[35] What counts here is not the verbal parallel, but the special thematic way in which Juvenal uses the figure to support Umbricius' jaundiced view of Rome as a place where one securely owns nothing so long as one is afflicted with *paupertas*.[36]

We may now pause to draw some conclusions about how Juvenal uses wit in this section of Satire 3, before extending our analysis to other passages.

1. Juvenal obviously knew Martial's epigrams well, prized their wit and used it.

2. Juvenal also drew his wit from many other sources in his extensive literary tradition, not only from witty writers of earlier times such as Horace and Ovid, but also dead-serious epic poets like Vergil.

3. Wit saturates this passage: every two or three lines exhibit an example.

[33] Martial 2.14.12.

[34] Cf. Horace *S.* 2.6.63 and Ovid *Met.* 15.75ff.

[35] The formula would be something like this: a noun or verb expressing ownership would be combined with an objective genitive or accusative object, which would define the thing owned in a phrase consisting of *unus* and a noun in the diminutive or itself denoting something tiny and insignificant (e.g., *unius lacertae*).

[36] Note the way *vilicus* in 228 acquires entirely different connotations from those in 195.

4. Juvenal uses a number of methods to introduce wit: (a) he brings a development to a neat close in a single hexameter, often in the form of a relative clause (229) or some surprising descriptive detail (207, 222); (b) he punctuates with hyberbole (231) or paradox (196); (c) he focuses attention on a single word in metonymy (193, 225) or a single resonant name (199, 205, 219, 221); (d) he manipulates a telling word like *nil / nihil* (208–209).[37]

5. Not only does each instance of wit enliven its lines, but it also serves the thematic purpose of the larger context.

6. The versatility of Juvenal's wit in respect of sources and mechanism, together with its crucial thematic functions, gives it a tone very remote from Martial's: it is either utterly angry or a blend of anger and humor, but never the naughty, basically tolerant *lascivia* which Martial rightly assigned to his *nugae*.

It seems to me that these conclusions place us somewhere between the positions occupied by Mason and Highet. Mason, conducting a polemical argument, tried to answer those like Highet who stress Juvenal's truth and moral sincerity, so he emphasized the factor of wit and depicted Juvenal as "a supreme manipulator of the Latin language."[38] This manipulator, according to him, negates the business of truth and moral fervor. However, his view of Juvenal's artistry is so confined as to be half-damning, for Mason feels obliged to deny the satirist any systematic themes and to insist on opportunism as Juvenal's dominant poetic strategy. Such a conception may, I think, arise from overemphasis of Martial's relevance. Although Mason rightly points out the common use of wit by Juvenal and Martial and frequently of the same witty situations, it does not follow that, because Martial's brief epigrams cannot develop themes and must limit themselves to mere verbal manipulation, Juvenal's broader scope must be similarly confined and represented as Martial set "to a different tune."

It is important to establish the fact of the special tonal and thematic qualities of Juvenalian wit, in opposition to Mason, and I shall first take another passage from this same Satire 3, then look at other

---

[37] Aside from Mason, few scholars have appreciated Juvenal's wit and humor openly. But R. Marache, "Rhétorique et humour chez Juvénal," *Hommages à Jean Bayet* (Brussels 1964) 474–478, without knowing Mason's work, makes some sensible comments on such devices as hyperbole.

[38] P. 176.

Satires. We have seen what Juvenal did to Martial's slight arson joke in order to make it pulsate with indignation and sustain the theme of the poor native Roman victimized by a now-hostile Rome. Although the wit continued to act as a final point, it fitted the angry character and speech of Umbricius. Now let us look back to the beginning of Umbricius' tirade.

He rages first (21–57) because there is no place in Rome for the native honesty which conservative, rigidly moral Roman upbringing bred in him. He is always being pushed aside by men more willing to adapt to circumstances and stoop to unscrupulous actions. Such men, we might reasonably infer, are Italians. Then, however, Umbricius continues at greater length (58–125) by attacking the scoundrels who most flagrantly succeed in worming their way into the confidence of the rich: they are Greeks, Levantines, and other "sewage" from the East. Now, commentators often cite a short epigram of Martial in relation to these hundred lines of Juvenal. Like the arson joke, it can help us appreciate the special features of Juvenal's wit.

> vir bonus et pauper linguaque et pectore verus,
>   quid tibi vis urbem qui, Fabiane, petis?
> qui nec leno potes nec comissator haberi
>   nec pavidos tristi voce citare reos
> nec potes uxorem cari corrumpere amici
>   nec potes algentes arrigere ad vetulas,
> vendere nec vanos circa Palatia fumos
>   plaudere nec Cano plaudere nec Glaphyro:
> unde miser vives? "homo certus, fidus amicus . . . ."
>   hoc nihil est: numquam sic Philomelus eris.   (4.5)

Martial imagines himself meeting Fabianus, an Italian of the good old type (as the first line indicates) who is coming to Rome to live, and he expostulates with the newcomer. Martial is clearly not angry; he is wryly amused, sympathetic but cynical at the purpose of this incredibly naïve "nice guy." What Fabianus *cannot* do is far more important than the simple virtue he possesses; hence the long list (3–8). The point is made succinctly at the end: for all his Italian honesty, Fabianus is doomed to starve in Rome because he is not Greek. The name Philomelus connotes not only riches, but also the unscrupulous devices by which alone a poor man can achieve wealth in Rome, devices that come instinctively to Greeks, not honest Italians. By restricting his point to the bare name, however, Martial avoids anger or any deep feeling against Greeks, and he keeps our attention trained on Fabianus, a comic figure in his unrealistic expectations.

Although this epigram covers the general contents of Juvenal's hundred lines, it does not follow that Juvenal has merely elaborated Martial in his specially witty manner, opportunistically manipulating his language regardless of theme. Again, for example, he has drastically altered the dramatic situation, as he did with the arson joke. As Satire 3 opens, Juvenal encounters Umbricius at the Porta Capena on the edge of Rome, but Umbricius is leaving, not arriving. He is a native Roman, born on the Aventine and raised in Rome; he is not an enterprising Italian with stars in his eyes. Having lived some thirty-five to forty years in the city, increasingly unable to survive by natural honesty and equally unable to compromise his conservative Roman standards, Umbricius has desperately decided to abandon this hostile environment, with vague hopes of making a go of it in a lonely rural region south near Cumae. All we know about Fabianus is that he is not Roman, a good man riding the crest of vain hope before being plunged into the sobering, disappointing realities of Rome. Fabianus speaks only four words, which help to define his simple-mindedness but gain him no sympathy; whereas Juvenal quickly yields to Umbricius, who dominates the Satire with his angry speech denouncing the Rome which has forced him out of his very home. Thus, the basic theme assumes shape: Rome is no place for the genuine Roman (119), for it has expelled, virtually exiled him.[39] Compare the angry tone of Umbricius, apparently fully approved by the silent satirist, with the amused cynicism of Martial who, by himself dominating the epigram, keeps us coolly distant from such passions as might be generated by the situation. Remember, too, that Martial always keeps his audience aware that he himself speaks as neither Roman nor Italian, but as a Spanish visitor.

In line with our earlier conclusions, we find that Juvenal's verses are saturated with wit, employed to elaborate the pathos of Umbricius' defeat in Rome and to create strong animosity against his successful rivals, above all Greeks and Easterners. Thus, what Martial

[39] I have analyzed Satire 3 in terms of this theme in "Studies in Book I of Juvenal," *YCS* 15 (1957) 55–68. See now Motto and Clark, "The Mythos of Juvenal 3," *TAPA* 96 (1965) 267–276.

cleverly implied in a single name requires, because of Juvenal's important changes, nearly seventy lines.

Umbricius says that he leaves his native Rome to the unscrupulous entrepreneurs who profit from it. These people, who once eked out their existence as hired attendants at the arena, now have the ill-gotten wealth to stage gladiatorial shows there and give the verdict of death with public approval (*occidunt populariter* 37). Then, from the dignity of the arena they go home to contract for building public latrines! These are the kind of sports that Fortune exalts when it jests (40). Now what can Umbricius do in a Rome like that? He lists a series of evil acts he neither knows how to nor can perform (cf. Martial) and concludes sarcastically: I am spurned like a useless cripple (48). Hyperbole follows: who is a friend these days unless also an accomplice? After amplifying this charge, he moves with particularly sparkling wit against the Greeks.

We all remember Umbricius' exaggeration in calling Rome a Greek city (61), then angrily qualifying his statement with the assertion that the Syrian river Orontes has flown into the Tiber and swept along in its polluted waters a series of vicious types. His list (63–72) develops in a variety of witty impulses. To represent the ingenious adaptability of these intruders, he comes to a point with the incredible assertion: "Tell one to fly, and he will" (78). He protests against yielding priority to someone who came to Rome imported for sale like other Eastern products, plums and figs (83). These people are past masters in adulation, he continues (86). Although he might speak the same words, only a Greek would be believed (92). After all, Greeks are consummate actors. They play female parts so convincingly that— gratuitous obscenity—you would expect to find on examination that they have a woman's anatomy (96–97). They are a nation of actors (100). Then follows a list of adulatory acts, concluding with pointed vulgarity: Greeks can lavish praise for a belch or good aim in pissing (107). Umbricius continues with a list of household members who are subject to the Greeks' indiscriminate lust, and he saves for the end the most flagrant example: the aged grandmother who is laid (112). At this line, we reach a precise parallel with Martial's list (cf. line 6 of the cited epigram). Juvenal's obscenity makes a conclusive angry point, whereas Martial drops in his similar comment about old hags almost indifferently among a series of unordered acts, the last of which is the trivial one of applauding Greek musicians.

Picking out a few of the above examples of Juvenal's wit, Mason objects that the satirist "is out to make any point he can regardless of consistency."[40] But *are* these points indiscriminate and inconsistent? I do not think so. These hundred lines, dramatically shaped to produce quite different effects from the slight ones of Martial's epigram, give a consistent impression of continuous anger and of the personality of the angry speaker, and the techniques of wit—the choice sordid details, the hyperbole, the sweeping generalizations, the vivid rhetorical language—all fit the violent mood of this self-styled Roman and his outrageous view of un-Roman Rome.

The wit of Satire 3, then, functions differently from the characteristic wit of Martial: it is subordinated to the angry speech and indignant themes of the Satire; its jokes enhance individual lines without destroying the dominant thematic concerns of the larger context. The next problem is to determine how far these conclusions, valid for Satire 3, can be extended to other Satires. Mason seems not to recognize the difficulties involved in making generalizations about Juvenal's wit, for he applies his ideas equally to Satires 1, 3, 6, 9, 10, and 13. But just as there is a temporal gap between the audiences of Martial and those of Juvenal which might well presuppose a *change* in tastes, so at least twenty-five years separate Satires 1 or 3 and 13, and in those years we know from observation that Juvenal changed his methods, including those of wit.[41] The most obvious change occurs between Book II and Book III, as is indicated by the opening of Satire 7, large parts of Satire 8, and the entire cast of Satire 9. It is then methodologically unsound to equate the wit of the later Satires with that of Satires 1 through 6. Mason is particularly unsound because he *starts* his analysis of Juvenal's wit and initiates his argument for regarding Martial as the key to Juvenal's art by developing an admittedly brilliant, but misapplied, analysis of wit in Satire 9. Satire 9 indeed can be profitably likened to much of Martial. However, if we are treating Juvenal's wit with due consideration for his own development as a poet, we should be able to appreciate the differences between the manner of Satire 9 and that of the earlier Satires, and, if we do start with Satire 9 as akin to Martial, the soundest move to make next would be to consider the early poem on a similar subject: Satire 2. Then we would encounter, not Martial's

40 P. 128.
41 See my article, "The Programs of Juvenal's Later Books," *CP* 57 (1962) 145–160.

383

wit, but the indignant, thematically relevant wit that, on the basis of our analysis of Satire 3, we should expect of Juvenal in Book I.

Satire 9 deals with a type familiar in Martial, and it gives him a name that occurs five times in Martial. We are introduced to one of those interesting "professionals" who hires himself out as both adulterer and satisfier of male homosexual desires. Naevolus' current employer requires his ambidextrous services for himself and for his wife.[42] To open the Satire, Juvenal uses a method reminiscent of Martial. Having bumped into Naevolus on the street (*occurras* 2), the satirist solicitously asks what is wrong, why Naevolus looks so badly. For about 25 lines he elaborates with seeming concern on his "friend's" condition, and only after this clever build-up does he surprise us by revealing the source of Naevolus' income: he is notorious throughout Rome as both *moechus* and *cinaedus*. This is precisely the tone of affected concern punctured by cynical realism that we met in the Tongilianus epigram and that can be found in numerous poems of Martial. Juvenal maintains that same tone of nonreproving realism to the end of the Satire, letting Naevolus dominate the conversation and voice his complaint in detail. I hardly need to note that Naevolus bears little resemblance to Umbricius of Satire 3, and the satirist's mockery in Satire 9 differs radically from his sympathy in the earlier Satire. But it is interesting and important to recognize that in Book I Juvenal does not touch such a versatile character as the *moechus-cinaedus*, ideal for a Martial-like display of wit as it would be. When he encounters an adulterer or a homosexual in Book I, he exchanges no words of solicitous concern with them; the mere sight of them and the awareness of what they are sends him into paroxysms of rage. This is clear from Satire 1 where, claiming that what justifies his indignant satire is the variety of depraved people he meets in his beloved Rome, he cites as illustration the professional gigolo who ministers to the lust of rich hags (39ff), the husband who connives like a pander with the adulterer of his wife (55), the man who seduces his own daughter-in-law (77), and the adolescent who sets out on his affairs sporting his juvenile robe (*praetextatus adulter* 78), already corrupted.

Adultery is among the vices that stimulate indignation in Satire 1. Although Juvenal's vignettes are phrased cleverly and memo-

---

[42] For similarly competent *cinaedi / adulteri*, see in Martial 10.40 and the jokes in 6.33, 11.45, 86, and 88 on the *paedico* who turns *fututor*.

rably, it is plain that he is not joking, like Martial, about the gigolo, husband-abetted adulterer, father-in-law, or juvenile adulterer. He leaves to Satire 6 more elaborate and lurid scenes that feature the adulteress, but his mood of indignation is essentially the same.[43] In Satire 2, he vents his rage on homosexuals without clouding the issue or attenuating the picture of corruption by amusingly combining *cinaedus* with *moechus*. Again, he expects us to picture him meeting people on the street, not conversing with them but erupting in anger as he realizes what they represent for Rome. "What Roman street," he asks, "is not crowded with perverts masquerading as strict moralists?" (*quis enim non vicus abundat tristibus obscenis?* 2.8–9). Even worse, as he strolls through the Forum and other public places, he must listen to these people orating piously against female adultery; for these are not just average perverts: they come from distinguished families and so exercise influence in Roman politics as Senators and Censors (29ff). Juvenal attacks them in two phases in Satire 2. First, he roars at the cryptohomosexuals who pose as Puritans; then, having stripped off their disguise, he pours his wrath on various homosexual acts which presumably are practised in secret by these same people, members of the "gay set" in Rome.

Martial treats these topics, as we would expect, with clever good humor. A favorite homosexual-joke in Rome exploited the unmistakable meaning of the verb *nubere*: to put on the marriage veil for another, that is, to marry. It must properly describe the act of a woman, a bride. Martial uses this topos in two epigrams published more than ten years apart, in each case to play with a situation that Juvenal in Satire 2 presents as outrageous. The first provides a useful contrast to the opening of the Satire:

> aspicis incomptis illum, Deciane, capillis,
>   cuius et ipse times triste supercilium,
> qui loquitur Curios adsertoresque Camillos?
>   nolito fronti credere: nupsit heri.   (1.24)

Martial points out to a companion a shaggy, severe-looking moralist who is apparently orating, denouncing contemporary corruption and citing the great virtuous Roman examples of the early Republic. The

---

43 On Satire 6, see Mason pp. 135ff and my article "Juvenal 6: a Problem in Structure," *CP* 51 (1956) 73–94.

three lines of build-up are then suddenly broken by the surprise of 4:
the "moralist" was married yesterday, to another man! Our amusement
is not disturbed by complicated feelings about the pervert, for Martial
has not identified his class.

Now compare the opening of Satire 2:

> ultra Sauromatas fugere hinc libet et glacialem
> Oceanum, quotiens aliquid de moribus audent
> qui Curios simulant et Bacchanalia vivunt . . .
> frontis nulla fides; quis enim non vicus abundat
> tristibus obscenis? castigas turpia, cum sis
> inter Socraticos notissima fossa cinaedos?   (1–3, 8–10)

Juvenal is indignant from the first line, ready to leave
Rome in disgust for the remotest spot beyond the limits of the Roman
Empire, and he makes no witty surprise of his reason. Line 3 is memorable and frequently cited, but it is significantly different from Martial's
line 3 and elicits a quite different response from the audience. Martial
has a "moralist" talking of two virtuous old patriotic types, and this
line forms part of his deceptive build-up to the surprise of line 4.
Juvenal epitomizes in his two phrases, each occupying half the line,
the outrageous paradox that provokes his indignation: people are
pretending to be virtuous according to ancient Curio, but in fact living
perversely. The same paradox is repeated neatly in *tristibus obscenis* and
Socraticos cinaedos. Juvenal brands the pretense from the start, and he
indicates, by the phrase about posing as a Curio, as well as by subsequent details, that he is dealing exclusively with the Roman upper classes,
whose perversion gravely affects the whole character of Rome.[44]

Martial's second epigram starts from the surprise use of
nupsit, develops the scene of marriage, then proceeds to an unexpected
final question.

> barbatus rigido nupsit Callistratus Afro
>   hac qua lege viro nubere virgo solet.
> praeluxere faces, velarunt flammea vultus,
>   nec tua defuerunt verba, Talasse, tibi.

---

[44] By contrast, Naevolus, about whom he expresses tolerant amusement in
Satire 9, is, like Martial's characters, no member of the aristocratic governing class. Juvenal
calls him *vernam equitam* at 9.10.

dos etiam dicta est. nondum tibi, Roma, videtur
hoc satis? expectas numquid ut et pariat?   (12.42)

Martial constructs his first line brilliantly: the pair of initial adjectives,
which imply that we have to do with a bearded moralist[45] and a stern
Catonian personality, are startlingly related by the verb, upon which
follow the pair of identifying names. Callistratus, who has grown a
beard so as to masquerade as a Cynic, has married Afer, a man as
seemingly stern as the proverbial *rigidi Catones* of Martial 10.19.21. It
has been a Roman ceremony, even though Callistratus has hardly been
the usual *virgo*. So Martial apostrophizes Rome and asks her what she
is waiting for, for Callistratus to have a baby? There is, I believe, some
impatience behind the question, but the incredible hyperbole manipulated into the final word shows that Martial's emphasis is, as usual, on
the joke. Callistratus appears a few epigrams earlier, also as a pervert,
upon whom Martial comments with his typical cool amusement, without
the slightest impatience.[46] Furthermore, in choosing a Greek name for
Callistratus, Martial has weakened the force of the appeal to Rome:
she is not being asked to punish one of her degenerate children, but to
drive out a foreigner who is polluting the scene. Afer, who has a Roman
name, receives little emphasis, and furthermore he plays the less
disgraceful role in this marriage.

    Juvenal breaks the elements of this epigram of Martial
into two dramatic sequences involving "marriages" between males
(2.117–142).[47] In the first (117–132), he gives a detailed description of
the marriage-ceremony, then angrily apostrophizes Mars without using
the special joke of Martial; in the second (132–142), he first listens to
someone else eagerly represent the occasion as one of the "society
weddings" of the season, then angrily denounces such corruption,
consoling himself with the thought that at least children cannot be

[45] Beards were worn in Martial's time only as a protest and indicated adherence to a Cynic-Stoic form of life. Only with Hadrian did ordinary men begin to allow
their beards to grow.

[46] See 12.35. In that poem, Martial assigns no beard to Callistratus because
his joke aims at a different point. A man of the same name appears also in 5.13, 9.95, and
12.80. Martial also makes frequent use of the name of Afer: see 4.37 and 78, 6.77, 9.7 and 25,
10.84.

[47] J. Colin, "Juvénal et le mariage mystique de Gracchus," *Atti Tor* 90,
(1955–1956) 114–216, claims that this marriage was a solemn act of ritual and that Juvenal,
misunderstanding it, twisted it into an obscene orgy. However, the common evidence of
Juvenal, Martial and Tacitus on such "marriages" gives no support to his hypothesis.

born from such unnatural unions. Juvenal's point is totally different from Martial's and entirely consistent with his stance in Satires 1 and 3 as an indignant Roman: Rome has become unmanned, and its once-heroic families now produce effeminates. The "bride" in 117ff is now not a Greek Callistratus but a Roman Gracchus, scion of one of Rome's most distinguished families. The groom, a nameless trumpeter, prob-ably a Greek or Easterner, further establishes the disgraceful qualities of this "marriage." And it is not by chance that Juvenal apostrophizes Mars. As he constructs the scene, the bridal attire of Gracchus forms a sharp antithesis to the military setting of the ceremonies in honor of Mars in which he participated as a Salian priest (124–126). So how can Mars ignore the disgrace? In disgust, he tells Mars to quit his own Campus Martius, for, if he permits this marriage, then he is no longer the warlike Roman Mars.

The second marriage involves no names, but every indica-tion suggests that the "bride" again is a "man of distinction." The first three lines (132–135) are organized as a rapid conversation which conceals its point until the end, and we might well see in them some of the successful touches of Martial.

> 'officium cras
> primo sole mihi peragendum in valle Quirini.'
> quae causa officii? 'quid quaeris? nubit amicus
> nec multos adhibet.' (132–135)

Somebody starts talking to Juvenal about the important *officium* which he just *must* perform the very first thing in the morning. It sounds important, cast as it is in the traditional Roman terms of public responsibility. So Juvenal inquires about the *officium*. The social butterfly replies without the slightest shame that he has been invited to an exclu-sive wedding where a male friend will be the "bride." That ends the Martial-like sequence. Note the difference, however: the shocking point is placed in the mouth of a despicable member of the "gay set"; it is not the amused observation of the satirist. As a result, Juvenal is free to comment, and the remainder of the passage consists of savage denunciation, in typical Juvenalian manner, of this perversion that threatens Rome itself. Instead of producing the incredible fantasy of Martial to end his scene, he consoles himself with the thought that at least these vile marriages can produce no offspring, no matter how much a Gracchus wishes to hold his/her "husband." Thus, Satire 2 establishes the typical tactics of Juvenal's angry wit, whereas Satire 9 (which Mason wrongly employed to define the standard of Juvenalian wit) reflects a later stage in Juvenal's development, when he was moderating his indignant manner and experimenting with the cynical humor of Martial.

Up to this point, my effort has been to answer Mason by describing the angry wit of Juvenal's poetry and showing its thematic function in the early Satires. We are to accept the statement of the satirist in Satire 1 that he is indignant; we should be able to feel the same indignation coursing through Satire 2; and Umbricius substitutes for the indignant satirist in Satire 3.[48] The indignation determines the immediate effect of the wit; hence, it cannot possibly resemble the wit which Martial uses to support his *lascivia*. However, despite the consistency of Juvenal's angry wit, the response of the audience is neither indignation nor anger. At this point, then, I wish to turn to Juvenal's audience, that of his time and of our time, in order to explain how the consistently manifested Juvenalian *ira*, his famous *saeva indignatio*, achieved its ultimately pleasurable effect. I shall continue to use Satire 3 as my touchstone, because that is the masterpiece of Book I and because Mason has provided us a hypothesis concerning its ultimate impression that fits his view of Juvenal's wit, but, I believe, does not adequately account for the different sensitivities of Martial's and Juvenal's audiences.

Mason makes the following suggestions with regard to Satire 3: "I am inclined to suspect and certainly hope that there is a special point in the external structure and the general tone: that, in a word, Umbricius is not Martial, but Juvenal himself recalling in verse the recitations he had so often delivered in prose and laughing both at himself in that rôle and at the attempt by contemporary writers of solemn hexameters to take themselves seriously. The poem in that case would be a genuine and witty drama and a piece of literary not social criticism."[49] Mason has earlier argued for the similarity between Umbricius (or Juvenal) and Martial; I have been arguing against that interpretation. Now, he attempts to give Juvenal some special credit by

[48] On Satire 5, see n. 8, supra. Martial jokes about a poor man's loss of liberty as he cadges a meal; Juvenal uses the same situation to wax furious because of the Roman relevance.

[49] P. 135.

suspecting and hoping that Juvenal himself functions through Umbricius, that the satirist mocks the style of prose recitations and solemn hexameters through the words of his character Umbricius. If so, Satire 3 would become witty drama and literary, not social, criticism. The audience would presumably recognize the literary mockery and so sit back and enjoy this Martial-like figure Umbricius.

Although I agree that Satire 3 did strike Juvenal's audience and should strike us as a witty drama, I believe that the mechanism of this drama and the actual impression it left (and leaves) is quite different from what Mason assumes. If I am correct in denying the close resemblance between Martial and Umbricius, then most of the details of Mason's hypothesis collapse. I should prefer to start from the observed differences between Martial and Umbricius (or Juvenal in the other Satires of Book I), from the evident fact that Juvenal subordinates wit to his announced mood of *indignatio*. Umbricius in Satire 3 and the satirist himself in the other Satires of Book I loudly declare their outrage over the degradation of Rome. It is my contention that these loud declarations in the form of Satires constitute self-consistent dramas, whose mood of rage is realistic enough to be accepted at face value. However, there is little doubt in my mind that Juvenal did not share the extremist ideas of his dramatic characters, Umbricius in 3 and "the satirist" elsewhere, and there is no doubt whatsoever that the sophisticated Roman audience repeatedly smiled and applauded at this superb display of "honest indignation." As I see it, then, in the interaction between Satire 3 and the Roman audience occurs the "dramatic effect." That effect depends upon the different personal experience of audience and Umbricius and the different attitudes that audience and indignant speakers draw from their experience of Rome. It is quite unnecessary to assume, as Mason does, that every indignant speaker is parodying somebody else and consequently that the dramatic participation of the audience is the merely supine experience of recognizing Martial smirking inside Umbricius.[50]

What I have in mind is that Juvenal devised angry satire in order to exploit the long moralistic tradition of Roman culture and to utilize the possibilities for ambivalence in the rôle of the indignant moralist. This is much more than literary criticism, although we are

[50] I am here outlining a theory which I have developed at length in relation to conventional Roman views on anger in my monograph "Anger in Juvenal and Seneca," *Calif. Publ. Class Phil.* 19 (1964) 127–196.

compelled to document this moralistic tradition by citing literature like Cato, Sallust, speeches in Livy, Seneca, Pliny the Elder, and others. Juvenal was involving his Roman audience with attitudes that were fundamental to their inherited and acquired idea of Rome. But since traditionalistic morality and the fierce appeal to it did not expire with Alaric's capture of Rome, since angry extremism is a phenomenon of all human experience, we should not be too distrustful of any inclination to react to Juvenalian indignation in the complicated way we react today to a speech in real life or, better still, in a work of literature or drama that waxes indignant and extremist over social and political issues.[51] When we and others are indignant, we know, we are often capable of superb touches of wit, which we mean angrily. The sweeping generalization, cleverly vicious character assassination, brilliant use of metonymy or obscenity to color the picture, hyperbole of all sorts— these and many other devices have long been recognized as features of angry speech. What we may say so tellingly in honest indignation does not necessarily strike our audience in the same simple manner; cooler listeners may register our indignation, but refuse to share it. Having so refused, they are open to other impressions, separate or combined: sympathy for our excitement, amusement at our hot language, condemnation of us as immature, irrational, or otherwise inadequate.

When a writer sets out to create an angry character for a drama, he relies on the complex response which people have to anger. We are never at ease with our own or others' anger, and yet anger is a basic passion. Formal drama regularly works with angry types or characters who express wrath on a particular occasion. It may be rash to risk the statement, but I would hazard the generalization that no good dramatist, no good drama, presents anger as an unqualified virtue. King Lear is one of the most magnificently angry characters in all tragedy, an angry father seething at the ingratitude of his daughters. Yet Shakespeare does not minimize the fact that Lear's fury springs from his own unwisdom and its consequences; the first outrage against innocent Cordelia betrays that. On the other hand, the anger of fathers in comedy, based as it is also on a foolish view of the behavior of children, is regularly represented as hilariously funny. Shakespeare could make tragedy or comedy out of the irate husband who feels he has been

---

[51] Modern drama, especially on television, is beginning to develop angry types in the campus rebel, the Southern reactionary, and the nouveau-riche resident of the suburbs.

deceived.[52] The misanthrope can be presented for laughs or sober reflection. From the monumental wrath of Achilles, so magnificently staged for our sympathetic condemnation by Homer, to the various soldier types of Menander, Plautus, and Terence, the steps were not difficult for the dramatist. Anger lies at the disposal of the creative writer, ready to serve a comic or tragic view, and consequently any sophisticated audience would be prepared instinctively to respond intelligently, not with an identically sympathetic passion, to anger in drama or dramatic satire.

It is not necessary to dispute the facts alleged by Umbricius or the angry satirist. No doubt there was a case or two of arson committed by a man like Persicus; no doubt some Greeks were uncommonly successful in getting ahead in Rome; and Tacitus himself tells us that Nero was "married" to a male. What counts, however, is not the sporadic facts of moral degradation but the way an Umbricius reacts to them. When Juvenal recited Satire 3 to his first audience in Rome, it knew Umbricius' facts, but his indignation did not correspond to the attitude of sophisticated Romans to isolated episodes of vice. I imagine that, as Juvenal concluded, he smiled and bowed, was roundly applauded, and that, as the audience filed out to get a drink, conversation developed enthusiastically over this new literary sensation in Rome, not so much about the moral charges of Umbricius as about the interesting way Juvenal achieved so convincing a presentation of a moral extremist. How could comfortable men of distinction, politicians accustomed to inspect angry words closely, literary connoisseurs who were steeped in the dramatic traditions of anger, citizens of Rome in the relatively comfortable, uncontroversial reign of Trajan, how could they muster much sympathy or credulity for the extremist conclusions of Umbricius? Could anyone possibly imagine them deciding to abandon their wonderfully cosmopolitan and active Rome?

To fix even more clearly the Roman audience's reaction to Satire 3 by invoking our own reactions, let me attempt to modernize Satire 3 for the reader.[53] We are not dealing with an ancient analogue

---

[52] Such dramas as the opera *I Pagliacci* and the ballet *Petrouschka* show further subtlety in their treatment of the angry lover. They deal with a clown who plays a cuckold in his stage role; but when this clown finds himself deceived in his real love, he becomes murderously furious.

[53] I am assuming my reader here is someone who has considerable experience of literature, and hence has the ability to back away and criticize what he reads or hears. I set no limits as to political or social sympathies.

for our common flight to the suburbs, nor would we be able to redupli-
cate Umbricius with ease. Umbricius and his decision, after all, are
extremist.[54] He is a man of the lower middle class who clings to the
moribund Roman system of patronage and refuses to adapt to the new
methods of earning a living. Yet he is well educated and cultured, and
he voices the conservative creed of what today would be a family with
a tradition (and usually affluent). Today we have no genuine counterpart to the talented Greeks and Orientals who replace this incompetent
Roman. First, then, we must put together a modern Umbricius who is
a composite of some contemporary disaffected types. From our Conservative Backlash, we might select a belligerent white worker who angrily
resists expansion of the union shops to include Blacks who might take
his job; a scion-of an old Eastern or Southern family which is losing
its money because of inability to adjust to the times; and an inhabitant
of an arch-conservative suburb who proudly proclaims the ideals of the
John Birch Society. Now we have our modern Umbricius. The modern-
ized scene should be the waterfront of San Diego, California, or some
place comparable. Our "friend" is about to leave the United States
forever. After he has denounced America with his raging half-truths,
hyperbole, and blind prejudice, he will climb aboard a 50-foot sailboat,
in which he has stowed his belongings, raise sail and set out heroically for
an uninhabited island in the South Pacific! I hardly need to define
our reactions to such extravagant behavior.

To conclude, wit is a vital element of Juvenalian satire,
but it stands in a different relation to Juvenal's purposes than wit does
to Martial's goals. In Martial, wit and *lascivia* operate in full agreement
with each other; the verbal manipulation and the manner that Martial
repeatedly professes have identical effects. The audience performs no
complicated process when it hears or reads the Epigrams, for Martial
does quite brilliantly exactly what he says he does.[55] Mason assumes
that the wit of Juvenalian satire constantly undermines the announced
mood of the speaker, who is quite apparently laughing at himself and
literary seriousness; that would mean that individual passages in the
Satires would operate generally in the manner of separate epigrams of

---

[54] Cf. Molière's Oronte, whose misanthropy and final decision to abandon
Paris for rustic solitude undoubtedly seemed more extremist and were easier for Molière,
who took the part, to play for laughs in the late seventeenth century than they are today in
modern revivals.

[55] I do not mean that Martial himself was so limited a character in his real
life. But his Epigrams are fully consistent with their claim of *lascivia*.

Martial, the sudden final surprise dispelling an initially affected serious-ness. His argument, however, as I have attempted to show, over-simpli-fies and hence falsifies the art of Juvenal. It tends to imply that wit is supreme in the Satires, that indignation is secondary, in fact, meretri-cious. If we read carefully the early Satires, the only ones which in fact proclaim *indignatio* or *ira* as their mood, and if we study the wit in context for its thematic and dramatic relevance, we discover that wit and anger operate, at the primary level, in full agreement with each other. That is, they produce a dramatically credible impression of a violently angry man who cannot distinguish between facts and his own extravagant reactions to them. However, this same angry wit functions at a second level with the audience, which can and must draw the distinctions that are not made in the Satires. Whereas Martial inclines us to like his witty picture of Rome, Juvenal inclines us by his extrava-gance to reject the distorted interpretation of what he claims is the real Rome. We enjoy the angry Satires, accordingly, by opposition to their wild anger; we treat Umbricius and the satirist who rage in the early Satires as dramatic characters whose indignation is part of the drama, not a requisite part of our response to the facts.

The contrast between the wit of Martial and Juvenal can be epitomized in their treatments of Rome's moralistic tradition. In the introduction to Book I of the Epigrams, Martial assumes an attitude that he maintains throughout Book XII. His poems are *ioci*, written with *lascivia verborum*, designed for an audience that enjoys the lusty humor of the Floralia. Therefore, he forbids Cato to enter his "theatre" in his conventional moral rôle; he may enter only as a "spectator," that is, prepared to enjoy himself. The short poem that concludes this Preface repeats the same ideas: where *licentia* is the mood, *Cato severus* has no place. Book XI announces a similar program in two poems. It rejects the severe brow of Cato and proclaims the wild deeds of the Saturnalian mood (11.2); it also dismisses Cato's wife from its audience, because it intends to be naughtier than all other books (*nequior omnibus libellis* 11.15.4). Book X has another variation: stiff Cato will be allowed to read the epigrams only if he has drunk well (10.19.21). For the poems of Martial, then, morality is ostensibly irrelevant. By contrast, Juvenal's indignation insists that morality is crucially relevant. The satirist repeatedly appeals to the venerable moralistic tradition of Rome, laments that it has fallen into disuse, and himself voices the anger of one who is out of touch with his own times. But whereas he takes himself seriously and denounces Roman vice with honest passion, the audience judges him to be a largely comic figure, full of irrelevancy. He is, in a sense, a Cato born 250 years too late. Thinking that his wit expresses the extreme extent of vice, he in fact rather exposes his own ridiculous extremism.[56] Nevertheless, correcting or laughing *at* moral extremism is not totally negating morality. Whereas Martial allows us to reject Cato and relax in witty amorality, laughing *with* him, Juvenal obliges us to achieve our amusement by adjusting to our moral awareness the extravagance of his Catonian speaker. The more complex operation of Juvenal's wit demands a more complex, less passive response from us in the audience.

[56] Laronia mockingly sneers at a hypocrite moralist in 2.40: *tertius e caelo cecidit Cato*. That alliterative irony could well be applied to the honest but extravagant moralist, too: he is something incredible, "out of this world."

Juvenal and Quintilian

IT HAS ALWAYS BEEN a tantalizing pursuit to attempt to establish relations between individual ancient writers, especially because so many of the connections ultimately depend upon conjecture. In some cases, a writer will facilitate the task by at least mentioning a contemporary or close predecessor; although even here a brief allusion may lead to divergent interpretations. When Horace refers to Catullus, he does so in such a way that commentators disagree as to his precise opinion of the poet. In other cases, a writer will borrow liberally from a predecessor and thereby reveal his high estimate of his source. So Vergil draws on Ennius and Lucretius, so Persius produces variations on Horatian phrases. But sometimes we are concerned not so much with the influence of one poet upon another as with the effect which a teacher of philosophy or rhetoric had upon a student who ultimately became a poet or prose writer. In this respect one thinks of Lucretius and Philodemus, two important Epicureans living in Italy at the same time, both familiar to Cicero, both inclined to literary endeavors. Yet how would one establish the likelihood that Philodemus exercised influence upon the poet, lacking necessary data? Another pair, this time rhetorical writers, exist a century and a half later: one, Quintilian, a highly successful lawyer, a teacher of rhetoric publicly maintained by the Flavians and finally promoted to consular rank for his services, the compiler of the most readable treatise on rhetorical education; the other, Juvenal, at this time a young man about to embark upon his career, the man who became the great rhetorical satirist. In this paper I shall consider the various strands of evidence which may be brought together to link the two and so explain more clearly the nature of Juvenalian satire.

1. Biographical Details

Since Quintilian was about thirty years older than Juvenal and had already attained prominence in Rome by the time that Juvenal began his education, since the satirist writes with a rhetorical flair, and since he refers to Quintilian by name, it is not impossible that the rhetorician influenced the rhetorical poet as his teacher, his particular *rhetor*. The evidence, entirely circumstantial, has never received a clear scholarly verdict, and some have argued that, far from revering Quintilian as a beloved teacher, Juvenal disliked the man as too successful and exhibits nothing in his work that he could not have learned from any rhetor. In this first section, I shall review the evidence and try to reach a tenable conclusion concerning the personal relation of Quintilian and Juvenal; in the second section, I shall discuss Quintilian not as the teacher of Juvenal, but in a more general sense, as a typical rhetorician whose writings can shed light on the concept of rhetorical satire.

Friedländer, in a passing comment, suggested that Quintilian had taught Juvenal.[1] Kappelmacher then investigated the possibility rigorously and concluded that Juvenal probably, though not certainly, had studied under the rhetorician.[2] Neither of his reviewers, Hosius and Helm, felt compelled by his arguments;[3] Schwabe and Vollmer, in their articles in Pauly–Wissowa, respectively on Quintilian and Juvenal, judged the question to be still undecided;[4] and the most recent studies of Highet and Serafini do not accept Kappel-

1. L. Friedländer, *D. Junii Juvenalis saturarum libri V mit erklären-den Anmerkungen* (Leipzig, 1895), Vol. 1, p. 16.
2. A. Kappelmacher, *Studia Juvenaliana*, Dissertationes Philologicae Vindobonenses 7 (1903), 159–99.
3. C. Hosius in *BPW*, 23 (1903), 1579; and R. Helm in *WKP*, 20 (1903), 1281–5.
4. Schwabe on Quintilian (1909); Vollmer on Juvenal (1919).

macher's thesis as proved.[5] A basic point of disagreement exists in the four references to Quintilian in the Satires and their potential significance. Twice in Satire 6, written perhaps fifteen years after Quintilian's death, and twice in Satire 7, written it seems after the accession of Hadrian,[6] the satirist introduces the rhetorician's name in a way that merits closer study.

The subject of Satire 6, the perversion of Roman women, would not seem to provide a context naturally appropriate to the name of Quintilian. The *Institutio Oratoria* insists upon the high moral standards of the *orator,* and Quintilian, in the role of *praeceptor,* expressly condemns sexual corruption of any sort in the education and manner of the ideal speaker. Juvenal first mentions the celebrated rhetorician as he reviews the abnormal passions aroused in women by various types of actors (6.60 ff.). In the whole theater, he insists, not one female deserves to be trusted as a wife.

> solvitur his magno comoedi fibula, sunt quae
> Chrysogonum cantare vetent, Hispulla tragoedo
> gaudet: an expectas ut Quintilianus ametur?   (73–5)

Obviously, the remark has little point unless Juvenal is making a striking contrast. For his purposes, Quintilian must possess associations that conflict sharply with those of Chrysogonus and the nameless tragic actor. Since the satirist has developed a composite picture of actors as sensuously corrupt Greeks who allow infatuated females to buy their favors, Quintilian should represent strict Roman masculine probity.

5. G. Highet, *Juvenal the Satirist: a Study* (Oxford, 1954), p. 238, note 22; A. Serafini *Studio sulla satira di Giovenale* (Florence, 1957), p. 366, note 59. Cf. the discussion in I. Scott Ryberg, *The Grand Style in the Satires of Juvenal,* Smith College Classical Studies, 8 (1927), 107 ff.

6. It is generally assumed that Quintilian died in the last years of Domitian's reign. Highet, p. 12, dates Satire 6 to 116; others prefer 110; Satire 7, on the basis of its apparent dedication to the new emperor, is usually placed shortly after 118 (cf. Highet, p. 14).

But of course, in asking his question, the satirist could also be exploiting an extreme type of unlovable man, so as to emphasize the extreme degeneracy of Roman women. Indeed, we know the rhetorician's moral principles from a treatise which he composed in the last years of his life, after he had retired from active pleading and public teaching and become, rather, a private tutor to Domitian's nephew. It would be proper, then, to add to the associations of his name the word "old" or "elderly." Now the contrast has changed character, for against the perverse seductions of the Greeks the satirist has posed the upright, retired old orator, a man who can neither perform publicly any more nor presumably offer sexual attractions. The sardonic quality of the allusion becomes even more powerful if we can accept the implications of a fact which Quintilian himself reveals about his own married life. In the preface to Book 6 he tells how he married a girl (although old enough to be her father) who gave birth to two sons before she was nineteen and died not long after. The marriage must have occurred in the early years of Domitian's reign, when Quintilian was about fifty, certainly not an impossible age, but most likely to provoke ironic remarks from contemporary Romans. After all, such a disparity in ages between husband and wife is a proverbial cause of adultery. Putting all these associations together, we have, in contrast to what Friedländer inferred,[7] a by no means flattering picture of an elderly Quintilian who was perhaps slightly ridiculous in his eagerness to be married. In other words, Juvenal asks in his typically hyperbolic manner: How can you expect a wife to ignore the attractions of the Greek actors when her husband is a retired old "performer," devoid of any power to interest her?

7. Friedländer's note on this passage shows that he interpreted all references to Quintilian as laudatory. But he was not unique. Cf. the note on 6.75 in A. J. Macleane, *Decii Junii Juvenalis et A. Persii Flacci satirae, with a Commentary* (London, 1857): "Juvenal had a great respect for Quintilian, who was his contemporary, and some say his master in rhetoric."

The second reference to Quintilian in Satire 6 exploits the associations of the rhetorician, but not so as to exclude those which we have adduced above. Nearing the middle of the Satire, Juvenal describes the wife in her totally shameless effrontery committing adultery and forcing the uxorious husband to accept it. When caught in the embrace of a slave or knight, the Roman matron calls upon Quintilian to contrive an effective argument of extenuation.

> Sed iacet in servi complexibus aut equitis: dic,
> dic aliquem sodes hic, Quintiliane, colorem!
> "haeremus; dic ipsa!"   (279–81)

We know both from Seneca Rhetor and Quintilian that *color* constituted a crucial element of legal cases and especially of *controversiae;* it amounted to twisting the evidence into a shape advantageous to one's position or to drawing slick deductions from a questionably employed general principle. So Quintilian, the expert on such devices, is called in by the wife to get her off. Unable to invent a satisfactory color in the face of such evidence, he throws up the case, telling the wife to argue it herself. And she does, inventing a color which would provoke the envy of many a declaimer and, for Juvenal's purpose, epitomizing the degeneracy of Roman wives. Again, the satirist has based his indignant point on the extreme contrast between the adulterous wife and Quintilian. Not merely the upright orator, the ideal *vir bonus,* Quintilian also represents the old husband, the rhetorician who could not defend his wife's infidelity, but whose uxorious devotion to her might well accept her color.

In Satire 7 Juvenal leaves behind the attack on Roman women and takes up a theme more directly relevant to our conventional concept of Quintilian as rhetorician. As he reviews the various occupations open to a man of good education but no means, the satirist comes to that of *rhetor* (150 ff.). It is his object throughout the Satire to force the conclusion that Rome affords no honest way of making a living, and he effectively shows that the rhetorician, while working under the most unpromising conditions, earns a pitiful salary and collects it with difficulty. A vigorous contrast suggests itself in a comparison of the sums spent on extravagant estates and those devoted to a son's education.

> quanticumque domus, veniet qui fercula docte
> componit, veniet qui pulmentaria condit.
> hos inter sumptus sestertia Quintiliano,
> ut multum, duo sufficient: res nulla minoris
> constabit patri quam filius.   (184–8)

In this case, Juvenal seems to cite Quintilian as a typical rhetorician, miserably paid despite his deserts. But before we can settle down with such an assumption, the satirist raises a question which leads to the exposure of Quintilian as the most atypical of rhetoricians.

>   "unde igitur tot
> Quintilianus habet saltus?" exempla novorum
> fatorum transi: felix et pulcer et acer,
> felix et sapiens et nobilis et generosus.
> [adpositam nigrae lunam subtexit alutae;]
> felix orator quoque maximus et iaculator,
> et si perfrixit, cantat bene.   (188–94)

Quintilian again represents a unique case, for, unlike other rhetoricians, he has no need of the miserable salaries which stingy parents dole out to their sons' instructors. He has achieved the miraculous success of winning Fortune's favor. For a man who is *felix,* everything goes well. As commentators observe, Juvenal plays on the Stoic paradox which, instead of *felix,* would read *sapiens:* nothing could be more opposed than the wise man and Fortune (cf. 10.365–6, 14.315–16). In referring to the foremost orator of the previous generation as *felix,* Juvenal inevitably implies criticism of his wisdom (understood in the Stoic sense) and obliges his readers to remember the source of Quintilian's prosperity. Quintilian was a state employee, possessing the coveted professorship of rhetoric throughout the Flavian regime; and, for Juvenal's purposes, most probably identified with the last and most hated of the three, Domitian. After all, he had acted as tutor to Domitian's nephews. Earning a handsome regular salary, Quintilian never experienced the privations of the average rhetorician; and Juvenal insinuates that part of such luck inhered precisely in his reputation as *orator maximus*. None of this serves to improve our opinion of the distinguished rhetorician.

Juvenal has not finished with Quintilian yet, but it might be well to introduce the corroborative evidence of Martial, generally assumed to be a close acquaintance of our satirist, at any rate a poet whose epigrams frequently take a satiric approach closely parallel to the ideas of Juvenal. I cite in full the epigram which he addressed to Quintilian in 92:

> Quintiliane, vagae moderator summe iuventae,
> gloria Romanae, Quintiliane, togae,
> vivere quod propero pauper nec inutilis annis,
> da veniam: properat vivere nemo satis.
> differat hoc patrios optat qui vincere census
> atriaque inmodicis artat imaginibus.
> me focus et nigros non indignantia fumos
> tecta iuvant et fons vivus et herba rudis.
> sit mihi verna satur, sit non doctissima coniunx,
> sit nox cum somno, sit sine lite dies. (2.90)

It is not clear whom Martial means by the indefinite *qui* (5), but, whether or not he makes a covert allusion to Quintilian's extravagant pretensions in his prosperity, he undoubtedly does establish a contrast between the highly successful professor of eloquence and himself, *pauper*. The goals which he defines as satisfying his needs, we can observe, closely parallel those implicit in the speech of Juvenal's ideal of Satire 3, Umbricius. As for what Martial says about *doctissima coniunx* (again similar to Juvenal's remarks in 6.445 ff.), we have no evidence to determine whether he refers to Quintilian's late wife. In any case, Quintilian's wealth constituted a commonplace, to which a Martial would contrast his modest means and which Juvenal would momentarily affect to overlook, only to expose in all its naked ignominy.

To return to Satire 7, Juvenal has one more remark to make before he lets Quintilian go, this time forever. The climax of the rhetorician's felicity was attained when, as an apparent reward for his good services as tutor of Domitian's nephews, he was honored with consular title.[8] Possessed of such a title, he became in all outward aspects the symbol of what Domitian could do to people, at least as Juvenal seems to interpret the situation; and we know well from Satire 4 what Juvenal could do with hangers-on of the emperor. The comments on luck and Quintilian continue in this sardonic vein:

> distat enim quae
> sidera te excipiant modo primos incipientem
> edere vagitus et adhuc a matre rubentem:
> si Fortuna volet, fies de rhetore consul;
> si volet haec eadem, fiet de consule rhetor. (194–8)

To summarize a man's career as the result of luck does not indicate a favorable opinion of his abilities. If we had doubts about the satirist's attitude toward Quintilian in Satire 6, they should no longer exist. He has gratuitously introduced the name of the rhetorician, in order to make patent the special favors enjoyed by the lucky man. Then Juvenal has proceeded to attribute everything about Quintilian to luck, in an invidious way that reduces even the consular rank to insignificance.

Just as Martial shared Juvenal's antagonism toward the wealth accumulated by Quintilian, so others seem to have made insinuations about his rapid advancement in the world.

---

8. The information that Quintilian gained consular rank comes from Ausonius, *Grat. Act.* 7.31, p. 23 Sch.

A letter of Pliny (*Ep.* 4.11) recounts the troubles of Valerius Licinianus who, after entering upon a promising career in Rome, fell under the disfavor of Domitian, was unjustly implicated in the case of a Vestal's adultery and forced into exile in Sicily, where he began to teach rhetoric as a means of living. Pliny's description of the reversal in Licinianus' career and of the disgraced man's bitter remarks bears close resemblance to the above lines of our satirist.

> praetorius hic modo inter eloquentissimos causarum actores habebatur; nunc eo decidit, ut exsul de senatore, rhetor de oratore fieret. itaque ipse in praefatione dixit dolenter et graviter: "quos tibi, fortuna, ludos facis! facis enim ex professoribus senatores, ex senatoribus professores."

Although Licinianus does not specify those who have advanced from professor to senator, Schwabe and Hanslik agree, I think correctly, that these remarks are directed at Quintilian.[9] While Licinianus suffered the hostility of the emperor and was reduced to the role of a humble rhetor in Sicily, he could not help sensing the irony of Fortune, who, debasing him, simultaneously advanced such people as Quintilian. The date of Licinianus' disgrace and that of Quintilian's attainment of consular rank are very close.

We may here conclude this portion of our inquiry, for the references to Quintilian in the two Satires of Juvenal have demonstrated effectively that Juvenal did not revere the rhetorician. He knew Quintilian well, but so well that he could employ him consistently, if my interpretation is correct, as the extreme type of rhetorician, the successful, affluent, and none too scrupulous one. To say this, however, implies nothing about the question whether Juvenal studied under Quintilian. But Friedländer assumed that Juvenal respected Quin-

9. Cf. Schwabe (note 4 above), and Hanslik, *RE,* art. "Valerius Licinianus" (1955).

tilian, on the basis of these four passages, and could move from there to the deduction that Juvenal did so because Quintilian had taught him. History abounds in examples of students who have honored their instructors and of students who have been impelled to react against their teachers, whether because the character of the master, when better known, offended them, or because the doctrine, when more fully understood, could not be accepted. Juvenal might conceivably have enjoyed the advantages of Quintilian as his rhetor, but logic forbids us to assume that familiarity with the more scandalous interpretations of a great man's career signifies any definite relation of master and pupil. We require more evidence.

It is of course possible to reason from the other side, namely that Quintilian knew Juvenal. If this were true, one might urge that the basis of such acquaintance, inasmuch as the rhetorician was too important to bother about unknowns, would rest on a prior relation of master to student. Fortunately, we do not have to resort to this dubious deduction, for nobody has succeeded in establishing the fact of Quintilian's references to, let alone acquaintance with, Juvenal. In reviewing the development of poetic satire (10.1.93 ff.) the rhetorician discusses the line of tradition extending from Lucilius through Horace and Persius down to his own day; and he adds that his own age boasts satirists who some day will be famous. From our perspective, it is tempting to treat this last remark as early recognition of the genius of Juvenal, for, after all, Juvenal did become the satirist of note within a short period. Herrmann starts from this passage and adds to it two other ambiguous comments of Quintilian, to conclude that Quintilian not only knew but praised Juvenal.[10] Now almost nothing is impossible, but Quintilian's putative attitude toward Juvenal plunges us into such a welter of conjecture and controversy that one should start with consider-

10. L. Herrmann, "Comment Quintilien a loué Juvénal," *Latomus,* 11 (1952), 451–3.

able skepticism. At the time when Quintilian was writing his celebrated *Institute,* Juvenal, according to one version of his biography, had departed for exile—one can choose between Britain and Egypt—because of a miserable lampoon directed against the actor Paris, a favorite of Domitian. We cannot automatically accept this particular exile, since another version banishes the satirist at eighty; nor can we be sure about the lampoon supposed to be embedded in Satire 7; nor can we really determine the type of exile, assuming it to have happened. However, if Juvenal had been exiled, Quintilian, in order to refer to him as clearly as Herrmann postulates, would have to be acquainted with the lampoon. To be sure, an attack on Paris which resulted in exile would constitute *libertas,* a basic quality of Roman satire; but a wide gap exists between political lampoons and Roman satire, even in the most brilliant representative of invective, Lucilius. One would have to suppose that Quintilian based his estimate on a sardonic set of verses of no great merit (which are also difficult to conceive of apart from their context in the much later Satire 7) or that he had read some of the early efforts of Juvenal (completely unknown, but perfectly conceivable) and recognized their promise. After that, one must imagine this tutor of Domitian's nephews, this adulator of Domitian, as the source of his inspiration (cf. Prol. 4), this highly paid rhetorician who owed his fortune to Vespasian, Titus, and now Domitian, as willing to risk the displeasure of the emperor by approving the genius and the personal attacks of the very man. whom Domitian had exiled, and in an ambiguous manner which would not deceive his Roman readers or his friend Juvenal, but would apparently escape the notice or at least the wrath of the emperor, who at this time was exhibiting frenzied suspicion of all his associates. Finally, we would have to regard Juvenal as a most ungrateful man. Satire 7 would contain an allusion to the satirist's exile and to Licinianus', and Juvenal would pointedly allude to the latter's sneer about Quintilian, feeling no compunction about attacking a dead man who had honored him so boldly. All this, it seems to me, amounts to a tissue of improbable conjecture. We do not know even whether Juvenal wrote much of anything under Domitian, or whether, as some biographies allege, he himself taught rhetoric, biding his time until the hated emperor had died. Quintilian may have known Juvenal; it is even remotely possible that he referred to Juvenal's immature satiric efforts in one place. Since, however, we cannot securely relate the two men directly by what they say of each other, we shall have to consider the possibility of connecting them through a third person, a mutual acquaintance.

One person whom Quintilian definitely knew as teacher and with whom Juvenal was certainly familiar as his own contemporary was Pliny the Younger. Sometime shortly before he died in the eruption of Vesuvius, Pliny the Elder entrusted his nephew to the celebrated rhetor to complete his education. Such reactions as we can detect in the letters of Pliny, written long after the event, do not give us a clear impression of Quintilian; but it is safe to conclude that Pliny enjoyed connecting his name with that of his master and deliberately related anecdotes that he had heard in the course of his instruction, in order to make his association with Quintilian more patent to his readers.[11] Although Pliny himself obviously hated Domitian, he never criticized his teacher for his role as imperial favorite; but this may be due more to Pliny's temperament than to his perception. Himself in comfortable circumstances and possessed of a great store of friendliness, Pliny did not often stoop to personal attacks. After all, Quintilian had not sunk to the level of those creatures of Domitian whom Pliny and his friends brought to justice after the tyrant's murder. One can detect the influence of the rhetorician in Pliny's style of speaking, which avoids the abuses of Seneca and re-

11. Pliny, *Epist.* 2.14.9, 6.6.3. Pliny did not entirely accept Quintilian's views on Seneca: cf. J. Niemirska–Pliszczynska, *De Elocutione Pliniana in Epistularum Libris Novem Conspicua Quaestiones Selectae* (Lublin, 1955), pp. 157 ff.

turns in part to Cicero; and of course Pliny's letters reflect the same high estimate of Cicero as pervades the *Institute*.

At the time when Pliny was studying under Quintilian, if Kappelmacher is correct, he would have had as schoolmate the young Juvenal. In the same Rome, though in different manners, the two would have commenced their careers. Both would have suffered under the literary and political repressions of Domitian, and both certainly breathed a sigh of relief when Nerva and then Trajan introduced a new era. Unfortunately, Pliny, who knew everybody else in Rome including Martial,[12] it seems, and who certainly shared some of the feelings, if with less intensity, exhibited by Juvenal, never refers to our satirist. And Pliny lived well into the period when the first book of the *Satires* was published. In Satire 1 Juvenal alludes to the notorious Marius Priscus, the corrupt governor whom Pliny prosecuted. In Satire 4 he sneers at the group of Domitian's courtiers and exposes the terroristic ways of the last Flavian, to a certain extent paralleling ideas in Pliny's *Panegyricus*. Considering the total silence of the otherwise loquacious Pliny, Mlle. Guillemin suggested an explanation in the possible existence of several different literary coteries in Rome, by which Pliny and Juvenal were decisively separated.[13] Whatever may be the reason, Pliny ignored Juvenal in his letters. Recently, Scivoletto has noted rhetorical themes common to the *Panegyricus* and Satires 4 and 8.[14] He does not go so far as to suggest that the common ground originates in the common influence of Quintilian; nor is such a hypothesis safe. While the two men may have

12. Pliny refers with regret to the death of Martial in *Epist.* 3.21, citing a poem (*Epig.* 10.20) which Martial dedicated to him. Martial therefore was familiar enough with both Pliny and Juvenal to address poems to them.

13. A.-M. Guillemin, *Pline et la vie littéraire de son temps* (Paris, 1929), p. 23.

14. N. Scivoletto, "Plinio il Giovane e Giovenale," *GIF*, 10 (1957), 133–46.

shared opinions about Domitian, they agree in little else; Juvenal continued to write indignant Satires twenty and more years after Domitian had died, but Pliny quickly relaxed in the relatively congenial atmosphere of Trajan's reign. Moreover, Satire 7 may provide us enough information to reveal how Juvenal felt toward Pliny, by now dead.

We have aleady considered Juvenal's sardonic references to Quintilian's consular rank and, as corroborative evidence, the remarks of Licinianus. It was Pliny who told the story of Licinianus, and yet he did not make any allusion to Quintilian. If Pliny were really attempting to save the reputation of his master and accordingly convert the specific epigram of Licinianus into a general one, Juvenal's lines would come as a distinct correction. Herrmann has also suggested an allusion to Pliny in the earlier lines about the rich man who spends all his money on his estate rather than on his son's teachers.[15] I am not convinced by his remarks, but I mention them as possibly relevant: he believes that the description of the rich estate parallels the one given by Pliny of his uncle's villa, that villa which Pliny himself inherited. Quintilian does criticize Pliny the Elder, not as a stingy man but as a rhetorical theorist.[16] If the allusion to Pliny's villa were conceded, Juvenal would be attacking the rich Plinys for neglecting the rhetoricians; then he would quickly shift his attack to their victim Quintilian, who after all was uniquely prosperous among rhetoricians through the tyrant's favor. In conclusion, Juvenal probably would not like Pliny for somewhat the same reasons that he sneered at Quintilian (whether or not he did make allusions to Pliny): he was too wealthy and able to enjoy life too easily. Since Pliny is the only definite pupil of Quintilian among the distinguished writers of the time, the radical difference in mood between the satirist and Pliny, their apparently different estimate of the rhetorician, and the total silence of the gossipy Pliny about a noted contemporary, if they prove

15. L. Herrmann, "Juvenaliana," *REA,* 43 (1940), 448 ff.
16. *Inst.* 11.3.143, 148.

409

anything, would imply that Juvenal and Pliny were not close, that Juvenal also lacked the advantages of the wealthy Pliny in enjoying the famous Quintilian's instruction.

Other noted writers of Juvenal's youth and early productive years, Statius, Silius Italicus, Tacitus, and the like lead us nowhere: none of them received training from Quintilian, Juvenal refers only to Statius by name,[17] and Quintilian mentions none of them. As a final resort, therefore, if we are to establish a clear relation of master and pupil between Quintilian and the satirist, we must consider whether Juvenal reflects the undoubted teachings of the rhetorician in his poetry. Kappelmacher used this method principally to support his argument, and accordingly it will be necessary to discuss the evidence which he adduced on its merits. In the first place, Kappelmacher argued that Juvenal and Quintilian differ from the general set of Roman rhetoricians in not indiscriminately disliking the Greeks. Helm has disputed this point, and, while we shall treat the matter under a different aspect later, it does seem proper to support Helm's criticisms. It is true, as Kappelmacher remarks, that Juvenal attacked the alien elements from the East rather than merely the Greeks, but the attack usually centered upon and derived its impetus from the prominent vices of the Greeks. Therefore, Juvenal, unlike Quintilian, did not avoid Greek words, especially those that were most disapproved by the rhetorician, which by their exotic sound emphasized their foreign quality.[18] One has only to examine the list in Kappelmacher of words rarely used in Latin before Juvenal or unique in the Satires to perceive the special character of his Hellenisms. Juvenal did not employ such striking vocabulary because he tolerated the Greeks or because he obeyed the rules set forth by his master Quintilian. As we shall see, the nature of Juvenal's satiric vision required a vocabulary radically different from that recommended and

17. In 7.83. Some have interpreted 2.102 as an allusion to Tacitus' work.
18. See below, pp. 54 ff.

employed by the lawyer. Whereas Quintilian more reasonably and dispassionately comments on the degeneration of his times, especially the sensuousness of eloquence, and blames his fellow Romans, Juvenal adopts one of the commonplaces perhaps first used by Cato the Elder, attributing Rome's moral decline directly to the conquered Greeks and their luxurious ways.[19] The satirist might have adopted his technique in reaction against Quintilian, although it is more likely that he understood the value of Hellenisms as used intermittently by his satiric predecessors; at any rate, any specific link in this respect between satirist and rhetorician quickly breaks down upon examination.

Kappelmacher then attempted deductions from the admitted familiarity with rhetoric shown by Juvenal. Juvenal uses a series of technical rhetorical terms, such as *color,* already commented on; in some cases, indeed, he seems to practice the rules set forth by Quintilian. To conclude, however, that such rules did not generally exist but were the unique invention of Quintilian, and that Juvenal must have heard them from Quintilian, fails to convince. In Seneca Rhetor many of the rules advocated by our rhetorician have long become standard. Kappelmacher also compares the satirist's analysis in Satire 7 of the plight of rhetoricians with scattered remarks of Quintilian. Again, little can justifiably be inferred from any supposed resemblance, especially because in that same section of the Satire, Juvenal so patently and ironically excepts Quintilian from the prevalent difficulties of his colleagues. As for the examples of famous men which Quintilian specifies in 12.2.30, Juvenal could just as well have heard the same thing from any rhetor—after all, such *exempla* were standard—or read it in some compendium like that of Valerius Maximus.[20]

19. Cf. Serafini, p. 375.
20. Cf. K. Alewell, *Über das rhetorische* παράδειγμα (diss., Leipzig, 1913), pp. 60 ff., 115 ff.; also, F. Gauger, *Zeitschilderung und Topik bei Juvenal* (diss., Griefswald, 1936), esp. pp. 46, 63, 71.

Juvenal and Quintilian mention some of the same people, notably Cicero. For Quintilian, of course, Cicero was the master who had paved the way, who in many cases could not be altered, and who was criticized only with great humility. For Juvenal, the respect attached less to the great orator and writer of rhetorical treatises than to the *novus homo,* the consul who crushed Catiline, and the senator who fearlessly braved Antony.[21] Some literary influence of Cicero on Juvenal is also demonstrable,[22] but this proves nothing about Quintilian and Juvenal. Others revered Cicero; others, like Tacitus (who cannot be connected with Quintilian either), show Ciceronian influence.[23] Juvenal and Quintilian refer to contemporary rhetoricians, too.[24] Both of them speak of Crispus' eloquence in terms of the adjective *iucundus.*[25] Juvenal goes on from that adjective and thus illustrates his difference from Quintilian, for the good humor of Crispus exposes by contrast the tyranny of Quintilian's patron, Domitian, who would let only an obsequious man like Crispus survive.[26] Again, no deduction is legitimate.

Finally, Kappelmacher reasoned that Juvenal derived his theories about satire and its tradition from Quintilian. Quintilian's review of Roman satire involves Lucilius, Horace, and Persius, the same three associated in the scholia usually attributed to Suetonius. Juvenal does not mention Persius, although he seems to have known his predecessor's work.[27] He

21. Cf. 8.235 ff., 10.114 ff.

22. Cf. H. F. Rebert, "The Literary Influence of Cicero on Juvenal," *TAPA,* 57 (1926), 181–94.

23. Cf. C. W. Mendell, *Tacitus* (New Haven, 1957), pp. 71 ff.

24. Cf. Kappelmacher, p. 188, who refers to Quintilian 5.13.48, 10.1.119, 12.10.11.

25. Cf. 4.81 ff.

26. We might note here the divergent tastes of Juvenal and Pliny with regard to the orator Isaeus, who appeared at Rome shortly after Quintilian's death. Juvenal associates him with the rest of the corrupt Greeks in 3.74; Pliny praises him highly in *Epist.* 2.3.

27. Cf. J. Van Wageningen, *Auli Persi Flacci Saturae* (Groningen, 1911), pp. lii ff.

refers to both Horace and Lucilius in his Program Satire, and some of his verses suggest the influence of earlier satirists. Quintilian modifies the Horatian criticism of Lucilius, and Juvenal clearly owes more to Lucilius than to Horace. On the other hand, contemporaries who have no known connection with Quintilian as pupils, Tacitus and Martial, refer to the current fashion for Lucilius or quote his work.[28] When Juvenal began to write satire, he needed no Quintilian to tell him about the canonic tradition. He would have to grapple directly with Lucilius and Horace and, to a lesser extent, with Persius to understand what potentialities satire possessed for his own abilities. I see no reason to believe that Quintilian alone recognized the satiric tradition in his time.

Enough has been said to show the nature of the evidence employed to associate Juvenal and Quintilian. Nothing can be argued from the references to the rhetorician by the satirist, for, if they possess any personal significance, they must be ironical, even sardonic. The context of Satire 6 implies the aged and pedantic nature of Quintilian and conceivably alludes to his ill-matched marriage. Satire 7 unmistakably brings out the extraordinary position of Quintilian, thanks to the patronage of the vicious Domitian, in a world where honest rhetoricians could not make a living. There are no definite references to Juvenal in Quintilian's *Institute,* and any attempt to connect the two by means of a common acquaintance, notably Pliny the Younger, fails. When Kappelmacher tried to demonstrate parallel elements in the practices of Juvenal and the teachings of Quintilian, he used inconclusive data. Whenever Juvenal does agree with the rhetorician—and in many cases he certainly does not—one could just as easily assume that another rhetor had provided the future satirist with the necessary instruction. Therefore, full examination of the relation between satirist and rhetorician cannot prove any as-

28. Tacitus mentions the current popularity of Lucilius in *Dial.* 23.2; Martial quotes a line from Lucilius' Book 22 in 11.90.4.

sociation between them. I see no reason to doubt that Juvenal had read Quintilian's *Institute*, but we must admit that nothing compels us to accept this as a fact. In any case, we certainly do not know whether Juvenal studied under the celebrated rhetorician.

2. JUVENAL'S SATIRE AND CONTEMPORARY RHETORIC

The length of this negative development has been designed to clear the ground so that once again we can return to Juvenal and Quintilian free from the biographical misconceptions which so easily becloud literary criticism. Near the end of his dissertation Kappelmacher indicated an approach to Quintilian which, differently adapted, can be fruitful.[29] He referred to *Inst.* 9.2.33, where the rhetorician recommends the vivid presentation of scenes, as though occurring before the audience's eyes, and compared the precept with the practice of Juvenal in Satire 1, where the satirist pretends to be standing on the street corner and reviewing the parade of degenerates passing before him. Kappelmacher used the resemblance, such as it is, to argue for his particular point. We have abandoned the possibility of proving that Quintilian taught Juvenal, but we can employ the resemblance also. Stress on vivid details, on direct participation in a scene or instantaneous reaction to it forms a basic element in the rhetorical manner of Juvenal. Whether or not he experienced all these horrors, the satirist obliges us to feel that he did; and that essentially is a rhetorical technique.[30] Quintilian can supply a great deal of information concerning the basic rhetorical theory of his age. Juvenal's Satires show how such theory has been adapted to a particular literary form and to the genius of a specific

29. Cf. Kappelmacher, p. 197.
30. This is a well-known technique, called *demonstratio* in *Ad Heren.* 4.55. For the Greek versions, cf. Caplan's note on this passage in his Loeb edition, p. 405; also Ryberg (note 5 above), p. 20.

414

poet. If we study the theory in connection with the practice, we can observe how the satirist set about his work and gave satire an entirely new direction in which to develop.[31]

A. De Inventione[32]

Nobody has ever successfully denied that Juvenal is rhetorical, but many have confused the implications of the term. All too often "rhetorical" has connoted artificial in the pejorative sense of the word. Much of De Decker's work betrays the prejudice that Juvenal's rhetorical or declamatory manner thwarts his poetic capacity, with the result that Juvenal is either declamatory or poetic, declamatory or honestly moral, never both at the same time.[33] The same tendency developed among Italian critics of the last generation under the influence of Croce. Most typical of this approach, Marmorale refused to rank our satirist as a poet because of rhetorical techniques and patent insincerity; instead, he invented the intermediate term "letterato" to epitomize the nonpoetic artistry that he perceived in Juvenal.[34] Highet has intermittently explained away the rhetoric in Juvenal by calling it profound emotion evident of the satirist's sincerity.[35] Recently, Serafini has examined the problem in two chapters on Juvenal as a

31. It will be observed that I owe much to the study of Mrs. Ryberg, both for its data and for its use of rhetorical theory as a means of defining the technique of our satirist. Where I differ from her, it will be seen, I place less emphasis on the Grand Style than on the rhetorical value of *indignatio* for satire. It seems to me that we must first grasp Juvenal's concept of satire before we can really understand why he resorted to the Grand Style—and he certainly employs that Grand Style intermittently at best. Longinus would have spurned Juvenal as any ideal.

32. A. Hartmann, *De Inventione Juvenalis* (diss., Basel, 1908), discusses entirely different aspects of inventio.

33. J. De Decker, *Juvenalis Declamans* (Ghent, 1913).

34. E. V. Marmorale, *Giovenale* (2d ed. Bari, 1950); cf. N. Salanitro, *Introduzione a Giovenale* (Naples, 1944).

35. Highet, pp. 97 ff., 172.

poet and as a rhetorical satirist. He, too, believes that Juvenal is poet and rhetorician, generally rhetorical but sometimes a poet when able to rise above rhetoric.[36] On the other hand, Serafini criticizes De Decker's prejudicial interpretation of the rhetorical elements of satire and attempts to show their positive effect.[37] Because, however, he instinctively accepts the premise that rhetoric undermines genuine moral opinions as well as poetic feeling, it is difficult to discover Serafini's criteria for positive rhetoric. To say anything new on the subject, therefore, one has to divest oneself of prejudices accumulated by years of Juvenalian scholarship, that rhetoric is false and bad, that exaggeration is immoral, that indignation is not a poetic emotion, and the like. It will help us, I suggest, to start with Quintilian, because we meet in his pages the firm conviction that rhetoric has unquestioned practical and moral value. It is a means by which a good man can ensure that good will prevail in the law courts especially, which he can also employ in summing up the character of a man and in discussing possible courses of action. As we begin, therefore, it will be well to propose a definition of rhetoric to which we shall attempt to adhere in the course of our inquiry: rhetoric, we may say, consists of the conscious use of techniques of speaking and writing so as to attain a specific end, usually considered a blend of pleasing and persuading the audience and of enhancing the otherwise unadorned speech. Depending on the ability of the speaker, rhetoric can be good or bad.

Definitions of rhetoric varied considerably in the ancient world. Cynics and unscrupulous realists emphasized the single purpose of persuasion regardless of moral factors, and Quintilian points out that the concept of rhetoric as *vis dicendo persuadendi* existed from the times of the Sophists—that is, from the earliest days of taught rhetoric.[38] Acting on the assumptions implicit in Socrates' and Plato's criticisms of the

36. Serafini, pp. 217 ff.
37. *Ibid.* pp. 229 ff., esp. note 1.
38. *Inst.* 2.15.10.

416

Sophists, the Stoics—Quintilian cites in particular Cleanthes and Chrysippus—devised a new definition in which the underlying moral purpose clearly emerges. Rhetoric would accordingly be *scientia recte dicendi,* or even better, *scientia bene dicendi.*[39] Quintilian strenuously argues for the moral definition, in this following the lead of Cicero.

> huic eius [i.e. rhetorices] substantiae maxime conveniet finitio, rhetoricen esse bene dicendi scientiam. nam et orationis omnes virtutes semel complectitur et protinus etiam mores oratoris, cum bene dicere non possit nisi bonus. (*Inst.* 2.15.34)

We do not need here to discuss the self-contradictions in the concept of rhetoric, for they emerge clearly enough in Quintilian's discussion.[40] Our concern is with this ethical definition and its extension, the requirement that an orator be *vir bonus.* In four words Cato the Elder summarized the ideal Roman view of the orator as *vir bonus dicendi peritus.*[41] As Quintilian develops his scheme of education, he assumes that his student has early acquired a firm moral background, both at home and with the *grammatici;* that, by the time the young man enters the classes of the rhetor, he is in fact *vir bonus.* The rhetor will devote his attention mostly to inculcating techniques of conveying the impression in speeches that, as *vir bonus,* one's word can be trusted.

39. *Ibid.* 2.15.38.

40. Quintilian finds himself facing the same dilemma forced on the Sophists by Socrates, and he honestly admits that the orator knows how to speak well, but does not know whether he speaks the truth (2.17.37). He also recognizes the moral problems that arise when the orator has to defend a guilty man (12.1.33). But he does not remove the inconsistency from his concept that the orator is *vir bonus.* M. L. Clarke, *Rhetoric at Rome* (London, 1953), p. 51, has criticized Cicero for similar inconsistency.

41. Quintilian cites this definition at 12.1.1, but from what he says in Pref. 1.9 it seems clear that he accepts Cato's definition from the beginning and works steadily toward it.

The ethical concept of rhetoric and of its product, the orator, runs throughout Quintilian's *Institute*. After the opening two books, in which the rhetorician treats the preliminary training of the young and the fundamental nature of the discipline which they will learn as rhetoric, he devotes five books to *Inventio,* the careful analysis and planning of typical speeches, mostly for the law courts; then he discusses the correlative problem of *Elocutio,* the stylistic technique by which the orator carries out his plans; and finally, in a last book, Quintilian produces a composite portrait of his perfect orator, starting from Cato's definition. Much of what is otherwise said *de inventione* does not affect our particular problem, inasmuch as it refers exclusively to legal issues. But arguing a case always involves more than merely presenting evidence for one's client. It is necessary to persuade the judges that one believes in one's case and that they should also, because it is right. To do so, the lawyer must to a certain extent assume a character,[42] not necessarily to deceive, but to make the most effective presentation of his points in view of the facts, the law, and the audience. At every stage of a trial, Quintilian teaches, the lawyer should react to the different circumstances and modulate his tone, organize his ideas with reference to appearing vir bonus. In short, planning out a case includes necessarily the conscious creation of a role appropriate to the legal context, designed to affect opinion about the facts.

Contemporary literary critics have observed a similar process of creation in biographical literature, especially poetry written in the first person or involving events allegedly experienced by the poet. A critical term, happily Latin, has arisen to denote the character assumed by a poet in a poem, as distinguished from the actual character of the poet in all

42. J. G. Cozzens' novel, *The Just and the Unjust* (New York, 1942), brings this fact out with typical irony: the district attorney loses a certain conviction on the charge of first degree murder, absolutely proved by the evidence, because he sternly refuses to descend to the emotional level of the defense attorney.

its complexity: I refer to *persona*.[43] Classical scholars have been less quick in accepting the term and its implications, particularly for Latin literature. But Roman elegy at least has found interpreters who exploit the concept of *persona*.[44] We now can recognize the fact that the passionate utterances of Propertius bear such conviction to a large extent because he so successfully created the impression of the tortured lover, not because he necessarily participated in all the experiences of which he writes. In a more obvious way and with a different artistic result, Ovid also assumes a character in his love poetry which we should not confuse with his own moral personality.[45] Satire, which is equally Roman and personal, has so far failed to share the benefits of this critical concept. We know that all Romans who engaged in literary pursuits, by the end of the second century B.C., studied rhetorical principles consistently in their formative years; but scholars have found it easier to grasp the elegist's use of a persona than they have the satirist's.

In his famous estimate of Lucilius (*Serm.* 2.1.30 ff.) Horace placed his stress on the total self-revelation of his predecessor. Whatever happened to him, whether good or bad, Lucilius is pictured as pouring it out in his writings, so that the reader gains as clear an impression of the satirist's life as though he were viewing a painting. This passage has become a commonplace by which critics still evaluate Lucilius. Unfortunately,

43. Cf. Maynard Mack, "The Muse of Satire," *Yale Review,* 41 (1951), 80–92, where he applies the concept to Pope. Others have perceived the value of the persona or mask in Swift: M. Price, *Swift's Rhetorical Art: a Study in Structure and Meaning* (New Haven, 1953), pp. 57 ff. (chapter on the mask of irony); also W. B. Ewald, *The Masks of Jonathan Swift* (Cambridge, 1954).

44. Cf. A. W. Allen, " 'Sincerity' and the Roman Elegist," *CP,* 45 (1950), 145–60. V. Pöschl, "Horaz und die Politik," *Sitzber. Heidelberg. Akad., Abh.* 4 (1956), 13, discusses the general use of the mask, "Spiel mit der Maske," in Horace's poetry.

45. Cf. R. M. Durling, "Ovid as Praeceptor Amoris," *CJ,* 53 (1957–58), 157–67.

we are not in a position to refute its implications absolutely. But if one thinks over the rhetorical influences operative in the Scipionic Circle, as carefully elaborated by Fiske,[46] and then considers the way in which Lucilius writes of his trip to Sicily, his sickness, his loves, or his political views, it becomes possible at least to modify the Horatian verdict. Lucilius did write of events in connection with himself, but, although he certainly lacked the restraint of Horace a century later, he did impose some limits on what he said, selecting anecdotes, subjects, details, even his very language, which would reveal an appealing character. It is ironic that he proved so successful that scholars have accepted the self-portrait (with the urging of Horace) as an exact three-dimensional photograph. When we proceed to Horace, we reach safer ground. As part of his irony, Horace continually poked fun at himself, hinting at qualities in himself which, if taken seriously, would convict him again and again of self-contradiction. When he discusses his satiric concepts or when he reports his troubles with the *garrulus* or, finally, when he permits his slaves to deliver diatribes against his morals, he allows traits of his to be impugned and forces us to reconcile the inconsistencies. Horace, therefore, creates a persona which, depending on the particular poem, whether epode, satire, ode, or epistle, conduces to the particular impression desired. Persius died young and did not fully perfect his artistic techniques. Still, the assumptions of Satires 1 and 5, that style does betray the essential man, suggest that we should be careful in picturing the young Persius, on the basis of his writings, as an innocent, bookish Stoic, much under the influence of women and his tutors, who spoke directly from his heart (as he pointedly insists in 5.19 ff.). He, too, has assumed the part appropriate to his special type of satire.

46. G. C. Fiske, "The Plain Style in the Scipionic Circle," *Classical Studies C. F. Smith* (Madison, 1919), pp. 62–105; *Lucilius and Horace: a Study in the Classical Theory of Imitation* (Madison, 1920).

Horace's and Persius' satiric personae do not conflict with the moral implications of their poetry, and the nice blending of the ironic and Stoic speakers with satiric themes attests to the care with which the persona has been created. This blending is less true of Lucilius, in Horace's opinion, and, as we shall see, critics have assailed Juvenal for similar defects in his persona. Throughout Horace's polemic against his predecessor, the assumption prevails that Lucilius' unreflective personal attacks lacked a firm moral basis. Lucilius would inveigh against some prominent figure, it appears, to vent personal or party spite rather than to achieve any positive moral improvement in his victims, himself, or his readers. Restraint in Horace, therefore, entails both moral and poetic improvement. This is not the place to defend Lucilius. Our purpose in discussing Juvenal's predecessors has been to show two things: first, that the poetic satirist, like the elegist, resorts to the technique of the persona, a created personality by which he enhances his moral doctrine; and second, that the more outspoken the persona seems, the less credit it earns among critics even in ancient times for being morally objective, morally and poetically honest. Juvenal, by adopting the attitude of indignation, has suffered more disfavor even than Lucilius.

If we insist on the rhetorical character of Juvenal's Satires, we should likewise perceive that Juvenal would adhere to one of the cardinal precepts of the rhetoricians, as stated by Quintilian, that the speaker must identify himself completely with his case and always maintain the appropriate character. We must ask, therefore, what would be the appropriate character for Juvenal and how far he has succeeded in achieving it. In his Program Satire Juvenal sets out to define his persona together with his general principles of writing satire. First, he tells us of his own rhetorical training, but of his total contempt for the standard themes of literature, obviously because myth and the genres of epic and tragedy appropriate to it have lost all relevance to the contemporary scene (1.1–18). In immediate contrast, he parades before our eyes his own themes, the flagrant degenerates who live in Rome. Repeatedly he punctuates his vignettes with excited interjections, to the effect that he must write of these people, that he could not possibly restrain his fury. This whole section comes to its climax in those famous and considerably misinterpreted lines:

si natura negat, facit indignatio versum
qualemcumque potest, quales ego vel Cluvienus. (79–80)

Juvenal goes on to claim that Rome has reached the farthest limit of degradation (87 ff.) and analyzes this moral collapse as due primarily to materialistic values, especially the sacrilegious apotheosis of Pecunia. Finally, voicing fury at the extent of Roman perversion, Juvenal implies that he cannot control the impetus to write; at which point an interlocutor succeeds in warning him of the dangers of attacking powerful political figures and persuades him to use the dead as his targets.

Satire 1 provides us with nearly all the information Juvenal feels we should know to appreciate his persona. It is to be observed that, unlike Horace, he does not talk about his home, parents, and friends; nor does he, like Persius, feel it necessary to specify his tutor in order to explain his own particular philosophic position. If we try to form a picture of our satirist, we will discover that we have no details to go on; we can hardly even infer his age.[47] Instead of precise facts about his background and present status, Juvenal displays his emotional reactions to prevalent scenes in Rome. Here are our vital facts, the only ones conducive to forming the proper persona: the satirist writes as a Roman appalled and indignant at the perversion of his beloved city. Rome has become *iniqua urbs* (30). In response, the satirist will describe the city as though writing tragedy. But he does not claim to be a skilled poet. No, his frenzied emotions could of themselves produce verse fit for this horrible subject. Had not a friend warned him at the last

47. Knoche, in his edition of Juvenal (Munich, 1950), deletes 25–6, from which otherwise we might deduce that considerable time has elapsed since Juvenal's youth.

moment, he would have completely lost control of his anger and attacked living politicians, who would crush him quickly. Such is our picture of our satirist. In other Satires, where additional details may promote the total effect, Juvenal will give us a few more facts: that he has an estate in Aquinum to which he, like Umbricius, retires; that the hated Crispinus, now so wealthy, used to shave him; that he visited Egypt and therefore can guarantee his angry indictment of the bestial Egyptians. But for the purpose of explaining his motives in writing satire—that is, in order to present himself in a light which will most support the mood and aim of his poems—Juvenal contents himself with this limited persona: the indignant Roman.

We do not have to inquire into the value of posing as a true Roman for the satirist; as such, it seems clear, he closely resembles the vir bonus of the rhetoricians. But when Juvenal qualifies himself as indignant, he stirs considerable controversy among those who question the merits of indignation in general as an ethical emotion and those who question Juvenal's indignation as being patently counterfeit, hence immoral.[48] I know of no commentator who has thoroughly discussed the Roman use and understanding of *indignatio,* so as to explain what Juvenal could expect his audience to infer from his assertion: *facit indignatio versum.* It therefore becomes important to consider *indignatio,* especially because Quintilian and his fellow rhetoricians show exceptional awareness of the emotion.

The verbal abstract *indignatio,* formed from *indignor,* denotes the feeling stirred by awareness that something is *indignum.* The Romans regarded it as one of the primary or basic emotions, almost on the order of an instinct. As soon as we realize the elemental, moral character of indignatio, we can see why rhetoricians began to appropriate it, for obviously it

48. E.g., De Decker, p. 186; Marmorale, pp. 27 ff.; and Serafini, pp. 97 ff.

enhanced the persona of the vir bonus to assume righteous anger at certain points in a legal dispute. Our earliest Latin treatise on rhetoric, *Auctor ad Herennium*, comments on the advantages of evoking indignatio through exclamations and provocative descriptive details.[49] At greater length Cicero analyzes the usage of indignatio according to the various circumstances in which plaintiff or defendant can profit from it.[50] Cicero's own speeches follow the practices recommended in his youthful treatise, and indignatio, we may infer, played a recognized part in the armament of any advocate or public speaker. When rhetorically trained men write history, careful application of the emotional word indicates the purpose of moving the reader as well as informing him. The pages of Livy have numerous significant instances of indignatio describing popular reaction (and hence suggesting the manner in which we should react) toward certain events.[51] Rhetorically educated poets also perceived the various applications of indignatio. One has only to read the speech of Sinon and his unscrupulous pretense of outrage at the murder of Palamedes (*indignabar Aen.* 2.93) to understand how sensitively this emotion could be exploited. Quintilian cites one of Juno's irate exclamations as an ideal example of indignatio in poetry.[52] The Augustan Period provides us with one poem which, whether or not it influenced Juvenal, certainly shows a conscious use of the word indignatio in almost the same context and meaning as Juvenal's word in Satire 1. Horace's Fourth Epode takes as its subject a nameless former slave who has promoted himself by patently unscrupulous methods to the rank of knight. As this man parades the Via Sacra, the poet imagines, passers-by look at him and erupt in honest fury (*liberrima indignatio* 10). Horace adopts this theme, appropriate to the generally aggressive tenor of his Epodes, and expresses the

49. Cf. 4.15.22, 39.51.
50. *De Inv.* 1.100 ff.; cf. *Orator* 131–2.
51. Cf. 2.37.9, 4.6.3, 4.24.9, 4.50.1, 4.50.5, 26.37.8.
52. In *Inst.* 9.2.10, he cites *Aen.* 1.48.

fury of Archilochus in terms of instinctive Roman indignation at the success of an unworthy man. The background of the Roman street, the Roman citizens, the figure of the alien risen over the head of native Romans—all this reminds one of Juvenal's dramatic presentation of his indignatio. Juvenal, however, assumes the character of indignant Roman for himself.

Passing over the intervening period,[53] we can now consider the rhetorical theory of Juvenal's time. Quintilian provides us with ample detail as to the value of indignatio, starting from the theories, as one would expect, of his beloved Cicero. By way of preface to his discussion of *pronuntiatio,* the rhetorician stresses the basic importance of exploiting the emotions— of impressing upon our presentation, that is, the feeling which is most appropriate to the circumstances. To do this, the speaker should be quite clear in his own mind about human emotions, and Quintilian proceeds to categorize feelings as either genuine or artificial. We shall concentrate on what he says about the genuine affections:

> sed cum sint alii veri adfectus, alii ficti et imitati, veri naturaliter erumpunt, ut dolentium, irascentium, indignantium, sed carent arte, ideoque sunt disciplina et ratione formandi. (*Inst.* 11.3.61)

Indignation bursts out of the heart directly, an immediate

53. It should be noted that Valerius Cato wrote an autobiographical poem entitled *Indignatio:* cf. Suet. *De Gramm.* 11.1. Since Cato was an editor of Lucilius and a theorist about the nature of satire, it is quite likely that he adopted satiric techniques for his poem; we know that he regularly indulged in polemic. In the next generation, Seneca Rhetor, while discussing *colores,* comments on the use of indignatio. To describe the orator's indignant manner he uses the terms *furiose* and *furiosissime* (cf. 10.5.21, 23). The orator also exploited indignatio in the same way as Livy, that is, to dramatize popular reactions against his infamous opponent (cf. *indignantium voces* and *publica indignatio,* 1.3.12). For indignatio considered as a necessary aspect of a successful speech cf. *Contr.* 7, Pref. 2, and 7.2.8.

reaction to some stimulus; fundamentally honest, it incurs the danger of seeming crude, of antagonizing the ear, and so must be brought under the control of reason and training. Quintilian continues by urging the student to counterfeit the other emotions so skillfully that they appear to be real *(tamquam veris moveri)*. In short, the orator exercises restraint at all times on his emotions, manipulating them knowingly, feeling indignation and disciplining it, counterfeiting indignation (and other useful sentiments) and successfully acting the part of outrage. Behind all this, we must recall, lies the basic definition of the orator, *vir bonus dicendi peritus*, with which at no time, in Quintilian's opinion, does the dramatization of such passions as indignatio conflict. An honest man would be affronted by injustice; therefore, the advocate as vir bonus should convey the appropriate effect of indignatio when the occasion demands.

The apparent emotional engagement of the speaker occupies Quintilian's attention at numerous points in his treatise, of which perhaps the most relevant to our specific problem is the following:

> summa enim, quantum ego quidem sentio, circa movendos adfectus in hoc posita est, ut moveamur ipsi. nam et luctus et irae et indignationis etiam ridicula fuerit imitatio, si verba vultumque tantum, non etiam animum accommodarimus.   (6.2.26)

How can we expect to arouse feelings on behalf of ourselves and our client, he continues, unless we convincingly express the very passions which we try to stir? It is a problem of identification: *nos illi simus quos gravia, indigna, tristia passos queramur, nec agamus rem quasi alienam, sed adsumamus parumper illum dolorem* (6.2.34). For this process of identification, for the selection of moments proper to indignatio, Quintilian affords much valuable advice. It can be employed as a color to palliate facts prejudicial to our case (3.8.45); it can provide a convincing motive for a useful digression (*velut*

erumpente protinus indignatione 4.3.5; cf. 15); it constitutes
a basic element in that device of provocatively vivid description known as δείνωσις (6.2.24); it can be conveyed by rhetorical questions (9.2.10) and by exclamations (9.2.26); it
demands a special quick rhythm when employed in the
exordium (*cum in accusatione concitandus est iudex aut
aliqua indignatione complendus* 9.4.138); we can enhance it
by a certain modulation of our voice (11.3.58), by the proper
inclination of our head (11.3.71), and by appropriate gestures
(11.3.103, 123); and finally indignatio seems to bear a close
relation to at least one aspect of the Grand Style (12.10.61).[54]
Such is Quintilian's doctrine on indignatio. The orator must
be aware of its potentialities in planning his case, and, once
he has decided to exploit it, he must know how to throw himself without reserve into the role of righteous anger. We need
only add that Quintilian characteristically uses the verb
erumpere with indignatio, thus showing his instinctive association of the emotion with violence and immediate reactions.
Other writers employ such expressive verbs as *cooriri* and *ob-
oriri*, again typical of surging passions, or metaphorical terms
like *ardere, exardere*, and *accendere*.[55] In short, indignatio
connotes exceedingly strong feeling.

Quintilian's treatise, supplemented by the earlier works of
Cicero and other surviving rhetorical theorists, demonstrates
that the importance of indignatio had long been recognized
in Rome as relevant to all aspects of rhetorical development,
whether oral or written, prose or poetry. Accordingly, when
Juvenal claimed to be motivated by indignatio in his writing,
he could expect that his rhetorically trained audience would
perceive the principles from which he operated. As a skillful
orator, Juvenal affects indignation even before he draws attention to it, so that he has already engaged the emotions of
his reader by the time he consciously announces his artistic
principles. He erupts in fury against contemporary poetasters

54. Cf. Ryberg, p. 43.
55. For verbs employed with *indignatio* cf. the *Thesaurus* s.v.

427

as though not only annoyed *(vexatus)* but outraged. His honor demands revenge (cf. *impune, clementia*). Since, however, the entire motivation of the satirist's fury cannot be appreciated by continuing in this vein, Juvenal shows his ability to bring his feelings under control. Momentarily, he affects a calm attitude and requests calmness of his audience *(placidi,* 21), as if he had in mind a tranquil, desultory conversation among friends *(si vacat);* then he begins on a new tack, to prove that his fury arises not so much against the incompetence of present writers as at their complete failure to discern a truly tragic theme there before their eyes in Rome. Instance after instance of un-Roman perversion piles up before us; the satirist dramatically conveys the increasing tension within himself; until finally he seems to shout: *facit indignatio versum.* He has carried us along with him, I maintain, even though any critic can point out the inconsistencies of such a self-conscious avowal of one's passion. The question, after all, is not what Juvenal feels, but what the *persona* of the satirist seems to feel. If the Satires continue, as the first eighty lines of Satire 1 have certainly done, to represent the irrepressible reactions of an honest Roman to the degeneration of his native city, then Juvenal has fulfilled his rhetorical duties, and simultaneously his moral duties—he has, indeed, chosen a theme of great moral interest—and his poetic function—he has, as we shall observe in greater detail later, integrated the precepts of the rhetoricians with the requirements of his particular form of poetry.[56]

56. Any reader of Juvenal knows that, with some exceptions, he did not maintain the impression of indignatio in the later Satires. Therefore, statements in this paper about the concept and style appropriate to indignation will apply to Juvenal's theme as announced in Satire 1 and to those Satires which more or less fulfill his original artistic purpose. After all, as a Program Satire, Satire 1 can be strictly referred only to its own Book 1. As Gauger observed (p. 100), we should not try to account for the changed character of Juvenal's poems by claiming that Juvenal himself loses his indignation in later years; but he does adopt an entirely new persona in Satires 9 and 11–14.

I shall continue throughout this paper to emphasize the rhetorical presuppositions of indignatio as the criterion by which Juvenal's satiric persona must be judged in concept *(inventio)* and in poetic presentation *(elocutio)*. So far, following the general methods of Quintilian, we have discussed the basic assumptions of the orator and the manner in which he steps forth into public life as vir bonus, an honest man who knows exactly the right emotions for the right occasion. Having given consideration to the facts of the situation and the emotional potentialities of certain arguments, the orator then proceeds to select the words and phrases, devices and gestures, which will most adequately achieve his purpose. I do not need to indicate the correlative functions and hence inseparability of the processes of inventio and elocutio; but for the present let us continue to follow the rhetorician's approach and study another topic that conventionally appears as part of inventio: namely, the process of analyzing the subject of an oration.

Quintilian divides the normal subjects of the speaker between general and particular questions (3.5) which may be exploited in any of the three main areas or *genera* of oratory. The general question cannot be restricted to time or place but, to use Quintilian's example, involves the issue whether Providence controls the universe; while the particular question confines its scope to specific people or places: for example, should Milo be condemned for killing Clodius? As the rhetorician notes, however, every particular question *(causa)* sooner or later involves a general question: in defending Milo the advocate will try to argue basic legal principles so as to leave no question in a judge's mind that premeditation must be essential to the definition of murder. Likewise, in arguing a general question (the Greek *thesis; propositum* in Cicero's terminology) the orator will necessarily resort to concrete arguments: for example, did or did not Providence act when Castor and Pollux announced the victory at Lake Regillus? Most commonly, the student trained himself for legal and political situations, thus concentrating on the *genus iudiciale* and *genus deliberativum*. The Roman teacher took over from his Greek predecessors the use of hypothetical problems, legal and political, which he set his pupils as rhetorical exercises. By the end of the first century B.C. these problems had acquired special designations: *controversiae* if they treated legal problems; *suasoriae* if they obliged the student to argue as if influencing some momentous political decision. Of the various ingenious topics devised to provoke the interest of the student, the selection in Seneca Rhetor affords a good example. One of the more popular suasoriae involved the abdication of Sulla and the reasons for or against that startling decision (*Inst.* 3.8.53, 5.10.71). When Juvenal claims that his rhetorical education equals that of the miserable contemporary poets, he cites this particular suasoria as one of the themes upon which he once declaimed (1.15–17).

Rhetorical categorizations such as the above have long attracted Juvenalian scholars. Significantly, one of the first to attempt defining the form of the Satires in terms of rhetorical topics was Friedländer—he designated Satires 5, 8, 10, and 14 as rhetorical theses[57]—the same man who proposed to make Juvenal Quintilian's student. Since his modest suggestions, others have taken up and elaborated his ideas. The most detailed discussion of this question is found in F. Gauger's *Zeitschilderung und Topik bei Juvenal.*[58] Gauger argued that Juvenal implicitly presents his theme at the beginning of each Satire, then proceeds to illustrate it by *exempla,* contrasts, and various rhetorical *topoi.* But Gauger found his problem more complex than Friedländer, inasmuch as he recognized the literary background of satire and its inevitable influence upon Juvenal. Accordingly, his categorization falls into three groups: to Friedländer's rhetorical theses he adds diatribes and satires. In Gauger's terms, satire involves the portrait of one's day, free from moral preaching; the moral element

57. Friedländer, p. 52.
58. Gauger, pp. 91 ff.

should never strike the reader as merely grinding an axe. For diatribe, he used the conventional definition: moral preaching. The thesis he regarded as mere rhetorical elaboration of some point; where Juvenal would employ historical illustrations, he would generally resort to events far removed in time from the reader. Following these principles, Gauger apportioned Juvenal's work as follows: A. Theses: Satires 1, 2, 3, 5, 6, 8, 10, 13, 14; B. Diatribes: Satires 11, 12, 15; C. Satires: Satires 4, 7, 9, 16.[59]

It may seem that Gauger has done violence to Juvenal by such categorization, but once we have accepted the fact that Juvenal is rhetorical, we can hardly be surprised when nine of his Satires are defined as rhetorical theses. On the other hand, since a thesis can involve many different types of oratory, the question arises whether Gauger has gone far enough. Would it be possible to narrow down the scope of the term "thesis" and so reach a more adequate estimate of the rhetorical purpose of the satirist? One possible approach would be to classify the thesis more precisely in terms of one of the genera of oratory; Highet has attempted this and discussed Satires 3, 5, 6, 8, and 13 as suasoriae. For the purposes of this paper, we shall concentrate on these five Satires, where both Gauger and Highet are in agreement, although Highet has attempted to go beyond the mere definition of rhetorical thesis.

It seems evident that Highet could safely eliminate from consideration the genus to which Quintilian devotes most of his attention, namely the *genus iudiciale;* similarly, we may disregard the practice version of the legal case, the *controversia.* Although Juvenal may employ techniques of the trial lawyer, his various Satires do not assume any such context as that so elaborately explained by Quintilian and illustrated in Seneca Rhetor; we certainly do not feel that the satirist is

59. O. Weinreich, *Römische Satiren* (Zurich, 1949), p. lxii, accepts Gauger's classification in entirety.

431

arguing a case in court. The real problem arises in determining the relevance of the *genus deliberativum* and its school version, the suasoria. Among rhetoricians, Quintilian observes, disagreement prevailed as to the orator's technique in this genus: should he argue in terms of honor or expediency? An orator who expatiated on honorable and dishonorable action would not be far from Juvenal's mind, it would seem. In any case, the suasoriae cited by Seneca and alluded to by Quintilian and Juvenal consisted of arguments for and against a specific action. Clearly, the satirist does not write suasoriae on the particular themes exemplified in Seneca and, to judge from Quintilian, more regularly set the student: problems from Roman history about Sulla, Caesar, Cicero, and the like; or from Greek history, especially the exploits of Alexander the Great. But Quintilian does recommend training in general questions also, and he cites as an example a subject directly relevant to Juvenal's Satire 6: *an uxor ducenda sit.* Unfortunately, the rhetorician does not demonstrate the method of arguing this suasoria or, for that matter, any general question. Certain facts emerge clearly, though. The orator organized his speech with care, perhaps a little less rigidly than the controversia but with constant reference to his main point. His method of argument consisted essentially of comparison; that is, one should marry because the bachelor lacked certain advantages, or one should avoid marriage because of the notorious difficulties of women.[60] The orator would undoubtedly define marriage in such a way as to support his case. At appropriate points he would introduce exempla about wives good or bad, depending on his viewpoint.[61] The basic criteria to which he would appeal would be honor and expediency.

Gauger stated that in Satire 6 Juvenal is arguing a suasoria against marriage, piling up twenty-four separate reasons in suc-

60. *Inst.* 3.8.34.
61. *Ibid.* 3.8.36.

cessive paragraphs; and Highet takes a similar view.[62] If so, Juvenal does a clumsy job, because, as all commentators note, he strays away from his subject by the middle of the poem and forgets the proposed marriage of Postumus, forgets even to talk about wives in his fascinated loathing of women in general.[63] At the middle of the poem the satirist pauses not to re-assert his views on marriage but rather to explain how Pudicitia has disappeared from the Roman scene. At the end of the Satire, Juvenal does not refer to Postumus or come to any decisive conclusion about marriage as being dishonorable or inexpedient; rather, he summarizes women in terms of the notorious tragic heroines who killed children or husbands, whose importance lies in their totally perverse effrontery. As I have argued elsewhere, Satire 6 treats marriage not so much for itself as to provide an insight into the perversion of Roman women. Juvenal may start from a concrete dramatic situation and seem eager to dissuade Postumus from marriage, but he quickly abandons his dramatic background to develop what is, after all, the theme which one would expect from indignatio. To argue against marriage, a rather purposeless pursuit in itself, one could employ indignation and rail away at women in general; but to deal with Postumus it would undoubtedly be more effective to make a specific attack on his intended. Most men think their bride an exception from the general male rule, that women are dangerous. But Juvenal never refers to the assumed bride. On the other hand, his indignation, to which he calls special attention in 6.634 ff. by his reference to Sophocles, does fit a general denunciation of

62. At least, Gauger states the theme as a suasoria, p. 35; Highet, p. 91, explicitly calls the Satire a suasoria, referring to Quintilian's version, p. 264, note 2.

63. Cf. my discussion, "Juvenal 6: A Problem in Structure," *CP*, 51 (1956), 73–94. I might add that the unimportance of Postumus seems quite clear from the fact that the satirist addresses his remarks in the first 100 lines to what appear to be three different people: Postumus (21 ff.), Ursidius (38 ff.), and Lentulus (80).

Roman women. We have something in this Satire essentially different in purpose and tone from the conventional suasoria.

Gauger and Highet agree that we should consider Satires 3 and 5 as theses, and Highet goes beyond to define them as suasoriae.[64] A brief examination of these two poems should reinforce our conclusion about Satire 6. In Satire 3, according to those who see it as a suasoria, Juvenal places in the mouth of Umbricius a speech essentially calculated to account for his abandonment of Rome, therefore to persuade Juvenal and the reader to forsake Rome likewise. Put in its technical form, the suasoria might read *an urbs relinquenda sit*.[65] Juvenal has organized this Satire carefully, and it might have been fairer to begin our discussion of satire and suasoriae with this poem, except that we know of no suasoria precisely on this topic. In any case, I question whether anyone reading Satire 3 really feels that we are deliberating a question or drawing persuasive contrasts. Umbricius has already made his decision. His justification, while it clearly assumes sympathy in his friend Juvenal, does not aim to persuade the satirist to join him; Umbricius knows that Juvenal will periodically retire from the city (cf. 318 ff.), but he nowhere speaks as though he were exercising conscious influence. Once again the occasion of the Satire, as in Satire 6, serves to introduce us to a deeper, more general theme worthy of Juvenal's indignatio, although the satirist has united the drama with his theme in a way that he does nowhere else, rendering this his masterpiece. Satire 3 epitomizes Juvenal's indictment of Rome. Umbricius' departure from the city is not the subject of a suasoria or of a comparison between country and city; it provides a

64. Highet, p. 84, calls Satires 3 and 5 "persuasions." Gauger states the theme of Satire 3, p. 25, as a comparison between country and city; of Satire 5, p. 33, as the question whether it is wise to become a client. The latter, as he expresses it, seems very close to a suasoria.

65. Gauger, p. 94, calls attention to a thesis mentioned by Quintilian 2.4.24: *rusticane vita an urbana potior?* and treats this as the theme of Satire 3.

symbol for all that the satirist has to say about his Rome. He lets Umbricius speak and become for us dramatically the ideal orator, *vir bonus atque Romanus*.[66] When Umbricius leaves Rome, all that is good and Roman in the city symbolically departs with him.

Basically, we are dealing here with a question of form and emphasis, a question which can be very nicely debated in relation to Satire 5. We must ask ourselves first whether Juvenal has adopted the form of a suasoria: to persuade an interlocutor (and indirectly us) or allow an interlocutor to persuade him that something should be done. We have seen that Satires 3 and 6 break down on this preliminary point, for Umbricius does not persuade to action, and Postumus disappears from sight before Satire 6 is half over. Secondly, even if the Satire formally approaches a suasoria, we must still determine the relevance of that fact to Juvenal's purpose as satirist: is he also trying to persuade the reader to the same action or avoidance of action? Or does he establish further reasons for his indignatio as citizen of the once-proud Rome?

Friedländer, Gauger, Weinreich, and Highet agree that Juvenal handles a rhetorical thesis, specifically a suasoria, in Satire 5. We might state the subject of such a declamation as *an cena divitis pauperi ferenda sit*. More than any other poem of Juvenal, this Satire follows the pattern of the rhetorical exercise in its main outlines. It begins by referring to Trebius' *propositum*, defined as *ut bona summa putes aliena vivere quadra* (2); and we recall that *propositum* can function as a technical term of rhetoric denoting the subject of a general question. Juvenal reviews the circumstances of the invitation (*primo fige loco*, 12), then concentrates on the *cena* itself and the invidious distinctions made during each course between Virro and his miserable guest; finally, he rounds off his argument by referring clearly back to the statements made in the introduction about the insults imposed on the *cliens*, which

66. Martial also comments on the intrinsic antagonism between the vir bonus and Rome: cf. 4.5.1–2.

reduce him below the status of the wretched buffoon. Now we do not know of any suasoria on this theme used in the schools, but it would not be entirely inaccurate to regard this as suasoria in form. When, however, the satirist devotes so much attention to a precise, though conjectural,[67] description of the banquet (132 out of 173 lines), we may justly ask whether he really concentrates his efforts on persuasion. The details do produce a cumulative verdict that such a banquet is dishonorable and inexpedient, criteria, we remember, which Quintilian teaches as fundamental to any suasoria. And yet the details seem to have a different purpose. Halfway through his description the satirist breaks in to address the rich man Virro, entirely ignoring the fact that he should be directing his arguments at Trebius. Shortly after, he makes a parenthetical remark in connection with the meat-carver: *ne qua indignatio desit* (120). Finally, the series of elaborate comparisons with mythical people and places, as a means of exaggerating the luxury of Virro's special dishes, promote persuasion less than the impression of *indignum* which motivates Juvenal's *indignatio*. Highet recognizes that Juvenal's purpose in Satire 5 consists of a biting analysis of the breakdown in the relationship between patron and client.[68] I would suggest that Juvenal achieves this purpose largely because he transcends the limits of the suasoria. As in Satires 3 and 6, he adopts a dramatic occasion, only to push deeper into the problem until he has denounced another salient aspect of Rome's degeneracy. Perhaps we might summarize the whole argument by suggesting that persuasion and indignation basically do not blend.

From what has been said about Satires 3, 5, and 6, it seems legitimate to conclude that Juvenal does not write a formal suasoria: only Satire 5 remains in character and maintains the dramatic organization around Trebius' proposed meal with Virro; none of the three confines its purpose to persua-

67. On the function of conjecture in the genus deliberativum, cf. *Inst.* 3.8.16.
68. Highet, p. 84.

sion; none of the three leaves its question universal as a mere thesis. I have commented on what I regard as Juvenal's purpose, namely, denunciation of the various aspects of Roman degeneracy, and I have suggested that the satirist's methods of argument, his provocative use of detail, and his tacit or express (in the case of Satire 5) exploitation of indignatio all imply a different use of the basic criterion of the suasoria: honor or dishonor. We turn now to the third genus, which both Cicero (*De or.* 2.88.333) and Quintilian (3.7.28) regard as closely related to the genus deliberativum, and I shall argue that if we must label Juvenal's satiric form in terms of a rhetorical genus—I do not think it an entirely safe way of defining poetry—we should pay considerable attention to the *genus demonstrativum*.

In our earliest Latin treatise on rhetoric, the third class of speaking receives the title genus demonstrativum (*Auct. Her.* 3.6.10), a name which has the advantage of defining the essential epideictic function rather than one aspect of it. The name which Quintilian uses, *genus laudativum,* probably assumed its place because of the relative importance of panegyric. The anonymous *Auctor,* Cicero, and Quintilian all state that epideictic oratory consists either of praise or of blame, *laus* or *vituperatio.* By *vituperatio* the rhetoricians translated the Greek term ψόγος, as we find it in Aristotle and succeeding Greek rhetorical writers.[69] The usage and the apparent etymology of vituperatio indicate that, when the speaker adopts this mode, he emphasizes *vitia.*[70] Cicero mentions a contem-

69. For Greek rhetorical theories on ψόγος or the εἶδος ψεκτικόν, theories which certainly stand behind and exist contemporaneously with those of Quintilian; cf. Aristotle, *Rhet.* 1.9; Anaximenes, *Rhet.* 3; Hermogenes, *Progymn.* 7–9; [Aristides], *Techn.* 1.12.8; Alexander, 3.3.22; and Nicolaus, *Progymn.* 9. All these will be found in Spengel. Hermogenes, [Aristides], and Alexander all belong to the second century A.D., shortly after Quintilian, and Hermogenes especially shows close resemblance to Quintilian on the genus demonstrativum.

70. For the etymology of *vituperatio* cf. Ernout–Meillet and Walde–Hofmann.

porary example of this genus, Caesar's *Anticato,* which clearly defines itself as such because it contradicts Cicero's own encomium of Cato.[71] Quintilian cites as examples portions of Cicero's speeches against consular rivals and legal opponents; of these, the speech *In Pisonem* survives to this day.[72] An even better example of sustained vituperatio would probably be the series of orations against Antony, the *Philippics.* In any case, we observe that vituperatio and panegyric most commonly took human beings as subjects. Quintilian adds to these themes many others (and we can find the same set of topics in the near-contemporary Greek rhetorician Hermogenes of Tarsus[73]): the gods, beautiful buildings such as temples, geographical regions (i.e. Sicily as praised by Cicero in the *Verrines*), and, especially relevant to our discussion, cities:

> laudantur autem urbes similiter atque homines. nam pro parente est conditor, et multum auctoritatis adfert vetustas, ut iis, qui terra dicuntur orti; et virtutes ac vitia circa res gestas eadem quae in singulis, illa propria quae ex loci positione ac munitione sunt. cives illis ut hominibus liberi decori.   (3.7.26)

When Juvenal has completed his Program Satire, he has defined his motivation and approach to Satire in terms of indignatio and the background of Rome. He does not call upon father Romulus until Satire 2 (126 ff.), but in other respects he seems to have covered the program for dealing with a city. The age of Rome provides many indirect comments on contemporary degeneracy throughout the Satires, and in Satire 1 allusions to the Trojans (100), Aeneas and his wars (162), and Lucilius (20, 154, 165) start this motif. As for *vitia circa res gestas,* that is Juvenal's main theme: *vitia Romana* and *cives indecori* meet his gaze wherever he looks in the streets, he

71. *Topica* 89 ff.
72. *Inst.* 3.7.2.
73. Quintilian and Hermogenes are nearly identical in their passages on the city-topos.

says. All the old values have disappeared, as symbolized in the virtual abandonment of the shrines dedicated to abstract qualities, once so highly revered (115–16). The most complete indictment of Rome (*iniquae urbis*, 1.30–31; *saevae urbis*, 3.8–9) comes in Satire 3, where Umbricius has things to say *de loci positione* or the equivalent, the crowded, noisy, dangerous streets, the fires, clumsy legionnaires, footpads, in brief all the things that set it off from the country and rural associations. If, then, we think of Juvenal's Satires as poetic equivalents of epideictic oratory, which aim at *vituperatio urbis*, we are likely to reach a closer approximation of his literary effect.

Quintilian comments that this epideictic genus and the deliberative genus have in common the use of comparison and largely ethical arguments. You determine to avoid an act because it is dishonorable, and you criticize a man or a city because their actions show them devoid of honor. Consistently, the orator bases his criteria on what is and is not *honestum*. To distinguish the two genera, it would be necessary to realize that the genus deliberativum persuades to some specific action or avoidance of action, while the genus laudativum persuades one of an attitude toward a person, place, abstract value, or the like. If we are right in claiming denunciation as Juvenal's satiric effect, both the mood and the manner of argument resemble that of the vituperatio. Quintilian does not explain the emotion to be impressed upon this genus; various examples from Roman literature and parallel discussion in the Greek rhetoricians amply demonstrate that the orator exploited passionate utterance.[74] The portion that we possess of

74. In addition to their comments on ψόγος, the Greek rhetoricians discuss a closely related usage which they regularly call ὁ κοινὸς τόπος: cf. Hermogenes, *Progymn.* 6; Theon, *Progymn.* 7; and Nicolaus, *Progymn.* 7. This topos differentiates itself from the genus demonstrativum in that it aims entirely at the emotions and prejudice, forming a calculated portion of a larger speech. In this sense it approaches the Roman use of *adfectus* and especially *ira, dolor, indignatio*. Longinus, on the other hand, seems to dislike epideictic oratory precisely because it lacks effective passion: cf. 8.3 and 12.5.

Cicero's *In Pisonem* abounds in all forms of invective: angry questions, emotional apostrophe, insulting epithets (*belua, Furia, monstrum, prodigium,* etc.), all based upon the vitia of Piso or, as Cicero summarizes them, his *indignitas*.[75] Cicero displays what Quintilian recommends, a shrewd awareness of his audience; and he appeals to basic Roman prejudices, especially in his attacks on Piso's Epicureanism. In short, as one might well expect, the proper vituperatio was conducted on a violent emotional level, for the orator, intent on his own role as vir bonus,[76] would necessarily be obliged to express aversion for the vices of his victim. In his denunciation of Piso and Antony, Cicero seems properly indignant, and his indignatio earns him credit, because it springs from a convincingly passionate concern for Rome and from a hatred of the monsters who have defiled it. A conceivable example of vituperatio in satire can be found in the *Apocolocyntosis* in Augustus' speech against Claudius. Augustus himself mentions his indignatio[77] and uses the techniques to be expected in the epideictic genus; so that we might well agree with Weinreich in describing the speech as *vituperatio Claudii*.[78] In Juvenal's own time, there must have been many formal vituperationes of Domitian, to judge from the official *damnatio memoriae* inflicted on the dead emperor, the destruction of his triumphal statue in the Forum, and particularly from the pale reflections of denunciation in Pliny's *Panegyric*. As a means of contrast with the *virtutes* of Trajan, Pliny repeatedly introduces the *vitia* of Domitian, his cruelty, the mood of terror that prevailed throughout his reign, his luxurious ways, the lack of freedom. Scivoletto has even found correspondences between Pliny's denunciations of Domitian and those of Satire 4,[79]

75. *In Pisonem* 99.
76. *Ibid.* 33.
77. *Apocol.* 10.2.
78. O. Weinreich, *Senecas Apocolocyntosis: Die Satire auf Tod/Himmel- und Höllenfahrt des Kaisers Claudius: Einführung, Analyse und Untersuchungen, Übersetzung* (Berlin, 1923), p. 106.
79. Scivoletto, note 14 above.

from which we may infer that the same rhetorical purpose motivates both men in the parallel sections. Juvenal implies that Domitian and his vicious predecessors have been responsible for the present perversion of Rome, especially in Satire 4, a miniature example of vituperatio on the order of portions of Cicero's *In Pisonem*.

In the preceding paragraph, I employed the word "invective" to denote some of Cicero's practices in his speech against Piso. Invective often appears in discussions of Roman satire as one of the defining qualities, especially when scholars treat Lucilius; and it might be suitable here to distinguish between vituperatio and Juvenal's version of it and, on the other hand, invective and its connotations. I do not need to elaborate the rhetorical presuppositions of invective in relation to Lucilius, since Fiske has presented the material fully,[80] nor do we have to go into the position which Horace took on the matter. It is sufficient to note that the Latin word for invective, *maledictio,* involves a whole range of connotations essentially opposed to those of *vituperatio.* Satire always ran the danger of being considered merely invective—*carmen maledicum,* as Diomedes actually does describe it—and the satirists before Juvenal seem to have worked out an adequate defense against the charge in terms of the theories of *sermo.* The conversational tone of the satirist, his claim to be interested in the opinion of only a few respected friends, his frankness about his own foibles—all this makes of the personal criticism in pre-Juvenalian satire ethical examples rather than maledictio. On the other hand, the ideal of satiric approach as represented in Horace in no way corresponds to Juvenal's rhetorical manner. Juvenal abandons *sermo* and orates; he refuses to lead us gently to an understanding of some fault, but denounces vice and forces an emotional attitude upon us. There is no question here of malice, of personal spite, inasmuch as the people introduced have long since escaped from life. Rather, as the

80. Fiske, *Lucilius and Horace,* esp. pp. 90 ff., 114 ff.

441

scholiast himself seems to realize intermittently, Juvenal appropriates the rhetorical vituperatio and adapts it to his purpose of delineating the downfall of Rome.[81]

Although, then, Quintilian and other Roman rhetoricians do not specify the mood appropriate to vituperatio, the examples we possess substantiate our assumption that vituperatio, essentially the consciousness and denunciation of *vitia*, would require a fairly continuous mood of indignatio. Here lies one of the basic differences from the suasoria. The second fundamental difference inheres in the method of argumentation or presentation employed by vituperatio and Juvenal as against the suasoria. Elsewhere I have commented on Juvenal's structural methods as follows: "Juvenal starts and ends with the same idea, having devoted the poem to its exposition. . . . Since Juvenal does not alter his theme, the scenes which he dwells upon must perform a parallel function of illustration, and an accumulation of such illustration forces the desired conclusion."[82] Such a technique closely approximates the technique of display employed in the genus demonstrativum. Pliny reviews various aspects of Trajan's career, the atmosphere of his rule, his personality and character, all as a means of illustrating what he says at the start: *at principi nostro quanta concordia quantusque concentus omnium laudum omnisque gloriae contigit!*[83] Illustration replaces logical argument, for, after all, Pliny does not need to argue a point that his audience generally accepts; instead, he tries to communicate his mood of enthusiasm by the aptness and pointed statement of his examples. Similarly, Cicero does not argue; the accumulated attacks on Piso force the desired conclusion, not by logic but by skillful exploitation of prejudicial instances,

81. Cf. the scholia on 1.155 and 4.2. On invective see also Ryberg, pp. 43 ff.

82. Cf. "Studies in Book I of Juvenal," YCS, 15 (1957), 89; also, Gauger's general description of the treatment of the thesis, pp. 91 ff.

83. *Paneg.* 4.6.

that Piso represents *odium populi Romani*.[84] On the other hand, if one really takes the genus deliberativum and its suasoriae seriously, one realizes that it had to be basically rational, intent on proving the value of a particular course of action, generally in a political crisis. It could exploit indignatio, but not continuously, inasmuch as high emotion generally connotes lack of self-control; and politicians are wary of emotional manipulation. The genus demonstrativum persuades only to the extent that it attempts to implant emotion, a specific reaction to a person, place, or whatever its subject may be. It exaggerates, calls on gods, digresses, asks rhetorical questions, exclaims, dwells on powerful pictures—using conventional topoi but not tied down to a rigid structure—and the final result consists of the original statement now backed by passionate feeling. Throughout the speech, feeling runs high, whether indignation or enthusiasm, so that the listener concentrates on the emotion and the dramatic credibility of the speaker's persona as manifested through illustration and striking detail and feels no great need to study the logical presuppositions of the arguments, as if some pressing political issue were being presented for his decision.

As I said at the beginning of this discussion of vituperatio, I do not wish to identify the structural form adopted by Juvenal with any particular *genus dicendi,* for Juvenal's Satires, by their very poetic nature, differ radically from the form defined for the rhetorical genera. It is important, on the other hand, to be clear in our own minds exactly how the rhetorical genius of the satirist operates. When he considered his theme, did he think of it as the equivalent of a suasoria and, with that purpose, adopt the *dramatis personae* for his declamations; or did he feel the similarity of some other genus? I have attempted to argue against the prevailing doctrine that Juvenal writes theses or, more specifically, suasoriae in many Satires, on the grounds that it does violence to both the mood and the

84. Cf. *In Pis.* 45, 64.

thematic presentation in these Satires. As a counterweight, I have advanced the claims to consideration of the genus demonstrativum in one of its two aspects, namely, vituperatio. Quintilian shows that a city could function as the subject of such oratory, and the requisite topoi recur in Juvenal's earlier Satires—especially those for which the Program Satire was written. Our examples of this genus in Roman rhetoric exhibit persistent recourse to passionate emotion and the rhetorical devices generally associated with such expression. Furthermore, the technique of display throughout Juvenal finds its best counterpart in this same genus demonstrativum, where argument always yields to illustration and provocative description. Satire and vituperatio both base their indignatio upon an appalled recognition of the flagrant vitia in the subject of discourse, and both derive much of their explosive power from their ability to connect individual vitia with the political conditions of Rome. In short, once Juvenal had consciously selected his persona in relation to his theme of Rome's degeneracy, he also had to choose a manner of presentation that fitted. No other genus, I would maintain, approximates so closely the persona and satiric purpose of Juvenal as vituperatio.

B. De Elocutione

Obviously, more could be said about the rhetorical process of planning one's speech as covered in inventio. In this paper, however, I do not expect to exhaust the general topic of Juvenal's rhetoric or the possibilities of applying Quintilian's precepts to the Satires. I have selected two important problems relevant to inventio, to illustrate some of the basic poetic presuppositions of our satirist. Now, just as all planning means little until it is put into practice, so inventio is meaningless without elocutio, the actual verbalization of the arguments and their enhancement by various rhetorical devices. In fact, when we analyze a speech, we cannot distinguish the process of inventio from elocutio, for we do not know what the

444

speaker planned apart from the results exemplified in the speech itself. We were, therefore, somewhat distorting the facts when we said that Juvenal adopted the role of the indignant Roman and chose the form of vituperatio. After all, we know Juvenal only through his Satires. On the other hand, while critics persist in emphasizing Juvenal's intentional insincerity and lack of true moral perspective, we can justly argue from the same evidence an entirely different conclusion: that Juvenal planned his Satires with an awareness of the problems involved; that he selected a certain role and a certain form to which he fitted a certain style. The product of this artistic process is the indignant Satire, an integrated whole poetically bringing out the satiric concept of Juvenal. In the following pages I shall discuss this product, working with the evidence that we actually possess, to determine to what extent the rhetoricians represented by Quintilian provided the poet with precepts applicable to his specific problems; also, to see how stylistically the satirist can fulfill his purpose of displaying an attitude toward Rome and showing that, if not actually made by indignatio, his verse is suffused with indignatio.[85]

Quintilian takes as the basic element of elocutio the proper choice of vocabulary. The orator should be highly conscious of the words he uses, to the extent that he can employ them accurately and effectively, but without falling into a precious overconcern with terminology. To put it briefly, Quintilian says: *nam cum Latina, significantia, ornata, cum apte sunt collocata, quid amplius laboremus?* (Pref. 8.31). Obviously, the orator is not conversing when he attacks a defendant or argues for a client, no more than when he uses the form of panegyric or deliberative discussion. Rhetoric has borrowed from poetry, Quintilian freely admits (Pref. 8.25), and the orator must maintain a stylistic level in keeping with the tenor of his

85. The following discussion of elocutio in Juvenal depends for its data upon, and has considerably abbreviated, a portion of my Ph.D. dissertation, "The Rhetoric of Juvenal," Yale, 1954.

subject. On the other hand, the rhetorician cannot accept some of the vices of his time, those, we may infer, which come in part from Seneca, summarized as *lenocinia*. Instead of effeminate ornament, Quintilian recommends vocabulary in keeping with an old maxim well stated by Cicero: *atqui satis aperte Cicero praeceperat, in dicendo vitium vel maximum esse a vulgari genere orationis atque a consuetudine communis sensus abhorrere* (Pref. 8.25). Here, then, are the principles by which a reputable, conservative orator of Juvenal's youth determined his choice of words.

In the case of style, the rhetorician could not and did not alone influence the budding satirist, because satire itself had acquired a traditional set of principles governing its choice of vocabulary. Most clearly stated in Horace's polemic against the cult of Lucilius, these rules were generally shared by Persius and familiar to Juvenal. Whatever Lucilius called his poems, they approximated in formal presentation, if not in tone, those poems which Horace so carefully named *sermones*. As Fiske demonstrated, Lucilius adopted many of the views of Panaetius, now surviving to us in Cicero's *De Officiis*.[86] Horace also conceived of his satire as a poetic version of conversation about moral topics among intelligent friends; he moderated the tone and diction of Lucilius to bring him into conformity with the current principles of literary correctness for sermo. In respect to vocabulary, sermo implied *sermo cotidianus:* easy use of the vernacular; witty command of poetic terms at times; general avoidance of words which would communicate the mood of grand poetry; caution in the use of Hellenisms; in short, effective but not affected adoption of words so as to reach an approximation of *Latinitas* or *urbanitas*.[87] Persius seems to have subscribed to Horace's prin-

---

86. Cf. works cited note 46 above.

87. For the most part, Horace leaves his rules implicit in the criticisms of Lucilius in *Serm.* 1.4, 10; but he does specify some of his key principles in 1.10.7 ff.

ciples, although his version of sermo, what he calls *verba togae,* represents something quite different in tone.

Juvenal does not subscribe to Horace's rules for sermo. If for a moment in Satire 1 he affects the calm conversational tone (*si vacat,* 21), he quickly dissipates it and flails away at the various people perverting Rome in a manner that he self-consciously calls indignatio. What change does this abandonment of Horatian sermo effect with respect to vocabulary? How does it reflect the current rhetorical theory? Horace and Quintilian, both wishing to restrict style to urbanitas, naturally criticize the flagrant adoption of an extravagant word, particularly the alien word. *hic non alienum est admonere ut sint quam minime peregrina et externa ... quare, si fieri potest, et verba omnia et vox huius alumnum urbis oleant, ut oratio Romana plane videatur, non civitate donata.*[88] By far the most common source of alien terms, at least from the third century B.C., was Greek; therefore, Horace uses only such Greek words as have become fully Latinized,[89] and Quintilian employs Greek terms in a perfectly correct manner, to render technical language usually invented by his Greek predecessors.[90] Kappelmacher claimed that Juvenal fully adhered to Quintilian's opinion of the Greeks and use of Hellenisms, perhaps the single argument on which his dissertation was most vulnerable. The fact is, as Serafini has rightly observed, Juvenal exploits Hellenisms in a largely new way, not as affecting his own Latinitas and his role as *vir bonus atque Ro-*

88. *Inst.* 8.1.2. Quintilian recognizes, of course, the Roman debt to the Greek language and discusses at considerable length the proper methods of declining nouns borrowed from Greek: cf. 1.5.58 ff.

89. Cf. M. E. Keirns, "The Use of Greek Words in Horace's Satires and Epistles," *TAPA,* 63 (1932), lvii. For an excellent review of the various usages and connotations of Hellenisms in Latin, cf. J. Perret, "Les Hellénismes du vocabulaire latin," *Information Litt.,* 3 (1951), 183–90.

90. Cf. J. Cousin, *Études sur Quintilien Vol. II: Le Vocabulaire grec de la terminologie rhétorique dans l'Institution oratoire* (Paris, 1936).

manus, but to enhance his attack on elements which, according to his satiric approach, most clearly have caused Roman degeneracy, at least in part. "Ma quel che importa notare è il fatto che quest'uso così abbondante di parole greche non significa che l'odiata lingua straniera si sia insinuata, nonostante tutto, nel lessico di G.; tutt'altro! Il poeta infatti se ne serve coscientemente proprio per esprimere il suo disprezzo per ciò che più detesta."[91]

In his exploitations of Hellenisms for a satiric purpose, Juvenal seems to have been fully aware of the rhetorical prejudice against *verba peregrina;* in fact, he uses these words in an entirely rhetorical manner, in keeping with the spirit of Quintilian, if at odds with the unwritten laws established by Horace for satire. For Horace opposed Hellenisms not only as un-Latin but as too striking; and, if anything, Horace attempted to influence the reason, not the emotions. Juvenal uses Hellenisms in 15.6 per cent of his lines, many of them highly significant because unusual.[92] In no sense does such usage approximate the clever manipulation of Greek terms illustrated by the letters of Cicero or those of Augustus which have come down to us; rather, Hellenisms convey the venom of the satirist. To achieve this effect, Juvenal willingly sacrifices the conventions of sermo: he is not conversing; he is furious. The Greek words, therefore, act as the sign and object of his indignation, now used to describe appropriately the conditions of Roman vice, now employed in the rhetorical purpose of *amplificatio.*[93] A few examples will suffice.

> haec sunt quae tenui sudant in *cyclade,* quarum
> delicias et panniculus *bombycinus* urit!   (6.259–60)

91. Serafini, p. 366.

92. A complete list of Juvenal's Hellenisms, with comparative statistics, will be found in A. Thiel, *Juvenalis graecissans* (diss., Breslau, 1901); a simple list occurs in P. Ercole, *Studi Giovenaliani,* ed. E. Paratore (Lanciano, 1935), pp. 146–8.

93. On *amplificatio* cf. *Inst.* 8.4.1 ff., and Ryberg, 36 ff.

One of the signs of the Greek word in Latin was the letter *y*, a letter whose sound was generally pleasing to the Roman ear.[94] Here, Juvenal sneers at the luxury and softness of Roman women, best represented in Greek articles of dress, which radically conflict with their gross interest in becoming gladiators. The Hellenisms, because they possess so forceful a connotation, render the passage angry.

sed nec structor erit cui cedere debeat omnis
pergula, discipulus Trypheri doctoris, apud quem
sumine cum magno lepus atque aper et *pygargus*
et Scythicae volucres et *phoenicopterus* ingens
et Gaetulus *oryx* hebeti lautissima ferro
caeditur et tota sonat ulmea cena Subura.   (11.136–41)

While the Romans liked the sound of *y*, they did not like the sound of *x;* and their own *p* and *g* were not considered particularly euphonious.[95] Here, then, Juvenal has taken words which, by their very sound, strike the Roman as alien and offensive. He places them in a context where he attacks luxurious dining habits, and by singling out the clearly Greek teacher Trypheros, he makes it emphatic that the Greeks have caused the introduction of such exotic tastes. Again, specific words focus the emotional feeling of the passage, and Juvenal will not allow us to reason the matter out. As far as he is concerned, all moral perversions, luxury in dress, food, building, sexual degradation, public amusement, everything comes from the East, the Hellenistic world. Such is his consistency that he gives Greek names to prostitutes.[96]

94. Quintilian constitutes a basic source on this point also: cf. 12.10.27 ff. Cf. also O. Weise, *Die Griechischen Wörter im Latein* (Leipzig, 1882), pp. 11 ff.; and E. H. Sturtevant, *The Pronunciation of Greek and Latin* (Chicago, 1920), pp. 36, 98 ff., 115.

95. J. Marouzeau, *Traité de Stylistique Latine* (Paris, 1946), pp. 92 ff.

96. For the practice of giving Greek names to prostitutes in Rome, cf. A. Cordier, *Le Vocabulaire épique dans l'Énéide* (Paris, 1939), p. 116. Juvenal uses Greek names for such women in 1.36, 3.136, 5.141, 6.123, 10.237.

The above examples have shown several Hellenisms used in a single passage, and although the satirist effects some *amplificatio,* his primary purpose seems to be evoking a general atmosphere of Greek corruption. In Satire 15 Juvenal exploits a rare Greek compound in a special metrical position, despite the fact that he could have achieved the same denotative meaning with a good Latin word.

> attonito cum
> tale super cenam facinus narraret Ulixes
> Alcinoo, bilem aut risum fortasse quibusdam
> moverat ut mendax *aretalogus.* (15.13–16)

Substitution of an expressive word for a neutral, perhaps more accurate term comes under one of the rubrics of amplificatio in Quintilian (8.4.1). With *aretalogus* Juvenal calls attention to the unscrupulous ways of the Greeks, even their moralists, and simultaneously stresses the incredible quality of the Egyptians' monstrous cannibalism.

Juvenal's indignatio integrates itself fully in his style. As a Roman, he takes a role of hating Greeks almost indiscriminately; as a rhetorical satirist, he makes Greek vocabulary speak for this hatred. This practice runs counter to Horace's employment of neutral terms and temperate reasoning, but it agrees entirely with the choice of expletives exemplified in Cicero's *In Pisonem.*[97] Juvenal the satirist has discovered a valuable use for *verba peregrina* in the very reasons that obliged Quintilian and his colleagues to disapprove of them.

Now let us look at other aspects of Juvenal's Latinitas, namely, the extent to which he will resort to *vulgare genus orationis* and *consuetudo.* I have already quoted Quintilian's approving citation of Cicero's comments in De or. 1.3.11–12 on the relative use of the vernacular. The rhetorician saw that

---

97. Cicero also exploits Roman prejudice against the Greeks by emphasizing Piso's association with that hated philosopher of Epicureanism, Philodemus (68 ff.).

if a speaker selected words conducive only to the ends of pure Latin and ornament, he might well leave the impression of affectedness. Therefore, choice of vocabulary must be determined not merely by linguistic prejudice but by the total function of a word. Quintilian draws a line at base, obscene terms (8.2.1), on the grounds that they interfere with the Roman concept of propriety; otherwise, the context determines usage.

> omnibus enim fere verbis praeter pauca, quae sunt parum verecunda, in oratione locus est. nam scriptores quidem iamborum veterisque comoediae etiam in illis saepe laudantur, sed nobis nostrum opus intueri sat est. omnia verba, exceptis de quibus dixi, sunt alicubi optima; nam et humilibus interim et vulgaribus est opus, et quae nitidiore in parte videntur sordida, ubi res poscit, proprie dicuntur.   (10.1.9)

The references to the writers of iambic verse and Old Comedy might well suggest the method which Juvenal will employ. Aware that obscene words affront the sense of propriety, the satirist exploits them in the same manner as Hellenisms: to focus his indignation. Similarly, he will use other vernacular terms, not to reproduce the easy informality of sermo, but to affect the feelings. Juvenal's satire, we may say, creates a new propriety, and he shows deep sensitivity to the demands of the context *(ubi res poscit)*.[98]

> lenonum ancillae posita Saufeiia corona
> provocat et tollit pendentis praemia coxae;
> ipsa Medullinae fluctum crisantis adorat;
> palma inter dominas, virtus natalibus aequa.   (6.320–3)

Juvenal's obscene terms are concentrated in Satires 2, 6, and 9, although they appear intermittently in other places: for example 1.37 ff.; 3.107, 112. By the very nature of the

---

98. Cf. the conclusion of Serafini, p. 276.

satiric subject, obscenity becomes proper as a means of precise and affective description. In the above example, Juvenal produces a scene of sexual perversion accompanying the notorious rites of Bona Dea, and makes it serve as symbolic of the corruption among women of the Roman nobility. The degrading "contest" among the females is portrayed with a careful blend of obscenity and highly honorific metaphorical words appropriate to Olympic games. That a Roman matron can defeat a prostitute in sexual prowess should horrify the imagination, and Juvenal summarizes the description with that acid phrase: *virtus natalibus aequa*. The accurate details serve a highly moral function, to make the scene all the more vivid and to expose the appalling contrast between the jaded interests of the matrons and the noble values *(corona, praemia, palma, virtus)* to which their high station commits them.

Juvenal draws from a wide range of vernacular words and forms: popular terms, whether in their primary or figurative sense; adjectives with a suffix that would conventionally make them common;[99] simple verbs that have been substituted for compounds;[100] loosely used superlatives; and diminutives.[101] Mostly they function to influence feeling, but they do so in various manners which merit some study.

> idem habitus cunctis, tonsi rectique capilli
> atque hodie tantum propter convivia pexi.
> pastoris duri hic filius, ille *bubulci*.   (11.149–51)

99. *Ibid.*, pp. 270 ff.

100. For the theory that such practice typifies the vulgar language, cf. F. Ruckdeschel, *Archaismen und Vulgarismen in der Sprache des Horaz* (diss., Munich, 1910), p. 25, and J. B. Hofmann, *Lateinische Umgangssprache* (2d ed. Heidelberg, 1936); for Juvenal's practice, cf. H. L. Wilson, "The Use of the Simple for the Compound Verb in Juvenal," *TAPA*, 31 (1900), 202–22.

101. For the vernacular implications of diminutives, cf. Hofmann, pp. 105 ff., and F. T. Cooper, *Word Formation in the Roman Sermo Plebeius* (diss., Columbia University, 1895), pp. 165 ff. For Juvenal's practice, cf. the list of Ercole, pp. 148 ff. and the comments of Serafini, pp. 264 ff.

consedere duces; surgis tu pallidus Aiax,
dicturus dubia pro libertate, *bubulco*
iudice. (7.115–17)

In Satire 11, portraying a modest banquet with great affection, Juvenal exploits the simple dress and origin of the servants as a means of capturing the reader's approval also. Conversely, *bubulco* in Satire 7 pointedly disturbs the context, Juvenal once again exploiting amplificatio to emphasize the point of his description. With reminiscences from Ovid's famous dispute between Ulysses and Ajax, the satirist envelops what is after all a sordid situation. By careful use of the metrical position, he forces the reader to linger over the explosive word before following the enjambement to the next line, to discover the extent of the horror: the cowherd is judge!

Both Juvenal and Horace use diminutives in about the same ratio.[102] Horace makes them blend into his context of gentle irony; Juvenal exploits them as rhetorically significant to his various moral attacks.

ni parere velis, pereundum erit ante lucernas;
si scelus admittas, dabitur mora *parvola,* dum res
nota urbi et populo contingat principis aurem.   (10.339–41)

qua nec terribiles Cimbri nec Brittones umquam
Sauromataeque truces aut inmanes Agathyrsi,
hac saevit rabie inbelle et inutile volgus,
parvola fictilibus solitum dare vela phaselis
et brevibus pictae remis incumbere testae. (15.124–8)

    o nummi! vobis hunc praestat honorem,
vos estis frater! dominus tamen et domini rex
si vis tunc fieri, nullus tibi *parvolus* aula
luserit Aeneas nec filia dulcior illo. (5.136–9)

I have chosen three instances of the diminutive adjective *parvolus,* to show how the satirist can vary the implications of a

102. Ruckdeschel, p. 13, and Ercole. It works out to approximately 3 per cent for each satirist (for Juvenal, 94 cases in about 3,800 lines).

word according to the passage, while consistently making it affective rather than vernacular. In Satire 10, Silius, facing the dilemma of whether to accede to Messalina's lust, learns that he can extend his life briefly by accepting "marriage." Since Juvenal aims to expose the vanity of physical beauty, the tiny delay in inevitable execution becomes almost pathetic, and we feel with the relatively innocent but too handsome Silius. To enhance the pathos, the satirist defines the extent of the brief respite by the time it takes the cuckolded old Claudius to learn his own shame. On the other hand, Juvenal attacks the Egyptians in Satire 15. The contrast of their cowardly ways and their miserable painted sailing vessels with their act of cannibalism emphasizes the enormity of their crime. Thus, the diminutive can serve as the basis for both affection and anger. Satire 5 provides us with an example of epic parody, where the diminutive actually comes from the Vergilian context. Juvenal, however, does make fun of epic conventions, and often by diminutives: for example 1.11 or 13.40. Dido made herself appealing in *Aen.* 4.328 by her desire to have a child by Aeneas. Now, the satirist implies, the world has changed, and, even if one has a child who promises to grow up a Roman hero, one earns no credit; all the *captatores* would abandon one, for friendship depends on available money, not on family honor. Serafini rightly concludes with respect to diminutives: "Ad ogni modo essi, sia perchè poco numerosi sia perchè quasi sempre espressivi ed artistici, non attestano affato una lingua popolaresca."[103]

Next, we turn to archaisms, which by definition conflict with the notion of everyday speech.[104] Archaisms became an important element of poetic diction quite early,[105] and in

103. Serafini, p. 270.
104. Marouzeau (note 95 above), p. 179.
105. Cordier (note 96 above), pp. 6 ff. B. Axelson, *Unpoetische Wörter: Ein Beitrag zur Kenntnis der lateinischen Dichtersprache* (Lund, 1945), pp. 25 ff., observes that, linguistically considered, the archaism and the poetic term fall into quite distinct categories; and, in this respect, we find a clue to Juvenal's usage.

Quintilian's time they were recognized as a permissible if infrequent part of the orator's vocabulary.[106] They served to lend the dignity of antiquity to a stately passage: *propriis* [i.e. verbis] *dignitatem dat antiquitas. namque et sanctiorem et magis admirabilem faciunt orationem, quibus non quilibet fuerit usurus* (8.3.24). The danger in archaisms consisted in obscurity and a taint of preciosity: *at obscuritas fit verbis jam ab usu remotis.*[107] It is in this context that Juvenal assails the woman who parades her exotic vocabulary:

odi

> hanc ego quae repetit volvitque Palaemonis artem
> servata semper lege et ratione loquendi
> ignotosque mihi tenet *antiquaria* versus. (6.451–4)

We may infer from the above passage that Juvenal knew as well as Quintilian the relative propriety of archaisms. Therefore, on the basis of his manipulation of other technically "improper" words, we might well expect that he will exploit archaisms to point up an attack on somebody or something.

> quondam hoc indigenae vivebant more, priusquam
> sumeret agrestem posito diademate falcem
> Saturnus fugiens, tunc cum . . .
> nulla super nubes convivia *caelicolarum*
> nec puer Iliacus *formonsa* nec Herculis uxor
> . . . nondum aliquis sortitus triste profundi
> imperium Sicula *torvos* cum coniuge Pluton . . .
> credebant *quom* grande nefas et morte piandum,
> si iuvenis vetulo non adsurrexerat . . .
> tam venerabile erat praecedere quattuor annis,
> primaque par adeo sacra lanugo *senectae*. (13.38–59)

106. Other writers of this time practiced archaism: for Statius, cf. A. Klotz, "Klassizismus und Archaismus—Stilistisches zu Statius," *Archiv für lat. Lex.,* 15 (1908), 401–17; for Tacitus, A. Schmidt, *De poetico sermonis argenteae latinitatis colore* (diss., Breslau, 1909), together with the remarks in *Dial.* 23.

107. *Inst.* 1.6.39. Cf. Seneca, *Contr.* 9.2.26.

Archaisms have been classified in several ways, and one can see an early classification in Quintilian (8.3.24–9): there are archaic endings for the infinitive or archaic declensions; archaic spelling may change the character of a word (e.g. *formonsa, torvos, quom*); some words had a vernacular form and a form fallen from regular use and adopted by the poets (*senecta* vs. *senectus*); some were obsolete in sense; and compounds of the type of *caelicolarum* smack of antique poetic vocabulary.[108] In the above passage I have accepted Knoche's use of orthographic archaisms.[109] If right, it fits the context very well. Attempting to evoke a picture of the primeval past, though with some irony, Juvenal comments on the moral uprightness of that long-gone era. The archaisms and the regretful tone of the passage work together to emphasize how irretrievably vanished such simple honesty is. On the other hand, archaism may serve the purpose of amplificatio, by exposing false pretensions. In Satire 10 we review the vain ambitions of men. In dealing with military glory the satirist describes a typical triumph, with considerable emphasis on the useless, broken items of plunder and the misery of the captives, then comments:

> ad hoc se
> Romanus Graiusque et barbarus *induperator*
> erexit. (10.137–9)

The archaism, we might say, constitutes the interpretation of the whole futile ambition; and Juvenal has especially called it to our attention by placing its five syllables at the end of a metrical line, in pointed violation of the conventional rules for the formal hexameter.

108. I have adopted, with some modifications, the classification of Cordier, pp. 4 ff.

109. Cf. U. Knoche, "Handschriftliche Grundlagen des Juvenaltextes," *Philol.*, Suppl. 31:1 (1940), 349. F. Cremer, *De grammaticorum antiquorum in Juvenale arte critica* (diss., Münster, 1913), pp. 3 ff., discussed errors that crept into the MSS as a result of unfamiliarity with Juvenal's orthography.

If archaisms conflict with the connotations of *sermo*, the liberal use of obviously poetic words utterly destroys any illusion of calm conversation. The rhetoricians, however, supported a moderate adoption of poetic terms for the same reason they approved of archaisms. When Juvenal makes liberal use of such words, we again infer that the contemporary rhetorical background influences him far more than the satiric tradition. From his earliest years with the grammaticus, a boy read and criticized poetry, learning especially to distinguish the poetic vocabulary and its special uses (1.8.13 ff.). When he went on to the rhetor, the student continued to read poetry for didactic and esthetic purposes. He soon had to realize that a line existed between poetry and oratory, across which it was dangerous for a speaker to advance. Quintilian severely cautions his pupils against copying the licentious manipulation of words permitted the poets (10.1.28–30). Similarly, he distinguishes the orator's from the poet's method of dealing with epithets: while the poet may employ what we call an ornamental epithet, the orator must take care to make every word count: *apud oratorem, nisi aliquid efficitur, redundat* (8.6.40). Juvenal, we shall see, knows this rule well: he makes all his epithets count, even the seemingly ornamental ones, in the latter case exploiting the very prejudice against redundancy. Quintilian also comments on the indiscriminate mixing of linguistic categories and specifies among other monstrous blends the practice of placing poetic and vulgar words in the same context (8.3.60). Here, again, is a rule made to order for Juvenal. He will commit the error deliberately, relying on the shock that it will cause, and make the mixture a means of expressing *indignatio*.

Since Vergil's inimitable epic provided the standard lexicon for the formal poet, in the opinion of Juvenal[110] as well

110. On Juvenal's thorough acquaintance with Vergil cf. G. Highet, "Juvenal's Bookcase," *AJP*, 72 (1951), 394. In commenting on the satirist, scholiasts cite Vergil more than any other writer.

as Quintilian,[111] we can discover the poetic elements in the satirist's vocabulary without too great trouble.[112] Some words are uniquely poetic in concept or association: for example, *dirus, letalis, priscus, trux, udus;* others have doublets which function in prose: *aequor* vs. *mare; tellus* vs. *terra.* And we have already discussed those compounds, basically archaic in form, which were appropriated to poetry. The length of the full list amply proves that Juvenal rejects any rules that restrict him to *sermo cotidianus.*

The poetic word can be affective because it stirs associations of an ideal world, or it can promote the satiric purpose of angry contrast between unreality and actuality.

> quis enim iam non intellegat artes
> patricias? quis *priscum* illud miratur acumen,
> Brute, tuum? facile est barbato imponere regi.   (4.101–3)

In Satire 4, Juvenal exposes Domitian against a background of epic values; and in this example he refers to the golden past when Brutus deceived the tyrannous Tarquin, awaiting the day when he would overthrow the king. That day lies far back in the legendary history of Rome, which the satirist stresses by the regretful, pessimistic epithet *priscum.* Brutus lived in a poetic atmosphere, which a degenerate, tyrannized Rome could never recapture.

> post omnis herbas, post cuncta animalia, quidquid
> cogebat vacui ventris furor, hostibus ipsis
> pallorem ac maciem et tenuis miserantibus *artus,*
> membra aliena fame lacerabant, esse parati
> et sua.   (15.99–103)

---

111. Just as Cicero represents oratory for Quintilian, Vergil represents poetry: no other Latin poet is cited so frequently.

112. I am particularly dependent upon Cordier, pp. 152 ff. My list of Juvenal's poetic vocabulary may be found in my unpublished dissertation, pp. 70 ff.

In contrast to the bestial and inexcusable cannibalism of the Egyptians, the satirist recounts the only analogous events of which he can think, to show that, in every other case, people became cannibalistic as a last resort, to escape starvation. Under tight siege, when all supplies and other substitutes for food had given out, the Vascones finally began to eat human flesh. To make the implications entirely patent, Juvenal describes how even the enemy pitied their emaciated victims; and he carefully inserts at the end of the line the poetic word *artus*, as if to stress the pitying feelings of the enemy and the piteous plight of the besieged. Not content with this, the satirist immediately juxtaposes to the poetic word its prose equivalent *membra*. As a result, he seems to lessen the impression of the act of cannibalism, to render it almost impersonal. From his perspective, we are to pity the starving defenders in general rather than the poor ones who were ultimately eaten.[113] A similarly clever use of poetic and prose doublets occurs in Umbricius' denunciation of the Greeks:

> quid quod adulandi gens prudentissima laudat
> sermonem indocti, faciem deformis amici,
> et longum invalidi *collum cervicibus* aequat
> Herculis Antaeum procul a tellure tenentis.   (3.86–9)

Such is the Greeks' skill in servility that they can compare the scrawny neck *(collum)* of a sickly rich man to the heroic neck *(cervix)* of Hercules imagined at a moment of special stress in his contest with Antaeus. The juxtaposition only emphasizes the audacity and outrageous success of their lies.

Quintilian regarded the poetic epithet as improper for the

113. It is of course permissible to object here that Juvenal does not achieve the effect described, but merely chooses his vocabulary *metri gratia*. I concede that my interpretation rests on a personal opinion; but I do think that the juxtaposition implies selection on the satirist's part, and the example which immediately follows illustrates the same technique in a context where there can be little doubt about the implications. Cf. 10.192.

orator. Juvenal exploits it as an ideal way of recreating the atmosphere of formal poetry for mock epic or epic parody.[114] I cite four examples from Satire 4, where, as if in an epic catalogue, the satirist introduces us to Domitian's advisors, one after the other:

> Rubrius, offensae veteris reus atque tacendae (105)
> et matutino sudans Crispinus amomo (108)
> Pompeius tenui iugulos aperire susurro (110)
> Fuscus, marmorea meditatus proelia villa. (112)

In each case but one, as regularly in Vergil, the epithet precedes its noun, and Juvenal places both in emphatic metrical positions, one before the central caesura, the other at the end of the line.

Quintilian disapproved of the mixture of poetic and vulgar words. Juvenal derives considerable emotional force from precisely such combinations.

> qualis tunc epulas ipsum gluttisse putamus
> induperatorem, cum tot sestertia, partem
> exiguam et modicae sumptam de margine cenae,
> purpureus magni ructarit scurra Palati? (4.28–31)

The satirist prepares the way for his mock epic by making patent in this carefully contrived rhetorical question, so typical of vituperatio, the sharp conflict between a gross concern with food and heroic ideals. The subject of the vulgar *gluttisse,* carefully delayed, strikes with special effect at the beginning of the line after enjambement, especially since *induperatorem* connotes archaic poetry. Similarly, the description of

114. Serafini, pp. 245 ff., discusses Juvenal's careful use of the adjective, but argues that such economy opposes current rhetorical practice (luxuriant use of adjectives). I do not feel that the point is well taken, because abundance of epithets typified only some orators. Certainly, Quintilian disapproves of such turgidity, as does Tacitus. Indeed, in Tacitus and Juvenal, it seems to me, we find the proper rhetorical application of epithets: to make a point.

Crispinus, by which Juvenal further taints Domitian, illustrates the ingenious blend of vulgar and poetic *(purpureus ructarit scurra)*. In the semantic conflict, the satirist finds the paradox which justifies his own righteous anger.

To summarize our discussion of vocabulary, we may say that Juvenal abandons the satiric convention of recreating sermo and, deeply imbued with the rhetorical doctrine of his day as well as an entirely new satiric approach, selects his words for their striking effects. The rigidly defined linguistic categories and the formal rules of propriety provide him with precisely the cultural prejudices he requires. He makes Hellenisms serve his purpose to stigmatize the demoralizing effect on Rome of the Hellenistic world; he makes vulgarisms affective, frequently to concentrate our attention on the base institutions of Rome; he uses archaisms to recall the dead past and place it in sharp contrast with the degenerate present; and he exploits poetic vocabulary in a series of ways to expose the crass lack of ideals in the city which once inspired the epic of Vergil. By using words "improperly" the satirist makes them explode in their contexts, for their semantic conflict consistently symbolizes his own personal conflict as *vir bonus atque Romanus* with the disgrace of Rome.

We turn our attention now briefly to transferred terms, tropes. Quintilian discusses them soon after he has given the rules for choosing words, and his reason soon emerges: tropes directly affect the vocabulary of a writer, being substitutes for the proper word. The rhetorician has provided us with the most elaborate discussion of such tropes now surviving, among treatises written up to his time. Indeed, his great interest in these rhetorical devices, by contrast with Cicero, indicates the probable concern of his period, hence a special influence operative on Juvenal during his early years. Quintilian discusses metaphor first, as the most common and beautiful of tropes, explaining the purpose of the trope as follows: *id facimus* [i.e. transferre], *aut quia necesse est aut quia significantius est aut (ut dixi) quia decentius* (8.6.6). Now, we can

461

be quite sure that Juvenal never felt under obligation either to necessity or to ornamentation, so that he will have aimed at significance. The very concept of *decor,* the rhetorical assumption that metaphor was the most beautiful of tropes, would tend to suggest an entirely different exploitation of the device: Juvenal would expose the ugly in Rome to affront his reader's preconceptions and thus bring out Rome's vicious state.[115]

> cum te summoveant qui testamenta merentur
> noctibus, in caelum quos *evehit* optima summi
> nunc *via* processus, vetulae *vesica* beatae?   (1.37–9)

Juvenal talks of himself being jostled out of the way by some wealthy upstart who has inherited the riches of an elderly lady because of his fine services for her. The metaphors, it will be noticed, work together both semantically and alliteratively to produce a rapid indictment of the city. In a sense, the very transfer illustrates the transvaluations that have taken place: it now is a way to exalted honor to become a gigolo! However, the satirist will not let us enjoy his irony for long; with the obscene metaphor *vesica* he shatters any illusions we may have had and bares the perversion in all its ugliness. In a similar manner, he can summarize a woman's efforts to make herself up:

> sed quae mutatis inducitur atque fovetur
> tot medicaminibus coctaeque siliginis offas
> accipit et madidae, facies dicetur an *ulcus?*   (6.471–3)

These are not beautiful metaphors that I have chosen. Juvenal has placed them in a position of emphasis to take advantage of the rhetorical preconception about metaphor, just as Cicero carefully placed his invective metaphors for Piso. In some

---

115. The only thorough inquiry into Juvenal's metaphors is the antiquated one, based merely on classification, of H. Jattkowski, *De sermone in A. Persii Flacci et D. Junii Juvenalis satiris figurato* (Allenstein, 1886). The dissertation of K. Heindl, "Bilder, Vergleiche, und Beschreibungen bei Juvenal" (Vienna, 1951), does not appear to have been published.

cases, the satirist will take more conventional metaphors, but the purpose will be approximately the same: he will show us that what once were conventions no longer exist. In Satire 2, he talks a great deal in terms of military prowess, a metaphor which conflicts radically with the effeminate interests of the homosexuals there discussed. Satire 15 employs much animal imagery which, by the end, ceases to function as tropical: men are beasts—worse than beasts, if they behave as the Egyptian cannibals. The significance, then, that Juvenal derives from metaphors contributes directly to his satiric preconceptions.

Another popular trope, metonymy, can sometimes be even more emotionally effective, because one sees the connection between it and the word it replaces. Juvenal forces that very connection upon us, the substituted word being the means whereby he calls attention to an evil condition.[116]

quid tam festa dies, ut cesset prodere furem,
perfidiam, fraudes atque omni ex crimine lucrum
quaesitum et partos *gladio* vel *pyxide* nummos? (13.23–5)

To say that murderous attacks and poisoning occur regularly would have served the same denotative purpose, but Juvenal forces us to visualize the instruments of these crimes. The result is precision and the revulsion that accompanies the vivid reference to the deadly weapons.

haec ego non agitem? sed quid magis? Heracleas
aut Diomedeas aut *mugitum labyrinthi*
et mare percussum puero fabrumque volantem? (1.52–4)

Quintilian observed that synecdoche and the closely related metonymy were more freely available to poets than to orators (8.6.19). Juvenal will use metonymy at will, but not like the conventional formal poet. In this case he deliberately undermines the grandeur of one of the most famous themes of

116. On metonymy cf. J. Strefinger, *Der Stil des Satirikers Juvenals* (Regensburg, 1892), pp. 35 ff., and Ryberg, p. 33.

poetry, Theseus and the Minotaur, and by the very device favored by poets. The most poetic use of metonymy, according to Quintilian (8.6.23), consisted in taking the name of an inventor or god and substituting it for the thing invented or governed. He specifically mentions the decorous propriety of replacing *coitus* with *Venus* (24). Compare with the rhetorician's ideas Juvenal's metonymous exploitation of *Venus:*

prima peregrinos obscaena pecunia mores
intulit, et turpi fregerunt saecula luxu
divitiae molles. quid enim *Venus* ebria curat?   (6.298–300)

Juvenal does not shrink from the proper word because of modesty, nor does Venus here stand for sexual intercourse. Rather, as the context shows, the satirist refers to any promiscuous woman who, under the influence of drink after a luxurious banquet, loses all moral perspective. The goddess serves to emphasize the enormity of the vice. Our satirist knows well how the poets use metonymy,[117] and he turns away from their licentious practice in order to make a savage, not a pretty, comment.

It is natural to think of antonomasia in connection with metonymy. It, too, Quintilian notes, occurs with particular frequency in poetry (8.6.29), while it is rare in oratory. Juvenal uses it extensively, again to make direct comments on poetic ideas and the total disappearance of the heroic ideal.[118] The passage above, cited from 1.52–4, illustrates the satirist's contempt for poetic subjects by contrast with real vice, and

117. Juvenal affords precise evidence of his acquaintance with the theory on metonymy in 3.198–9. There, he takes Vergil's famous *iam proximus ardet/Ucalegon* (*Aen.* 2.311) and rewrites it *iam frivola transfert/Ucalegon,* having already made clear that the house is burning. Juvenal makes the change because Vergil's phrase constitutes an outrageous example of poetic metonymy. As such, it receives rather severe comment from Quintilian in 8.6.25. In other words, Juvenal and the rhetorician agree entirely in their interpretation of this trope.

118. On antonomasia cf. Strefinger, p. 28; Friedländer in notes on 1.61 and 5.45; Ryberg, pp. 30, 70 ff.; and Serafini, p. 283.

he adopts metonymy, as I noted, but also antonomasia: in *fabrumque volantem* he strikingly undercuts the romantic picture of the winged Daedalus. At other times, the satirist uses a familiar name from legend to describe a vicious person of the present:

> ut cessit, facili patuerunt cardine valvae;
> exclusi spectant admissa obsonia patres.
> itur ad *Atriden*. (4.63–5)

When a patronymic replaces a name, antonomasia occurs; and when a mythical name replaces that of a real person, antonomasia occurs. Here, Juvenal has combined both processes, to refer to Domitian in terms of the son of Atreus. The tremendous gap between the heroic leader of the expedition against Troy and the gourmet Domitian becomes focused in the single word. Juvenal achieves precisely the opposite of poetic ennoblement, so implying that there is no poetry in the regime of Domitian. Antonomasia becomes even more significant when one substitutes for a name the name of a real, but more famous, prototype:

> occurrit matrona potens, quae molle Calenum
> porrectura viro miscet sitiente rubetam
> instituitque rudes melior *Lucusta* propinquas
> per famam et populum nigros efferre maritos. (1.69–72)

Juvenal affects to take a great heroine, whereas he cites the notorious poisoner of the Claudian line. In this respect, *melior* illustrates the transvaluation of Roman honor: heroes no longer stand as models for the youth; they have been replaced now by monsters such as Lucusta. Antonomasia, with its poetic associations, provides the most savage imaginable comment on an unpoetic situation.

Periphrasis has two main functions according to Quintilian: to skirt around a ticklish, generally obscene subject and to ornament a passage, the latter being especially favored by the poets (8.6.60). Juvenal, who calls a spade a spade with great effect, would not try to cloak a description of sexual depravity; he would exploit the poetic associations of the device to make his typical comment on the lack of poetic ideals in contemporary Rome.[119] To reinforce the attack, he regularly begins the relative clause by which he characteristically presents periphrasis at a metrical position which pointedly defies the rules of the formal hexameter. For instance, in 6.7–8, he refers contemptuously to Catullus' Clodia: *nec tibi, cuius/turbavit nitidos extinctus passer ocellos.* A relative should never end a line. Later on in the same Satire, he refers to Clodia's brother:

sed omnes
noverunt Mauri atque Indi quae psaltria penem
maiorem, quam sunt duo Caesaris Anticatones,
illuc, testiculi sibi conscius *unde* fugit mus,
intulerit.   (6.336–40)

The circumlocution for the rites of Bona Dea actually seeks out the obscene, and, with that jolting rhythm at the end of the line, so sharply in contrast with the heavy force of *Anticatones,* makes amply evident the extent of female corruption. A mouse might shun the rites, not Clodia's brother.

Quintilian considers hyperbaton a trope, so we shall treat it here. This device of moving words from their expected position has, as the rhetorician notes, a special value in making a speech more rhythmical and more pleasing in structure (8.6.62–5). For various reasons, especially the requirements of meter, hyperbaton occurs even more commonly in poetry, though the example of tmesis which Quintilian cites (66) should not be regarded as typical. Let us admit that Juvenal did have to make some concessions to meter; he certainly did not use hyperbaton to beautify his verse.[120] When he employs

119. On periphrasis, cf. Strefinger, p. 30; Friedländer in his note on 1.25; Ryberg, p. 30; and Serafini, p. 283.
120. Serafini, pp. 286 ff., discusses hyperbaton well, using the term "disgiunzione."

a typical epic hyperbaton, with the epithet at the caesura and the noun at the end of the line or variations thereof, he does so to produce a mock-epic setting. Often he achieves a sharp effect, as one sees in the first lines of Satire 1:

> impune diem consumpserit ingens
> Telephus aut summi plena iam margine libri
> scriptus et in tergo necdum finitus *Orestes?* (4–6)

By the time the reader reaches *Orestes*, he is nearly breathless; he realizes just how long the dreary play must be.

As the last trope, I shall discuss hyperbole. Juvenal has suffered severe criticism on this point,[121] and we should attempt to discover what the satirist was doing with this device, what reactions he could anticipate in his rhetorically trained milieu. Quintilian defines hyperbole succinctly as *decens veri superiectio* (8.6.67). The examples he adduces give us some help: five poetic ones from Vergil, one from a humorous epigram of Cicero; three Ciceronian periods in the style we have called vituperatio (one from the *Verrines*, two from the *Philippics*). The Vergilian examples do not exaggerate a passion but enhance a scene. However, we have but to recall Dido's attacks on Aeneas' honor in *Aeneid* 4 to realize that hyperbole can have more than ornamental functions in poetry. But Quintilian's distinction serves our purpose of illustrating the characteristic difference between poetical and oratorical hyperbole: ornament vs. expression of passion appropriate to indignatio and vituperatio. In this respect, Quintilian's final comments should be quoted in full:

> tum est hyperbole virtus, cum res ipsa, de qua loquendum est, naturalem modum excessit. conceditur enim amplius dicere, quia dici, quantum est, non potest, meliusque ultra quam citra stat oratio. (76)

Here we discover precisely what Juvenal seeks to express,

---

121. Cf. De Decker (note 33 above), pp. 142 ff.

that Rome has exceeded all limits and that its degeneracy can be implied only by hyperbole.[122] The Roman world is out of joint. Juvenal does not, therefore, enhance a touching scene to make us appreciate its poetic beauty; he describes the real world: *nunc ad quas non Clodius aras?* (6.345). Is there any less moral vigor in this, for all its exaggeration, than in Cicero's description of Verres, and later Antony, as Charybdis? One Clodius symbolized the corruption of Roman matrons at the end of the Republic; numberless copies of Clodius now show how far Rome has degenerated even since 62 B.C.

In summary, tropes in Juvenal work with exceptional rhetorical effect, precisely because Juvenal skillfully adjusted their functions to those rhetorical conventions current in his time. In the examples which we have studied, we have seen that the satirist exploited tropes usually considered "poetic" in order to make particularly indignant comments on Roman degeneracy, not to be poetic. With a device like hyperbole, he adopts an entirely rhetorical manner to demonstrate that Rome has gone beyond all rational limits of vice and to fit this emotion to the style which a man like Cicero would appropriate in scathing *vituperatio*.

Quintilian immediately proceeds from tropes to figures of thought, which he defines as an artful shaping of speech (9.1.4 and 14). Such figures seem to have a primary function in arousing feeling: *iam vero adfectus nihil magis ducit* (21); and consequently, in every passage of high emotion, figures will be found (24). Quintilian goes on to list a wide variety of such devices, of which I shall discuss four in reference to Juvenal. When a figure achieves its effect by indirection (for example irony or insinuation), it interferes with the expression of *indignatio* and evokes an image of a rather wily speaker, an

122. For Juvenal's practice cf. De Decker; Strefinger, p. 11; Ryberg, p. 34; and Serafini, pp. 290 ff. The latter argues, I think incorrectly, that Juvenal actually experiences these emotions, and thus he excuses Juvenal.

image which Juvenal strenuously avoids. One thinks of rhetorical questions as typical figures, for, as Quintilian observes, it is a basic instinct in us which makes us inquire. Among the various passions which such questions can connote, the rhetorician specifies indignatio and cites an angry complaint of Juno from *Aen.* 1.48 (9.2.10). Almost any paragraph of Cicero's speech *In Pisonem* contains similarly irate questions, as do the more spirited sections of the *Philippics*. Juvenal uses this figure without hesitation and totally in keeping with rhetorical presuppositions.[123] Just as Cicero makes it serve to express his outrage, so Juvenal in Satire 1 makes it lead directly to his statement *facit indignatio versum*. He begins with a series of questions, and, when he actually starts to explain his satiric creed, he repeatedly erupts: Who could have a heart of iron to endure the depraved city and not launch out at its vices (30 ff.); or, Should he not use satire to denounce the vices he sees (51 ff.); or, Would not anyone be impelled to fill a book right on the street corner, when people flaunt their perversions so openly (63 ff.)? These questions, I maintain, fall in the same class as those conveying Cicero's indignatio: they form a carefully designed portion of the satirist's persona, fully appreciable to a contemporary reader at least.

Figures designed to rouse emotions depend on *simulatio*, Quintilian observes (9.2.26), so that *exclamatio* functions as a figure when the orator designs the outburst. Again, among the emotions conveyed by the device, he specifies indignatio, but he so compresses his examples that it is difficult to determine which one serves this particular passion: I would suspect the most appropriate *exclamatio* to be Cicero's famous *O tempora, o mores!* Again, we find the device in our model of vituperatio, *In Pisonem*. Cicero fulminates *O di immortales;*[124]

---

123. A formidable list of Juvenal's rhetorical questions will be found in De Decker, pp. 180 ff.; he regards this figure as clear evidence of Juvenal's insincerity. Cf. also Ryberg, p. 24, and Serafini, p. 243.

124. *In Pis.* 41; cf. frag. 1, 45.

or he cries out: *miserum me! cum hac me nunc peste atque labe confero!*[125] and later: *O scelus, o pestis, o labes!*[126] In all these, the orator simulates indignation, the exclamation forming part of the general denunciation of Piso. So, too, Juvenal gives his indignant persona expressions appropriate to its role, but cases of true *exclamatio* occur rarely.[127] More often than not, Juvenal directs the general expostulation at a particular person or thing, so as to convert it to apostrophe. The resultant precision of reference produces an implicit emotional contrast between the person evoked and the vice which has provoked the outcry. I cite one example of *exclamatio* approaching apostrophe:

declamare doces? o ferrea pectora Vetti,
cum perimit saevos classis numerosa tyrannos! (7.150–1)

The very difficulty of the rhetorician's task incites the satirist to a rhetorical exclamation. Juvenal may also have felt that this device too obviously depended upon *simulatio* and accordingly did not want to taint his persona. At any rate, he comments on Cicero's famous *O fortunatam natam me consule Romam* in 10.122[128] in a manner that shows his amusement at Cicero's exaggeration (by comparison with the *Philippics*) as well as at the jingling structure of the verse.[129]

As I have said, Juvenal prefers the closer, more specific connections of apostrophe to the undirected outbursts of ex-

125. *Ibid.* 3.
126. *Ibid.* 56.
127. The Scholia frequently comment on a passage with the single word "exclamatio": cf. 3.60; 6.97, 277. However, the scholiast uses the word not in its technical meaning, but with a loose reference to the emotional feeling which he senses in the passage.
128. For the most recent discussion of Cicero's line cf. Walter Allen, Jr., *TAPA,* 87 (1956), 130 ff.
129. Again, we find Juvenal agreeing with the verdict of the rhetoricians represented by Quintilian: Quintilian pronounces Cicero's line entirely inappropriate and as such cites it twice: 9.4.41 and 11.1.24.

clamatio.[130] Quintilian discusses the special affective quality of the figure in three respects, one of which he defines as an appeal that brings our opponents into disfavor: *invidiosam implorationem* (9.2.38). If this were not sufficiently suggestive, the example would dispel any doubt, for Quintilian cites an angry apostrophe from the *Verrines,* in which Cicero cries out to those laws which Verres has so flagrantly broken. In his attack on Piso, Cicero calls up the spirits of the great Roman *triumphatores,* to shame his victim who has implicitly scorned a triumph.[131] This usage I have singled out fits well with the righteous wrath of our satirist, who also will expose the vicious against the ideal background.[132] He calls upon Mars to do something drastic with the effeminates who now disgrace Rome (2.126 ff.); he demands of Janus whether he can endure the degrading prayers of a woman seeking victory in a musical contest for her lover (6.393 ff.); and, with considerable irony, he allows the pervert Naevolus to appeal to his Lares to secure his future prosperity (9.137 ff.). A different contrast by apostrophe may be seen in Satire 1:

> exul ab octava Marius bibit et fruitur dis
> iratis: at tu victrix, provincia, ploras!   (49–50)

Marius Priscus has been condemned for plundering his province, but he enjoys his loot. Juvenal directs our emotions by suddenly shifting from a dispassionate description of the situation to a sympathetic address to the province itself, brought directly before our eyes in its anomalous position, successful in prosecution but unable to receive compensation for its losses.

Our final figure of thought epitomizes Juvenal's technique

130. On the function of apostrophe cf. Ryberg, p. 25.

131. *In Pis.* 58.

132. Juvenal's use of apostrophe is discussed by Ryberg; De Decker, pp. 174 ff.; and Serafini, pp. 243, 293 ff. De Decker criticizes the satirist severely.

in most of his rhetoric: I refer to antithesis. Quintilian hesitates whether to regard it as a figure of thought or of speech and so discusses it cursorily under both heads.[133] The distinction, essentially a quantitative one, does not concern us especially: antithesis can reside in a phrase, in adjacent clauses, in related sentences or paragraphs; and the examples which the rhetorician adduces do not really differ in effect. As will be recognized, I have consistently suggested that the underlying result of nearly every rhetorical device in Juvenal is contrast or, in other words, antithesis. The satirist produces linguistic mixtures, where vulgar and poetic vocabulary conflict or where Hellenisms affront the reader's conventional expectations, and the conflict symbolizes the moral conflict in Rome. Tropes also create paradoxical concepts: consider the use of metonymy or antonomasia. Now, we have observed that Juvenal's figures of thought exploit emotional reactions against a national degradation that provokes rhetorical questions, exclamations, and apostrophes. Such antithesis fits the persona of the indignant satirist, because, as an honest Roman, he abhors what has happened to his Rome: everything in the city contradicts his noble ideals. As Umbricius says: *non est Romano cuiquam locus hic* (3.119).

Juvenal exploits several standard moral antitheses which became popular with rhetoricians long before his time, especially the opposition of present to past.[134] For the satirist, however, such contrasts do not function merely as commonplaces. His affection for the past stems directly from his moral revulsion from the present. In a sense, as Serafini justly observes, the persona in the Satires strikingly resembles some of the attitudes of the Elder Cato.[135] Like Umbricius, he appears as a man living in an age and an environment that can

133. *Inst.* 9.2.100, 9.3.81.
134. For Juvenal's use of antithesis see the divergent comments in Strefinger, p. 13; De Decker, pp. 117 ff.; and Ryberg, pp. 39 ff.
135. Serafini, p. 375.

no longer accommodate him. Antitheses form an essential aspect of the organization of each Satire. In Satire 1 the satirist's reaction against contemporary dabbling in unreal poetic themes contributes directly to a definition of his own literary concepts. In Satire 3 several pauses to describe the idyllic attractions of the country serve to bring out the fact that at least some Roman values survive outside Rome, so that Umbricius is justified in seeking a rural retreat. Elsewhere I have argued that the basic theme of every Satire of indignation resides in a sharp antithesis, a paradox.[136] Lesser contrasts support the major thematic ones. One of the most effective vignettes of Satire 3 consists of a street scene (239 ff.) in which we compare the movements of a rich and a poor man. The rich floats over the heads of the mob, generally asleep in his sedan chair; the poor struggles along, jostled by everyone he meets, kicked by passing legionnaires, bruised by timbers that others are carrying, and always running the danger of burial under the load of a collapsing wagon. Juvenal carefully selects the details to bring out with the maximum power this contrast; in turn, this antithesis emphasizes the theme of the whole Satire, the hostility of Rome to a native Roman. The celebrated passage in Satire 10 on the fall of Sejanus uses similar techniques. Once Sejanus was second only to Tiberius and his statues met the gaze wherever one went; now the corpse of Sejanus has been dragged to the Tiber, his statues have been demolished, and his former associates tremble for their lives. From this brilliant antithesis Juvenal derives his comment on the vanity of political ambition.

Within lesser limits, yet essentially accomplishing the same results, the satirist produces antithesis by oxymoron and striking juxtapositions.[137] To take a few examples from Satire 1:

cum *tener uxorem* ducat spado, Mevia Tuscum
figat aprum et nuda teneat venabula mamma . . . (22–3)

136. "Studies in Book I of Juvenal," *YCS*, 15 (1957), 86 ff.
137. On oxymoron cf. Strefinger, p. 10.

cum verna Canopi

Crispinus Tyrias umero revocante lacernas
ventilet aestivum digitis sudantibus aurum
nec sufferre queat *maioris pondera gemmae* . . . (26–9)

cum leno accipiat moechi bona, si capiendi
ius nullum uxori, doctus spectare lacunar,
doctus et ad calicem *vigilanti stertere* naso . . . (55–7)

We would normally expect *uxor* to be qualified with *tenera;* the satirist juxtaposes these normally associated words, but grammatically dissociates them to show the enormity of the marriage here arranged. Similarly, he focuses our outrage against Crispinus on the savage detail that the Egyptian upstart cannot even lift his ring because of the excessive weight of its jewel. When a husband prostitutes his wife, when he pretends to be asleep in order to facilitate the arrangement, we have another illustration of moral degradation in Rome, here emphasized by the use of *doctus*. In fact, it will be found that nearly every person mentioned in that parade of vice (22–78) has his perversion impressed on our imagination by some express verbal or tropical antithesis. The verbal contrast symbolizes the fundamental moral tension between degraded Rome and the ethically sensitive satirist. It simply cannot be stressed enough that the basic rhetorical approach of Juvenal inheres in a tissue of contrasts, small and great, totally adapted to the assumptions of indignatio.

Our discussion of antithesis provides a good transition to figures of speech which, according to Quintilian, lend charm and vigor to a passage (9.3.28). He begins with the various types of verbal arrangement by *adiectio*—that is, by repetition of some sort. Elaborate classifications existed at the time, so that, depending on the position of the repeated word, one called the device *geminatio, repetitio, anaphora,* or some other fit name. Because the process is essentially the same and the effect varies but slightly, Quintilian treated such figures together, and we shall follow his lead. The first poetic example he cites (28) shows, as he remarks, *geminatio* exploited to arouse pity: *A Corydon, Corydon.* Juvenal, well aware of the possibilities of the device and what Vergil achieved in his context, shamelessly parodies it in Satire 9, where Corydon becomes the pervert Naevolus, and the pity dissolves into irony (cf. 102 ff.). More frequently, geminatio operates as amplificatio to emphasize the word it repeats; and Quintilian uses an example from Cicero's defense of Milo. Juvenal exploits amplificatio consistently in these devices, but he achieves added emphasis by utilizing metrical possibilities also.[138]

> liceat modo vivere: *fient,*
> *fient* ista palam, cupient et in acta referri!   (2.135–6)

The satirist has just told us that two males are about to celebrate their marriage. Here is the way in which he conveys his indignant reaction. He might permit the homosexuals to live, but they wish to flaunt their deeds. Whereas formal poets do not punctuate between the fifth and sixth feet of the hexameter, Juvenal pointedly sets *fient* off at the end of the line. Then he repeats the word in the emphatic first position of the following line. These outrageous acts will be committed, he drums into our consciousness![139]

The difference between repetitio and geminatio consists in the slight separation of the repeated words. Juvenal uses repetitio even more freely, and one can see how, in this case, the poet would find it easier to deal with the hexameter.[140]

> iubet a praecone vocari
> ipsos Troiugenas (nam vexant limen et ipsi
> nobiscum): "da praetori, da deinde tribuno!"
> sed libertinus *prior* est: *"prior"* inquit "ego adsum."
> (1.99–102)

---

138. For Juvenal's use of geminatio cf. Strefinger, p. 7, and De Decker, p. 187.
139. For a similar use of an emphatic verb cf. 5.112–13.
140. Strefinger, p. 8, lists some instances of repetitio.

Again, the effect depends upon amplificatio. The traditional order for handing out the sportula would follow the social scale: the nobility and elected officials would naturally come first. As the satirist stresses in this instance, the social classification has collapsed and a freedman, merely because he arrived first, can confidently claim his right to receive the sportula before the aristocrats. Thus *prior,* repeated by the freedman himself, becomes a means of portraying the general destruction of Roman values; nowadays, priority bears no relation to honor.

I do not mean to imply that the satirist always uses emphatic verbs and adjectives for repetition. Quite frequently he will repeat adverbs, conjunctions, and relative pronouns which in themselves have no special denotative value, but whose very usage connotes the close emotional connection between parts of sentences or paragraphs. Particularly when he employs anaphora, which he does often, Juvenal will use relatively colorless words for repetition.[141] One has only to think of the number of parallel *cum*-clauses in 1.22 ff. I do not think, however, that we should consider the anaphora devoid of effect. The very repetition serves to present these separate instances of vice as a single cumulative impression: the satirist sees these people at the same time and forces us to imagine them simultaneously. Juvenal also employs standard technique in piling up angry rhetorical questions, regularly beginning in anaphora with the same interrogative (cf. 1.77–8). And he achieves a similar effect by repeating negatives such as *non, nil, nullus,* implying that the true values of Rome are now utterly negated (cf. 3.22). De Decker has dismissed this type of anaphora as of no rhetorical value,[142] so I have devoted special attention to it. But Juvenal also picks out words

141. For Juvenal's use of anaphora cf. Strefinger, pp. 5 ff.; De Decker, pp. 193 ff.; and Ryberg, pp. 27 ff.

142. De Decker regarded his case as proved if he had statistics on his side; but he consistently quoted anaphora, as well as the instances of other rhetorical practices, out of context.

which, possessing intrinsic significance, can be advantageously stressed by amplificatio.

> haud facile emergunt quorum virtutibus obstat
> res angusta domi; sed Romae durior illis
> conatus: *magno* hospitium miserabile, *magno*
> servorum ventres, et frugi cenula *magno*. (3.164–7)

The satirist, through Umbricius, emphasizes the huge expenses of the city by repeating *magno,* always exploiting metrical position. The third *magno* he deliberately unbalances and instead of placing it at the beginning of the phrase, puts it at the end, also at the end of the line. As a result, we are left with a final impression of the high living costs in Rome. Characteristic examples of such repetition, used to convey the speaker's outrage, will be found on every page of Cicero's attack on Piso.

Another common figure of speech, which assumes roused emotions in the speaker, is asyndeton and its opposite, polysyndeton.[143] Of their rhetorical value Quintilian says *fons quidem unus, quia acriora facit et instantiora quae dicimus et vim quandam prae se ferentia velut saepius erumpentis adfectus* (9.3.54). That is, their distortion of regular connections in the sentence symbolizes the distorted feelings of the orator. The word *erumpentis* should remind us of the characteristic word in Quintilian for the operation of indignatio[144]—like all genuine passions, it erupts. Asyndeton, then, can convey the mood appropriate to Juvenal's persona.[145]

> ingenium velox, audacia perdita, sermo
> promptus et Isaeo torrentior: ede quid illum
> esse putes. quemvis hominem secum attulit ad nos:

143. Cf. Longinus 19 ff., and Ryberg, p. 26.
144. Cf. above, pp. 33 ff.
145. On Juvenal's use of asyndeton cf. L. O. Kiaer, *De Sermone Juvenalis* (Copenhagen, 1875), pp. 60 ff.; and H. P. Wright's edition of Juvenal (Boston, 1901), p. xxiv.

grammaticus rhetor geometres pictor aliptes
augur schoenobates medicus magus, omnia novit
Graeculus esuriens. (3.73–8)

Two sets of asyndeton occur here, first of phrases describing
the qualities which make the Greek so adaptable, then of
titles which illustrate his versatility. Umbricius has already
indicated his passionate hatred of the Greeks (cf. 60–1). Now,
we can see that his hatred depends upon something more than
prejudice; it is indignatio roused by the success attendant on
unscrupulous ingenuity.

As a last figure I discuss ellipsis. Quintilian gives it a brief
treatment (9.3.58), stressing the values of *brevitas* and *novitas*,
and he cites as a prose example a letter of Cicero. It is true that
ellipsis serves the concision of vernacular speech,[146] but it
possesses an equally valid function in impassioned oratory. We
find it commonly in rhetorical questions after *quid, quo, unde*
or in angry conclusions after the connectives *hinc, inde, unde*.
In none of these cases does ellipsis run the risk of obscurity.
From the context, the omitted verb, more often than not a
form of *esse,* can quickly be inferred, and the process, which
reverses that of *adiectio,* has approximately the same value, to
emphasize the missing word and even more the emotion that
lies behind the omission. Thus in Cicero's vituperatio of Piso,
several examples occur. He introduces a detail about his foe
and comments *quid hoc turpius?*[147] or he describes the depraved character of Piso by anaphora and ellipsis: *nihil apud
hunc lautum, nihil elegans, nihil exquisitum—laudabo inimicum—quin ne magno opere quidem quicquam praeter
libidines sumptuosum.*[148] Juvenal uses the device to achieve
something very close to the effects of Cicero's vituperatio.[149]

146. Ruckdeschel (note 100 above), p. 153, treats Horace's ellipsis
properly as an element of popular speech.
147. *In Pis.* 49.
148. *Ibid.* 67.
149. On Juvenal's ellipsis cf. Kiaer, pp. 108 ff., and Wright, pp. xxx ff.

The most striking of all instances of ellipsis occurs significantly in Satire 1, precisely at the point where the satirist
defines his manner and his subject matter:

> quidquid agunt homines, votum timor ira voluptas
> gaudia discursus, nostri farrago libelli est.
> et quando uberior vitiorum copia? quando
> maior avaritiae patuit sinus? alea quando
> hos animos? (85–9)

Asyndeton serves to present the subject matter of satire in a
formidable series. In immediate reaction to his relatively calm
table of contents, the satirist bursts into a question in ellipsis.
He follows on with anaphora, giving the second clause a verb.
Then, apparently completely losing control of himself and
logical discourse, he produces an elliptical question for which
we do not know the verb at all. Of course, the subsequent
context quickly explains the obscurity in a vivid picture of
gambling, but the fact remains that the satirist has chosen
to express his feelings in this striking manner. He has, in effect, given us a vivid illustration of his recent assertion: *facit
indignatio versum*.

After this rapid survey of Juvenal's style, in which we followed the general approach of Quintilian, we can see how well
the satirist grasped the rhetorical principles of fitting elocutio
to inventio. His style cannot be separated from his conscious
poetic purposes; his persona lives and functions through his
vocabulary, his tropes, and his various figures. Where Horace
avoided figures because they would interfere with his modest,
unaffected persona or used such devices as anaphora only for
special effects,[150] Juvenal abandons the satiric tradition so
heavily influenced by Horace and adapts his style to an entirely new and rhetorically consistent persona. The models
that exist for impassioned oratory conveying indignatio, es-

---

150. Cf. E. Fränkel, *Horace* (Oxford, 1957), p. 206: "Horace is not
a writer to use anaphora idly. Whenever he uses it he does so to stress
something which he has very much at heart."

pecially the example of vituperatio cited by Quintilian, Cicero's *In Pisonem,* show the same integration of style and attitude and mostly the same stylistic features, although Juvenal devised some new practices with regard to vocabulary and of course achieved special emphasis by his careful disposition of important words in salient metrical positions. Quintilian discusses other points relevant to style, notably the selection of rhythms suitable to one's speech and the use of gestures as a dramatic aid to the mood of the oration. The choice of rhythms might sound analogous to the poet's work with meter, but, even if true, Quintilian's rules have small bearing upon Juvenal's purposes as a metrician. Accordingly, I leave Juvenal's meter for another paper. Naturally, the satirist could not exploit gesture, even though certain movements, as Quintilian observed, implied indignatio. If he expected to convey emotion, Juvenal had to depend entirely on the appropriate union of style and satiric concept. So long as his theme can evoke indignation, I maintain, Juvenal's rhetorical style succeeds.

CONCLUSION

After thoroughly discussing the two principal concerns of rhetoric, namely inventio and elocutio, Quintilian returns in his final book to the concept of the ideal orator, starting with these words: *sit ergo nobis orator, quem constituimus, is, qui a M. Catone finitur, "vir bonus dicendi peritus"; verum, id quod et ille posuit prius et ipsa natura potius ac maius est, utique vir bonus* (12.1.1). He goes on to argue that unless a man possesses the moral integrity of the vir bonus, he cannot possibly be conceived of as a proper orator. This moral integrity, he continues (12.2), cannot be divorced from moral consciousness: one must know and understand *virtus.* Not that a man of honor needs to adhere closely to a particular philosophic sect;[151] in fact, Quintilian suggests that the orator will

151. Cf. the attitude expressed by the satirist in 13.120 ff.: he carefully dissociates himself from Stoics, Cynics, and Epicureans and takes a broad position of common sense.

rise above particularism in his pursuit of an illustrious public career. Quintilian probably has himself in mind as he develops his ideas, especially when he deals with the retired orator. In addition, he cherishes the image of Cicero and, behind him, of the great Cato. One of the finest appreciations of Cato occurs in this book, as our rhetorician reviews the career of that great Roman whose definition for the orator he has accepted.[152] Emphasis on the vir bonus who must possess virtus runs throughout the early history of Rome; and certainly Vergil's Aeneas, with his frequent approximation to Augustus, represented one of the finest efforts of Augustan Rome to recapture that past. To Vergil and Horace, Cato was also a great model of virtus. Those who, like Varro or Columella, wrote on the principles of agriculture, and Vergil, who transmuted them into poetry, shared the moral preconceptions evident in the preface to Cato's treatise on agriculture:

> maiores nostri sic habuerunt et ita in legibus posiverunt, furem dupli condemnari, feneratorem quadrupli. quanto peiorem civem existimarint feneratorem quam furem, hinc licet existimare. et *virum bonum* quom laudabant, ita laudabant, bonum agricolam bonumque colonum.

In these lines and what follows we have the associations proper to Cato's definition of the orator. If one were ever to achieve the moral ideal, it would be necessary to be thoroughly imbued in the fundamental Roman values: to esteem the country and direct contact with the land, with the production of food; to prize Roman citizenship and honorable service to Rome; to scorn those practices connected with the pursuit of wealth, desperate mercantile ventures, and unscrupulous moneylending. When one possessed such a moral core as vir bonus, skill in speaking could never lead to dishonor.[153]

152. *Inst.* 12.11.23.
153. Cato's patent effort in his definition to confine the orator within a moral framework may well arise from his reaction to sophistic attitudes taken by the Greek rhetoricians. The relativistic arguments of Carneades

It is significant that Seneca the Elder cites Cato's definition as the ideal for his sons to follow in an age of corrupt eloquence[154]—significant and also ironic, in that Seneca the Younger became the model of debased style against which Quintilian struggled. In Quintilian's day also, orators existed who defined their function differently and who represented the same effeminate taste for sensuous display which so offended the Elder Seneca. But there were rhetoricians like Quintilian, those who contributed to the education of Tacitus and Juvenal, who continued to stress the ethical basis of rhetoric. It is from such a background, now represented for us only in the invaluable treatise of Quintilian, that Juvenal emerges, to dominate the stage as the indignant satirist. Casting aside the Horatian traditions of satire, Juvenal accepted with alacrity the methods of the ethical rhetoricians and, at least to a certain extent, incarnated in his persona the ideal orator: *vir bonus dicendi peritus*.[155]

Serafini has discussed the similarities between Cato and Juvenal, on the grounds that both have the same moral purposes.[156] They both take a stand on traditional morality: Cato refers to *maiores nostri;* Juvenal constantly uses as *exempla* the great Republican heroes of Rome, who lived in Cato's time or before. They take a similar attitude toward the country, toward luxury, toward the Greeks, toward the military virtues; and, above all, they speak in much the same manner. Serafini refers to the fragments of Cato's orations suffused with that attitude of frankness which Juvenal affects in Satire 1 and which must be the first impression left by the vir bonus. I would supplement this with a quotation from

---

in Cato's own Rome might well have struck him as the epitome of degeneracy, something against which the Romans should guard themselves at all costs.

154. *Contr.* I Pref. 9.

155. Serafini, p. 248, reaches a similar conclusion: "Si verifica in G. il saldo connubio tra l'*orator* e il *vir bonus,* secondo l'ideale quintilianeo."

156. Serafini, pp. 375 ff.; also p. 117.

Cicero, who greatly admired Cato as a man and orator, especially as a master of the genus demonstrativum: *quis illo* [i.e. Catone] *gravior in laudando acerbior in vituperando, in sententiis argutior in docendo edisserendoque subtilior?*[157] In short, Cato defined the ideal orator, as we might expect, in terms of principles which he himself practiced in an era that already, according to him, was destroying the essence of Rome. I do not feel that the one reference to Cato in Juvenal (11.-90)[158] justifies us in asserting that the satirist masqueraded as *Cato alter.* When, however, we observe how Cato carried out his ideal definition and how it was honored throughout succeeding centuries, we can perhaps understand why such a definition, by its rich associations, would seem perfectly appropriate to the rhetorical satirist. The image of Cato practicing his vituperatio of luxurious Romans, of corrupt Greeks, of equally corrupt Carthage; the image of Cicero attacking Piso as the epitome of foreign-influenced degeneracy, Antony as a totally dissolute brute with no right to political power; perhaps the poetic use of vituperatio in works like Horace's Epode 4, where *liberrima indignatio* erupts against an upstart—all these provide a background to Juvenal's persona. In all such cases, the speaker acquires power over us because it is as a Roman concerned for the well-being of Rome that he denounces his opponent.

What we know about Quintilian would not lead us to compare him with Cato; as the favorite of the Flavians and one of the few successful rhetoricians of his time, he would hardly have spent his time denouncing the corrupt ways of the powerful. On the other hand, his teaching concentrated on legal oratory; and in a lawsuit the attorney can, to a large extent, divorce himself from his own faults and assume an attitude. Quintilian himself shows some embarrassment in dealing with the axiom that the good orator, the man who

157. *Brutus* 65.
158. The reference in 11.90 patently idealizes Cato. There is another, less clear because of its heavy irony, in 2.40, to *tertius Cato.*

can properly be identified as an orator, must always be vir bonus, not only in appearance but in essence. More often, he tacitly assumes the exercise of simulatio, whereby the orator produces a convincing show of honest feeling to fit his style. When the orator speaks, it must be admitted, it matters very little whether he is in fact an honest man skilled in rhetoric or whether, for the purposes of the occasion, he successfully simulates such an ideal. The fact remains, as Quintilian notes, that it is hard to convince intelligent men when arguing a dishonest cause.

Regardless of Quintilian's personal morality—and we cannot justly treat him harshly—he advocated Cato's concept of the ideal orator. If he, the leading rhetorician of his time, did so, many another less successful rhetor must have done the same. The remarks Juvenal makes about Quintilian must, I have argued, be interpreted as deprecatory. But although our satirist may have disapproved of Quintilian, especially for his prosperity under the hated Domitian, we must avoid inferring anything about their personal relations: Juvenal might have reacted against a man whose life so conflicted with his ideal for the orator, whether or not he studied under him. In fact, if we must conjecture, we could suggest that a spiteful rival rhetor might have pointed to Quintilian as a living anti-type to Cato. Since we cannot spend our lives in conjecture that has little chance of substantiation, it seems safer to leave the precise relation between Juvenal and Quintilian in doubt; for it really interferes with the unprejudiced investigation of a more important problem: what does Juvenal owe to rhetoric and what values could he assume in adopting rhetorical principles?

In this paper I have treated Quintilian not as a man writing about his own private opinions, but as a rhetorician whose doctrines presumably parallel those of many other contemporary teachers. This general doctrine is familiar to Juvenal: he knows the technical language of rhetoric; he has argued suasoriae; and, above all, he writes his Satires with a skill that exploits many of the advantages of rhetorical teaching. I have called attention to his self-conscious comment: *facit indignatio versum;* for I believe that here we can detect the satirist's inventio, his careful planning of the mood appropriate to a vir bonus who will castigate Rome's perversion. When we considered next the rhetorical genus which indignatio and Juvenal's particular method of presentation seem to assume, I attempted to dispute the usual definition of many Satires as rhetorical theses on the order of suasoriae, the practice version of the genus deliberativum. To think of Juvenal's themes as persuasive arguments is to misinterpret the principle of indignatio and its method of operation. Of the three rhetorical genera, by far the closest in mood to indignatio, and in subject and presentation to Juvenal's denunciation of Rome, proves to be the genus demonstrativum in the capacity of vituperatio. The classic example for vituperatio, to Quintilian, among orations surviving today, is Cicero's speech *In Pisonem.* Study of this tirade reveals that Cicero operates from the same assumptions as Juvenal: he attacks the un-Roman qualities of Piso, namely approval of Greek ways, Epicureanism, luxury, avoidance of all that a good Roman would accept without question; in short, as the orator sums it up at the end, Piso's *indignitas.* The stylistic techniques adopted by Cicero to convey his hatred of all that Piso represents—and Cicero here exhibits his mastery of simulatio—constitute prose analogues to what Juvenal employs in his Satires. As he planned his satiric method, Juvenal appears to have formed a persona based on the general rhetorical requirements of indignatio and on the formal limits of vituperatio, as translated into poetic terms.

Since in poetry concept and poetic product quickly fuse, we considered aspects of Juvenal's style as adequate vehicles for indignatio and vituperatio. Here, particularly, Quintilian proves helpful, for Juvenal patently abandons most of the Horatian conventions to adopt new ones based on rhetoric. He rejects Horace's whole doctrine of creating a style close to conversation, namely sermo; instead, he uses words in an explosive manner, making them attract attention and carry emotional weight. Regularly he resorts to linguistic conflicts or tropical paradoxes that serve to symbolize the moral paradox of Rome. Figures of thought avoid any pretense of subtlety and convey the most patent of emotions: anger, fury, outrage—in short, indignation at the state of things. Figures of speech convey the same meaning, emphasizing by *adiectio,* emphasizing by leaving out connectives or obvious verbs. Style and concept go together, we conclude, in an adequate expression of indignatio. Some have stressed Juvenal's Grand Style and his Tragic Satire,[159] and these terms provide helpful insights into the workings of Juvenal's genius. But the Grand Style is too broad a definition of the satirist's rhetorical technique; and Tragic Satire merely emphasizes one aspect of Juvenal's abandonment of Horatian sermo. If we expect to understand what Juvenal is doing, we have to start with his Program Satire and his own poetic definition of his purpose. When we accept the rhetorical assumptions of indignatio, we read with greater understanding that verse in which the satirist succinctly explains his principles: *facit indignatio versum.*

159. Cf. the thesis of Mrs. Ryberg and Serafini's chap. 5, "La satira tragica ed alta," pp. 249 ff.

INDEX

Accius, 24, 323
Aeschylus, 115
Alcaeus, 60n, 62, 73
Alewell, K., 411n
Alexander, rhetorical theorist, 437n
Alexander, W. H., 56n
Alexandrians, 5
Allen, A. W., 419n
Allen, Walter, Jr., 470n
Allers, W., 340n
anaphora, 239, 474, 476, 478-479
Anaximenes, rhetorical theorist, 437n
Andrewes, M., 115n
antonomasia, 119, 303, 307, 464-465, 472
apostrophe, 280, 282, 287, 388, 470-472
Apuleius, 90n
archaisms, 454-458
Archilochus, 60n, 114
Aristides, rhetorical theorist, 437n
Aristotle, 317, 320, 332, 340n, 437
Augustan (English) satire, see English satire
Augustus, letters, 448
Ausonius, 403n
Axelson, B., 267, 276n, 454n

Babrius, 132n
Bäker, F., 101n, 115n
Barbu, N. I., 370n
Best, E. E., Jr., 56n
Bion, 28, 343
Birt, T., 275n
Boissier, G., 368n, 370n
Britannicus, 103
Brugnoli, G., 365n
Buchheit, V., 80
Buchholz, V., see Buchheit, V.
Büchner, K., 60n
Buecheler, F., 267, 276n, 346

Caecilius Statius, 24, 356n

Caesar, Julius, 90n, 91n, 97n, 99n, 291n, 438
caesura, 25, 27, 187-189, 238-239, 467
Calderinus, 103
Callimachus, 76n, 77, 106n
Caplan, H., 414n
Carneades, 481n
Cartault, A., 154n
Casaubon, I., 154n, 158n, 166n
Castagnoli, F., 87
catachresis, 186, 190
Cato the Elder, xiv, 14, 343, 391, 411, 417-418, 472, 480-484
Catullus, 15, 58n, 106, 266, 369n, 396, 466
chiasmus, 189-190, 205n
Chrysippus, 340n, 417
Cicero, 18, 21, 92n, 100n, 106, 164n, 165n, 276n, 291n, 340n, 341, 356n, 359, 377, 396, 408, 412, 414n, 417, 424-425, 427, 429, 437-438, 440-442, 446, 448, 450, 458n, 461-462, 467-471, 475, 478, 480-481, 483, 485
Cinna, Helvius, 18
circumlocution, see periphrasis
Ciresola, T., 191n
Clark, J. R., 374n, 381n
Clarke, M. L., 417n
Clausen, W. V., 164n, 346
Clauss, R., 268
Cleanthes, 106, 177, 179, 181, 191, 417
Coccia, M., 340n
Colin, J., 276n, 387n
Colton, R. E., 367n
Columella, 481
comedy, xiii, 24-25, 356, 451
Commager, Steele, 63n
concinnitas, 21-22
Cooper, F. T., 452n
Cordier, A., 449n, 454n, 456n, 458n
Cousin, J., 447n
Cozzens, J. G., 418n

487

491

Library of Congress Cataloging in Publication Data

Anderson, William Scovil, 1927-
Essays on Roman satire.

(Princeton series of collected essays)
Includes index.
1. Satire, Latin—History and criticism—Collected works.   I. Title.
    PA6056.A56   877'.01'09   81-47906
        ISBN 0-691-05347-2 AACR2
        ISBN 0-691-00791-8 (pbk.)